CRITIQUE
OF
PATRIARCHAL REASON

To interpret is to create a kind of world.

CRITIQUE OF PATRIARCHAL REASON

By Arthur Evans

With Artwork
By Frank Pietronigro

White Crane Press
San Francisco

Text © 1997 by Arthur Evans
Artwork © 1997 by Frank Pietronigro
All rights reserved.

White Crane Press
P.O. Box 170152
San Francisco, CA 94117-0152
Robert Barzan, Editor

Cover artwork: *Energy Interceptors* (detail)
by Frank Pietronigro
Acrylic on canvas, 32" x 32", 1996

Printed in the United States of America
on recycled, acid-free paper.

Publication of this book has been supported by a grant from the San Francisco Art Commission's Cultural Equity Grants Program. Opinions expressed herein are those of the author, not the commission.

Evans, Arthur (Scott), 1942-, and Frank Pietronigro, 1954-
    Critique of Patriarchal Reason
    Includes illustrations, bibliographical references, glossary, and index.
    Library of Congress Catalog No. 97-90047
    ISBN 0-9645384-1-5
    1. Logic. 2. Analysis (Philosophy). 3. Wittgenstein, Ludwig, 1889-1951. 4. Philosophy and Science.
    5. Humanism. 6. Art, Abstract. I. Title.

In memory of my mother,
Helen Clara Klingel Evans

CHAPTER CONTENTS
(Notes follow each chapter.)

Introduction. What is Philosophy? 1
1. One and Many 7
2. Right and Wrong 43
3. The Myth of Mathematics 69
4. The Illogic of Antiquity 91
5. The Illogic of Early Modernity 125
6. The Illogic of the 20th Century 151
7. Logic and Misogyny 173
8. Logic on Stilts 193
9. The Descent to Language 219
10. Logic vs. Language 241
11. The Logic of Dr. Strangelove 259
12. The Metaphysics of Science 283
13. The Science of Dr. Frankenstein 301
Epilog. Beyond Logic, Mathematics & Science 331
Cited Titles 343
Glossary 351
Index 363

ARTWORK
BY FRANK PIETRONIGRO

Energy Interceptors ....Cover

Passing Bodies..*x*

Triadic.. 6

Source 68

Sacra 1 90

Doxa 150

Hey Bud Xerox That Head.. 172

Sacra 3 191

Documents 192

Being of Service 217

Ron 218

Abstract Returned... 239

Inner Vision... 240

Technophilia 282

Hey Faggot 300

Talismans 330

Sacra 2 341

Spatial Relativity... 342

Costanza 350

THE WRITER AND THE ARTIST

ARTHUR EVANS studied chemistry and political science at Brown University, and philosophy at the New School for Social Research, the City College of New York, and Columbia University. He is the author of *The God of Ecstasy* (1988). The book explores the ancient rites of the Greek god Dionysos and includes Evans' new translation of Euripides' play *Bakkhai*. Evans also wrote *Witchcraft and the Gay Counterculture* (1978), a study of the sexual dimension of the European witch hunts. He was born in York, Pennsylvania, is a veteran activist of the gay/lesbian liberation movement, and has lived in San Francisco since 1974.

FRANK PIETRONIGRO studied fine art at the Philadelphia College of Art and holds a Bachelor of Fine Arts degree, in interdisciplinary arts, from the San Francisco Art Institute. By appointment of the San Francisco Art Commission, he has directed the San Francisco Arts Festival, and twice produced San Francisco's popular "Art in the Park." His recent work includes traditional and nontraditional modes of expression, using painting, public art, multimedia, and installations. He has lived in San Francisco since 1977 and grew up in Philadelphia.

ACKNOWLEDGMENTS

My heartfelt thanks to the many people who contributed to this book. For preserving intact, for more than a decade, my entire collection of philosophy books after I abandoned graduate school in 1972, I am deeply indebted to Morty Manford (deceased) and his mother, Mrs. Jeanne Manford. For financial help given during the writing process, I am indebted to Billy Amberg (deceased), Assunta Femia, Rand Gillen, Marty Robinson (deceased), Marc Rubin, and Paul Stewart. For providing me with a computer, printer, and paper supply, John Behrens. For help in finding a critical reader in philosophy, James Walsh. For criticism of the text, D. Allen, Bob Barzan, Reid Condit, Jim Gordon, Paul Gross, Wilfrid Koponen, Bart Kosko, Norman Levitt, Peter Limnios, Mary Mothersill, Andrea Nye, Dan Smith, Phil Tryon, and Tundra Wind. For supporting my grant proposal to the San Francisco Art Commission, Tom Ammiano, Bob Barzan, Claudia Card, Ron Lanza, and Adam Nagourney. For granting an award for the book's printing costs, and for supporting the effort to reclaim philosophy for the arts, the San Francisco Art Commission. For practical advice in following grant-making procedures, Art Commission personnel Lawrence Thoo and Katie Bell. For grants and loans to supplement the Commission's grant for production costs, Carolyn Amberg, David Axel, Charlie Bufis, Ron Gold, John Paul Hudson, Toby Johnson, Arnie Kantrowitz, Larry Mass, Ken Miller, José-Luis Moscovich, David Roggensack, Charley Shively, Robin Souza, and Eric Thorndale. For help in managing the project's finances, Ben Gardiner of the Community of St. Matthew. For assistance with layout and book design, Jack Kendrick. For advice with cover design, Michael Starkman. For help in producing galley copies, Joey Cain. For practical tips on book production, Bert Herrman. For the fine images used throughout the book, my collaborator Frank Pietronigro. And for the gift of philosophy, Athena and the Muses.

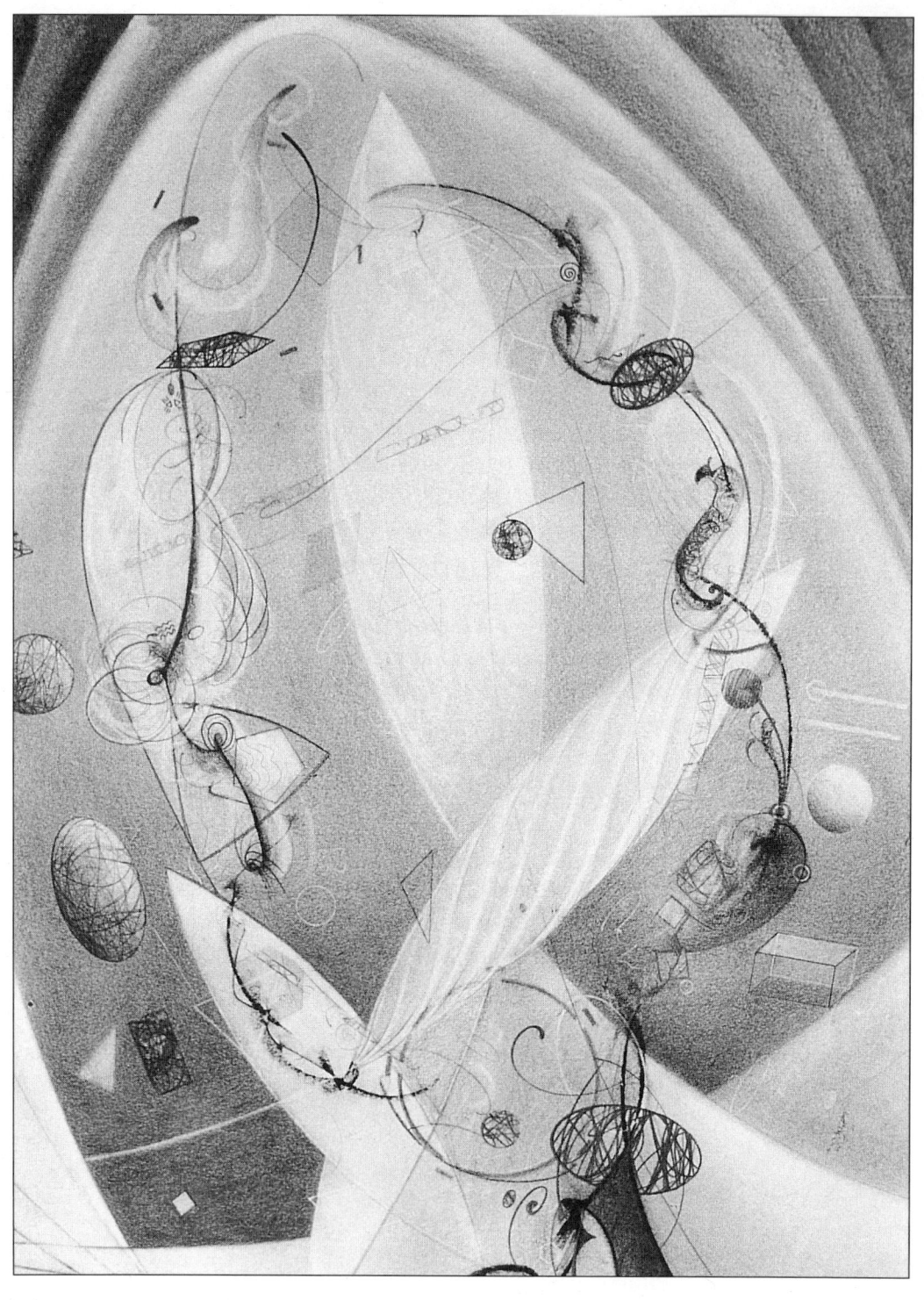

Passing Bodies, Detail
Graphite, 21" x 15", 1996

Introduction

What Is Philosophy?

SUMMARY: This chapter reclaims philosophy as an art, against the scientific model that now mesmerizes many academic philosophers. The chapter also outlines the book's overall goals: to expose the patriarchal mythology embedded in scientific "rationality," and to develop a more humane and inclusive view of reason.

The Greek roots from which the word "philosophy" is derived imply that philosophy is a matter of both passion and intellect: "philo-" from the verb *philein*, which means to attend to, care for, nurture, and love; "-sophy" from the noun *sophia*, which means skill, learning, cleverness, knowledge, and wisdom. *The passionate pursuit of knowledge or wisdom*—this is the literal meaning of our word "philosophy."

Like all human passions, philosophy is restless. It is never satisfied, but ever looks beyond the partial to the more complete, beyond the taken-for-granted to the not-so-obvious. Unceasingly and everywhere, it relentlessly asks all comers, like Socrates in ancient Athens, "Why?" Without such restless passion, philosophy would have no great motivation and so no great accomplishments. In fact, it would soon be reduced to a mere mental game. Mental games certainly have a role to play in human experience, but they are not philosophy.

Conversely, philosophy draws on the ability to think—rationally, critically, and systematically. Without such critical thinking, philosophy would soon be reduced to enthusiasm for some belief system or social movement. Belief systems and social movements certainly have a role to play in human experience, but they are not philosophy.

The philosopher is passionately motivated but critically discerning, a man or woman who yearns for the whole truth while yet remaining skeptical of any purported example of it. Confronted with any assertion or any form of activity, an inquiring mind can always ask "What does this assume?" and "What follows as a consequence from this?" The motivation to do so systematically for the sake of greater knowledge is philosophy.

Through the critical and systematic examination of assumptions and implications, philosophers sometimes succeed in creating whole new systems of their own, but they can never remain completely satisfied with such systems. If they do, either the passion has failed or the critical thinking been blunted. In either case, the system may indeed continue, but philosophy has ended.

So then, we may define philosophy as the critical and systematic examination of presuppositions and implications, motivated by a passion to know. As such an endeavor, philosophy can obviously be applied to any area of inquiry and to any question. Over the past few millennia it has in particular often been applied to certain basic, recurring questions, a practice that has given rise to certain specialized names for philosophy when these questions are asked. When applied to the question "What is being?," philosophy is called ontology; when "What is knowledge?," epistemology; when "What is right?," ethical theory. But in all these cases, philosophers are really asking the same questions: "What are the presuppositions?" and "What are the implications?"

The Narrowness of Anglo-American Academic Philosophy

During the last century a number of academic philosophers in Britain, North America, and elsewhere have taken the position that philosophy is of a much narrower scope than I have just outlined. They see philosophers as paid professionals exercising technical expertise on subjects of special interest. Accordingly, philosophy should not tread on the toes of other disciplines that are equally specialized. "Who am I as a philosopher to ask critical questions in nuclear physics?" advocates of this school typically ask. "I'll leave that to the nuclear physicists, who are much better qualified than I am on that score."

Ironically, but not surprisingly, many of these same philosophers have found that the special fields allegedly appropriate to philosophical inquiry have been steadily shrinking. So, for example, with all the sciences and arts now removed from their purview, these philosophers typically spend most of their time debating only questions about language and logic, and regard anything else as "not philosophical." But one could use their own criteria to object even to these fields. Why not yield language to linguists? Why not yield logic to mathematicians? Aren't they better qualified in these fields than philosophers? Indeed, why even have departments of philosophy at all in universities?

The great fallacy of much recent Anglo-American academic philosophy is its refusal to see that one can *always* ask substantive questions. For example, even if a person is not learned in nuclear physics, he or she can still ask "Is nuclear physics worthwhile?" This is a question *about* nuclear physics but one that cannot be answered *within* nuclear physics. There is no theory or set of experiments that a nuclear physicist can point to in order to answer this question, since the question is about the very propriety of such experimentation and theorizing in the first place.

To answer the question of whether nuclear physics is worthwhile, we first have to specify what we mean when we say something is "worthwhile." Next we have to compile the salient historical record of nuclear physics. Finally we have to evaluate that record according to our criterion of what is worthwhile. Now, describing the historical record of nuclear physics can be done through observation, but developing a criterion of what is worthwhile is a question of *value*. We have to examine various standards of "good" and "bad" and then decide which of these standards we will use to judge the effects of nuclear physics. In other words, there is no way to answer the question "Is nuclear physics worthwhile?" without making some value judgment as to what we mean by "worthwhile."

Is it possible to make such value judgments? Yes. Who, then, is to make them? Anyone who wishes to! Can these value judgments in turn be systematically analyzed for their presuppositions and implications? Yes. And what do we call doing *that*? Clearly not nuclear physics, though such analysis may have implications for nuclear physics. What then? What, indeed, if not *philosophy*?

The above example with nuclear physics can be applied by analogy to any human endeavor. Hence a great many important and interesting questions remain to be asked about meaning and value, touching every aspect of human life. Yet these questions generally go unaddressed by most Anglo-American academic philosophers, who all the while agonize over what they regard as the steadily narrowing field appropriate to philosophical inquiry. In their quandary they have forgotten the great lesson of the philosopher Socrates. He taught that everything human involves a basic question of value and that the examination of such values constitutes the mission of philosophy. Socrates encapsulated this broad view of philosophy with the remark that has ever since been associated with his name:

> For human beings, a life unexamined is not worth living.[1]

Philosophers with the narrow, modern view have another failing: they underestimate the historical role of philosophy as a generator of *new sciences*. If philosophers throughout the ages had followed the advice of recent Anglo-American academics, most of the sciences themselves, which these academics so admire, would never have arisen in the first place. Physics and astronomy, for example, were once known as *natural philosophy* and were initiated by Greek and Latin philosophers speculating about things not yet known with precision. What are now called sociology and psychology are offshoots of more recent philosophical speculation. However clumsy the original speculations of these philosophers may appear in hindsight, they nevertheless addressed human attention and imagination to new avenues of knowledge. Should we assume today that no new sciences will ever appear? If not, isn't it possible that philosophic speculation may yet pave the way for them as it has so often in the past? And if that is so, what becomes of the notion that philosophy must be limited to language and logic?[2]

Alienated from much of philosophy's past rich history and in massive retreat from the most pressing of contemporary issues, Anglo-American academic philosophers increasingly find that they have nothing of substance to say. Within the last half century, only a few academic philosophers have undertaken to buck this trend. Those who have done so have generally been marginalized by other academics.[3]

More recently, a ray of hope has appeared: many women in the field, moved by feminist concerns, are now insisting that philosophy once again take up issues of substance. An outstanding example is Andrea Nye's lucid, groundbreaking book *Words of Power*. The book argues that formal logic, seemingly the most objective part of philosophy, actually embodies patriarchal values.[4]

Many of Nye's academic male peers have reacted with dismay to her claim. "If sheer logic is not absolute," they exclaim, "then what is?" Despite their umbrage, Nye is right. This present work confirms and builds on her pioneering insights.

The Popular Hunger for Meaning

Despite the current sterility and insularity of Anglo-American academic philosophy, the general public remains highly responsive to the raising of what are basically philosophical questions. Just look at the great abundance of popular books on meditation, metaphysics, science fiction, the occult, reincarnation, etc. Naturally enough, academic philosophers look down on such books, regarding them as unprofessional and not really philosophical. But when judged in terms of Western philosophy's varied currents during the past 2,500 years, these topics are indeed philosophical. In fact, the history of philosophy shows that the narrowness of modern academic philosophy is untypical.

As to the fact that the popular books are "unprofessional," the academics are right. But they overlook the reason: those who have formal training in philosophy are schooled to disdain such topics. Hence a gap has developed, with those having an interest in the great substantive questions of philosophy on one side, and with those having the greatest formal training on the other. Thus has philosophical substance been sundered from philosophical technique, a breach that has served to diminish both.

A Personal Example

I myself have experienced first-hand the narrowness of Anglo-American academic philosophy, an experience that is directly related to the writing of this work. From 1967 to 1971 I was a graduate student in the doctoral program in philosophy at Columbia University in New York. By the spring of 1969 I had completed all course requirements and qualifying exams for the Ph.D. degree and had begun writing a dissertation in ancient Greek philosophy.

Judged by my academic record of the time, I was swimmingly "on track." But by 1971 numerous factors had led me to feel disenchanted with both Columbia University in general and the philosophy department in particular: the complicity of the university's administration in the Vietnam War; a violent police assault on the campus, engineered by the administration; the narrowness and dogmatism of the sect of "analytic philosophy," which then prevailed (and still does) at Columbia; and the uninspiring personal example set by many of my own professors.

In early 1972 I withdrew from Columbia, gave away all my books in philosophy, left New York for the West Coast, and became an auto mechanic. In the meantime, I also wrote two books on gay history and culture. In 1986, fourteen years after I withdrew from Columbia, I wrote a letter to the philosophy department, inquiring if I still had any options with them. To my surprise, the department generously responded that it would re-admit me, and that if I finished my dissertation, I would be granted the degree.

A serious problem, however, remained. Although retaining my doctoral research notes after leaving Columbia, I had no further interest in my original dissertation topic. Instead, I wanted to develop a whole new approach to philosophy that would be congenial to feminism and gay liberation, reflecting my own personal and philosophical growth during the 14 years since I had left Columbia. No one in the philosophy department, however, was willing to sponsor such a dissertation. So I have written this present work instead, both for my own personal fulfillment and as a contribution to the common good.

Opening the Doors

This book is the initial installment of an intended three-volume series dealing with certain basic themes in Western philosophical consciousness in light of the approach of a new millennium. The general aim of the entire series is to help heal the breach between substance and technique that now characterizes much of Anglo-American academic philosophy. To that end, the series forthrightly seeks for truth in the face of some of the great philosophical questions still asked in popular works, such as "What is the difference between reality and illusion?," "How can we distinguish knowledge from opinion?," "What happens when we die?," and "What does it mean to live a worthy human life?" But in discussing such substantive questions, the series also draws on formal methods of argumentation, as well as past developments in the history of philosophy. In this way, the series seeks to cull what is best both from the popular interest in the substantive questions of philosophy and from the specialized techniques of the professionals.

This installment in particular, *Critique of Patriarchal Reason*, focuses on two questions: "What does it mean to experience reality?" and "What does it mean to be rational?" The main argument developed here is this: formal logic, higher mathematics, and science have all fostered a crippling concept of human rationality that fails to do justice to the richness of human experience. The book demonstrates how these biases have emerged historically, and illustrates their harmful impact on women, gay people, indigenous Third-World cultures, and the natural environment. Many philosophers are discussed in detail, with a special emphasis on Ludwig Wittgenstein, a crucial transition-figure in 20th-century philosophy. (Chapters seven through ten uncover a surprising connection between Wittgenstein's theories of logic and language on one hand and his conflicted attitude toward his homosexuality on the other.) On the basis of its examination of the life and thought of these various philosophers, the book concludes with an appeal: let us jettison the crippling ideal of patriarchal reason and open ourselves to a more inclusive understanding of human rationality.

Patriarchal Reason

Why, the reader might wonder, does the book call this crippling concept of reason "patriarchal"? The history of the noun "patriarchy" provides the answer. From antiquity to the present, this word has had various meanings: "the rule of the fathers," "the rule of the male founders of the tribes of Israel," "the rule of the early Christian bishops," and "the dominance of men in the family and society." Behind these various meanings lies a simple historical fact: *men have been in charge*. Accordingly, this book uses the adjective "patriarchal" in a simple and broad sense, as a synonym for "male-supremacist."

But why the term "patriarchal reason"? Because in 1781, the German philosopher Immanuel Kant published one of the most influential works in the history of philosophy, *Critique of Pure Reason*. Hoping to reconcile the possibility of religious belief with the methods of the new sciences, Kant undertook to map out both the powers and the limits of human reason. In doing so, Kant just assumed that the highest manifestations of human reason occur in a rather limited area—the fields of formal logic, higher mathematics, and natural science. This narrow assumption about what is most rational represented a significant break with the broader views of the Renaissance humanists before Kant, and was also at odds with notions found in many non-Western societies. Although later Western philosophers typically rejected many of Kant's dogmas, most have unthinkingly adopted his narrow assumption about the highest manifestations of human reason. This book will show that so-called "pure reason" is actually only one band on the spectrum of human rationality, and a narrow, male-oriented band at that.

I have tried to make the material presented here as accessible to the general reading public as possible, without at the same time oversimplifying the questions at issue. Every chapter beings with a summary of its contents and a recapitulation of the last chapter, and there is a glossary of philosophical terms at the end of the book. Nonetheless, certain sections may at first seem intimidating to readers who are unaccustomed to sustained intellectual argument. As with any skill, however, so the skill of thinking philosophically improves with practice. The key to understanding in philosophy, as in life, is patience and perseverance.

Because this work discusses, in a new light, the thought of numerous past philosophers, it may prove useful as a resource book for introductory philosophy classes. Nonetheless, readers should not expect to find here some sort of authoritative overview of the thoughts of others. To the contrary, what follows is an original philosophical work in its own right, dealing with the nature of human experience and rationality, and developed with an eye toward the approach of a new millennium.

One might object here, of course, that a millennium is a very artificial thing. For example, if our number system were based on 8 instead of 10, the year we now symbolize by "2000 A.D.", which is the last year of the present millennium, would instead be "3720 A.D." But for all that, anniversaries of any kind are important to human beings because they provide us with an opportunity to reflect on our past accomplishments and future goals. If a great many people begin to think that a certain kind of anniversary is especially important, then in fact it will be, and for no other reason than that people so regard it. A millennium, then, is much more than so many rotations of the earth around the sun, counted in a number system that happens to be based on 10. A millennium is also a cultural and psychological construct in the consciousness of the people for whom it is important. If that importance succeeds in generating a philosophical discussion, then a millennium has philosophical significance.[5]

The Art of Philosophy

If you have studied philosophy before, you may want to sit down and read this book through from beginning to end as you would a novel. But if you do not have such a background, you may want to skip around, concentrating at first on those chapters that are initially of most interest to you. Alternatively, you might just let the book fall open at random, read a paragraph or so, close the book, and then *think* and *feel* about what you have just read. Do you agree or disagree? Does it ring true to your own experiences and feelings? How would you frame an objection to the argument, then an objection to the objection, etc.?

As with all works on philosophy, there will probably be only a small part of this one that you completely agree with. In fact, if you should find yourself agreeing with much of what you read in this book, it probably means that you are not thinking critically enough. Ironically, although philosophy at its best attempts to give substantive answers to substantive questions, the real value in any given work of philosophy does not lie in the particular answers it offers but in its ability to stimulate a worthy dialogue with its readers. In the end, the *process* of thinking and feeling is what is most important, and not any particular argument in itself. Therein does philosophy differ from the sciences, and to its greater credit, for philosophy is an *art*.

As part of its effort to reclaim philosophy as an art, this book displays a number of paintings and photographs by San Francisco artist Frank Pietronigro. What is the connection between these images and the text? The best way for you, the reader, to answer this question is to ask yourself these further questions: What are the feelings that underlie the various shapes and lines in these images? What are the feelings that underlie the various words in the text? How do the feelings expressed in the one medium relate to those expressed in the other? What new ideas of my own come to mind after I reflect on this interplay of feelings, images, and words?

In asking yourself these questions, you will mirror the creative process that gave rise to this book. Whenever I write, even on the most abstract of matters, I always begin with feelings, which I seek to articulate in concepts and words. When I succeed in doing so, the result is a text. Likewise, many visual artists first begin with feelings, which they seek to express in shapes and colors. When they succeed in doing so, the result is a painting or drawing. Although using different media, both the writer and the visual artist partake of a common process, the creation of a meaning that is rooted in feeling.

Although artist Frank Pietronigro and I use different media, we share a certain common sensibility in looking at human experience. As you trace out the connections in this book between images, words, and feelings, you will encounter this common sensibility through different lenses. If you persevere in making these connections, you will likely make an interesting discovery: the common experiential content that lies behind both visual art and text, although quite meaningful, is not something that can be easily captured by any logical or scientific formula. And *that* is part of the message of this book.

The Personal is the Philosophical

The philosophical interpretations presented here have arisen from decades of reflection on my own personal experiences and on the major historical events happening in the world around me. Hence they have been influenced (although not determined) by the fact that I am a white, 54-year-old gay man, born and raised in a working-class family, and formally educated in philosophy. In addition, I am a 60s-inspired rebel and an American citizen, to name but a few of my personal circumstances. But regardless of my own particular background, I seek, like every thinking person, an understanding of the greater world around me and of the role of the human species within it. This book has emerged as a result of that greater seeking.

I invite you to come with me now for a journey into the world of philosophy. My hope is that in taking up these pages you will find yourself stimulated to raise questions in your life that you might not otherwise have asked and, even more, to conceive of entirely new ideas of your own that go beyond those presented here. If that should come to pass, then regardless of whether we agree on the specific arguments presented here or not, we will have participated in a worthy dialogue.

---

[1] Plato, *Socrates' Defense*, 38a.

[2] John Horgan, a widely read commentator on science, predicts that "science is unlikely to make any significant additions to the knowledge it has already generated. There will be no great revelations in the future comparable to those bestowed upon us by Darwin or Einstein or Watson and Crick." Horgan brings to mind the misplaced confidence of the ancients in Ptolemy's astronomy, and of the Enlightenment in Newton's physics. See his *The End of Science*, Helix Books, New York, 1996, p. 16.

[3] Three notable examples: (1) Susanne Langer's *Philosophy in a New Key* (first published 1942). Langer reclaims music, metaphor, and ritual for philosophy, arguing that each is rational in its own right, although formal logic cannot easily capture this rationality. (2) Paul Feyerabend, *Against Method* (first published 1975). Feyerabend denounces the effort to enshrine the scientific method as a criterion of rationality for all human inquiry. (3) Richard Rorty, *Philosophy and the Mirror of Nature* (1979). Rorty views philosophy as an ongoing "conversation," not a science-inspired mirroring of the nature of reality.

[4] Andrea Nye, *Words of Power*, Routledge, New York, 1990. For a general overview of current feminist philosophy, see Nye's *Philosophy and Feminism*, Twayne Publishers, New York, 1995.

[5] Throughout this series, I have used the conventional abbreviations "B.C." and "A.D." for dates, instead of the newer "B.C.E." and "C.E." The latter are open to objections as serious as those against the older. For example, does the so-called "Common Era" include the era of the residents of the Americas before Columbus? If so, then "0 C.E." should refer to a point in time substantially earlier than it now does. But if the Indians are to be excluded, why call this era "Common"? The truth is that we need a whole new way of conceptualizing the last half-dozen millennia.

Triadic, Detail
Graphite, 15" x 15", 1996

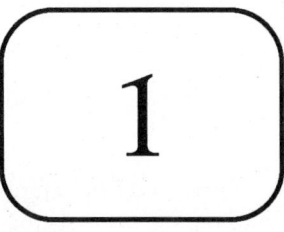

One and Many

SUMMARY: This chapter shows why there can be no such thing as absolute objectivity, only relative objectivity. Contrary to the claims of science, the interpreter (that is, the subject) cannot be ripped out of the knowing process. Understanding this point clarifies many philosophical conundrums, such as the puzzle of one and many, the question of the relationship between reality and language, and the problem of universals.

What does it mean to be a rational human being? Would everybody come to the same conclusions about things if everybody had the same information? Does the world have a knowable, objective nature independent of the various ways that people interpret it? Is it possible to have a purely subjective experience, completely independent of the way the world really is? Is reality essentially one thing or essentially many?

At first glance, these various questions seem like a hodgepodge. What could the nature of human rationality possibly have to do with the question of whether the world is essentially one or many? How do these two questions relate to understanding the difference between objectivity and subjectivity? And—most important of all—*who cares anyway?!*

In this chapter, we will begin our journey into philosophy by exploring the way these various questions all hang together. They are important questions because the way particular individuals and entire cultures answer them can have an enormous practical impact on other people and the natural environment. Ancient tribal societies, for example, give answers to these questions that are quite different from those of societies dominated by science and technology. Indeed, as the reader will see later, one of this book's principal contentions is that patriarchal-industrial civilization has promoted a set of assumptions about rationality and reality that are quite irrational, with devastating consequences for all. But more of this heady contention later.

We will begin our inquiry by using one of philosophy's favorite methods, a "thought experiment." That is, we will consider certain abstract concepts, and note how things turn out differently depending on what elements in the concepts are varied. Using this method, we can at least discover that *if* certain things are true, then certain other things must be true as well. The question then boils down to whether certain initial things are true or not, which can simplify our search for a solution to the larger problem.

The thought experiment that we are about to begin will lead into a discussion of the nature of knowledge, a discussion that will occupy the first half of this chapter. In particular, we will explore the respective roles of subjectivity and objectivity in the knowing process. Once we clarify these roles, we will be in a better position to evaluate the conflicting claims of various philosophers about the nature of knowledge, reality, and language. Our evaluation of their claims will occupy the second half of the chapter.

Because this chapter lays the foundation for the remainder of the book, it necessarily begins with certain concepts of wide scope. Although some of the arguments concerning these concepts may at first seem abstract, they will be much easier to handle if you consider them at an unhurried pace. Speed has become a high priority in the modern era; nonetheless, there is no fast lane on philosophy's road.

Where Do Parts and Wholes Come From?

Let us begin our thought experiment by considering a concept of great generality, namely the concept of *anything* (no matter what) that may be given as an object of someone's sense perception or thought processes. Notice that whatever happens to be given as an object of perception or reflection to someone can equally well be regarded either as one or as many, depending on that person's particular interests. To illustrate this point, consider the following geometrical example: suppose that there are three straight lines on a plane arranged in such a way that any end of any line touches one end, and only one end, of another line (fig. 1, next page). These lines can be regarded as one thing (a

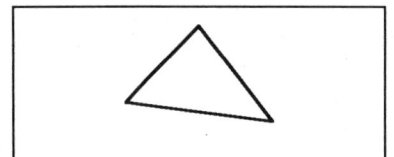

Figure 1
Three Lines on a Plane

"triangle"). Propositions can be made that are true for the triangle as such but which are inapplicable or false for the individual lines as such. For example, the proposition "It has three angles" is true for the triangle but false for each of the lines. Similarly the three-sided figure can be regarded as several lines, and propositions can be made that are true for each of the lines but which are inapplicable or false for the triangle as such. For example, "It is straight." Whether a person makes propositions in this case about one triangle or about several lines depends on that person's particular interests.

An interesting question arises here: what is more basic or more real in our example, the lines that constitute the triangle, or the triangle that is exemplified by the lines? In a certain sense, the three lines are more basic than the triangle—after all, they could just as well be arranged in some other way and yet still exist as lines, although the triangle would be no more. But the triangle is not a nothing, either; it is more than each line or even the mere aggregate of the lines. Consider: if a triangle were nothing more than a mere aggregate of lines, every arrangement of the lines would be a triangle—but that's false! Therefore, although the triangle depends for its existence on the existence of the lines, it is recognizable as an entity above and beyond any or all of the lines as such.

Another interesting question arises: what is it that enables the formation we call a triangle to be a triangle, above and beyond just being a mere aggregate of certain individual lines? Answer: the formation's capacity to have a particular shape, as constituted by the arrangement of certain lines. What, then, enables the formation to have a particular shape? The fact that the lines all exist on a plane. But what is a plane? A flat surface, of course. But what is it about a flat surface that enables lines to constitute something more than mere lines as such? Simply the fact that a flat surface makes it possible for lines to have definite and distinguishable *relations* to each other. Once the range of possibilities for such interrelations is given, lines can form any number of shapes that are more than mere aggregates of lines as such. Among such possible shapes is our triangle. In other words, the triangle can be more than the mere aggregate of its lines because of the range of possibilities for the interrelations of the lines.

Our reflections above on the triangle, its constituent lines, and the way these lines can or cannot be related to each other, raise other questions as well: what makes any whole a whole, and any part a part? And how, in general, are wholes and parts interconnected? To proceed further in dealing with these questions, we need to have clear definitions. Accordingly, any unity that is more than the mere aggregate of its many parts I call a "system," from the Greek word *systema*, meaning an organized whole. The many parts from which the one system is created, and apart from which the system cannot exist, I call its "elements." Finally, the range of possibilities for interrelations among the elements I call their "relational range."

Bearing these definitions in mind, we see that we can completely specify any system as follows: identify its elements, and then indicate which one of the definite and distinguishable possibilities in the relational range the elements exemplify. In the above example, the triangle is the system; the lines, the elements; and the geometry of a two-dimensional plane, the relational range. The system is completely specified by identifying three lines formed into the triangular shape in question.

The elucidation we've just made about systems, elements, and relational ranges is pertinent to our earlier mention of one and many. We found that what is one and what is many is related to the interests of the subject that is perceiving, or reflecting on, the matter at hand. Analogously, the same object of perception or reflection can equally well be regarded as an *element* from one point of view, as a *system* from another.

To develop this point further, consider a slightly more complicated geometrical example. Suppose that 12 straight lines on a plane are so arranged that the following two requirements are met: (1) any end of any line touches one end (and only one end) of another line; and (2) neither more nor less than three lines at a time are ever connected in this way (fig. 2, below). Anyone who views the 12 lines so arranged can regard them as one system of four elements (that is, one system consisting of four triangles); but the viewer can also view each triangle in turn as one system of three elements (that is, one system consisting of three lines). In other words, each triangle can be *both* a system *and* an element: a triangle-system of three line-elements, and a triangle-element in a system of four triangles.

Which of these two ways of viewing, or thinking about, these lines correctly captures reality? Both! If the observer describes what is seen in terms of the interrelations of triangles, triangles will be the elements. If the observer's interest is to describe the relations between the lines in each triangle, then the lines will be the elements. Neither sort of element is more "real" than the other.

This same display of lines could equally well be analyzed in an entirely different way. For example, someone might, for whatever reason, regard the twelve lines as divided into two separate sets consisting of two three-sided figures in each set; the observer would then regard each set itself as an element. The observer might even decide to give sets of this sort their own new name. Let's suppose that the observer calls these new sets "bifurcated sextangles." In this case, the twelve lines is a system of two bifurcated sextangles, not a system of four triangles.

Of course it seems more reasonable to describe this display of lines as a system having four triangles as its elements, rather than two bifurcated sextangles. Why? Because the former description represents the way the display of lines immediately appears to the human eye. But is the way a thing first appears to the human eye necessarily the most useful way of analyzing it? Surely not! For example, it might be useful to describe a bar of gold as a system consisting of billions of interacting atoms. Nonetheless, no atom, either of gold or of any other substance, has ever appeared immediately to the human eye. To the contrary, atoms appear only indirectly, through sophisticated instruments and in the context of an elaborate, presupposed theory of matter.

This example reveals something important: the decisions about what constitute systems and elements in any data scene involve contextual considerations on the part of the observer or thinker. They are not just *given*.

Can we ever be guaranteed of hitting some sort of rock-bottom foundation in dividing systems into elements? No. For any given system of elements, it's always logically possible to regard each element itself as a system of elements, since there is nothing in the notion of element itself that says it must be indivisible. A logically indivisible element would be something so small that we could never conceive of anything smaller. But we can always conceive of something smaller.

Likewise for any given system: it is always logically possible to regard the system as an element in a larger system, for there is nothing in the notion of system itself that says it must be the largest. The largest system, logically speaking, would be something so large that we couldn't conceive of anything larger. But we can always conceive of something larger.

Of course, as a matter of empirical fact, we might come upon an element that cannot be further analyzed because of the limits of the process of empirical observation. Likewise, as a matter of empirical fact, we might come upon a system that is all-inclusive because nothing additional can be observed. But these observational limitations do not imply a *logical* limit to the concept of element and system.

Enter the Interpreter

The above thought experiments have led us to a significant insight, whose implications will reverberate throughout the remainder of this book:

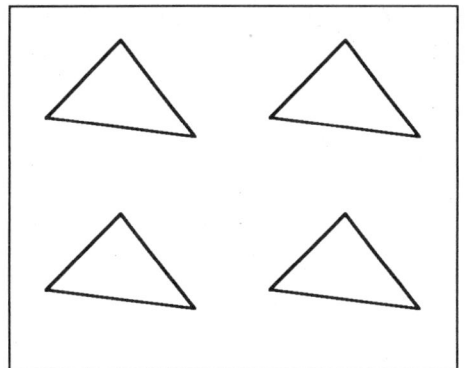

Figure 2
Twelve Lines on a Plane

For any given data scene, what is to be regarded as an element and what is to be regarded as a system depend both on the data scene and also on someone's decision; the data scene in and of itself is insufficient to yield such a determination.

This is *not* to say that the decision determines what is given in the data scene prior to the decision; but the decision does determine what in the data scene is to be classified as system and what is to be classified as element. In the absence of such a decision, a data scene lacks any sort of whole-part structure. The entity (whether human, animal, or machine, etc.) that makes such a decision about element and system for any data scene I call "the interpreter." (Note: I am *not* referring here to the concept of interpretation as it appears in recent deconstructionist literary theory.)[1]

The interpreter's decision about what constitutes system and element in a data scene is not made in a void. For one thing, this decision affects, and is affected by, decisions the interpreter makes about the system's relational range. In the case of our triangle above, the relational range was that of plane geometry (Euclidean geometry); however, there are other kinds of geometry as well (such as Riemannian geometry). The type of geometry we presuppose will affect the way we think about particular objects.

Without a relational range, elements cannot form a system, because a relational range specifies the possibilities open to elements in the manner in which they form a system. Without elements, the possibilities of a relational range cannot be exemplified, because a relational range specifies only what is possible, not what is. Range-decisions and system-decisions mutually affect each other because what *is* is limited by what *can be*, and what *can be* is inferred by interpreters from their observations and reflections upon the varieties of what *is*.

Relativity of Descriptive Analysis

The things we have discovered above about one and many, and about system and element, are important because they illuminate the nature of knowledge. All empirical knowledge of whatever sort depends at some point on descriptive analysis: that is, all empirical knowledge involves at some point propositions made about the way some elements relate to each other in some systems according to some relational ranges.

Without such a scheme of element and system, any data scene is structureless. Why? Because apart from a division into system and elements, nothing has boundaries. (To be bounded *means* to be an element in some system.) Consider this: even to mention an object, we must somehow indicate (that is, somehow *point to*) what that object is. But an object cannot be pointed to apart from any and all context (that is, apart from any and all systems, and hence apart from system-decisions). Pointing, without some background context, either physical or mental, is literally pointless. A solitary finger suspended in a total void has no direction in which to point. (Imagine an eye at the end of the finger in the void. How would it know what direction it is looking in?)

Whenever any object, of whatever sort, is mentioned, some interpreter has already made some decision about elements, systems, and relational ranges; therefore, all empirical knowledge presupposes the making of some such decision. Conclusion:

The interpreter cannot be meaningfully excised from the knowing process.

The *Interpretandum*

So far we've been focusing on the role of the interpreter and its decisions in giving structure to data scenes. But, of course, there's a whole other side to the coin. Any decision made about elements and systems also presupposes the existence of something that is to be interpreted. This thing that confronts the interpreter and elicits a response I call, because of the conciseness of Latin, an *interpretandum* (*interpretanda* in the plural). This word literally means "that-which-is-to-be-interpreted." Whenever interpreters render decisions about elements and systems, they always do so in regard to some pre-given *interpretandum* that confronts them. Without such a reference point, interpretation would have no way to hook onto the world beyond itself, and so would cease to be an interpretation *of* anything.

This concept of an *interpretandum* represents a fine-tuning of our earlier concept of "data scene." Throughout this book, we will return again and again to the conceptual components of interpretation, further fine-tuning them each time. Thus does philosophy proceed (as Aristotle somewhere says) from the obvious and simple to the recondite and complex.

The essential link between interpretation and the *interpretandum* is what keeps interpretation from sailing off into unreality. That is, interpretation, by the very meaning of the term, is always *about* something and always *prompted by* something (at least about, and prompted by, some aspect of the interpreter itself, if nothing else). If the interpreter were in every respect strictly identical with the *interpretandum*, interpretation simply would not occur in any meaningful sense of the term. The very concept of interpretation, therefore, invites further inquiry into the nature of the *interpretandum* that confronts the interpreter.

In sum, once any interpreter makes any decision about systems and elements, the mere act of doing so implies two things: (1) there is an *interpretandum* (data-scene) that is not strictly the same as the interpreter; (2) the *interpretandum* has evoked a response from the interpreter.

Where, then, has all this abstract theorizing gotten us? We've made an important discovery: to analyze is at least to divide some *interpretandum* in accordance with some scheme of part and whole; and to describe is to make propositions at least specifying some interrelations among the elements. We have also discovered that the very possibility for the existence of any such scheme of element and system depends on three irreducible factors: an *interpretandum*, an interpreter, and a decision.

Empirical knowledge, therefore, is not a matter of an objective world existing completely independent of all interpretation, nor is it a matter of pure subjectivity. Rather, empirical knowledge necessarily involves both a given *interpretandum* for, *and* an interpretive decision by, some interpreter. Remove either the *interpretandum* or the interpreter, and empirical knowledge disappears.

We can now see the error of those who say that there can be some sort of absolute empirical knowledge valid for all, at least in theory, if only the tools of observation be precise enough. In fact, the above considerations show that empirical knowledge is always knowledge relative to some interpreter or some group of interpreters. We can also see the error of those who say that reality is of their own making. In fact, whenever we make any kind of interpretation, we assume the existence of some *interpretandum* given to us prior to interpretation. Contrary to both these erroneous claims, all knowledge rests on interpretation, and all interpretation involves *both* an interpreter *and* an *interpretandum*.

The Interpreter's Response Patterns

What sorts of things affect the way in which an interpreter makes a decision about the scheme of elements and system? The *interpretandum*, of course, is crucial—a fact often overlooked by deconstructionists, as noted earlier. Interpreters, by continually knocking their heads against *interpretanda*, proceed to construct for themselves a view of the world. By virtue of such knocks, the *interpretandum* naturally affects the decisions that any interpreter may make about elements and system, and for a very simple reason: any interpreter that cannot adapt its decisions to these knocks is not likely to survive.

But there is a whole other side to interpretation. What is often overlooked, especially by admirers of science, are factors that stem from the side of the interpreter. One such factor is the physical structure of the interpreter. For example, a computer has certain definite capacities, depending on its internal electrical components. Likewise a human being has definite quantities of different kinds of cells in his or her brain and central nervous system. In the case of both the computer and the human, there will be both capacities for, and limits to, decision-making determined by the entity's given physical structure. The same is also true for other life forms. Consider the many different ways in which different animals spontaneously interpret the flux of impressions as elements and system. A dolphin, for example, can "see" inside the bodies of other dolphins by virtue of its in-built sonogramming abilities; a fly, on the other hand, has compound eyes; and an octopus, one eye. For any given interpreter of any kind—whether natural or artificial, human or animal—certain parameters of interpretation are preset by the physical structure of that interpreter.

An interpreter's own physical structure thus sets limits for what may be called the interpreter's primary response pattern. In the case of a new-born human being, the primary response pattern is a system of instinctive physical reflexes. All subsequent interactions of the human being with his or her environment build on this initial system of reflexes.

Humans also have secondary response patterns, namely those learned cultural patterns of response that are so common and ingrained in the dominant culture as to become automatic in the individual. These secondary response patterns can vary considerably. For example, popular Greek culture in the early first millennium B.C. viewed natural phenomena as if they were embodiments of living entities with whom humans could personally communicate (animism).

A memorable example of this type of responding appears in a scene of Homer's *Odyssey*. The shipwrecked Odysseus, struggling to keep his head above swirling ocean waves off the rugged Phaiakian coast, catches sight of an inland stream descending to a calm sea inlet. As the current moves him along, he speaks to the stream as he would to a living being:

> Hear me, oh lord, whoever you are.
> With a great imploring do I come to you,
> In flight from the scourge of Poseidon's sea.
> Even immortals show their respect
> To whoever of men may come as wanderers,
> As I myself, having suffered much,
> Come now to your stream and invoke your aid.
> Have mercy, lord. Accept your suppliant.[2]

By way of contrast, patriarchal-industrial cultures of the late second millennium A.D. typically regard other living beings as if they were nonliving or dead (mortism). For example, experimentation on living animals—often involving excruciating pain to these subjects while under the unfeeling eyes of human experimenters—has become a regular feature of this epoch, not to mention the driving into extinction of entire species, and the general befoulment of air, water, and soil. All these phenomena presuppose an underlying cultural response pattern whereby humans respond to other animals and the earth itself as mere things. From the point of view of the surrounding natural environment, the "nature" of human interpreters has thus been as effectively defined by dominant cultural conditioning (secondary response pattern) as by genetically triggered reflexes (primary response pattern).

In addition to the primary response pattern determined by genes and the secondary pattern imposed by culture, human beings also have the capacity to develop their own idiosyncratic response patterns. These emerge from their unique life experiences. Hence it is quite possible that a merchant, for example, will interpret the same *interpretandum* quite differently from a visionary poet, as William Blake describes with characteristic wit and insight:

> "What," it will be Question'd, "When the Sun rises, do you not see a round disk of fire somewhat like a Guinea?" O no, no, I see an Innumerable company of the Heavenly host crying, "Holy, Holy, Holy, is the Lord God Almighty."[3]

Common response patterns (such as those occasioned by one's genes or culture) promote the likelihood of common decisions among interpreters in regard to systems, elements, and relational ranges in the *interpretanda* that confront them. To the extent that different interpreters respond to *interpretanda* with common decisions, to the same extent will they experience a kind of interpretational commonality. Common response patterns followed by common decisions thus allow for the creation of a commonly accepted system of reality—in short, a public world.

Although the sharing of primary and secondary response patterns promotes the likelihood of common interpretations, there is no guarantee that most interpreters will make the same decisions in every case. Indeed, it is possible for there to exist a considerable variety of interpretational systems within the same overall culture. Some will be nearly the same, some generally overlapping, and some irreconcilable. In our own culture, for example, we see on one hand the fundamentalist Christian view that the universe is a hierarchy consisting of God, angels, humans, animals, and demons. We also see the contrary view of many 20th-century physicists, that all reality is reducible to energy fields and subatomic particles. Barring a subsequent concurrence on basic interpretational decisions, these two views of reality are not likely to find common ground.

As noted earlier, the possibility for commonality of interpretation does not all stem from the side of the interpreters. The *interpretanda* themselves also provide bases for such commonality. There is, however, a catch. If a commonality among *interpretanda* exists before interpreters make any interpretations, that commonality cannot be known to be such until the *interpretanda* are actually interpreted. The reason, as we saw above, is that no interpreter can extract actual knowledge from any *interpretandum* without first interpreting it. Because we all behold so many different creatures interactively inhabiting one great common world of nature, we are justified in presupposing that deep commonalities exist in reality prior to any interpretations we might make of it. In any particular case, however, we can never delineate with absolute precision how much of the commonality comes from the side of our interpretations and how much from the side of the *interpretandum*. This limitation introduces ineradicable complications into any effort to apprehend the nature of reality.

We are now in a position to see that the commonly used phrase "the real world," in the sense of one, absolute, universal standard for all, regardless of interpreters' particular circumstances, is an over-simplification. *Interpretanda* are certainly real, but we can know them only insofar as we interpret them. As a result, there are as many irreducibly different views of reality as there are separately constructed interpretive interplays between interpreters and *interpretanda*. To the extent that such interpretive constructions happen to overlap (as, for example among human beings, and particularly so among human beings commonly enculturated) there will, of course, be common world-views. Even so, however, there will always also remain a genuine plurality with varying degrees of overlap. Far from being a monolithic monochrome, "the real world" (to push the metaphor a bit) is rather more like a rainbow. It contains various bands of color that gradually fuse into each other to form one great spectacle, yet these colors are also clearly distinguishable in their own right.

Reality Maps

Whenever any interpreter consciously makes any decision about a given *interpretandum*, the making of that decision always presupposes some previously made set of decisions about elements and systems. The scope of these previous decisions is either expanded, diminished, or redefined by the new decision. Without some such previously made set of decisions (at least preconsciously made), no conscious interpretive act is possible. The reason is that the interpreter, if completely lacking any prior context of interpretations, would simply have no criterion of differentiation vis-à-vis the flux of impressions encountered, and to lack the ability to differentiate is to lack the ability to interpret. Any interpreter in this fix would have no sufficient cause or adequate criterion for "seeing" any given part of the *interpretandum* as one thing rather than another—which means that everything within the *interpretandum*, and indeed the *interpretandum* itself in its entirety, would remain a blur to the interpreter.

As discussed above, the interpreter's previously made set of decisions about systems and elements is fashioned by layered influences—on the surface by idiosyncratic response patterns, and more deeply by secondary (cultural) and primary (genetic) patterns. That most basic (in the sense of least changing and most arresting) set of decisions which any interpreter has made about systems, elements, and relational ranges I call the interpreter's "reality map." By "least changing" here I mean most deeply embedded in, and most basic to, the complex of all previously made interpretations; and by "most arresting" I mean most emotionally gripping (for interpreters, that is, that are capable of experiencing emotions).

In regard to the last point, it is quite possible for a human interpreter to make a decision about *interpretanda* that is so emotionally colored (as in a "conversion experience") that it will influence most subsequent interpretations as much as an older but less intensely felt set of decisions. And even short of such an extreme instance, most human decisions have emotional associations that in some way determine for the interpreter what is important or interesting or exciting or threatening in subsequently encountered *interpretanda*. Indeed, without such an aptitude for emotional associations, human beings would have a most difficult time getting through a day of ordinary life, let alone creating a great work of art or scholarship. We arrive, then, at an important insight:

For interpreters that are capable of having emotions, reality maps always have an emotional charge; therefore, reality for them always has an irreducible emotional content.

Hence we can see how short-sighted it is for any philosophical system to attempt to construct a model either of knowledge or of reality that is utterly separate in principle from feeling. The human capacity to know anything is of a piece with the human capacity to have emotions.

Like any other map, one's reality map is a guide used for getting around in the world, but in this case "getting around" means making sense out of the flux of feelings and sensations that are encountered when interacting with any and all *interpretanda*. Again like any other map, this one also is a *construction*; that is, it is created in time from a long series of interactions between interpreter and *interpretanda*, and is constantly subject to changes and revisions as a result of these interactions. More so than other maps, however, one's reality map contains a large section determined by previous decisions arising from the interpreter's genetic structure and from uncritical decisions arising from dominant cultural patterns. It is unique in the sense that it is the map of last resort, the guide for answering all questions about the kinds of things that ultimately exist in the world and about what is possible and impossible.

But as it is important with other maps not to confuse the map with the terrain, so with one's reality map. The most basic and arresting set of decisions that an interpreter makes about elements, systems, and relational ranges is not the same thing as either the *interpretanda* themselves or the process of overall interaction between interpreter and *interpretanda* that first gives rise to that basic set of decisions. The pre-interpreted interactions of any organism with its environment can never be fully interpreted by a finitely interpreting organism, that is, by any organism whose interpretations do not themselves constitute the whole of its possible interactions. Hence it follows that for any finitely interpreting organism, its reality map is incomplete and fallible. As a result, there can never be, as some philosophers have longed for, a knowledge that is completely certain and a world that is completely objective. Like the oceanic deep, life itself will always elude the farthest cast of our intellect's finest nets, however interesting at times may be the catch these nets bring to the surface.

Conflicts Between Reality Maps

Since it is possible for differing interpreters to have different reality maps, the question naturally arises as to how conflicts between these different maps are to be resolved. If the differences are extreme, it may not be possible to reach any kind of resolution. In the most extreme cases of all, the interpreters may come to view each other as insane. Unless at least one of the interpreters makes accommodating changes in his or her map, the "resolution" that results may be the violent imposition by one interpreter of his or her map on the other.

If an entire group of interpreters shares a reality map that is at odds with that of a given individual, the group may try to coerce the individual into changing his or her map, especially if the non-conforming individual is perceived as dangerous to the group. If, on the other hand, an individual interpreter has a position of power over a group as a whole, he or she may try to coerce the group, especially if the interpreter perceives the group's reality map as subversive to his or her power. Hence radical differences in reality maps can be contributing factors (among many others) to the tension between peer group and individual dissident, and between insulated ruler and populace.

In the case of radical differences in reality maps between entire groups, especially when occurring in the context of a struggle for power, the matter is often resolved by an appeal to mass violence, however much such violence may be masked in the language of law, morality, religion, or mental health. In such cases, that reality map is most likely to prevail of the group that is most effective in applying violence in forwarding its own self-interests. For example, the dominant reality map of 20th-century North America has proved to be that of the white European invaders of the last few centuries, not that of the indigenous Indians. The reason is that most of the Indians were exterminated.

These considerations show that reality maps do not exist in a vacuum but always in the context of real individuals and groups who are interconnected through a complicated maze of historical forces. As the example above of the

European-Indian conflict shows, the question of which reality map is to prevail is sometimes resolved by massive violence—which may or may not have anything at all to do with a given reality map's intrinsic value (whatever that may mean).

In most cases, however, conflicts between differing reality maps are neither so grave that each side considers the other insane nor so laden with mutual fear that each tries to destroy the other. Most often it turns out that those in conflict actually share a considerable overlap of their respective reality maps, which is to be expected for interpreters who are members of the same species and raised in the same culture. For conflicts in this context, dialogue is possible based on the shared portion of the overlapping maps. Starting from a jointly-agreed-upon body of propositions describing systems, elements, and relational ranges, each side will try to show the other that any further proposition with which it disagrees is inconsistent with the propositions thus jointly accepted. Such dialogue can become enormously complicated, as witnessed by the historical debates between philosophers. This complexity runs deep, since many of the decisions made in constructing a human reality map are preconscious, and since every reality map, reflecting the complexity of life itself, is necessarily incomplete and even contradictory.

Group conflicts involving reality maps have been essential ingredients even in the case of science, as noted by Thomas Kuhn in his classic study *The Structure of Scientific Revolutions*. Kuhn shows that science is not just a straightforward matter of testing hypotheses against empirical data, as is commonly assumed. Rather, the actual history of science demonstrates that any particular science always involves what Kuhn calls a "paradigm." By this term he means (in the widest sense) some core system of beliefs and values about reality that are shared by a particular community of scientists:

> It [the paradigm] functions by telling the scientist about the entities that nature does and does not contain and about the ways in which those entities behave. That information provides a map whose details are elucidated by mature scientific research. ...That map is as essential as observation and experiment to science's continuing development. Through the theories they embody, paradigms prove to be constitutive of the research activity.[4]

Kuhn demonstrates that great breakthroughs in science have always involved what he calls a "paradigm shift." That is, some particular community of scientists will typically encounter serious anomalies that cannot be accounted for by their existing paradigm. Eventually this community will convert to a new paradigm (as in the shift from Newtonian to Einsteinian physics). This paradigm shift, however, is not itself a matter of "normal science." Why? Because the criteria of scientific normality are themselves the question at issue in a paradigm shift. How, then, is such a question to be resolved? Kuhn never fully answers this question, but his book rightly emphasizes an important irony: the greatest breakthroughs in science have always involved crucial interpretive decisions about reality that are not themselves scientifically normal at the time they are made.

The fact that science depends on paradigms does not mean that science is a mere social construct, as social-constructivists sometimes intimate.[5] On the contrary, science certainly does reveal certain aspects of reality. Nonetheless, science, like every cognitive endeavor, is able to disclose reality only through some set of interpretational lenses. Even in the case of science, the interpreter cannot be excised from the knowing process.

Correlativity of Objectivity and Subjectivity

Even if all human interpreters, of whatever sort, agreed on one reality map, there would be no guarantee whatever that such a map would be "objectively correct," as that phrase is commonly understood. For example, if it could somehow be shown that every human being on the earth shared a certain core system of interpretations, would such a common reality map necessarily agree with that of an interpreter from another galaxy who might happen to land here? No, especially if the visiting interpreter possessed a radically different gene system and came from a radically different type of culture, both of which would be likely. There might be some or no overlap with the map of such a being, but anything approaching unanimity would be unlikely.

The very notion that one reality map must be "objectively correct for everybody" is a fallacy, since every reality map emerges as a complex result of some interpreter's history of interactions with some *interpretanda*; that is, every reality map is a reality map *for some interpreter or for some group of interpreters*, created through the previous interpretations, both preconscious and otherwise, of the interpreters. Of all the interpretations that a given interpreter has made, there will be some that the interpreter is most inclined to take for granted (for humans, this means genetically determined and culturally conditioned interpretations). These least-questioned interpretations will be "objective"—*for that interpreter*. All other interpretations for that interpreter will be contingent, fanciful, impossible, etc.

Furthermore, there can be no such thing as a knowable world completely independent of interpretation; as we have seen, to be known is to be interpreted, at least to the extent of having some elements, systems, and relational ranges specified. Ironically, if anything were completely objective, it would also be completely unknowable, since complete objectivity means the absence of interpretation.

Likewise there can be no such thing as a completely subjective interpretation, since interpretation is always *of* or *about* something. If an interpreter has absolutely no interaction with any pre-existing *interpretandum* (at least the interpreter itself as a *interpretandum*), then there is no interpretation *of* anything. Therefore, there cannot be any subjectivity, at least if subjectivity means having one's own interpretation of something. If a human interpreter were completely subjective, he or she could never even use, either explicitly or implicitly, the word "I," since an awareness of "I" presupposes an awareness of the correlative "not-I," and vice-versa. Just as there can be no pure objectivity that is knowable, so there can be no pure subjectivity that is meaningful.

Since "I" and "the world" are strictly correlative, it is impossible to maintain that either of these is "more real" or "more basic" than the other, or that one is the mere after-effect of the other. If, moreover, one posits some kind of radical dichotomy between "I" and "the world," the problem immediately arises as to how any parallelism can exist between the spheres thus separated, and hence how any interpreter can interact with and know any world. To solve this last problem, one might resort to arguing either that the world is merely the idea of the "I", or that the "I" is a mere mechanical result of the world. But both these arguments run afoul of the inescapable logical correlativity of "I" and "the world," as noted above.

These considerations show that those philosophers are wrong who begin with "the objective world" as the first fact of reality, just as those philosophers are wrong who begin with "the subjective ego." The former can never establish the reality of subjective experience, since for them all reality derives from externality; the latter, on the other hand, can never reach the external world, since for them all reality comes from within. Contrary to both, we insist on this truth:

> The first fact of known reality is always some interpreter interacting with some *interpretandum*.

To remove any of these three—the interpreter, the *interpretandum*, the interaction—is to remove all three, since they are all correlative notions. Hence either there is no knowledge and no world, or else there is at least some interpreter, some *interpretandum*, and some interaction. (And if there is no knowledge, then there can be no knowledge that there is no knowledge.)

Here, then, is our major conclusion so far:

> Objectivity and subjectivity, although real, are but two sides of that which is the major coin in the realm of knowledge—interpretation.

First Interpretations

Although plausible, the above account of knowledge involves a serious difficulty, which might be called the problem of first interpretations. We have noted the key role played in all interpretation by the interpreter's reality map, which emerges from genetic, cultural, and idiosyncratic influences on the interpreter. In rendering any interpretation, the interpreter in effect applies, either consciously or preconsciously, some pre-existing reality map to some pre-given flux of impressions in order to divide the latter into systems and elements. It would seem then that, until such time as the interpreter applies a reality map, any given flux of impressions is completely uninterpreted.

Here is the problem: if a pre-given flux of impressions is absolutely indeterminate and devoid of all characterization (that is, completely uninterpreted), how can the interpreter even be aware of its presence in the first place? To say that something is absolutely devoid of all characterization is to say that it can be neither perceived nor conceived, since both perceiving and conceiving are always of *something*, that is, of that which is in some way characterizable. To be utterly devoid of characterization is the same as to be nothing. Hence we must conclude that the presence of a completely uninterpreted flux of impressions could not be detected by an interpreter. Even if the interpreter could be minimally aware of the presence of a completely uninterpreted flux of impressions, another problem emerges: how could he or she possibly pick out any features in the terrain of this flux and then compare them to his or her reality map, when the terrain, apart from the map, is considered to be utterly featureless?

Impressions

To answer these questions, let us examine the very first steps of the interpretational process. In order for any interpreter to make a first interpretation, certain conditions must be met. As we saw above, the interpreter must have something that is to be interpreted—an initial *interpretandum*—since an interpretation is always an interpretation *of* something. This initial *interpretandum* must provide the interpreter with something that the interpreter can latch onto, even though the *interpretandum* has as yet no structure; otherwise, interpretation would never have a foothold. But this something cannot be anything that itself presupposes an act of interpretation. What, then, is this initial, pre-interpreted something?

To answer this question, we need to understand the distinction between interactions and impressions. Any entity at all can have interactions with its environment. When, however, some entity has interactions with its environment that it can use for making decisions about systems and elements in its environment, then, and only then, is that entity an interpreter. Let us focus on these interactions that an entity has with its environment, and by which the entity characterizes its environment. We will call these interactions "impressions."

For interactions that are impressions, the affected entity has the ability to manipulate the effects of the change to itself in a way that is independent of the control of the source of that change. At the same time, however, the entity is also able to relate the effects of the change back to their source. So impressions are the kind of interactions that leave a lasting mark or aftereffect of their source on the entity. This characteristic of impressions is aptly suggested by the Latin noun *impressio* (the source of our English "impression"). *Impressio* literally means "the-leaving-of-a-mark" upon something, derived from the Latin verb *imprimere*, "to press into."

There is more: the mark that is left on the entity from an impression must be such that the mark has some sort of referential function; that is, the mark must somehow have the capacity to point back, beyond itself, to the source from which it came. An entity, by the very act of using its impressions to make decisions about what constitute systems and elements in the *interpretandum*, presupposes that these impressions have such a referential function; otherwise, the entity would not be making a decision *about* anything; it would merely be interacting, not interpreting.

Without the presupposition of some kind of referential function, we could conclude only that the entity has interactions, never impressions. Therefore, we are led to this conclusion: either (1) there are no such things as impressions and interpretations (but only interactions); or (2) if impressions and interpretations exist, there must also be some kind of after-effects or marks with some kind of referential function.

Why, then, should we suppose that impressions and interpretations exist in the first place? As discussed above, if knowledge and a knowable world are assumed to exist, then an interpretational process must also be assumed; an interpretational process, in turn, presupposes the existence of impressions. Therefore, we conclude: either there is no knowledge and no knowable world, or else impressions with referential functions exist.

Now if there is no knowledge and no knowable world, then there can be no knowledge that there is no knowledge and no knowable world. (To know that we know nothing is a contradiction in terms.) In sum: if we claim to have any knowledge at all, we must have at least some impressions with some referential functions. These impressions that have a referential function constitute our sought-after "something" that the interpreter can latch onto when making first interpretations.

How does this referential function work? Three factors are involved: (1) the source (the environment of the entity), which is able to generate an effect from itself; (2) the effect, which is able to become (or leave) an after-effect on the entity; and (3) the entity, which is able to respond to the after-effect as a thing that *arises from* the environment and that somehow *points to* the environment.

Of the above three factors, the most important, in regard to distinguishing interactions from impressions, is (3). The receiving entity must have the ability to act *as if* the after-effects both arise from and point to the environment. I say "act as if" because there cannot be any question of knowledge on the part of the entity at this point, since we are here examining the presuppositions for having the very first bits of knowledge.

The only way, at the very beginning, for an affected entity to know that an after-effect has a kind of referential function is simply for the affected entity to act in such a way that the after-effect has such a function. Any interaction that occurs between the environment and the affected entity, and which precedes the entity's first use of the after-effects of that interaction, must forever fall below the threshold of knowledge for that entity. Hence we reach this conclusion:

> The ultimate nature of the root connection between interpreter and *interpretandum* is unknowable.

This conclusion is just another way of saying that all knowledge presupposes interpretation. It still leaves this question: What does it mean for the receiving entity to act in such a way that the after-effects have a referential function? Answer: The entity must so act that it uses the after-effects to begin constructing, either consciously or preconsciously, either with effort or spontaneously, a view of the world.

But how can the entity *know*, during its very first interpretations, that the after-effects do in fact point to a world? The entity cannot, and for two interconnected reasons: (1) as discussed above, there is no sense in speaking of an absolutely objective world that exists independent of the interpretational process; and (2) there cannot, by definition, be any knowledge prior to the emergence of the prerequisites for knowledge.

In the beginning, the interpreter simply *acts*. Through this primal action, the interpreter first engages a world whose structure it cannot yet see. From this first engagement flows all subsequent interpretation, and therefore all knowledge. Whatever deep connection there may be prior to this first engagement must remain forever unknowable.

Up to this point, the word "impression" has been used somewhat ambiguously, to denote both the process whereby an environment leaves an after-effect on an entity, and also the after-effect that is left. To avoid possible confusion in what follows, the word "impression" will have a more restricted sense, to denote only the process of leaving the after-effect, and not the after-effect itself. The latter, as that which *points to* the environment from which it was generated, we will call the "sign."

Using this terminology, we summarize our conclusion this way: Entities are affected by interactions with their environments. Some entities have the capacity to use some after-effects of these interactions as if they were signs. Those that do so have the potential for interpretation.

Anticipations of Experience

One further qualification is necessary: The mere capacity for having a flux of impressions (or, more accurately, a flux of signs) is not in itself sufficient to allow an entity to interpret. Why? Because at this point in our analysis, there is as yet no sufficient cause within the signs themselves for the entity to divide them into one particular system of elements rather than any other. Since no sign has as yet been interpreted, and so no causal context of any kind established, how could it be otherwise? In order to take the first step in the interpretational process, therefore, an entity must initiate, on its own, some decision, however arbitrary, as to systems and elements.

Having acted thus, an entity must also *remember* this arbitrary decision, for only so will it have an interpretational context for continued interpretations of signs coming from the environment. That is to say, only so will the environment become a continuous *interpretandum*, and the entity, a continuous *interpreter*. Otherwise, all that remains is a flash, so to speak, of a momentary environment and an equally momentary proto-interpreter. Henceforth, however, after having not only made but also remembered this initial arbitrary decision, the entity will not only interact but also interpret. Why? Because the entity will be able to put its successive interactions into a continuous interpretive context, which can in turn be changed by these successive interactions. In this way the entity becomes a continuous interpreter, and its interpretations, a continuous world-view.

But what does it mean "to put into an interpretive context," when speaking of a future *interpretandum* that is previously unknown? How can that which is utterly unknown be put into any context at all? Only if in some way it is tentatively assumed or guessed to have some features, and if this assumption or guess can subsequently be tested. In other words, for an interpreter with a memory to put an unknown future *interpretandum* into context can only mean this: to anticipate at least some features of the unknown *interpretandum* by means of some features in the interpreter's memory. Unless such anticipation is presupposed, there is no way for an interpreter to apply its memory to a new, uninterpreted *interpretandum*, and hence no way to extend the interpretational process to the future or to a changing environment.

Hence every interpreter initially encounters a new, unknown *interpretandum* through a filter of experiential anticipations. These phenomena are "anticipations" because they prefigure the new *interpretandum* (both in the sense of coming before and giving shape to); and they are "experiential" because they derive from past experience and also apply to future experience.

Experiential anticipations can vary widely, depending on the particular circumstances of the interpretive encounter. As an example of a rather limited kind of anticipation, consider a human interpreter who is accustomed to be awakened every morning by the sound of an alarm clock ringing at 7:15. On one particular morning, this interpreter's central nervous system is stimulated by the sound of a bell ringing at 7:15. She awakens and interprets the *interpretandum* as follows: "The alarm clock is ringing. I will reach over and turn it off." She does so, only to discover that she has forgotten to set the clock the night before. How, then, can the alarm be ringing? A moment of confusion follows until, reinterpreting the *interpretandum*, she realizes that it is her phone that is ringing.

In the above case, the pre-given flux of signs (the stimulus to the interpreter's central nervous system at 7:15 a.m.) is not devoid of all characterization to the interpreter. On the contrary, because of the interpreter's anticipations derived from past experiences, the *interpretandum* presents itself for interpretation with certain familiar features (the alarm clock is ringing). But in this case, the interpreter, after interacting with more features of the total *interpretandum*, makes a reinterpretation: the phone, and not the alarm clock, is ringing.

The above example of an interpretive encounter is not unusual. In every act of interpretation for human interpreters, from carrying out daily wake-up functions to developing theories in subatomic physics, the pre-given *interpretandum* is always to some extent pre-interpreted by virtue of the interpreter's experiential anticipations derived from his or her past history and genetic constitution. The interpreter will always have these experiential anticipations because he or she will always have had some previous experience, whether genetic, cultural, or idiosyncratic. Interpretation, therefore, is really a matter of a never-ending process of *re*interpretation.

In some cases, the experiential anticipations can be of a much grander scope and be far more deeply entrenched than in the above wake-up scene. For example, in all cases of ordinary human interactions with a day-to-day environment, *interpretanda* are anticipated to be unidirectionally ordered in time and to contain objects positioned in mutually exclusive positions in space. (That is, time moves forward, and no two objects can be in the same place at the same time.) These considerations, however, are not some kind of *a priori* conditions for the possibility of human experience, as some philosophers have held, but merely well established experiential anticipations for human interpreters in ordinary situations. There is no reason in the nature of things why humans may not find certain kinds of experiences at odds with these anticipations, however seemingly well founded they may be in ordinary daily experience. As a matter of fact, late twentieth-century quantum mechanics holds that in certain subatomic interactions particles may be logically interpreted as moving backwards in time. This interpretation, though consistent with the current findings of physics, is clearly contrary to previous "common sense." Nonetheless, it may yet turn out to be correct.

The Imaginative Basis of All Objectivity

The fact that experiential anticipations are a necessary part of every interpretation means that an act of *imagination* is likewise a necessary part of every interpretation. Such a consequence follows from the very meaning of experiential anticipation: to anticipate experientially means to have at hand, for the purpose of imparting order to an oncoming flux of signs, some interpretational structure derived from past interpretations. Depending on the outcome of subsequent interpretations, the interpretational structure at hand may then be modified and as such made available for ordering additional fluxes of signs.

This very act of creating, keeping available, and changing structures for the ordering of fluxes of signs is what constitutes an act of imagination; that is, to imagine is to have the ability to construct, remember, and modify hypothetical interpretational structures. In the case of ethical ideals (discussed in chapter two), acts of imagination play a different role than in empirical description. The reason: in ethics the imagination creates hypothetical interpretational structures against which actual *interpretanda* themselves are judged (rather than vice-versa). Nonetheless, both ethics and empirical description, however much they may otherwise differ, share this commonality: they both involve an irreducible element of imagination.

From previous considerations, we have seen that all empirical knowledge is based on interpretation. From the immediately foregoing, we have seen both that all interpretation involves experiential anticipations, and that all experiential anticipations involve acts of imagination. Therefore, an important conclusion follows:

> All empirical knowledge involves an act of imagination.

There remains a crucial and irreducible element of the interpreter's imagination in every depiction of "the objective world." Hence any effort to erect an absolute wall between knowledge and imagination, as some philosophers have tried to do, is a fatal misunderstanding of the interpretational process.

To say, however, that there remains an irreducible element of imagination in every depiction of the objective world is *not* to deny a meaningful distinction between "the objective" and "the imaginary." "The objective," in a public sense, always means "that which is objective for some group of interpreters"; moreover, "the imaginary" can be of widely different degrees, from the minimal level in the analysis above to the purely fanciful, say, in drug-induced visions.

Group Objectivity

To appreciate the importance of these distinctions, we need to bear in mind the nature of group-defined objectivity. Groups of interpreters, when confronted by *interpretanda*, construct shared reality maps and criteria for propositional evaluation. These maps and criteria are influenced by the *interpretanda*, and also by the shared genetic structures and enculturated values of the interpreters. Using these shared maps and criteria, groups construct a common view of the *interpretanda* that confront them. That is, they construct a world-view that is objective—for *them*.

For example, human interpreters who also happen to be professional subatomic physicists share a view of the world based on the atomic data that confront them, and also on the following: their common possession of a peculiar type of central nervous system (that of the animal *homo sapiens*) and a peculiar set of enculturated values (the reality map and criteria for propositional evaluation taught in professional schools of physics). Using their central nervous systems, reality maps, and criteria for propositional evaluation, professional subatomic physicists interpret atomic data, and evaluate proffered propositions descriptive of these data. They accept some of these descriptive propositions as valid and reject others. By so doing, they necessarily create and use, through acts of imagination, experiential anticipations that have in the past been derived from, and that will in the future be modified by, interpretations of *interpretanda*. Hence they use *imagination* for the construction of a shared view of the world. Hence also their shared view of the world is *objective*—for them.

Of course, as has been frequently noted before, there is no guarantee that the world that is objective for human beings who happen to be subatomic physicists will also be objective for other groups of interpreters who are neither humans nor subatomic physicists. "Objectivity," in a public sense, is just another word for group interpretation, and all interpretation, whether by groups or individuals, is based in part on imagination. Trudy the Bag Lady sums up the matter like this:

> After all, what is reality anyway? Nothin' but a collective hunch.[6]

Imagination and Artistic Interpretation

Although imagination has a certain role to play in mathematics and the sciences, it finds a more ample stage for itself in the arts, and particularly so in the fine arts as they have developed since the Romantic period. In writing a novel, performing a concerto, or sculpting a statue, interpreters generally make a more playful use of their experiential anticipations than they do in proving a logical theorem or conducting a scientific experiment.

In artistic endeavors, interpreters are "imaginative," as that word is now popularly understood. Artists allow themselves more leeway for *modifying* their repertoire of experiential anticipations (that is, the resultant structure of experience that has presented itself to them from their previous history of interpretations). As a result, experiential anticipations in the arts can be valued for their playful innovativeness, rather than regarded as ideals by which to judge further behavior (as in ethics) or as hypotheses to be tested against further observation (as in the sciences).

Hence those philosophers are wrong who maintain that the artistic endeavor is merely one of "imitation." And they are wrong to say that the artist, as one who merely imitates nature or reality, is somehow inferior to those who truly behold the real world as it is in itself (the philosopher or the scientist). On the contrary, the artist is not merely imitative but also *expressive*: he or she creates a kind of new world, as it were, in every new piece made, because the new piece creates, to some extent, its own rules for giving context to feelings, perceptions, and reflections.

This "giving context to" is the very nature of every interpretative process; however, in the arts the giving-of-context is a more flexible process, since the artist is often less limited by group standards of interpretation ("objectivity") than is the moralist or the scientist. As a consequence, the artist is more free to draw on idiosyncratic abilities and experiences to create a new standard of reality, the work itself. At their best, artists personify the interpretative process at its most creative, a striking demonstration of the fact that to interpret is to create a kind of world.

On the other hand, however, artists are also historically and genetically conditioned; therefore, they have reality maps and values reflective of their particular genetic structure and enculturation. Like achievements in the sciences, works of art are also part of the weave of history and so are reflective of many historical contexts, apart from which they cannot be fully appreciated or even minimally understood. Without years of diligent study, no composer could ever write a serious piece of music that is intelligible to his or her contemporaries.

Ironically, therefore, the more an artist strives for interpretational autonomy, the less likely will he or she be understood or appreciated by contemporaries, since most human interpreters in any historical period interpret all reality, whether artistic or otherwise, through prevailing conventions. On the other hand, the more an artist strives for conventionality of interpretation, the less likely will he or she be remembered by later ages, since the ordinary tends to be forgotten, unless it is retrospectively viewed as a kind of generic sample. Accordingly, works of art that are of the most lasting influence tend to be those that are sufficiently conventional in interpretation to appeal to some influential segment of the public at the time of their making (thereby surviving the present) but also sufficiently innovative to break through or redefine those conventions (thereby finding their way to the future). When successful in redefining conventions, a work of art then becomes itself part of a new set of conventions, which later works likewise both use and in turn redefine, and so on for the life of any definable artistic movement.

Impossibility of Absolute Artistic Standards

It should be clear why there can never be absolutely objective standards of "good art" or "bad art." Artistic conventions are constantly changing, and every work of art can only be fully appreciated by understanding the context of conventions in which it emerged and the manner in which it either adopted or redefined these conventions.

Despite the changeability of convention, however, rational dialogue concerning works of art is still possible. Groups of interpreters can have a common understanding of conventions and styles and can debate the manner in which individual works of art exemplify, deny, or change the same. But all such artistic criticism can only be comparative, descriptive, or expressive, never *pre*scriptive in an absolute sense.

To assume that there is a realm of absolute objective standards for "the beautiful" is as irrational as to claim that there is a self-subsistent "realm of ideas," and for the same reason: interpretation, of whatever nature, is always historically conditioned, in that it presupposes the existence of interpreters, and interpreters always have a particular history and a particular memory.

Indeed, artistic criticism can itself become an art form and so have conventions and redefinitions of convention in its own right, just like any other art form, and thereby become subject to a kind of meta-criticism (as in the foregoing paragraphs). Moreover, as has been often implied above in other contexts, that which can be evaluated and criticized cannot by definition be an unchanging, absolute standard. But all things can be evaluated and criticized; hence there cannot be any unchanging, absolute standard, either in the arts or in any other interpretive endeavor.

The fact, however, that there are no unchanging, absolute standards does not mean that there cannot be standards that are relatively objective. As an essential part of living and creating, groups of interpreters develop standards by which they evaluate other people's works and their own. Their standards are real and important, but they are not eternal.

Fallacies of Monism and Pluralism

The foregoing thought experiments and discussions have disclosed the inherent correlativity of one and many, system and element, objectivity and subjectivity. Consequently, we are now in a better position to evaluate the claims of various conflicting schools of philosophy about the underlying nature of knowledge, reality, and language. In particular, we can see the fallacy of any philosophical system that would seek to depict the universe as a mere after-effect of some underlying unity or some underlying plurality that is regarded as somehow "more real" than everything else in the universe.

By grasping on to either "the one" or "the many" as the alleged real basis of everything else, these philosophical systems overlook two considerations: (1) "one" and "many" are correlative, not absolute, concepts; and (2) *any* application of the one-and-many schema ultimately represents a decision conditioned to some degree by some interpreter's physical structure, cultural conditioning, and idiosyncratic life experiences.

A group of interpreters may very well succeed in constructing a relatively objective world-view for themselves based on their special regard for either "one" or "many"; nonetheless, they have no rational grounds for expecting agreement from other interpreters who succeed in constructing other relatively objective world-views using other applications of the same schema. To have absolute expectations for either "one" or "many" is analogous to arguing that "up" is more real than "down," or vice-versa, whereas in fact "up" and "down" are correlative concepts.

Plotinus' Absolute Monism

A classic example in the West of the attempt to give oneness a privileged status as the real basis of everything is the thought of the Greek-writing Egyptian philosopher Plotinus (205-270 A.D.). According to Plotinus, everything both exists and is conceivable only in virtue of being some kind of one; therefore (he argues) the One must be that which ultimately makes all existence and knowledge possible. For example, in a famous passage Plotinus argues as follows:

> All beings are beings owing to the One, both those that exist in a fundamental way, and those that are in any way predicated of things that exist. What else indeed could anything be, if it could not be one? When stripped of the One that is predicated of them, they are not what they are. An army does not exist, unless it exists as one, nor does a chorus, nor a herd, except as one. Why, not even a house or a ship exists

without the One, since the house exists as one, and also the ship. If they should cast off the One, the house would no longer be a house, nor the ship, a ship.[7]

Plotinus correctly points out that any entity exists and is conceivable as such because it is a unity; however, he overlooks the fact that any *interpretandum* can be variously analyzed as consisting of any number of different kinds of unitary entities, depending on the interests of the interpreter. He also overlooks the equal importance of plurality, which is the necessary logical correlate of unity and without which no *interpretandum* can be interpreted. If it is true to say that a ship is one thing because of its unity, it is equally true to say that the many parts that constitute the ship are such precisely because they exist and are conceivable as a plurality. Every existing object in ordinary life is in fact a unity in plurality or a plurality in unity, and cannot be conceived apart from these two equally important correlative concepts.

Relying (in part) on these logical fallacies, Plotinus develops an elaborate philosophical structure on which to proclaim the alleged ethical and ontological supremacy of the One. All that seems to exist independently in the universe is but a kind of overflow that issues forth effortlessly from the One.

By its very nature, says Plotinus, the One generates maximal perfection. Accordingly, things that appear to be evil in the universe are so because of the effects of the existence of plurality. The more any being in the universe falls away from unity into plurality, the more removed it finds itself from its source, the One, and hence less good. In effect, evil is a kind of lack, the lack that stems from distance from the One.

However tenuously conceived, plurality (and hence apparent evil) thus finds a grudging niche for itself in Plotinus' universe. But this most minimal of concessions entangles Plotinus in an impossible contradiction. He can never adequately explain how the One, conceived as unity in the most absolute sense and as the source of all being, could possibly have generated or given rise to plurality, which by its very definition is not-One. Contrary to Plotinus, if plurality is in any way conceded to exist or function in the universe, then its logical opposite, the One, cannot be regarded as the sole source of all reality. This is the stone on which Plotinus stumbles.

Relying heavily on his monistic philosophical system, Plotinus develops an elaborate quasi-religious ethical system. He advocates withdrawal from the many (which he identifies with sensation, the body, and sexuality). Instead, he emphasizes commitment to an introspective "flight of the alone to the Alone."[8]

Plotinus' system contains much insight when interpreted metaphorically or psychologically. It fails, however, as a form of philosophical analysis when taken too literally, for the reasons noted above. Plotinus' virtue lies in the elaborate metaphorical expression he gives to the sublime "peak experiences" (as they would be called today) that he experienced as a contemplative philosopher; his weakness lies in the belief that such experiences can be articulated as an objective system of thought equally valid for all.

Leibniz' Absolute Pluralism

The philosophical mistake of going too far in the opposite direction, of regarding plurality as an absolute category, can be found in the works of the German philosopher Gottfried Wilhelm Leibniz (1646—1716 A.D.). Leibniz was both a Christian and an enthusiast for the new sciences of his time. Accordingly he wanted to develop a system of philosophy that would preserve the principal philosophical implications of Christianity while at the same time providing room for new concepts of matter. The result was an ingenious, but highly contrived, philosophical system that eventually estranged both theologians and scientists.

According to Leibniz, the entire universe consists of an infinite aggregate of metaphysical entities he calls "monads" (derived from the Greek *monades*, meaning "units"). Each of these monads is a living, incorporeal, self-determining center of energy and activity, the whole of whose history emanates from its own inner nature, independent of all other monads. What seems to our senses to be a material object is really the macroscopic material consequence of a great conglomeration of monads. In addition, what appears to be a human being is one dominant monad (the soul) in control of a great mass of subsidiary monads (manifest through the body). The order that is perceived to exist throughout the universe is not the result of any real interaction between such "windowless" monads. Rather, it is a pre-established harmony of synchronized parallel activities that God has programmed into all monads when he first created them. Hence the universe really consists of but two kinds of being: God and an infinite number of autonomous monads. The objects that science measures and tests are "well founded phenomena." They are grounded in the eternal, living monads that are their immediate source of being and definition.

Leibniz's monads are really kinds of atoms, except that they are eternal, immaterial, and totally self-evolving. In this, they contrast to the atoms of twentieth-century physics, which are mortal, material, and interactive. Although God had an important place in Leibniz's affections, he ended up on a rather remote ontological shelf in Leibniz's actual philosophy. Leibniz's God was a kind of philosophical *deus ex machina*, used to explain the possibility of apparent order among non-interactive, absolutely autonomous monads.

Leibniz turned Plotinus on his head, multiplying Plotinus' One into an infinite number of monads. Each of these autonomously generated its own reality and history from its inner nature, just as the One of Plotinus had generated the whole universe from *its* nature. As a result, Leibniz ended up with an infinity of autonomous, unrelated universes. These could only be unified by appealing to a transcendent creator-God who pre-programmed a later history of harmonious interaction into each monad at the time of its creation.

The basic fallacy of Leibniz's approach is the absolute status he gives to plurality. Once plurality ceases to be relative and becomes instead a base reality in its own right from which every natural phenomenon is constituted, then unity, which by its very definition is non-plurality, cannot be accounted for. In groping for some source of unity, Leibniz found himself with the mirror-image problem of Plotinus, who could not account for plurality. Leibniz's attempted solution—appealing to God as a kind of remote monad of monads—is as weak as Plotinus' nebulous emanationism: if God preprograms the natures of monads at creation in order to make the best possible world (as Leibniz believed), then monads are not really autonomous causes after all. Rather, they become attributes of one universal underlying substance, which was the position of Leibniz's contemporary philosophical opposite, Benedict Spinoza. Hence there is a certain unintended irony to Leibniz's celebrated remark that, were it not for the monads, his philosophical system would be the same as Spinoza's.

Contrary to both Plotinus and Leibniz, neither unity nor plurality is absolute in any real sense. Both are correlative concepts (neither having meaning without the other) and applicable to *interpretanda* only by virtue of the decisions of interpreters. Insofar as the universe is rationally accessible to us, it is not definable as the mere effect of either an exclusively existing underlying one or an exclusively existing underlying many. Rather, the known universe is an interpretational construct resulting from the decisions of human interpreters interacting with *interpretanda* and using correlative concepts. And in so far as the universe is not rationally accessible to us, all human concepts fail, including those of unity and plurality.

Language

Among the various types of interpreters that exist are those that are capable of making descriptive statements ("propositions") about the *interpretanda* with which they interact. Such an interpreter has the ability first to make a decision that such and such elements and systems exist and interact in a certain manner, and then to describe their existence and interaction through the use of a system of conventional signs ("language").

Whenever an interpreter makes a proposition about a given *interpretandum* to the effect that certain elements and systems exist and have certain interactions, at least three questions always arise: (1) Does the proposition correctly express the interpreter's interpretive interaction with the *interpretandum*? (2) Is the proposition consistent with the interpreter's previously made propositions (both observational and inferential), including propositions expressive of the interpreter's reality map? (3) Do these previously made propositions likewise correctly express the interpreter's interpretive interactions with *interpretanda*?

If the interpreter comes to the conclusion that the answer to all three of these questions is yes, then the interpreter will regard the original proposition as "true." If the interpreter concludes that the answer to (1) is no, or else that the answer to (2) is no while the answer to (3) is yes, the interpreter will regard the original proposition as "false." If the interpreter concludes that the answer to (1) is yes, while the answer to (2) and (3) is no, the interpreter will alter some previously made proposition or propositions. If the interpreter is undecided about the answer to any of these questions, the truth of the original proposition will likewise be undecided. If the interpreter concludes that the answer to (1) is yes, (2) is no, and (3) is yes, the interpreter will be unable to render a propositional interpretation.

The use of language necessarily evolves after other types of interpretation. In addition, linguistically-capable interpreters evaluate their propositions against non-linguistic interpretations. Therefore, interpreters who use language (and the world that they so interpret) cannot be completely understood through linguistic analysis alone. For human interpreters in particular, both "subjective experience" and "the objective world" are more than mere linguistic constructs. In short, the use of language is far more than a linguistic phenomenon. Language always presupposes for its use a much greater interpretational reservoir that cannot itself be captured in language.

We saw earlier that there is no such thing as an absolute reality for everyone. In the same way, there is no such thing as an absolute truth for everyone. Rather, there is only the truth of a certain proposition or propositions for a certain interpreter or certain group of interpreters. To seek to establish an absolute truth for all, unconditionally, overlooks the very nature of the process whereby propositions are judged truthful—that is, interpreters using language to express interpretive decisions about their interactions with *interpretanda*.

Indeed, even this claim—that there is no absolute truth for everyone—cannot claim for itself any sort of absolute validity. In effect, anyone who makes this claim really says this: "I assume that you are a certain sort of interpreter having certain kinds of presuppositions and values; if so, and if you reason in a way that is consistent with these presuppositions, you will conclude that the only absolute truth is that there is no absolute truth except this one."

The question will always remain open, however, as to whether some given interpreter is of the sort presupposed, and whether this interpreter shares certain kinds of presuppositions. A fundamentalist Christian, for example, would never concur with the view of truth I have just outlined. In the face of such a basic disagreement, there is no broader argument to which either I or the fundamentalist can appeal in order to convince the other. We simply disagree, and there is nothing further to be said. Hopefully, neither one of us will seek to impose his or her views on the other.

Although truth always has a relative aspect, it nonetheless remains a very real thing. It is *not* a mere collection of personal opinions or fancies. To the contrary, any given human interpreter will judge only a certain limited number of propositions as: (1) correctly expressive of his or her interpretive decisions about *interpretanda*; and (2) consistent with those previously made propositions that are likewise judged as correctly expressive of *interpretanda*. The interpreter will conclude that all other propositions are false, uncertain, impossible, meaningless, etc. Moreover, just as there can be shared reality maps, so there can be shared truths.

We have seen that when interpreters seek to determine the truth or falsity of any proposition, they do more than merely test whether these propositions correspond, like pictures, to the world (the "correspondence theory of truth," discussed below). They also do more than merely test whether these propositions cohere with a greater body of previously accepted propositions (the "coherence theory of truth," also discussed below). Instead, what is involved at all times is a complex set of relations between interpreter, *interpretandum*, language, and system of previously made interpretations (including, at some point, prelingual interpretations).

The *interpretandum* is given independently of both interpreter and language; in and of itself, however, it is not linguistically interpretable. Application of the predicates "is true" or "is false" must wait upon an interpreter who is able to do the following three things: (1) use his or her language to describe the *interpretandum*; (2) evaluate the expressive competence of his or her descriptive propositions; and (3) compare propositions so made to other propositions based on, and evaluated against, other *interpretanda*. If any of these factors is wanting—*interpretandum*, interpreter, language—there is no making of propositions and no interpreting of such propositions as "true" or "false."

A corollary of the above is that no proposition can be explicitly judged true by an interpreter if that interpreter has not first judged, at least implicitly, some other proposition true. Hence if there is truth, there must always be some proposition or propositions that are *assumed* to be true. A second corollary is that the making of true propositions is limited by one's capacity for interacting with *interpretanda*, facility in using language, depth of experience in interpreting previous *interpretanda*, etc.

Wittgenstein's Correspondence Theory of Truth

One of the most famous examples of the correspondence theory of truth (which, as noted above, differs substantially from the account presented here) is that of the Austrian philosopher Ludwig Wittgenstein (1889-1951). While in his late twenties, Wittgenstein wrote an essay destined to exercise a lasting influence on subsequent Anglo-American academic philosophy. He called it *Logisch-philosophische Abhandlung* ("Logical-Philosophical Treatise"). In 1922, Wittgenstein published an English translation of this book, but bearing a Latin title, *Tractatus Logico-Philosophicus*. This is how it is now commonly known.[9]

In later chapters, we will see that Wittgenstein's *Tractatus* was greatly misinterpreted by those whom it most influenced; moreover, he himself later repudiated much of it. For now, however, we will limit our attention to Wittgenstein's early correspondence theory of truth as expressed in *Tractatus*.

According to Wittgenstein (at least at this stage of his life), the world of empirical reality and the world of language have a parallel structure. Each world is ultimately reducible to minimal elements that can be correlated to the minimal elements of the other. The minimal elements of the empirical world are "states of affairs" (*Sachverhalte*), and those of language are "elementary propositions" (*Elementarsätze*). Actually, states of affairs are further divisible into "objects," and elementary propositions into "names." Nonetheless, elementary propositions are minimal in the sense that they are the least things that can be *asserted* about the world. Likewise, states of affairs are minimal in the sense that they are the least *knowable facts* in the world.

Regardless of how complicated any proposition or set of propositions may be, argues Wittgenstein in *Tractatus*, they can ultimately be reduced to combinations of logically independent elementary propositions. These in turn either correspond, or not, to respective independent states of affairs. If the elementary propositions correspond to states of affairs, then the propositions are "true," and otherwise "false." Further, since all complex propositions can be viewed as mere chains of elementary propositions, the truth or falsity of these complex propositions is a direct function of the truth or falsity of their elements. For example, let some complex proposition p be a combination of four elementary propositions q, r, s, and t. In this case, p is true if and only if q, r, s, and t are all true. In technical terms, p is a "truth function" of q, r, s, and t.

How can we know when propositions, whether elementary or otherwise, correspond to states of affairs or larger facts constituted by states of affairs? According to Wittgenstein, we use language to make pictures for ourselves of facts (*Wir machen uns Bilder der Tatsachen*).[10] In effect, this means that amid the chain of names that constitutes any elementary proposition we perceive a certain logical form. We then compare this logical form, like a picture, to the logical form we perceive in a state of affairs. If the form of the picture matches the form of the fact, and if to each object in the fact there corresponds a name in the elementary proposition, then the elementary proposition is true, otherwise false. Thus it is that language is "the great mirror" of the world.

The strength of Wittgenstein's correspondence theory of truth is that it insists on both the extra-linguistic reality of the world and the importance of language, allowing neither to be simplistically absorbed into the other. But as he himself later came to realize, his theory is nonetheless riddled with serious flaws. For example, he assumes that the meaning of a name must be the object it refers to. This must be so because meaning comes either from having logical form, or from referring to an object, and because names as such have no logical form. But this assumption means that if an object ceases to be, the name becomes meaningless, which is absurd. For example, the name "Ludwig Wittgenstein" is still meaningful even though the bearer of that name died in 1951. But what object or fact now corresponds to the name "Ludwig Wittgenstein?"

Further, if we use propositions as pictures, it would seem that there could be various degrees of similarity between any given proposition-picture and its corresponding depicted fact. After all, there can be varying degrees of similarity between various portraits of a person and the person portrayed. But if that's the case, then it's a mistake to think that a proposition must be absolutely true or absolutely false. To the contrary, there could be a degree of truth in any proposition, answering to the degree of correspondence between the logical form of the proposition and the logical form of the fact. But if truth is a matter of degree, then the traditional logical calculus that can see only "true" or "false" is inadequate. On the other hand, if correspondence between the two logical forms is not one of degree, how can we know when there is exact identity? Are there certain criteria of exact identity above and beyond logical form? If so, how can we maintain that meaning is solely a matter of either logical form or reference to an object?

More seriously, our earlier analysis has shown that in any *interpretandum*, element and system are correlative notions resulting from the decision of some interpreter or group of interpreters. Hence the following interconnected assertions are all *fallacies*: (1) complexes can in principle be reduced to simples that are absolute for all systems and all interpreters (the fallacy of absolute reductionism); (2) simplicity is a meaningful concept independent of context (the fallacy of non-contextual simplicity); and (3) there is a realm of things that is absolutely objective (the fallacy of absolute objectivity). Wittgenstein's correspondence theory of truth embodies all three fallacies. He maintains that both the world and language are reducible to the absolute simples consisting, respectively, of states of affairs and elementary propositions. He also assumes that definitive names and objects meaningfully exist prior to the formation of any propositions or any states of affairs. Finally, he argues that there exists in both the world and language an absolute logical form unambiguously knowable to all interpreters in all contexts.

Wittgenstein also overlooks something else: the interpreter's assessment of whether presently considered propositions are consistent with previously made propositions, particularly those expressive of one's reality map. In effect, an interpreter in Wittgenstein's eyes has no *history*. But the meaning of every human interpretation depends, in part, on the history of the person who makes it.

The many difficulties with the theories propounded by Wittgenstein in his *Tractatus* eventually led him to disavow the book. In his later years he developed an entirely different approach to language that appeared in his posthumous *Philosophical Investigations*.[11] Of course, philosophers are entitled to change their opinions, but Wittgenstein's great shift is ironical in view of the grand initial claims he made for the *Tractatus* when it was first published in 1922:

> The *truth* of the thoughts that are here set forth seems to me unassailable and definitive. I therefore believe myself to have found, on all essential points, the final solution of the problems.[12]

Bradley's Coherence Theory of Truth

Nearly the exact opposite of Wittgenstein's correspondence theory of truth can be found in the coherence theory propounded by the English philosopher Francis Herbert Bradley (1846-1924). The fourth son in the second marriage of an evangelical minister (who fathered 20 children in all), F.H. Bradley was admitted to Oxford in 1865, where he studied philosophy. In 1870 he was awarded a fellowship for the purpose of conducting philosophical research and writing, free of the duties of teaching, and terminable at his marriage. Since Bradley, like Wittgenstein, never married, he was thus able to devote his entire life to philosophical writing in an academic environment, but unencumbered by the usual professorial obligations. About his personal life, little is known except that he was rather reclusive and afflicted with some chronic health problem. He devoted all his books to a certain "E.R.," thought to be an American woman living in France who had no interest in philosophy.

By the latter part of his life, Bradley, influenced by the German philosopher Georg Wilhelm Hegel, had become the most influential British philosopher of his time, having published, among other works, *The Principles of Logic* in 1883 (2nd edition, 1922), *Appearance and Reality* in 1893, and *Essays on Truth and Reality* in 1914. Despite Bradley's former fame, however, modern English-speaking students of philosophy rarely read him. The reason is that he was the great critic and opponent of those philosophical traditions that later developed into analytic philosophy, which today holds sway in most philosophy departments of Anglo-American universities. In fact, when analytic philosophers cast aspersions on what they regard as "metaphysical nonsense," they usually have the philosophy of Bradley or Hegel in mind. Despite his fall from current official academic favor, however, Bradley was a solid, articulate philosopher. Given the zigzag history of past academic fads, perhaps he will some day enjoy a revival. In any case, he is certainly still worth reading.

According to Bradley's developed thought, a correspondence theory of truth, such as advocated by Ludwig Wittgenstein, is adequate for only a limited part of human experience, such as the routines of daily life or the rudiments of science. Once, however, we move beyond these areas and begin to reflect on the full implications of things, we need to define truth in terms of systematic coherence and comprehensiveness. Otherwise, Bradley argues, we will find ourselves entrapped in impossible paradoxes.

Bradley arrives at this conclusion by minutely analyzing the process involved in rendering a judgment about any particular subject matter. For example, consider a seemingly simple observation statement such as the following (to update Bradley a bit): "I look out the window of my inner-city tenement and see the police doing a drug deal in the alley." I might at first be tempted to think that my statement here is a simple picture of reality, and that all my knowledge is merely a piling up of similar simple statements that happen to truly mirror reality. But, we could imagine Bradley making this point: What do you mean by the word "I" here? Is this "I" really such a simple unconnected reality? If so, then it cannot refer to the simple unconnected reality you referred to with the word "I" half an hour ago. But if not, then what is the underlying connection that permits you to use the same word for both these unconnected realities?

Again, Bradley would likely ask questions about the verification of this observation statement. For example, suppose that in taking in a wider view of the scene in the alley, I now notice movie cameras and a film crew around the corner, and hence realize that it is not true that police are doing a drug deal in the alley but that actors are rehearsing the roles of police doing a drug deal. As a result of this new realization, I now regard my first statement as false, but not because I compared it directly with some little piece of reality. Rather, I see it as inconsistent with another, larger description of a more comprehensive reality.

Arguing on the basis of such examples as these, Bradley maintains that *any* subject about which we may wish to render a judgment always presupposes some surrounding context of meaning. Only by virtue of this context does the subject possess its identity. However minute or discrete any given subject of discourse may seem to be—

> It has always edges which are ragged in such a way as to imply another existence from which it has been torn, and without which it really does not exist.[13]

Furthermore, even after we take a larger view, that view itself will also have ragged edges, and so on, until at last we reach that which includes all that is and which is not itself conditioned or dependent on anything else. This encompassing reality Bradley calls "the Absolute."

Seen in this way, truth is not absolute in itself but rather relative to a greater Absolute. Any judgment is true to the extent that it coheres with other accepted truths and encompasses reality, and false to the extent that it fails to do so. Hence there is a degree of truth and falsehood to *every* judgment. Moreover, there is no irreducible dichotomy between me and my truths, since we are all in some sense contained within, and conditioned by, the Absolute. Indeed, in a sense both my truths and I are manifestations of that Absolute. Therefore truth is neither an alien intrusion into my being nor a lifeless objectification that I have created. In

Bradley's celebrated remark (with a pun on the word "premises"):

> Truth does not break into my premises like a burglar, nor again like a corpse does it suffer my anatomy.[14]

My truth and I are *related* through our mutual contexts, including in the end the Absolute, which is the context of all contexts. In addition, since there is but one Absolute behind many appearances, truths that are seemingly subjective or individual must eventually lead into one that is true for all, if only sufficient comprehensiveness and coherence be obtained. To the extent, therefore, that we attain such comprehensiveness, we not only find a greater degree of truth but also a greater expanse of shared truth.

The search for truth, then, is but the "ideal" (that is, the intellectual) aspect of our deep-seated longing for wholeness as a finite center in a vast universe. First in our lives we experience the immediacy and wholeness of undifferentiated feelings. Whenever we seek to express these feelings in words, we immediately gain a degree of clarity from definition but also leave something out. In pursuit of what has been left out, we create ever larger and more complicated intellectual structures, yet something always eludes us. But even if we could somehow encompass all of reality that human cognition can grasp, we would still have to step beyond cognition, indeed beyond truth itself, and, abandoning all definition, including our own self-definition, find wholeness through sublime union with the Absolute. In sum, all of human life is spent in a kind of "mid-world" between two kinds of wholeness: that of immediate feeling and that of the yearned-for Absolute, partially manifested to us through our pursuit of truth.

The great value of Bradley's coherence theory of truth is that it emphasizes the contextual nature of any alleged system of elements, which is glossed over by Wittgenstein's correspondence theory of truth in *Tractatus*. Contrary to Wittgenstein, Bradley shows that it is *meaningless* to assert that there are any entities that are utterly elemental in their own nature apart from any and all context. Bradley highlights the very contextuality of the knowing process that Wittgenstein (at least in *Tractatus*) cannot account for.

But Bradley's account also has many deficiencies. For example: since the Absolute exceeds every finitely-comprehending proposition to an infinite degree, no finitely-comprehending proposition can be truer than any other. One way to get around this difficulty would be to define overall coherence in terms of a comparison among finite propositions themselves. But such a comparison would require that at least one such proposition be regarded as a standard in and of itself. Bradley, however, will not countenance any finite standards as final.

In addition, on Bradley's account it is inconceivable for an entire system of encompassing propositions to be jettisoned because a newly made single proposition might happen to be inconsistent with it. Yet there doesn't seem to be anything in the ordinary understanding of the word "truth" to require this impossibility. Quite the contrary: Albert Einstein, drawing attention to just a few anomalous observations, overthrew the vast system of Isaac Newton. In response, Bradley could claim that the result of Einstein's efforts was a more encompassing system, which is true; nonetheless, the old encompassing system was made to accord with a few new facts, not vice-versa. Bradley's weakness here is a consequence of something he underestimates: the importance of assessing the expressive competence of certain propositions vis-à-vis immediate *interpretanda*. This type of propositional assessment is the very thing that is most resistant to a coherence theory of truth.

Bradley also faces a problem in regard to the Absolute. By his account, everything that we know (including ourselves) is a finite construction arising out of interactions with reality. The Absolute, on the other hand, is not constructed but rather transcends and includes all constructions; but if that is so, how can we ever know there is an Absolute, much less talk about its nature? When pressed with this difficulty, Bradley seems to vacillate between saying either: (1) some context must be presupposed in order to explain the meaningfulness of elements; or (2) I accept the Absolute as an act of faith. But the most he can claim on the first point is the existence of some context or contexts, not a universally transcending absolute context; and on the second point, although he is certainly entitled to his own acts of faith, it remains unclear why they should be compelling to others.

Indeed, it is precisely the penchant of Bradley and other idealist philosophers to talk about what they claim is ineffable that led Wittgenstein to make the famous remark with which he closes *Tractatus*: "That whereof we cannot speak, over that must we pass in silence."[15]

The underlying problem with Bradley's entire approach is this: although he recognizes the relativity of elements with respect to systems, he is blind to the relativity of systems themselves. As we have seen above, what constitutes system and element for any *interpretandum* depends, in part, on the decision of some interpreter or some group of interpreters. Hence, although there must always be some system-context in interpretation, there is no reason in logic or in fact why there cannot be one or more finite systems among the same interpreters, of which some are mutually consistent and others overlapping.

As suggested by the analysis earlier of interpretation, the following three interrelated assertions are all *fallacies*: (1) all elements can be encompassed in one system that is in principle absolute for all interpreters (the fallacy of absolute encompassment); (2) system decisions are interpreter-independent (the fallacy of purely objective systematization); and (3) there is an Absolute (the fallacy of absoluteness). Bradley's philosophy embodies all three of these fallacies, for he maintains that regardless of what elements may exist in any interpreters' systems, such interpreters, elements, and systems are all encompassed in one Absolute system that is in principle valid for all. In adhering to these fallacies, Bradley in effect takes the fallacious ontological monism of Plotinus, discussed above, and gives it an epistemological twist, just as Wittgenstein takes the fallacious ontological pluralism that he inherited from Leibniz via Russell and gives it a linguistic twist. But contrary to Bradley and Wittgenstein, Plotinus and Leibniz, we have found the following to be true: one and many, system and element, whole and part are all correlative concepts depending, in part, on the decisions of interpreters or groups of interpreters. Neither One nor Many is Absolute, either in being or knowledge or language.

Subject to the qualifications discussed earlier in this chapter, we make this (relatively) absolute claim: the only absolute is that there are no absolutes, at least in so far as reality is interpretable. This claim, it should be noted, does *not* mean that absolutes cannot exist; rather it means that, even should they exist, they cannot be adequately captured by perception, cognition, or language.

Universals

An understanding that unity and plurality are correlative concepts, applied by the decisions, both conscious and otherwise, of interpreters, will help clarify an issue that has bedeviled Western philosophy for more than two thousand years: the question of the nature of "universals." Derived from the Latin word *universalia*, which literally means "commonalities," the philosophic term "universals" refers to those entities that can have more than one instance. For example, I have in my purse some red lipstick, and I see on the street a red fire hydrant. Both the lipstick and the fire hydrant are separate, particular things. But what about the redness that is shared in common by these two particulars? Clearly this redness cannot be a separate, particular thing like a piece of lipstick or a fire hydrant because these two things can exist only in one place at one time, whereas the redness is *common*—it exists in *both* the lipstick and the fire hydrant at the same time.

Aside from colors, a great many other important things in human experience are universals: justice, triangularity, the number five, etc. Are these universals something real in their own right, mere conventional creations of behavior or speech, or something else? And how do particulars and universals interact? The answer that one gives to these questions will have powerful implications for every aspect of one's thought. Indeed, the issue of universals is one of the most important ever raised in philosophy.

Plato's Theory of Forms

Perhaps the most memorable answer to the question of universals was provided by the ancient Greek philosopher Plato (427-347 B.C.). Before developing as a philosopher in his own right, Plato had been the pupil of Socrates, who stressed the importance of using proper definitions, especially in ethical matters. Whenever anyone in ancient Athens began pontificating about any particular virtue that people should exemplify in their personal lives (such as piety to the gods), Socrates would relentlessly push his seemingly modest question, *Ti esti?* ("What is it?"). Generally the person asked could at best give individual examples of the virtue in question, not a coherent account of the virtue in and of itself (that is, of the virtue as a universal). Socrates' emphasis on definition impressed Plato, who eventually concluded that universals, not particulars, were the core realities of the universe.

According to Plato's maturely developed thought, universals are eternal, incorporeal "Forms" or "Types" (*ideai*) that exist in and of themselves, and in which temporal, sensible particulars "participate" (*metekhein*). To Plato, the world of the senses was but a passing flux; reality, and therefore true knowledge, pertained to the world of the Forms, which could only be apprehended by pure intellect. Moreover, the Forms constituted a great hierarchy among themselves, the highest and most inclusive of which was a kind of Form of Forms—the Form of the Good.

Drawing out the educational, ethical, and political implications of this doctrine, Plato came to hold a number of dogmas that have ever since typified the philosophic tradition bearing his name. These Platonic dogmas are the following: mathematics is the most worthy subject of human study; the artist is but a clumsy imitator of the shadows of higher realities; self-perfection consists in transcending materiality and the body, and particularly sexuality; democracy is only a little better than tyranny; and nations should be ruled by philosopher-kings. In later times, Christian thinkers incorporated many Platonic themes into their theology, regarding the Forms as ideas existing in the mind of God, and viewing the historical Jesus of Nazareth as the incarnation of God's Idea-Word (*Logos*).

The strong point of Plato's theory of Forms is that it affirms the reality of universals. Although the ideal of Justice, for example, is not palpable in the sense that a hammer is, such an ideal has nonetheless inspired great masses of people to overthrow entire political regimes, a feat obviously beyond the capacity of any hammer. So if the capacity to bring about great social changes is a sign of reality, then the ideal of Justice is at least as real as any hammer. Furthermore, if non-sensible commonalities are not real, what becomes of the reality of mathematics and the sciences, all of which would be impossible without non-sensible abstractions? Clearly, at least some universals must be conceded at least some reality.

There are, however, many fatal problems with Plato's theory, as classically pointed out by his most famous pupil and critic, Aristotle. For example, consider the case where a universal has the same quality as the particulars that participate in it, as with Goodness. Goodness is that by virtue of which particular things may be said to be good. But isn't Goodness itself also good? If not, how can it make particulars good? But if so, mustn't there then be yet another Form to account for the fact that *both* Goodness and its many particulars are good? And then another Form beyond that, and so on, so that we have to postulate an infinite sequence of Forms to explain how particulars can be good. But what is the explanatory value of generating such an infinite series of Forms, all to explain just one quality?

Other problems also exist for Plato: how can a particular that is temporal and corporeal participate in (or in any way interact with) that which is immortal and incorporeal? And if only the Forms are truly real, how can materiality then have any existence at all? But if materiality has reality in its own right, is there a source of reality independent of the Forms? If so, what is the relationship of that source to the source of the reality of the Forms? And how can there be a common source of two such disparate things? But without such a common source, how can there be a common world? Plato himself was acutely aware of these difficulties, and discussed them at length in his dialogues; nonetheless, he was never able to adequately resolve the difficulties.

Aristotle's Theory of Essences

In attempting to save the reality of universals, Plato in effect developed a philosophy that lost the reality of particulars. In his reaction against such a philosophy, Aristotle (384-322 B.C.) placed a renewed emphasis on the particular. In Aristotle's philosophy, that which is primarily real is *tode ti*, "this something here"; for example, this human being now standing in front of me. But this particular that now confronts me is not an undifferentiated something (otherwise I could never recognize it as anything). Hence it must have something that makes it a definite thing, and this defining thing is what Aristotle calls *to ti en einai*, a highly condensed Greek expression difficult to translate fully into English. Literally, *to ti en einai* means "that which pertains to what it is." Latin writers later translated this difficult Greek phrase by the word *quidditas*, meaning a thing's "whatness" (or that which makes it what it is). When viewed in the context of Aristotle's fully developed thought, *to ti en einai* means "the defining and definable nature of a thing"; hence it is equivalent to what he elsewhere calls "essence" (*ousia*).

Although Aristotle believed that particulars are the base realities, he also believed that some essence inheres in every particular, defining both it and every other particular of the same type in which it likewise inheres. In examining particulars, the human mind is able to abstract out, as it were, concepts of the inhering essences that define classes of particulars, and these conceptual classifications become in turn the objects studied by the sciences. In other words, essences only exist by inhering in particulars, every particular has an essence, and to know is to use both the senses and reason to see and organize conceptual classes modeled after the parallel orderings of real essences.

The virtue of Aristotle's theory of essences is that it strives to strike a balance between real universals and real particulars. Universals are real, but, apart from the particulars that embody them, vacuous. Particulars are real, but, apart from the universals that define them, indeterminate and unknowable. As a result, the pursuit of knowledge requires a balanced use of both sensation and intellectual insight, neither of which is more important than the other in any ultimate sense.

Despite this philosophical balancing act, however, Aristotle's theory is also open to fatal objections. Since essences remain incorporeal by Aristotle's account, he is faced with the problem of explaining how they can interact with material bodies. Here he finds himself with the same sort of problem as Plato, but from the opposite end of the stick. Whereas Plato stumbles on explaining how particulars can participate in Forms, Aristotle stumbles on explaining how essences can inhere in particulars. For Plato the principal focus is on Forms; for Aristotle, on the concrete particular; but for both the underlying problem is the same: there can be no real interaction between universal and particular if each is defined as the antithesis and absence of the other.

Aristotle's attempted solution to this problem is to argue that essence is to particular as form is to matter. But this attempted solution slides over a crucial difficulty: if each particular's essence is its particular form, how can differing particulars be said to have the *same* essence-form? Clearly, only if the essence-form is something above and beyond each thing in its particularity. But then the essence cannot be to each thing as the thing's form is to its matter, because real differences in the forming of matter can always be discovered between two material objects, however similar they may at first glance seem to be, and precisely because of unique variations in each one's particular matter. Hence if the defining essence is general and incorporeal (as Aristotle always claims), it cannot be analogous to the form of a specific material object. At best, it can be analogous to a form in some kind of general or universal matter. But that still fails to explain how a general and incorporeal form can inhere in what is particular, which is the problem at hand.

William of Ockham's Nominalism

Both Plato and Aristotle are called "realists" or "essentialists" in their approach to the question of universals, since both believed that universals are real things (Forms, essences), as opposed to mere concepts or words. In sharp contrast to this approach, the 14th-century English Franciscan philosopher William of Ockham (1300-1349 A.D.) was a "nominalist." That is, he argued that universals are merely names (Latin *nomina*) that we invent and use to classify particular phenomena.

According to Ockham, the real universe consists only of individuals and God (who is also a real individual). So, for example, the fact that we can meaningfully talk about "humanity" does not mean that we need assume the existence of some kind of universal being—namely, Humanity—which somehow inheres in all particular human beings and which is the object of our discourse. To the contrary, the word "humanity" here is merely a convenient name or term that we use for the sake of abbreviation to stand for all individual human beings. To say "Humanity is mortal" is just a shorthand way of saying this: "If there is an individual being that happens to be human, then that individual being is also mortal."

Ockham argues that we have been deceived into thinking there must be universals by the subject-predicate form of our language. Once we properly analyze the underlying logical functions of the linguistic terms we use, we will come to see that the vexing problem of universals disappears. Instead of ghostly universals mysteriously inhering in particulars, we end up with a non-nonsense world of human beings using language to refer to particulars, and nothing more.

Of course, one might object here that even if universals are no longer required to explain our linguistic or logical usages, they may still have some kind of real existence in their own right. To this objection, Ockham would reply with his famous dictum ("Ockham's razor") that the simplest explanation is always the best. Since philosophers first conceived of universals in order to explain definition, classification, and other logical relations, there is no reason to continue holding onto them now that they are no longer needed for that explanatory purpose. Unless we adhere to an economy of explanation, maintains Ockham, we will always be faced with an endless series of new principles and entities. After all, someone can always offer a more complicated explanation for something, whereas there is only one explanation that can explain all the facts in the simplest way.

The great virtue both of Ockham's nominalism and his "razor" is that they cut through the tangled overgrowth of abstractions in medieval thought. This overgrowth resulted from the attempt to reconcile Aristotelian metaphysics (as interpreted by Thomas Aquinas) with Christian theological dogma. By using his new methods, Ockham clarified many logical conundrums of his time and paved the way for the development of later logical theory and the methodology of the sciences.

Despite, Ockham's seemingly elegant solution to the problem of universals, however, it remains open to fatal objections. For example, consider the phenomenon that bears the name "the United States of America." According to Ockham, this phenomenon, like all phenomena, must be either a real individual or an aggregate of real individuals. If it is a real individual, what then are its millions of citizens? Surely, they are real individuals, if anything is. If so, can they combine to form a bigger real individual? In that case, the bigger individual could exist in several places at once (for example, in San Francisco and in Dubuque), unlike the smaller individuals that belong to it, which cannot. But that which can exist in several places at once is a universal. Therefore universals would turn out to be real individuals, which Ockham denies. Hence on Ockham's account, "the United States of America" cannot name a real individual; rather, it can only name a mere aggregate of individuals.

Let us agree, then, with Ockham and say that "the United States of America" is a mere name referring to some particular aggregate of individuals. But suppose these millions of citizens were suddenly dispersed throughout the rest of the world, subject to different laws, speech, and customs. Would the United States of America still exist? According to Ockham's concept, it would, even though there would no longer be any commonly observed federal or state laws, for example, or public rituals of state. But surely there is some real, and not merely nominal, difference between millions of unconnected people scattered about the planet, and the same people living in geographical contiguity, observing the same laws, speaking the same language, and practicing the same customs. But if geographical contiguity, law, language, and custom can make such a real difference to real individuals and yet not themselves be real individuals (as they are not, under Ockham's view), what, then, are they?

Again, if "the United States of America" is merely an abbreviation for the set of all individuals who happen to have been born in a certain part of the globe, what happens tomorrow when a new individual is born in this part of the globe? On Ockham's account, this part of the globe will then consist of two entirely separate entities, the United States of America and the individual who has just been born. Clearly, however, the new-born individual is part of the United States of America.

If Ockham's definition is amended, so that "the United States of America" refers to all individuals who *may* be born in a certain geographical area, then it simply begs the question at issue. Why should we have a common name ("The United States of America") for people who may be born in certain areas and not for those who may be born in other areas? Why don't we have a common name, say, to cover any individual who may be born in either the Amazon basin or the Crimea? For example, "Amacrimea."

Clearly, individuals born in the fifty states of the American Union have something in *common* that is lacking by the set constituted by individuals who may be born in either the Amazon or the Crimea. But if these commonalities are important enough to affect our use of names, then aren't they as real as individuals?

Analogously, consider your own identity as a person. According to Ockham you are a real individual, and not just an aggregate defined by a name. But what of the billions of atoms of which you are composed? Are they not also real individuals? If so, are you then nothing more than the mere aggregate of such atoms? In that case, there would be no difference between you in the form of, say, ashes and smoke after your cremation, and you as you are now. But clearly there is a real, and not merely nominal, difference between a living human body, and the matter and energy that exist after such a body is cremated. Hence in the case of the human body, as in the case of a body politic, some real general thing—that is, some real universal—exists over and above the mere aggregate of its parts.

Ockham's nominalism actually contains a hidden premise: there exist real, basic, sharply defined individuals in the world that are immediately and unambiguously identifiable as such to everyone. But as shown earlier in this chapter, what is regarded as element or system in any *interpretandum* is relative, depending in part on the decision of some interpreter or group of interpreters, apart from whose interpretation there is no structured world. Ockham and all the empiricist philosophers later influenced by him are wrong: the world does not have the simple palpability of a pile of marbles.

Ockham's great philosophic error consisted in grasping for too great a simplicity. Although it is true that a simple explanation that accounts for all the facts is better than a more complicated one, an overly simple explanation that fails to account for some essential facts is also inadequate. This is the case with Ockham's assertion that all universals are simply names. In using his razor to cut away the callus of his day's encrusted philosophical presuppositions, Ockham overcut into the quick of the very phenomena he sought to explain.

Ludwig Wittgenstein's Family Resemblances

In the twentieth century, the question of universals was approached in a novel way by the Austrian philosopher Ludwig Wittgenstein (discussed earlier in regard to the correspondence theory of truth). According to Wittgenstein's mature thought (as reflected in his posthumous *Philosophical Investigations*), the peculiar forms of our language bewitch us into drawing the wrong conclusions about such things as universals. For example, we use the word "game," and so conclude that there must be something common to all the different things that bear this name. But in fact such a conclusion is nonsense, for if we actually *look* at all the things we call games—board games, Olympic games, etc.—it's just not so. Whenever we think we may have found some commonality among games (such as "being amusing"), we can nonetheless always find some counter-example that lacks this quality. For example, is a game of "chicken," played with oppositely aimed cars on a one-lane highway, "amusing"?

What really underlies our varied applications of the word "game" is not some kind of mysterious essence but a complicated network of overlapping and crisscrossing "similarities" (*Ähnlichkeiten*). No one similarity extends throughout the entire range of the word's use. Hence the alleged commonality behind the word "game" is really like a cord composed of many interwoven threads. No one thread extends for the entire length of the cord, but all of them, through their mutual overlap, perform a certain function, namely that of constituting this particular cord.

Far from being essences, these overlapping continuities are merely *Familienähnlichkeiten* (usually translated as "family resemblances," but literally "family similarities"); that is, they are like the collection of various physical resemblances that one can recognize, but never quite precisely define, running through numerous members of the same family. Since, therefore, a common word like "game" really denotes such a *family of things*, we can apprehend the meaning of such a word only by looking at the many different living contexts in which it is actually used. Once we behold these various usages, we know all we can of the meaning of the common word. Beyond that, there is simply nothing else to understand.

The value of Wittgenstein's analysis is that it seeks to bring philosophy back to earth, by focusing on the actual way we use words in real-life situations. Language does not exist of its own accord in some kind of privileged vacuum, but rather as a tool deeply rooted in the behavior and practices of a particular life-form, namely that of human beings. Wittgenstein rightly argues that to lose sight of these contexts runs the risk of falling into all sorts of misconceptions and paradoxes.

Despite the value, however, of Wittgenstein's emphasis on functional linguistic contexts, his treatment of the question of universals is superficial. Even if we can resolve the apparent commonality behind the word "game," as he claims, into a complex of overlapping "similarities," we are still faced with an insistent question: just what is meant by the word "similarity"? If the meaning of this word, like that of "game," lies in the overlapping similarities of its actual use, then we are stuck in a loop: in order to understand the meaning of similarities, we have to understand the meaning of similarities. But how can we look for such similarities in functional contexts when we don't even know how to recognize what a similarity is in the first place?

Just how do we know when we are faced with a "similarity"? Do we have some kind of innate idea of it? Does it exist objectively in things that are similar? Is it a mere name? In other words, in trying to understand Wittgenstein's "similarity," we are faced with exactly the same questions that have arisen in the traditional philosophical debate over universals. And for good reason, because in the later philosophy of Wittgenstein, similarity is a crucial universal that is at the base of his entire theory of language, although he nowhere explicitly acknowledges it as such or attempts to analyze it. In effect, Wittgenstein just shuffles the universal card behind other cards in the philosophical deck that are of more interest to him, but which in turn inevitably lead back to this basic unresolved question.

Ironically, the unresolved difficulties implicit in Wittgenstein's approach bring us right back to square one on the philosophical game board. It was precisely such challenging questions about the nature of family resemblances and identity that first prompted Plato to set out on the long intellectual journey that ended with his theory of Forms, as discussed above. Indeed, one of the terms used by both Plato and Aristotle to denote universals is the Greek word *genos*, which literally means "family" or "clan."

Ironically, if Wittgenstein's attitude toward family resemblances had prevailed in the very area from which he took the metaphor (genetic development), science would have been seriously impeded. The reason is that scientists would have been slow to discover that such differences *do* in fact have an essentially defining basis—genes.

Relativity of Universals

As in the myth of the blind men, each of whom felt part of the elephant and interpreted it as the whole, so with the great historical debate on the nature of universals: each of the major schools of thought mentioned above is partly right and partly wrong, although none has had sufficient breadth of vision to see how each of its rivals has also had a handle on the truth. The key to gaining such an overall perspective lies in understanding the *relativity* of universals, which in turn depends on understanding the correlativity of unity and plurality in the interpretational process.

As discussed earlier in this chapter, all empirical knowledge depends on descriptive analysis, which in turn depends in part on interpreter-made decisions as to what in any *interpretandum* constitutes systems and elements. These decisions in turn are defined by the interpreter's decisions about one and many. Now to say that any entity x is a universal in regard to some particulars a, b, c... etc., means at least this: there is some distinguishable similarity among a, b, c... that is named "x." Further, to say that there is some distinguishable similarity among a, b, c... is equivalent to saying that a, b, c... constitute a set, namely the set of those particulars having that distinguishable similarity, in contrast to all other particulars, if any, that do not. But to say that particulars constitute a set means that such particulars constitute in some sense a unity, for a set is that which is one by virtue of some definition or circumstance or function.

Here we should note that even in the most minimal sense of the word, a "set" is more than a mere aggregate—the "more" being the unity, occasioned by the decision of some interpreter, that constitutes the set as a set. Therefore, it is possible to regard *every* interpretable entity as a whole greater than the sum of its parts (even if it has but one part), since every interpretable entity can be viewed as a set (a set of at least one member), and since every set, as a set, is more than a mere aggregate. Moreover, for any interpretative system that contains such a set as an element, the set will be a *real object* in the context of that system (although not necessarily so in the contexts of other systems). The full implication of these considerations will emerge later in chapter three, in a discussion of the nature of mathematics.

To see how these considerations apply to universals, consider the universal named "chess piece." Contrary to what we might at first think, a chess piece is not just a piece of wood having a particular shape, because *any* object placed on the chess board can be a chess piece if it moves according to certain rules. In fact, the different shapes of chess pieces are mere artistic conventions to aid players in recognizing them during play. No, a chess piece is more than a kind of material or a kind of shape. Rather, any material object may be regarded as a chess piece provided that it move in a board game in accordance with rules prescribed by the International Chess Federation located in Paris.

In terms of the formula given previously for a universal, x is chess piece; a, b, c... are any finite material objects; and the distinguishable similarity is movability by a material object in a board game whose rules are prescribed by the International Chess Federation located in Paris. Although the many material objects that satisfy this stipulated distinguishable similarity may be diversely scattered throughout the world, fashioned from different materials, and possessed of different shapes, nonetheless they all constitute a set (and therefore a unity) by virtue of their satisfying the stipulated distinguishable similarity. In short, they are the particulars of which chess piece is the universal.

As the above example shows, the key factor in determining what constitutes a universal in regard to certain particulars is a decision about one and many made by some interpreter. In the case at hand, the decision is conscious and explicit, resulting from a deliberate, rational analysis of the game of chess and its constituents. But the earlier sections of this chapter have shown that many, indeed most, decisions about what constitutes one and many in any *interpretandum* are made preconsciously or semiconsciously, and are determined or highly influenced by the interpreter's primary and secondary response patterns. But whether preconscious, semi-conscious, or conscious, whether determined, influenced, or autonomous, all such decisions remain *decisions*, which means in effect that there is nothing in the *interpretandum* as such that logically requires the particular decisions that happen to be made; therefore, there is no logical impediment to the *interpretandum's* being analyzed into a different system of universals and particulars. It all comes down to this:

Universals and particulars are *correlatives*, resulting from the decision of some interpreter interacting with some *interpretandum*.

As a result of this analysis, we can see that the so-called "problem of universals" is equally the problem of particulars, or rather the problem of universals *and* particulars; that is, the existence of universals is neither more nor less problematic than the existence of particulars, since no interpreted *interpretandum* exists that is devoid of both, and since the two are defined relative to each other by the decisions of some interpreter. Hence particulars do not "participate in" self-subsistent Forms as Plato argued, nor do self-subsistent essences "inhere in" particulars per Aristotle, nor are universals "mere names" per Ockham, nor are universals "family resemblances" per Wittgenstein. Contrary to all, *both* universals *and* particulars are perceived, felt, or inferred to exist partly as a result of the *interpretandum* itself, and partly as a result of the decisions of some interpreter or some group of interpreters.

Particulars and universals are both partly nominal, because both partly result from the decisions of the interpreter. But both are also partly objective, because they are evoked by an *interpretandum* that is not the same as the interpreter. Most important of all: no absolute trench can be dug between knowledge and world, or between subject and object. The ultimate constituents of knowledge/world are interpretational events. These have an interpreter-*interpretandum* polarity (not dichotomy). They cannot be meaningfully subdivided into any subunits that are more basic. In the beginning was interpretation.

Even if one insists that the uninterpreted can be said to exist, nonetheless, it remains unknowable to any particular interpreters until they in fact interpret it. Remove all interpretation, and you remove the world insofar as it is knowable.

Since universals and particulars partly depend on the decisions of interpreters or groups of interpreters, it's not surprising that there can be a great variety of humanly-created universal-particular schemata. For example, consider subatomic physicists. They construct a universe of interpretation where quanta are particulars and fields are universals. Sociologists, on the other hand, construct a universe of interpretation where human beings are particulars and societies universals. Neither of these schemata is more real, in any absolute sense, than the other. Both are universes of interpretation that constitute a field of relative objectivity for certain kinds of interpreters examining certain kinds of *interpretanda*. To atomic physicists, when they are pursuing physics, quanta and fields are real elements and real universals. To sociologists, when they are pursuing sociology, human beings and societies are real elements and real universals. And for both atomic physicists and sociologists, there will be different particulars and universals when they do other things, such as shop for groceries or make love. Whether as an atomic physicist or as a sociologist or otherwise, all human beings function with a multiplicity of universes of interpretation and hence with a multiplicity of schemata for particulars and universals.

How, then, are these different universes of interpretation to be related to each other? Can there be one definitive way of interrelating them that makes one such universe of interpretation more basic than all the rest? For example, can we derive all other universes of interpretation (such as sociology, economics, etc.) from the universe of interpretation we call "atomic physics"?

To the extent that any interpreter or group of interpreters succeeds in reducing several shared universes of interpretation to one basic universe of interpretation, to the same extent will that basic universe of interpretation possess a greater relative reality for the interpreter or interpreters who so succeed. Nonetheless, there is no commanding reason to think that such a reduction must, or must not, be possible. Therefore, the claim of certain twentieth-century logical positivists that all the sciences are in principle a unity, expressible through one formalized scientific language, is at best a pious hope, not at all a necessary principle. Such a hope can be useful as a kind of hypothetical guide, if it encourages interpreters to search for underlying commonalities in various universes of interpretation in order to simplify them into fewer, more encompassing systems. But the same hope can also be harmful, if it encourages interpreters to overlook or suppress essential differences in various universes of interpretation in order to force them into one overly-simple mold.

Every human interpreter on the planet lives in a many-mansioned reality. In the course of a lifetime, he or she participates in numerous universes of interpretation. Some of these overlap. Some of them conflict. None is the exclusive root of which all the others are mere appendages. In addition, it remains an open question whether striving for some overall unity of interpretation is socially desirable. The closest approximation in the West to such an ideal was the dominance of the Christian myth system over all aspects of life in medieval Europe. Would we be any better off today if a similar domination were achieved by the myth systems of logical positivists or nuclear physicists?

Whether nuclear physicists, sociologists, and poets will someday agree on common particulars and common universals, and hence on a common universe of interpretation, remains to be seen. But even if they could, indeed even if every human interpreter came to agree on one common universe of interpretation, there would still be no necessary agreement with universes of interpretation of other species on the planet, to say nothing of species in other galaxies.

Still, the nagging question recurs: can't we somehow get around behind these schemata? Can't we behold, not some particular universe of interpretation, but the universe as it really is, in and of itself? As discussed earlier, there is no pure objectivity that is knowable, just as there is no pure subjectivity that is meaningful. We know reality only insofar as we interpret it, and there are many ways to interpret it. The universe was not created by a fundamentalist.

Normative Communities

Granted the limiting conditions on interpretation previously discussed, we *can* reasonably ask this question: Is it possible for there to be a kind of exemplary interpreter? That is, can there be an interpreter so perceptive of *interpretanda*, so linguistically capable, so comprehending of present and past experience as to set a standard for the process of making true propositions? The answer is a qualified yes.

An exemplary interpreter, or at least the ideal of a hypothetical exemplary interpreter, can exist by implication for any group of interpreters. The test is whether they agree about the criteria for perceptiveness, linguistic capability, depth of experience, etc. Given the existence of such shared criteria, interpreters can examine any proposition and compare the circumstances of its making (including observations, inferences, etc.) to those specified by the criteria. They conclude with a judgment as to how closely the propositional process in the particular case approximates to the ideal. In doing so, the interpreters judge the proposition through the eyes of a hypothetical exemplary interpreter.

Any group of interpreters that shares such criteria for the evaluation of propositions (and so shares, by implication, an ideal of a hypothetical exemplary interpreter) I call a normative community. One example of such a normative community is the international group of interpreters currently doing research on the physics of subatomic particles. Although living in different countries and speaking different languages, these interpreters nonetheless share by implication an ideal of a particular kind of hypothetical exemplary interpreter. Their ideal interpreter is one who is knowledgeable of previous and current research, who adheres to certain standards of experimental methodology, and who is adept at expressing new discoveries in the language of advanced mathematics.

As a result of their agreement concerning such criteria, these interpreters are often able to agree on the value of the descriptions of reality made by their members. When so agreed, they judge these descriptions through the eyes of the hypothetical exemplary interpreter that is implicit in their criteria for propositional evaluation. At the same time, there other groups of interpreters (such as Christian fundamentalists) that have radically different criteria for propositional evaluation. Not surprisingly, they may come to radically different conclusions about what constitutes a proper description of reality.

The fact that Christian fundamentalists happen to dismiss a set of propositions held dear by nuclear physicists, or vice-versa, does not mean that the dismissed propositions lose their truth-value. To the contrary, normatively established propositions remain true and valuable for the normative community that evaluates them as such. To the extent that there may be a mutual desire among disparate normative communities for common dialogue or even cognitive agreement, to the same extent will they endeavor to find propositions deemed true and valuable for both. Otherwise, however, they will continue to define themselves cognitively by the contexts of their own relatively-established objective worlds.

As shown above, there is no possible way for any interpreter or any normative community of interpreters somehow to "get around" interpretation and so behold "the objective world as it really is." All any interpreter or normative community can ever know is the world as interpreted by that interpreter or by that normative community.

In the end, we come to an ineradicable complexity at the very heart of the knowing process. All interpretations of the world remain both partly conventional and partly revelatory of reality. There is no way in principle to draw an absolute and final distinction between the two.

Epistemological Crisis

When, for whatever reason, deep divisions develop *within* a normative community over what constitutes the ideal of its hypothetical exemplary interpreter, that community undergoes a crisis of self-definition. A good example of this effect can be found in the history of astronomy. For the normative community of European astronomers prior to the 16th century A.D., the hypothetical exemplary interpreter was one who regarded Christian scripture, papal decrees, and the writings of Ptolemy as authoritative for evaluating astronomical questions. By the 18th century A.D., however, the hypothetical exemplary interpreter in astronomy had become one who regarded only the evidence provided by telescopes as authoritative.

Corresponding to this radical change in the nature of the ideal of the hypothetical exemplary astronomical interpreter was an equally radical change in the normative community of astronomers themselves. And both changes in turn were part of a much larger pattern of change in religion, economics, politics, and general culture. As in the case of individual interpreters, so with normative communities: their interpretations do not exist as absolutes in a vacuum but are contingent threads interwoven in a far larger fabric of complex historical forces.

Since conflict can arise both between and within normative communities as to the nature of the hypothetical exemplary interpreter, how are such conflicts finally to be resolved? As in the case of individual interpreters, if there is little or no overlap in reality maps, a resolution will not likely be forthcoming. But what if there are shared areas of their differing reality maps and a mutual interest in dialogue? In that case, each side will seek to show that the other's dissenting criteria for propositional evaluation are inconsistent with the mutually shared part of their respective reality maps, with shared criteria of propositional evaluation, etc. The greater the overlap among conflicting normative communities in regard to reality maps and criteria for propositional evaluation, the greater the likelihood of reconciliation and agreement. But there is no guarantee that conflicts of this nature can be resolved.

Let us grant that it is not possible to behold the universe except through the eyes of some interpreter. Even so, we can ask this question: Is it at least possible that all interpreters that are *rational* could share, despite other differences, a reality map and criteria for propositional evaluation based on commonalities inherent in rational interpretation as such? In other words, can we posit the ideal of a universal hypothetical exemplary interpreter for rationality in and of itself? And, even more, can we posit the actual existence of any such universal exemplary interpreter?

Immanuel Kant's Transcendental Philosophy

The ideal of a universal hypothetical exemplary interpreter for rationality as such is reasonable only if there is some constant factor of interpretation for all rational interpreters, regardless of their genetic structure, cultural conditioning, and idiosyncratic life experiences. The desire to establish the possibility for such an ideal exemplary interpreter, at least among human beings, was a principal motivating force behind the work of the German philosopher Immanuel Kant (1724-1804), the greatest Western philosopher since classical antiquity.

According to Kant, we cannot explain, merely by examining sensation, how we are able to have an ordered knowledge of stable objects in the world, for the senses report to us only a constant flow of unconnected, changing impressions. Nor can we discover the cause for this stability in reasoning, since reasoning merely re-directs and manages the flow given to it by the senses. In order to explain the possibility of our knowing a stable world, we have to go further and examine the logical and philosophical presuppositions for the existence and functioning of human consciousness as such.

Kant called such a philosophical endeavor "transcendental" because it did not seek to establish any empirically verifiable facts, but rather looked beyond empirical facts to inquire into the purely formal conditions for the very possibility of their existence in the first place. By pursuing this line of inquiry, Kant hoped to show that in order even to be conscious of sensations we have to assume a common underlying structure of rational interpretation for all human beings. In a great stream of thick books throughout his life, and most memorably in his magnificent *Critique of Pure Reason*, Kant strove mightily to prove this point: although we can never know "things in themselves" precisely as they are in themselves, we can nevertheless have a well grounded interpretation of their phenomenal appearances due to the nature of the human mind. The reason is that the common parameters of the mind's functioning *define* what it means to have such knowledge as is available to us.

Despite Kant's claim that transcendental philosophy could reveal only the purely formal aspects of such interpretational constancy, he nonetheless sought throughout his life to establish an ever growing list of substantial claims based on these underlying formal necessities. By the time of his death in 1804, Kant had come to argue that the formal conditions for rational human interpretation as such require that we accept, either theoretically or practically, the necessity of the following: Euclidean geometry, the irreversible forward movement of time, the doctrine of substance, a strict causal nexus among all physical phenomena, the establishment of all morality on a sense of impersonal duty, the immortality of the soul, and the existence of one, all-powerful God. Alas for Kant, however, later physicists rejected the necessity of the first four points, just as later philosophers undermined the seeming necessity (although not the possibility) of the remainder.

Kant's work had a great merit: it forthrightly faced up to the realization that we can only know our own interpretation of the universe, never the universe as it is in and of itself. Moreover, Kant attempted to do justice to the correlativity of objectivity and subjectivity, thereby preserving the relative reality of both. By so doing, he was able to clarify many of the philosophical anomalies that his age had inherited from both continental rationalism and British empiricism. In effect, Kant attempted to create a grand synthesis of the best insights of Western philosophy in his day. To a considerable degree he succeeded, a feat for which he deserves lasting fame.

Kant, however, had a great weakness: attempting to buttress beliefs that were peculiar to his own personality and his own historical epoch on a purely formal analysis of the interpretative process as such. In particular, Kant simply could not accept the possibility that the principles either of Isaac Newton's new physics or of traditional monotheism might be contingent.

Although we can indeed analyze the formal requirements of interpretation as such, as Kant claimed, this analysis provides an understanding only of the correlativity of one/many, system/element, and subject/object, as outlined above. Such an analysis, however, does *not* provide the basis for making substantive claims of the nature Kant hoped for. Nor does it guarantee the existence of any universal standard of rational interpretation, except for the requirement that such an act of interpretation be characterized by the correlative polarities just noted.

After Kant's death, a great split developed in Western philosophy between two camps: the idealists and the positivists. The former, abandoning altogether Kant's limiting function of things in themselves, concluded that both nature and history reflect the workings of some kind of higher consciousness; the latter, suspicious of all forms of subjectivity, concluded that the inner person is just a mechanical after-effect of external phenomena. In effect, each camp grabbed onto half of Kant and tried to cut off or explain away the other half. In so doing, they turned their back on Kant's greatest philosophical achievement: the realization that interpretation requires a mutually entailing polarity (not dichotomy) between subject and object. Contrary to those who have sought thus to sunder Kant, this book is largely an attempt to rehabilitate his basic insight, while also peeling away the extraneous accretions with which he himself eventually loaded it.

Universal Exemplary Interpreters

Although Kant tried mightily to demonstrate the reality of constant, constitutive factors in all rational interpretation among humans, the only such common factors that exist are empty and purely formal, not substantive. Furthermore, it is risky to assume that what has been defined as rationality by some (or even all) human cultures must hold for every other rational interpreter in the universe. A universal hypothetical exemplary interpreter for rationality *may* exist, but no one, not even Immanuel Kant, has successfully shown that it *must* exist.

The assertion of the existence of a special kind of exemplary interpreter, namely one that is actual (not just hypothetical), and one that is universal in every sense, is implicit in the assertion that there exists an omniscient and omnipotent God. The proposition that this type of interpreter exists may be true. Even so, however, such an interpreter cannot be construed to have the power to make interpretations that must in and of themselves be valid for every other interpreter in the universe. Why? Because the most that *any* interpreter can do is make interpretations that are valid in terms of that particular interpreter's own reality map. Even if a universal exemplary interpreter had some kind of universal reality map, all other interpreters in the universe would still have only their own partial reality maps, in accordance with which they must make all their interpretations. Therefore the mere fact that a universal exemplary interpreter renders a judgment is no reason in and of itself for other interpreters to accept (or even understand) that judgment. To argue otherwise is to misconstrue the entire nature of interpretation.

The proposition that an actual universal exemplary interpreter exists also runs into another complication: in order to rationally evaluate the claim of any entity in the universe to be that interpreter (that is, to know *whose* version of God is the right one), one must have the capacity to approximate in interpretive power just such a universal exemplary interpreter. Only an interpreter so powerful can rationally interpret if some particular candidate satisfies the necessary conditions for God's nature and power. The situation is analogous to that of an interpreter who is a physicist. He or she must be able to approximate the interpretive power of the hypothetical exemplary physicist in order to know whose hypotheses in physics most closely fulfill the criteria for truth and reliability in that discipline. In the case of God, however, the degree of interpretive power to be approximated is infinitely beyond all human ability, at least if God is to be understood as infinite. Regardless of how much interpretive power a human interpreter has, he or she will always be surpassed to an infinite degree by the power and nature of an infinite God.

Therefore if God exists, only an interpreter whose interpretive power approximates that of God's can rationally interpret which entity in the universe *is* God. For every other interpreter, interpretations on such a question—in the absence of a direct revelation from God—must be a matter of conjecture, guess work, hypothesis, or faith.

Consider, then, the case of someone who has not previously received a direct revelation from God and who utters a prayer to God. Although it is logically possible that this person is praying to an entity that is in fact God, it is also logically possible that the object of his or her prayer is a misconception, fantasy, hallucination, obsession, cultural construct, etc. As we have seen, no mortal who prays to an entity he or she regards as an infinite God can rationally interpret, without receiving a direct revelation, that that entity is God.

Furthermore, even a belief in God that might arise from a direct revelation from God provides no logical basis whatever for imparting that faith to others, however convincing it may be to the recipient. Lacking such a direct revelation, other interpreters can only rely on rational interpretation, which is inadequate to the task for the reasons just mentioned. Consequently if a religion bases its belief in God on an alleged direct revelation from God, it is irrational for that religion to condemn others for not believing in God if they have never had such a direct revelation. On the other hand, if a religion does *not* base its faith in God on an alleged direct revelation from God, it can never rationally assert that the object of its faith is really God. In either case, human beings who believe in a particular version of an infinite God have no rational basis for condemning those who do not. The most such believers can reasonably claim is this: "I have had a direct revelation from God that is valid for me."

Moreover, if the highest standard of human life is to live according to the dictates of rational interpretation (as Socrates, among others, apparently maintained), one cannot give the highest value to the putative dictates of a God one cannot rationally understand. On the other hand, if the highest standard of human life is to be found in the judgments attributed to such a God (as Jesus of Nazareth, among others, apparently maintained), one cannot give the highest value to the putative standards of rational interpretation.

How do we know that the voice that speaks to us is really God's? This question is the stumbling block of all "revealed" religion. How can we interact with the universe without presupposing much more than merely rational interpretation? This question is the stumbling block of all "rationalism." Is it possible to leave room in one's life for the more-than-rational while at the same time avoiding the grossly irrational behavior characteristic of most organized religion? To this last question we will return in later chapters.

The Great Dialog

We are now in a position to answer some of the questions concerning reality and knowledge with which we began this long chapter. Our elucidations have shown that it is not possible, even in principle, to cut an absolute swath between objectivity and subjectivity. Although the capacity to distinguish between the two is obviously essential to human life, it is a fallacy to presuppose that the separating process can be carried out exhaustively, or that every human endeavor requires the same degree of such separation. Neither objectivity nor subjectivity is the final standard by which to judge the reality of any phenomenon. Objectivity and subjectivity are, rather, but two sides of a more fundamental coin, interpretation. Insofar as the world is knowable, it emerges from the interactions of interpreters with *interpretanda*. Once the link between the interpreter and the *interpretandum* is cut, the most that remains is a chaotic flux of impressions. Should objectivity shed all subjectivity, it would be unknowable; should subjectivity shed all objectivity, it would be meaningless. The fount of all knowledge and meaning lies in the very thing that links objectivity and subjectivity, that is, interpretation.

To say that objectivity and subjectivity are ultimately inseparable, however, is not to say that there can be no standards. To the contrary, objective standards really do exist, but they are always *relative* objectivities, that is, they always presuppose some interpreter or some group of interpreters for whom they are objective. To pretend otherwise usually represents an effort to fob off the objectivities of one's own particular group onto other groups. Historical examples of this sort of fobbing effort are abundant: the attitudes of the invading white Europeans toward the American Indians; of monotheists toward pagans; of Christians toward non-Christians; of heterosexuals toward homosexuals; of men toward women; and of scientists towards poets, artists, and spiritual visionaries.

A philosophy that acknowledges the interpretational source of knowledge and reality firmly resists all those who would force their own monumental objectivities onto others. In place of such intellectual bullying, interpretation-based philosophy calls for the opening of a great dialog on this question: *What does it mean to lead a rational and worthy human life?* Interpretation-based philosophy invites as prospective participants in this great dialog all persons of good will from every avenue of human experience. In the spirit of furthering such a dialog, we will turn in the next chapter to a discussion of the nature of ethics.

---

[1] Some deconstructionists say there is nothing outside the text, in terms of which the text may be judged. But on this account, interpretation becomes a hopelessly drifting boat, throwing away the nonlinguistic anchor that it needs to moor itself at the ports of reality. For a concise philosophical critique of the deconstructionist view, see T.K. Seung, *Structuralism and Hermeneutics*, Columbia University Press, New York, 1982.

[2] Homer, *Odyssey*, 5, 438-450.

[3] William Blake, "A Vision of the Last Judgment" in *The Poetry and Prose of William Blake*, ed. by David Erdman and Harold Bloom, Doubleday & Co., Garden City, NY, 1968, p. 555.

[4] Thomas S. Kuhn, *The Structure of Scientific Revolutions*, 2nd edition, The University of Chicago Press, Chicago, 1970, p. 109.

[5] Their sometimes-excessive claims are rightly criticized by Paul Gross and Norman Levitt, *Higher Superstition: The Academic Left and Its Quarrels with Science*, Johns Hopkins University Press, Baltimore, 1994, p. 44 ff. This book has an excess of its own, however: it is quick to dismiss as "superstition" any critique of the dogma that science is our best window on reality.

[6] Lilly Tomlin in Jane Wagner's *The Search for Signs of Intelligent Life in the Universe*, Harper & Row, New York, 1986, p. 18

[7] Plotinus, *Enneads*, VI, 9, 1.

[8] *ibid.*, VI, 9, 11.

[9] Ludwig Wittgenstein, *Tractatus Logico-Philosophicus*, bilingual edition of by D.F. Pears & B.F. McGuinnes, The Humanities Press, New York, 1961.

[10] *ibid.*, 2.1; original's emphasis.

[11] Ludwig Wittgenstein, *Philosophical Investigations*, trans. by G.E.M. Anscombe, the Macmillan Company, New York, 1953.

[12] Wittgenstein, *Tractatus*, p. 5; original's emphasis.

[13] F.H. Bradley, *Appearance and Reality. A Metaphysical Essay*, 2nd edition, 9th impression, The Clarendon Press, Oxford, 1930, p. 156.

[14] F.H. Bradley, *Essays on Truth and Reality*, The Clarendon Press, Oxford, 1914, p. 327, n.2.

[15] Wittgenstein, *Tractatus*, 7; my translation.

Right and Wrong

SUMMARY: This chapter shows how the interpreter (that is, the subject) is essential to moral judgment. Understanding the interpreter's role helps clarify the conflicting ethical claims made by different individual philosophers, both ancient and modern. It also illuminates the nature of group morality.

In the beginning was interpretation. From interpretation have emerged one and many, system and element, objectivity and subjectivity, interpreter and interpreted, world and knowledge. As discussed in chapter one, these concepts are all correlative; that is, the meaning of each depends on the meaning of its respective opposite, and on interpretation, which is the fount of them all.

As we have seen, some interpreters have only a simple ability: to interpret what is, or is not, in their immediate environments, and to express these interpretations in descriptive propositions. Other interpreters, however, also have a higher-order ability: to *evaluate* propositions according to certain standards. This chapter will examine in greater detail what it means to evaluate interpretations according to standards, an examination that will naturally lead to an inquiry into the nature of ethics.

At the beginning of this inquiry, we will look at both the personal lives and the conflicting ethical theories of certain well-known Western philosophers, noting what is valuable in the ethical views of each. This overview will enable us to bring into better focus the common interpretative basis that underlies all ethical systems. We will then integrate this insight into what we have already discovered in chapter one about the interpretative basis of empirical knowledge.

To begin, let us recall that interpreters who evaluate propositions according to standards are often members of a normative community; that is, they are part of a group of interpreters who share a common reality map and a common set of criteria for propositional evaluation. Interpreters engaged in such an evaluational process make interpretations about two distinct kinds of things: (1) systems, elements, and relational ranges in a given data scene (that is, about what is); and (2) hypothetical ideal data scenes (that is, about what might be or what ought to be). Any interpreter having this twofold interpretative ability I call a normative interpreter. When such interpreters are members of a similarly interpreting group, they constitute a normative community of interpreters.

Different normative communities pursue different ways of evaluating data scenes, depending on their own particular group interests and standards. Consider, for example, the normative community that consists of physicists engaged in the study of subatomic particles. What happens when they encounter any proposition proffered by any of their number concerning the behavior of subatomic interactions? They evaluate such a proposition according to their established criteria for experimental methodology, deductive rigor, mathematical elegance, etc. When members of the normative community of subatomic physicists make these evaluations, their principal interest is to establish the most complete and consistent description possible of subatomic reality, and they develop and apply all criteria of evaluation pursuant to this interest.

In the example just given, the normative interpreters have a cognitive interest. Many other kinds of interest are also possible, as are many other kinds of normative interpreter. One such possible interest is that which pertains to what is called "moral value."

What does it mean to say that an action has "moral value"? We can find a clue from etymology. The adjective "moral" derives from the Latin *moralis*, a word coined by the Roman orator and philosopher Marcus Tullius Cicero in the first century B.C.[1] Cicero found it necessary to coin the adjective *moralis*, meaning "that which pertains to mores or personal character," while he was translating certain philosophical treatises from Greek. The Greek word that *moralis* translated (*ethikos*) had originally meant "pertaining to the haunts of an animal." Later this Greek word meant "pertaining to mores or personal character." Cicero combined his new adjective *moralis* with the Latin noun *philosophia*, so that *philosophia moralis* meant "that branch of philosophy dealing with mores or personal character." The contemporary English phrase "moral value" means "the adjudged merit of conduct or behavior in terms of its goodness or rightness."

These linguistic considerations suggest a number of parallel historical developments. First, the late expansion in meaning of both the Greek word *ethos* and the Latin word *mores* from "custom" and "habit" to "conduct" and "character" implies that what we today call "moral philosophy" or "ethical thinking" is a fairly recent development in the history of human consciousness. When judged by the linguistic evidence, the earliest speakers of Greek and Latin (and, indeed, of many other languages) seem not so much concerned with personal ethical values as with collective *custom*. When they began to reflect on personal ethical values and behavior, however, they found it necessary to create a new terminology with which to do so. In general, they first reached for old words that meant "custom" and then expanded their meanings, initially viewing the individual as a kind of microcosm of the surrounding society, having his or her own personal "custom" or "habit" analogous to the way in which the encompassing society had *its* collective custom. Only after a long process of historical change and linguistic clarification did the idea appear that the individual human being is an autonomous moral agent in his or her own right.

At least for the last several thousand years, most adult human beings have routinely evaluated human behavior in moral terms. For much of the same period, a great debate has raged among philosophers as to what is involved in this evaluational process. For example, some philosophers see moral judgments as evaluations of one's duty to God; others, as judgments about duty in the abstract; others, as calculations about what is useful; and yet others, as expressions of one's feelings.

None of these interpretations has succeeded in winning widespread support among other philosophers. Indeed, there has been but little progress among philosophers in clarifying the nature of moral judgment since the time of Socrates. Before we undertake our own analysis of moral judgment, we will take a brief look at some of these earlier views of the matter, noting what is valuable in each.

Augustine of Hippo

The first of the four viewpoints noted above is the belief that moral judgment means evaluation of one's duty to God. Probably the most influential effort in the West to build a philosophical and religious system based on this view was that of the African Christian philosopher Augustine (Aurelius Augustinus). Born into the Roman-controlled region of Numidia in North Africa in 354 A.D. to a Christian mother and pagan father, Augustine experimented with a succession of ascetic religious movements. These included Manichaeanism, Neoplatonism, and finally Christianity.

Under the influence of Bishop Ambrose of Milan, Augustine moved ever closer to embracing Christianity; however, he still felt great inner turmoil over the issue, partly because of his previous history of extra-marital sexual relations. In 386 A.D., while in the garden of his house, Augustine underwent a celebrated conversion-experience, occasioned by hearing a child's voice coming over the wall, repeating *Tolle, lege, tolle, lege* ("Take, read, take, read").[2] Opening the letters of Paul of Tarsus at random, Augustine alighted on Paul's Letter to the Romans, where he found it written (as translated by *The New American Bible*):

> Let us live honorably as in daylight; not in carousing and drunkenness, not in sexual excess and lust, not in quarreling and jealousy. Rather, put on the Lord Jesus Christ and make no provision for the desires of the flesh.[3]

The above passage, defining Christianity in terms of asceticism, became the final catalyst that triggered Augustine's conversion. Although commentators on Augustine often refer to this celebrated passage, they generally overlook the fact that it not only promotes asceticism but also alludes to (and condemns) a specific Greco-Roman religious tradition. This alternate tradition, repudiating the asceticism of Manicheanism, Neoplatonism, and Christianity, was the religion of the ancient Greek god Dionysos, "the God of Ecstasy." Celebrations to this god were renowned for wine-drinking, dancing, transvestism, and sexual acts, including homosexuality.

The English translation cited above obscures the allusion to Dionysian religion by its use of the general English words "carousing and drunkenness" for the Latin phrase *comisationibus et ebrietatibus*. These Latin words actually transliterate Greek words that refer to the ritual wine-drinking and revelry found in the ancient worship of Dionysos.[4] Other words in the passage also have Dionysian allusions. Bearing in mind these allusions, we would do better to translate the above passage from Romans as follows:

> Let us live honorably as in daylight; not with the drunken bouts of Dionysian bands or with licentious sex acts, not with quarreling and jealousy. Rather, put on the Lord Jesus Christ and make no provision for the desires of the flesh.

The full significance of this passage is not merely that it condemns the joys of the flesh, but that, by implication, it also repudiates the religious and cultural forces that had previously validated them in the Greco-Roman world. Indeed, more: this passage offers in place of the personal god Dionysos, who was the patron of these delights, the personal god Jesus Christ, who is the patron of their abandonment.

This passage had a powerful impact on Augustine because it crystallized an important realization for him: not only was he turning his back on his own personal past but also on an entire religio-cultural epoch. Indeed, his agonized life was one of the living, self-conscious hinges on which the great door of history was then turning as it swept out of the classical era and into the middle ages.

After his conversion to Christianity, Augustine rapidly rose in the church hierarchy of North Africa, becoming Bishop of Hippo in 396 A.D. Although deeply involved in the minute details of day-to-day church administration, he nonetheless found time to write voluminously. By the time of his death in 430 A.D. (while the Vandals were besieging Hippo), he had created a highly developed system of religious philosophy. It would serve as the definitive intellectual statement of Christian belief in the West until the work of Thomas Aquinas in the 13th century.

The Role of God in Ethics

According to Augustine, all moral judgments are to be understood as evaluations of one's duty to obey the will of God as revealed in the Old and New Testaments and as interpreted by the church hierarchy. The God that is the author of this moral obligation is the transcendent, omniscient, and omnipotent ruler of the universe, which he created by his own free will. A human being, in turn, is to be understood as an immortal soul using a mortal body. Because the body perishes while the soul persists, the purpose of human life cannot be found in this world but only in the everlasting world to come. Hence to follow, as an end in itself, any desire or pursuit that does not point or lead to the life to come is a perversion. Hence, also, to suffer any deprivation or pain in this life is justified, provided that to do so promotes the likelihood of everlasting union with God in the afterlife.

Augustine viewed the human personality as subject to the pressures of numerous conflicting forces that he called *amores*, meaning "loves," "desires," or "passions." He compared these *amores* to physical elements in nature that, moved by their own "weight" (*pondus*), tend to seek out their own proper places, as when fire moves upward, and stones downward. Hence his famous statement:

> My weight is my love; by it am I borne wherever I am borne.[5]

By this remark Augustine meant that the love or passion to which one gives oneself is never a neutral, inert thing, but rather a force that will tend to lead one either upward (to Heaven) or downward (to Hell). The implication is that every love or passion must be evaluated by one criterion: its capacity for leading one to eternal blessedness in the life hereafter.

Because the soul is pulled in various directions by the weights of its various *amores*, it must repeatedly make decisions by free choice (*liberum arbitrium*) concerning the directions it wishes to follow. By consistently choosing those *amores* that lead heavenward, the soul brings to them a kind of order patterned after God's will. Hence the prime emphasis of Augustine's ethical philosophy is on *obedience*: God has expressed his will to us through certain commands; our obligation to obey these commands requires that we impose order and direction on our capacity to love; otherwise, we will go to Hell.

Augustine's emphasis on obedience to God seems to contradict the spirit of his most often quoted remark—

Love and do what you will.[6]

But there is no contradiction here. Augustine presupposes that believers have already structured their emotional lives according to the dictates of orthodox Christian dogma. So what his remark means is love *properly* (that is, in accordance with God's commands) and then do what you will.

Augustine's emphasis on obedience as the basis of ethics represents an extraordinary shift in Greco-Roman philosophical thinking. Previously, most classical philosophers based their ethical theories on the concept of happiness. (*Eudaimonia* in Greek; hence such theories are called "eudaemonistic.") Although these philosophers argued about the nature of human happiness, they generally agreed that the purpose of human life is its attainment. Accordingly, they sought to help people find the most rational methods of obtaining happiness. Augustine, on the other hand, combined the other-worldly idealism of late Neoplatonism with the unyielding monotheism and prudery of Judaism. The result was to bring classical ethical theory's emphasis on happiness to an end.

Despite his emphasis on obedience, however, Augustine was aware of the emphasis on happiness in his philosophic predecessors. To find some role for happiness in the new ethical theory, he argued that only one object, God, could really satisfy the soul's deepest and most powerful longings. If only a soul would come to terms with its own deepest longings, said Augustine, then it would discover that true release can be found only in the arms of God. Hence, according to Augustine, the quest for human happiness coincides with obedience to God's commands, for only the latter can make possible the former. Despite this (literally) happy coincidence, however, God's commands remain the crucial factor. We must obey God's commands because they come from God, who can command anything he wants; fortunately for us, according to Augustine, he has commanded those things whose observance will, in the long haul, make us happy.

The great importance of obedience in Augustine's thought is reflected in his behavior toward those who disagreed with him. When he became Presbyter (and later Bishop) of Hippo, the majority of the inhabitants of that city were "Donatists," followers of a reform movement led by Donatus, Bishop of Carthage. According to the Donatists, the moral life of priests should not be separated from the validity of their ecclesiastical functions. Hence if a priest were guilty of mortal sins, any sacraments of the church he happened to administer while in that state were invalid. Some Donatists also called for separation of church and state.

Augustine argued that such beliefs were heresy. He also appealed to the state to suppress them, invoking the famous saying of Jesus in the third gospel:

> Go out into the highways and all along the hedgerows and force them to come in. I want my house to be full.[7]

Under the guise of commenting on the concept of love (in the first letter of John), Augustine wrote a famous attack on the Donatists. This attack is where Augustine made his famous remark (quoted above) about loving and doing what you will. The context of his attack on the Donatists makes it clear that Augustine's peculiar notion of "love" or "charity" had a zealous, doctrinaire meaning. For example, Augustine insists that love or charity is not to be confused with "a sort of gentle mildness." To the contrary, he proclaims:

> You are not to suppose that you love your servant when you do not beat him. ... That is not charity, but weakness. Let charity be zealous to set right, to correct faults. ... Love the man, not his errors.[8]

In the name of such a "love," Augustine called on the civil authorities to suppress the Donatists, rebuking them with these words:

> Back, brigands! Back, usurpers of Christ's estate![9]

In response to Augustine's plea, imperial troops attacked the Donatists, who responded with equal violence. After a brief civil war, the heresy was suppressed, and Augustine's position prevailed.

In the later Middle Ages, Christian inquisitors appealed to Augustine's example in order to justify the arrest, torture, and execution of alleged heretics and witches, all the while claiming to act out of love. These inquisitors based their behavior on three interrelated assumptions in Augustine's moral theory: (1) human destiny can only be fulfilled in the life to come; (2) the essence of any particular human being is his or her immortal soul, which will outlive its temporary domicile in the body; (3) to be good is to obey God, which, practically speaking, is the same as to obey the teachings of the church. Accordingly, Augustine's spiritual successors concluded that it is reasonable for the state to torture, mutilate, or destroy the bodies of those who refuse to obey the church, if that should be necessary in order to save their immortal souls for the life to come.

Granted Augustine's assumptions, conclusions like these are easy to draw. To this day, some Christians are still prepared, if only they could once again capture control of the state, to repeat such historical patterns. (Fundamentalist attitudes toward lesbians and gay men come to mind.) Other Christians, however, have been horrified by these implications, and so have rejected one or more of Augustine's assumptions.

Immanuel Kant

The second moral viewpoint mentioned above—that moral judgments pertain to duty in the abstract—finds its classical expression in the work of the German philosopher Immanuel Kant (1724-1804). Kant was born in Königsberg, then an important Prussian trading center and university town, but today the dilapidated Russian city of Kaliningrad. At an early age, Kant was exposed to the influence of Lutheran Pietism, which emphasized the importance of personal piety over external ritual and dogmatic conformity. At the age of 16 he was admitted to the University of Königsberg, where he studied mathematics, the sciences, and philosophy, eventually becoming one of the most learned men of his age. In 1770, at the age of 46, he was appointed professor of logic and metaphysics at the university, where he continued to teach for most of the remainder of his life. Until his death in 1804 at the age of 80, Kant hardly ever ventured beyond the environs of Königsberg, although he read avidly of events in other parts of the world and maintained communication with visiting foreigners. He never married, and so strictly did he keep to daily routine in his living habits that local residents were said to set their clocks by the punctuality of his daily walk.

Kant came of age during the peak of the Enlightenment, an era of great intellectual and artistic energy motivated by faith in the power of human reason and by an eagerness to challenge the established institutions of Europe. In his famous essay *What is Enlightenment? (Was ist Aufklärung?)*, Kant sympathized with the American and French Revolutions and the growing popular belief in liberty, equality, and the rule of law.

Kant was widely read in the major philosophical traditions of his day, which then tended to fall into two main groups: empiricists like David Hume, who argued that only the senses provided a basis for knowledge, and even then only tentatively so; and rationalists like Christian Wolff, who argued that abstract reasoning could reveal the true nature of the world. Kant attempted to cull the best of each tradition and to synthesize the results in a new system of philosophy that would redefine and transcend the major issues previously debated by both. His major work was *Critique of Pure Reason (Kritik der reinen Vernunft)*, first published in 1781 and revised in 1787. This book is probably the single most important philosophical work published in the West since the time of Aristotle. Most modern Western philosophers take as their starting point concepts or issues that *Critique* addresses, often borrowing Kant's terminology even when disagreeing with him.

Importance of Duty

Kant's *Critique* presented suggestive outlines for his theory of moral judgment, which he later developed more fully in *Foundations of the Metaphysics of Morals (Grundlegung zur Metaphysik der Sitten)* and *Critique of Practical Reason (Kritik der praktischen Vernunft)*. In Kant's mature view, an action has positive moral value ("is good") only if it is an expression of the will to do one's duty *because* it is one's duty. For example, if I treat members of different races respectfully in order to minimize social friction in my daily life, my behavior has no positive moral value according to Kant (although it's not a form of bad behavior, either). If, however, I treat people respectfully because I regard it as my *duty* to do so, then my behavior is good.

But what is duty? According to Kant, it is a special kind of necessity, but differing from the logical necessity found in the operations of reasoning or the causal necessity presupposed in all observed phenomena. This third kind of necessity is that which is felt by any rational being as a result of its respect for lawfulness as such. Whenever a rational being wills that its actions exemplify "conformity to universal law as such" (*die allgemeine Gesetzmässigkeit überhaupt*), then that rational being is acting out of duty, and its will may be called "good" without further qualification.

How, then, does a rational being make such a determination? According to Kant, two stages are involved: first, the rational being formulates a proposed action's "maxim," that is, the implicit principle of conduct of which the proposed action is an example; second, the rational being considers whether this maxim can reasonably be willed as a universal law for all rational beings or for nature.

For example, is it right for me, being indigent, to borrow money from another person and promise to pay it back, while yet knowing that I will never be in a position to do so? Here Kant would say that the maxim of my considered action is, "In seeking a loan, promise to pay back money when you know you can't." Now, can I will that this maxim be a universal law? That is, can I reasonably say, "*All* rational beings seeking loans should promise to pay back money when they know they can't"? Clearly not, Kant would say, because if everybody acted thus, promises concerning money would no longer have any value. As a result, no one would ever be able to borrow any money, including me. Hence my action, considered in a universal manner, is self-contradictory, and therefore morally wrong.

A rational being that consistently acts with such a regard for the universal legislatibility of its various maxims possesses what Kant calls a "good will." Such a will acts with moral consistency because it continually decides to act in accordance with its high regard for universal law as such. Hence such a will is the defining fount of all morality; hence also the famous opening lines of the first chapter of Kant's *Foundations of the Metaphysics of Morals*:

> Nothing in the world—indeed nothing even beyond the world—can possibly be conceived which could be called good without qualification except a *good will*.[10]

Kant says that one can also conceive of a "holy will," that is, a kind of will that, by its very nature, wills only what is in accord with universal law as such. A will of this nature is possessed by God. Hence (contrary to Augustine) we should obey God's commands, not because God has decreed them, but rather because God always acts in accord with duty by virtue of possessing a holy will. If God did not possess a holy will, then it would be conceivable that we might rightfully oppose him in certain instances in the name of morality. But in Kant's eyes, God is God precisely because he possesses such a will.

The Categorical Imperative

Kant's elucidation of the concept of a good will in terms of universal law leads him to restate his theory in terms of *imperatives*. These are principles that are binding on the will of a rational being (that is, statements that can be expressed with the word "ought"). Among such imperatives, Kant distinguishes two kinds: (1) hypothetical (those that command actions that serve as a means to some other action that is good in itself); and (2) categorical (those that command an action that is good in itself). But we have seen that in Kant's view only one action is good in itself, namely the act of a will conforming itself to universal law as such. Hence there is only one categorical imperative: act only on those maxims that you can will to be general laws.

The categorical imperative means that every rational being must regard his or her own desires and needs with the same impartiality as those of every other rational being. Therefore, the categorical imperative can be expressed in a second, more practical, form: so act as to treat all human beings, both yourself and others, as ends, never as mere means.

In developing such a theory of moral valuation, Kant implicitly makes a very important assumption: a rational being possesses a free will by which it can choose between various courses of conduct. However, in his philosophy of science, Kant assumes that all knowable things are causally determined. If that is so, what becomes of the concept of free moral choice? It would seem that Kant's great philosophical system is a house fatally divided against itself.

Phenomena and Noumena

Kant went to great lengths to resolve this paradox. His solution, which was a take-off on Plato, was to distinguish between *phenomena* (literally, "things that appear") and *noumena* (literally, "things that are intellected"). *Phenomena* are the direct reports of the senses. These the intellect gathers up and arranges, thereby creating science. *Noumena*, on the other hand, are things as they are in themselves. These science can never know; nonetheless, they must be presupposed in order to explain the realities of moral experience and religion, which are just as important as the realities of science.

Among such *noumena* is the human soul. It never appears directly to science, because science, by its very methodology, can see only the empirical self (the self as a causally determined effect). As a *noumenon*, a human being is free and the maker of autonomous moral judgments, but as a *phenomenon*, a human being is subject to the laws of matter, unfree, and the object of scientific study.

The upshot is that moral freedom is real but empirically indefinable, while the empirical objects of science are real but not the same as things in themselves, which are empirically unknowable. Every human being is thus one being having two polarities: ethically autonomous noumenally, but causally determined phenomenally. This polarity is rooted in the nature of reality, argues Kant. It must be acknowledged, but it can never be fully understood.

Rigid Formalism

One of the greatest virtues of Kant's ethical theory is his determination to account for the conflicts involved in moral decision-making, without attempting to explain them away. So, much like the ancient Stoics by whom he was influenced, he frankly faced the conflict between duty and desire, acknowledging the inescapable inner turmoil that can accompany the making of a moral judgment. In addition, he was unwilling to sacrifice the human sense of inner moral autonomy to external scientific necessity or vice-versa.

Even so, however, Kant's moral theory is liable to serious objections. For one thing, it provides no way to distinguish between actions that are morally neutral and those that are positively bad. The most that he can show for any proposed action is that if it logically contradicts law in the abstract, it is not good. But there is no further test to distinguish between the morally neutral and the morally bad, unless one arbitrarily assumes that the two must always be the same, which is contrary to actual human experience. Kant is also unable to account for degrees of goodness and badness, since an action either logically contradicts, or not, conformity to universal law as such.

A more serious objection to Kant's approach is that it slights the role of personal feeling and social utility in moral judgment. For example, suppose a mother is at home, with her child in the next room in a crib. She smells smoke, sees flames coming from the room, and realizes it is on fire. Without giving the matter any thought at all, she dashes into the room, fights off flames, plucks her crying child out of the crib, and runs out of the house, thereby saving the child's life, at great risk to her own. According to Kant, this action has no moral value because it was the result of unthinking impulse: the mother acted not for the sake of any abstract duty but *to save her particular baby*, which is all she cared about, the rest of the world be damned if need be. In most people's eyes, the mother's action would have positive moral value, but Kantian presuppositions cannot account for it.

Again, Kantian theory implies that the more difficult it is for one to follow the dictates of duty in the face of contrary feelings, the more moral value one's action will have if duty is in fact followed. But this implication entails the paradox that someone who positively loathes humanity, but nonetheless supports some charitable projects out of a commanding sense of duty, is morally better than someone who does much more, but out of a feeling of love.

In the end, Kant's moral theory, like that of Augustine's, comes down to a question of *obedience*. For Augustine, the commanding entity is a transcendent God, while for Kant it is universal law as such. For both philosophers, human passions and instincts are treacherous seducers leading people away from the path to goodness. To be good means to turn away from their influence and, by a conscious act of will, to obey, in the one case God, in the other, duty.

Influenced by the Enlightenment and Isaac Newton's new physics, Kant could no longer accept the mysterious (and seemingly irrational) God of Augustine. But neither was he prepared to abandon the compelling claims of moral and religious experience. His solution, as mirrored by the highly convoluted structuring of his writings themselves, was to find refuge in rational order and structure for its own sake. As in physics, so in ethics and religion, Kant basically believed that that which is real, important, and valuable is that which is law-like. All the rest he regarded as unknowable, morally neutral, uninteresting, or bad.

Jeremy Bentham

The third interpretation of ethics mentioned above regards moral judgment as a kind of calculation about what is useful (utilitarianism). This view found classical expression in the writings of the English jurist and philosopher Jeremy Bentham (1748-1832).[11] Born in Houndsditch, London, to a prosperous bourgeois father with literary interests, Bentham was a precocious child, learning Latin and Greek at the age of six from a private French tutor, and later entering Oxford University at the age of twelve. After his graduation in 1763, he entered Lincoln's Inn for the purpose of studying law, and in 1768, at the at the age of twenty, was admitted to the bar.

Not long after becoming a lawyer, Bentham came to regard the English law of his time as a muddled heap of socially harmful practices, buttressed by a theoretical structure of preposterous fictions. Repelled by the prospect of working in such an environment, he decided instead to devote the rest of his life to the advocacy of legal and political reform. In 1776 he published, anonymously, *Fragment on Government*, a short attack on Sir William Blackstone's widely hailed *Commentaries on the Laws of England*. Later, in 1789, he published his most important philosophical work, *An Introduction to the Principles of Morals and Legislation*. In 1802, an admiring editor published a collection of his French-written articles in Paris (*Traités de Législation Civile et Pénale—Essays on Civil and Penal Legislation*). As a result of this work, Bentham quickly achieved fame in France as a major thinker and reformer, although still relatively unknown in his native England.

After the turn of the century, latent forces working for social change finally came into their own in England. An increasingly powerful bourgeoisie challenged the monopoly on state power then in the hands of the Crown and the old landed aristocracy. During the same period, Bentham found natural allies in the philosopher James Mill, his philosopher-son, John Stuart Mill, and others. These thinkers fused various progressive ideas in ethics, law, economics, and politics into one coherent philosophical system; and they buttressed this new philosophy with a sophisticated political machine designed to elect its supporters to public office.

Bentham and company were variously known as "Utilitarians," "Benthamites," "Philosophical Radicals," and "Radicals." Bentham's goals were sweeping for the time: abolish the monarchy and the House of Lords, disestablish the Church of England, transform the House of Commons into the supreme organ of government, establish universal adult male suffrage, simplify the law code, reform the prisons, provide universal compulsory education, and establish free trade. In 1832, as Bentham lay dying, the British parliament passed the Great Reform Bill, which incorporated a number of important reforms he and his friends had long advocated.

Bentham's philosophy, Utilitarianism, is an analysis of the way individual human beings behave (that is, a psychology), which is used as the determinant for the way human beings *ought* to behave (that is, an ethics). The connecting link between Bentham's psychology and his ethics is his view of the way pleasure and pain function in human life, as he declares in the following famous passage:

> Nature has placed mankind under the governance of two sovereign masters, *pain* and *pleasure*. It is for them alone to point out what we ought to do, as well as to determine what we shall do. On the one hand the standard of right and wrong, on the other the chain of causes and effects, are fastened to their throne.[12]

According to Bentham's psychology, whenever individual human beings contemplate performing a certain act, they do so with regard to the likelihood of the act's contributing to their benefit, advantage, or pleasure. The likelihood (or "property" as Bentham calls it) of any act's so doing he defines as its "utility." For example, even an ascetic monk who practices self-flagellation (a pain) does so in the hope that such an act will be conducive to an eternal life of bliss hereafter (a greater pleasure).

Likewise, whenever human beings assess individual actions or public policy, they do so in terms of estimating the utility of such actions or policy—at least if they are rational. Those actions or policies that are rationally assessed to have utility are "good," and those contrary to utility, "bad." Indeed, apart from this utilitarian context, Bentham asserts, the words "good" and "bad" have no meaning.

According to Bentham, those who insist that the words "good" and "bad" have another, non-utilitarian, meaning are faced with an insuperable difficulty: if good and bad were non-utilitarian, why would human beings ever be *motivated* to do anything good? They wouldn't. Therefore, Bentham concludes, if the terms "good" and "bad" are meant to apply to real human behavior, they must be definable in terms of utility.

The Felicific Calculus

Having founded both psychology and ethics on a consideration of pleasures and pains, Bentham addresses the further question of how such pleasures and pains are to be evaluated. First, we can conceive of a sort of elementary unit of pleasure or pain—the least amount of pleasure or pain required for human beings to be aware of it. Further, for any particular human being, the final value of some particular pleasure or pain will be a multiple of this minimal amount, depending on various circumstances: the intensity of the pleasure or pain, its duration, etc. Finally, in the case of *several* human beings, the value of some pleasure or pain will depend on the number of persons affected.

Hence it is always logically possible to make a quantitative comparison of utility for various alternative courses of action. Therefore, we can reduce all moral evaluation, both for individuals and for societies, to a series of mathematical calculations about pleasures and pains. Bentham calls this type of evaluation "the felicific calculus" (from the Latin *felix*, meaning "happy").

In regard to national policy, Bentham continues, we must always be guided by the felicific calculus, just as we are in our private lives. Now a nation, says Bentham, is nothing more than a collection of individuals. Therefore, the utilitarian approach to public affairs reduces to the practical requirement of "the greatest happiness principle." In other words, the only criterion of right and wrong in public affairs is promotion of the greatest happiness of the greatest number.

Attack on Aristocratic Privilege

Bentham's utilitarianism had a great merit: it provided progressives with a sharp-edged tool for cutting through all the obscurantist defenses thrown up in defense of arbitrary aristocratic privilege. The great defender of this privilege was the reactionary orator Edmund Burke. He had argued that the institutions, practices, and even "prejudices" that had been long established in Britain were worthy of respect merely in virtue of their long existence.

In defiance of Burke's assumption that time of itself confers worth, Bentham in effect said this: Let's take a look at the social consequences of any institution. Who is benefiting from its continuation, and how? And who is suffering? Do the overall benefits outweigh the overall costs? If not, what can be done to correct the imbalance?

In response to Bentham's challenge, conservatives found that they themselves were forced to point out the social utility of criticized institutions in order to save them. As a result, they implicitly came to endorse Bentham's contention that rational evaluation of utility, not reverence for longevity, should be the ruling criterion in forming social policy.

Even though Bentham and his followers often failed to win the particular reforms they advocated, they nonetheless succeeded in redefining the nature of the debate over public policy. Moreover, Bentham's approach encouraged the development of the new sciences of economics, sociology, and political science. These called for the accurate observation and quantification of social data in order to test general hypotheses about social behavior. As a result, Bentham furthered his long-standing dream of doing for social phenomena what Isaac Newton had done for physical phenomena.

Tyranny of the Majority

Despite these accomplishments, however, Bentham's philosophy is open to serious objections. For one thing, the position of personal rights is precarious in his concept of utilitarianism. Since all law and morality are based on social utility, there can be no such thing as the enshrinement of personal rights over and above the necessities dictated by utility. Bentham regarded any such rights as "nonsense on stilts," and scorned their affirmation in both the American Declaration of Independence and the French Declaration of the Rights of Man. In Bentham's eyes, if the existence of personal rights happens to promote the greatest happiness of the greatest number, then the state should create and observe these rights; otherwise, not. Indeed, more: by Bentham's logic all statements of the following form are meaningless or contradictory: "I recognize that act x promotes the greatest happiness of the greatest number; nonetheless, x is wrong." So Bentham's philosophy is blind to what later came to be called "the tyranny of the majority." In fact, by Bentham's assumptions such a phrase is a contradiction in terms.

The authoritarian possibilities in Bentham's thought are a reflection of his own personal temperament. Throughout his life, he displayed a marked concern for security and order, albeit rationally planned, as opposed to personal freedom (except in economic matters, where he advocated laissez-faire capitalism). Before the outbreak of the French Revolution, his great hope was to find an enlightened despot (such as Empress Catherine of Russia) to implement some of his political and legal experiments. He was particularly obsessed with erecting a kind of model prison building, the Panopticon ("all-seeing"). It would be so structured that guards, centrally located within concentric tiers of cells, could oversee the behavior of all prisoners at the same time. Only after the French Revolution, and then largely due to the influence of James Mill, did Bentham begin to emphasize the utility of personal political freedom.

Homogeneity of Pleasure

Another problem with utilitarianism is the assumption that all pleasure is qualitatively the same. According to Bentham, the value of any particular pleasure is due only to the number of lumps that it contains of some underlying, generic pleasure-stuff. By this account, the difference between the pleasure of performing Mozart's *Clarinet Concerto in A* and that of hitting a volley ball over a net is purely one of quantity, not quality. So Bentham would have us ask such odd questions as this: "How many times must the ball go over the net in order to equal one play-through of the adagio movement?"

Despite such odd consequences, Bentham did not shrink from his quantitative assumption. An example is his famous quip, "Quantity of pleasure being equal, push-pin [a child's game] is as good as poetry." And, indeed, Bentham could not logically do otherwise, since comparing pleasures qualitatively immediately raises the question, "By what standard?" But to posit any such standard by which to evaluate pleasures is to say that they themselves no longer function as the standards of all value. So if all value is reducible to pleasure and pain, particular pleasures and pains *must* vary only quantitatively, not qualitatively. Conversely, if pleasures and pains can be compared qualitatively (as Bentham's revisionist follower John Stuart Mill later believed), then goodness and badness cannot be reduced to mere units of pleasure and pain.

Motivation

Bentham's theory also runs into difficulties in regard to considerations of motive. As noted above, he argues that all notions of good and bad must at base be utilitarian because otherwise no one would ever have a motive to perform an action because it is good. But his argument here overlooks the position of Immanuel Kant, discussed above. Kant argued that a rational being can be moved to do good for the sake of making its will conform to universal law as such. Of course, one can disagree with Kant's position, but it won't do simply to ignore it or to dismiss it as meaningless. Bentham, however, rejected Kant's entire philosophical approach as the work of a muddleheaded metaphysician.

Even apart from Kant, Bentham's theory of motivation runs into a paradox: if we always choose to do something for the sake of some utility, and if utility in turn defines goodness, then it follows that there can be no such thing as a bad motive, only bad effects, as judged by the overall impact of the act on society. Suppose, however, that one maintains that the phrase "a bad motive" is meaningful and substantive regardless of its overall social impact. In this case, one cannot accept a theory of ethics based solely on utilitarianism, which logically excludes such a phrase.

The Idolization of Bourgeois Males

Underlying Bentham's philosophy is a premise that he never examines critically but which colors his every thought: all human motivation is at base an expression of self-interest. For example, when, in his *Principles of Morals*, he analyzes the different kinds of "simple pleasures" into fourteen different classes, all of them eventually resolve either directly or indirectly into self-interest. Even the pleasure he calls "benevolence" turns out to be that which we may hope to gain for ourselves by having others become emotionally or materially indebted to us.

Behind this presupposition of universal egoism lies an implicit model of human behavior–that of the self-seeking, aggressively-calculating bourgeois male. This was the very type of person whose political and economic agenda Utilitarianism as a political movement was then promoting in the face of entrenched resistance from the Crown and the old landed aristocracy. In effect, Bentham took a model of the bourgeois male and made it into the human norm. As a result, moral goodness and political utility became a matter of satisfying this norm's needs.

In the immediate contexts of Bentham's day, his thought was progressive, challenging a system of class oppression based on reverence for the past. But in the historical long-run, his thought eventually became regressive, overlooking the needs of the working class and women. It's no accident that in Bentham's philosophy the phenomenon of a human being selflessly loving another for the other's sake (exemplified above all by a mother's love for her child) is totally incomprehensible. Nor is it an accident that one of the most contemptuous denigrations Bentham could think of was the word "sentimental," which he hurled at women. Nor is it an accident that his "universal suffrage" omitted women, or that he rejected the idea of governmental support for poor workers. These omissions are all the more remarkable because existing literature of the time called attention to these needs. Examples are Mary Wollstonecraft's essay *A Vindication of the Rights of Woman*, published in 1792, and the writings of her anarchist husband, William Godwin. To Jeremy Bentham, however, to be human primarily meant to be a male member of the rising European bourgeoisie, and to be moral meant to promote the historical self-interest of such men.

A.J. Ayer

A recurring theme in the ethical systems of Augustine, Kant, and Bentham is the notion that moral judgments must be *objective*. To Augustine, the ground of this moral objectivity is God; to Kant, the rational will's conformity to law as such; to Bentham, the greatest happiness of the greatest number. Although differing in the way in which they happen to ground ethical objectivity, each of these three thinkers shares a tacit underlying assumption: if moral judgments are not objective, then morality can have no validity. As a result, all of these writers share a genuine sense of urgency in finding some universal, objective basis for morality in the face of the obvious variety of conflicting moral opinions that prevail among humans. Otherwise, these three fear, the entire edifice of human moral evaluation must collapse.

A stunning break with this entire approach to moral thinking occurred in the writings of the English philosopher Alfred Jules Ayer (1910-1989). In 1936, Ayer published his book *Language, Truth and Logic* (later revised in 1946). This book argued that moral judgments are literally meaningless, serving merely to express the emotions of those who use them.[13] Although Ayer was not the first philosopher to advocate an emotive theory of ethics, he *was* the first to develop such a view rigorously in the context of logical positivism, a new school of philosophy destined to exercise significant influence in 20th-century Anglo-American thought.

A.J. Ayer was born in England in 1910, the only child of Jules Ayer, a wealthy immigrant from Switzerland, and the Belgian-born Reine Citroen, twenty years her husband's junior. The name of Citroen (which literally means "lemon") later became renowned, when her uncle, the French weapons maker André Citroën, founded the famous car company that bears his name. A.J. Ayer's own first name, Alfred (which he never used until he was knighted many years later), derived from his godfather, the fabulously wealthy Alfred Rothschild, a personal friend of Britain's King Edward VII.

Following a typical educational track for those of his social class, Ayer attended first Ascham St. Vincent's, then Eton, then Oxford, eventually specializing in philosophy. While at Eton and Oxford, indeed throughout his life, Ayer seems to have been ill at ease in situations involving displays of emotion, even more so than might be attributed to the general emotional shriveling that is characteristic of WASP cultures. For example, he notes in his autobiography that while at Oxford he found that so many of the young students were having homosexual liaisons that a student was made to feel guilty if he did not participate in them. Although believing that homosexual practices were not bad (and even supporting homosexual law reform), Ayer reports that he steadfastly withstood the social pressure of his peers toward these practices. Instead, he remained nobly devoted to his girlfriend (and later wife) Renée Lees.[14] By his own account, however, Ayer was slow to become sexually involved with this same Renée Lees. Indeed, Lees called Ayer "Monk" (because of his "innocence", as Ayer claims, and his physical resemblance to the 19th-century Dominican monk Jean Lacordaire).[15]

Ayer's claim of disinterest in Oxford homosexuality is paradoxical in light of an earlier incident in his life: while at Eton, he had a friendship with another student, David Hedley, who was later to become head of the Communist Party in California. Significantly, Ayer admits to having had "a romantic attachment" to Hedley, even causing some raised eyebrows on the part of Hedley's parents. Yet Ayer declined to respond to Hedley's overt expression of such feelings:

> On the one occasion on which he [Hedley] put his arms around me and said he loved me I was embarrassed and disengaged myself.[16]

The point here is not whether Ayer was homosexual but rather his tendency to regard *any* display of emotion as embarrassing or misplaced. When reading his autobiography, one often gets the impression that whenever he was in a situation where emotional displays might occur, his basic impulse was to pull back, saying, "I was embarrassed and disengaged myself." Not that he was incapable of experiencing passion, but rather that its occurrence was something he perceived as a nuisance. As we will see later, this psychological quirk is related to his dim view of the role of emotion in human cognition.

Logical Positivism

While a student at Oxford, Ayer had heard of a new approach to philosophy formulated by "the Vienna Circle." This was an informal group of logicians, physicists, and mathematicians meeting in Vienna in the 1920s. Members of the Circle dedicated themselves to rebuilding the bridge between philosophy and science, which they felt had been corroded by the Romantic movement and by idealist philosophy. After finishing his studies at Oxford, Ayer visited the Vienna Circle, which impressed him deeply. In time, he became a leading proponent of its philosophical viewpoint, logical positivism.

Except for the interruption of World War II, Ayer spent much of his adult life as a professor of philosophy, principally at Oxford University and the University of London. In recognition of his great influence on British philosophy, he was knighted in 1970. By the time of his death in 1989, he had become an icon of the new type of 20th-century philosopher. This new type of philosopher was a career specialist in logic and language, someone who stayed within the confines of formal academic institutions, and who promoted the scientific mentality as the paradigm of human rationality.

Logical positivism, the tradition in which Ayer embeds his theory of moral judgment, is a theory of language and logic. It asserts that all meaningful statements fall into two mutually exclusive classes: (1) formulas of logic; and (2) descriptions of fact. The first class, formulas of logic, are formal deductions based on the meanings of constituent terms, assumed axioms, and rules of transformation. If correctly stated, formulas of logic are always true, regardless of any observed phenomena. For example:

> If X is longer than Y, and Y is longer than Z, then X is longer than Z.

The second class, descriptions of fact, refer to conditions in the physical world; they are contingently true or false, depending on what actually happens to be the case. For example:

The majority of American males are anxiety-ridden about the length of their penises.

Verifiability Criterion of Meaning

The uniqueness of logical positivism lies in its assertion that *all* statements, if they are meaningful, must fall into one or the other of these two classes. In addition, logical positivists claim that the meaning of any statement of the second class is the method by which the statement can be empirically verified. This doctrine, the verifiability criterion of meaning, found its most notable defender in A.J. Ayer.

According to Ayer, any statement other than a deduction of pure logic is meaningful if and only if the person who asserts it can say how it can be empirically verified. As an example, consider the statement above about the anxiety American men feel concerning the length of their penises. It is possible to construct a scientifically designed survey of opinion concerning penis-length anxiety among randomly selected American males. Therefore, the proposition concerning penis-length anxiety is meaningful.

Other kinds of statements, however, become meaningless. For example, the statement "Waiter, this music is frozen!" There is no way in principle to measure the temperature of music. Another example is "The Absolute manifests itself in time." What kind of physical test could possibly detect the temporal manifestations of absolutes? Yet another example is this: "You ought to do this." Although descriptions of a person's actual behavior can be verified, what test can there be for use of the word "ought"?

The Emotive Theory of Ethics

In *Language, Truth and Logic*, Ayer points out that "normative ethical symbols," such as the word "ought," cannot be reduced to empirical descriptions. For example, to say "X is morally good" is not the same as to say "X is approved of," since not all things approved of are morally good. Nor is it the same as to say "X is useful," since not all useful things are morally good. More generally, we cannot equate "X is morally good" with "X has such and such observable property."

An ethical judgment, Ayer continues, never adds any new information to the action that is judged. For example, consider the following three statements: (1) "Brutus plotted Caesar's death"; (2) "It is good that Brutus plotted Caesar's death"; and (3) "It is bad that Brutus plotted Caesar's death." The last two statements do not add any new information concerning Brutus' part in the conspiracy against Caesar beyond what the first statement already describes. Since (2) and (3) are neither statements of pure logic nor empirical descriptions, they are meaningless. But surely sentences like these have some role to play in human life! Quite so, Ayer agrees. But that role is merely to indicate the *feelings* of the person who utters these sentences.

Since ethical judgments are mere expressions of feeling, Ayer concludes, there can be no rational debate about morality other than to establish the facts of the action itself, or to clarify the linguistic terms that each party uses. Hence the idea of an objective ethical standard is an illusion; indeed, nearly all ethical discourse is illusory, based on pseudo-concepts. I have certain feelings; you have certain feelings. Beyond that, there's not much else to be said.

In his later years, Ayer came to feel that the theory of ethical judgment he developed in *Language, Truth and Logic* was a bit crude, and he recast his views in more behavioristic terms.[17] Instead of seeing an ethical judgment as a mere expression of feeling, he now saw it as the expression of a "moral attitude." This "attitude" he defined as that aspect of a behavior pattern that results in moral judgments. But for all that, Ayer continued to adhere to a modified form of the verifiability criterion of meaning.

Ayer's philosophy was an important contribution to both linguistic analysis and ethical theory. In the former area, he brought newly developed methods of formal logic to bear on numerous linguistic muddles, thereby helping to redefine in startlingly new ways many old philosophical issues. In the latter area, he succeeded in demonstrating that moral discourse could not be subsumed into either purely deductive reasoning or contingent empirical description. More generally, the logical positivist movement that Ayer promoted proved to be a refreshing antidote to the dogmatic rigidity into which much European philosophy had frozen at the turn of the century.

Back-Door Metaphysics

Despite these accomplishments, however, logical positivism in general and Ayer's philosophy in particular are fatally flawed. As a rather obvious example, consider the central thesis of logical positivism:

> Any proposition that is neither an expression of formal logic nor a description of empirical reality is nonsense.

What is the status of this proposition itself? Clearly it is not an expression of a logically necessary truth because one can meaningfully deny it, nor is it a description of any kind of empirical reality (if it is, which one?). In reality, this statement is a sort of practical guide for inquiry or a rule for classifying propositions. But by the terms of this proposition, any such practical guide or rule must be nonsense analogous to the manner in which moral judgments are held to be nonsense. If an exception is to be made from the requirements of this proposition for the proposition itself, why can't exceptions be made for other propositions as well? And if there are criteria for the making of such exceptions, then aren't these criteria themselves of a higher logical order than this proposition? The obvious fact is that this proposition is as meaningful as any proposition can be, yet it is neither a logical truth nor an empirical description. The entire system of logical positivism is based on a self-canceling assumption.

An analogous objection can be made for the second major assumption of logical positivism:

> For any proposition that is not a necessary logical truth to be meaningful it must in principle be verifiable by some description of physical reality.

As with the first proposition listed above, this one also is neither a necessary logical truth nor an empirical description. Moreover, there is a further complication: to date, no one, including A.J. Ayer, has succeeded in giving a detailed, logically satisfactory account of what constitutes empirical verification. A reader who examines Ayer's new introduction to the second edition of *Language, Truth and Logic*, as well as numerous other articles over the years by other logical positivists, will see that every attempted account of verification ends in paradoxes. Even more interesting: when logical positivists discard apparent solutions as inadequate, they typically do so in the name of "scientific methodology" or "common sense." In effect, scientific methodology and common sense become the real criteria for defining the verifiability of propositions. But the assumption that scientific methodology and common sense set the parameters of propositional verifiability is itself unverifiable. Indeed, this assumption is ethnocentric, since the phenomena called "science" and "common sense" are, in part, culturally constructed. As such, they are vulnerable to rational criticism of a very trenchant sort, as future chapters will show in detail.

Despite its loudly proclaimed disdain for "metaphysics," logical positivism is itself filled with numerous metaphysical pronouncements. In addition to those noted above, logical positivism presupposes the following dogmas: (1) all of science constitutes a unity, expressible through one unified scientific language; (2) any data scene can in principle be analyzed into absolute, non-contextual elements, expressible through absolutely elementary propositions; (3) there exists one objectivity that is absolute for all interpreters. Of these three dogmas, the first is at best a pious hope, while the second and third embody three fallacies previously discussed in chapter one: the fallacy of absolute reductionism, the fallacy of non-contextual simplicity, and the fallacy of absolute objectivity.

In trying to introduce these dogmas into their system, logical positivists sometimes say they are engaged in "metalogic" or "metaphilosophy" or "metamathematics" or "metaethics." In fact, however, they are simply engaged in old-fashioned metaphysics, but through the back door. Despite all their boasts to the contrary, logical positivists have been forced in practice to acknowledge an inescapable fact: whenever anyone says "I maintain that...," he or she is at once committed to certain metaphysical doctrines, for no reasoning is possible without unproven presuppositions of a very general nature.

Dichotomy of Emotion and Meaning

In his treatment of moral judgment in *Language, Truth and Logic*, Ayer uncritically postulates an irreducible barrier between emotion and meaning. As a result, he is at a total loss to explain how any human phenomenon in which emotion predominates can be meaningful. This metaphysical presupposition encourages him (abetted by his own personal psychology, as noted above) to relegate emotion to nebulous second-class citizenship in the realm of cognition. As a result, the rendering of moral judgments and the expression of esthetic taste become "meaningless."

Ayer simply averts his eyes from the role of emotion in cognition, unable to bear the thought that the light of truth might enter our lives through the windows of ethics and esthetics. Closing these venues tightly to any such possibility, he insists that we view the nature of reality through only two lenses, science and common sense.

Emotional Expressions vs. Judgments

Ayer runs into insuperable paradoxes as a result of his reduction of moral judgment to emotional expression. For example, if we assume that to render a moral judgment is merely to express an emotion, we are naturally led to this knotty question: "Exactly *what* emotion? Fear? Anger? Lust? Empathy? Or perhaps some special as-yet-unnamed emotion unique to the giving of moral pronouncements?" Surprisingly, Ayer devotes but little attention to this crucial question. His best answer is that moral judgments represent the expression of feelings of approval and disapproval. This, however, is no answer at all. Despite the fact that the phrase "feeling of approval" occurs in the English language, approval and disapproval are not emotions or feelings at all but rather *judgments*.

To understand this point, consider the following two formulas: (1) "I approve of X," where X is any action; and (2) "I feel E in regard to X," where E is some emotion. According to Ayer, there must be some value or values that can be substituted for E in the second formula that render it identical with the first. But what is that value or values?

Consider this possibility: "I feel giddy in regard to Brutus' participation in the slaying of Caesar." But this is not at all to say "I approve of Brutus' participation in the slaying of Caesar." Nor, again, is it the same to say "I feel happy in regard to Brutus' participation in the slaying of Caesar." I can feel happy about an action and still disapprove of it. ("I'm glad he killed him, but it was wrong.")

For *any* emotion that is substituted for E in the second formula, there will always be a real difference in meaning between the statement created and a statement of approval. The reason is obvious: one can always express some feeling in regard to an action and yet not approve of it.

Ayer's only remaining option is to argue that there is some peculiar emotion that is *unique* to the rendering of moral judgments. To see why this argument, too, must fail, imagine a situation where a judge had to deliver a sentence in a murder trial strictly by using first-person emotion statements, and nothing else. We would certainly be able to see how the judge felt about various aspects of the case from this emotional display. But how would we ever know his or her *verdict*? For example, a verdict of second-degree murder vs. a verdict of accidental homicide. Even more, how would we be able to know and evaluate the judge's *reasons* for reaching this verdict? We couldn't, because there is simply no sure way to infer "I judge such-and-such" from "I feel such-and-such." Expressing an emotion—*any* emotion—is just not the same as rendering a judgment, whether the judgment is moral, judicial, or otherwise.

Ayer faces the same problem in his later analyses of moral judgment. There, instead of emotions, he speaks of "attitudes." Regardless of what attitude one may have in regard to a certain action, he or she can always, independent of that attitude, express either approval or disapproval. Attitudes are no more judgments than emotions are. To its credit, Ayer's analysis of moral judgments draws attention to the importance of emotion in their formation; to its discredit, it ignores every other factor.

The Boorishness of Logical Positivism

In view of logical positivists' dismissal of the cognitive meaningfulness of emotion, it's not surprising that they often display a boorish attitude toward the arts. For example, Ayer seems to have regarded the difference between poetry and prose as the use of rhythmical devices in the former. Good poets, he seemed to believe, were those who made "sense," despite their recourse to such devices.

Acting on Ayer's presuppositions, we would naturally dismiss as both meaningless and bad poetry such a phrase as "frozen music." What, then, would we make of Goethe's celebrated remark that "Architecture is frozen music"?[18] This statement is clearly meaningless in terms of Ayer's metaphysical assumptions (especially the assumption that linguistic elements can be meaningful independent of overall linguistic contexts); nonetheless, Goethe's remark splendidly exemplifies the human capacity to convey truth through metaphor. Ayer, alas, simply had no understanding of the cognitive value of metaphor. His way of thinking was to ethics and esthetics what fundamentalism is to religion.

Neoscholasticism

Logical positivism can be viewed as a kind of mirror image of Platonism, a metaphysical system much derided by logical positivists themselves. Both Plato and the logical positivists dogmatically insist that the real world is an all-encompassing unity, definitively describable through philosophically refined language. They also both agree on an irreducible gap between logic and mathematics on one side, and empirical observation on the other. Plato, however, seeks for "the real" (*to on*) in logic and mathematics, and views the material world as a muddy flux. The logical positivists, turning the coin, regard the formulas of logic and mathematics as formally vacuous, and seek for the real in the findings of empirical science. As Karl Marx was said to have turned the German idealist philosopher Georg Hegel on his head, so the logical positivists, and particularly A.J. Ayer, may be said to have turned Plato on his head.

Again, logical positivism (and its historical heir, analytic philosophy) can be viewed as a kind of secularized neoscholasticism. In the late middle ages, philosophy primarily became the province of institutional hacks associated with the church and the university, hacks who showed a special fondness for logical quibbles. In more recent times, logical positivism and analytic philosophy have also largely become the province of academic hacks who show a special fondness for logical quibbles.

One might object here that late medieval philosophy conceived of itself as the handmaiden of theology; logical positivism and analytic philosophy, on the other hand, conceive of themselves as the handmaidens of science. Even this difference, however, betrays a commonality, for science in the era of patriarchal industrialism plays much the same ideological role as did theology in the Christian Middle Ages.

There is, finally, this parallel: The ossified scholasticism of the high Middle Ages got its first start, ironically, from innovative philosophical pioneers. Likewise, obstreperous philosophic outcasts originally created logical positivism and analytic philosophy. In the end, however, analytic philosophy likewise hardened into a dogmatic sect pushed by academic careerists. In both medieval and modern times, the same factor undermined the creativity of philosophy—academic professionalization.

The Complexity of Moral Judgment

Each of the four interpretations of moral judgment we have thus far examined (and there are many others) has some truth to it. Throughout history, human beings have in fact judged certain things morally right because they regarded them as in compliance with the divine will, or consistent with duty, or useful to humanity, or validated by certain feelings. However, humans can also feel a *conflict* between these factors when making a moral judgment, and so end giving more weight to one factor at the expense of the rest. Nonetheless, such a judgment remains a moral one. The possibility of such a weighted decision shows that moral judgment is not strictly the same as judgment in accordance with some one of these factors in and of itself.

Philosophers who claim otherwise often find themselves in an ironic bind. After saying that moral judgment necessarily involves this or that factor, they commonly slip into the habit of saying or implying that moral judgment *ought* to involve this factor, and that other interpretations of moral judgment are misguided. Philosophers who fall into this pattern are really making two incompatible arguments: "X is logically Y," and "X ought to be Y." The second kind of argument makes sense only if it is logically possible for X *not* to be Y, since use of the word "ought" presupposes at least the logical possibility of an alternative choice. But if it is logically possible for X not to be Y, then these philosophers cannot first argue that there is some logical necessity in saying "X is Y."

Despite sometimes-Herculean efforts, no philosopher has yet convincingly demonstrated that all considerations of, say, duty can be logically reduced to those of utility, or vice-versa. Such reductive efforts only trivialize the complexity of the human moral experience.

If moral judgment is something more than a judgment pursuant to the divine will, duty, utility, or feeling (or all of them for that matter), what is this "something more"? Is it perhaps a quality of a certain class of propositions, namely those propositions we call moral judgments?

The answer is "no." Despite many words written on the subject, no one has yet isolated the alleged distinguishing mark of a proposition that expresses a moral judgment—except for the word "ought" in place of "is." But this observation is of little help, since the whole question concerns what this little word "ought" means. If the word "moral" in "moral judgment" represents some as-yet-undiscovered quality of a certain class of propositions, its presence there has been as elusive as a ghost's.

The Three Factors in Moral Judgment

The something more in moral judgments (the meaning of "ought") is not to be found by a mere linguistic analysis of a certain sequence of words. Rather, we have to understand the nature of the interaction of human interpreters with data scenes (*interpretanda*) when they use the word "ought." In all such cases, the interpreter does at least three things: (1) renders a judgment of fact; (2) imagines an ideal; and (3) compares the fact to the ideal.

Consider this hypothetical example: An investigative newspaper reporter discovers that the leading candidate for President of the United States has used his prior connections with certain elements in the F.B.I. to have a political opponent assassinated, all the while running on a platform of "law and order." The reporter first renders a judgment of fact: the presidential candidate had his opponent killed. Next she imagines an ideal: it is immoral to kill, and immoral to act contrary to one's professed values. Finally she compares the fact to the ideal: the presidential candidate has acted immorally. Whether the reporter chooses to take any particular action as a result of this process of judgment is another question entirely, but such are the minimal steps that she goes through in reaching her moral judgment.

The key step in the above process is number two, the act of imagining. In the case of statements of fact (propositions), interpreters make judgments about what exists and also compare existing data scenes. In the case of moral judgments, however, something more is involved: the construction of a hypothetical ideal. Any interpreter (of whatever kind) that can only perceive or infer the existence of actual data scenes can never make a moral judgment. The only thing such an interpreter can do is note differences and similarities among various data scenes without making the value judgment that "this one is *better*." For the latter kind of judgment, the interpreter must also have the ability to apply some kind of standard.

Stated more fully, the interpreter must have the ability to imagine a hypothetical ideal data scene, and then to recognize the degree to which an actual data scene resembles this hypothetical ideal. Lacking such interpretational abilities, an interpreter is limited to judging that "this data scene is like that one," without any notion of "better" or "worse."

Note that a "hypothetical ideal" is not merely a concept but a concept that the interpreter uses as a standard of value. Lacking the interpreter's interest in it as a standard of value, any hypothetical ideal collapses into a mere description or consideration of possibility. Only because of some interpreter's interest, can any concept be said to be a "hypothetical ideal."[19]

As noted in chapter one, the capacity to imagine hypothetical ideal data scenes is a requirement for *any* interpretation that is evaluational, and hence for any normative community of interpreters, be they physicists or moral deliberators. What, then, distinguishes the hypothetical ideal data scenes of the moral deliberator from those of other kinds of evaluational interpreters?

The Moral Interest of the Interpreter

The distinction we are looking for between evaluational processes is to be found in the interest of the interpreter who does the evaluating. Atomic physicists are interested in developing a description of atomic data scenes that are as complete and consistent as possible. To this end, they construct a set of criteria for evaluating proffered propositions about atomic data scenes. As we have seen in chapter one, such criteria implicitly define a kind of *hypothetical exemplary interpreter* through whose eyes individual physicists attempt to make their evaluations. In this case, the hypothetical exemplary interpreter is that of the ideal physicist.

Just as an ideal can be constructed for doing atomic analysis, so it can be constructed for any type of human activity and, in fact, for human activity considered as such. For example, there can be an ideal of a good flute player, a good lover, a good baseball player, etc. In all of these cases, however, the word "good" in "a good X" actually pertains more to a kind of technical skill than to moral value. This difference is strikingly apparent when the phrase pertains to something obviously regarded as morally wrong, as in "a good liar" or "a good torturer."

Nonetheless, the shift from technical to moral goodness in phrases such as "a good X" is gradational rather than absolute. In general, the more inclusive of human activity any such hypothetical ideal becomes, the less technical and the more moral it likewise becomes. For example, the phrase "a good American" clearly has more than a merely technical meaning, yet it does not denote unqualified moral goodness, since it is inapplicable for the goodness that might be found, say, among Russians or Japanese.

Consider the case where human interpreters imagine a hypothetical exemplary interpreter in order to evaluate what is good, not for a physicist or a flute player or a male or an American, but for a human being as such. The evaluational interpretations that are made in light of this type of ideal are what we call moral judgments. Why? Because whenever any interpreter says that such-and-such an action is morally good, the interpreter judges that the action is consistent with, or required by, his or her hypothetical ideal of a human being as such. In other words, to say "That action is morally good" is to say "Under those circumstances, that is what a good person does." To say "In my opinion, she's a good person" is to say "She acts in accordance with my ideal of a good person."

The Naturalistic Fallacy

Certain philosophical schools deny that an interpreter need appeal, either implicitly or otherwise, to a hypothetical ideal of humanity in the making of moral judgments. Their position, however, overlooks a crucial point: unless an appeal is made to at least some kind of hypothetical ideal, there is simply no way to pass from "is" to "ought." Consider: how else can "ought" be introduced except by means of some comparison to that which is not in fact the case? Furthermore, unless the hypothetical ideal is that of a human being as such, any evaluational judgments rendered will have a technical and partial, rather than a moral, scope (pertaining to a good physicist, for example, as opposed to a good person). Our conclusion:

> Either there are no moral judgments or else moral judgments presuppose a hypothetical ideal of a human being as such.

Of course one can argue for the first alternative, simply denying the existence of moral judgments as such. In other words, one might argue that every occurrence of the word "ought" can in fact be meaningfully reduced to an occurrence of the word "is." This is the same as to say that all moral judgments can be meaningfully reduced to statements of fact. This move, however, involves a complication: in order for the reduction of value to fact to be possible, there must be at least one natural thing or activity that by itself meaningfully constitutes no less and no more than what the word "good" in its moral sense conveys; otherwise, value will always be different from fact.

The putative existence of such a natural fact of moral goodness runs afoul of telling objections raised against it by the British philosopher G.E. Moore (1873-1958), who termed belief in such a notion "the naturalistic fallacy."[20] To understand Moore's point, consider the following formula (which restates Moore somewhat): X *in and of itself is morally good*, where X is some natural object or activity.

This formula represents a *stipulated* definition of moral goodness in and of itself in terms of a natural object or activity; that is, this formula stipulates the natural object or activity that sets the standard by which all other ancillary goods are to be judged good.

How can we know when this *stipulated* definition of the word "good" will do justice to our *usual* use of the word "good"? Only if we can find some value for X that will land us in a contradiction if we say, according to our *usual* use of the word "good," "X is *not* morally good."

For example, suppose we let X = "pleasure." In this case, we generate the *stipulated* definition "Pleasure in and of itself is morally good." Despite this *stipulated* definition, however, we do *not* land in a contradiction if we say, according to our *usual* use of the word "good," "Pleasure is *not* morally good." Accordingly, "pleasure" fails as an adequate value for X in the stipulated definition. And, in fact, any other value for X that is a natural object or activity will likewise fail in the stipulated definition. Why? Because it will always remain an open question whether such an object or activity is morally good in terms of our usual use of the word "good." (Hence this is called "the open-question argument.") Therefore, "ought" cannot be meaningfully reduced to "is," and values cannot be reduced to facts.

Another problem with the naturalist reduction of ethics is that it does not do justice to a whole group of well-known human phenomena: the many cases throughout history where people have insisted, even to the point of their own deaths, that their moral values and the decisions based thereon were real and important, yet different from the world of empirical facts.

The reductionist approach also seems implausible in view of the many other kinds of activities that involved evaluational judgments (as in research in atomic physics, noted above). If normative interpretation in general is conceded to exist among humans, then why not the making of moral judgments, which are simply another form of normative interpretation?

The Formation of Moral Values

How do interpreters come to form their moral ideals? Some philosophers have argued that value formation is purely a matter of creating *concepts*: in the course of our lives we develop, either consciously or unthinkingly, certain abstract concepts of right and wrong; these abstract concepts are the things that become our values. There is, however, a problem with a purely conceptual theory of value formation: it fails to explain the special "pull" that our ethical ideals can have on us. We are constantly forming all sorts of abstract concepts in everything we do. Why is it that certain of these concepts have the power to influence our behavior, while others do not? Certainly there is a conceptual element in value formation, but that element alone cannot account for the special power of values in affecting human behavior.

The answer is that in addition to concepts, an important *emotional* factor is also involved in the formation of moral values. We do not experience everything in our lives with the same degree of feeling. Certain kinds of experiences—seeing another human being suffer, being loved, loving others—elicit strong feelings in us. The concepts that become associated with such feelings are the ones most likely to influence our behavior. Among such emotionally colored concepts are our moral ideals. Like all hypothetical ideal data scenes, they have a conceptual component. In addition, they also exercise a special power on our behavior because of their emotional coloring.

Moral Debate

Human interpreters come to form their moral ideals in the same way they form reality maps: by virtue of having certain genes, a certain enculturation, and certain idiosyncratic life experiences; in short, by having a life. Hence there is no guarantee that interpreters will agree on such hypothetical ideals. In fact, we find the same overlap and conflict in the case of moral ideals as in the case of other evaluational criteria. Moreover, those who dispute moral issues among themselves do so in a manner analogous to those who argue over disparities in reality maps. Each side attempts to show that dissenting conclusions on the opposing side are inconsistent with mutually-shared values, or that the other side has misrepresented certain facts to be judged by moral evaluation, or that the other side's values are inconsistent among themselves, or that the other side's actions are inconsistent with his or her own stated values, etc. If the division of opinion hangs on certain irreconcilable base values, then, short of one side's simply being silenced, it cannot be resolved.

As with reality maps and propositions of fact, so with moral judgments: the interpreter (with a tip of the hat to Protagoras) is the judge of all things. To say, however, that moral judgments result from interpretation is not to dismiss them as "merely subjective" or unreal. To the contrary, as in chess, so in life: one *must* move, or else lose the game by default. Death is the loss of the ability to interpret. As long as we live, we interpret, and that means we constantly form values as best we can, using them to guide and assess *how* we live. Although subjectively rooted, these values nonetheless have a very real impact on the way we interact with the external world.

Just as there can be normative communities in other areas of human concern, so too there can be such communities in the area of rendering moral judgments. Consequently we often find widespread areas of agreement in morals among human interpreters, especially where the interpreters experience the same enculturation and have similar life experiences. Where great disagreements in moral judgments appear, they are most likely to reflect great differences in enculturation and in idiosyncratic life experience. Consider, for example, the moral disagreements that might be found between two white, male, middle-class, 20th-century suburban American Protestants. They are likely to be less than those between such persons and an 18th-century Navaho shaman.

The Relativity of Morals

Which system of moral judgments, then, is the "right" one? As should be obvious by now, this question is unanswerable when asked in this way. Moral judgments are always judgments for some interpreter or for some group of interpreters. To be answerable, the question must be rephrased thus: Which system of moral judgments is the right one for some particular interpreter?

The answer to the latter question depends on the interpretations of the particular interpreter in question, if he or she is asked the question directly. If, however, the question is asked of some second-party observers *about* this first interpreter, then the answer depends on *their* evaluations of the original interpreter's evaluations. To the extent that yet others share the ideals of these second-party evaluators, to the same extent will the second-party evaluations gain wide acceptance. Hence in all cases the answer to the question of who is "right" about what presupposes the existence of some interpreter or some group of interpreters who evaluate data scenes according to hypothetical ideals.

Even if all human interpreters agreed on a basic core system of moral judgments, there would be no guarantee that they would agree with the moral judgments of beings who might come to the Earth from elsewhere. The only way such agreement would be possible is if some trans-species evaluational criteria of an exemplary interpreter of morals could be established. The question, however, of the extent to which such a cosmic exemplary interpreter is possible cannot be decided with certainty in the absence of actual interplanetary contact. Even on the Earth itself, few if any moral values have prevailed in all human cultures at all times. Further, as noted above in chapter one, it is doubtful (despite the heroic efforts of Immanuel Kant) that there can be any kind of universal criterion of rationality as such. Therefore, no universal moral values can pretend to hang from such a criterion.

Among human interpreters, some identify the hypothetical exemplary human as one who obeys divine laws; others as one who follows the dictates of rational duty; others as one who promotes the greatest happiness of the greatest number of people; others as one who acts in accordance with certain kinds of feeling. And others have ideals different from these. From this complexity has arisen the great variety of moral systems found among philosophers. There remains, however, an implicit assumption common to all these interpretations: There is some hypothetical ideal of the human being as such in light of which actual human behavior and motivation can be compared and judged. The rendering of judgments through the application of such an ideal is what we call "moral judgment."

Enlightenment

All moral judgment eventually boils down to particular interpreters acting according to particular values. This fact means that every human interpreter is ultimately responsible for his or her own values. The unthinking acceptance of values from some established "authority" or institution is no exception. To the contrary, the assumed worthiness of the pre-packaged values is itself the result of a personal value judgment on the part of the interpreter who accepts them. Consider, for example, Christians who claim that, by following the New Testament's value system, they are obeying objective moral directives ordained by God. Even so, these believers have first decided that the New Testament's value system defines the hypothetical ideal of a human being as such. Their initial decision in this regard is no less personal and existential than that of interpreters who become atheistic hedonists.

Moral judgments reflect the full genetic, cultural, and idiosyncratic natures of the interpreters who make them. Consequently, the more any interpreter is conscious of his or her own being, the more informed will be his or her decisions as to value systems. Naturally, those interpreters who place a high value on knowledgeability in interpretation will have as a principal goal of life the cultivation of full self-awareness; they will also tend to resist all external social forces that would impede such a cultivation. This process of consciously rooting one's values in expanded self-awareness I call self-authentication.

The affirmation of the importance of self-authentication in the face of all external social, political, or religious impediments was one of the great rallying cries of the European Enlightenment. This cry found its most succinct articulation in the opening lines of Immanuel Kant's famous essay *What is Enlightenment?*:

> Enlightenment is man's release from his self-incurred tutelage. Tutelage is man's inability to make use of his understanding without direction from another. Self-incurred is this tutelage when its cause lies not in lack of reason but in lack of resolution and courage to use it without direction from another. *Sapere aude!* "Have the courage to use your own reason!"—that is the motto of enlightenment.[21]

Despite this stirring opening, the remainder of Kant's essay promotes a rather modest claim: scholars should be free to publish their scholarly findings without government censorship. The reason Kant blunted the thrust of his own essay was that he identified humanity's essence with the capacity for abstract reasoning. This assumption easily led him to the conclusion that the practice of formal scholarship was the epitome of human fulfillment. But suppose we take a more encompassing view of human capacities for interpretation—including not only the rational, but also the sensual, emotional, and sexual. In that case, it is quite easy to take Kant's opening declaration to a far more radical conclusion: Dare to know and develop your full being, and resist all arbitrary efforts to impede that quest.

Suppose we adopt the value judgment that the attainment of enlightenment is one of the purposes of human life. Suppose, further, that we regard enlightenment as natural maturation of the self when grounded in authentic living. Then it follows that part of the purpose of life is to fully develop one's natural interpretive capacities—intellectual, emotional, and sexual. I, for one, accept such presuppositions and therefore draw such conclusions. Readers who have different presuppositions will come to different conclusions.

The Motivation to Be Moral

However the hypothetical ideal of humanity may be interpreted, there is no guarantee that action in accordance with one's moral ideals will promote one's well being or happiness. In fact, human history abounds in cases where interpreters have suffered because of adherence to their moral values. Furthermore, those people who pay little or no heed to moral values often seem to be the very ones who accumulate the greatest wealth and power in any society. Both the frequently observed inconvenience or suffering of those who adhere to moral values and the apparent success of those who do not, raise an obvious question: Why be moral anyway?

Despite the observed chasm between morality and success, it remains a remarkable fact that throughout history even the most unscrupulous of connivers, when publicly challenged, often seek to justify (or at least cloak) their actions by invoking some moral principle. Why is there this commonly felt need among even the most unscrupulous to put up at least some pretense of moral principle? Why should they care at all about moral values?

Some may think that the answer is simple: the unscrupulous believe it will be easier for them in the long run to get what they want if others are not aware of the real extent of their amorality. But this answer just pushes the question back one notch further. Why should public disclosure of their amorality make things harder for the unscrupulous? After all, humans commonly ignore or contradict their moral values, and the amoral tend in general to be the more successful.

The answer is that in every society there always exists at least a minority of people who do in fact generally act in accordance with moral values, either their own or those dominant in the culture. They are prepared to take issue with those who do not, even at the risk of great personal suffering. Under the right conditions of access to the public ear, this moral minority can have an impact far out of proportion to their small number.

The potentially great influence of morally-minded minorities is due to an important psychological cause: history shows that many human beings feel ill at ease, sometimes acutely so, at the prospect of seeing their moral values publicly flaunted, even if they themselves often do so in private. Moreover, many humans can be deeply affected by the personal example of someone faithfully adhering to such values in the face of obvious impediments or threats. In fact, the more cynical the prevailing social and political ambience, the more telling can be the impact of such a personal example. Twentieth-century examples of this effect are the lives of Mohandas Gandhi and Martin Luther King.

Many, perhaps most, human beings apparently desire to see the idea of morally motivated action validated in principle even if they themselves in their individual lives often fail to act in accordance with such a principle. This desire can sometimes be strongly aroused, with far-reaching social and political consequences, by the example of individuals who make a point of acting with such consistency. Hence it would appear that the ability and desire to make moral evaluations is something deeply rooted in the human condition, however inconsistent such an ability and desire may at times be with the attainment of personal success and happiness.

Moral Happiness

How does it happen that moral abilities and desires can sometimes have such a strong impact on certain individuals, even leading them to jeopardize their own happiness and survival? Those who are morally motivated often report a sense of inner happiness and inner success, stemming from morally motivated action, that is at least as important to them as other kinds of success. Among some, this morally-related inner happiness is felt to outweigh any possible external happiness; among many, it is felt to be a factor that can at least sometimes influence their behavior. Only among a minority of human beings does it seem to be completely lacking as a factor influencing behavior.

The state of inner happiness that stems from morally consistent action seems to be of the type that is related to self-affirmation. When I know that I act in accordance with my moral values, I feel focused, inwardly strong, and at peace with myself. Hence, in a sense, I affirm myself. But when I know that I fail to act in accordance with my values, I feel inwardly weakened and at odds with myself, and the greater my feelings about the values violated, the greater my self-alienation. In a sense, I repudiate myself. In other words, for me to act in accordance with my values is for me to be self-affirming, while to act contrary to these values is for me to deny or be at odds with myself.

When I am divided against myself, I feel discomforted or pained, but when I am a focused and integrated self, I feel a certain satisfaction and pleasure. The extent to which these inner feelings arising from self-repudiation or self-affirmation are important to me is the very extent to which I am likely to act in accordance with my moral values. This correlation is to be expected, since values in the abstract can never apply themselves directly to the world; they become applicable only through the agency of specific interpreters with specific motivations and feelings. Without evaluational interpreters who have motivations and feelings, the world of "ought" would never impinge on the world of "is." This is *not* to say that such motivations and feelings are identical with the moral values affirmed, but it is to say that such motivations and feelings are necessary.

So we see that there is an important connection between being morally motivated on one hand and placing an importance on a certain kind of self-affirmation through self-consistency on the other. In effect the likelihood of being a moral person turns out to be the natural and expected consequence of the degree to which one has a positive sense of self-esteem and a developed degree of self-knowledge. In this one particular regard at any rate, not only is there no conflict between moral action and self-fulfillment, but even an essential harmony.

Of course, the mere fact that one acts with the greatest of sincerity in accordance with one's moral values is no guarantee whatever that he or she is "right" in any absolute sense, as discussed above. It is quite possible for two human beings, both of whom are highly motivated, self-consistent, and convinced of their own moral rectitude, to be in irreconcilable moral conflict with each other. Their moral conflict may even lead to the death of one or both of them, or of others around them. From this possibility arises much of both the pathos and the grandeur of human life, as the ancient Greek tragedians well understood.

Ethical Communities

In addition to rendering individual moral judgments, human beings also have the ability to establish group-wide criteria of right and wrong. Any group having such criteria is but an extension of the normative community, as discussed earlier. When a normative community's standards consist of ideals of the human being as such, and when the objects the group evaluates are human motives and actions, then the normative community becomes an ethical community.

Groups (such as tribes) that judge by received custom and groups (such as states) that judge by created law are both ethical communities. The reason is that both have the capacity to share ideals of the human being as such. In the first case, the ideals are embedded in custom; in the second case, in laws.

Two sets of distinctions are at work here: customary/critical, and implicit/explicit. When customary, group-wide criteria of moral evaluation are called "mores" in English, derived from the plural of the Latin noun *mos*, meaning custom. When explicit, especially in written form as the result of some decision-making process, these criteria are called "laws." When individuals within the group critically reflect on shared values, whether customs or laws, the values become morals. On the basis of these distinctions, we find three distinct, albeit related, types of ethical-community phenomena: customs, laws, and morals. All involve the capacity of individual interpreters to share group evaluational criteria, but they differ in the degree of critical reflection and explicitness. As we will soon see, they also differ in the degree and type of their coerciveness.

Although history has provided many instances of societies having mores but having few or no laws, the reverse has never been observed. In addition, no being that is recognizably human has ever been found who had the ability to render personal moral judgments but who had not first been enculturated in some society's mores. Although personal moral judgments and group laws are something more than mores, they presuppose for their historical emergence the existence of some group with some mores.

From this consideration, a number of important corollaries follow. First, although human beings can deliberately form new groups with new laws, at some previous point all the contracting parties were enculturated in some group's mores. In other words, there never existed in the remote past a number of individual human interpreters who subsequently contracted together to form the first human society, as some philosophers have suggested. Historically, society has pre-existed individuality, not vice-versa.

Another important corollary: no human mores and laws are absolute, but all have emerged as the result of groups of various sizes, types, and origins interacting with various environments. These corollaries mean that any particular individual's system of evaluational judgments has emerged against the backdrop of the interpretive activity of some ethical community. Personal consciousness emerges out of group consciousness, and all consciousness is relative.

The Coerciveness of Law

As noted above, two features distinguish laws from both social customs and personal values: the greater explicitness of laws, and the role of a formal decision-making process in their making. A third and more notable feature of laws is their coerciveness. Whereas customs hold sway through social pressure (shame, for example), and personal values motivate through individual feeling (guilt, for example), laws coerce through governmental or judicial machines set up to enforce them.

A certain arbitrariness is likewise involved in the making of laws. For example, under parliamentary regimes the law is that which a majority of the voting members in the legislative chamber (or chambers) decrees to be the law. Here the law is essentially a command, even though a number of voices constitute the commanding entity (parliament). When the entity that commands is one person, the government is an autocracy; when a few, acting on behalf of the privileged, an oligarchy; when a few, elected at large, a representative democracy; when all, present and voting in person, a participatory democracy. In all cases, however, regardless of the nature of the commanding entity, the law is imperious, in that it bears the threat of sanctions against those who would disobey. It is also arbitrary, in that whatever the commanding entity decrees, is law. Hence in both their creation and execution, laws are arbitrary and coercive: in their creation, because they are dependent upon the decision of some commanding body; in their execution, because they are dependent upon the running of some judicial machinery.

A corollary of the above is that laws need not have anything at all to do with considerations of right and wrong. This fact may seem surprising, since laws first made their historical appearance as a result of the human need and ability to make evaluational judgments. A law, however, is whatever the commanding entity decrees it to be; that entity, whether autocratic, oligarchic, or democratic, may indeed take moral judgments into consideration in making laws, but it also may not.

Legislative decisions by the commanding entity result from complex pressures brought to bear on that entity by competing interest groups, institutions, and economic classes. In order to remain in power, the commanding entity must placate those groups, institutions, and classes that are its chief supporters. Not to do so runs the risk of being replaced by another commanding entity (revolution). Hence in actual historical practice, the most widely sought legislative goal is the placation of the principal backers of the commanding entity, not the implementation of moral values for their own sake. Of course, commanding entities usually take care to clothe their laws in moral values, just as individuals do in regard to private behavior.

In the case of an autocratic commanding entity, the chief backers are usually the army and the secret police; for oligarchies, the circle of richest families; for representative democracies, business corporations and the middle class; for participatory democracy, the lower classes. In each case, the principal backers of the commanding entity pursue their own self-interest, and the laws decreed by the commanding entity reflect that interest, regardless of the ostensible moral language in which they may be clothed.

Even when laws are passed to enforce supposedly universal values, they often turn out to re-enforce the value system of the principal backers of the commanding entity. And when a revolution occurs in which there appears to be a triumph in law of new values, the latter reflect the rise to power of a new class of principal backers. Just as individual values cannot impinge on the world apart from the actions of an individual motivated by those values, so social values do not become law without the action of interest groups, institutions, and economic classes influencing the commanding entity.

Priority of Interpreters Over Ideas

As a result of the above considerations, we can see that it is erroneous to speak of the great tumults of human history as simple "clashes of ideas." Without an interpreter or group of interpreters acting in their behalf, ideas have absolutely no impact whatever on the real world. Behind every "idea whose time has come" there stands a group of interpreters whose time has come.

Historically only those ideas and values have survived or triumphed whose supporters have survived or triumphed. Consider the idea systems of the various Indian nations that once occupied what is now called the United States. Although these idea systems existed time out of mind in North America, they completely disappeared as a serious historical influence within a very short interval after the onslaught of the white invaders from Europe. Were the ideas and values of the invaders somehow "better"? Not at all; rather, the invaders had more effective methods of male-inflicted violence (guns and nation-states). As a result, pictures of the white slave-owner George Washington, not the Indian rebel Sitting Bull, now routinely adorn the walls of American classrooms.

Of course ideas and values vary in the success with which they attract influential adherents, and in that sense certain ideas and values do influence history. But why is it that some ideas and values have greater "pull" than others? That question really asks this: why do certain historically influential interpreters or groups of interpreters imagine and act pursuant to certain hypothetical ideal data scenes? The answer to this question is complex, depending on the configuration of existing historical forces at the time in question, the needs and feelings of the specific interpreters involved, etc. The important point is that in all cases it is the *interpreters* who are the prime movers, since they first imagine hypothetical ideal data scenes and then act pursuant to them.

Some philosophers (most notably Plato) have postulated the existence of a self-subsistent realm of ideas in order to explain human concepts and values. No one, however, has ever been able to demonstrate the existence of such a realm or satisfactorily explain how it could interact with the world of material things. As we have seen above, appeals to such an alleged realm are unnecessary. All that is needed in order to explain human concepts and values is to postulate the existence of human interpreters, data scenes, and acts of imagination.

We are led, then, to these general conclusions: Moral values cannot be reduced to facts, but ultimately rest on hypothetical ideals of the human being as such. Moreover, moral values are not merely conceptual but also involve imagination and subjectivity, reflecting the particular life circumstances and feelings of those who hold them. Nonetheless, moral values also possess a relative objectivity. Individuals, acting on their own particular moral values, make real differences in the world. In addition, groups and entire societies often share common moral values, a circumstance that can affect the course of human history. Finally, the capacity to act morally is an essential part of what it means to be a human being, contributing to both the majesty and the pathos of the human condition.

On a personal level, it comes to this: I am responsible for my values. As a moral person, I may someday need to stake everything, including even my life and that of others, on these values. Yet I can claim no more ultimate foundation for my values than my own judgments and feelings in adopting them. My core values express who I am and how I live. When I act pursuant to them, I help to create a certain kind of world.

Although one may readily concede that imagination and subjectivity play crucial roles in moral interpretation, many would no doubt balk at a similar prospect in the seemingly hard-nosed disciplines of formal logic, higher mathematics, and natural science. The remainder of this book, however, will show that those who balk at this prospect are wrong. We will see that the most that these hard-nosed disciplines can reasonably claim for themselves is a sort of relative objectivity. In science as elsewhere, to interpret is to create a kind of world.

---

[1] Marcus Tullius Cicero, *On Fate*, I, 1.
[2] Augustine of Hippo, *Confessions*, 8, 12, 29.
[3] Romans, 13:13-14, *The New American Bible*, P.J. Kenedy & Sons, New York, 1970.
[4] The Greek phrase is *komois kai methais*; on Dionysian religion in general, see my *The God of Ecstasy*, St. Martin's Press, New York, 1988.
[5] Augustine of Hippo, *op. cit.*, XIII, 9, 10.
[6] Augustine of Hippo, *Ten Homilies on the First Epistle General of St. John*, VII, 8; trans. by John Burnaby in *Augustine: Later Works*, The Westminster Press, Philadelphia, 1955.
[7] Luke, 14;23, *The New American Bible*.
[8] Augustine of Hippo, *Ten Homilies*, VII, p. 318.
[9] *ibid.*, p. 319.
[10] Immanuel Kant, *Foundations of the Metaphysics of Morals*, trans. by Lewis White Beck, The Liberal Arts Press, New York, 1959, p. 9; original's emphasis.
[11] For a good overview of Bentham's life and thought, see Elie Halévy, *The Growth of Philosophic Radicalism*, translated by Mary Morris, Beacon Press, Boston, 1966.
[12] Jeremy Bentham, *An Introduction to the Principles of Morals and Legislation*, in Edwin A. Burtt, *The English Philosophers from Bacon to Mill*, The Modern Library, New York, 1939; 1, 1; original's emphasis.
[13] A.J. Ayer, *Language, Truth and Logic*, first published 1936; 2nd ed., Dover Publications, New York, 1946.
[14] A.J. Ayer, *Part of My life. The Memoirs of a Philosopher*, Harcourt Brace Janovich, New York, 1977, pp. 70-71; 91-92.
[15] *ibid.*, p. 68.
[16] *ibid.*, p. 59.
[17] See "On the Analysis of Moral Judgments," chapter ten in his *Philosophical Essays*, St. Martin's Press, New York, 1965 (reprinted from 1954); and "Freedom and Morality," chapter one in his *Freedom and Morality and Other Essays*, Clarendon Press, Oxford, 1984.
[18] Cited and discussed by Friedrich Waismann in "How I See Philosophy" in *Logical Positivism*, ed. by A.J. Ayer, The Free Press, New York, 1959, p. 367.
[19] Strictly speaking, the word "hypothetical" is redundant when used with the word "ideal." I have retained "hypothetical," however, because it emphasizes the difference between natural objects and ideals. The etymology of the word is vivid: "hypo-" comes from the Greek adverb *hypo*, meaning "up before one," and "-thetical" from the Greek verb *tithenai*, meaning "to place." Literally, "hypothetical" means "placed up before one," an apt image for the status of an ideal that is hanging, as it were, in the imagination of some interpreter.
[20] G.E. Moore, *Principia Ethica*, Cambridge University Press, Cambridge, 1966 (reprint of 1903 edition), p. 10 ff.
[21] Immanuel Kant, "What is Enlightenment?" in *Foundations of the Metaphysics of Morals* and *What is Enlightenment?*, trans. by Lewis White Beck, The Liberal Arts Press, New York, 1959, p. 85.

Source, Detail
Acrylic on Canvas, 32" x 32", 1995

3

The Myth of Mathematics

SUMMARY: This chapter shows how the interpreter (that is, the subject) is essential even to mathematics. Although many people are not aware of it, modern mathematics is in the midst of a philosophical crisis because it has failed to make good on its absolutist claims. This chapter examines these claims in their historical context and shows that mathematics contains a mythological core.

Formal logic, higher mathematics, and natural science have long made absolute claims for themselves. They boast that, unlike ethics or esthetics, they are free from the taint of subjectivity, and so provide us with an objective picture of the world as it really is. In the last chapter, we saw that ethics and esthetics do, indeed, contain an irreducible subjective element; nonetheless, they are hardly alone in this regard. In the remainder of this book, we will turn our attention to the boastful claims of absolute objectivity made on behalf of scientific pursuits. We will begin in this chapter with the field of mathematics, and continue on with logic and empirical science in later chapters. We will see that the conceptual foundations of the absolutist boasts made for science are spongy and mythical, having been derived from patriarchal religious beliefs. Despite the enthusiasm of those who genuflect at the name of science, nobody has a corner on the rational interpretation of reality. To the contrary, rationality is a wide spectrum containing many different colors. Although logicians, mathematicians, and scientists do enjoy special access to certain parts of this spectrum, a great many colors extend beyond their purview. In raising our eyes to take in this greater expanse, we will come to view both the scientific endeavor and much of recent history in a radically new light.

Many people today continue to believe that mathematics in particular constitutes a coherent system of absolute, proven truths. The fact of the matter, however, is otherwise. Despite the self-assured way that many schools and colleges now teach mathematics, the field is actually in a state of intellectual crisis.[1] The major reason for the general public's lack of awareness of this crisis is the way most people have learned the subject. Introductory courses often depict mathematics as a collection of rote techniques for performing various kinds of calculation; they simply slide over the deep philosophical assumptions that underlie such methods. Even advanced-level courses usually ignore the historical and cultural contexts in which basic mathematical concepts have emerged and which continue to condition both their abstract meaning and their practical application. People trained in this way come to view mathematics as a kind of absolute that transcends history and culture. Although mathematics, like every rational endeavor, reveals something about the nature of reality, it is also, in part, conditioned by the circumstances of its practitioners.

The absolutist attitude in mathematics is analogous to the fundamentalist attitude in religion. For example, biblical scholarship has established that none of the authors of the New Testament knew Jesus personally and that Jesus probably did not regard himself as the Son of God. Yet fundamentalist Christians continue to view the New Testament picture of Jesus in absolutist terms. In the case of both mathematics and religion, a widespread method of popular teaching that is both uninformed and uncritical has created what may be called the fallacy of misplaced absoluteness.

The existence of these teaching flaws does not mean that either mathematics or religion is without merit. The point, rather, is that we need to use critical and informed thought when evaluating where their merit actually does lie. Bearing this need for critical thought in mind, we will examine in this chapter a few highlights in the history of mathematics as well as certain contemporary philosophical issues pertaining to its development. We will see that the main threads of Western mathematical thought are part of a much larger fabric: the historical and philosophical contexts of the interpreters who created mathematics.

Before beginning our inquiry, we need to have a working definition of "mathematics." This word is derived from the ancient Greek *ta mathematica*, meaning "the mathematical sciences." To the Greeks, these were arithmetic, geometry, and astronomy. Why did the Greeks regard these three as constituting some sort of unity? Because they all shared a principal concern with quantitative relationships; that is, they all basically sought to answer, in one way or another, the question "How much?" (*Poson?*, in Greek; in Latin, *Quantum?*).

The most immediate way to answer this question is simply to resort to counting or measuring. A more indirect way, but one no less powerful, is to make calculations about what has in fact been counted or measured. An even more indirect way is to make abstract deductions about the basic concepts themselves that are required in order to count or measure. Despite the increasing level of abstraction, however, the root question remains the same—"How much?"

Since the days of the ancient Greeks, many more sciences have been added to the mathematical list besides arithmetic, geometry, and astronomy. Although constituting a diverse lot, all these sciences nonetheless share three core interests: the attainment of knowledge, formal reasoning, and the quantitative relations of things. Accordingly, we will understand by the term "mathematics" in this chapter any science that seeks for knowledge primarily through the formal analysis of quantitative relations.

The Practical Thrust of Ancient Mathematics

In the earliest human societies of which we have record, the concept of number, which is one of the essentials of mathematics, seems to have been of a straight-forward and strictly practical nature. In some of these societies, there are no separate words for numbers as such, but one word for, say, *two coconuts* and another word for *two stones*. Again, some early societies that do recognize number as such use only three numbers, *one*, *two*, and *many*. A survival of this practice is seen in the grammar of ancient Greek, which has declensions and conjugations for three grammatical numbers—singular, dual, and plural. Early societies that developed an extended series of numbers seem originally to have calculated with fingers and toes; hence the great number of societies that use five, ten, or twenty as the numerical base for recording large sums. If human beings had twelve rather than ten fingers, Euro-American civilization would today use twelve as its base. As a result, the number we today designate by the symbol "144" (reading, from right to left, 4 units + 4 tens + 1 ten-times-ten) would instead be designated by the symbol "100" (0 units + 0 twelves + 1 twelve-times-twelve).

These facts, although simple, have an important implication: the ability of any interpreter to do mathematical calculations presupposes a special kind of interpretational capacity. This is the capacity to imagine a certain type of hypothetical ideal, namely the hypothetical ideal of number in and of itself.

To understand this point, imagine that you were transported into an early human society that thus far had no concept of number. In order to teach the members of this society the number *two*, you might point to a pair of recently killed brown boars, at the same time uttering a word previously unknown in this society, for example, "grezhd." As a consequence, the members of the society would probably think that "grezhd" was your word for boar. Then you might point to a pair of brown stones, again uttering "grezhd." Comparing this with the last gesture, they might think that "grezhd" meant brown. Again, you might point to a pair of scarlet parrots, likewise uttering "grezhd," and so on. Eventually someone in the society would have an "Aha!" experience; that is, someone, by a leap of the imagination, would be able to conceive of the hypothetical ideal of twoness and to understand that your word "grezhd" corresponded to this hypothetical ideal.

Anyone in this society who was capable of such a minimal interpretation of numerosity would likewise be capable of engaging in at least some mathematics. On the other hand, anyone in this society who was incapable of such a minimal interpretation would likewise not be able to understand or engage in mathematics. Their situation would be like that of someone who was totally color blind and so could never coordinate colors.

We come, then, to an important realization: the possibility of doing mathematical calculations of any kind depends on the existence of some interpreter or some group of interpreters that is capable of a certain leap of the imagination. This leap is that which is involved in the minimal interpretation of numerosity.

The fact that certain interpreters with certain abilities are necessary in order for there to be mathematics does *not* imply that numbers or mathematical formulas are in any sense unreal. Nonetheless this fact *does* imply that numbers and number functions, whatever reality they may have, cannot be considered in absolute isolation from the conditions and behavior of the interpreters who create and use them. Like all human tools, numbers reflect the circumstances of the tool makers.

The concepts of number invented by early human societies were eminently practical and reflected the special needs of these societies. This practical thrust is evident in the succession of civilizations that emerged in the geographical area called "Mesopotamia" (literally, "the land between the rivers," referring to the area between and around the Tigris and Euphrates rivers). Beginning about 3500 B.C., Mesopotamia was settled by the Sumerians, and later infiltrated or conquered by numerous other ethnic groups. Around 1800 B.C., Hammurabi, ruling from Babylon, established a kingdom of great renown that eventually passed to Assyrian rule. Although various peoples rose and fell in Mesopotamia, the priestly scribes of successive ruling dynasties succeeded over the ages in developing and codifying a fairly coherent system of mathematics that is today known as "Babylonian."

In the Babylonian system, the base number for small numbers was ten, and that for large numbers, sixty (hence our own sixty-based angular measurements in terms of degrees, minutes, and seconds). Babylonian mathematics represents the most sophisticated ancient mathematical system known prior to that of the ancient Greeks. Much of it, at least judging by surviving cuneiform tablets, consisted of tables, formulas, and practical rules of thumb designed to help merchants in conducting commerce, builders in constructing buildings, and astronomers in designing calendars.

Insofar as Babylonian mathematics could be said to reveal reality, it did so through the eyes of Babylonian merchants, builders, and astronomers. Certainly such a perspective revealed something important to them about the world's nature. But would anyone today argue that ancient Babylonian methods embodied a privileged angle on absolute truth that must be equally important, interesting, and valid for everyone in every culture? Of course not. Yet very much the same claim is often made for the methods of currently-practicing mathematicians. Being human, however, modern mathematicians remain as culture-bound as their ancient predecessors, although they typically remain oblivious to this fact. Water is invisible to the fish that swim in it.

Another system of ancient mathematics, that of the Egyptians, was also practically oriented and culturally conditioned. Egypt was first united about 3100 B.C. by Menes, and the great pyramids built around 2500 B.C. As with the residents of Mesopotamia, the Egyptian people were really a mix of various ethnic groups who managed to maintain, over millennia, a coherent identity as a civilization. Egyptian mathematics seems to have been primarily concerned with problems of monument building, land measurement, and grain storage. As with the Babylonians, Egyptian mathematics thus represented a specific set of tools used by a specific culture dealing with specific problems. No one today would claim that these methods possessed an absolute validity for all peoples at all times.

The Shift to Theory in Greek Mathematics

A momentous shift in the thrust of mathematical interest toward the theoretical and the philosophical occurred among the ancient Greeks. In antiquity, they occupied not only the peninsula today called "Greece" but also western Turkey, southern Italy, and other areas in the Mediterranean. Sometime in the sixth century B.C., Pythagoras, a native of the island of Samos, moved to Crotona in southern Italy and there founded a quasi-religious society, the Pythagoreans. They believed in reincarnation, advocated ascetic living, opposed the growing movement for democracy in Greece, and held that the universe ultimately consists of numbers. According to tradition, it was Pythagoras who invented the word "philosophy," a compound of the roots "philo-" and "-sophia," literally meaning "the love of wisdom" or "the love of knowledge." Pythagoras was also said to be the first to call the universe by the Greek word *kosmos*. This word literally means "beautiful ornament," and emphasizes the beautiful mathematical proportionality that Pythagoras thought held the world together. Although Pythagoras and his followers were eventually expelled from Crotona after a democratic revolution, the Pythagorean movement continued to spread throughout the Greek-speaking world.

Even though the Pythagoreans had a philosophical and even religious attitude toward mathematics, they did not view numbers as incorporeal abstractions, as do modern mathematicians. Rather, the Pythagoreans regarded numbers as point-like substances that determined the geometric shapes of objects. For example, they believed that there existed tiny triangular shapes, which they regarded as a form of the number ten, consisting of successive lines of four points, three points, two points, and one point. Again, they held that there existed tiny squares, which they regarded as a form of the number sixteen, consisting of four points on a side. Believing that everything we see and know to be constituted of geometric aggregates of such tiny physical numbers, the Pythagoreans put much effort into measuring and understanding the mathematical attributes of music, the motions of the heavenly bodies, and everyday physical shapes.

In effect, Pythagorean number theory was a combination of an early form of physical atomism with a form of mathematical realism. (Mathematical realism is the belief that numbers constitute a realm of reality in and of themselves.) Later, even though Pythagoreanism itself continued as an identifiable school of thought, this tradition broke into two separate halves: on the one hand, the strictly-physical atomism of Leucippus (5th century B.C.) and Democritus (460 B.C.-370 B.C.); on the other, the non-physical mathematical realism of Plato (427 B.C.-347 B.C.).

Plato's Idealization of Mathematics

Plato distrusted all sensory knowledge as deceptive or illusory. He held that true knowledge (as well as the moral purpose of human life) consisted in the contemplation of a realm of pure, incorporeal Forms (*ideai*), and particularly mathematical Forms. Plato scorned pleasure as at best irrelevant to the purpose of human life, and regarded democracy as but one step above tyranny. He advocated the rule of an elite circle of philosopher-kings who would be highly educated in mathematics and abstract reasoning.

In his early days, Plato was the devoted follower of Socrates. As judged by contemporary accounts, Socrates seems to have been a person of wit, sensual humor, and a determinedly anti-dogmatic, even skeptical, bent of mind. Plato imputes these characteristics to Socrates in his earliest dialogues. Some time after Socrates' death, however, Plato "got religion"—the religion of Pythagoreanism, noted above. As a result, Plato's later writings progressively hardened into a series of philosophical justifications for three dogmatic motifs that have ever since been associated with his name: (1) the quest for knowledge is the quest for absolute certainty, which is ultimately grounded in a realm of incorporeal Forms, including mathematical Forms; (2) all human souls possess this knowledge before they reincarnate, but forget it once they fall heir to the flesh; and (3) by casting off the concerns of the flesh in general and the pursuit of physical pleasure in particular, the soul has the best chance of experiencing a "recollection" or "remembering" (*anamnesis*) of the pure knowledge it possessed before it became incarnate.

In his dialogue *Meno*, Plato associates this process of recollection with abstract geometrical reasoning; indeed, the dialogue depicts an uneducated slave as recollecting abstract geometrical principles after being properly questioned on the matter by a character Plato names "Socrates."

Plato's attitude toward knowledge, especially his quasi-religious attitude toward mathematical knowledge, represented a profound shift in the thinking of the ancient world. Whereas previous mathematics had generally been this-worldly and practical (even when the heavens were the object of study), Plato in effect removed mathematics from the empirical world and elevated it into a realm of absolute being beyond the contingencies of culture and history.

In addition, Plato drew a sharp distinction between "opinion" (*doxa*) and "knowledge" (*episteme*). He identified the latter with absolute certitude grounded in the transcendent realm of

Forms. As a result, Plato implicitly made the seeming rigor of abstract mathematical deduction into the standard by which to judge all other claims to knowledge. Many later Western mathematicians have adopted, either consciously or otherwise, this same metaphysical bias.

Aristotle, Plato's most famous pupil, tried to temper his master's other-worldly approach to knowledge. Aristotle argued that a thing's Form (or "essence" in Aristotle's terminology) could only be known by abstraction from the particular object itself (*tode ti*). In this way Aristotle validated an empirical approach to the pursuit of knowledge; nonetheless, he retained the goal of deductive rigor, modeled after mathematics, as the ideal for the final organization of knowledge empirically obtained. As a result, ever since the time of Plato an underlying philosophical leitmotif has often prevailed uncritically in Western thought:

> Sensation and feeling are merely subjective and therefore epistemologically suspect; the road to certitude and objectivity passes through the realms of the abstract and the impersonal.

The Historical Impact of Euclid and Ptolemy

In 332 B.C., Aristotle's own most famous pupil, Alexander the Conqueror, occupied Egypt and founded there the famous city named after himself, Alexandria. Within a few years, Alexandria became one of the greatest centers of learning in the world, a home to those steeped in the intellectual traditions of Egypt itself, Greece, Babylonia, and even India.

In approximately 300 B.C., Alexandrians witnessed the publication of what was to be the most famous and influential book in the history of mathematics—Euclid's *Elements*. This was a thirteen-book treatise on geometry, geometric algebra, and number theory, all deductively derived from ten axioms. (In Euclid's terminology, there were five "postulates," dealing with geometry proper, and five "axioms," dealing with other mathematical or logical notions.)

Euclid's *Elements* had a sensational historical impact because he seemed to have succeeded in organizing the entire body of known geometrical knowledge into a coherent deductive system derivable from a handful of axioms. As a result, most Western philosophers, mathematicians, and scientists down to the 20th century came to believe that the physical world had to be governed by these very axioms as if they were objective laws of nature; otherwise, they argued, one could not explain the amazing correspondence of the deductions made from them with measurable geometric findings. The world had a mathematical structure, and Euclid had been the one to discover it!

Unfortunately, those who argued thus had forgotten the historical and cultural conditions under which geometry actually arose. For a thousand years before Euclid, the ancient Babylonians and Egyptians had been painstakingly measuring various configurations of land as part of their farming, irrigation, and construction efforts. In the process, they noted and recorded various relations between parcels of land shaped in the form of triangles, squares, etc. The Greeks, later coming upon this body of accumulated empirical knowledge, called it *geometria*, which literally means "earth measurement." Euclid thus had at his disposal a whole body of findings already derived from actual physical measurement—the *geometria* of the Babylonians and Egyptians—which he proceeded to arrange in the most elegant manner possible, forming it into a deductive system derivable from a few axioms.

Why did the world of physical measurements turn out to agree with deductions from Euclid's axioms? Not because Euclid had amazingly discerned the mathematical skeleton of the great body of nature; rather, because Euclid first culled these axioms themselves out of a great mass of such measurements. Later believers in the priority and universality of Euclid's axioms completely reversed the order of their actual historical evolution!

The contingent and empirically fallible nature of Euclid's *Elements* was not fully appreciated until 1905. In that year, an obscure patent clerk named Albert Einstein proved that Euclidean geometry was inadequate for explaining both astronomical and atomic phenomena. For such purposes, Einstein turned to another geometry invented in the 19th century by the German mathematician Georg Riemann.

There was another Alexandrian writer whose erroneous theory was destined to have a lasting impact on the West. This was the 2nd-century-A.D. mathematician and astronomer Ptolemy

(Claudius Ptolemaeus). Drawing on the theories of many predecessors, Ptolemy's *Great System of Astronomy* (*Megale Syntaxis tes Astronomias*) presented the classic arguments for the view that the sun and the planets revolve around the Earth. After the decline in learning in the West occasioned by the Germanic invasions and by the rise of Christianity, Ptolemy's work was preserved and recopied by Arabic-writing scholars under the name of *Almagest* (from the Arabic-Greek coinage *al megiste*, meaning "the greatest"). When Ptolemy's *Almagest* later reappeared in the West via Arabic scholarship, it came to exercise an authoritative influence comparable to that of Euclid's *Elements*.

The Revolution of Copernicus and Galileo

Like Euclid's work, Ptolemy's *Almagest* was later found to be in error, despite the nearly sacrosanct status it had obtained for itself in the Christian academic establishment. Indeed, so great was the official academic and clerical support for Ptolemy's view that the Polish astronomer Nicolaus Copernicus delayed publishing his famous refutation of it until he was on his deathbed in 1543 A.D., when he knew he would be safe from persecution. A later defender of the Copernican view who was more outspoken in his own lifetime, the Italian astronomer Galileo Galilei (1564-1642 A.D.), was subsequently forced by the Office of the Holy Inquisition at Rome to recant. But although the Inquisition successfully coerced Galileo into retracting his professed doctrine, it failed to stem dissemination of his newly improved version of the telescope. As a result, people were able to observe the heavenly bodies themselves and so draw their own conclusions.

Some opponents to the new astronomy were genuinely puzzled by anomalies it seemed to introduce. For example, they objected that if the Earth rotated eastwards, there should always be a strongly blowing wind from the east, which is not the case. Despite such theoretical qualms, however, the great intellectual crisis provoked by Copernicus and Galileo involved far more than a dispute over the movements of the heavenly bodies. Any historical account that limits itself to this narrow astronomical issue cannot explain the furious outbursts of passion that occurred. Nor did the ferocity of the debate stem, as many subsequent commentators have erroneously claimed, from the displacement of the human race from its privileged central position in the universe. To the contrary, the traditional Christian view has always been that *God*, and not the human race, is the proper central focus in the life of the cosmos. To make the Sun, and not the Earth, the center of the solar system detracts nothing whatever from God's centrality in the life of the cosmos. No, at stake was a far more touchy issue: the claim of the great academic and clerical hierarchies of the time to exclusive epistemic privilege; that is, their claim to have a monopoly conduit to truth by virtue of their sacrosanct institutional status.

In Medieval and Renaissance Europe, both the clerical and the academic hierarchies claimed credibility and deference in virtue of their respective roles as agents of revelation. This revelation was of two kinds, pertaining to the truths about God (the clergy's specialty), and pertaining to the truths about nature (the university faculty's specialty). Any person who was validly coopted into either hierarchy was presumed to have, in virtue of this institutional status, a special access to truth.

Contrary to this entire epistemic system, Copernicus and Galileo came along and said that anybody can know the truth simply by looking through telescopes and using mathematics. The implication of this claim was not only that the clerical and academic hierarchies were wrong about astronomy but something far more explosive: these hierarchies' claim to exclusive epistemic privilege was bogus. Hence their further claim to credibility and deference, based on their alleged epistemic privilege, was likewise bogus. If Copernicus and Galileo were right, then the whole institutional network of political and economic privilege, justified by claims of epistemic privilege, would be undermined. This concern about privilege and power, far more than any abstract qualms about "the central place of mankind in the universe," is what led the authorities of the day to cry "Heresy!" and to bring into play the machinery of the Holy Inquisition.

Ironically (but predictably) a secular version of this medieval fantasy about institutionalized truth has entrenched itself in many patriarchal-industrial societies in the twentieth century. We no longer find academic hierarchies appealing to the authority of Christian scripture or certain writings of Alexandrian scholars. Instead, we find them appealing to a new breed of "authorities"—the established professional journals in their respective fields. To have work published in these journals means to be presumed to have access to truth; otherwise, one is a crank or (even worse!) a popularizer. Although the great cultural construct called "science" has now replaced religion in the West as the ideology of last appeal, an underlying motif has persisted from medieval to modern times: the notion that great, educationally-validating hierarchies as such somehow possess a privileged window on truth. This motif in turn justifies their claims to influence, prestige, and the consumption of economic resources. These industrial-age institutions, like their Christian predecessors, may in fact succeed in making certain kinds of contributions to human knowledge; nonetheless, truth has nothing whatever to do with institutional validation.

The Cartesian Revolution

Copernicus and Galileo contributed mightily to overthrowing the pretensions of existing ecclesiastic and academic hierarchies to be privileged conduits of truth. This overthrow led in turn to a quest among European thinkers for a new and more reliable theoretical foundation for human knowledge. The new foundation to which many turned, inspired by a renewal of interest in the writings of Plato, was mathematics.

The epoch's most influential effort in this direction was that of the French mathematician and philosopher René Descartes (1596-1650 A.D.). In 1637 and 1641 Descartes published two works that represented a revolutionary shift in European thinking: (1) *Discourse on the Method of Rightly Conducting Reason and Seeking for Truth in the Sciences*; and (2) *Meditations on First Philosophy*.

In these works, Descartes professed to begin his inquiry into truth independently of the perspective of any existing institution or even the presumption of any objectively existing realm of being. Instead, Descartes professed to begin with *himself* in his own pure subjectivity, rejecting, at least initially, any assertion or dogma that could conceivably be doubted.

In following this method of doubt, Descartes concluded that although he could doubt everything, he could not doubt that he was doubting. Indeed more: every time he asserted "I doubt," the very act of making this assertion required him to be aware of the existence of the "I" that is the assertion's subject. More generally, he could never make the assertion, "I think" (where "think" refers to *any* form of consciousness) and not also be incontrovertibly aware of his own existence. Hence Descartes' famous dictum: *Cogito, ergo sum* ("I think; therefore, I am").

Commentators sometimes criticize Descartes for his use of the word "therefore" in this dictum. This word, they claim, actually presupposes the validity of the traditional syllogistic logic of Aristotle, despite Descartes' pretense of absolute doubt. If their criticism of Descartes is valid, then the alleged independent certitude of his dictum is, of course, destroyed. Descartes makes it clear, however, that the word "therefore" in his dictum is not to be understood as a syllogistic term, but rather as expressive of a certain kind of necessity stemming from the very possibility of meaningfully saying "I doubt" or, more generally, "I think."

Updating Descartes' terminology a bit, we might say that the words "I am" are part of the logical grammar of "I think"; that is, one cannot have the ability to meaningfully use the words "I think" without also being able to truthfully assert the words "I am." The reason is that it just makes no sense for me to say "I think" (even if this statement is false) if at the same time it is false for me to say "I am." In short, the following combination of words is just plain *nonsense*: "I think, and I am not." Therefore, if my doubt is meaningful, then I am real, and if my doubt is not meaningful, then it is meaningless for me to doubt—which is precisely Descartes' point.

There is a certain circularity here, in that Descartes simply *presupposes* himself as the doubter. But he is entitled to this circularity in virtue of his initial claim that *he* is going to doubt everything. If one were to demand by what right he can make this presupposition, Descartes could simply reiterate, If I cannot doubt without thereby being certain that *I* am the doubter, then it is meaningless for me to doubt my own existence; therefore, either my doubt is meaningless or else I cannot doubt that

I am the doubter. This response again establishes the dictum *Cogito, ergo sum*, or at least, *Nequeo dubitare quin sim* ("I cannot doubt that I am").

The real problem for Descartes is not justifying his own existence in terms of his method of doubt but justifying the existence and knowability of a world external to himself. He is able to build such a bridge only by a twofold appeal to God: (1) Descartes claims he has an innate idea in his mind of a perfect being (God), which therefore must exist, for otherwise such a perfect being would not be perfect; and (2) Descartes' clear and distinct perceptions of the external world must be true, for otherwise God would have been deceptive in creating Descartes, which is impossible since that would mean that God is not good and hence not perfect.

As many subsequent commentators have shown, Descartes' arguments here are filled with questionable or fallacious assumptions. (For example: that there are innate ideas; that the phrase "the idea of a perfect being" denotes an unambiguous concept; that to exist is more perfect than not to exist; that for God to deceive Descartes is not in the interest of a greater cosmic good, etc.). In fact, Descartes' God is just a philosophical *deus ex machina*. It allows Descartes to make an otherwise impossible jump from the ontological priority of pure subjectivity to the existence of an objective external world.

Once Descartes lands on his feet in the objective world, his standard of truth and reality turns out to be mathematics; or, more precisely, it turns out to be analytic geometry (the geometry of Euclid as refined and corrected by new algebraic techniques invented and applied by Descartes himself). In Descartes' objective world, human beings are conceived as immaterial souls interacting with bits of extended matter called their bodies; everything else in the universe is this mere extended matter (*res extensa*). The crucial point is that by "extension," Descartes means that which is geometrically analyzable. The upshot of the Cartesian revolution, then, is this:

> The applicability of higher mathematics is the guarantor of objective truth, replacing the validation of sacrosanct hierarchies.

Like his ancestors in the Middle Ages, Descartes thus still believed in universal objective truth and in God. But whereas previously God validated clerical and academic hierarchies, which in turn validated truth, now God validates Cartesian mathematics, which in turn validates truth, or at least truth in the natural world. Despite, therefore, a seemingly radical subjective turn in his philosophy, Descartes quickly seeks refuge in the arms of an alleged objectivity, but one guaranteed by mathematics, not by theology. His revolution of European thought, therefore, may be viewed as a kind of mathematicization of the quest for absolute certitude. In this, Descartes turned his back on the Aristotelian tradition as interpreted in the West by Thomas Aquinas. In its place, he returned to the tradition of Plato, whose shadow looms large over much of Descartes' thinking. But contrary to Plato's own bias against physical reality in favor of a transcendent realm of pure Forms, Descartes sought to explore the beauty and certitude of mathematics in the physical. It was precisely this bringing down of mathematics from the Heavens to the Earth and its subsequent wedding with empirical research that has ever since constituted the professed ideal method of "modern science."

As Susan Bordo has shown, Descartes' new mathematical philosophy represented a "flight from the feminine." Prior to the triumph of Cartesian thinking, European philosophers often used female metaphors in describing nature, and validated a role for subjectivity and empathy in the knowing process. After Descartes, European philosophers increasingly came to view nature as a machine, and regarded thinking as calculating. In the end, subjectivity and empathy declined in status to the level of bodily impurities. In their place stood the shiny new tools of mathematics and the hard-nosed scientists who used them.[2]

Kepler's Religious Mathematicism

Descartes' grounding of certitude on a kind of higher mathematics, thought of as endorsed by God, was quite in accord with the spirit of the various emerging sciences in 17th and 18th-century Europe. For example, the German astronomer Johannes Kepler (1571-1630 A.D.) was obsessed by the belief that mathematics revealed the mind of God, and that the motions of the planets in particular were physical manifestations, in their mathematical regularity, of God's nature. Driven by an almost religious zeal to collect great bodies of recorded astronomical measurements and to subject them to mathematical analysis, Kepler eventually discovered the three laws of planetary motion that have since been named after him: (1) the orbits of the planets are not circles, as Copernicus thought, but ellipses, with the sun at one focus of the ellipse; (2) the planets do not move at constant speeds, as Copernicus thought, but faster the closer they are to the Sun (more precisely, an imaginary line joining any planet and the sun sweeps out equal areas in equal times); and (3) for every planet, the time it takes to make one complete orbit of the Sun is a function of its mean distance from the Sun.

Newton's Consummate Mathematical System

By the middle of the seventeenth century, Galileo, in addition to improving the telescope and arguing for the astronomical theories of Copernicus, had developed a convincing mathematical model for many previously misunderstood terrestrial physical interactions ("terrestrial mechanics"). Kepler had developed a convincing mathematical model for the motions of the planets ("celestial mechanics"). Finally, Descartes had argued that mathematics was revelatory of objective truth and reality in the natural world. The crowning achievement of this entire trend of thinking came in 1687. In that year, the English mathematician and natural philosopher Isaac Newton (1642-1727 A.D.) published the single greatest book in the history of science—*Philosophiae Naturalis Principia Mathematica* (*The Mathematical Principles of Natural Philosophy*).

Inventing a new kind of mathematics for the occasion (calculus, or theory of "fluxions" as he called it), Newton deduced Kepler's laws of planetary motion from an antecedent mathematical description of the universal force of gravity; he also integrated both terrestrial mechanics and celestial mechanics into one seamless and coherent mathematical system. From the dropping of an iron ball from atop the tower of Pisa to the motion of the planet Jupiter around the Sun, all material objects in the universe seemed to move, whatever their spheres of action, according to the grand mathematical vision of Newton. As a result, the universe came to be viewed as one great clock that God had distantly set in motion and which continued to run according to unvarying mathematical principles discovered and described by Newton. For so awesome a feat, most of Europe heaped praise on Newton. The French mathematician Joseph Lagrange summed up the spirit of this praise when he remarked that the basic laws of nature could be discovered but once, and that it was Newton's great fortune to have been the one to do so.

Despite this outpouring of adulation, however, not everyone in Europe was enthusiastic about Newton's accomplishments or the philosophical presuppositions on which they rested. Among the most noteworthy of these dissenters stood the English visionary poet William Blake (1757-1827 A.D.). Today Blake is renowned for the mythic sweep of both his poetry and his engravings (including his illustrations in 1791 for the works of the English feminist writer Mary Wollstonecraft). In his own day, he was noted as a fierce voice of passionate and visionary prophecy against the entire intellectual tradition of which Isaac Newton was the culmination. Surveying the extent to which the Newtonian world-view had become entrenched in the European academic establishment, Blake lamented—

> I turn my eyes to the Schools & Universities of Europe,
> And there behold the Loom of Locke, whose Woof rages dire,
> Washed by the Water-wheels of Newton.

Blake was a great defender of the integration of sexuality, spirituality, and reason in the individual person, and of peace, equality, and harmony in social relations. In the name of this integration, Blake denounced Newton's new mathematical science as the intellectual prop of a new system of social oppression that was destroying nature in Europe and elsewhere, subjugating native peoples in newly found lands, fomenting ever larger and more devastating wars, and fragmenting and twisting the emotional and sexual lives of Europeans themselves. Viewed in the context of the historical and ecological cataclysms that were to follow him, Blake appears as one of the earliest and most passionate prophets against the burgeoning horrors of patriarchal-industrial civilization.

Despite the beauty and power of Blake's prophetic warnings, however, they have had but little influence on subsequent Western philosophers. To the contrary, philosophers have typically embraced mathematics and science as paragons of knowledge and social utility. As a result, modern Western philosophy has become the handmaiden of science, just as medieval Western philosophy became the handmaiden of theology. As the latter part of this book will argue in detail, Western philosophy, if it is to have any relevance to the early decades of the coming millennium, must rise and free itself from the shackles that both theology and science have heretofore imposed on it.

Newton and Leibniz

At about the same time that Newton invented calculus, the German mathematician and philosopher Gottfried Wilhelm Leibniz (1646-1716 A.D.) did likewise. Leibniz's symbols are the ones in use today, despite dogged resistance from the British school of mathematics, who long clung to Newton's. From the time of Newton's death until the appearance of Einstein's theory of relativity over 175 years later, a theory of physics thus prevailed in the West that was essentially a melange of Newtonian findings dressed in Leibnizian symbols.

Leibniz's derived both his method and his symbols from two metaphysical assumptions: (1) science is a unity that can be expressed in one common mathematical language; and (2) all reality ultimately consists of an infinity of metaphysical points ("monads," discussed in chapter one). These two metaphysical assumptions later exercised an enormous influence on Anglo-American academic philosophers. This influence was transmitted via Leibniz's great 20th-century admirer and commentator, Bertrand Russell, and Russell's star pupil, Ludwig Wittgenstein (in his earlier period). More than any other figures, therefore, Isaac Newton and Gottfried Wilhelm Leibniz proved to be the principal influences on mathematical and logical philosophizing in the West from the 18th to the early 20th century.

Cracks in the Mathematical Monolith

Despite the stirring impact by Newton and Leibniz on European philosophers, the ironic fact is that Western mathematics itself was in a chaotic state, particularly in regard to the questions of logical foundations and overall logical consistency. Typically, mathematicians invented new concepts or operations on an "as needed" basis. Or they extrapolated from a particular body of empirical findings, justifying proof in terms of "intuition" or "metaphysics." In the process, they sometimes came upon puzzling conclusions that they had difficulty accepting.

This process of making puzzling deductions stimulated by *ad hoc* empirical needs is as old as mathematics itself. Indeed, it is clearly illustrated in the bedrock of all mathematics, number theory. For example, ancient Greek mathematicians originally based their number theory on *counting* (that is, on whole positive numbers and, later, on fractions consisting of whole positive numbers). So they were quite flustered when they ran up against an entirely different kind of number when *measuring*. Consider, for example, a right-angle triangle whose width and height is each one unit. Its hypotenuse is equal to the square root of two, a number that cannot be expressed in terms of whole positive numbers or fractions consisting of whole positive numbers.

At first reluctant to admit that there could be such numbers, the Greeks called them *aloga*. This word literally means "incommensurable" but also, by a pun in Greek, "unspeakable" or "irrational." Later mathematicians experienced a similar discomfort when "negative," "imaginary," and "hyper" numbers were introduced. In each of these cases, there were distinguished mathematicians who insisted that the new kind of number was bogus, refusing to countenance calculations with it. Eventually, the crucial factor that won acceptance for the new kind of number was some practical interpretation; for example the use of negative numbers in financial record-keeping, or the use of imaginary numbers in vector analysis.

Up until about 1800 A.D., not only number theory, but most of mathematics in general, was a theoretical patchwork consisting of a rough mixture of both abstract deduction and empirical analogizing. In fact, the only branch of mathematics seemingly well grounded and cleanly deduced in 1800 A.D. was that of Euclid's geometry, created some 2,100 before (and that monolith itself was soon to crack). Mathematical historian Morris Kline compares the mathematics of the time to a big business corporation that ostensibly had been spectacularly successful. Actually, however, unknown to its customers and creditors, the venture was on the verge of bankruptcy:

> Of course, the customers—the scientists who bought and used the mathematical merchandise—and the creditors—the public which invested unhesitatingly in the stock of mathematics—were unaware of the true financial state.[3]

Non-Euclidean Geometries

An important development prodded mathematicians into tackling the question of the logical foundations of mathematics: a sensational discovery concerning Euclidean geometry by the Russian mathematician Nikolai Lobachevsky (1793-1856). Ever since Euclid had first published his results in 300 B.C., mathematicians felt uneasy with his fifth postulate, which said, in effect, that through any given point P on a plane outside a given line L there is one and only one line parallel to L. (Euclid himself used a much more complicated formulation for this postulate.) This, Euclid's famous "parallel postulate," implies that if two finite parallel lines on a plane are drawn out to infinity they will never cross. Because of the complicated way in which Euclid had formulated his original version of this postulate, some of the greatest mathematicians in history had tried to prove that it could really be derived from Euclid's other four postulates, but in 2,100 years no one had ever succeeded in doing so. As a result some began to suspect that perhaps it could not be deduced from them.

In 1829 Lobachevsky suggested a novel approach: let us *change* the fifth postulate, he said, to state that through a point outside a given line on a plane at least two other lines can be drawn that are parallel to the given line, and then proceed to deduce theorems based on this and the other traditional postulates. If, by so doing, we can deduce a theorem that logically contradicts other deduced theorems, then we know that Euclid's parallel postulate is logically dependent on the other four postulates. Why? Because to say that the parallel postulate is logically dependent on the other postulates is the same as to say that the parallel postulate is itself just a theorem; and all theorems, by the meaning of the term, are logically consistent with each other, provided the postulates from which they are derived are consistent.

To everyone's great surprise, Lobachevsky's new geometry proved to be logically consistent; that is, his new parallel postulate, together with the other four postulates, generated a new batch of geometrical theorems that were consistent with each other, however difficult it might be to try and visualize such a geometry.

From this discovery, two important corollaries followed: (1) because denying Euclid's fifth postulate did not result in a contradiction, the fifth postulate was in fact logically independent of the other four, which is why no one in 2,100 years had been able to deduce it as a theorem from them; and, far more important, (2) logically consistent geometries can be developed on the basis of purely arbitrary postulates, without regard for what actually happens to be observed in the real world. In other words, mathematical systems in and of themselves tell us nothing about the empirical world; only when interpreted in terms of empirically observed regularities do mathematical terms and formulas have predictive value. Even then, it is by no means obvious when a mathematical system has in fact been given a correct empirical interpretation.

As a result of Lobachevsky's example, the German mathematician Georg Riemann (1826-1866) later developed a system of geometry based on yet another parallel postulate: through a given point P outside a given line L there is *no* line parallel to the given line. (That is, any two finite lines on a plane extended to infinity will eventually cross.) In the early years of the 20th century, Albert Einstein showed, as part of his theory of relativity, that Riemannian geometry, not Euclidean, correctly describes actual physical space. (More precisely: space and time constitute one continuum, and this continuum is curved by virtue of the matter within it.) With Einstein's *coup de grace*, the monolith of Euclidean geometry, and with it the alleged objective reality and infallibility of mathematics, cracked.

As a result of these developments, the 19th and 20th centuries witnessed numerous efforts to establish mathematics, viewed as a purely formal system, on a logically rigorous foundation. In particular, the Italian mathematician and linguist Guiseppe Peano (1858-1932) succeeded in showing that a new symbolism for formal logic could be used to express mathematical postulates. He also showed that an arithmetic for positive whole numbers could be logically deduced from five postulates about the qualities of such numbers. The German philosopher and mathematician Gottlob Frege (1848-1925) went even further, attempting (unsuccessfully) to derive the notion of number itself from formal notions used in formal logic. His efforts inaugurated "the logicist school" of mathematics.

Russell's *Pincipia Mathematica*

Frege's quest to reduce formal mathematics to logic was later taken up by the British philosopher Bertrand Russell (1872-1970), assisted by Alfred North Whitehead (1861-1947). From 1910 to 1913, the pair published the three volumes of their monumental *Principia Mathematica* (*Mathematical Principles*), the most famous work on mathematics in the 20th century. It attempted to show that arithmetic could be rigorously derived from purely logical notions independent of any notion of number as such. In the eyes of its authors, *Principia Mathematica* was to do for mathematics what Newton's similarly named *Philosophiae Naturalis Principia Mathematica* had done for physics; that is, it was to provide a solid foundation for a grand synthesis of all that was known on the subject.

The key to Russell's effort to reduce the notion of number to logical relations lay in his concept of class (or set), class membership, and class relation. According to Russell, any given number may be defined as the class of all classes in the universe having that quantity of objects in it. For example, what we mean by the symbol "2," claimed Russell, is really the class of all pairs.

To the charge that this definition is circular, since it seems to sneak in the notion of number in the definition, Russell responded that this circularity only appears in the English paraphrase of the strictly formal logical concepts he used. More formally stated, two classes may be said to have the same number if and only if there is a one-to-one correspondence between the members of the two classes; or, more formally still, classes X and Y have the same number if, and only if, given any member a of class X, there is some member b of class Y such that a has a certain relation to b and to no other member of Y, and such that b has the same relation to a and to no other member of X.

For example, consider a bag of some marbles (class X) and another bag of some coins (class Y). Suppose that I remove a marble from its bag and then pair it with a coin removed from its bag; again, I do the same thing for another marble and another coin, and so on, until both bags are empty. At the end of this process, I find, say, that I have five sets, each consisting of a marble and a coin. In this case, Russell would say that, according to their understanding of class, class membership, and class relation, both marbles and coins may be said to have the same number (namely, 5). Further, they have been determined to have this number without any appeal to a prior concept of number. Since this process can be extended to the determination of any number, however large, the concept of number can be reduced to that of class, class membership, and class relation, which are logical, not arithmetic, concepts.

The Nature of Classes

Despite claims to the contrary by Russell, however, this definition of number still turns out to be circular. As discussed in the beginning of chapter one, no data scene, whether perceived or conceived (that is, whether empirical or conceptual), can become interpretable except in virtue of the decision (either conscious or preconscious) by some interpreter or some group of interpreters in regard to what constitutes one and many for that data scene. In other words, apart from some interpreter's decision about one and many, no data scene is interpretable, and apart from interpretation there is neither perception nor cognition. As a consequence, there can be no awareness whatsoever of any classes or any members of any classes that is not based on some interpreter's decision about one and many, because a class is that which, despite its plurality, is regarded as one. Even in the case of a class that has no members (the null class) or has only one member (the unit class) or has every member (the universal class), the class is still something over and above its members or lack thereof—namely, that unity by virtue of which it is a class. This unity is always, in part, interpreter-dependent.

Russell himself stressed the distinction between the members of a class and the class itself in his "theory of types." According to this theory, classes are of a different and higher type than their members. That which can be predicated of any or all class members is not necessarily predicable of the class itself to which they belong. Russell correctly understood that apart from the postulation of such a theory of types their entire mathematical and logical system would collapse into hopeless paradoxes.

Priority of One and Many

Even on Russell's terms, a class is always something over and above its members. But we have seen that that thing, by virtue of which any class is not merely identical to its members, is the fact, stemming from the decision of some interpreter or group of interpreters, that the class makes some many, one. In other words, a class is many, regarded by some interpreter or group of interpreters as one. As a result, the claim of Russell and Whitehead that they succeeded in reducing mathematics to logic by defining numbers as classes of classes is false, because the notion of class itself inescapably presupposes the notion of number, at least the numbers one and many. Russell got it backwards. An implicit application of number, or at least the numbers one and many, is a necessary presupposition of the notion of class—and indeed, as we have seen, of all interpretation whatsoever.

Readers may be puzzled that the word "many" is regarded as the name of a number. But this puzzlement only arises because of a peculiarity of the English language; namely, that it has no separate numerical symbol for that quantity denoted by the word "many." As we saw above, some societies use the numerical scheme of *one*, *two*, and *many*. Let us learn from these societies and assign some symbol, say "Þ," to represent the number *many*. Having done so, we can then say that all interpretation and all class formation presuppose at least an implicit application by some interpreter or some group of interpreters of the numbers 1 and Þ. Therefore, the attempt by Russell to reduce numbers to classes of classes is circular, because classes themselves presuppose at least an implicit application of the numbers 1 and Þ.

The ancient Pythagoreans, then, were right after all: in a certain sense all things are composed of numbers, at least the numbers 1 and Þ. Contrary to the Pythagoreans, however, these numbers are not absolutes; rather, they depend for their applicability to any data scene on the decision of some interpreter or some group of interpreters.

The logicist approach of Russell is also open to other objections. The most significant is this: in order to avoid logical paradoxes he was forced to introduce a number of axioms which, although possibly true, are certainly not self-evident. For example: (1) "the axiom of choice" (for any collection of classes, it is always possible to choose one object from each such class and so form a new class); (2) "the axiom of reducibility" (any proposition for some higher logical type is logically equivalent to some proposition for the first-order type); and (3) "the axiom of infinity" (the universe consists of an infinite number of objects). There are mathematicians that have challenged the truth of each of these axioms.

In his later years, Russell backed away from many of the categorical claims he had made for *Principia Mathematica*. He still remained committed, however, to the Platonic ideal of absolute logical certitude and the Leibnizian goal of a universal mathematical language; nonetheless, he admitted that *Principia Mathematica* had failed to realize such ideals.

Although *Principia Mathematica* failed to demonstrate what it set out to prove, no other 20th-century book on logic and mathematics has come close to matching its scope and power. And, in fact, the very shortcomings of *Principia Mathematica* did succeed in proving something of great importance, although not at all what Russell had intended: the greatest logicians of the age could not deduce arithmetic from logic.

In addition to the objections raised above, set theory (the theory of what classes are) has been bedeviled by paradoxes. Accordingly, a number of logicians and mathematicians have tried to reformulate the system of axioms on which set theory is based. An example was the work of Ernst Zermelo and Abraham Fraenkel. Their aim was to allow for the existence of a sufficient variety of sets in order to ground the complexities of mathematics but to preclude the sorts of sets that lead to paradoxes. The success of their program, particularly in view of Gödel's proof (discussed below), has been limited; in any case, their elementary concept of set, like the logicist concept of class, is incomplete, for it fails to acknowledge the role of the interpreter in creating sets.

Because no set can be rigorously defined without reference to some interpreter, it is a theoretical simplification when mathematicians say that certain objects by themselves constitute a set. Nonetheless, mathematicians can get away with this sort of simplification in many practical applications. After all, applied mathematics (as opposed to pure mathematics) is the art of knowing what simplifications you can get away with in actual practice. When pushed to its theoretical limits, however, this simplification generates the type of paradoxes that stumped Russell and his successors. The only hope for comprehensively solving these paradoxes is to come to terms with this fact: to be a member of a set is to be a member of a set *for some interpreter*.

The Formalism of David Hilbert

As the failings of the logicist approach of Russell became apparent, mathematicians and philosophers turned to other strategies in the hope of establishing mathematics on a rigorous logical foundation. In particular, the German mathematician David Hilbert (1862-1943) initiated what has come to be known as "the formalist school" of mathematics. In Hilbert's view, the grounding of mathematics is not merely a matter of reducing mathematics to logic, as Russell had attempted to do, but an endeavor requiring the use of *both* mathematical and logical axioms. As part of this widening of the theoretical base, Hilbert acknowledged that any formalization of mathematics presupposes an irreducible intuition of number. (Hence his approach was not an absolutely formalist one, as the later name "formalist school" misleadingly implies.)

However, once having made these initial concessions to mathematical intuition, Hilbert maintained that one could abstract from the basic elements and relations of arithmetic a system of symbols that are purely formal, that is, that have no meaning other than as strings of marks on a piece of paper. Certain of these strings are designated as "axioms" (pre-given strings). In addition, rules are stipulated that define the following: (1) what constitutes a "well formed" string (those strings that are to be admitted in deductions); and (2) what constitutes a valid deduction (how well-formed strings are to be generated from the axioms). In Hilbert's approach, proof becomes a purely mechanical operation, conducted according to formally stated transformation rules, of symbols that are in themselves vacuous.

In effect, Hilbert wanted to look at the elements of arithmetic with X-ray eyes, then take out the skeleton of arithmetic's logical structure, and finally manipulate and study this skeleton as the object itself of formal analysis. The effort to do so, to make the formal structure of mathematical proof itself an object of study, is called "metamathematics."

According to Hilbert's approach, the formal system to be analyzed is an abstraction from arithmetic elements and relations; consequently, there can always be various ways of making such an abstraction. The natural question arises, then, as to which formally abstracted system is the best. And, even before that question, this: what must characterize any formalization in order for it to be adequate? At the time, everyone seemed to agree that any adequate formal system for arithmetic must have two qualities, consistency and completeness; that is, there must be no logical contradiction among the axioms, and it must be possible to deduce from the axioms every true arithmetical theorem.

Gödel's Proof

It was within the context of these expectations that the Czech-born mathematician Kurt Gödel (1906-1978) dropped a bombshell from which mathematics has never recovered. In 1931 Gödel published an ingenious and shocking paper with the seemingly innocuous title of "On Formally Undecidable Propositions of *Principia Mathematica* and Related Systems."[4] The argument of this paper, together with a number of later corollaries, is known as "Gödel's proof." It states that *any* formal logical system that is powerful enough to express the elements and relations of arithmetic cannot be *both* complete *and* consistent. In other words, regardless of how sophisticated or complex any formal logical system for arithmetic may be, if the axioms are logically consistent, there will always be some true arithmetic proposition that cannot be proved within that system.

Gödel's proof pulled the rug out from under the entire axiomatizing approach to mathematics. It did so because it showed that no logically consistent formal system, precisely in virtue of being a logically consistent formal system, can demonstrate all that is true in arithmetic. The same limitation, of course, also applies to any branch of knowledge that incorporates arithmetic. Higher mathematics, it turns out, has this resemblance to the empirical sciences: it is not just a matter of making correct deductions from axioms.

Brouwer's Intuitionism

In reaction to the entire axiomatic approach, the Dutch mathematician L.E.J. Brouwer (1881-1966) emphasized the importance of mathematical intuition, whose power, he felt, extended beyond that of any kind of deductive proof. According to Brouwer, the human ability to form mathematical concepts is ultimately connected to the ability for distinguishing separate, successive events in time. In the context of such temporal experiences, said Brouwer, humans develop an intuition of numbers and simple mathematical operations that cannot themselves be further reduced to any other kind of reality. In Brouwer's view, the intuition of numbers and minimal mathematics is even more basic than what are called the laws of logic, so that any effort to derive mathematics from logic is doomed to failure. In fact, the opposite is true: logic is a branch of mathematics.

Since all mathematics derives from intuition, Brouwer argued that any effort to extend mathematical operations beyond what is possible to intuition is meaningless. Hence he rejected those parts of 19th and 20th century mathematics that assumed the existence of infinite sets, for it is impossible to construct an infinite set by making a finite number of additions to a finite set. In addition, Brouwer challenged use of "the law of excluded middle" in infinite-set proofs (the principle that if a proposition is proved false, then its denial must be true).

The virtue of Brouwer's intuitionism is that it avoided the conundrums of infinite-set theory and was immune to the devastating implications of Gödel's proof. Its weak point (a fatal one in the eyes of many mathematicians) is that it ruled out of court a great body of abstract 20th century mathematics that had proven to be of great practical importance in applied science. If this body of mathematics was to be rejected as inherently unsound, how could one explain its great practical usefulness?

Historicity of Mathematical Proof

As the above developments show, mathematics in the 20th century has spawned competing schools. Among these schools has been the logicism of Russell, the set-theoretic approach of Zermelo and Fraenkel, the formalism of Hilbert, and the intuitionism of Brouwer, to name only the most noteworthy. The real significance of the emergence of these various schools is not merely that there have been differences of opinion concerning the nature of mathematics. Rather, the crucial point is this: there have been, and continue to be, irresoluble differences about the nature of mathematical *proof*. The fact that one group of highly trained mathematicians accepts a certain kind of proof can no longer be taken to mean that another group of highly trained mathematicians will do likewise—even though both groups of mathematicians clearly understand the terms, premises, and reasoning in such a proof. This divergence in regard to the criteria of proof is the crux of the crisis in modern mathematics, for such criteria in effect define what constitutes mathematics; that is, mathematics is that body of knowledge which is proved in a certain way. But there is no longer agreement about what that way is. Hence it is quite feasible for there to develop different kinds of mathematics, each with its own methods and conclusions, and each claiming to be the one true mathematics.

In chapter one we saw that whenever any group of interpreters shares agreement about the criteria of evaluation for certain kinds of propositions, then that group of interpreters constitutes a normative community; furthermore, such a group also always shares, by implication, some ideal of a hypothetical exemplary interpreter that is implicitly defined by their common criteria. As a result of their agreement concerning criteria for the evaluation of propositions, interpreters in a normative community are able to reach common agreement among themselves on the value of propositions proffered by their members. When so agreed, they all in effect judge these propositions through the eyes of the hypothetical exemplary interpreter that lies implicit in their criteria for propositional evaluation.

We also saw in chapter one that when, for whatever reason, deep divisions develop *within* a normative community over what constitutes the ideal of its hypothetical exemplary interpreter, that community undergoes a crisis of self-definition. One of the most famous examples of this effect involved the normative community of European astronomers. During the Renaissance, a crisis developed concerning the criteria of astronomical proof and hence the ideal of the hypothetical exemplary astronomer. Moreover, this crises was part of a much larger pattern of change in religion, economics, politics, and general culture. The changing definition of astronomical proof was affected by the historicity of the particular interpreters who practiced astronomy.[5]

An analogous situation now exists in mathematics. The normative community of mathematicians at the end of the second millennium is undergoing a crisis of self-definition similar to that of European astronomers during the Renaissance. In both cases, there has been a profound disagreement over what constitutes each science's ideal hypothetical interpreter, as implicitly defined by each science's standards of proof. Like human astronomy, human mathematics is, in part, a cultural and historical construct.

Suppose that all or most mathematicians living today shared the same criteria of proof. Even so, history shows that what seems certain and rigorous to one generation of mathematicians often seems less so to their descendants. In fact, even for mathematical proofs that have been used for generations, there are few that have not been modified over the ages. Every mathematical proof, however rigorous it may seem at the time it is first propounded, always presupposes certain unexamined assumptions that its proponents simply take for granted. With the passage of time, other mathematicians, either because they live in another age with different assumptions, or because the proof has led to certain unexpected anomalies, realize that the original work was not really rigorous after all. As a result, the proof is amended (sometimes discarded), until yet another group of mathematicians takes it up and re-examines it, and so on.

Hence the common observation among historians of mathematics that one generation's proofs is the next generation's fallacies. Hence also the cynical, but often true, quip that in mathematics proof is the assertion of error with confidence.[6]

Individual working mathematicians rarely make new discoveries in their field simply by deducing new theorems from old axioms. To the contrary, they typically begin with a vague hunch or a flash of insight that they struggle to make more precise through successive symbolic formulations, some of which they may eventually discard, while retaining others. Any new concept that they may eventually proffer to their colleagues is always embedded in a formally deduced argument in its final form, but that final deductive formalism masks an imaginative process of creation that is anything but rigorous. Indeed, some of the most innovative mathematicians have been known to concede in private that they believe or disbelieve in certain theorems *despite* proof to the contrary that their colleagues accept as rigorous. A similar situation exists in physics, the most famous example of which was Albert Einstein. He rejected statistical quantum physics till his dying day, dismissing proofs in its support with the quip that God does not play dice with the universe.

Ambiguity of Applied Mathematics

Not only are there different schools of mathematics, but even those parts of mathematics accepted by all schools do not apply unambiguously to the real world, despite popular notions to the contrary. For example, most people would probably assert without any hesitation that the following mathematical proposition is always unambiguously true of the real world: "1 + 1 = 2."

Is popular confidence in the empirical applicability of this formula justified? Yes—in many cases; however, not in all. For example, let us put one marble into the same bowl and then another, cover with a lid and shake, then remove the lid. The bowl will contain a total of two marbles. But what if we put one quart of alcohol into the bowl and then one quart of water, cover and shake? If we actually conduct this experiment, when we remove the lid we will see that the bowl actually contains a total of approximately 1.9 quarts of fluid, not 2 as expected, due to an interaction between alcohol and water molecules. Again, if we put one mouse into the same bowl and then another, cover with a lid and then check one week later, we will find one very large mouse left and only four little feet and a tail from the other.

Perhaps someone will make this objection: It is true that mixing one quart of water and one quart of alcohol in the same bowl yields less than two quarts of fluid. Nonetheless, the following is incontrovertible: if I put one quart of alcohol and one quart of water in the same bowl, then I put one quart of alcohol and one quart of water in the same bowl.

Our objector has a point—assuming an unambiguous understanding of what the phrase "the same bowl" refers to. In most everyday activities, no disagreement on this matter would arise. But let us consider the case were the lapse of great periods of time may be involved, or great expanses of distance, which are not uncommon circumstances in modern science. In these cases (as Heraclitus would remind us), there may indeed be disagreement as to exactly what the phrase "the same" refers to. (Will the molecules that now constitute my body constitute "the same body" 1,000 years from now?) Our objector overlooks a crucial fact: abstract mathematical formulas, to the extent that they truly describe the real world, *always* presuppose a vast network of prior empirical interpretations about sameness and difference. In most cases, we just take this complex of interpretations for granted, and so it becomes oblivious to us, as the water is to fish in the sea. Nonetheless, this complex of prior interpretations is always there; without it, a mathematical formula is just a string of empty symbols.

In view of these complications, should we perhaps alter the above mathematical proposition to the effect that 1 plus 1 *usually* equals 2? Or should we regard the results of these experiments as evidence that the material world is just one of illusion? *Both of these alternatives are genuine logical possibilities*. In fact, we adopt neither alternative, but say instead that "1 + 1 = 2" is always true, except that its applicability "depends on circumstances." This solution is like saying "I always tell the truth—except when I don't."

Why do we make this rather self-serving choice about mathematics? Answer: because of purely practical considerations. We find it much easier to get things done in the world if we *decide* both that mathematical equations shall be invariable and true, and that the material world shall not, on the whole, be one of illusion. But however practical the consequences of such a decision may be for us, it must never be overlooked that it remains a *decision* and that it is made by some *group*. There is no logical necessity whatever for supposing that such a decision could not be made otherwise, especially if interpreters of a radically different nature should constitute the group. The practical applicability of abstract mathematics is always a matter of a previous decision by some interpreter or some group of interpreters. This circumstance is yet another example of the principle that to interpret is to create a kind of world.

The reason we can get away with making such a self-serving decision is that much of mathematics is not really so purely abstract, as often thought. To the contrary, both mathematics and mathematicians have a history. In fact, the most useful concepts of abstract mathematics generally turn out to be those that were first abstracted from numerous empirical examples. As a result of surveying such examples, mathematicians create abstract concepts, from which, in combination with certain axioms and rules of transformation, they deduce certain definite consequences. As a result, these deduced consequences often have practical applications, which is not at all surprising, considering the mode of their original formation.

Naturally, mathematicians are also free to play with abstractions far removed from empirical experience and to deduce from them certain other definite consequences. As might be expected, these "purer" forms of mathematics generally show less practical applicability; indeed, "pure" mathematics is full of concepts that no one has the slightest idea how to apply to the real world. Nonetheless, they sometimes find an unexpected application by empirically-oriented scientists looking for new conceptual tools to handle unusual phenomena. Einstein's use of Riemannian geometry is an example. But even Riemann's unusual concepts were an outgrowth of the empirically influenced geometry of Euclid.

In sum: human mathematical propositions, however abstract, always have empirical feet. They are always true for the empirical world because the human interpreters who use them have decided that either they shall always be true or else they shall be inapplicable (and you can't beat that).

From the various issues raised above, both historical and otherwise, it should be clear that mathematics is, in part, *subjective*; that is, mathematics cannot be meaningfully separated in any absolute sense from the physical structure, cultural conditioning, and the idiosyncratic lives of the interpreters who practice it. If human beings had the ability to perceive in five dimensions, or if the Renaissance or the Industrial Revolution had never happened, or if long periods of abstract, objectifying study caused incapacitating emotional breakdowns in human beings, human mathematics would today be quite different from what it is.

We have seen that despite 2,300 years of development since the time of Euclid, no one has yet succeeded in grounding mathematics on a solid logical foundation. Furthermore, no commonly accepted standards for rigorous mathematical proof exist. Finally, the alleged universal applicability of mathematics to the real world holds only by a kind of conventional courtesy. Although human mathematics has undeniably attained a high degree of abstraction, precision, and practical applicability, it remains nonetheless a form of human interpretation. We cannot remove the mathematician without losing mathematics, just as we cannot remove the artist without losing art.

Relative Objectivity of Mathematics

Despite its subjectivity, however, mathematics also possesses a certain relative objectivity. As pointed out in chapter one, absolute objectivity is a meaningless concept; the only meaningful objectivity is that which is relative to some universe of interpretation for some group of interpreters. For those interpreters engaged in doing mathematics, numbers or other formal constructions constitute the basic elements in an interpretative system. Within the context of that universe of interpretation, numbers and such formal constructions are *real*, as real, say, as movements on a battlefield are for a general while conducting a campaign, or as chess moves are for a chess player while playing chess. But to seek absolute objectivity beyond such contexts, that is, to try somehow to get behind interpretation, is futile, since objectivity itself is a creation of interpretation.

Furthermore, all the elements and constructions within mathematics' universe of interpretation are *universals*. As shown in chapter one, all universals (like all particulars) are in part nominal—deriving from the decisions, whether conscious or unconscious, whether spontaneous or calculated, of some interpreter or group of interpreters. They are also in part real—deriving from some given data scene (at least an ideal data scene) and functioning in the context of some universe of interpretation. Mathematical objects, like all objects, have a bipolarity of nominality and reality. Apart from this bipolarity, they cease to be a part of interpretation and therefore a part of knowledge.

Even so, one might ask whether mathematics is not in some sense *more* real or *more* objective than other human endeavors. This question really resolves itself into another, namely, whether various other universes of interpretation can be reduced to functions within the universe of interpretation of mathematics. In fact, some other universes of interpretation have been so reduced to, or at least made partially to overlap with, that of mathematics, such as that of quantum physics. Others, however, seem far removed from such a reduction. One example: my delight while watching the Cowardly Lion in *The Wizard of Oz*.

One can certainly adopt as a guiding principle the goal of trying to reduce as much of reality as possible to mathematical interpretations. The virtue of such a goal is that it may lead one to discover mathematical reductions where they might not otherwise have been suspected (as in Galileo's treatment of terrestrial mechanics). This approach, however, also has a drawback: it may lead one to force other universes of interpretation into arbitrary reductions, thereby diminishing and even trivializing the richness of human experience (as in the writings of the logical positivists). There is simply no way to know for certain in advance whether all human universes of interpretation can be reduced to one, all-encompassing universe of interpretation, whether that of mathematics or any other.

Certainly to date no interpreter or group of interpreters has convincingly succeeded in doing so.

Because mathematics has proven to be so effective in certain of our dealings with the world, we are quite justified in surmising that reality has a mathematical aspect. Whether, however, this aspect is the most important, basic, or interesting of all the aspects of reality is another question entirely. In any case, this question is not one that can be answered within mathematics itself; that is, this is a *philosophical* question.

Mathematics As a Myth System

When viewed in terms of its full historical, cultural, and interpretational contexts, mathematics takes on the features of a kind of socially conditioned myth system. Lest mathematicians choke at the mere thought of such a thing, I want to clarify the meaning of the word "myth." Many people in patriarchal-industrial societies, especially those who have never seriously studied mythology, use the word "myth" in a derogatory sense, meaning a popular misconception or vague delusion. In this sense, myth is far removed from mathematics. The word, however, has another, far more serious meaning. Derived from the Greek *mythos*, which originally meant "word" or "speech," and later "story" or "narrative," the word "myth" refers to a certain kind of communications tool—a system of symbols that depicts supra-empirical beings or entities, and which is socially created, historically transmitted, and explanatory of archetypal aspects of reality. If we review the various aspects of mathematics heretofore examined in this chapter, we will see that it falls within this definition of myth.

For one thing, both mathematics and myths are a matter of special symbols, specifically designed for the unique social contexts in which they are used. Mathematics relies on special written signs that are chosen or invented precisely because they are not in common use (or "profane," in the language of myth). Significantly, these symbols are commonly derived from dead languages, especially ancient Greek, or previous occult traditions, such as alchemy or astrology. Moreover, the meaning, use, and interpretive power of these symbols are not casually available to all members of the society at large but must be learned from initiated experts ("shamans" or "wizards" in myth) who have spent many years examining their mysteries. Those initiates who suitably master such symbols demonstrate their agility to other members of the confraternity of the learned by creating rigorous proofs ("rituals") that must be correct down to the least detail ("auspicious"). In the creation and use of these symbols, the mathematician, like his or her cultural analog, the shaman, relies both on flashes of personal intuition and on a received public system of symbolic interpretation.

Furthermore, the mathematician, when manipulating his or her symbols, does not depict this or that particular object but rather invisible conceptual entities or forces ("daimones," "mana" in myth) of which visible material objects are but so many tokens or effects. Such symbols and their depictions, when adapted to ever larger wholes, and when more fully interpreted by fellow mythologists in the empirical sciences, come to tell great stories ("epics") about the nature of the world and of the origin and functioning of the human species within it. These stories are in turn handed down from age to age, with each generation making some further contribution of its own. Eventually the system of symbols so interpreted crystallizes into the primary cultural matrix that the society uses in order to organize and understand the underlying archetypes of its collective experiences of life. Any set of humanly contrived symbols so established and so interpreted constitutes a myth system.

Now one might object here that these parallels are superficial, in that mathematics, despite esoteric qualms over its logical foundations and objective reality, is both practically objective and cumulatively correctable. That is, mathematics as a practical matter has proven to be of enormous utility in our dealings with the real world; furthermore, although each generation admittedly makes its share of mathematical blunders, the next generation corrects them, with the result that the overall body of mathematical knowledge is continually augmented and fine-tuned from generation to generation. Hence mathematics is far more substantial than "mere myth."

But this objection, far from undermining the analogy of mathematics with myth, actually reinforces it further, since these two traits—great practical applicability and cumulative correctability—are also typical of myth. In many so-called "primitive" native societies around the globe, myth embodies, validates, and ritualizes much of the society's technical and spiritual capacities needed for survival. Through myth each generation learns not only the practical skills needed for day-to-day living but also the complex of expected patterns of behavior and of emotional expressiveness that work to promote the society's survival as a whole. In addition, each generation transforms and augments the society's received body of myths with contributions from its own unique experiences, thereby continually preserving both its long term continuity and its immediate relevance. Myth, like mathematics, is both enormously practical and generationally cumulative.

"Well," our objector might add, "you also have to look at the overall historical and cultural accomplishments of the societies in question. It's one thing to have a few dozen half-naked people running around eating roots and bark, and quite another to have a civilization of hundreds of millions who have harnessed most of the resources of the planet and repeatedly accomplished astounding technical feats. Modern civilization and all its accomplishments could not have been possible without mathematics as we know it. How can you possibly compare primitive myth to that? To do so is to trivialize very real differences."

The underlying premise of this objection is that the mode of life and the technical accomplishments of patriarchal-industrial civilization are in some meaningful sense *better* than those, say, of the original inhabitants of North America, whom industrial civilization (aided, incidentally, by mathematically enhanced technology) destroyed. But one might reasonably ask our objector, "Better by *what standard*?" As indicated by eyewitness reports and surviving evidence, the original inhabitants of North America had, at least prior to the final white onslaughts, a form of life that on the whole they much enjoyed; in fact, they fought ferociously on its behalf. The few judgments of these early people that have been preserved in their own words show that they viewed the white invaders as twisted and highly destructive *savages*. Are we, then, to embrace unthinkingly the standards of the white invaders simply because they proved most capable of destroying existing civilizations? And if not, by what other standards shall we conclude that such conquering civilizations are superior?

As to patriarchal industrialism's great technical accomplishments, we also have to take into account the horrifying destructiveness that such technology has also made possible, such as genocide, holocausts, repeated wars of global scope, and ecological catastrophe. When both accomplishments and horrors are put in the scale, it is by no means obvious that the triumphant civilization of Euro-American whites has on the whole been better, either intrinsically or practically, than all the native societies around the world which such a civilization has enslaved, impoverished, or annihilated for the sake of its own well-being. Hence we cannot conclude that modern mathematics is superior to the myths of nature societies merely because it has empowered patriarchal-industrial civilization. In fact, as we will later see in chapter thirteen, there are good reasons to argue that this empowerment should lead to exactly the opposite conclusion.

What is called "modern mathematics," like any dominant myth system, is the historical outgrowth of a certain kind of civilization, in this case the patriarchal-industrial civilization. As with any myth system, modern mathematics is partly subjective in nature, owing much to individual imagination—the imaginative leap, first, in making a minimal interpretation of numerosity, and then the imaginative leap in envisioning new concepts and systems. But like other dominant myths, mathematics also possesses a relative objectivity—that of a publicly transmitted view of reality in which idealized concepts find both their appropriate symbolic formulation and their empirical interpretation. Again as with myth systems, mathematics cannot be given any kind of absolute logical foundation, since it rests on an endless number of implicit presuppositions, most of them invisible to its practitioners, which have arisen from the historical peculiarities of the culture in which it appears. Such justification as it may claim for itself must rest, first, on the satisfaction it provides to its individual practitioners; second, on its overall usefulness to its home culture in its dealings with reality; and finally on the manner in which that culture itself is judged in terms of the human race as a whole.

Partially subjective and partially objective; generated by, and supportive of, a certain kind of culture; illuminative of certain aspects of reality; transmitted with both continuity and change from one generation to the next; contributory to the historical merit or blame of the culture that uses it—such is the system of symbols that may be called on the one hand mathematics, and on the other myth.

When pressed with this analogy between mathematics and myth, our objector has one final argument to make: "If mathematics were just another set of symbols, you would be right. But mathematics possesses a remarkable characteristic that uniquely distinguishes it from all other sets of symbols: its presuppositions and methodology define, in the end, what it is logical and what is not. If you deny that Zeus is the king of the gods, you do not thereby undermine the possibility of speaking logically. However, if you deny that one plus one equals two, logic comes to a halt, and nothing further can be said. This is a trait of mathematics that does not appear in any myth system."

Here our objector seems to have played a trump card. Who, after all, could deny that the special force called "logical necessity" prevails in mathematics in a way not found in any other form of human communication? Shall we, then, throw up our hands at this point and concede the game to our objector? The temptation to do so may be strong. Nonetheless, two little nagging questions remain: (1) What does it mean to say that a statement is "logical"? and (2) What is this thing called "logical necessity"?

Most people would no doubt brush these questions aside. The whole business of logic, they would say, boils down to a simple rule: whenever you say anything, make sure you're consistent. But this facile response merely raises other nagging questions: Consistent in terms of *what* language? And according to *whose* criteria of consistency?

Most of the remainder of this book is devoted to answering questions such as these. As readers will discover, formal logic—the great robe in which mathematics drapes itself while holding its imperial pose—is itself a culturally-woven fabric. As we proceed to unsheet mathematics of this last pretense, we will discover that, even in logic, to interpret is to create a kind of world.

---

[1] For an excellent discussion of the nature of this crisis and its historical background, see Morris Kline, *Mathematics: The Loss of Certainty*, Oxford University Press, New York, 1980.

[2] Susan Bordo, *The Flight to Objectivity: Essays on Cartesianism and Culture*, State University of New York Press, Albany, NY, 1987. Bordo attributes the great historical impact of Descartes' views to psychological causes (collective European anxiety over separation from nature). However, we will see in chapter thirteen that the real causes were political and economic (the usefulness of the new scientific mentality to the creators of the Great Devastation).

[3] Kline, *loc. cit.*, p. 169.

[4] Kurt Gödel, "Über formal unentscheidbare Sätze der Principia Mathematica und verwandter Systeme I," *Monatshefte für Mathematik und Physik*, vol. 38, 1931, pp. 173-198.

[5] Thomas Kuhn calls such a change in a normative community of scientists a "paradigm shift." See his *The Structure of Scientific Revolutions*, 2nd edition, The University of Chicago Press, Chicago, 1970.

[6] Quoted by Kline as, "Logic is the art of going wrong with confidence," *op. cit.*, p. 197.

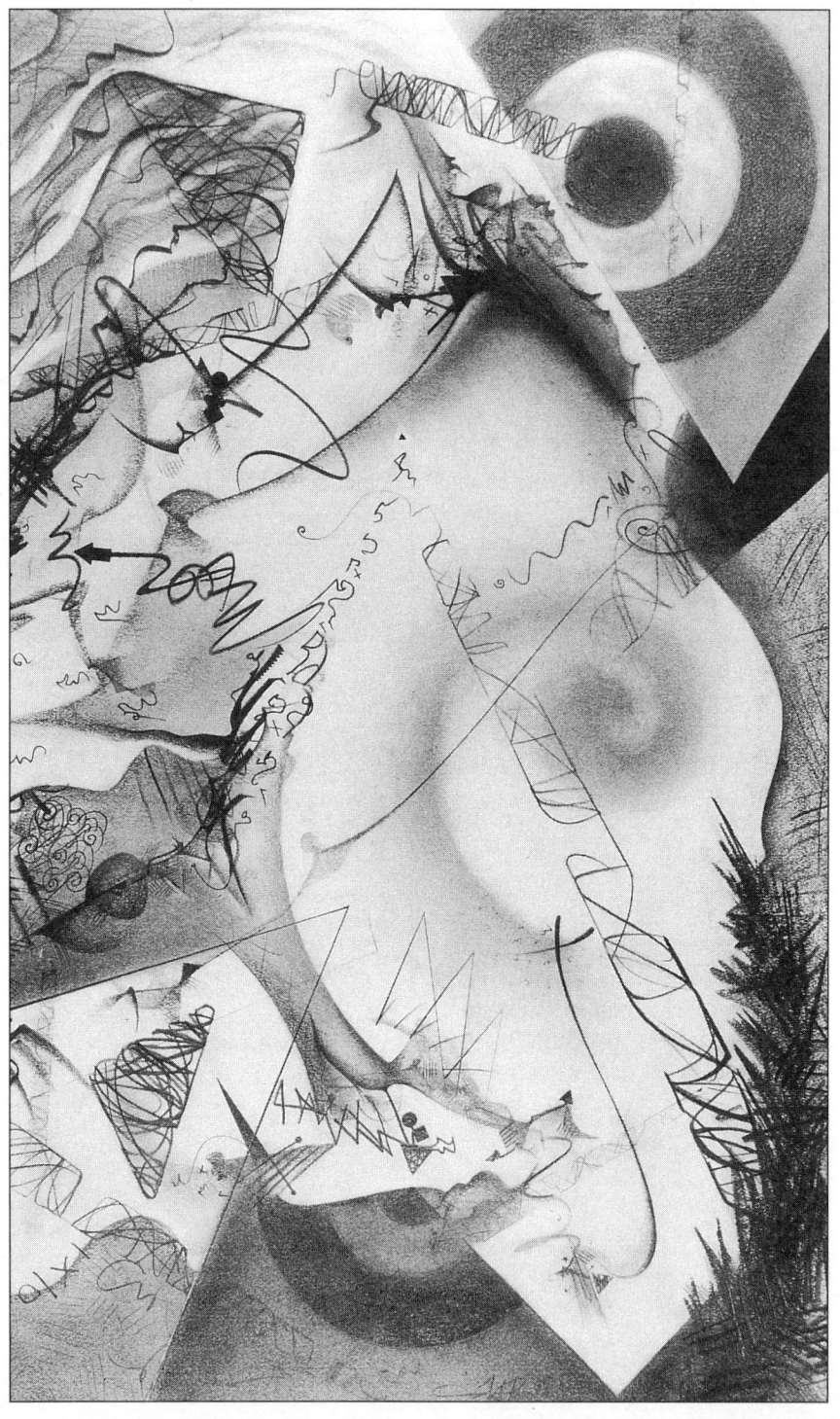

Sacra 1, Detail, Graphite, 30" x 22", 1990

4

The Illogic of Antiquity

SUMMARY: This chapter challenges the claim that mathematics transcends myth because of its special relationship to formal logic. The chapter shows that formal logic itself first emerged from a myth system (the Parmenidean myth), which in turn derived from patriarchal religious beliefs. The development of this myth system is explored in the case of various Greek, Roman, and medieval logicians. Subsequent chapters follow the transmission of this myth-system down to modern times.

Popular belief regards mathematics as a timeless system of absolute, proven truths, existing independently of the peculiar circumstances of its creators. In the last chapter we saw that this popular belief is mistaken on two counts. First, mathematics, like all human tools, has a *history*, and so reflects the needs and attitudes of the particular culture that happens to shape and use it. Second, modern mathematics in particular is in the midst of an identity crisis precisely because of the repeated failure of those who believe in its absoluteness to prove their point. When its historicity is taken into account, mathematics loses its quasi-religious aura and comes into focus as a socially constructed tool. The use of this tool, like the use of any tool, tells us something about the nature of reality; nonetheless, every human tool remains, in part, conventional.

As we have seen, many choke at this assessment, insisting that mathematics possesses a unique characteristic: an inner process of development that is determined by logical necessity. Like a sort of unseen, providential hand, logical necessity is said to guide the growth of mathematical systems, insuring that in the long run the mathematical world is the best of all possible worlds (logically speaking, that is).

The Burden of Absoluteness

Those who hold this belief in effect take the burden of absoluteness off the shoulders of mathematics and place it instead on logic, or, more accurately, on formal logic. Such a shift is not surprising in view of the natural affinity of mathematics and formal logic: the former is a matter of making valid deductions about quantitative concepts and their formal relations, while the latter is the study of the formal grounds of valid deduction as such.

Is it in fact true that formal logic embodies some sort of ahistorical absolute? Most Western academic philosophers would answer with a resounding "yes." Despite this confident reply, however, the next several chapters will critically examine the growth of formal logic in the West, beginning with its origin in ancient Greece, and concluding with some of its latest developments in the United States and Japan. This overview will show that at the heart of formal logic lies a myth system that was originally derived from patriarchal religious beliefs, and which has been handed down from one generation of logicians to another. We will find not only that this core is mythical but, even more important, that its principal presuppositions are also *false*.

As usual in doing philosophy, we need to begin with a definition. What is formal logic, as opposed to ordinary logic? In our daily lives, we participate in all sorts of discussions with other people, as well as holding a silent inner dialog with ourselves. In the course of these discussions, we constantly make judgments as to what is logical and what is illogical. In practice, the grounds for our making these judgments can be quite complex.

Consider the many different factors that may be involved when we conclude that another person is speaking illogically. It may be that we just have an uneasy feeling that what the other says doesn't add up, without, however, being able to pinpoint the exact problem. Or we may feel that the other person's ideas are too vaguely expressed. Or we may disagree with certain of the other person's basic assumptions. Or we may think that the other person's conclusions simply don't follow from his or her assumptions. On the basis of such factors as these, we say "that's illogical."

Formal logic, as opposed to ordinary logic, takes a much stricter view of the entire process of evaluating the logical merit of statements. Formal logic maintains that we can take any possible argument and restate it in such a way as to display certain formal features that are typical of entire groups of arguments, regardless of what their particular subject matters may be. On the basis of examining these formal features alone, says formal logic, we can *calculate* whether any statement that embodies them is always true, always false, or neither.

For example, consider this proposition: "If all men are self-centered and sexually compulsive, and if Mr. Jagger is a man, then Mr. Jagger is self-centered and sexually compulsive." In the hope of revealing this proposition's formal structure, logicians restate it thus: "If all x's are both p and q, and if a is an x, then a is both p and q." Here x stands for any sort of object; a stands for some particular object; and p and q stand for any particular attributes. This type of formula is called a propositional function. Logicians can easily calculate that *any* proposition generated by this propositional function has to be true, including the particular proposition where a = Mr. Jagger.

Formal logic, then, is the technique of distilling formal structures from particular arguments, with an eye toward deciding questions about validity of inference. As such a technique, formal logic rests on a prime assumption: the study of such formal structures provides a reliable guide as to whether the arguments so analyzed are always true, always false, or neither.

Is this prime assumption reliable? Clearly, this question cannot be answered *within* formal logic, for the question is *about* formal logic. To understand this distinction, consider the following simple formula: "p is a false proposition," where p designates any proposition. Considered purely formally, this formula would appear to be quite unremarkable. What happens, however, when p = "this proposition"? When we plug this value for p is into our logical formula, the generated statement becomes self-canceling. (More accurately: the generated statement is of a different order from other statements generated by other values of p.) How can we deal with this anomalous result, if we restrict ourselves to the assumption that the reliability of logical formulas is decidable by formal methods internal to formal logic itself? We can't.

Despite their effusive lip-service to formalism, logicians in actual practice constantly test the alleged rationality of their concocted formulas against some assumed greater standard of rationality (usually "common sense," or "ordinary language," or "science"). How, then, can formal logic presume to establish a formal standard of rationality in its own right? And how do we know that the standards actually appealed to in practice by working logicians (such as "common sense") are worthy standards? To date, no logician has succeeded in satisfactorily answering these embarrassing questions. Indeed, most college textbooks on formal logic never even raise them.

Despite such weaknesses, logicians, mathematicians, and scientists commonly assume that formal logic lays bare the universe's skeleton of rational possibility, both for physical events and for concept-formation. Although human beings may differ genetically, culturally, and idiosyncratically, they and everything else that exists are subject (according to the logicians) to a peculiar kind of unequivocal, universally encompassing necessity discoverable through formal logic.

The problem with this absolutist concept of formal logic, as with the absolutist concept in regard to higher mathematics, is that it overlooks two crucial factors: (1) the historicity of human logical development in particular; and (2) the complexities of the human interpretational process in general. Once these two factors are taken into account, formal logic, like higher mathematics, displays a culturally conditioned and humanly featured face.

Parmenides and the Uniformity of Being

The history of Western formal logic begins with the fifth-century-B.C. Greek philosopher Parmenides of Elea (then a Greek colony in southern Italy). Unlike many of his philosophical contemporaries, who sought for an explanation of nature in terms of various interacting factors, Parmenides held that logic proves that "what is" (*to on*) must be one, indivisible, timeless, and unchanging. Therefore, all our notions of plurality and change are a delusion resulting from the false testimony of the senses. We must not be deceived by the seductive power of the senses, Parmenides argued. Instead, we should heed the better testimony of reason, which alone can apprehend the true nature of reality.

Parmenides presented his conclusions in an epic poem entitled *On Nature*. At the poem's beginning, Parmenides appears as a young man traveling in a chariot, guided by the Daughters of the Sun, to the abode of a great goddess, "far-constraining Order" (*Dike polypoinos*). After Parmenides is admitted to the goddess's sacred precinct, she reveals to him a "mighty Necessity" (*Kratere Anagke*). This Necessity manifests itself in a grand principle: *That which IS, simply IS; all else IS NOT*. Here is how Parmenides sums up the goddess's message:

> But come, and I myself will tell you, attend and hear this tale.
> Behold, two paths alone exist in all pursuit of knowledge.
> The first, when "Is" is said and "Cannot be but be."
> This is the road Conviction takes, she who follows Truth.
> The next, when the words "Is not" are used and "Cannot be."
> Now this second path, heed me here, cannot even be conceived,
> For what "is not" you cannot know (how could you?),
> And neither can you say it.[1]

In plainer language: any claim about the nature of the world that refers to what "is not" is illusory. For example, consider the claim that there are individual things that come to be and pass away. If there really are such things, then there must have been a time when they "were not." But if and when they "were not," then at that very time they were part of non-being. Not being real at that point, how could they ever come to be at a later point, since being is only that which *is*? In fact, they were nothing, and from nothing comes only nothing. If, on the other hand, they "were" before they came to be, they could not have come to be, since only that which at some point was not and later is can be said to have come to be. Therefore, logic proves our senses wrong: the common notion that there are individual things coming to be and passing away is an illusion.

Parmenides concludes that the world is really a static, eternally present oneness, comparable in its fullness and simplicity to a great homogeneous sphere. For such an entity, the most accurate description is merely to say "it is" (*esti*).

At times Parmenides fudges his argument by playing on different meanings of the word "is." Nonetheless, his main point is correct. As long as existence and non-existence are construed as two absolute, mutually exclusive categories, then either there is nothing at all (a possibility Parmenides does not consider) or else everything that exists always has and always will exist; therefore, there can be no real change or development. But if, contrary to Parmenides, we are committed to a belief in the reality of change, then we must allow for some kind of aperture between existence and non-existence.

Parmenides' philosophical contemporaries, jolted by the implications of his logic, devoted themselves to finding such an aperture between existence and non-existence. In general, they favored the solution of allowing for different *degrees* or *kinds* of existence (or "being" in Greek). For example, Empedocles and Democritus argued that objects in the material world are really short-lived, changing configurations of underlying elements that are themselves eternal and unchanging. Plato, on the other hand, argued that there is a realm of immaterial, eternal Forms in which the ever-changing flux of matter participates. Aristotle, Plato's pupil, held that there is both a potential and an actual kind of being. Whatever solution particular philosophers adopted, Parmenides succeeded in setting the terms of philosophical debate for generations of his successors. Although not very many people agreed with Parmenides, no one could afford to ignore him.

Persistence of the Parmenidean Myth

The basic motifs in Parmenides' mythical poem *On Nature* came to exercise an extraordinary fascination on many subsequent generations of Western philosophers, especially logicians, even down to the present day. Of these mythological motifs, the most important is that the whole of reality is bound by some kind of great, all-encompassing order or necessity connected with logic. As we have seen, Parmenides calls this ruling logical principle the goddess "far-constraining Order" (*Dike polypoinos*) or the force "mighty Necessity" (*kratere Anagke*). Invisible to those bewitched by the senses, and manifest only to those initiated into the correct use of deductive reasoning, this goddess extends her great power throughout the entire cosmos, unyieldingly determining its nature everywhere.

Under the sanitized name of "logical necessity," this same mythological bird has continued its flight in the stratosphere of much Western philosophical thought until well into the twentieth century. Although commonly, indeed unthinkingly, admired today by those who regard themselves as the most hard-nosed of scientific rationalists, this bird remains a myth nonetheless, as this and following chapters will show.

Closely connected to the motif of the goddess far-constraining Order is that of the absolute dichotomy between "is" (*esti*) and "is not" (*ouk esti*). According to Parmenides, only those initiated into the proper understanding of the absolute dichotomy between these two can ever understand the true nature of being. This presupposition—that correct deductive thinking consists in judging descriptions of reality in terms of two mutually exclusive categories or values—has also survived into twentieth-century formal logic under the guise of "the principle of bivalence." In modern terms, logicians say that any given proposition is either true or false, depending on whether the state of affairs it describes exists or not. Despite the change in terminology, the underlying mentality is the same: either "is" or "is not," and no other choice.

A third mythological motif of Parmenides' poem is that the objective necessity established by correct logical thinking ("the Way of Truth") is immune to any contradiction from the evidence of the senses ("the Way of Opinion"). Even though inundated with evidence from the phenomenal world validating movement and change, Parmenides steadfastly refused to concede any reality to change. The world, he insisted, is a timeless, motionless, homogeneous One—because that's what logic says it must be!

The underlying bias here is this: knowledge that is deductive and patterned after a timeless, impersonal model of reality is inherently superior to knowledge that is dependent on personal subjectivity, feeling, and change. This bias has likewise been a principal factor in the later development of much Western logico-scientific thinking. Subsequent chapters will show that this bias has never been justified theoretically and that it has proven to be disastrous practically.

These three motifs, then—the universal force of logical necessity, the principle of bivalence, and the inherent superiority of an impersonal, static model of knowledge and reality—I call "the Parmenidean myth." We will eventually see that the Parmenidean myth, like the myth of mathematics as discussed in chapter three, is both the product and the prop of a certain kind of society, namely patriarchal society.

Zeno of Elea

Parmenides' teachings were taken up and defended by his younger male pupil and lover, Zeno of Elea. Against scornful critics who claimed that Parmenides' teachings led to impossible paradoxes, Zeno reversed the tables by formulating a series of devastating arguments that attempted to demonstrate the impossibility of plurality and motion ("Zeno's paradoxes"). These arguments have succeeded in stumping many succeeding generations, down to the present day. Because of his great skill in framing these paradoxes, Zeno was regarded by the ancient Greeks as the founder of logic (*he dialektike*—"the art of logical disputation").

Among the most famous of Zeno's paradoxes is that of the arrow, argued from the following two simple assumptions: (1) an arrow is shooting through the air; and (2) at any given moment, everything that exists is located in some definite place and nowhere else. Now if the second assumption is true, then the arrow mentioned in the first assumption must also, at any given moment, be located in some definite place and nowhere else. So take any moment you choose—at that precise moment the arrow will be in one definite place and nowhere else. But if that is the case, the arrow can't be moving at that precise moment, since it is located in one definite place and nowhere else. The same is likewise true for any other moment you might choose. Hence, whatever moment you may choose, the arrow can't be moving at that precise moment. Therefore the arrow can never be moving, and the first assumption above is false. Furthermore, since any supposedly moving thing can be analyzed in the same way, all motion is impossible. Hence our everyday perceptions of motion must all be illusions.

If one rejects the assumption that at any given moment everything that exists is located in some definite place and nowhere else, the paradox of the arrow dissolves. But if something is not always located in a definite place at a definite time, where, then, is it? In two different places at once? In no place at all? Apparently this assumption cannot be meaningfully denied.

Despite the efforts of many, some of Zeno's paradoxes remained unsolvable down to the twentieth century. The break finally came with the development of modern quantum mechanics, which challenges the assumption that subatomic particles must always be in a definite given spot at a given time, and that space is an infinitely divisible continuum. When these assumptions fall, Zeno's paradoxes fall with them—but at the price of an interpretation of nature that is quite contrary to "common sense." Indeed, if quantum mechanics proves anything, it's the falsehood of the old adage that science is just a continuation of common sense.

Throughout the ages, the great majority of learned Western minds simply ignored the practical implications of Zeno's paradoxes, even though they could not refute them logically. However, many of these very same learned minds still pretended to regard "logical necessity" as a kind of final arbiter of the nature of reality. In clinging to this belief in theory while acting contrary to it in practice, they resembled commonplace religious hypocrites. Parmenides would have laughed them to scorn.

The Sophists and the Varieties of Becoming

In contrast to Parmenides and Zeno, who emphasized the uniformity and unchangeability of *being*, a group of practical-minded thinkers appeared in 5th-century B.C. Greece who directed their attention to the variety and changeability of *becoming*. A thinker of this type was generally known as a "sophist," from the Greek noun *sophistes*. This word originally meant "wise one" or "expert," and later, due to unflattering depictions by Plato and Aristotle, "intellectual quibbler" and "cheat."

Despite the negative views of Plato and Aristotle, the sophists in their time were quite popular, especially with the emergent middle class, which is one of the reasons the aristocratic Plato disliked them. This popularity was the result of political upheavals that had turned 5th-century Athens and many other Greek cities into democratic regimes. Athens in particular had become the wealthy head of a powerful alliance of democratically run Greek city-states. In many ways Athens fell short of the democratic ideal, as in its oppressive treatment of women and its use of slave labor. But for all that, the Athenian alliance was quite different from most other states then existing in the Mediterranean and the Near East. Like Athens, these other states were misogynist, slave-owning, and imperialistic; in addition, they also concentrated power in the hands of a monarch or a small group of aristocratic land-owners or generals. In the case of the Athenian alliance, for the first time since the patriarchal revolution four millennia before, states existed where all free-born males had a genuine voice in the conduct of public affairs. The Athenian ideals of "liberty" (*eleutheria*) and "equality of political rights" (*isonomia*) were a reflection of genuine political practices.

As power in Athens passed from the old landed aristocracy to the leisured middle class, a need arose for new methods of education. Previously, to be educated meant to possess the skills necessary to function as a well-bred gentleman. But now, with the rise to power of the Assembly of the People and populist law courts (conducted like debating societies), there was an intensely practical need to be able to speak well in public. The man whose speeches could best sway his fellows, whether through logic or emotion, was the man whose political agenda would prevail in the Assembly. Such a man could also repel assaults in the populist courts, where partisans commonly attacked their political opponents with bogus criminal accusations.

This need for a new kind of education appropriate to the rough and tumble of democratic political life promoted the popularity of the sophists. Traveling from one city-state to another, they taught, for a fee, many practical skills, particularly the professional secrets of how to speak well in public. They found abundant buyers wherever they went, particularly among the younger generation eager to prove its political mettle.

In honing their skills, the sophists studied the meanings and emotional colorings of various kinds of words, the effectiveness of verbal rhythm and sentence structure, and—most important for the subsequent history of Western philosophy—the different kinds of logical arguments and logical fallacies. As a result, the political ambitions simmering in the cauldron of ancient Athenian democracy stimulated what later came to be called the disciplines of rhetoric, grammar, and logic.

The great intellectual opponent of the sophists was the aristocratic philosopher Plato, ancient Greece's most articulate critic of democracy. He yearned for a return of the old aristocratic regime, but in an intellectually purified form. Plato wanted the state to be governed by an intellectual elite of philosopher-kings. These were to be educated in ascetic morality, mathematics, and abstract reasoning. Plato viewed the methods of the sophists with disgust, as is clear in his famous diatribe, *Sophist*. This work, veering back and forth between satire and seriousness, describes sophists as mercenary, pugnacious, predatory, lying hucksters of false ideas. Alas, this depiction caused Plato an embarrassing problem in regard to his beloved mentor and friend Socrates. At the time, all Greeks, except for Plato and his circle, regarded Socrates as the sophist *par excellence* (more on this below).

Protagoras

Aside from Socrates, the most famous sophist of the age was Protagoras from Abdera, Thrace (490-421 B.C.). Like many other sophists, Protagoras traveled from city to city, eventually spending a considerable time in Athens. There he enjoyed the friendship of Pericles, Athens' most famous democratic statesman. Like the Greek atomic theorist Democritus (also from Abdera), Progatoras was a defender of democracy. In fact, he appears to have written one of the first philosophical justifications for democratic government (which has not survived).

Judged by its few surviving fragments, Protagoras' philosophy was of a type that would naturally lead to democratic conclusions. In contrast to Pythagoras and Parmenides, who argued for one absolute standard of truth for all, Protagoras held that there is no such thing as absolute objectivity. Rather, every view of reality is determined by the individual circumstances of the particular interpreter who experiences it. Protagoras expressed this idea with his famous dictum—

> The individual person is the measure of all things: of things that are, that they are; of things that are not, that they are not.[2]

As a result of the relativity of knowledge, Protagoras taught the concept of "differing accounts" (*dissoi logoi*). He meant that there can always be more than one account of anything. Although Protagoras' actual arguments for democracy have not survived, we may reasonably speculate that he built on the idea of "differing accounts" like this: There is no self-validating criterion of reality or justice. Therefore, no one individual or class of individuals can claim to establish standards for society at large. Instead, out of an ongoing dialogue of all with all, workable laws can be passed that embody society's most widely held opinions.

Protagoras presented a number of logical views in a book entitled *Contrary Arguments* (*Antilogiai*). Apparently it argued for something like this: Different human beings have different sets of sense experiences. Each of these is a criterion of truth in its own right. Therefore, there can be two or more conflicting accounts of the same matter. All these accounts are true in a *relative* sense, which is the only truth there is.

Protagoras' approach to philosophy is thus the diametrical opposite of Parmenides'. In particular, Protagoras' philosophy undermines the principle of bivalence, which says that something either "*is* or *is not*." Instead, Protagoras suggests that human discourse is too complicated to be reduced to a simple matter of affirming or denying an allegedly objective state of affairs. There are many different ways of sensibly perceiving reality. Consequently, it is both meaningful and true to say "the same wind is both warm and cool." A statement of this sort later vexed both Plato and Aristotle. Their entire logical systems, inspired by the Parmenidean myth, were designed to rule out statements like this.

The value of Protagoras' philosophy was that it validated the complexity of human language in the face of the reductionist trend initiated by Parmenides and Zeno. Protagoras reminded their followers that their works were of an artificial nature, since he could continue to uncover counter-examples from real human life that violated their would-be universal laws. However useful in certain contexts formal logic may be (we might imagine Protagoras saying), we must never forget that logic's roots lie in actual human experience. The complexities and richness of this experience transcend all humanly made artifices, including those of formal logic.

There are also problems with Protagoras' approach. For example, when he says the same wind is both warm and cool, by what right can he use the phrase "the same wind"? To refer to the same *anything* for different human interpreters presupposes the possibility of some kind of unity of object that transcends the particularity of individual sense experience. But if all that we can know are our own individual sense experiences, then we can never meaningfully speak of objects that are common or real to several different interpreters. The most that we can say is "warm" or "cool."

In order to make a leap from pure subjectivity to some kind of relative objectivity, Protagoras must provide for a platform of commonality in interpretation. As noted earlier in this book, various possibilities to this end are a common physical structure in interpreters, common cultural conditioning, etc. Protagoras may have found such a platform for relative objectivity in language itself, since he was known to have made important strides in grammatical analysis; however, the surviving fragments of his work are too scanty to know for sure.

Even if Protagoras did find some platform for a commonality of interpretation, he still had to face another problem: if there are common objects, then to that extent it must also be possible for there to be a common logic. After all, logic is part of the process of abstracting the general and the formal from the particular and the idiosyncratic. Hence Protagoras would be wrong to claim that the nature of human subjectivity must preclude the possibility of objective logic. The most he could reasonably claim for subjectivity would be this: Although some aspects of human experience are subsumable under the laws of abstract logic, other aspects are not. Logic has a *relative* objectivity, depending on the interpretational context.

The Rise of Relativism

Although the sophists had many differences, most shared a common desire: to eke out an independent living by teaching their own special techniques, especially language-related techniques relevant to the competitive conditions of fifth-century Greek democratic life. As a result, the sophists had a vested interest in promoting a critical attitude toward language, existing political and social institutions, and other rival sophists. By promoting these separate agendas, the sophists as a whole inadvertently encouraged a new common world-view: critical relativism.

This new attitude of questioning all authority and tradition, reinforced by the rise to power of the middle and lower classes, alarmed reactionaries like the comic playwright Aristophanes, and exhilarated radicals like the tragedian Euripides. In response, the reactionaries—always secretly hoping for the overthrow of the democratic regime, even through foreign invasion if necessary—occasionally scapegoated the sophists, arguing that they were blaspheming the gods and corrupting youth. Such attacks could be quite successful, particularly during times of great public crisis.

Socrates

The person who was the most significant heir both of Parmenides' interest in the uniformity of being and of the sophists' legacy of critical relativism was the Athenian philosopher Socrates (470 B.C.-399 B.C.). Socrates combined and transformed both these factors in such a way as to give a whole new thrust to Western philosophy.

In his youth, Socrates associated with the circle of radical intellectuals patronized by the democratic statesman Pericles. One of the thinkers in this group was the naturalist philosopher Anaxagoras of Clazomenae, renowned for his effort to find a natural explanation for all phenomena.

While Anaxagoras was at Athens, certain political plotters sought to discredit Pericles by attacking the intellectual radicals he patronized. They initiated a prosecution against Anaxagoras, charging him with irreverence to the gods (*asebeia*) because he had said the sun was a huge burning stone. Despite a personal plea for clemency by Pericles, Anaxagoras was convicted and banished from Athens. Later, Anaxagoras' views were expounded by his pupil Archelaus, and by Archelaus' pupil (and lover) Socrates.

In his middle years, Socrates became the butt of a fierce attack by the reactionary satirist Aristophanes in his famous play *Clouds*. The play depicts Socrates as the odious epitome of both naturalist philosophers like Anagaxoras and relativist sophists like Protagoras.

In the play, Socrates spends most of his time uselessly speculating about heavenly bodies, teaching his pupils how to undermine ancient traditions, and encouraging lustful anal receptivity in young men.[3] In the last scene of *Clouds*, Aristophanes has an angry mob burn down Socrates' house, a not very subtle clue as to what the playwright himself thought Socrates should suffer in real life.

Socrates' Trial and Death

Despite the wrath of Aristophanes and other traditionalists, Socrates survived to an old age. By then he had abandoned his interests in scientific speculation and devoted himself instead to understanding ethics and questions of value. However, a fatal reversal came to him at the age of 71, during a time of political upheaval in Athens. Certain individuals stepped forward and accused him of the familiar charge of "irreverence to the gods" (*asebeia*), alleging that he did not believe in the gods of the state, but instead had introduced strange new ones. This charge was an allusion to Socrates' claim that he was inspired by his own personal divinity, which he called his "spirit-guide" (*to daimonion*). The indictment also claimed that Socrates was corrupting the young men of Athens, echoing the depiction of him made years earlier by Aristophanes.[4]

At his trial, conducted before several hundred jurors, Socrates claimed that his life was exemplary of the best of Athenian values; nonetheless, he was convicted and sentenced to death. Rather than flee into exile, as persons in his situation were routinely expected to do, he stunned both his friends and his enemies by choosing instead to remain and drink the poison hemlock prescribed by the jury. Thereby he gained for himself in both history and myth a position unequaled by any other philosopher.

Plato's Portrait of Socrates

Throughout his life, Socrates associated with persons of all different social classes and points of view. After his death, his immediate followers formed a number of different philosophical schools, most in conflict with each other, and each claiming to be his legitimate philosophical heir. Today we possess mere fragments from most of these schools, with the exception of the works of Plato, nearly all of which have survived.

Because of this imbalance in evidence, modern readers often mistakenly take Plato's philosophical views as those of Socrates. Especially in the later Platonic dialogues, Socrates appears as an ascetic, anti-democratic believer in the theory of other-worldly Forms. The earlier Platonic dialogues, however, paint a different portrait, one more consistent with the non-Platonic evidence. This Socrates is witty and sensual. He is critical of injustice under all forms of government and claims no special expertise for himself (except in erotic matters). Above all, he views himself as a kind of intellectual midwife, helping others to bring their own philosophic viewpoints to birth.

The earlier, rather than the later, Platonic depiction is probably closer to the historical Socrates. Indeed, Socrates' reluctance to push any philosophic line of his own, coupled with his eagerness to examine the views of others, made it easy for his survivors to project their own favorite opinions back onto him after he was dead. And so the later dialogues of the other-worldly Plato show us a Socrates who is an ascetic, whereas the fragments of the hedonist Aristippus depict Socrates as an advocate of the joys of physical pleasure. The truth common to both Plato and Aristippus is that Socrates was a successful midwife, enabling each of them to bring to birth his own particular philosophy of life.

In his earlier dialogues, Plato strives to show that Socrates was not one of the sophists. It is hard to see, however, how Socrates differed from at least the more distinguished of their number. For example, although Socrates did not charge his pupils, he accepted "contributions." And although there were many sophists who were unscrupulous hacks, there were also some, like Protagoras, who were highly principled. Contrary to Plato, many Athenians felt that Socrates epitomized the sophists.

Socrates' Emphasis on Definition

In his later years, Socrates' typical practice was to confront anyone who claimed to be knowledgeable about something, especially any of the virtues (filial devotion, justice, etc.). Socrates would ask for a definition of the virtue in question. At first, the respondent would usually just list specific examples. When pressed by Socrates, the respondent would come up with some make-shift definition. Socrates would then conduct a cross-examination (*elegkhos*), leading the respondent to see that his definition was inadequate or contradictory. Socrates himself would not, except hypothetically, offer any definition of his own. The discussion would typically end with an admission by the bewildered respondent that he didn't know what he was talking about.

This effort to make people aware of their own ignorance was one of Socrates' principal goals. He stated at his trial that the only thing he knew was that he knew nothing, but that in this regard he was wiser than all the others, since they all mistakenly thought they actually knew something. Although Socrates believed that by enlightening others of their own ignorance he would make them better people, the practice naturally caused many to resent him, especially those who boasted of their own virtue. The young men who attended Socrates, and with whom he was enamored, enjoyed this spectacle of the cross-examination of moral know-it-alls. In imitation of Socrates, they often tried out the same technique on their own moralizing elders. They were not amused.

In effect, Socrates told his contemporaries this: Whatever you may have been taught to believe, you alone are responsible for your own values. How do you justify them rationally?

Once anyone took this challenge seriously, the natural tendency would be to critically evaluate *all* of life's circumstances, including social and political institutions. In following this tendency, therefore, people strengthened the new spirit of critical relativism at Athens.

Socrates' contribution to the spirit of relativism was, however, unintended. In cross-examining other people, he did not seek to unsettle their opinions as an end in itself; rather, he sought to guide his respondents to an understanding of the various virtues as they are in and of themselves, independent of any accidental circumstances. Although his contemporaries (except for Plato) did not realize it, Socrates was motivated by belief in a realm of absolutes, a belief he had ultimately inherited from Parmenides.

Socrates believed that every virtue was a real, unchanging, uniform entity in its own right, which rational dialogue could reveal "in and of itself" (*auto kath' hauto*). It was this real, unchanging entity that Socrates sought whenever he confronted anybody who professed some virtue, and asked "What is it?" (*Ti esti?*). In effect, Socrates replaced Parmenides' famous statement "It is" (*Esti*) with a question, "What is it?" (*Ti esti?*). For Socrates, that which provides the correct answer to the question "What is it?" is being (as opposed to becoming).

As Aristotle later correctly observed, what Socrates had done was to invent the notion of definition. Indeed, the Greek phrase that Aristotle himself later used for that which a correct definition reveals, comes from Socrates. (The Greek phrase is *to ti esti*, which literally means "the what-it-is.")

In terms of the future history of Western formal logic, Socrates' crucial contribution lay in linking together three important assumptions: (1) there is a radical dichotomy between the real and the non-real; (2) the real corresponds to what is abstract, impersonal, and unchanging, while the non-real corresponds to what is individual, personal, and changing; and (3) the real can be definitively captured in language.

As should be apparent, Socrates' three assumptions are thus a modification of the Parmenidean myth, discussed above. Socrates' second assumption, that there is a radical dichotomy between the real and the unreal, is simply a restatement of Parmenides' version of the principle of bivalence. Socrates' third assumption, that the real corresponds to the abstract and the impersonal, mirrors Parmenides' bias in favor of the static model of knowledge. Socrates' own special contribution lies in his third assumption, that language can definitively capture a plurality of real entities. This assumption departs from Parmenides' view that the real is a pure simplicity that can only be described by the phrase "it is."

For Socrates, language's ability to capture reality stems from the fact that both language and the world are dominated by a common force, logical necessity (the first principle in Parmenides' myth). In practical terms, this necessity makes its power felt through the search for contradictions (the Socratic *elegkhos*, or "cross-examination").

In sum, the knowable world for Socrates consists of a plurality of real, unchanging entities. Each of these entities is accessible through rational dialogue. All are in principle unambiguously definable, thanks to the force of all-reigning logical necessity that manifests itself in the search for logical contradictions.

Fallacies of the Socratic Approach

Socrates' assumptions, reformulating somewhat the Parmenidean myth, provided the basic philosophical scaffolding on which generations of subsequent thinkers built the grand edifice of Western formal logic. But however deeply these assumptions may now be embedded in Western thinking, they remain assumptions nonetheless, and not very obvious ones at that.

Consider Socrates' first assumption, that there is a radical dichotomy between the real and the non-real. This assumption ignores the possibility that there may be *degrees* of reality or being. Yet, as noted earlier, one interpretation of modern quantum mechanics argues for just this possibility, at least in the case of subatomic particles.

Socrates' third assumption, that the real can be definitively captured in language, seems little short of a miracle if one reflects on it even momentarily. How is it that formulations in ancient Greek, or in any human language for that matter, are capable of capturing the essential features of reality in and of itself? Contrary to this grand claim, we saw in chapter one that all linguistic interpretation depends in part on prelinguistic interpretation, which in turn depends on the genetic structure, cultural conditioning, and idiosyncratic life experiences of particular interpreters. Human interpreters using various languages can attain a relative objectivity. There remains, however, a vast world of uncaptured reality above and beyond any interpretation in language.

The most troubling of Socrates' assumptions is the second, that the real corresponds to what is abstract, impersonal, and unchanging, while the non-real corresponds to what is individual, personal, and changing. I say "troubling" not only because of this assumption's wobbly philosophical legs but also because of its damaging historical and social consequences.

The philosophical weakness of this assumption lies in its illogical attitude toward what is momentary or uniquely individual. According to this view, the intense rush of love that a mother feels when first seeing her newborn child is inherently less revelatory of reality than, say, the medical profession's model of a properly functioning human offspring. Or again, a poem sung by William Blake is held to express a vision of nature inherently less real than a mathematical equation deduced by Isaac Newton.

To denigrate a mother's rush of love or Blake's poetic passion merely on the grounds of their individuality or transitoriness is illogical. Definition itself (which is the basis of all abstract knowledge) is merely a generalization derived from what is individual and transitory. The definition, by abstracting from the individual and the transitory, grasps onto only what can be reduced to a common formula, and ignores all the rest. How can the definition ever know for sure that "the rest" that it ignores is not really relevant? Just because the definition is abstract, impersonal, and timeless is no reason whatever to accord the definition any sort of epistemological superiority.

Socrates was right to point out the great power of definitions for accumulating abstract knowledge. He was wrong, however, to ridicule the poets because they could not express their visions in definitions rather than poetry.

Socrates' equation of the real with the impersonal and the abstract has had troubling historical consequences. Acting in the name of this equation, powerful institutions in patriarchal civilization have repeatedly bludgeoned others with their agendas for power and their views of reality (the two reinforcing each other). We have a greater window on truth, they claim, because we are, as great institutions, more impersonal, abstract, and long-lasting.

For example, the great institutions of patriarchal civilization have routinely ignored or maligned the views and feelings of women, homosexuals, the poor, Jews, artists, and racial minorities. The experiences of these groups are merely partial, personal, and transitory, claim the patriarchs, when compared to the grand, synthesizing realities of the state, the church, the university, the party, or the *Volk*.

When such an attitude is carried to its extreme, as in medieval Christian Europe or in 20th-century Nazi Germany, it views the expression of any world-views contrary to those of dominating institutions as a sign of subhuman behavior, justifying ferocious violence against the nonconformists. In fact, however, neither impersonality, nor permanence, nor abstraction, nor institutional validation, nor indeed all of these together, is any guarantor whatever of truth. An entire phalanx of ruling institutions can be unanimous for generations and still be wrong. The lone individual, isolated and trembling in his or her own personal subjectivity, can still be right—as every self-affirmed gay person who survived the United States in the 1950s, to name but one historical example, clearly knows.

Plato

Although Socrates invented the concept of definition, he never explained the nature of the entities that language captures in its definitions. Particular virtues like justice, courage, filial devotion, etc., were real entities, each of which rational dialogue could capture "in and of itself" (*auto kath' hauto*). But what kind of bird is this in-and-of-itself entity?

The question "What is the nature of the thing that definitions define?" became the central interest of Socrates' most famous pupil, the Athenian aristocrat Plato (428-348 B.C.). But whereas Socrates emphasized a tentative, even skeptical, approach to finding philosophical answers, Plato developed an elaborate system of quasi-religious dogma. This system came to exercise an extraordinary influence on all subsequent Western formal logic and, indeed, on nearly all Western philosophical thought in general.

Plato Gets Religion

The turning point came some time after the death of Socrates when Plato "got religion," the religion of Pythagoreanism. As previously discussed in chapter three, Pythagoras was an earlier Greek philosopher who had founded a religio-philosophical community in southern Italy. He opposed the rising democratic movement in Greece, believed in reincarnation, and argued that all reality consists of numbers. Years later, at a time when democratic institutions were deteriorating throughout Greece, Plato embraced Pythagoreanism, but with a twist of his own that he derived from Socrates' interest in definition.

Whereas the Pythagoreans held that numbers were actual material objects, Plato maintained that a realm of incorporeal Forms exists consisting both of numbers and of the exemplars of all other material objects. For Plato the objects to which Socratic definitions apply are these eternal, incorporeal Forms, which only the pure intellect can apprehend. This concept triggered the long-standing philosophical debate over the nature of "universals" (discussed in chapter one).

According to Plato's dogma, people enjoy a direct apprehension of the Forms in the periods of time between their various earthly incarnations. After birth in lowly matter, however, they forget their previous knowledge and are led astray by the seductive reports of the senses (including sexual feelings, which are particularly distractive). If, however, people practice a certain kind of ascetic, intellectual technique, they can begin to see in material objects the faint images of the Forms above. Practicing this technique triggers a "remembering" (*anamnesis*) of what people knew prior to their current incarnations. In this way, people can ascend intellectually out of the realm of the senses. Like a person emerging from a cave, they can at last behold the true light of real knowledge streaming down from above.

Division and Collection Into Classes

The technique that leads to this sublime result is the study of logic and mathematics. An essential part of this technique is the art of "division" (*diairesis*). According to this art, when we seek a definition for anything we should first consider the broadest class to which it belongs, which corresponds to some encompassing Form. We then divide that class successively into ever smaller, mutually exclusive subclasses, each of which corresponds to a Form of lesser scope. Eventually we reach the thing itself.

Another part of this technique is the art of "collection" (*synagoge*). Using this art, we start out with a plurality of specific individuals, collecting them into ever-larger classes, corresponding to Forms of ever-greater compass. As the art of division starts with the one and divides downward to the many, so the art of collection begins with the many and collects upward to the one. Plato regarded the ability to organize knowledge on the basis of an encompassing hierarchy of classes and Forms as the supreme intellectual skill. Those who possessed this skill ("the logicians"—*hoi dialektikoi*) he called godlike.

Plato engrafted his reinterpretation of Pythagoreanism onto the Parmenidean myth as he had inherited it from Socrates. A good example of Parmenidean influence is his dialogue *Soph-*

ist. Here a protagonist named (significantly) the Stranger from Elea discusses the nature of logic with Theaetetus. In the following exchange, the Stranger defines logic in terms of a hierarchy of timeless Forms, and regards the study of them as a spiritual quest:

> *Stranger:* "What do we mean by the science of logic? Isn't it the ability to divide things into their Types, without confusing one Form with another, but distinguishing them properly?" *Theaetetus:* "That's right." *Stranger:* "So someone who is trained in this science is good at discerning among many things one Form that is situated separately from them, but which orders them all. And he sees that many different Forms are reciprocally contained by another, external Form. And also that one Form among the mass of Forms joins them into a whole, although the many Forms remain quite apart and distinct..." *Theaetetus:* "Exactly." *Stranger:* "Well then, it seems to me that our logician has to be the type of person who seeks for knowledge in a pure and honest way." *Theaetetus:* "How could he not be!"[5]

The style of thought from Parmenides through Socrates to Plato displayed a consistent bias against the personal, the immediate, the transitory, and the sensual in favor of the alleged higher value of the impersonal, the abstract, the permanent, and the rational. The positive side of this bias is that it validated and encouraged abstract human cognitive endeavors like mathematics and the sciences; its weakness was that it undervalued immediate personal experience as found, say, in artistic creativity or sexual ecstasy or the myth systems of allegedly "primitive" peoples.

The reality that mathematics and the sciences reveal to humans is obviously important and certainly possesses a relative objectivity. But the reality that sensation, feeling, or other immediate personal experience reveals to humans is likewise important and just as certainly possesses a relative objectivity for those interpreters who have these experiences. To validate one-half of the human experiential spectrum while denigrating the other half represents a *value judgment*. This value judgment may indeed be relatively valid for some interpreter or group of interpreters; however, it can lay no logical claim to be a principle of reality objectively valid for all interpreters. The persistent effort to establish such a universal claim on behalf of logic by means of the Parmenidean myth represents the ingrained illogic of Western formal logic.

The invidious dichotomy between the abstractly rational and the immediately sensual was destined to cast a long shadow over subsequent Western thought. Largely as a result of the confluence of Pythagoreanism and the Parmenidean myth in Plato's writings, an elaborate justification existed for identifying reality with the abstract, and for identifying the abstract with what can be expressed in mathematical formulas.

Aristotle's Essences

In the 4th century B.C., the kings of Macedon created an expanding military state that destroyed democracy in Greece and reached eastward as far as India. It was in the context of this Macedonian military expansionism that classical Greek logic reached its culmination in the works of the philosopher Aristotle (384-322 B.C.), born in the Macedonian city of Stagira. Aristotle's father had been court physician to King Amyntas of Macedon, and Aristotle himself was for several years the personal tutor of Alexander the Conqueror.

Aristotle built on the Parmenidean myth that he had inherited from Plato, his long-time teacher. The corner of both Aristotle's logic and his metaphysics was his theory of "essences" or "substances" (*ousiai*), which was a modification of Plato's theory of Forms. Plato had held that language connects to reality through definitions modeled after a realm of separately existing, non-corporeal Forms. Aristotle argued that definitions refer to essences that inhere in concrete particulars, which in turn are the bases of all reality.

Aristotle brought Plato's Forms down from the heavens and attempted to ground them in the particularity of observed objects. This change corresponded to Aristotle's greater interest in the sciences as compared to Plato's focus on pure mathematics. Aristotle rightly criticized Plato for his inability to explain how material objects can participate in separately existing immaterial Forms. Aristotle himself, however, was never able to explain how immaterial essences can inhere in concretely existing particulars. Clearly there must be some kind of a link between reason and the abstract on one hand and sensation and the concrete on the other. Neither Plato nor Aristotle, however, was ever able to account for what that link might be. (Previous chapters have shown that the missing link is the interpreter.)

Aristotle often describes the inhering essence of a thing with a rather convoluted Greek phrase, *to ti en einai*, which is difficult to translate. As noted earlier, one of Aristotle's phrases for that which a definition captures is *to ti esti*. This phrase literally means "the what-it-is." It is derived from Socrates' famous question, "What is it?" (*Ti esti?*). Aristotle's phrase for a thing's essence, *to ti en einai*, is a modification of this Socratic-derived phrase and literally means "that which pertains to what-a-thing-is." This phrase denotes both that which defines what a thing is and also that which is itself definable in language. A passable English translation is "the defining and definable nature of a thing."

Building on this phrase, Aristotle postulates that human reason can intuit, in aggregates of concretely existing beings, a defining and definable nature (their "essence"). Reason abstracts this essence from its concrete existence and uniquely express it in a verbal definition. For Aristotle, all knowledge is a knowledge of such abstracted essences verbally defined. As with Socrates and Plato, so Aristotle in effect assumes that the real and the knowable is that which is general and rationally intuitable or abstractable. That which is uniquely individual, especially insofar as it is manifested through individual sensation and personal feeling, is in and of itself cognitively valueless.

Logic and Aristocratic Bias

Aristotle's philosophy of essences, like Plato's theory of Forms, echoed an old Greek aristocratic bias, ultimately derived from the heroic values of Homer. This aristocratic bias had a suspicious attitude toward emotionality, sensuality, or sexuality, especially as manifested in the behavior of slaves or women. By contrast, the aristocratic bias lauded the values and behavior of the old Homeric warrior clan (*genos* in Greek, the same word Plato and Aristotle use for "genus"). In the heroic period, the ruling aristocratic clans established group norms and concepts, based on their own prerogatives. These norms defined essential reality for the entire society. What lay beyond these norms was dismissed as merely individual, idiosyncratic, or accidental. The world-view abstracted from the aristocratic class was thus the essence; the circumstances of the individual, especially the individual from the slave classes or from the feminine sex, were the accidents.

This old aristocratic bias contrasted to a contrary Greek tradition, equally old, associated with the god Dionysos. The Dionysian tradition celebrated the personal feelings of the moment as the revelations of a god. Its most enthusiastic followers were women and slaves. No greater gulf could be seen in ancient Greek consciousness than that between Dionysos on one hand and Aristotle and Plato on the other.[6]

Aristotle's Syllogisms

Aristotle's contribution to formal logic lay in the use he made of his philosophy of essences as a foundation on which to build a new theory concerning the drawing of valid inferences. According to Aristotle's logic, reasoning consists in making assertions about various possible relationships that may exist between three kinds of entity: the *individual*, the *species* (determined by "essence"), and the *genus* (*genos* in Greek, originally meaning "aristocratic clan," as noted above). For Aristotle, the crucial link between these three kinds of reality on one hand, and language on the other hand, is the syntax of ancient Greek.

Drawing on the grammatical studies of many previous philosophers and sophists, Aristotle stresses two important features found in ancient Greek: (1) every meaningful proposition in the language contains, at least implicitly, a subject and a predicate; and (2) the separate linguistic functions of subject and predicate are indicated by separate grammatical conventions for each. As Aristotle analyses the case, the predicate is that part of the proposition containing a word inflected according to time. (Greek verbs are elaborately conjugated according to tense.) The subject is that part of the assertion which contains words not inflected according to time and which is described by the words in the predicate.

Aristotle makes the crucial leap of his logical theory when he fuses his grammatical analysis of ancient Greek with his philosophical theory of essences: The subject is to the predicate as the individual is to the species, or the species to the genus. For example, in the proposition "Socrates is a human being" the word "Socrates" is the grammatical subject. It denotes a particular individual. The words "is a human being" are the grammatical predicate. They indicate that the particular individual just named is a member of the human species.

If we now assume that some propositions that we assert are true, under what circumstances will we be justified in saying that a certain other proposition is also true by virtue of them? This question Aristotle addresses in the strictly logical portion of his philosophy. To lay the groundwork for his answer he first specifies the following: (1) there must be a consecutive sequence of three propositions, each in subject-predicate form; (2) there must be some "middle term," that is, a word or phrase common to both the first and second propositions (the premises); this term must denote a class that links some term from the first proposition with some term from the second proposition; and (3) the third proposition (the conclusion) must express this linkage. Any sequence of propositions conforming to these requirements Aristotle calls a "syllogism," from the Greek work *syllogismos*, meaning "calculation."

For example, consider the following argument, consisting of three propositions:

> (1) Socrates is an Athenian. (2) All Athenians are human beings. Therefore, (3) Socrates is a human being.

The words "an Athenian" in (1) and "All Athenians" in (2) can be understood as alternative expressions for the same middle term, namely, "the class of Athenians." This middle terms links Socrates and the class of all human beings. The third proposition expresses this linkage. Because the third proposition cannot be false while the first two propositions are true, the sequence of propositions constitutes a valid syllogism.

The important point is this:

> Validity of inference for Aristotle is a matter of class inclusion as expressed in subject-predicate propositions, regarded as denoting relations between individuals and real essences.

According to Aristotle's presuppositions, any form of reasoning that does not embody this syllogistic paradigm is, strictly speaking, invalid. The world consists of individuals and essences, whose relations are reflected in subject-predicate propositions. Truth is a matter of classification, of knowing or inferring what individual thing belongs to what class. Beyond such classification and inferences lies only ignorance and non-being.

Historicity of Aristotle's Logic

Aristotle died in 322 B.C. For more than 2,000 years after his death, most of those acquainted with his writings regarded his logic as the quintessential expression of universally necessary laws. Both reality and human thought are bound by a parallelism of necessary connections, the argument went, and Aristotle had discovered them once and for all in his theory of the syllogism. Until the dawn of the twentieth century, the study of logic in the Christian West was, with only a few exceptions, synonymous with the study of Aristotle.

Such an uncritical belief in the alleged universal validity of Aristotle's logic is easy to challenge on both historical and philosophical grounds. As we have seen, his logic and the greater philosophical outlook of which it was a part were products of historical circumstances peculiar to ancient Greece, a rather small portion of the habitable globe. And even in Greece itself it was not until the fifth and fourth centuries B.C., a rather late date in the context of the whole of human history, that logical principles as such first came to be articulated. Moreover, these principles were not suddenly handed down from on high to the Greeks; they *emerged* during a lengthy and complicated series of historical processes in which orators, sophists, and philosophers struggled toward clarification in certain of their linguistic usages. These struggles were molded both by political contexts (such as the rise and fall of Greek democracy) and by peculiarities of the Greek language (such as its high degree of inflection). Furthermore, powerful culture-specific myths heavily influenced the formation of Aristotelian logic, the most notable being the Parmenidean myth.

If Aristotle's logic embodied universal principles of human reasoning, it would seem likely that non-Western cultures with long, developed traditions of philosophic inquiry would sooner or later come to similar conclusions. This development, however, has generally not taken place.

To give but one example, in the entirety of Chinese philosophy there is no body of thought comparable to Aristotle's theory of logic. With the exception of a few peripheral figures in antiquity, Chinese philosophy knows very little of what Western philosophy calls "logic." Most Chinese philosophers have disdained their country's few logicians with the sentiment expressed by the 4th century B.C. philosopher Chuang Tzu:

> They are able to subdue other people's mouths, but cannot win their hearts. This is where their narrowness lies.[7]

There are many reasons for this difference of interest, not the least of which is the fact that Chinese grammatical syntax, unlike that of Greek, is not a function of the inflection patterns of various parts of speech; hence Chinese linguistic preoccupations are of an entirely different order from those which absorbed Aristotle and his predecessors. Much of Aristotle's analysis of being and logic is patterned after an analogous analysis of the structure of the Greek language; his basic work on the subject, *Categories*, is equally a treatise on grammar and on metaphysics. If Aristotle's native language had been Chinese, his *Categories*, and all his other logical works based on its presuppositions, would either never have been written or else written much differently.

One could argue that just because Aristotelian logical principles had a historical origin does not mean that they cannot have a validity that transcends history. True enough, but we will see later that logicians in the twentieth century, using a powerful notation unknown to Aristotle, have been able to create alternate systems of logic that Aristotle would have regarded as quite illogical.

Philosophical Presuppositions of Aristotelian Logic

Apart from considerations of historical relativity, the logic of Aristotle, and indeed much Western logic in general, is based on a number of dubious philosophical presuppositions. For example, Aristotle's entire methodology hangs on the following three implicit "laws of logic," which have often been touted as essential to all thought: (1) no given thing can both be and not be x (called "the law of contradiction"); (2) any given thing must be either x or *not-x* (called "the law of the excluded middle"); and (3) If any given thing is x, then it is x (called "the law of identity").

These so-called "laws" are an outgrowth of the Parmenidean myth, as that myth was amplified by Socrates, Plato, and Aristotle. Moreover, exceptions can be found to each. For example, consider the first one, the so-called law of contradiction, asserting that no given thing can both be and not be x. Suppose, that two students studying at a culinary institute taste a blackberry tart they have just jointly made. One says "This tart is too sweet," while the other responds "No, it's not too sweet; it's just sweet enough." In terms of the law of contradiction, with x = "too sweet," we get the rule "A blackberry tart cannot both be and not be too sweet." Accordingly, if we observe the law of contradiction, we cannot meaningfully say that both of these students are right; rather, we must say that one student is right and the other is wrong. Clearly, however, any rational human being witnessing such an exchange between the students would conclude that both students were right in a relative sense, according to his or her own taste, regardless of any alleged law of formal logic.

At this point, an advocate of the Parmenidean myth would likely make two objections to our example: first, that we should amend our formulation of the law of contradiction so that it states that the same tart cannot both be and not be too sweet *to the same taster at the same time*; or, alternatively, that we should understand that the real, defining features of what constitutes "the same tart" are those that are *quantitatively measurable*, and that the remaining features are merely subjective and hence irrelevant to the issue at hand.

Despite their seeming reasonableness, however, both these Parmenidean objections are spurious. The first objection, by acknowledging the importance of the taster, reformulates the law of contradiction in general to read "No given thing can both be and not be x to the same interpreter at the same time." If admitted, this reformulation of the law of contradiction will in fact overthrow Aristotelian logic (and, indeed, all formal logic). Why? Because the entire methodology of formal logic assumes that one can meaningfully ignore both the interpreter and time in making logical calculations. If these two factors cannot be meaningfully ignored, then the process of making deductions becomes, in practice, far more complicated than any system of formal logic can handle. Indeed, an entirely new kind of logical calculus would be required, complicated beyond anything imagined by Aristotle or any other logician. Although it is certainly possible in theory to develop such a calculus (and some partial efforts in this direction have at times been undertaken), to do so is self-defeating, since the whole point of having the simplified logical calculus has been its ease of use. But as we have just seen, the simpler the logical calculus, the shakier its foundations.

In addition, even when the law of contradiction is amended to refer to the interpreter and to time, there are still instances where it fails. For example, consider the case where someone has just helped his boyfriend, long sick from AIDS, commit suicide. For the last several months of his life, the boyfriend had been feverish, emaciated, bed-ridden, blind, incontinent, covered with cancerous skin lesions and bed sores, and subject to fits of delirium. Now, at last, he is out of his misery. In contemplating the shriveled body of his boyfriend who now lies dead before him, the survivor feels both relieved and burdened at the same time as a result of the same incident: relieved, because his boyfriend is finally free of all suffering; burdened, because he is dead.

According to the amended form of the law of contradiction, the survivor in this example can never find himself in this particular situation for two reasons: (1) to feel relieved means at least not to feel burdened; and (2) the same person cannot both feel and not feel burdened at the same time in regard to the same thing. Despite the strictures of the amended law of contradiction, however, any rational person would at once understand the reality and meaningfulness of the survivor's ambivalent emotional state here.

In response, a defender of formal logic might argue that these feelings are not really contradictory because the *reasons* for them are different. That is, whereas the survivor feels relieved because he knows his boyfriend is free of suffering, he feels burdened because he knows his boyfriend is dead. However, this response only gets formal logic into deeper trouble. As noted above, the whole concept of formal logic is based on the assumption that the state of mind of the interpreter is irrelevant to logical calculations. But here formal logic finds it must appeal to the state of mind of the interpreter in order to save the law of contradiction.

This is a case where formal logic can save the law of contradiction only by pulling the rug out from under itself. The reason for this predicament is simple: wherever reality is at least partially constituted by the feelings and thoughts of the interpreter, the law of contradiction cannot be assumed to apply in an unequivocal manner.

Formal logic simply assumes that an absolute cleavage can always be made between reality on one side and the feelings and thoughts of the interpreter on the other side. That is, formal logic assumes that inference is simply a matter of calculation. In a great many cases, such an assumption can be made to work; but not in all, and there's the rub. Like an over-stretched rubber band, this assumption ruptures when logicians try to expand it into a universal law that admits of no exceptions. The logicians' attempt to constrain human reasoning within their overstretched dogmas constitutes the illogic of formal logic.

There was another Parmenidean objection raised above, namely that the identity of the blackberry tart in our example is definable only by what is quantifiably measurable. This objection assumes that primary qualities, not secondary qualities, define reality. (Primary qualities depend on the object alone; secondary qualities depend on the circumstances of the observer.) This argument is particularly inappropriate in this case. After all, one of the prime reasons for making a blackberry tart is to enjoy its *taste*; that is, its taste is one of the things that makes a blackberry tart what it is. Remove the question of taste here, and you remove part of what it means to be a blackberry tart.

The so-called law of contradiction is true by a kind of courtesy, adopted because of its great utility in certain circumstances. No great harm arises from such a convention—*provided we bear in mind the limited scope and the arbitrary presuppositions of the convention's original formulation.* Serious problems arise, however, when such a convention is stripped of its historicity and elevated to the heavens as a kind of universal law.

The Law of the Excluded Middle

The second allegedly universal law implicit in Aristotelian logic is that of the excluded middle: any given thing must be either x or *not-x*. As in the case of the law of contradiction, we can find instances where this alleged law fails. For example, in logical theory an important instance of the law of the excluded middle is the case where "any given thing" is a *proposition*, and where "x" stands for "true," and "*not-x*" for "not-true" (understood as equivalent to "false"). The law of the excluded middle in this form, stating that any proposition must be either true or false and nothing else, is merely a restatement of the Parmenidean principle of bivalence, and as such is one of the most dearly held principles of Western formal logic.

Despite the longevity of this principle, however, chapter one has shown that we can assign many additional values to a meaningful proposition besides "true" and false," such as the following, to name but a few: "improbable," "partially true and partially false," "highly likely," "true in one context but not in another," etc.

As with the law of contradiction, so the law of the excluded middle represents an oversimplification of actual human linguistic use, made in the interest of simplifying logical calculations. In some contexts, this simplification may indeed prove to be useful. There is no justification, however, for regarding such a simplification as a basic law of either language or reality. In fact, chapter twelve will show that a whole new system of formal logic has recently emerged that explicitly rejects the law of the excluded middle.

The Law of Identity

The third Aristotelian law noted above, that of identity, states that if any given thing is x, then it is x. In the crucial case of propositions, the law asserts that if a proposition is true, then it is true. Consider, however, the following proposition, uttered during the occurrence of an earthquake: "We are now having an earthquake." Although this proposition is true when uttered by us while experiencing an earthquake, it is not true when we utter it only a few minutes after the earthquake has subsided, nor is it true even during the earthquake itself when uttered by persons in other parts of the world who are not then experiencing an earthquake. In order for the law of identity to hold here, this proposition must be reformulated so as to remove all self-reference to the interpreters who utter it and to the time in which they do so. For example, if the proposition is reformulated as "So and so experienced an earthquake at such and such a time," then it will obey the law of identity.

As with the laws of contradiction and the excluded middle, the law of identity is based on the assumption that both the interpreter and time can be ignored for purposes of rendering logical inferences. As we saw above, this assumption is practical in some cases but not in others, which means we are not dealing with a law after all. We should have expected the failure of this law as a consequence of the previous failure of the law of contradiction, since the law of identity is simply a restatement of that law. (To say "If x, then x" is the same as to say "Not both x and *not-x*.")

In sum, the so-called universal laws implicit in Aristotelian logic turn out to have only a relative validity. Historically, they emerged as a result of an unusual combination of social, political, and linguistic forces at work in ancient Greece. Philosophically, they were (and are) conventions that are useful in certain situations.

Although formal logic is partially conventional, we mustn't fall off the other side of the boat and claim that formal logic is *merely* conventional. To say that the laws of traditional logic have a conventional and relative validity is *not* to say that they have no validity at all.

Because formal logic is useful in many contexts, we are justified in surmising that it reveals something of reality. So the logicians are right, up to a point: formal logic works (often enough). A problem arises, however, when logicians jump to further conclusions, claiming that what formal logic reveals is the most important or interesting part of reality. Formal logic is one lens that human beings can use to interpret reality; there are other lenses as well.

Formal Logic's Theory of Types

It's no accident that Aristotle's system of formal logic relies on a theory of essences. *All* formal logic, and not just Aristotle's, requires some theory of types. (I am *not* speaking here of Bertrand Russell's more particular "theory of types," as developed in *Principia Mathematica*.)

To appreciate this point, consider the modern "formalist" school of logic, which has now displaced Aristotelian logic. This school claims it can construct a system of formal logic free of any metaphysical assumptions, such as Aristotle's theory of essences. A system of formal logic, the formalists say, need merely consist of the following parts: a set of undefined physical marks on paper that can be combined to form formulas; certain assumed formulas (axioms); rules for defining what constitutes a well-formed formula within the system; and rules for generating additional well-formed formulas (theorems) from the axioms.

Formalists claim that a logical proof is nothing else than a formally structured set of physical marks made on a piece of paper. The proof is valid if well-formed strings have been generated from assumed strings according to the rules of transformation.

Despite their disclaimers, however, formalists actually make a hidden metaphysical assumption: any symbol "x" that occurs in one string of some proof is the same as the symbol "x" occurring in another string of the same proof. For example, if "x" occurs both in line 1 and in line 3 of the same proof, formalists just *assume* that these are the same symbol. But if a logical proof merely consisted of marks on a piece of paper, as the formalists claim, then clearly the "x" on line 3 could not be the same thing as the "x" on line 1; that would mean that the same physical mark is in two different places at the same time, which is impossible.

Contrary to the formalists, the only way that physical marks can constitute a logical proof is if certain repeated, similarly-made physical marks are assumed to be tokens of the same symbol-type. Only under the assumption that the "x" that appears on line 1 is in some sense the same as the "x" that appears on line 3 can one interpret both lines 1 and 3 as referring to the same thing, and therefore as being part of the same logical proof. But the only way that these two separate physical marks can be the same is if some interpreter or some group of interpreters *interprets* them as physical tokens of the same symbol-type. (As shown in chapter one, all conceptual definition presupposes interpretation.) Without some such assumed theory of types, physical marks made on a piece of paper constitute scratches, not logic.

In addition, some assumed theory of types is also needed if logical proofs are to have a relationship to reality. This need arises because the most that one can claim for any logical proof in and of itself is that it is *valid*; that is, that the conclusions follow from the premises according to the rules of transformation. It is quite another matter, however, to claim that such a valid logical proof is *true*; that is, that the premises themselves correctly express reality. If the premises are false, then a valid inference from the premises is still false; only where the premises are true and the inference from the premises valid is the proof both true and valid.

The connection of a logical proof to reality is through its premises. How, then, do these premises express or describe reality? Clearly, at least certain elements in the premises must be interpreted as representing certain features of reality. This requirement means that certain elements of the premises be *type-symbols*, corresponding to certain *types in reality*.

To understand this point, consider the following two premises: (1) "A human being is a rational biped"; and (2) "Socrates is a human being." In both these premises, the phrase "a human being" is a type-symbol. If the first premise is true, then there exists in reality a *type* of entity that can be characterized as both rational and a biped; and if the second premise is true, then there exists in reality a particular being, namely Socrates, who is an instance of that type. Interpreters judge both these premises to be true because they judge that there is a type as described, and that the individual Socrates, whom they know, is an instance of the type. Therefore, they are able to infer from these premises that Socrates is a rational biped, resulting in a logical proof that is both valid and true.

The above example illustrates that all inference in formal logic involves some sort of *generality*; in this case, the generality implied by the phrase "a human being." Without some such generality, there would be no connection between the premises, only unconnected particularity, and hence no way of getting beyond the premises as individually stated.[8]

The elements in the premises that denote generality are what I have called the type-symbols. But if the premises are interpreted as true, then there must also be some generality in reality that is interpreted as corresponding to the type-symbols in the premises; otherwise, there would be no connection in this regard between formal logic and reality. The features in reality that are thus interpreted to be general and to correspond to the type-symbols are the types. Therefore, all inference in formal logic, if it is assumed to relate to reality, is in fact a kind of type-inferencing that presupposes the existence of at least some types and at least some type-symbols.

As readers should by now realize, the "types" in question here are the same as the entities called "universals" in chapter one. As that chapter demonstrated, both universals and individuals are correlative concepts, each in part nominal and in part real, and both meaningless apart from some interpreter or some group of interpreters acting in some universe of interpretation.

From the considerations here and in chapter one, it follows that no valid inference in formal logic can ever be regarded as absolutely true. Why? Because formal logic (as opposed to ordinary logic) essentially depends on formulas, and we can never be sure that our formulas cover all the ground in reality that needs to be covered.

A Reminder from Heraclitus and Walt Whitman

Formal logic ignores both time and the interpreter, and defines identity in terms of abstracted generality; thus does it slide over the radical indefinability and changeability of actual particularity. In light of this weakness, Aristotle and his modern successors should have taken more seriously the remark of the philosopher Heraclitus of Ephesus that you can't step into the same river twice. Contrary to the entire Parmenidean approach, Heraclitus argued that the real identity of anything lies precisely in its unique particularity, which constantly changes from moment to moment.

In many practical contexts we can get away with treating an abstracted generality *as if* it were a thing's real identity; therein lies the great practical power of formal logic. Nonetheless, if we lose sight of the initial relativity of formal logic's foundation, then we will eventually stumble into paradoxes that only the insight of Heraclitus can resolve.

Contrary to the pretensions of the logicians, there are essential parts of reality that can be found only in the concrete passions of here and now. These are our "native moments," as they were dubbed by the 19th-century gay American poet Walt Whitman:

> Native moments—when you come upon me—ah you are here now,
> Give me now libidinous joys only,
> Give me the drench of my passions, give me life coarse and rank,
> To-day I go consort with Nature's darlings, to-night too,
> I am for those who believe in loose delights, I share the midnight orgies of young men.[9]

The Sexual Politics of Aristotelian Logic

Although Aristotle's logic seems far removed from politics, it nonetheless has served to validate hierarchies of power in patriarchal societies. Its historical role in this regard has been forcefully exposed by the feminist philosopher Andrea Nye in her book *Words of Power*.[10]

Although she does not actually use the phrase "the Parmenidean myth," Nye suggests that some sort of myth-complex, first invented by Parmenides and later augmented by Socrates, Plato, and Aristotle, has influenced Western formal logic. Nye persuasively argues that this myth-complex reflects an abiding fear of the mutability of nature, the immediacy of personal feeling, and "feminine" subjectivity—a fear that has historically obsessed the patriarchal male in the West.

As Nye sees it, Aristotelian logic in particular created a "bracketing of the truth."[11] That is, Aristotelian logic so emphasized the formal nature of logical proof as an end in itself that it lost sight of the substantive questions first asked in the pursuit of truth, thereby turning logic into an impediment to truth.

Nye recounts how the agents of rising Macedonian imperialism viewed a formal education in logic and the sciences as the defining characteristic of men who were "civilized" and thus worthy to conquer and dominate their "barbarian" neighbors. She points out how later European conquerors used a similar line of reasoning in the 16th- and 17th-centuries to justify their conquest and enslavement of the native residents of the Americas.[12] As Nye rightly concludes, Western formal logic in all historical periods has served as an intellectual tool for men in furthering their institutional domination over women and nature.[13]

Zeno of Citium, the Founder of Stoicism

As a result of the rise and spread of Macedonian imperialism, the educated classes in most Eastern Mediterranean societies turned to Greek culture as a resource for developing their own ideas and to the Greek language as the vehicle through which to express them. Among important new thinkers entering the ambit of Greek letters was a certain Zeno from the town of Citium in Cyprus, who lived roughly 336-264 B.C. (He should not be confused with the earlier Zeno of Elea, the lover and pupil of Parmenides.)

A man of Phoenician descent, and possibly Black, Zeno of Citium moved to Athens to study the various philosophic schools established there. Breaking off on his own philosophic path around 300 B.C., he held discussions of his ideas in the "Painted Porch," a renowned public walkway. Because of their wonted meetings on the Painted Porch (*Stoa Poikile* in Greek), Zeno and his followers became known as "the Stoics."

Breaking with both Plato and Aristotle, Zeno of Citium argued that there are no such things as transcendent Forms or inhering essences, but that all reality consists of nothing but particular material bodies. Furthermore, Zeno denied that reason in and of itself can directly apprehend any kind of special realm of things; to the contrary, Zeno regarded the senses as the sole windows on reality. Reason can compare and order the information that it receives from the senses, Zeno maintained, but apart from the senses that are its conduits, there is no other information to order.

According to Zeno, the mind is a very fine material substance; and perception, which is the basis of all knowledge, happens when an external material object makes an imprint on the mind, in the way that a signet ring makes an impression on wax. An imprint made on the mind is a "representation" (*phantasia*). When such a representation is so clear and striking as to prompt us to consent to it, it is a "comprehending representation" (*phantasia kataleptike*). To Zeno such a representation "grasps onto" (*katalambanei*) reality, and as so constitutes the criterion of what truly exists in the world.

Whereas Plato and Aristotle had explained the common features of things by postulating the existence of Forms or essences, Zeno argued that the mind at birth is a blank page. Only later does it create common notions of its own from repeated sense impressions, and from certain "anticipations" (*prolepseis*) of experience that stem from its natural structure. To Zeno, therefore, the "universals" of Plato and Aristotle became mere subjective notions created by the mind; the only things that are objectively real in themselves are concrete material bodies, including the human mind.

Zeno's successor as head of the Stoic school at Athens was Cleanthes (c. 331-232 B.C.). Today he is remembered largely on account of a majestic hymn he composed to Zeus. He viewed this patriarchal Greek god allegorically as a symbol for the rule of universal law in nature.

Chrysippus, "the Second Founder of Stoicism"

Zeno and Cleanthes were not much interested in logic. Nonetheless, the Stoics were eventually forced to take up the subject on account of scathing criticisms directed against their teachings by the Skeptics, a contemporary school in Greek philosophy. The Skeptics ridiculed the Stoic notion that any representation of the senses could be a criterion of truth, since one can always doubt whether any given representation is true. The Skeptics also tore into the Stoic claim that the universe is absolutely determined by one common law, and that morality consists in carrying out what is "appropriate" (*kathekon*) to one's station in life.

In response to the Skeptics, the third head of the Stoic school, Chrysippus (280-206 B.C.), reorganized the whole body of Stoic teaching. He sharpened his defenses with a new method of logic that he himself developed. Because of this reorganization, he became known as "the second founder of Stoicism," and it became a common saying that if there had been no Chrysippus, there would be no Stoicism.

Chrysippus was one of the greatest logicians in antiquity, and indeed in the entire philosophical history of the West. However, because of the influence of Aristotle's logic in the Middle Ages, later generations had difficulty understanding Chrysippus' alternative system of logic, dismissing it as unimportant. Not until the twentieth century did Chrysippus' reputation come into its own. Modern logicians, while developing a counter-logic to Aristotle's, realized that many of their new insights had been anticipated more than 2,000 years before by Chrysippus. (This modern re-evaluation of Chrysippus appeared in 1953 in the work of Benson Mates, who was trained both as a classical scholar and as a logician.[14])

Chrysippus' Propositional Calculus

Aristotle, as we saw, based his logic on syllogistic *terms*, which he claimed expressed class notions grounded in real essences. Chrysippus, rejecting the entire Aristotelian theory of class-defining essences, based his logic on *propositions*. Chrysippus excised the entire metaphysical debate over universals from the study of logic. Instead he began with propositions, which he defined functionally as those things that are either true or false.

As an example of Chrysippus' methods, let us use the letter "*p*" to represent the proposition "Socrates is a human being." Now consider some composite proposition made from *p*, such as this: "*p or not-p or p.*" We can see, just by looking at this composite proposition, that it must be true. Furthermore, it's true regardless of any class-designating terms that may appear in "*p.*"

Chrysippus *algebracized* logic. First, he symbolized propositions by variable letters. (He actually used the phrases "the first," "the second," etc.) Next, he assigned truth values to these variables. Finally, he analyzed how the truth value of any composite proposition is determined purely formally by the manner in which its constituent propositions are combined. This algebraic approach to logic is precisely what distinguishes 20th-century symbolic logic from the long-standing Aristotelian tradition that it supplanted.

Again anticipating modern logic, Chrysippus postulated certain basic types of undemonstrated arguments, together with certain rules of transformation, by means of which he deduced additional propositions. In fact, Chrysippus claimed that *all* valid logical arguments could be understood as so many manipulations carried out on these five undemonstrated argument types; the process of reducing any argument to these five basic types he called "analysis."

Signification

As part of his new logic, Chrysippus developed a theory of signification (that is, an explanation of propositional meaning). He analyzed propositions into three elements: (1) the sound or verbal expression (*phone*); (2) the meaning (*lekton*); and (3) the external object (*ektos hypokeimenon*). For example, consider the three words "This is Socrates." According to Chrysippus, the conjunction of these three word-sounds is a "statement" (*logos*). The "proposition" (*axioma*) is the meaning conveyed by these word-sounds. The external object to whom the proposition applies is Socrates. A proposition, then, is a kind of meaning; it is not just a sound pattern. It is, as Chrysippus aptly observes, what foreigners do not understand when they hear the sounds of a language they do not speak. By this theory, Chrysippus anticipated the modern distinction between sense (attributed meaning) and reference (that to which meaning is attributed).

Chrysippus' concept of the meanings of statements runs afoul of the traditional Stoic doctrine that all reality consists of material objects and their interactions. Are meanings merely material objects or interactions between material objects? If so, how do they differ from "sounds" and "external objects"? If not, what happens to the materialist hypothesis?

The problem of the materiality of meaning also arises with the Stoic concept of "representation," discussed above. As we saw, Zeno had argued that a representation occurring to the mind is like the image of a signet ring made in wax. But a physical impression in wax considered purely in and of itself has no *meaning*, just as a verbal sound uttered in a language one does not understand also has no meaning. For this reason, Chrysippus felt uncomfortable with Zeno's original definition of a representation. Instead, Chrysippus said that a representation is not "the making of an impression" (*typosis*) in the mind but rather "the altering" (*heteroiosis*) of the mind. But even so, a problem remains: How can something that is material, considered in its purely material aspect, ever be a meaning?

Chrysippus' theory of signification implies a concept of immaterial meaning. Chrysippus skirted the issue, however, because this was the very thing that prompted Plato and Aristotle to believe in immaterial Forms and essences. What is it that permits separate material sensations to have a unified meaning? Forms and essences, said Plato and Aristotle. The Stoics answered with their "notions" and "anticipations," which they viewed as creations of the mind. But if these notions and anticipations are merely material, what is the ground of *their* unity and meaning? The Stoic answer just pushed the whole question one step further back. They never really answered it.

Because he rejected any theory of Forms or essences, Chrysippus was at a loss to explain how any proposition that makes a universal empirical claim can ever be regarded as true or false. For example, consider the proposition "All human beings are mortal." If reality does indeed consist of nothing but concrete material bodies and their interactions, then no one to date can ever have known whether this proposition is true or false. The reason: no one to date has ever examined the life spans of all human beings, especially the life spans of all those human beings who have yet to be born.

The question of universal empirical propositions is where the theory of universals in Plato and Aristotle is at its strongest, whatever criticisms may otherwise be leveled against such a theory. We can know the truth of these propositions, Plato and Aristotle argue, because with the eye of reason we can apprehend the immaterial Forms or essences that define the real nature exhibited by families of individual bodies. In particular, we know that it is true that all human beings are mortal because we know through the eye of reason that mortality is part of the essence of humanity.

Chrysippus' logic also stumbles on a notorious counter-example to his definition of a proposition as that which is either true or false, but not both. Known as the paradox of the liar (*ho pseudomenos*), this counter-example is the deceptively simple proposition, "I am now lying." If this proposition is true, it is false, and if false, true. So here we have a proposition that is both true and false at the same time.

The currently accepted solution is to lay it down as a rule that no proposition may specify its own truth conditions. Such a rule works well enough, but it shows the degree to which logical theory is based on conventional, *ad hoc* presuppositions. It is inconvenient and paradoxical for formal, two-valued logical calculuses to allow for propositions that specify their own truth conditions; therefore, they are simply banished. Such *ad hoc* methods may indeed permit the creation of logical calculuses that are convenient in certain contexts; however, they provide no justification for regarding such constructs as expressive of any kind of necessity inherent in reality itself.

Every system of formal logic, like every system of higher mathematics, rests on a mass of *ad hoc* conventional stilts. The tendency, however, has always been to forget about the wobbly foundation, once the steely upper structure is complete. For example, in 1787 Immanuel Kant, the greatest philosopher of his age, surveyed the then hoary system of European logic derived from Aristotle. Kant thought it inconceivable that so grand a structure could ever be thrust aside, as it would be in a little over a hundred years. He declared:

> It is remarkable that to the present day it [Aristotelian logic] has not been able to make one step in advance, so that to all appearance, it may be considered as completed and perfect.[15]

After Chrysippus developed his new system of logic, the ancients were faced with two sharply competing logical systems, the Stoic and the Aristotelian. As we have seen, after the collapse of Greco-Roman civilization, the writings of Chrysippus were mostly lost, whereas the works of Aristotle, although scattered, later re-emerged in the West during the Christian Middle Ages. The result was that the syllogistic logic of Aristotle became the established standard in the West until the early part of the twentieth century, when it was overthrown by a new propositional logic similar to that of the lost logic of Chrysippus. These events demonstrate the degree to which formal logic, like higher mathematics, is a historically conditioned artifact.

Although Aristotle and Chrysippus had many differences, they nevertheless also shared a common store of root beliefs, ultimately derived from Parmenides. They both assumed that propositions are either true or false (the principle of bivalence) and that the real world is ruled by logical necessity, two important tenets of the Parmenidean myth. And although Zeno, the founder of Stoicism, had argued that there is an empirical criterion of truth (the comprehending representation), the logical system of Chrysippus implied that logic is a higher-order criterion than sense experience (the third major tenet of the Parmenidean myth). This shift became explicit when later Stoics declared that the criterion of truth is not the comprehending representation itself but the comprehending representation that does not encounter any obstacle from reasoning.

The Zeus-Logos

The mythical, even religious, underpinning of Stoic logic is apparent in the manner in which they justified the idea of logical necessity. As Parmenides felt it necessary to invent the myth of the goddess "far-constraining Order" (*Dike polypoinos*) in order to ground logical necessity, so the Stoics revised the received myth of Zeus, the king of the gods, to do likewise.

Prior to the Stoics, the traditional Greek concept of Zeus was largely that of a swaggering Greek patriarch writ large. Reacting against this tradition, the Stoics stripped Zeus of his anthropomorphic quirkiness and spiritualized him into the embodiment of the rule of cosmic law.

According to the religious philosophy of the Stoics, the universe is one great living organism. The source of its movement and structure is Reason or Rational Order (*Logos*), a kind of intelligent fire that permeates everything. This Reason the Stoics worshipped as the mind of Zeus. Later, Christian theologians, combining the Zeus-Logos idea with certain Platonic notions, created their own doctrine of the Logos as the second person of the Holy Trinity.

According to the Stoics, what we perceive as logical necessity is simply another manifestation of the Zeus-Logos that controls everything. Those who study logic, therefore, are devoted to a religious endeavor, for they disclose forms of necessity that express the mind of the living universe.

The most noteworthy expression of the Stoic concept of Zeus-Logos is a famous hymn written by Cleanthes, the teacher of the logician Chrysippus and his predecessor as head of the Stoic school. Cleanthes begins and ends his hymn by stressing the essential interconnection between three important traits of Zeus: his rule as the mighty king and father of the gods; the pervasiveness in nature of a kind of universal field of energy (symbolized by Zeus's lightning bolt); and the universal supremacy of Reason or Rational Order (*Logos*).

In effect, Stoic religion made rational behavior for human beings into a kind of conformity. That which demanded such conformity was overwhelming cosmic power in its capacity as the law-like, the universal, and the abstract. As Cleanthes himself expressed it:

> Exalted of the gods, lord of many names,
>   Zeus forever almighty,
> Nature's prince who guides all things with law,
> Hail! That we should all invoke your name is right,
> For from your Reason are we born, alone of those
> That, being mortal, live or crawl upon the earth.
> And so I sing your hymns and will ever praise your rule.
> Yours is the will this vault entire of heaven,
> Turning 'round the earth, obeys as you direct,
> Glad to serve your rule.
> How great a tool in adamantine hands you hold—
> Jagged, fiery, ever living—the lightning bolt!—
> Whose strikes make all of nature shudder, through which
> You further Reason's common order, extending everywhere,
> Mingled with the stars, both great and small ...
> Oh, dark-wrapped in clouds, bright in the lightning flash,
> Source of all gifts, Zeus—
> Deliver mortals from their sorry want of knowledge.
> Father, dash this ignorance from their souls!
> Allow us to share the Wisdom you yourself require,
> Along with Law, to govern all that is,
> That, so honored, we may respond with honor back to you,
> Never failing to praise your works, as befits a mortal soul.
> For either gods or mortals no greater boon exists than this—
> Ever to praise in righteousness the common law for all.[16]

By one of the great flukes of history, the school of philosophy founded by Zeno, Cleanthes, and Chrysippus found itself in ideal accord with the emerging spirit of a new world order, as a ruthless and relentless form of political and military imperialism began to sweep across the entire Mediterranean Basin—the Roman Empire. By the middle of the 2nd-century B.C., the Romans had conquered all of Greece, whose defeated inhabitants were far superior to their victors in cultural accomplishments. Accordingly, Greeks soon became the slaves of choice for staffing skilled managerial posts throughout the burgeoning imperial bureaucracy. As a result, the influences of Greek culture, language, and philosophy quickly swept westward across the Mediterranean, eventually making intellectual converts (or at least intellectual imitators) of Rome's own ruling classes.

Of the various schools of Greek thought that the Roman rulers encountered, Stoicism in particular lent itself to a world-wide imperialist mentality. Stoic logic and religion stressed the notion of a universal, abstract law emanating from one supreme divine will, regarded as expressing the common rational order of the universe. Roman emperors were quick to invoke this concept as a metaphor for validating their own absolutist claims to power. I and my law are to the empire, the emperors in effect said, as Zeus and his law are to the cosmos. Later, Christian emperors continued the same analogy, when "Father Zeus" (*Dzeus Pater* in Greek) gave place to "God the Father" (*Deus Pater* in Latin).

Stoic ethics defined moral duty in terms of mental resignation to what is appropriate (*kathekon*) to one's particular station in life. According to the Stoics, everything in the universe, including all human action, is absolutely determined according to universal natural law. The sphere of moral decision, therefore, is limited to our *attitude* toward our actions and the world around us. Either we can mentally and emotionally fight against what is objectively required of us, or else, using philosophical study to cultivate a sense of emotional indifference (*apatheia*), we can acquiesce to the inevitable. To the Stoics, the latter attitude is the fitting moral choice and the mark of the wise man, whereas the former is the mark of the fool.

These quiescent ethical values recommended themselves to the Emperors, because it was easy to control subjects that were so motivated. Indeed, Stoic ethical theory proved to be the perfect system of values for the type of obedient, emotionally-neutralized institutional functionary required by the huge new imperial bureaucracy. Later, the authoritarian values preached by Christianity served the same purpose for Christian emperors.

The whole thrust of Stoic philosophy was to reinforce the same underlying message: acquiesce to the powers that be, whether in the great world of nature ruled by the Zeus-Logos, or in the world-state administered from Rome. Andrea Nye is right, therefore, to characterize Stoic logic as "the scaffolding for a ruling culture" which helped support the building of a new "idiom of control."[17] Thanks to the Stoics, to be logical and philosophical now effectively meant to be obedient to Rome.

The Legacy of Greek Logic

Greek logical inquiry culminated in two schools of logic, on the one hand the syllogistic term-logic of Aristotle (indebted to the prior thought of Socrates and Plato), and on the other the algebraic propositional logic of Chrysippus (indebted to the prior thought of Zeno and Cleanthes). Despite significant differences between them, however, both these logical systems traced a common philosophical pedigree back to Parmenides. Aristotle's pedigree came through the influence of Parmenides on his teacher Plato and on Plato's teacher Socrates; the early Stoics' pedigree came through the influence exercised on them by the logicians of Megara, who were likewise heavily influenced by Parmenides.

The common philosophical influence emanating from Parmenides expressed itself through what I have called the Parmenidean myth. Although modified somewhat at the hands of each of its successive recipients, this myth in its final form was basically the same for both Aristotelian and Stoic logic: there exists a kind of invariable necessity that rules both the objective world of nature and the subjective world of human experience; a comprehensive system of formal logic can be developed through application of the principle of bivalence to the uses of human language; and the system of impersonal knowledge that is revealed through such applications is inherently superior to knowledge revealed by sensation or subjectivity.

As we have seen, the formulation of each of these elements in the Parmenidean myth was historically conditioned by circumstances peculiar to ancient Greek culture, politics, and language; moreover, the truth of each element remains open to serious philosophical objection. In the final analysis, both systems of Greek logic, despite their seeming rigor of development, remain intellectually rooted at their deepest levels in the soil of myth. Behind all the dry prose in Aristotle's analysis of the syllogism there looms the implicit assumption of Parmenides' goddess "far-constraining Order." Likewise, behind all the algebraic formulas of Chrysippus' propositional calculus there looms Cleanthes' god "Zeus forever almighty," himself a masculinization of Parmenides' original goddess. Moreover, we should not lose sight of this fact: the definitive expression of both these systems of logic was made by men, not women, and by men often expressing anti-democratic biases in the context of a society that was itself becoming increasingly regimented and militaristic.

The logical systems of Ancient Greece, like their later counterparts, proved to be useful tools in certain contexts. To that extent, these systems possessed a relative objectivity that expressed certain aspects of reality. To claim more for these systems, however, is another matter altogether, particularly the claim that these systems' windows on reality were in some absolute sense better than other windows in human experience. A claim of this sort rests on both a value judgment about what is epistemologically "better" and "worse," and on a certain interpretation of reality as such. In other words, such a claim rests upon a system of metaphysical assumptions, and ones that are by no means obvious, at that.

Anyone has the right, of course, to develop a theory of knowledge and being, based on some such metaphysical assumptions (this book itself is based on certain metaphysical assumptions of its own). The important thing, however, is to *acknowledge* that one is doing metaphysics, and not try and hide this pursuit under a pretended cloak of absolute objectivity.

Once admitted, all metaphysical assumptions are immediately open to critical assessment, as they should be. Critical assessment has shown that the metaphysical assumptions of Aristotle and the Stoics involve very serious problems. Even so, however, both Aristotle and the Stoics had the merit of frankly acknowledging that their respective logics were metaphysically grounded. In this regard, they contrast favorably to more modern approaches to logic. As we will see, the moderns loudly disclaim any involvement in metaphysics, while yet relying on implicit assumptions that are every bit as mythical as those of Aristotle and Chrysippus. In this sense at least, the formal logic of modernity has proven to be even more illogical than that of antiquity.

Like its modern counterpart, ancient Greek logic was an inseparable part of the civilization that created it. To evaluate that logic in any full sense must hang on an evaluation of the greater civilization of which it was an integral part. Therefore, the critique of formal logic, higher mathematics, and science is ultimately part of a greater critique, one that may be called, for lack of a better term, civilization-critique. Whatever else it may be, this greater critique is not itself a logical, mathematical, or scientific inquiry. What shall we call it, then, if not "philosophy"?

The Triumph of Christian Authoritarianism

Beginning in the late third century A.D., the Roman imperialist system entered a phase of marked decline, eventually collapsing, at least in the West, by the latter fifth century A.D. Before its final dismemberment, the empire witnessed the birth within itself of a new, aggressively proselytizing myth system, the Christian religion.

Although fitfully persecuted in its formative years, the Christian religion nevertheless managed to survive and spread throughout the first-century A.D. Roman Empire. Gradually, various congregations accumulated wealth and power, especially after it became fashionable for members of the Roman upper classes to convert. In time, the church evolved into a wealthy, hierarchically structured corporation consisting of people born into the faith for generations, and headed by powerful, aristocratic bishops commanding professional staffs.

By the end of the third century A.D., certain farsighted Roman officials recognized that the Christian Church had become an oasis of stability, power, and wealth in the midst of a society otherwise suffering decay and disintegration. Accordingly, in 313 A.D the Emperor Constantine, ever seeking to shore up the sagging fortunes of the empire, decreed full religious freedom for Christians. He also began appointing Christians to many high-level posts in the civil bureaucracy and the army. Eventually he adopted the cross as a military symbol for his troops, and on his death bed converted to the new religion. Except for the brief reign of the Emperor Julian, Constantine's successors continued, for similar reasons, the policy of favoring Christianity. In 391 A.D. the Emperor Theodosius banned all pagan cults, effectively making Christianity the state religion of the empire.

Despite the state support given to Christianity by Constantine and his successors, the great majority of the empire's population, particularly the masses of rural slaves and serfs, remained pagan. The continuing decline in the central authority of Rome, combined with the massive territorial infiltration by Germanic tribes, served to check the church's ambition for a universal ideological grip on the populace.

After Rome's decline, newly arriving Germanic chieftains secured various duchies for themselves in the western half of the former empire. They too, like Constantine before them, converted to Christianity, using the existing Christian ideology and institutional infrastructure to consolidate their spheres of control. Because the rural classes clung to paganism, the Germanic chieftains often resorted to violence to maintain at least the facade of a Christian regime.

Over the course of generations, two different Europes came into being within the same continent. On top was a tiny minority of Christian-identified male rulers and ideologues. They controlled the coercive institutions of state, church, and university, communicated with each other in Latin (at least on formal occasions), and regarded themselves as the bearers of all learning, culture, and religion worthy of the name. On the bottom was a huge majority of illiterate country dwellers, politically disenfranchised, economically exploited, speaking various local dialects, and often practicing broken-down strains of the old paganism under a Christian veneer. Once established, this fundamental bifurcation of European life remained entrenched until the rise to power of the bourgeoisie in the 18th century and the emergence of the industrial proletariat in the 19th.

The triumph of Christian authoritarianism had a profound impact on the style of learning in general and on philosophy in particular. Pagan Greece had possessed a polycentric belief system and, during its most creative period, even democratic political structures. Medieval Christian Europe, on the other hand, was subjected to ranks of aristocratic popes, emperors, kings, bishops, and petty warlords. These authorities all professed allegiance to one common religious ideology that brooked no deliberate dissent. The teachings of Christ as interpreted by his one holy church were the one true religion; any consciously competing intellectual alternative was heresy.

A typical sign of the new religion's attitude occurred in 529 A.D. In that year, the Christian emperor Justinian closed the ancient pagan schools of philosophy at Athens, the oldest of which had been founded some 900 years before. As the city's resident philosophers fled eastward to the kingdom of Persia, the Western tradition of philosophy as the autonomous exercise of reason came to an end. That autonomy would not appear again in the West until a thousand years later.

The Emergence of Europe

After about 1000 A.D., a distinct European civilization in its own right began to emerge. As intellectual preoccupations gradually reappeared in subsequent centuries, Christian authorities carefully subordinated the learning process to the control of bureaucratic institutions (a style of learning that has continued into the industrial era). Unlike the independent schools of ancient Greece in its most creative period, the medieval center of higher learning was viewed as an institutional tool for training new teachers as inculcators of established values. Although the chief governing body within the university was usually the faculty (sometimes both faculty and students), authorities always maintained a careful watch that no idea be espoused or book read that might be subversive to the faith. Although latitude existed for a certain range of interpretations for received texts, anyone who genuinely challenged basic assumptions (one of the principal historical roles of the philosopher) quickly found himself or herself in serious trouble.

Although initially hostile to pagan philosophy, Christianity was eventually forced to have recourse to surviving fragments of the great philosophical systems of Greek antiquity, for it had no intellectual tools of its own to make the dogmas of faith rationally accessible. Of the great systematic philosophers of early Greece, the one who was most alienated from the spirit of Greek democratic relativism and this-worldliness was Plato. He was followed in a not-too-distant second place by his revisionist pupil Aristotle. Hence it was no accident that it was these two thinkers who provided the Christian religion, at different periods of its development, with the intellectual building blocks for both its metaphysics and its system of logic.

The Transmission of Boethius

An important link between the last vestiges of ancient thought and the revival of learning in the later Middle Ages, especially in regard to logical studies, was the Roman aristocratic philosopher Boethius (roughly 480-524 A.D.). One of the most highly educated men of his time, Boethius was also deeply involved in politics, serving in effect as the prime minister to Theodoric, the warlike East Gothic chieftain in control of Italy. In 522 A.D. Theodoric had Boethius arrested on a charge of treason (apparently without foundation) and subsequently had him executed in 524 A.D.

While in jail awaiting his execution, Boethius wrote his most famous work, *The Consolation of Philosophy*. The work is remarkable in that it makes no reference to Christ, although Boethius was a professed Christian. Instead, Boethius receives consolation in his misery from a vision of Philosophy personified, who appears to him as a goddess-like figure with whom he conducts a philosophical dialogue.

Boethius composed a number of translations, including his own commentaries, of certain works of Plato and Aristotle. Of particular importance later, he translated certain of Aristotle's treatises on logic, along with a celebrated introduction to Aristotle's logic by the third-century A.D. Neoplatonic philosopher Porphyry. Boethius also composed several original logical treatises of his own. As a result of these endeavors, medieval philosophers of the 11th and 12th centuries largely viewed ancient philosophy, especially ancient logic, through Boethius' eyes.

The logical tradition that Boethius bequeathed to the later Middle Ages was saturated with the spirit of the Parmenidean myth. For one thing, the logical fragments of Plato and Aristotle that Boethius transmitted ultimately derived from that myth, as discussed above. Second, Boethius' own philosophy constantly reaffirms the Parmenidean myth. As noted, *The Consolation of Philosophy* tells the story of a mythical encounter, with many sections written in poetry, between Boethius and the mighty, goddess-like figure Philosophy. The scene brings to mind Parmenides' mythical encounter with the goddess "far-constraining Order" (*Dike polypoinos*). Boethius explicitly describes himself as a man "nourished in the lore of Eleatics [Parmenides and Zeno] and Academics [Plato and company]."[18] In the style of Parmenides and Plato, Boethius expresses contempt for democracy ("the many-headed people"), artists, and human sensuality.

For Boethius, the truly real is the One that far transcends the mere shadow-world of appearance. Humans can attain access to the One only by an abstract reasoning process that is devoid, as much as humanly possible, of all sensuality and subjectivity. Accordingly, Boethius regarded formal logic as the most divine of human studies.

Like all the contributors to the Parmenidean myth that preceded him, Boethius latched onto a style of interpretation typical of certain privileged males in patriarchal society and idolized it as the epitome of all worthy human interpretation. Such a bias came easy to someone like the patriarchal, aristocratic Boethius, for whom women, artists, and the lower classes were second-rate human beings.

The Rise of Scholasticism

Beginning in the 12th and 13th centuries a style of philosophy emerged in Western Europe that was stimulated initially by a few transmitted fragments of Aristotle's logic, and later by the recovery of much of Aristotelian philosophical writings. Because this philosophical tradition mostly involved professionally trained teachers of theology or philosophy working within universities or monastic orders, it came to be known as "scholasticism" (from the Latin noun *schola*, meaning "school"). As noted above, both bureaucratic control and ideological narrowness served to confine medieval philosophical inquiry within the bounds set by orthodox Christian dogma. As a result, philosophers naturally tended to focus their work on safe, technical issues, such as the study of formal logic, which flourished during the scholastic era.

Peter Abelard

Medieval Christian logic first came into its own in the 12th century with Peter Abelard (1079-1142 A.D.), the first great medieval logician. Abelard was born in Palais, Brittany, and in his youth studied logic in Tours, and theology in Paris. His adult life was a well-publicized mix of brilliance and catastrophe.

At age 36, while a lecturer in Paris, Abelard seduced one of his pupils, the 17-year-old Héloïse, niece of an ecclesiastical official with whom Abelard was then lodging. After Héloïse gave birth to their child, the two secretly married, handing over the child to Héloïse's sister. Following an argument with the uncle, Abelard conducted Héloïse to Argenteuil, where she became a nun, and returned to his lodging in Paris. Relatives of the uncle, furious at Abelard's handling of the whole affair, broke into his room and castrated him. After the castration, Abelard followed Héloïse's example, becoming a monk at the abbey of St. Denys, where he established a school of logic. Later, he came to view his castration as a blessing in disguise, enabling him to free himself from his earthly passions and to devote himself more fully to logic and theology.[19]

Like modern logicians, who view logic as the handmaiden of the prevailing orthodoxy of their time (science), so Abelard viewed logic as the handmaiden of the prevailing orthodoxy of the Middle Ages (Christian theology). In fact, Abelard was the first to use the word "theology" in its modern sense. (Prior to Abelard, "theology" effectively meant Christology.)[20]

Fully devoted to theological orthodoxy, Abelard undertook to use the power of logic to discredit those whom he regarded as heretics, especially in regard to the doctrine of the Trinity. Ironically, however, he himself ran afoul of other self-appointed defenders of orthodoxy, notably Bernard of Clairvaux, who attacked Abelard for letting logic step on the prerogatives of theology. As a result of Bernard's incessant scheming, ecclesiastical authorities twice condemned a number of Abelard's theological views as heretical. In his later years, after a forced retraction of his condemned views, Abelard lived unassumingly as a monk until his death in 1142 A.D. Although humiliated by his theological opponents, Abelard nonetheless exercised a lasting influence in philosophy because of his brilliance in logic.

Abelard's great accomplishment was to forge a Christian reconstruction of the fragmentary Aristotelian logical tradition as it had been transmitted to his age by Boethius. As it happened, the works of Aristotle that Boethius had transmitted dealt with the nature of substance, species, and genus. Prompted by his study of these works and by certain commentaries by Boethius, Abelard devoted himself to the question of "universals." He argued that universal terms such as "human being" do not denote any kind of general *thing*, as some of his contemporaries had argued, but rather a kind of general *meaning* that is based on similarities among specific individual things. According to Abelard, the general terms that we use, although subjective, are nonetheless objectively true when based on real similarities among things. These real similarities, in turn, depend on ideas in the mind of God, which Abelard associated with the Logos, or second person of the Holy Trinity.

Abelard derived this doctrine from Augustine of Hippo, who had earlier identified the Logos of the Stoics and the Neoplatonists with the "Word" or "Reason" (*Logos*) mentioned at the beginning of the fourth gospel. In a development that was to influence Western logic for centuries, Abelard took up this concept of the Logos as God's incarnate Reason and made it into the foundation stone of logic as the most sublime of human sciences. From Christ as the incarnate Logos, Abelard claimed, logic derives both its sublime power and its name:

> Since, therefore, our Lord Jesus Christ, the Father's Word, is called *Logos* [Reason] in Greek, and since he is also named the Father's *Sophia* [Wisdom], that science above all clearly belongs to him whose very name is connected to him—the science which, by a certain derivation from *Logos*, is called 'logic.' And it is clear that just as Christians are properly named after Christ, so logic is properly named after *Logos*.[21]

Like all logicians, Abelard was confronted by the problem of how to account for logical necessity. Since, as a good Christian, he could not ground such necessity on the goddess "far-constraining Order" of Parmenides nor on the Zeus-Logos of the Stoics, he turned instead to the Christ-Logos. According to Abelard, when we as human beings apprehend individual things created via the divine mind, we can abstract from them general meanings ("universals"), which approximate to the original divine ideas after which things have been patterned. When, further, we use linguistic terms to express correctly these universals and combine them in such a way as to conform with logical necessity, we make true statements. Logic, therefore, is a kind of divine activity, since by examining and elucidating linguistic terms and their applications, we uncover a kind of necessary order in language and the world that is ultimately grounded in Christ as God's Logos.

In effect, Abelard traced the whole validity and power of formal logic back to the myth of the Christ-Logos. That is, he took the Parmenidean myth as it had been modified by Aristotle and Christianized it by assimilating it to the myth of the Christ-Logos as presented in the prologue to the fourth gospel.

Western logic from ancient to medieval times thus rests on a direct mythological succession from the goddess of Parmenides to the Logos of the Platonists and the Stoics to the Christ-Logos of the Christians. Far from being a culturally-independent apprehension of objective reality, Western formal logic has repeatedly demonstrated its dependence on persistent, underlying myth systems of a religious nature.

The Aristotelian Crisis

After Abelard's death in 1142 A.D., the West began recovering most of the lost works of Aristotle, including translations of commentaries made on Aristotle by Arab-writing Islamic philosophers. This recovery of the full works of Aristotle provoked a major intellectual crisis.

As noted above, Plato in particular and Aristotle to a lesser extent had been the two ancient Greek philosophers most akin in spirit to Christianity. Both these philosophers, however, and Aristotle especially, were nonetheless affected by the prevailing humanist spirit of their times.

When the full implications of Aristotle's recovered works became apparent, medieval Christian thinkers experienced a nasty jolt: the greatest intellectual system that the world had ever known reached numerous carefully reasoned conclusions that were completely contrary to the basic dogmas of their own faith. Among other disturbing conclusions, Aristotle had argued (or assumed) that the world is eternal and not created, that there is no personal immortality, that the highest expression of human life lies in the untrammeled exercise of critical reason, that the purpose of virtue is to promote human happiness in this life, and that God is a kind of remote unmoved mover for whom it is irrational to feel any kind of personal affection.

The Taming of Aristotle by Thomas Aquinas

As a result of the naturalistic thrust of the recovered works of Aristotle, a number of medieval thinkers regarded his philosophy as dangerous to the faith. Others, however, believed that important elements could be extracted from Aristotle's philosophy that would be useful for buttressing Christian dogma and institutions. The most famous member of the latter camp was the theologian-philosopher Thomas Aquinas (c. 1224-1274 A.D.).

The son of the high-placed Count of Aquino, Thomas Aquinas received one of the best educations of his day, studying at the University of Naples and the University of Paris, and with Albert the Great in Cologne. Even in his earliest years, he showed a strong religious bent, which moved him to enter the Dominican Order in 1244. After receiving his doctorate in theology from the University of Paris in 1256, he spent most of his life as a professional teacher at various schools and monasteries. Deeply impressed by the intellectual power of Aristotelianism, he sought to reconstruct it in a way that would be consistent with his equally deep religious belief.

Aquinas met much opposition in his own lifetime to his proposed synthesis of Aristotelianism and Christian dogma. In 1277, a few years after Aquinas' death, the Bishop of Paris condemned a number of philosophical propositions commonly associated with Aquinas' name, and the Archbishop of Canterbury banned the teaching of his works at Oxford. The Dominicans, however, proud of Aquinas, took up the cause of Thomism, which gradually won over many influential theologians. In 1323 Pope John XXII proclaimed Aquinas a saint, and five centuries later, in 1879, Pope Leo XIII declared

Thomism to be the official philosophy of the Roman Catholic Church.

Aquinas achieved his grand synthesis by frankly acknowledging a distinction between theology and philosophy. He regarded the first field as that which pertains to "revealed truth" (that is, the dogmatic pronouncements of the church hierarchy) and the second as that which pertains to the search for truth when unaided by revelation (as in the philosophic system of Aristotle). According to Aquinas, the final criterion of truth is always theology, so there can be no such thing as two conflicting truths existing side by side. But on questions where the church hierarchy has not proclaimed definitive dogma, one is free to rely on critical reasoning as an avenue to truth. Moreover, even in areas in which dogmatic theology has spoken, Aquinas thought it might be of interest to inquire how close to revealed truth the human mind could approximate by using reason alone.

As with Aristotle, Aquinas begins his strictly philosophical inquiry with the world as it exists in concrete particulars, an approach that offended some theologians. Again like Aristotle, Aquinas maintains the celebrated dictum "There is nothing in cogitation that was not first in sensation." (*Nihil in intellectu quod non prius fuerit in sensu*.) Many of his Platonic-influenced contemporaries regarded this dictum as scandalous. On the other hand, contrary to Aristotle, Aquinas maintains that the most important feature of reality is not "essence" (*essentia*) but rather "the sheer fact of existence" (*ipsum esse subsistens*).

Focusing on existence rather than essence, Aquinas concludes that in every particular thing that exists the human mind discovers contingency; hence it is naturally led to seek out that which exists by necessity, or, in other words, that whose essence *is* existence, and this is what we mean by God. As a result, the philosophy of Aristotle can stimulate the rational mind to reach the limits of human cognition, at which point, in order to find the highest truths, it must make the leap of faith. Hence the works of Aristotle, once rightly understood, can serve to point one in the direction of God, but without actually getting one to the goal. To Aquinas such an accomplishment is about the most that one can reasonably expect of human thought unaided by divine revelation.

Although often invoking the name of Aristotle, Aquinas was also deeply indebted to Augustine and to the Christian mystic Dionysius the Pseudo-Areopagite (the second most quoted authority in Aquinas after Aristotle). Evidence of Augustine's influence is Aquinas' belief in the existence of ideas in the mind of God that serve as exemplars for the creation of actually existing things. As noted above, this belief is also found in Peter Abelard.

Logic and the Logos, Again

The fact that, philosophically, Aquinas defines God as that which necessarily exists leads him to assimilate the principle of contradiction to God. According to Aquinas, if something were a logical contradiction, it could not exist. The source of this impossibility is not any lack of power on the part of God, but rather a lack of capacity (or potency) on the part of the self-contradictory thing:

> The reason God's power can't do what is impossible in the sense we are discussing is because it [the self-contradictory thing] lacks possibility; so we don't say God's power is limited by not being able to do it.[22]

But what is it that determines the potency of anything for existing? Its idea in the mind of God, who is the act of existing *per se*. The divine mind is "the Word" (*Logos*), who proceeds from the Father, and who expresses what may and may not exist:

> Because the Son is a word that perfectly expresses the Father, the Son expresses all creatures. This sequence is outlined by the words of Anselm, who said that by uttering Himself the Father uttered all creatures. ... The Word is not merely that by which the arrangement of all creatures take place; it is the arrangement itself which the Father makes of things to be created.[23]

Because God's essence is existence itself, and because each particular thing exists only in virtue of its idea in God's mind, to say that something is a logical contradiction is to say that the idea of the thing cannot exist in the mind of God. Because of this impossibility, the self-contradictory thing can never exist in the world. Like all his Christian predecessors, Aquinas thus invokes the myth of the Logos to justify the logical necessity which he believes prevails in the world.

Although Aquinas was himself an innovator, the system of medieval scholasticism to which he gave classical expression, as well as alternate systems such as that of John Duns Scotus, served to promote intellectual conformity in Medieval and Renaissance Europe. Among literate Christians (a tiny minority of the population) academic and ecclesiastical authorities repeatedly used the philosophy of Aquinas and other scholastics as intellectual bludgeons for knocking down any serious attempts towards a radical rethinking of basic Christian dogma. Among illiterate country-dwellers (the overwhelming majority of the population), authorities added the force of scholastic philosophy to canon law and the machinery of the Holy Inquisition in systematically hunting down, torturing, and executing large numbers of "heretics" and "witches." Andrea Nye rightly observes that medieval logic became the tool of choice used by aristocratic, institution-bound males for the purpose of turning theology into "a self-consistent body of forced belief."[24]

William of Ockham

The last great logician of the Middle Ages was the English Franciscan William of Ockham (1285-1349 A.D.). He was the most brilliant philosopher of the 14th century and, in the eyes of some, of the entire medieval period. Although educated in the Aristotelian tradition, he developed a new theory of logic reminiscent of that of Chrysippus, the great Stoic logician, and anticipatory of that of later 20th-century philosophers.

As might be expected in an age of enforced religious dogmatism, a philosopher of Ockham's originality was bound to incur the wrath of the established authorities, both academic and ecclesiastical. In 1323, after finishing the formal requirements at Oxford for a degree in theology, Ockham was blocked from receiving his degree by John Lutterell, the Chancellor of the University, who regarded him as a heretic. In 1324, at the instigation of Lutterell, Ockham was summoned to defend himself before John XXII (Jacques d'Euse), the opulent French puppet-pope then residing at Avignon.

In response to the Chancellor's complaint, John XXII appointed a commission to evaluate Ockham's writings, which at length recommended that some of them be condemned. In any case, during the four years of his stay at Avignon, Ockham became embroiled in a further argument when the opulent pope criticized the Franciscan Order, of which Ockham was a member, for teaching the heresy that Christ and the apostles had practiced a life of poverty. Ockham argued in support of his Franciscan brothers against John XXII, appealing to statements favorable to their cause made by a previous pope.

Aware that their situation at the papal court was becoming precarious, Ockham and a number of his associates fled Avignon in 1328, taking up residence in Munich, under the protection of Ludwig IV, the Holy Roman Emperor, a fierce enemy of John XXII. In response, the Pope excommunicated Ockham. In the meantime, Ludwig invaded and captured Rome, installing there his own anti-pope. In 1347, Ockham lost his protection when Ludwig unexpectedly died. As a result he began to take steps towards an accommodation with the church, but died himself from the plague in 1349.

Ockham's Razor Cuts Off Aristotle's Essences

Ockham's philosophy was radical in that he seized upon the horns of a logical dilemma that Aquinas had inherited from Aristotle, and proceeded to tear it apart, discarding one of its horns entirely. To understand this dilemma, we recall that Aristotle had brought Plato's postulated Forms down to earth. Aristotle agreed that incorporeal essences exist, as Plato had claimed, but only by inhering in concrete particular substances, which consist of matter and form (the latter being the essence). Again borrowing from Plato, Aristotle argued that knowledge must be of essences, not of matter. The reason is that matter is contingent and ever changing, and as such unknowable. Aristotle also stressed the notion that the principle of individuation for any concrete substance is its matter, not its essence. For example, Socrates and Plato are different individuals by virtue of the particular matter possessed by each, not by virtue of their essence, humanity, which is common to both.

Beginning with these assumptions about essence, matter, and individuality, Aristotle concluded that knowledge consists in the use of the mind to abstract from any group of perceived particulars their commonly-defining essence. This theory of knowledge, alas, immediately generates a paradox: if knowledge must begin with concrete particulars, as Aristotle insisted against Plato, it can never abstract from them any essence, because the only difference between essence and particulars is matter, and matter in an of itself is unknowable. Hence the Aristotelian dilemma: all knowledge must begin with the concrete particular, but the concrete particular, as such, is unknowable. This dilemma is really just the epistemological side of an ontological problem: how can incorporeal essences inhere in corporeal substances?

Although Aquinas partially modified Aristotle's theory of essence, he was never able to solve the core problem of how there can be knowledge of the concrete particular, when all knowledge derives from form. In practice, Aquinas tended to side-step the problem by emphasizing existence rather than essence. Aquinas' neglect in dealing with this Aristotelian dilemma was noted by a rival 13th-century scholastic theologian, John Duns Scotus. He attempted a solution by proposing an additional metaphysical premise, namely that matter as such has its own essence, "the form of corporeality" (*forma corporeitatis*).

In a stunning break with the Aristotelian metaphysics of Aquinas and Duns Scotus, William of Ockham came along and offered a far simpler solution: he took up Aquinas' distinction between existence and essence and simply threw out essence. According to Ockham, the world consists of nothing but individual existing things and their interactions. What the Aristotelians call the universal or the essence is merely the meaning (*significatio*) of certain terms used in propositions, namely those terms whose reference (*suppositio*) is a group of particular individuals.

The universal or essence, therefore, is not any kind of reality in its own right, as Aristotle maintained, but rather the meaning that answers to a name that we use. Individual things, the only realities that exist, are knowable as such, said Ockham—through sensation and reason. From individual things we abstract general notions that are represented in propositions by terms. But these general notions are nothing more than a kind of mental abbreviation for the various individuals for which they stand, nothing more. So Aristotle's dilemma dissolves; there is no need to explain how we can move from individuals to essences because there are no essences.

Drawing on new trends that had been developing for some time in medieval logic, Ockham moved toward replacing Aristotle's theory of syllogistic inference with a propositional calculus (although he never completely broke with the syllogism). In the manner of the ancient Stoics many centuries before, he stressed the importance of certain types of propositional implications (*consequentia*). According to Ockham, we combine terms in propositions to express both our direct intuition of individual things and the more indirect knowledge that we abstract from such intuition. On the basis of certain rules of valid propositional inference, we eventually deduce those great complicated systems of propositions that constitute science. In the end, all natural knowledge arises from only two founts: the immediate sense perception of individual things and the force of logical necessity.

Ockham's philosophical method is commonly paraphrased by a principle known today as Ockham's razor: "Entities should not be multiplied more than necessary" (*entia non sunt multiplicanda praeter necessitatem*). Although this paraphrase correctly captures Ockham's spirit, it nowhere occurs in exactly these words in his extant writings.

God, the Savior of Logic

Among the particular individuals that really exist Ockham places God, whom he believes in as required by church dogma. God, however, is different from every other particular individual being, in that he is all-powerful; in fact, Ockham defines God as that individual being who is all-powerful. Apart from the volitional acts of rational beings such as humans and angels, everything else in the created universe is absolutely determined, according to Ockham, and the source of this determinism is the will of that all-powerful entity called God.

Since everything that exists depends for its existence on the free will of God, which might be otherwise in any given case, everything that exists does so contingently. Hence the question of whether any supposed particular thing exists always remains open in theory and can only be decided practically through an act of direct intuition (that is, through immediate perception).

Ockham insists that to say that God is all-powerful does not mean that God can act contrary to logic. According to Ockham, the phrase "the power to act contrary to logic" is meaningless. To have some power *means* to have some power that is logically possible. But Ockham's view has a catch: an irrefutable proof of the logical possibility of something is its actual existence, which is a matter of observation. Because God by definition is that omnipotent being who creates all things, and because an irrefutable proof of the logical possibility of anything is its observed existence as a created entity, Ockham in effect fuses logical necessity with the divine nature. As a result, he argues that one cannot establish a meaningful order of precedence between the requirements of logic on one hand and the boundaries of God's power on the other:

> The inability to do the impossible is not something that God has prior to the impossible's inability to be done by God. Neither is the impossible's inability to be made by God prior to God's inability to do the impossible.[25]

Reviewing passages such as this one, many commentators have argued that Ockham grounds logic on divine *power*. A more careful reading, however, shows that Ockham's real basis for logic is God's *mind*. As noted above, a confluence of pagan and Christian concepts encouraged medieval Christian philosophers to view the *Logos*, mentioned in the fourth gospel, as God's mind. God creates and sustains the world, said the philosophers, according to eternal ideas in his mind. Like his predecessors, Ockham took up this old belief in the divine ideas, but gave it a new twist: he rejected the identification of these ideas with *forms*. Insisting that only *individuals* are real, Ockham concluded that the divine ideas are of individuals, not forms.

Regardless of whether they pertained to forms or individuals, ideas in the mind of God remained for Ockham, as for all medieval Christian philosophers, the basis of the conceptual structure of reality. On this foundation of the *Logos* as the mind of God, containing eternal ideas, Ockham grounded his concept of logical necessity and logical possibility. Ockham scholar Marilyn Adams, using the symbol "*p*" to stand for any proposition, rightly observes:

> On Ockham's view, it is objectively existent divine ideas that make propositions of the form "It is possible that *p*" true.[26]

In the end, Ockham divides all reality into two parts: on one hand is a world of contingently existing individuals whose existence is ascertainable only through acts of direct intuition. On the other hand is God, the all-powerful individual, whose boundaries of conceptual efficacy coincide with those of logical necessity.

Ockham represents an important turning point in the history of philosophy because his logic moved in the direction of regarding reasoning as a propositional calculus. At the same time, his metaphysics moved in the direction of dividing all reality into two mutually exclusive realms, the empirically contingent and the logically necessary. Those thinkers immediately influenced by Ockham justifiably called their approach "the modern way" (*via moderna*), as opposed to the methods of the Aristotelians, which they called "the ancient way" (*via antiqua*).

The later logical positivism of the 20th century, with its great stress on the unbreachable dichotomy between logical necessity and empirical contingency, can be viewed as an updated version of Ockhamism. The major difference is that the logical positivists stripped logical necessity of its connections to the mind of God. As we will see later, however, this maneuver left them facing an embarrassing question that they were never able to answer: Just what makes logical necessity so necessary?

However hard-nosed and "modern" Ockham may seem, he nonetheless found it necessary to ground his logic on the religious dogma of the Logos. As a result, his propositional logic—including his theory of logical necessity, his theory of propositional reference, and his theory of truth values—represented a Christianized reworking of the ancient Parmenidean myth.

The Illogic of Antiquity

The history of Western formal logic from the "way of truth" of Parmenides to the "modern way" of William of Ockham reveals a common pattern. Logicians, although regarding themselves as paragons of reason, have repeatedly invoked mythical, and even religious, motifs in order to ground their claims about logic. Although their systems have had practical value in certain contexts, the logicians themselves are guilty of illogic, the illogic of making the following grand claim:

> The methods of formal logic are in some absolute sense better or more revelatory of reality than other forms of human discourse that embrace subjectivity and time.

For example, logicians have traditionally argued that the syllogisms of Aristotle tell us something more important about reality than the love poems of Sappho. In fact, however, any such claim quickly collapses in the face of rational analysis, as we have seen.

The basis of the logicians' illogic is the Parmenidean myth. The following chapters will show how this myth has wormed itself into the core of all modern systems of formal logic as well. Not surprisingly, therefore, we will see that as the illogic of antiquity has receded into the mists of history, it has done so only to make room for an equally irrational successor, the illogic of modernity.

---

[1] Parmenides, *On Nature*, fragment 2, as cited in Greek by G.S. Kirk & J.E. Raven, *The Presocratic Philosophers*, Cambridge University Press, Cambridge, 1963, p. 269.

[2] Protagoras, *Panton khrematon metron anthropos...*, cited, among others, by Diogenes Laertius, *Lives of the Famous Philosophers*, 9, 51. Anthropos should *not* be translated as "man." This word gives the misleading impression that Protagoras is talking about either the male sex or else the whole human race. He is not talking about the male sex. *Anthropos* is a gender-neutral word, in contrast to *aner* (*andros* in the genitive). Nor is he talking about the whole human race. The whole point of his philosophy is that reality is variable because of the variability in *individual* sense perceptions. Ancient Greek commentators correctly took *anthropos* here to mean "the individual person."

[3] The last point is usually lost in prudish translations. For example, *euruproktos* is often translated as "adulterous." It really means "having a loose asshole."

[4] In the indictment, the Greek verb for "to corrupt," *diaphtheirein*, has a sexual connotation, usually overlooked by commentators.

[5] Plato, *Sophist*, 253de.

[6] Regarding Dionysos, see my *The God of Ecstasy*, St. Martin's Press, New York, 1988.

[7] Chan, Wing-Tsit, ed., *A Source Book in Chinese Philosophy*, Princeton University Press, Princeton, NJ, 1963, p. 233.

[8] It should be noted that the word "this," when used by itself in a premise, is often mistakenly regarded as a particular. In fact, when so used, it is the most general type-word in the English language, standing for "this entity."

[9] Walt Whitman, "Native Moments" in *Leaves of Grass*.

[10] Andrea Nye, *Words of Power. A Feminist Reading of the History of Logic*, Routledge, New York, 1990.

[11] *ibid.*, p. 47.

[12] See also Lewis Hanke, *Aristotle and the American Indians*, Indiana University Press, Bloomington, 1959.

[13] Nye errs in her assessment of Greek homosexuality, repeating the old chestnut that Greek male homosexuality was the result of the subjugation of women (Nye, *op. cit.*, pp. 15; 36-37. In fact, male homosexual relations enjoyed the highest esteem in ancient Greece in those cities in which women had the greatest degree of social freedom and political power. Like many commentators, Nye mistakenly takes Plato's particular views on sexuality as typical of those of his contemporaries, and overlooks evidence from the Dionysian tradition. See my *The God of Ecstasy*, St. Martin's Press, New York, 1988.

[14] Benson Mates, *Stoic Logic*, University of California Press, Berkeley & Los Angeles, 1953.

[15] Immanuel Kant, *Critique of Pure Reason*, 2nd Edition, trans. by Max Müller, Macmillan, New York, 1925, p. 688.

[16] Greek text as in A.C. Pearson, *The Fragments of Zeno and Cleanthes*, C.J. Clay, London, 1891; reprinted by Arno Press, New York, 1973, pp. 274-275.

[17] Nye, *op. cit.*, pp. 74-75.

[18] Boethius, *The Consolation of Philosophy*, trans. by W.V. Cooper, The Modern Library, New York, 1943, p. 4.

[19] J.G. Sikes, *Peter Abailard*, Cambridge University Press, Cambridge, 1932, p. 13.

[20] *ibid.*, p. 27, n.1

[21] Peter Abelard, *Exposition of Romans*, xiii, col. 355 BC, quoted in Latin by Sikes, *op. cit.*, p. 49, n. 1.

[22] Thomas Aquinas, *Quaestiones disputatae de potentia*, Question 1, Article 3, in *Selected Philosophical Writings*, selected and translated by Timothy McDermott, Oxford University Press, New York, 1993, p. 247.

[23] Thomas Aquinas, *The Disputed Questions on Truth [Quaestiones disputatae de veritate]*, vol. 1, questions I-IX, trans. by Robert W. Mulligan, Henry Regnery Company, Chicago, 1952, pp. 186 & 192.

[24] Nye, *op. cit.*, p. 94.

[25] Quoted by Marilyn McCord Adams, *William Ockham*, vol. II, University of Notre Dame Press, Notre Dame, IN, 1987, p. 1079.

[26] *ibid.*, p. 1082.

5

The Illogic of Early Modernity

SUMMARY: This chapter shows how the mythological motifs of ancient and medieval logic influenced later logicians and philosophers. It describes how Gottfried Leibniz, George Boole, and Gottlob Frege created modern formal logic by drawing on these ancient myths.

Since its beginnings in Greece in the fifth century B.C., Western formal logic has professed to be an objective science. In reality, however, formal logic has been based on certain mythological and religious motifs, which I have called "the Parmenidean myth." As discussed in the last chapter, this myth consists of three claims first put forward by Parmenides of Elea and later amplified by numerous Western logicians: (1) there is a divinely grounded necessity that rules both human discourse and the external world (the myth of logical necessity); (2) correct deductive thinking consists in judging descriptions of reality in terms of two mutually exclusive values (the myth of bivalence); and (3) a timeless, static model of knowledge is inherently preferable to one that is dependent on personal subjectivity and feeling (the myth of absolute objectivity).

We saw that the Parmenidean myth was taken up and developed by other Western logicians and philosophers, including Socrates, Plato, Aristotle, Chrysippus, Boethius, Peter Abelard, Thomas Aquinas, and William of Ockham. This chapter will follow the Parmenidean myth as it continued into the early modern period.

The Father of Modern Logic

The first great logician of the modern era, and the one who set the basic tone for the development of much subsequent logical theory, was the German philosopher and mathematician Gottfried Wilhelm Leibniz (1646-1716).[1] Leibniz's father, a professor of moral philosophy, died when Leibniz was a young child, after which his mother married a Lutheran minister. The philosophical and religious interests of his home environment instilled in Leibniz a lifelong preoccupation with metaphysics and religion, which in turn deeply molded his philosophy of logic. Even so, however, Leibniz always retained an independent, critical perspective, as witnessed by his disdain for formal church ritual. (He refused to take communion on his death bed.)

Like many other prominent Western philosophers, Leibniz was a bachelor. Although maintaining a lively philosophical correspondence with a number of aristocratic women, he seems to have had little or no romantic interest in them. His most intimate friend was a certain John Ker of Kersland, about whom little is known.

In 1676 Leibniz became the librarian to the Duke of Hanover, Johann Friedrich, of the House of Brunswick. Leibniz continued to hold this same post throughout the remainder of his life, eventually serving the Duke's successor, Ernst August, and *his* successor, Georg Ludwig, who in 1714 became King George I of England.

During his long tenure as librarian to the Dukes of Hanover, Leibniz was unable to devote as much time as he wanted to philosophy because of his employers' insistence that he research the genealogy of the House of Brunswick, of which they were members. Despite this demand on his time, however, Leibniz was one of the most prolific writers of his age, although little of his work was published during his own lifetime. Ironically, when he died in 1716, his funeral went practically unnoticed. As with the death of Mozart in 1791, so with Leibniz in 1716, contemporaries underestimated the extraordinary genius the world had just lost.

Leibniz's most memorable accomplishment was probably the invention of the differential and integral calculus in 1676. In fact, Isaac Newton, who had invented calculus independently in England, was "scooped" by Leibniz, who published his results first. The ensuing controversy over who was the "real" inventor of calculus stirred up national passions in England and Germany. In the end, the notation developed by Leibniz turned out to be far more "user friendly" than Newton's and continues in use to this day. The English, however, stubbornly clung to Newton's clumsy symbols. As a result, most mathematical progress during the next century occurred on the continent, which had converted to Leibniz's system.

This nationalist controversy over calculus was no doubt a reason why Duke Georg Ludwig of Hanover refused to take Leibniz with him to London when he became King George I of England, and why the ducal family downplayed the importance of Leibniz's death. It was embarrassment enough that the new King of England could hardly speak English, let alone that the chief documenter of his claim to the throne was the arch intellectual rival of an English national hero.

Leibniz's philosophical work consists of a great mass of scattered essays and letters rather than one great *magnum opus*. Moreover, much of this material was not published until the 19th century; in fact, a substantial amount still remains unpublished. As a result, students of philosophy are usually exposed only to highly abbreviated résumés of Leibniz's thought, as in his *Monodology*, and rarely explore the intellectual development that underlies that essay.

Despite the diffuse format of his work and the lateness of its publication, Leibniz exercised an extraordinary influence on modern philosophy and logic, beginning in his own lifetime. Initially this influence was exercised directly, through personal contact and letter-writing. After Leibniz's death, Christian Wolff popularized a version of Leibniz's thinking in the Germany university system, which influenced Immanuel Kant.

Later, the 20th-century movements called "logical positivism" and "analytic philosophy," although reacting against German metaphysics, inherited concepts and terminology that Kant had borrowed from Leibniz. Finally, the publication of Leibniz's essays and correspondence in the 19th and 20th centuries exercised a latter-day influence on such important later logicians as Giuseppe Peano, Gottlob Frege, Bertrand Russell, and (through Russell) Ludwig Wittgenstein.

The Priority of Metaphysics

Since the time of Bertrand Russell, most modern commentators have regarded Leibniz's logical theory as the core of his thought. His metaphysical views, they say, are just a muddled extrapolation from that core. The evidence alleged for this view is that in his correspondence Leibniz often explains his metaphysical views in terms of logical concepts, giving the impression that his metaphysics is based on his logic. This interpretation, however, overlooks an important point: when Leibniz is explaining his metaphysics in terms of logic, he is usually writing to *logicians*. So it is not clear whether he is basing his metaphysics on his logic or rather just using the language of logic because that is familiar and accessible to his correspondents.

Contrary to the currently prevailing view, there are good reasons for concluding that the reverse is actually true, that is, that Leibniz's logic is actually an outgrowth of his metaphysics. For one thing, Leibniz bends or changes his logic whenever there is an evident conflict between it and his metaphysics. An example is his theory of logical relations, where he maintains that there is no such thing as a purely external relation. (That is, Leibniz argues that any relation that involves a substance can in principle be explained in terms of that substance alone, without regard to other substances.)

Modern logicians generally scoff at this notion, claiming that Leibniz simply did not understand the logical properties of relations. In fact, however, Leibniz was an admirer of the logician Joachim Jungius, whose book, *Logica Hamburgensis*, promoted a view of logical relations similar to that of the modern critics of Leibniz. Despite his admiration for Jungius, however, Leibniz rejected his view of relations.

The best evidence for the priority of Leibniz's metaphysics to his logic is a short intellectual autobiography he wrote in 1695 entitled *A New System of the Nature and the Communication of Substances*. In this essay, which is little read today, Leibniz explains how he came to hold the notions that seemed so odd both to his contemporaries and to later commentators. In most instances, he indicates that he was struggling to solve underlying metaphysical and religious questions.

Leibniz's logical theories did not just pop out of a vacuum; they were an integral part of his larger view of the nature of reality. His reflections on logic contributed to the formation of this larger view, to be sure, but there was also quite a significant flow of influence in the other direction as well. In the first part of this chapter, we will see just how close the fit was between Leibniz's logic and his metaphysics.

The Intellectual Crisis of Leibniz's Era

In order to understand Leibniz's metaphysical presuppositions, we have to know something about the intellectual crisis that confronted the Europe of his time. Beginning with the Renaissance, a string of new scientific developments had appeared that were well grounded in observation and advanced by geniuses of the caliber of Nicolaus Copernicus, Galileo Galilei, Johannes Kepler, and Isaac Newton. These developments all undermined the established academic philosophy of scholasticism that had been fashioned in the Middle Ages by Thomas Aquinas and other theologian-philosophers.

The new developments, based on plainly observable phenomena, implied that nature is mechanical and deterministic. The old scholastic tradition, however, advocated two notions of a different tenor: (1) in every kind of material substance there inheres a certain invisible "essence" or "substantial form"; and (2) individual instances of each kind of material substance act so as to exemplify the invisible essence that is peculiar to them. In other words, there exists in every kind of material substance something that is analogous to a purposive mind.

Whatever its theoretical value, the older view proved to have very little explanatory value in concrete cases. While the new mechanical theorists continued to develop impressive new systems of ever greater scope and rigor, the older scholastics seemed to flounder helplessly in an intellectual quagmire of invisible essences. The best minds of Europe increasingly came to view these essences as ghostly illusions.

Enter Descartes

Despite the mountain of ridicule heaped on the scholastics, European thought remained disturbed under its bright new veneer of modernity by certain ominous implications: if nothing exists but observable phenomena, and if all these phenomena are mechanically determined, what becomes of the inner life of the spirit? How can there be any free will? How can there be a God?

A notable effort to resolve this intellectual crisis was the work of the French philosopher and mathematician René Descartes (1596-1650). As noted in chapter three, Descartes believed there were two separate kinds of substance: *res extensa* ("extended reality" by which he meant the spread-out-ness of observable phenomena) and *res cogitans* ("thinking reality," by which he meant any form of consciousness). To Descartes, most of reality was a vast machine. He viewed human minds, on the other hand, together with God, angels, and demons, as immaterial souls. As to the knotty question of how an immaterial human mind could interact with a material body, Descartes vaguely speculated that the interaction occurred in the pituitary gland.

Believing that he had provided a convenient philosophical shelf for God, angels, demons, and human minds, Descartes proceeded to devote his attention to his real interest, extended reality. His most memorable accomplishment in this regard was his invention of analytical geometry (a combination of algebra and geometry), which he intended as a mathematical tool for analyzing extended reality. The basis of this new system of analysis, his famous "Cartesian coordinates," are well known to everyone who studies mathematics to this day.

Leibniz's Rainbow

Leibniz was dissatisfied with the entire intellectual scene of his time, including the old teachings of the scholastics, the unwelcome implications of the new mechanical theories, and Descartes' theories. As an alternative to them all, Leibniz turned to the atomic theory of matter, which had been propounded in antiquity by Leucippus and Democritus, and more recently by the French philosopher Pierre Gassendi. Leibniz was disturbed, however, by the claim that atoms were physically indivisible. (The Greek word *atoma* means "indivisibles.") In Leibniz's mind, any bit of physical matter, regardless of how small, could always be conceived as being further divided; therefore, to claim that there were tiny bits of matter that could no longer be divided was to posit the existence of something for which no sufficient reason could be given. On the other hand, though, there must be *some* principles of minimal unity somewhere; otherwise, there would be no definition of parts among phenomena, and all reality would dissolve into an undifferentiated flux.

Leibniz concluded that we must assume the existence of some kind of grounding principles for the unities we observe among physical phenomena, but that these principles could not themselves be physical; otherwise, *they* would have to be explained by other grounding principles of unity, and so on, *ad infinitum*. These postulated immaterial atoms Leibniz called "monads" (from the Greek word *monades*, meaning "units").

Leibniz reasoned that because monads, by definition, had no parts, they could not exhibit any physical changes; they either existed or not. But if this was true, then monads could never be affected by any external physical objects either. (To be affectable by a physical object means to have the capacity to show some physical effects from that object.) So if there are monads, they must be immaterial. Even more, each monad must be a complete universe unto itself, since to be part of a greater physical system means to have some interaction with it. Monads, however, have no such interactions. In Leibniz's famous metaphor—

> The monads have no windows through which anything could come in or go out.[2]

Leibniz also reasoned that monads could not come to be and pass away, because for a thing to be generated means that certain constituent parts come together to form it, and for a thing to perish means that the thing dissolves back into parts. Each monad, then, must be a separately existing universe in its own right, immaterial and eternal.

Now if monads are not physical, what are they? In a decisive break with Descartes, who believed that nature was one huge machine, Leibniz argued that everything that existed was in some degree alive and conscious. The source of this life and consciousness were the monads—an infinite number of atoms of consciousness permeating every part of the natural world. What appear to our senses as solid physical objects are mere phenomena, concluded Leibniz. They are well grounded on underlying aggregates of monads, but nonetheless derivative. Leibniz compared the seeming hardness and reality of such physical objects to the effect of a rainbow. What we see is a spectrum of colors in the sky; however, the underlying realities are innumerable drops of rain, each of which is colorless.

Although all monads exhibit consciousness, not every monad does so to the same degree. Those that do so to the highest degree, at least on the planet Earth, are human minds. As a form of self-consciousness, I am a monad, the dominant monad of a huge aggregate of monads whose collective physical appearance (like that of the rainbow) is my body. Since monads are eternal, I have always existed in some body, but not always with the same degree of consciousness I have now. And after my seeming death, I will continue to exist in some body. This continuity of my existence, however, is not some kind of reincarnation; rather, it is the world history of one and the same monad that has a continually altering body manifestation exhibiting varying degrees of consciousness.

A factor in prompting Leibniz to discard Descartes' machine-view of nature was the invention of the microscope by the Dutch scientist Anton van Leeuwenhoek. Peering through a microscope, Leibniz was amazed to see that every bit of matter he examined, regardless of how small, contained living organisms. He was particularly impressed to see that human sperm contained self-moving spermatozoa, which he thought, with typical male chauvinism, were tiny, pre-conception human beings. (He regarded the ovum as a kind of nutritional yoke.)

In view of the microscope's revelations, Leibniz rejected Descartes' view of matter as mere extension, because extension by itself cannot account for points of energy and movement, which are found in every bit of matter. Furthermore, Leibniz realized that Descartes' mathematical method, analytic geometry, was inadequate to give a quantitative description of such energy points. It was this train of metaphysical reasoning that motivated Leibniz to invent the differential and integral calculus, which *can* quantitatively describe point forces in matter.

Despite these theories, Leibniz was still faced with the knotty mind-matter problem: how can monads, which are immaterial, have any interactions with the material phenomena that are well-founded on them? With great intellectual candor, Leibniz acknowledged that they could not, just as he acknowledged that monads could not interact with each other. How, then, can there exist a coherent universe?

As discussed in chapter one, Leibniz found his bridge from "the many" to "the one" via his concept of God, whom he regarded as the original monad—the omniscient, all-powerful, all-good, necessarily existing monad. According to Leibniz, God miraculously creates and sustains from eternity two separate realms of being, that of monads and that of material phenomena, each unfolding independently according to its own kind of necessity. (The former unfolds according to reasons, the latter according to causes.) But God also establishes, pre-temporally, a harmony between these two realms, analogous to the way in which a watch maker might initially set two perfectly accurate watches to the same time, so that they will always agree thereafter. In reality, there is no real interaction between monads and phenomena, but to us mortals it always seems as if there is because of the harmony pre-established by God.

Even more, God has a concept in his mind of every monad he creates. That concept includes, down to the most minute detail, everything that will ever happen to that monad throughout the entire course of its existence. The life history of any monad, therefore, is simply the unfolding of its essence as conceived in the mind of God. Monads *appear* to interact with each other because God in his creation of them has chosen those concepts whose unfoldings are all mutually compatible in their consequences.

God also creates each monad so that it is a kind of microcosmic mirror of the entire universe, both temporally and spatially. As a result, if each monad could become completely conscious of itself, it would in the process also become completely conscious of the entire past history and future development of the universe as a whole.

Despite the mirroring power of my own consciousness, however, nothing ever really *happens* to me in my capacity as a mind. My seeming experiences both of other monads and of material phenomena are simply a string of thoughts, desires, feelings, and perceptions that unfold according to my inner nature as conceived in the mind of God. Strictly speaking, therefore, the only real relation I ever have is with God. "Every soul," Leibniz insists, "is a world apart, independent of everything else except God."[3] Without God, I and all the other monads, assuming we could still somehow exist, would constitute an infinity of separate, hermetically sealed universes totally oblivious to each other.

Although Leibniz developed his theory of monads in reaction against the various theories of the scholastics, the Cartesians, and the physical atomists, he was indebted to each of these schools. From the atomists, he borrowed the concept of material atoms, as noted above. However, he turned these atoms into monads by spiritualizing them and identifying them with the "substantial forms" of the scholastics. Against the scholastics, however, he added the proviso that the monads could have no direct explanatory value in the realm of physical phenomena. From the Cartesians he borrowed the concept of a radical dichotomy between extension and thought. Against the Cartesians, however, he added the proviso that extension has an inherently dynamic quality ultimately due to a hidden world of spiritual monads. In this way, Leibniz drew on the dominant intellectual traditions of his time in order to solve the problem of how God and the human soul could be reconciled with the new mechanistic concept of nature.

Necessary Necessities

How can Leibniz account for free will? In the realm of physical phenomena, everything is determined by mechanical causes; in the realm of spirit, everything happens according to concepts of monads in the mind of God.

In order to extricate himself from this metaphysical quandary concerning free will, Leibniz developed a theory of different kinds of necessity. This theory, *which he developed for metaphysical and religious reasons*, served as a bridge between his metaphysics and his logic. After Leibniz developed this theory of necessity, it exercised a lasting influence, directly and indirectly, on all subsequent logical theory. Eventually, logicians simply began taking this concept of necessity for granted, forgetting its metaphysical and religious origins.

To account for free will, Leibniz distinguished between four types of necessity: physical, moral, metaphysical, and hypothetical. The first type, physical necessity, is that which pertains to the chain of causes among physical phenomena. As noted, this realm is independent of the realm of monads and only appears to be its cause because of a pre-established harmony between the two realms. Hence we can put aside physical necessity as irrelevant to the question of the soul's free will.

Of the remaining three types, moral necessity is that which stems from the obligation to be morally good. Metaphysical necessity consists of the basic principles assumed by logic. Hypothetical necessity (a sort of extension of metaphysical necessity) is that which requires certain things to be the case *if* certain other things are assumed to be the case. The interplay between these three kinds of necessity—moral, metaphysical, and hypothetical—is the key to Leibniz's solution to the problem of free will, both for God and for mortals.

How did Leibniz get the rabbit of free will to pop out of the hat of four-fold necessity? The trick was not an easy one. Leibniz began by making a distinction between the *mind* and the *will* of God. In Leibniz's view, God freely exercises his *will* in choosing to follow the dictates of moral necessity, whereas moral necessity itself is something he apprehends in his *mind*. That is, God is good because he freely chooses to follow moral necessity; it is not the case that certain things are good merely because God happens to choose them.

As a result of his free choice for goodness, argues Leibniz, God decided to create the best possible world, which is the world among all possible worlds that contains the maximal amount of perfection. As part of the creation process, God examined in his mind various different possible worlds, each of which was a separate collection of logically compatible concepts of monads. (Leibniz calls them "compossible" concepts.) When God beheld the one collection of monadic concepts that included the greatest amount of perfection of all such collections, he willed that that collection should become real. In this way, God created the actual world we live in, which for this reason is the best of all possible worlds. So God acts out of free will, but his actions are necessarily good.

In his account of the way God conceptualizes monads while creating the world, Leibniz drew on old Platonic and Stoic traditions that were subsequently modified by Augustine and William of Ockham. As discussed in the last chapter, Plato had argued that there was a separate world of immaterial Forms that gave shape to the flux of reality. Augustine, Christianizing Plato, said the Forms were ideas in the mind of God which God contemplated when he freely chose to create the world. Ockham, nominalizing Augustine, said that God had ideas only of individuals, not of universals. Now Leibniz, a great admirer of Ockham, in effect asked himself this question: What do you get when you eliminate divine ideas of universals but keep divine ideas of particulars? Answer: concepts of monads. God freely chooses to create the best possible world while contemplating various possible sets of compossible concepts of monads.

Among the set of monads that God actually created are human souls. As with all monads, whatever any human soul does or experiences throughout its entire existence follows by necessity from its complete concept (or essence) in the mind of God. But what kind of necessity is this? In a certain sense, it is metaphysical necessity, since the fact that the whole contains its parts is a principle of logic. But in another, more important, sense the necessity is hypothetical, since if God had not chosen to make real a certain monad's complete concept, that monad would not exist. Therefore a human soul and its actions are hypothetically, not absolutely, necessary.

How does this view save the soul's freedom of the will? Suppose I am about to make some decision. God already knows my choice from eternity because he beholds my complete concept in his mind. As I experience my choice, it will be genuinely free; nonetheless, this choice is hypothetically necessary because God chose to create a certain monad (me) who would make just this free choice. Indeed, the fact that God created me, knowing that I would make this free choice, is the reason why my free choice contributes to making this the best of all possible worlds. So there is a certain necessity (moral) in God's creation of the world, although God acts out of free will, just as there is a certain necessity (hypothetical) in my choices, although my choices are free.

Does Leibniz's trick succeed in pulling the rabbit of free will out of the hat of necessity? Hardly. For one thing, Leibniz's principal metaphysical premise is that all reality is a product of God's consciousness and will. If this is so, however, what is the difference between God's concept of a monad and the monad as actually existing? Leibniz would say that the difference lies in

God's free choice to bring the monad into existence, after conceiving of its concept in his mind. But how does an actual monad differ from its concept in the mind of God *after* God has chosen to bring the monad into existence? There can only be a real difference here if existence itself is something that is not strictly the same as God. But this distinction Leibniz denies, for he believes, with Aquinas, that God is that being whose essence *is* existence. The upshot is that Leibniz muddies the difference between a monad and its concept in the mind of God, and so reduces existing things to mere manifestations of God. (In this respect, he resembles his philosophical opposite, Spinoza.)

Another problem is Leibniz's assumption that it is meaningful to speak of complete concepts for entities that are functioning in time. If, in the example above, my choice is genuinely free, then it is unclear how there can be a complete concept of me *before* I make such a choice. The concepts that we make of things in actual life cannot be complete unless the things captured by the concepts are past or timeless or dead. For things that are still functioning in time, we require *open* concepts, that is, concepts that are tentative and subject to further amendment, depending on what actually happens. To say there must be complete concepts for temporally functioning entities, because such concepts exist for nontemporal entities in mathematics, is like saying there must be colored objects for blind people because they exist for people who can see. In reality, what Leibniz has done is to take a mathematical idea (closed concepts) out of its ordinary context and made it bear extraordinary philosophical weight in contexts where it is not at all appropriate. Perhaps such a new usage can ultimately be justified, but Leibniz cannot simply assume it is with further ado, especially when doing so yields such paradoxical results.

Logic and the Logos, Again

Of the four kinds of necessity postulated by Leibniz, the most important, both for his own system and for the future development of logical theory, are metaphysical necessity and hypothetical necessity. As we have seen, hypothetical necessity is merely the metaphysical necessity that obtains *if* certain things are assumed to be the case. The crux, therefore, is metaphysical necessity. But what makes metaphysical necessity so necessary?

Like all his great predecessors in logic since the time of Parmenides, Leibniz grounds the force of metaphysical necessity (or logical necessity, as it later came to be called) in the divine nature. In particular, he draws on the metaphysics of his hero William of Ockham. As noted, Ockham had argued that the Logos, or second person of the Holy Trinity, is the ultimate ground of logic, containing eternal ideas of all individuals (but no universals).

Drawing on this metaphysical tradition, Leibniz declares that the mind of God contains and determines the grounds of all necessity. This assimilation of all necessity to logical necessity, and of logical necessity to the mind of God, comes easy to Leibniz, because he regards all reality as a manifestation of the mind of God.

In particular, Leibniz says there are certain logical principles (such as the laws of contradiction, excluded middle, and identity) that are inherent attributes of the mind of God. As such, these principles necessarily determine what is possible and impossible for all thought and all being. They are the parameters of what God thinks, and what God thinks is reality. As Leibniz says in his *Monadology*:

> The divine understanding is the region of the eternal truths and of the ideas on which they depend, and without them there would not be anything real in the possibles... If there is to be any reality in the essences or possibles, that is, in the necessary truths, this reality must be founded in the existence of the necessary being whose essence implies its existence.[4]

In short, logical necessity is necessary because it is divine. Previous chapters have shown that this is the same basic answer given in one form or another by Western logicians from Parmenides to William of Ockham. In fact, Leibniz's version is simply another Christianized restatement of the old Parmenidean myth.

Two Kinds of Proof and Truth

Leibniz combines this traditional view of logical necessity with his own peculiar theory of complete monadic concepts to develop a distinctive theory of logical proof. Since, by definition, a monad's complete concept includes all that can be truly predicated of the monad, the proof of any theorem involving the monad's concept must be analytic. That is, the proof must be true by virtue of an analysis of the meanings of the terms involved. The proof must also be *a priori*. That is, true regardless of particular facts that happen to be observed in the world. In addition, Leibniz believes the whole history of the universe is contained in the concept of every monad. The implication of all this: anything that occurs in the universe can in principle be deductively proven from the complete concept of any monad.

Leibniz, then, is the quintessential "rationalist." He believes that it is possible in principle (although not necessarily practical) to dispense with knowledge about particular contingent facts in order to know the truth about reality.

Despite his rationalist bias, however, Leibniz admits empirical observation through the back door. His escape clause: only the infinite mind of God can know the complete concept of any monad. We human beings must rely on induction in addition to deduction when we pursue the truth (because of our limitations, not because of the nature of reality). Hence our proofs concern existing physical phenomena, not monadic concepts, and are based on observation. They are at most probable, never certain.

Despite these limitations, however, when we reason about formal logical principles themselves, we can attain the same deductive certainty as God attains in his knowledge of monadic concepts. Why? Because in this area, says Leibniz, God illuminates our minds, enabling us to behold the metaphysical binding-power contained in such formal principles. Illuminated in this way, we can know that any proposition of the form "*AB is A*" is true in all possible worlds. However, a true proposition about some particular existing monad is true because a certain possible world happens to exist, namely, the world that God actually created.

This analysis of necessity and truth leads Leibniz to his famous dictum that all truths are either truths of reason or truths of fact. That is, from the standpoint of any finite mind, any true proposition is true because it falls into one of two mutually exclusive categories: either (1) it is a principle of logic or follows analytically and *a priori* from some principle of logic; or (2) the state of affairs that it postulates happens to be observed to be the case. (From God's viewpoint, as just noted, every truth is a truth of reason.)

Now to say that truths of reason are either principles of logic or deducible from truths of logic is the same as to say to that they are tautologies. (Their truth depends solely on the formal relations among their terms.) Therefore, Leibniz concludes that any true proposition is either a tautology or the description of a particular empirical fact. This classification in turn implies that mathematics, which consists of deductions about formal relations and not about particular facts, is reducible in principle to logic.

Back to Leibniz?

Immanuel Kant later amended Leibniz's classification of propositions. Kant argued that there exists a third kind of proposition. Like tautologies, these propositions are necessary, but like empirical descriptions, they are not deducible from logical principles. Kant called them "synthetic *a priori* judgments." An example: "Everything that we perceive is in space and time."

Later, logical positivists rejected Kant's amendment with their famous battle cry of "Back to Leibniz!" In making this cry, they did not intend to embrace the baroque metaphysical system that led Leibniz to articulate his distinction in the first place. Nonetheless, any such distinction rests on a host of underlying metaphysical presuppositions, as we have just seen.

The Dream of an Ideal Logical Language

Leibniz's metaphysics of complete monadic concepts led him to postulate a certain kind of knowing process as an ideal for the human mind. Although we cannot, like God, ever know any monad's complete concept, we *can* form nominal concepts of certain classes of phenomena, and from these nominal concepts deduce certain necessary logical consequences. Following the example of William of Ockham, Leibniz argues that the "universals" that these nominal concepts represent are not any kind of real being, since only individuals (that is, monads) are real beings; nonetheless, the nominal concepts are useful because they serve as "abbreviations of speech" (*compendia loquendi*). On the basis of these nominal concepts, we can draw conclusions about the world, compare the conclusions to actual experience, and further refine the concepts, depending on what we observe.

For example, suppose we postulate a class of phenomena named "human being," and characterize it as "the class of featherless bipeds." We conclude (with correct logic but erroneous original definition) that plucked chickens are human beings. Comparing this conclusion to what we actually observe in the world, we are naturally led to revise our original characterization of "human being" to, say, "the class of animals dominated by war-making males." From this characterization we draw certain other conclusions that we compare with additional observations, and so on.

Using such a method, we can construct deductive scientific systems, provided we bear in mind that the initial concepts on which such systems are based are nominal and incomplete, and so open to further revision. The more knowledgeable we become by using this method, the more closely our nominal concepts approximate to complete monadic concepts. This process, if carried to infinity, would gain for us God's knowledge of the world.

Leibniz's emphasis on nominal-concept formation and deductive reasoning in science led him to examine the role of human language in carrying out these functions. He came to the conclusion that the linguistic grammar of any natural human language is quite different from its logical grammar, and that the former typically obscures the latter. For example, the proper use of case endings for Latin nouns follows a bewildering pattern of *ad hoc* rules that bear little relation to the actual logical relationships in which the concepts denoted by these nouns occur.

Inspired by the ideal of God's analytic knowledge of complete concepts, Leibniz decided to try and invent an artificial language whose syntax would mirror logical relations, and whose primitive terms would denote simple nominal concepts. A language so structured, Leibniz thought, would be universally applicable to all the sciences, since all reality and all human reasoning are governed by patterns of necessity existing in the mind of God.

Leibniz dubbed this proposed ideal language a "universal sign-system" (*characteristica universalis*). Leibniz's own experiments in this direction show that he was groping toward what is today called "symbolic logic" (that is, the fusion of algebraic symbolism with logical analysis).

Leibniz's beliefs in these matters have influenced most modern logicians. Like Leibniz, they make the following three assumptions: (1) there is ultimately but one reality; (2) this reality is describable, at least in principle, by one comprehensive science; and (3) there is one pattern of humanly-expressible necessity common to both reality and science. The principal difference between Leibniz and his modern imitators is that Leibniz himself examined these underlying mythical assumptions explicitly and critically. His modern successors, on the other hand, generally take these assumptions for granted as if they were obvious truths. Contrary to the hopes of logicians, however, the first several chapters of this book have shown that these assumptions are all false.

The Ghost of Leibniz

Leibniz inherited and reinforced the Parmenidean myth as it had been modified by William of Ockham, but gave it his own special twist. His twist represents a major turning point in the history of Western thought, and has had a tremendous impact on modern thought.

To understand the Leibnizian twist, we recall from the last chapter that prior to William of Ockham the Parmenidean myth included the three sub-myths of logical necessity, bivalence, and absolute objectivity. Ockham embellished this mythical system by repudiating Aristotle's essences as useless fictions. In addition, he argued that a truth-functional logical calculus is possible, and that all human knowledge derives from only two kinds of direct intuition, that of empirical facts and that of logical necessity.

Leibniz, for his part, sought to develop an all-inclusive metaphysical ground for Christianity, the new mechanistic sciences, and mathematics. He also sought to include in this synthesis as much of an Ockhamist-style logic as was compatible with this system's basic metaphysics. Faced with this daunting project, Leibniz believed he had found a golden key: the notion that reality consists of ultimate simples defined by concepts in the mind of God, a notion first suggested by Ockham.

These metaphysical presuppositions led Leibniz to emphasize the overriding importance of *analysis*. Since all reality consists of ultimate simples, Leibniz reasoned, the knowing process must be a matter of analyzing seeming complexities into their constituent simple elements. If we only had enough intellectual power and enough time, our analyses would eventually lead us to an understanding of those concepts that define both the mind of the one true God and the objective nature of the one true reality. Even so, however, we can make ever closer approximations to this ideal by having clear perceptions of ever more distinctly defined phenomena, and by using a truth-functional logical calculus that displays logical form.

Leibniz's twist, then, to the Parmenidean myth is the extraordinary stress he placed on *analysis*. In maintaining this stress, he put his finger on what was to become one of the deepest pulse-beats of patriarchal-industrial civilization—the bias that to divide and specialize is to know and conquer reality. From assembly lines with precisely defined repeatable chores, to universities with endlessly subdivided specialties, to alienated human souls fragmented into isolated, competing desires, the brave new industrial world that the mind of Leibniz helped inaugurate relentlessly applied the principle of divide and conquer to every aspect of life.

In contrast, say, to the great philosophical systems of ancient India or the beliefs of the American Indians, Leibniz's new style stressed the importance of analyzing wholes into parts as *the* key to understanding all reality. The other half of the coin, the importance of integrating parts into encompassing wholes, disappeared from view. Combined with the ancient Parmenidean myth onto which it was grafted, the Leibnizian twist strongly reinforced the emerging world-view of modernity: there is one objective reality for everyone, and this reality is best captured through dissections carried out by unfeeling, technically trained specialists.

The philosophical presuppositions that Leibniz provided for the growth of modern logical theory were thoroughly mythical and even religious; in addition, they were also *false*. Despite its flaws, however, Leibniz's system remains worthy of study and reflection. It represents a great intellectual achievement that has had a lasting historical impact, and that is the best that can be said for any philosophical system.

The baroque metaphysician Gottfried Wilhelm Leibniz has, ironically, turned out to be the single most important influence on 20th-century Anglo-American academic philosophy. I say "ironically" because many of the philosophers influenced by him have been loath to acknowledge his intellectual paternity, behaving in this regard like the young Hamlet when first confronted with stories about his father's ghost. This reluctance is in part due to plain ignorance, since many modern Anglo-American academic philosophers are poorly read in the history of philosophy. But to an equal degree this reluctance is also due to a sense of embarrassment. After all, these same philosophers are the ones who have most loudly and hard-nosedly proclaimed the death of metaphysics; yet many of their most cherished assumptions were first given classic expression by this *grande dame* of Western metaphysics. Seeking to dissociate their intellectual pedigree from the embarrassment of Leibniz's metaphysics, these modern academic philosophers resemble the family of George I of England. They were equally embarrassed that the great intellectual enemy of Newton had been the one to authenticate their own claim to the English throne. Despite the ingratitude of both these groups of parvenus, the ghost of Leibniz continues to haunt the corridors of Western thought until this very day.

A Boolean Bump on the Leibnizian Twist

The first serious attempt to realize Leibniz's dream of a precise mathematical notation for logic occurred 131 years after his death, in 1847. In that year, the English mathematician George Boole (1815-1864) published his essay *The Mathematical Analysis of Logic*, followed in 1854 by *An Investigation of the Laws of Thought*. These works influenced many subsequent logicians and mathematicians, becoming the basis for the various calculuses later known as "Boolean logic" or "Boolean algebra."

Although an admirer of Leibniz, Boole was apparently unfamiliar with the details of his predecessor's suggestions for a system of logical notation. Nonetheless Boole endorsed the new spirit imparted by the "Leibnizian twist" to the old Parmenidean myth, namely, the enthusiasm for *analysis* as the golden key for understanding reality and human thought. As we are about to see, however, Boole managed to impart to the Leibnizian twist a special turn of his own.

Like all his predecessors on the subject, Boole grounded the presuppositions of his logic in the realm of myth and religion. In the spirit of Leibniz in particular, Boole held that the Parmenidean myth was true because of pre-established harmonies rooted in God:

> It consists with all that we know of the uniformity of Nature, and all that we believe of the immutable constancy of the Author of Nature, to suppose, that in the mind...there should exist a harmony and uniformity not less real than that which the study of the physical sciences makes known to us.[5]

But once having made this dutiful obeisance to God, Boole proceeded to make an important break with his predecessors: although God in theory is the ground of all order, for all practical purposes the basis of the order in logic is the human mind. Quite apart from what we may believe about God, Boole argued, we can know for certain, merely by examining our own thought processes, that some things must necessarily be true in logic. Therefore a sufficient working foundation for our belief in the basic principles of logic is our own immediate intuition of the workings of our own minds. As a result of such reflections, Boole called his work on logic *An Investigation of the Laws of Thought*, since he believed that logic merely clarifies the laws by which we think.

In practice, then, although not completely so in theory, Boole replaced the mind of God with the human mind as the foundation of logical necessity. Despite this change, however, Boole still believed that some absolute foundation had to be found for logical necessity.

Some later logicians have accused Boole of "psychologism"—that is, of mistakenly basing the verities of logic on empirical generalizations about the human mind. In fact, however, Boole did not regard his "laws of thought" as the equivalent of empirical generalizations. To the contrary, Boole held that we possess a unique cognitive ability, that of directly intuiting the general truths of logic—*even from one particular instance.*

As noted, Boole believed that the laws of logic have a divine source above and beyond their particular manifestations in the human mind. Following the example of Leibniz and Augustine, Boole claimed that we possess an inner God-given light. This light enables us to behold the workings of logical principles in our own minds, even from one particular instance. This view is not psychologistic at all, but one based squarely on traditional Platonic-Christian metaphysics.

The Bridge from Mathematics to Logic

In the spirit of Plato, Boole considered mathematics to be the ideal model of knowledge. As we have just seen, however, he also regarded logic as an absolute. There must then be some link, he concluded, between mathematics and logic, since both are absolutes, and since all absolutes eventually converge in the unity of God.

Boole believed he found the connecting link between mathematics and logic in the principle of bivalence. Specifically, he realized that if the elementary equations of algebra are restricted to only two values, 0 and 1, then many known algebraic operations can be used as a calculus for doing logical deductions.

An example: let 0 equal the null class (the class with no objects in it), and let 1 equal the universal class (the class with every object in it). Then if we let x stand for any class at all, $1-x$ will represent its complementary class (the class of all other objects not contained in itself). The product of these two classes (the class consisting of the objects common to both) will be represented by the formula $x(1-x) = 0$. From this formula, we obtain $x^2 = x$, which means that if a second class is formed consisting of nothing but members of a first class, the second class will have as members only the members of the first class.

Boole foreshadowed the abiding interest of many later Anglo-American academic philosophers in "ordinary language." As we have seen, Boole was committed to a belief in God and the absolute operations of the human mind as the foundations of logical necessity. Nonetheless, Boole felt that we could study the underlying forms of "ordinary language" or "the language of common discourse" in order to uncover instances of these universal laws. In actual practice, Boole commonly used "ordinary language" as the standard against which to test the adequacy of his own logical formulations, much as his successors have done. As a working logician, then, Boole tended to slide down the metaphysical pole from God to the human mind to "ordinary language."

The Myth of "Ordinary Language"

That which Boole and many of his successors have revered as "ordinary language" is actually an amalgam of cultural eccentricities specific to some particular historical epoch. This amalgam is littered with the debris of broken-down metaphysical systems from the past.

For example, consider the English word "quality" and its equivalents in other European languages. Today this word is widely regarded as a member in good standing of the ordinary-language club. Prior to the fifth century B.C., however, the ancient equivalent of this word was unknown in the West. Both the word and the concept it covers were first *invented* by the philosopher Plato in his dialogue *Theaetetus*. Anyone who reads this work can see that Plato had great difficulty in explaining this new word to his puzzled contemporaries.[6]

In the "ordinary language" that existed before Plato wrote *Theaetetus*, the word "quality" did not exist. Therefore, any logical system that might have developed based on "ordinary language" before *Theaetetus* would have been seriously lacking. How, then, do we know that there will not yet be other Platos in *our* future who will invent words and concepts that will render our current ordinary-language logic outmoded?

There's another side to the problem. Modern philosophers who assume that formal logic must answer to the word "quality" take for granted the complicated metaphysical arguments offered by Plato to justify this new word and the concept it covers. Indeed, broken-down strains of ancient Greek metaphysics *saturate* contemporary Western "ordinary language." To take this "ordinary language" as a standard is to validate the inherited metaphysical debris on which it is based. To most logicians, this debris is invisible, as water is to fish.

There is nothing wrong with taking some "ordinary language" as a datum of experience, and then trying, as a kind of intellectual game, to express its basic concepts in logical formalism. But neither Boole nor his successors have been satisfied with such a modest description of their work. Uncritically accepting a mishmash of inherited broken-down metaphysical prejudices, they proclaim their logical systems as standards of right-reasoning.

The myths of logical necessity, bivalence, and absolute objectivity can no more be validated by "ordinary language" than they can be by the goddess far-constraining Order, Zeus, the Logos, God, or the nature of the human mind. And for good reason, since all these myths are fallacious.

Boole's Piecemeal System

Although Boole made progress in adapting some mathematical methods to logic, his overall system was of a piecemeal, *ad hoc* nature. For one thing, he created two parallel, tenuously connected, logics: on the one hand, a logic of *classes*; on the other, a logic of *propositions*, itself based on a scheme of classes of time-periods. Another weakness of his system was that it could not express relations (as opposed to simple subject-predicate propositions) or the basic theorems of arithmetic.

Despite these drawbacks, however, Boole's system had the merit of using an existing set of familiar algebraic symbols. Consequently, his system was easily accessible to both logicians and mathematicians. Ironically, however, this congeniality of symbolism caused a problem: Boole's system long overshadowed a far superior system developed by the true intellectual heir to Leibniz, and indeed the greatest logician since Aristotle, Gottlob Frege (1848-1925).

The Life and Values of Gottlob Frege

Gottlob Frege was born in the northern German town of Wismar, located by an inlet of the Mecklenburg Bay, in 1848. This was a time of great revolutionary upheaval in Europe, whose legacy he later opposed. His parents were petty-bourgeois Lutherans, both teachers. Inspired by the example of his parents, the young Frege adopted the life of an academic careerist. First he studied science and mathematics at the Universities of Jena and Göttingen. Later he became a mathematics instructor in Jena in 1873, where he remained for most of his life.[7]

While teaching at Jena, Frege acquired the reputation of being an authoritarian and uncommunicative instructor. The remarks of one of Frege's most celebrated pupils, the German logical positivist Rudolf Carnap, attest to this fact:

He seldom looked at the audience. Ordinarily we only saw his back, while he drew the strange diagrams of his symbolism on the blackboard and explained them. Never did a student ask a question or make a remark, whether during the lecture or afterwards. The possibility of a discussion seemed to be out of the question.[8]

While at Jena, Frege married Margaret Lieseburg. After all their children died young, the couple decided to adopt a boy, Alfred, in 1900, when Frege was 52. After Frege's death in 1925, Alfred took pains to collect and preserve his adopted father's papers, and was himself killed during World War II while fighting on behalf of the Nazis.

Although many Anglo-American academic philosophers admire Gottlob Frege for his contributions to logic, there is a darker side to his personality. British Frege scholar Michael Dummett has revealed incriminating parts of Frege's personal diary. Its contents were withheld by Frege's German editors from his published collected works:

> The diary shows Frege to have been a man of extreme right-wing political opinions, bitterly opposed to the parliamentary system, democrats, liberals, Catholics, the French, and, above all, Jews, who he thought ought to be deprived of political rights and, preferably, expelled from Germany.[9]

Today most Anglo-American academic philosophers argue that these views are irrelevant when Frege is considered as a logician. We will see later, however, that the issue is not to be so tidily resolved.

Taking Up the Dreams of Leibniz

Frege was impressed by Leibniz's unfulfilled dream of creating a new logical notation that would serve as a "universal sign-system" (*characteristica universalis*, as discussed above).[10] Although Leibniz and Frege used slightly different terms, the underlying idea was the same: to create an artificial language that would clearly depict the logical form of any argument expressed in it. Such a language was to be not only a "logical calculus" (*calculus ratiocinator*) but also a universal means for expressing the propositions of mathematics and the natural sciences with absolute clarity.

Frege was also impressed by a second dream of Leibniz's, that of reducing arithmetic to logic. Frege hoped to demonstrate in detail how the concept of number and numerical properties in general could be deduced from purely logical concepts, an aspiration now known as "logicism." When Frege began work on this dream, he realized that the existing logical notation of his day was inadequate for expressing the required logical proofs. So he set about inventing an entirely new type of logical notation. In the process, Frege created the first comprehensive system of what is today called "symbolic logic." Here again Frege paralleled the example of Leibniz. Just as Leibniz had invented the infinitesimal calculus while trying to ground the study of physical dynamics, so Frege invented symbolic logic while trying to ground arithmetic. Behind both endeavors lay a common assumption: reality ultimately consists of one single, absolutely-objective system, ruled by a small set of supreme logical principles, and expressible in one universal formal language.

Logicism vs. Psychologism

Frege was eager to reduce arithmetic to logic because of a growing anti-Leibnizian intellectual current of his time. He regarded this current, which he called "psychologism," as a subversive threat to both logic and mathematics. This threat, as perceived by Frege, was the failure of empiricist philosophers to distinguish the objective, public content of logical concepts from the subjective, private impressions that might be associated with them.

Frege vehemently insisted that the content of any assertible concept is different from the circumstances of its emergence; therefore, the concept is judgeable independent of time and subjectivity. Frege sharply distinguished between "ideas" (*Vorstellungen*), which are private and subjective, and "concepts" (*Begriffe*), which are shared, objective, and judgeable as true or false. Frege regarded these shared, objective, and judgeable concepts as the proper province of logic, mathematics, and the sciences.

Frege was especially upset at the British empiricist philosopher John Stuart Mill and the German psychologist and historian Benno Erdmann. Contrary, however, to what many Anglo-American academic philosophers today believe, Frege never made such a charge against the

English logician George Boole, although he criticized Boole for the technical deficiencies of his logical notation. The reason Frege did not accuse Boole of psychologism is that Boolean logic, as we saw above, claims an absolute, metaphysical basis for logic; it is *not* based on psychological or empirical principles, although modern commentators often misconstrue it to that effect.[11] In fact, as we will later see, there is actually a parallel between Boole's and Frege's concept of the intuition of logical truth.

Concept-Script

In 1879 Frege published an epochal book *Begriffsschrift*, meaning *Concept-Script* (also translated as *Conceptual Notation* or *Ideography*).[12] Apparently impressed by the use of simple strokes in Chinese ideograms to convey meaning, Frege reduced all the operations of logic to five elemental operations, each represented by its own stroke or symbol set. For example, he used an elbow-shaped stroke for material implication ("if *a*, then *b*"). Again, he used a concave stroke combined with Gothic letters for universal judgment (as in "for all *a*, *a* is such and such").

Combining these strokes and symbol sets in various ways, Frege constructed elaborate, two-dimensional logical proofs that were read from the bottom up, and which resembled electrical diagrams. And in fact, Frege's approach to logic paved the way for the later development of programming languages for computers, for these languages are nothing more than various systems of formal logic embodied in electrical circuitry.

Because of Frege's novel symbolism, which is forbidding at first but simple once mastered, critics of the day generally ignored or panned *Concept-Script*. Those who deigned to mention it compared it unfavorably to Boole's system, which was more "user-friendly" because of its reliance on familiar algebraic symbols. Moreover, Frege had failed, perhaps because he was ignorant of Boole's work, to show how his notation could express important logical relations that were impossible in Boole's. Hence what is today regarded as one of the most significant works in logic since the time of Aristotle went for years practically unnoticed.

Disappointed by the unenthusiastic response to *Concept-Script*, Frege wrote a number of follow-up papers for scholarly journals, showing the superiority of his system over Boole's. His disappointment only deepened when editors rejected the papers as below the professional standards of the time, even though they are now regarded as far superior to anything that was then appearing in print on the subject. (Then, as now, the last place to find genuinely innovative work in philosophy was in professional philosophical journals.)

Later Works on Arithmetic

Despite indifference from his colleagues, Frege persisted in the pursuit of his logicist dreams. In 1884 he published *The Foundations of Arithmetic*. The book aimed to show, in general terms, how all the concepts and operations that seem to be distinctly arithmetical can be reduced to strictly logical concepts and operations.[13] Finally, in 1893, he published the first of his monumental two-volume work, *The Basic Laws of Arithmetic*. The work sought to prove, step by step and with absolute rigor, how arithmetic could be deduced from five logical axioms. Four of these axioms he held to be self-evident, and the fifth, although seemingly complicated, he called "a law of pure logic."[14]

This last axiom, Frege's famous "Basic Law V," states that two different concepts define the same class of objects if and only if it is the case that whatever object is characterized by one concept is also characterized by the other. For example, consider the following two quite different concepts: (1) "animal whose male sex is the most violent sex of any species"; and (2) "talking, featherless biped." Although differing from each other, each of these concepts in reality defines the same class, namely the class of objects that are human beings. Why? Because (apparently!) if any particular object is characterized by one of these concepts it is also characterized by the other.

Basic Law V implies that we can arbitrarily define any class by stipulating some concept. This law is crucial for Frege because the particular proofs he uses for reducing arithmetic to logic require that he be able to equate speaking about concepts with speaking about their associated objects, and this law allows him to do just that.

Chapter Five

A Fly in the Logicist Ointment

With the publication of volume one of *The Basic Laws of Arithmetic*, Frege felt he was well on the way toward providing a logical foundation for arithmetic. He was convinced that no one who understood his concepts could deny his conclusions. With great bravado he challenged anyone to do a better job, spelling out what he meant by "better":

> As a refutation in this I can only recognize someone's actually demonstrating either that a better, more durable edifice can be erected upon other fundamental convictions, or else that my principles lead to manifestly false conclusions. But no one will be able to do that.[15]

Unfortunately for Frege, however, one of the few people who recognized his greatness, a then obscure British philosopher named Bertrand Russell, was able to rise to this challenge. Just as Frege was preparing to have the second volume of *The Basic Laws of Arithmetic* printed in 1902, he received a short letter from Russell informing him that Russell had been able to deduce a contradiction from Frege's Basic Law V.

Russell's famous objection, now known as "the Russell paradox" goes like this: Frege's Basic Law V implies that we can arbitrarily define any class by stipulating some concept. If this implication is correct, then it must be possible for us to define a class, say, by the concept "class that does not belong to itself." (For example, the class of wife-battering men is not itself a wife-battering man). Likewise, it must be possible for us to define another class, which we will call "class x," by the concept "the class of all classes that do not belong to themselves." Having defined these two classes by concepts, let us also ask ourselves this further question: "Does class x belong to itself?" If so, then class x does not belong to itself, which is a contradiction. But if not, then class x does belong to itself, which is also a contradiction. Here we have found a case where the definition of classes by concept-stipulation leads to a contradiction. Basic Law V cannot be a basic law.

Frege was devastated by Russell's letter and hastily added an appendix to the second volume, trying to patch things up. In his effort to do so, he implied that he originally had some doubts about Basic Law V after all:

> I have never concealed from myself its lack of self-evidence which the others possess, and which must properly be demanded of a law of logic, and in fact I pointed out this weakness in the Introduction to the first volume.[16]

This is a self-serving misrepresentation, however. Frege had earlier claimed that even if other logicians might be hesitant about Basic Law V, if they pondered the matter, they would see that it is "a law of pure logic." In any case, Frege used the appendix to propose various changes in his system in order to circumvent the Russell paradox, none of which really worked. Interestingly, one solution that would have worked—abandoning the law of the excluded middle—Frege could not bring himself to adopt, since he feared it would make logic too complicated.

In his later years, Frege abandoned the logicist position. Instead, he adopted the quasi-Kantian view that numbers are derivable from geometry, which in turns depends on a direct intuition of a mode of reality. Ironically, however, Frege's original logicist position was then taken up by Bertrand Russell, his critic. Russell correctly regarded Frege as the greatest logician of the age, and believed that the uncovered paradox was correctable.

From 1910 to 1913, Russell, assisted by Alfred North Whitehead, published the magnificent three-volume series *Principia Mathematica*. The series sought to fuse the logical insights of Frege with the symbolic notation of Giuseppe Peano in a new effort to deduce arithmetic from purely logical principles.

Principia quickly established Russell as the greatest English-writing philosopher of the twentieth century; nonetheless, it too was eventually found to contain fatal flaws. In fact, the work falls short of the rigor displayed earlier by Frege's *Basic Laws*. The collapse of this, the second great attempt to realize the logicist dream, is largely responsible for the philosophical crisis that continues to haunt contemporary mathematics (discussed in greater detail in chapter three).

The Function of a Function

Although Frege failed in his efforts to reduce arithmetic to logic, he achieved great success in clarifying certain basic notions in logic and mathematics. Ironically, Frege himself viewed these clarifications as merely subsidiary preparations toward the greater goal of establishing arithmetic on indubitable foundations. To later generations, however, these preparatory clarifications are what have proven to be of lasting value.

The key to Frege's clarification of logic lay in his concept of *function*. He took this concept from mathematics, refined it, and then applied it to logic. In order to understand Frege's revolution in logic, we need first to examine his refinement of the notion of mathematical function.

In simplest terms, a mathematical function can be understood as a relationship that is specified by a formula containing a symbol or symbols for unknown quantities. For example, the formula "$y = x^2$" specifies a certain relationship between two unknown quantities: the first quantity is always the square of the second.

Mathematicians often employ a loose terminology in speaking of functions, referring, for example, to the x in x^2 as an "indefinite number" or a "variable." Against this looseness of terminology, Frege insisted that there is no such thing as an indefinite or variable number. Every number has its own definite and unique properties.

Frege argued that the "x" in "x^2" is a placeholder for inserting some definite number. When a number is inserted into "x", another number is generated according to a rule. The result is that a sequence of pairs of numbers is generated: (1,1); (2,4); (3,9); etc. None of these numbers is indefinite or variable.

Frege called the definite number that is put into the place marked by "x," the "argument"; the number that is specified as a result of this placement, the "value"; and the sequence of correlated numbers thus obtained from the relation, the "course of values" (*Werthverlauf*).

Are We Saturated Yet?

Frege argued that the essential feature of any function is that it is "unsaturated" (*ungesättig*), whereas everything else that is not a function is "saturated" (*gesättig*). Frege borrowed these phrases from chemistry, where they are used to indicate the chemical bonding properties of atoms.

An atom that has lost one of its electrons is said to be unsaturated. Its search for an electron to restore its overall neutral electrical charge leads it to combine with other atoms. A saturated atom, on the other hand, is a previously unsaturated one that has gained a missing electron by sharing the electron of another atom. This bonding process creates a stable chemical unit with properties of its own over and above those of its constituents.

Just as an unsaturated atom can bond with other atoms to yield different chemical results, so a mathematical function can bond with various numbers to yield different numbers. This metaphor has persisted into current English usage, with the saying that arguments "satisfy" functions. In fact, the German verb *sättigen*, from which both *ungesättigt* and *gesättig* are derived, also means "to satisfy."

This was Frege's revolution: he expanded the concept of function beyond the limits of mathematics, and applied it to objects and sentences in logic. For example, consider the sentence-formula "x is homophobic" (Frege did not actually use this example). This formula is unsaturated, just like a mathematical formula. When we substitute the name of some object in the place marked by "x," the sentence-formula becomes saturated, as in "Pope John Paul II is homophobic."

What, then, is the *value* that corresponds to each name that is substituted for "x"? According to Frege, any sentence that is created this way must be either true or false, and nothing else; therefore, the value of such a generated sentence is what Frege calls a "truth-value," or, more accurately, "the True" or "the False." So our sentence-formula "x is homophobic" will generate a series of paired, determinate values, just like a mathematical function. For example: (Pope John-Paul II, the True); (Walt Whitman, the False); (Adolf Hitler, the True); (Gertrude Stein, the False); (Anita Bryant, the True); etc. In sum: we can construe all concepts as functions, and we can construe the relation of an object's falling under a concept as that object's saturating a function.

A functional analysis of sentences allows us to deal with sentences that are not strictly of the subject-predicate form, which is difficult in Aristotelian logic. For example, the sentence-formula, "x is bigger than y but smaller than z" is inadmissible as such in Aristotelian logic. It must be converted into a clumsy, fictitious form, part of which is arbitrarily designated as the subject, and the remainder as the predicate. Under a functional analysis, however, this sentence-formula is straightforward, generating truth-values for the various sets of object-names that are substituted in place of "x", "y," and "z."

As this example suggests, a functional analysis of sentences permits a logical analysis of arithmetical sentences, which is impossible under Aristotelian logic. And, in fact, it was precisely because Frege wanted to have a logic powerful enough to express arithmetical relations (for the further purpose of reducing arithmetic to logic) that he turned to a functional analysis of logic.

Sense and Reference

In his fully developed logical theory, Frege made a distinction between "sense" (*Sinn*) and "reference" (*Bedeutung*). He came to this distinction through his efforts to clarify the nature of identity sentences.

Consider the following identity sentence: "The morning star is the evening star." What is the nature of the identity asserted by this sentence? To answer this question, Frege replies that we must distinguish between that which is asserted by any phrase (the sense) and the thing about which an assertion is made (the reference). In our example, that which is asserted is the conceptual content of the phrases "the morning star" and "the evening star." The thing about which the assertion is made is the planet Venus. The word "is" indicates that the conceptual contents of "the morning star" and "the evening star" refer to one and the same thing, namely the planet Venus. The identity of our sentence is provided by the reference, which anchors the senses of two different phrases.

Ironically, Frege's distinction between sense and reference is more lucid in English translations than in the original German. The reason is that the translation of "reference" for *Bedeutung* is really an over-simplification; that's why readers may see the word translated as "meaning," "significance," etc. The German verb *bedeuten*, from which the noun *Bedeutung* is derived, has two different meanings: (1) "to signify," in the sense of "refer to" (hence the usual English translation of *Bedeutung* as "reference"); and (2) "to be of importance" or "to be meaningful."

Frege often plays on this double meaning of *Bedeutung* as both that which is referred to and as that which is important or meaningful. He does so because of a crucial assumption underlying his entire approach to mathematics: a concept's *reference*, as opposed to the concept itself, is the thing that is really *important* or meaningful. Therefore, says Frege, we can replace assertions about concepts with assertions about their corresponding references.

Only on the basis of this assumption can Frege's logical system deduce certain needed sentences about numbers and arithmetical functions. Since Frege is eager to move from concepts to the objects they refer to, he easily slips into the fallacy of thinking that because a concept (such as a logical description of number) has a *sense* (*Sinn*), it therefore has a *meaning* (*Bedeutung*), and because it has a *meaning* (*Bedeutung*), it therefore has a *reference* (also *Bedeutung*). It is precisely this tendency to slide from concepts to objects, while playing on the double meaning of the *Bedeutung* of a concept, that leads him to postulate his troublesome Basic Law V.

On These Rocks Shall I Build My Logic

Frege argues that entire *sentences*, and not just the descriptive phrases within them, must possess both a sense and a reference. As we saw above, the individual names or descriptive phrases within a sentence all have their own particular references. What, then, is the reference of the sentence as a whole? Is it the collection of objects referred to by the sentence's constituent names and descriptive phrases?

To this question, Frege responds with an emphatic "no." Instead, he argues that the basic unit of assertible meaning in any language is not any of these constituent parts, or even all of them, but rather a *sentence*. The reason: only a sentence (that is, that which can be asserted) is true or false. But what is this object referred to by the sentence as a whole?

Frege seeks for the answer in his analysis of functions. As we saw above, Frege views a sentence as a saturated function having a determinate truth-value (either the True or the False). Indeed, having such a truth-value is precisely what constitutes a sentence as a sentence. The object referred to, then, by a sentence cannot be the collection of objects that happen to be the references of its constituent names or descriptive phrases; otherwise, there would be no difference between a sentence and a mere collection of such names and phrases. The object referred to by a sentence must be that which only a sentence, as a sentence, can refer to and which is uniquely determined by that particular sentence. Conclusion: the object referred to by a sentence must be its truth-value, because only sentences, not names or phrases, have truth-values, and because each sentence's truth-value is a function of just that sentence.

From these assumptions, it follows that any given sentence can have only two possible references, the True or the False. Moreover, all true sentences refer to only one object, the True, and all false sentences refer to another object, the False. It is precisely in virtue of making such a reference to either the True or the False, argues Frege, that a concatenation of words becomes a sentence. Therefore, to understand what constitutes a sentence as such (and thereby to understand logic) is to elucidate the roles played by the True and the False in language.

For Frege, the True and the False are the two rock-bottom, indefinable realities that distinguish, on the one hand, sentences from mere words, and on the other, logic from psychology. Any being in the universe that uses words to refer to the True or the False uses sentences and presupposes the laws of logic, and any being that does not do so is either nonliterate or insane.

Inheriting Truth-values

Not only do all sentences have truth-values, but the claim of certain sentences to have their truth-values depends solely on their form. For example, let "A" and "B" stand for definite sentences. Then the complex sentence "If A, and also if A, then B, then B" is true regardless of *what* sentences the letters "A" and "B" stand for; that is, this complex sentence is true by virtue of its form alone. Likewise, the complex sentence if "If A and B, then *not-B*" is false regardless of what "A" and "B" stand for.

In mathematics and the sciences, arguments can occur that are true or false by virtue of their form alone, but the arguments may be so complicated that their truth-values are not self-evident. It is at this point that logical notation becomes useful. A notation that displays the logical form of an argument can reveal in a straightforward, mechanical way whether such an argument has a truth-value in virtue of its form alone. This ease of mechanically displaying truth-values is the purpose of Frege's concept-script.

How is the truth-value "the True" demonstrated for the form of an argument? — Derive its form from axiomatic forms by repeated applications of explicit definitions and rules of inference. This logical methodology is said to be "truth-functional," in that the truth-value of the argument's form is a function (in Frege's strict sense) of the manner of deriving the argument. In effect, this methodology gives the rules for determining how truth-values are *inherited* by forms of arguments from given presuppositions.

Frege's concept-script also provides a truth-functional definition of its elementary logical symbols. For example, Frege understands the elementary logical relation exemplified by the sentence-formula "If A, then B" to mean "It is not the case that both A and *not-B*." He represents this relation between sentences with an elementary logical symbol, the elbow stroke. According to Frege's theory of functions and courses of values (as discussed above), the elbow stroke represents a function. That function has the following course of values (where A and B are definite sentences, T = the True, and F = the False):

Course of Values for Elbow Stroke

A	B	Elbow Stroke
T	T	T
T	F	F
F	T	T
F	F	T

This understanding of simple logical symbols as functions that correspond to courses of truth-values helped inspire Ludwig Wittgenstein's later "truth tables" (as Wittgenstein's imitators called them). We will see, however, that Wittgenstein also drew on another, less well known source in developing this idea.

Public vs. Private

Frege was led to his functional analysis of logic because of certain metaphysical views he held about the nature of language, thought, and reality. According to Frege, the capacity to communicate presupposes a dichotomy between public and private consciousness; in addition it shows the overriding importance of the former.

If everything experienced were purely private to the experiencer, Frege argues, it would be nonsensical for anyone to assert *anything*, even

"I assert that all experience is private." In such a case there would be no commonality or continuity to justify a meaningful use of the word "I."

Language exists, and people use it to communicate; therefore, there is shared consciousness. But what is this shared thing that makes language possible? This is the question that prompts Frege to postulate two distinct areas of consciousness, the public and the private. To the former area belong concepts and the workings of reason; to the latter, feelings and anything created by sensation or imagination. Accordingly, Frege distinguishes between "ideas" (*Vorstellungen*), which are purely private and subjective, and "concepts" (*Begriffe*), which are public and objective. When the latter are combined to make assertions, we obtain "thoughts" (*Gedanken*). When these are expressed through a sensible medium such as the written word, we obtain "sentences" (*Sätze*).

For Frege, all communication that is not a mere display of feelings is a matter of thoughts and concepts. Language, therefore, is essentially conceptual, not emotive, sensible, or imaginative. The various sounds, gestures, and written marks used in language function like a pliant drape fitted over a marble statue: they both reveal and conceal the underlying hard reality, which is the thought or the concept.

Not only do thoughts and concepts constitute the essence of language; they also define objectivity. To say that something is objective requires that it be communicable, says Frege. Otherwise, we couldn't think or talk about it. In that case, the thing couldn't be defined; but without definition, there is no objectivity. But if the thing is communicable, it must be something that is public and sharable. Anything private, precisely insofar as it is private, cannot be communicated. Therefore, objectivity consists of that which is public and commonly shared. If so, then objectivity must consist of thoughts, since thoughts are just those public, shared things that we grasp with our minds and assert through sentences about the nature of things.

Surely, one might object here, there is a big difference between a thought and something that actually exists. True enough, Frege responds, but he argues that this difference is due to actuality (*Wirklichkeit*), not objectivity. According to Frege, although we use pure reason to grasp thoughts (and therefore objectivity), it is through sensation that we perceive what is *actual*.

Whenever we say that something actually exists, what we really do is say that we have perceived something through our senses, and then judge that it is an instance of some concept. That is, all judgments about reality are judgments that assert that some object falls under some concept. Through sensation we perceive the object; through pure reason we grasp the concept (or thought, which is the joining of concepts to make assertions). What we call "the real world," therefore, is a matter of *both* actuality and objectivity, the former arising from sensation, the latter from reason.

The connections that Frege traces out between language, thought, and reality form the first premises of his whole philosophy. According to these premises, the crucial connecting link between logic and the world is *language*. It is language that embodies the concepts which grasp what is objective. It is language that expresses our concepts in words. Indeed, the only strictly non-linguistic factor in our interpretive relations to the world is sensation. Its role is limited to presenting us with impressions of things, which we judge according to concepts in order to admit them into reality. Frege regards sensation, in and of itself, as anarchic, private, and (strictly speaking) meaningless. This philosophic position puts Frege squarely in the camp of continental "rationalism." (The opposing camp is "empiricism," as in the philosophy of John Locke).

Frege's great emphasis on language has earned for him the distinction of inaugurating "the linguistic turn" in modern philosophy. As we are about to see, however, Frege had a radically ambivalent attitude toward language, seeing it as both divine and devilish. This ambivalent attitude was the very conduit through which he passed on to his later philosophical heirs the great metaphysical juggernaut he had inherited from Leibniz, the Parmenidean myth.

Language as God

Frege was the first great Western logician to develop a system of logic free of any appeal to God as the guarantor of logical necessity. In effect, Frege adopted the basic view of logic as suggested by William of Ockham and as greatly elaborated by Leibniz, but he stripped it of everything religious. Frege was Leibniz made palatable to a secular age.

Without God, where does logical necessity come from? Frege found the answer in his analysis, outlined above, of what it means to communicate. As we have seen, Frege argued that communication is possible only on the assumption that there is something in language that remains over and above the privacy and subjectivity of language-users. This linguistic commonality is universal because it constitutes the core of linguistic meaning. To say that signs have any meaning is to say that common concepts exist and that the words that represent them are combined according to certain laws. Any attempt to deny these presuppositions is impossible, because without them there can be no assertion, including the assertion of their denial:

> If other persons presume to acknowledge and doubt a law in the same breath, it seems to me an attempt to jump out of one's skin against which I can do no more than urgently warn them.[17]

What if we should some day encounter a form of life whose language is not based on these commonalities? We can only assume that the linguistic behavior exhibited by these strange beings is incoherent:

> I should say: we have here a hitherto unknown type of madness.[18]

In his search for the ground of logical necessity, Frege took one aspect of language itself, that which he regarded as its universal and objective part, and put this in the place of God as the savior of logic. In effect, he took the medieval philosophers' *L*ogos (with a capital "*L*," meaning the second person of the Holy Trinity) and turned it into the modern analytic philosophers' *l*ogos (with a small "*l*," meaning "language"). This transition from "Logos" to "logos" reflected a great shift in the historical role of Western philosophy. No longer was philosophy the handmaiden of theology; now it was the handmaiden of science.

The Two

Although Frege regarded the replacement of "Logos" by "logos" as a liberation from metaphysics, his reasons were just as metaphysical as Leibniz's. As noted, Frege's whole linguistic analysis rests on the assumption that there exist two ultimate, indefinable objects, the True and the False. Although not existing in space and time, these two objects are as real as two rocks, because they make a crucial difference in the world: their existence must be presupposed in order to explain how linguistic communication is possible. Moreover, according to Frege's theory of sense and reference, all true sentences refer to one of these objects, the True, while all false sentences refer to the other, the False. This theory implies that every true sentence ever made is simply a different way of talking about one and the same object, the True.

The True, existing above and beyond the infinite diversity of material objects in the universe, is that single entity by virtue of which all knowledge can be coherently expressed in language. The True, therefore, performs a unifying role with regard to individual sentences analogous to the unifying role played by God in Leibniz's system with regard to monads.

Because the True and the False exist as primal, nonmaterial objects, Frege is able to conclude that there is an irreducible dichotomy between logic and psychology. Logic is that science which deals with these two objects as such, whereas psychology deals with the temporal conditions pertaining to the genesis of ideas and concepts.

By virtue of the objective existence of the True and the False, Frege is also able to make a sharp distinction within language itself: on the one hand, language as the expression of clean, determinate, objective thoughts that refer to the True and the False, providing the basis for reliable knowledge; on the other hand, language as the expression of messy, vague, subjective, private feelings that are eternal stumbling blocks to all truth-seeking philosophers.

For Frege, that aspect of language that refers to the True and the False is precisely where we find the ground for logical necessity. Once we strip away the gunk that has accrued to language from sensation, privacy, and subjectivity, we behold with the eye of pure reason the "primal truths" (*Urwarheiten*). These regulate the manner in which language must refer to the True and the False in order for language to be intelligible, and for the world to be knowable. The True and the False, therefore, are the eternal anchors that keep language from sailing adrift in the treacherous sea of human sensual experience. They permit language, in its purely objective form, to replace God as the source of the common necessity that rules in both logic and the world.

As part of this theory of truth, Frege postulates the existence of two modes of knowledge. Whereas we perceive material objects with the senses, with pure reason we "grasp" (one of Frege's favorite words) the primal truths of logic, even though these are embedded in the particularity and concreteness of language. We are able to accomplish this feat, independent of any kind of intuition, because pure thought (*reine Denken*) is simply confronted by its own nature:

> Pure thought (regardless of any content given through the senses or even given a priori though an intuition) is able, all by itself, to produce from the content which arises from its own nature judgments which at first glance seem to be possible only on the grounds of some intuition.[19]

This view is similar to Boole's. As noted earlier, Boole did *not* claim that the laws of logic are derived from empirical generalizations. Like Frege, Boole believed that the mind can, of its own nature, recognize abstract laws of truth even when presented with only one concrete empirical example. This doctrine smacks of ideas that go back to Augustine and Plato. They enjoyed a renewed popularity in Protestant circles during the Enlightenment.

Frege traded in the idea of God for the idea of language in its objective, conceptual aspect; then he identified objective language with the workings of the rational mind as such. On this basis, he transmuted the old idea of divine illumination into the new idea of linguistic-conceptual illumination.

The upshot is this: Frege took one part of the Parmenidean myth, the principle of bivalence, and made it into the foundation for the other two parts, the myth of logical necessity, and the impersonal, static ideal of knowledge. This change of emphasis enabled Frege to sever the logical insights of Leibniz from the theological trunk that had first sprouted them.

Despite Frege's efforts at theological pruning, however, his system clearly remains metaphysical and even mythical. The root of his system, the doctrine of the True and the False, is reminiscent of the metaphysics of the ancient Pythagoreans (also mathematicians). They spoke of the mystical dyad of the Limited and the Unlimited.

Adamantly committed to bivalence, Frege refused to concede the possibility that propositions could be, say, partially true or partially false, or true for some interpreters in some contexts but not for others, or neither true nor false. For Frege, bivalence reflects the need for absolute determinacy of concepts. (An object either falls under some concept or it doesn't.) Should bivalence fail, the result for him would be the impossibility of all conceptual communication.

Contrary to Frege's approach, earlier chapters of this book have offered another account of human communication, one that assumes only *relative* objectivity and that acknowledges a *multiplicity* of truth-values. As those chapters demonstrated, the concept of absolute objectivity is incoherent, and the principle of bivalence is an arbitrary over-simplification.

Frege claimed to have freed logic from psychology. Behind his approach to logic, however, there lies a deep, almost compulsive need to constrain all reality to a rigid system of laws based on the transcendent command of either/or. Ironically, this same psychological need eventually caused his supposedly objective reduction of arithmetic to logic to collapse from its own paradoxes. Frege explicitly acknowledged that the Russell paradox could be avoided by dropping the law of the excluded middle, but he could never take that step. In the end, his fierce anti-psychologism reflected his own psychological deficiencies.

Language as the Devil

As just noted, Frege takes what he regards as the objective and conceptual part of language and uses it to replace God as the savior of logical necessity. Likewise, he disdains the subjective, sensual, and emotional aspects of language as a kind of Devil. At times sounding like a fundamentalist preacher, Frege repeatedly warns the innocent reader to beware of the dangerous seductiveness of the non-conceptual element in language. He compares this aspect of language to a trap, a diversion, a set of fetters, a source of contamination, a bewitchment, and an intellectual bog. The role of philosophy is to seek out, purify, and display the conceptual jewels hidden away in the dregs of language. Philosophy must cut away all the ugly excrescences due to sensuality, subjectivity, historicity, and personal feeling:

> We can see from all this how easily we can be led by language to see things in the wrong perspective, and what value it must therefore have for philosophy to free ourselves from the dominion of language.[20]

Underlying Frege's dichotomy between the divine and the devilish in language is his devotion to that which is "lawlike" (*gesetzmässig*). The public and objective in human experience is most worthy because it is that which most easily lends itself to lawlike formulation in a formal language. Knowledge means acknowledging objective laws of truth and constraining one's cognitive and linguistic experience accordingly, just as ethics means acknowledging objective laws of goodness and constraining one's behavior accordingly. For Gottlob Frege—the petty bourgeois German Lutheran academic—law, order, and regularity are everything. That which is un-lawlike is dangerous and a temptation into the abyss.

Frege's adulation of the "lawlike" led him, as it has many of his intellectual heirs, to underestimate the significance of the subjective, temporal, and emotional in human interpretational experience. Like the logical positivists and analytic philosophers who have followed in his steps, Frege had a very poor understanding of poetry, the arts in general, visionary religious experience, and ecstatic sexuality. For Frege and his successors, these are nothing but "displays of feeling" (a phrase always spoken with a slight snarl).

Frege and those of his mind-set have had a predictable reaction when encountering entire peoples who value idiosyncratic, subjective experiences as roads to truth, as in the many native cultures around the world that Western civilization has conquered and destroyed. Shaking their heads at such "primitive" cultures, Frege and company typically mutter "We have here a hitherto unknown type of madness."

We see, then, that Frege's great accomplishments in logic and philosophy were as much a matter of religion and mythology as of science. In effect, Frege took the prime myth of Western patriarchal religious consciousness—that of God and the Devil—and transmuted it into a paradigm for analyzing language. The sensual, subjective, emotional, and anarchic—the old realm of the Devil—now became language in its bewitching aspect. The non-sensual, objective, cognitive, and law-like—the old road to heaven—now became language in its conceptual aspect, the aspect that leads to truth. Purified of its sensual impurities and chastened by the discipline of a new analytic philosophy, language finally re-connects with a transcendent source of its own in the dyadic demigods of the True and the False. With this divine pair, language negotiates a renewed lease on life for the hoary logical myths ultimately derived from Parmenides.

Analytic Philosophy's Misanalysis

Although Frege was largely ignored or misunderstood for most of his life, his mythology of logic eventually came to exercise an extraordinary influence in Western philosophy, and especially so in that Anglo-American academic tradition known as analytic philosophy. His influence on later generations was conveyed, among others, through Bertrand Russell, Ludwig Wittgenstein, and Rudolf Carnap, all of whom were deeply indebted to Frege for the formulation of their own philosophies.

Ironically, however, although contemporary analytic philosophy owes much to Frege, a number of the adherents of that tradition have blundered in assessing the historical significance of Frege's thought. In a certain sense, this blundering is understandable, since analytic philosophy has a strong anti-historical bias (influenced in this very respect by Frege himself); as a result, its proponents tend in general to be poorly read in the history of philosophy.

The classic example of analytic philosophy's historical misreading of Frege is the work of Michael Dummett, until fairly recently regarded as Frege's leading English-writing interpreter. Himself an analytic philosopher with a degree from Oxford, Dummett wrote the article on Gottlob Frege for *The Encyclopedia of Philosophy*.[21] Later, Dummett also published an enormous single volume on Frege entitled *Frege, Philosophy of Language*.[22] In these works, Dummett completely misconstrued Frege's basic philosophical motivation, a blunder he himself later admitted.

According to Dummett, Frege's philosophy was a non-nonsense, science-inspired reaction against German idealism. In fact, however, as Hans Sluga later proved, Frege was actually reacting *against* the tradition of scientific naturalism in his day. That tradition viewed logic and mathematics as natural, temporally-conditioned phenomena, and not as the conceptual absolutes that Frege held them to be.[23] Far from approaching logic and mathematics as an empirical scientist, Frege was in fact motivated throughout his career by deep philosophical presuppositions that he believed to transcend all the sciences. It has been very hard, however, for modern analytic philosophers, who pride themselves on being "hard-nosed" and "scientific," to swallow the fact that one of the principal founders of their tradition was really a metaphysician or, even worse, a mythologist.

Again, the Ghost of Leibniz

Although Hans Sluga was right, against Michael Dummett, to stress Frege's anti-naturalist biases, Sluga was wrong to argue that Frege's basic goal was to correct and complete the philosophical enterprise of Immanuel Kant.[24] Although Frege accepted Kant's views on geometry, his entire approach to logic and arithmetic was a vehement rejection of Kant's notion that arithmetic consists of "synthetic *a priori* judgments." (Kant held that arithmetical theorems are necessarily true, but *not* in virtue of their logical form alone.) To the contrary, Frege appealed to the opposite view of Leibniz that arithmetical theorems are analytic *a priori* judgments. (Leibniz held that arithmetical theorems are necessarily true precisely in virtue of their logical form.)

Only near the end of his life, when he came to the conclusion that his entire approach was a failure, did Frege undergo a kind of Kantian conversion, arguing that the concept of number depends on an intuition of space. But this last phase of Frege's intellectual life was also his least creative one, practically devoid of interest to his great philosophical heirs, such as Russell, Wittgenstein, and Carnap. For them, the name "Frege" always meant the brilliant author of *Concept-Script* and *The Basic Laws of Arithmetic*.

Frege's rejection of Kant's view of arithmetic was hardly a mere correction to the Kantian philosophical enterprise, as maintained by Sluga. To the contrary, the most characteristic elements in Frege's system everywhere resonate with the profound influence of another philosopher, the one whose name Frege invokes the most in his writings—Gottfried Wilhelm Leibniz.

That Frege's system was actually a completion and correction of Leibniz, not of Kant, is easily seen by comparing the principle interests and doctrines of the two. For example, compare Leibniz's dream of a universal sign-system to Frege's book *Concept-Script*. Or compare Leibniz's belief that mathematics can be reduced to logic to Frege's book *The Basic Laws of Arithmetic*. In many cases, Fregean concepts that seem to be purely logical turn out to be variations on previous Leibnizian metaphysical themes. For example, for Leibniz all commonality is due to a transcendent One; for Frege, the significance (*Bedeutung*) of all true sentences is one nonmaterial object, the True. For Leibniz, all existing things are exemplifications of concepts in the mind of God; for Frege, to exist is to fall under a concept. For Leibniz, no finite individual thing can be said to exist in its own right; for Frege, the statement "this object exists" is meaningless. For Leibniz, reality is ultimately a common form of consciousness; for Frege, objectivity is grounded in the common, formal aspects of language.

There are many concepts that are identical in both Leibniz and Frege: all truths are either truths of reason or truths of fact; two things are the same if, when one is substituted for the other in different propositions, they both generate the same truth-values; linguistic grammar disguises logical grammar; all the sciences are in principle parts of one great science; and analysis is the golden key to knowledge.

Although Frege certainly did not adopt Leibnizian positions blindly, he nonetheless paid homage to the creative stimulus that Leibniz, uniquely, had provided to his own thinking:

> In his writings, Leibniz threw out such a profusion of seeds of ideas that in this respect he is virtually in a class of his own.[25]

The most striking distinction between Leibniz and Frege lies, as noted previously, in Frege's rejection of Leibniz's philosophic appeal to God. It is precisely here that the influence of Immanuel Kant worked itself on Frege, for Kant had shown that the so-called "ontological argument," to the effect that existence must be part of the essence of God, is based on a fallacy. Leibniz, on the other hand, had defined God as that being that necessarily exists. Frege, recognizing the cogency of Kant's argument against Leibniz in this matter, was thus prompted to reject the use of the concept of God as the ultimate validator of logic.

Confronted with the need to find a new ultimate foundation for logical necessity as a result of Kant's critique of Leibniz, Frege turned to language, or rather to that aspect of language that is formally expressive of the True and the False. Thus did Frege, through his celebrated "linguistic turn," bequeath to future generations the Parmenidean myth as it had been amplified by Leibniz's concept of analysis, but freed of Leibniz's appeal to God.

Frege and the Male Reality Principle

Is there a connection between the spirit of Frege's authoritarian, racist politics and his motivation in developing a more rigorous, objective, and quantifiable kind of logic? Most contemporary analytic philosophers would respond with a resounding "no," and for two reasons: first, Frege's politics and his logic are conceptually independent systems in their own right; and second, modern logicians who have been inspired by Frege's logical work have generally proven to be apolitical, moderate or liberal, not authoritarian, reactionary, and racist. Real human beings are often quite contradictory, these analytic philosophers observe, and the fact that a person is repulsive in one area of life does not preclude the possibility of being admirable in another. Indeed, there are examples even more striking than Frege, such as Martin Heidegger, the celebrated existentialist philosopher who was also the Nazi rector of the University of Freiburg.

Recently this conventional opinion has come under a scathing attack from the feminist historian of logic Andrea Nye.[26] Nye rightly points out that behind Frege's entire approach to logic there lay a very deep-seated fear of the emotional, the sensual, the personal, the subjective, and the undefinable. Himself inept at emotionally expressive communication, Frege sought to develop an artificial language that would eliminate, as much as possible, any connection to the subjectivity and feelings of those who used it. Further, he claimed that such an artificial language was an inherently superior vehicle for discovering the truth, and for the very reason that he regarded the truth itself as impersonal, public, and quantifiable. Indeed, for Frege all reality consists of functions and objects, and so persons themselves are simply a kind of object. This view later influenced the American neoscholastic philosopher Willard Van Orman Quine, who championed the chilling principle that the real is that which is the value of a variable.[27] This whole line of thinking simply *assumes* that what is public and quantifiable is somehow more real or important than what is not. But as we have seen in this and previous chapters, such an assumption is both mythical and false.

As Nye points out, 20th-century totalitarian regimes have been especially fond of the view that the real is the public and the quantifiable. Hitler, Stalin, and Mao all justified their episodes of mass murder in the name of an objective, public, quantifiable reality. In pushing their monumental objectivities, they treated citizens like so many replaceable values that they could just plug into the variables of the state's collective functions. What right does the Jew have to practice a peculiar religion? Or the homosexual to express a peculiar kind of love? Such peculiarities stand in the way of the state's massive, public, quantifiable mission. Many scientists and engineers in totalitarian societies bought into the same rationale in order to justify their collaboration with the leadership.

Much of the personal degradation and environmental devastation characteristic of patriarchal-industrial civilization has also been justified by an appeal to the myth of quantifiable objective reality. The rights of the North American Indian tribes to their ancestral lands, the right of human beings in general to meaningful labor, the right of animals and plants to live and thrive—how can such rights presume to stand against the massive, public, quantifiable reality of "progress"? They can't, and so in the name of quantifiable objective reality (the male reality principle), industrial civilization has crashed its way across the stage of history, everywhere leaving in its tracks ghastly episodes of genocide, war, and environmental rape.

Loss of the Mystical and the Personal

Frege was Leibniz without God. In peeling a personal God away from logic, Frege took the objective reality on which he believed logic to be based and made it into a kind of impersonal god in its own right. Prior to Frege, even though God was viewed as the validator of logic, one could always claim that God himself was above logic, since God was conceived as a transcendent *person*. So there always remained a transcendent personal ground to which one could appeal in justifying the claim that subjective, idiosyncratic personal experience had a significant conceptual content. After Frege, however, this transcendent personal ground disappeared. Henceforth the ultimate ground of meaning lay in two impersonal objects, the True and the False. These could be reached only by sentences that themselves were instances of public, objective functions. Therefore, to claim any kind of cognitive validity for purely private, subjective experience became absurd. To be meaningful, all speech must be that of the publicly knowable, which in its most ideal form is the language of mathematics and the sciences. All else is "the mere expression of feeling."

The logic that Frege bequeathed to patriarchal-industrial civilization was essentially a "logic of domination" (in the words of Herbert Marcuse).[28] Not only did it celebrate the objectification of persons and nature as a basic principle of reality, it also validated the worst qualities of the human male. Since the triumph of the patriarchal revolution in the West some six thousand years ago, men have increasingly come to view spontaneity of feeling, emotional identification with others, and subjective playfulness and creativity as female traits, and therefore as unworthy of "real men." One of the reasons men are superior to women, the old patriarchal argument goes, is that men are more in touch with reality. Frege's logic gave this old argument a newer, sharper definition: "being in touch" means using the methods of abstract conceptualization and quantification, and "reality" means the monumental objectivities of patriarchal modernity.

The iron logic that Frege forged on the anvil of male values raised an old patriarchal prejudice to the level of a philosophic principle and celebrated it as an ideal of the life of reason. But for all that, this logic remained in its core a mythical rationalization motivated by the pathetic inability of the human male to love and feel, an inability reinforced over millennia by both genetic factors (testosterone poisoning) and the traditional male social roles of patriarchy.

Although Frege was quick to make absolutist claims for his logical methods, we saw that his entire philosophical house of cards collapsed from a puff of paradox from the then-obscure Bertrand Russell. In making this challenge to Frege's system, Russell was not motivated by the desire to subvert the logicist agenda; rather, he wanted to make the best possible argument for that agenda. After Frege collapsed, Russell himself took up the logicist banner with renewed vigor. In the next chapter, we will watch as Russell's own monumental efforts to find an absolute foundation for logic and mathematics likewise faltered. Even so, however, Western academic philosophers continued to resist the obvious implication: formal logic and higher mathematics are grounded in myth.

---

[1] For various aspects of Leibniz's thought, see the following: Hidé Ishiguro, *Leibniz's Philosophy of Logic and Language*, Cornell University Press, Ithaca, NY, 1972; Benson Mates, *The Philosophy of Leibniz: Metaphysics and Language*, Oxford University Press, New York, 1986; G.H.R. Parkinson, *Logic and Reality in Leibniz's Metaphysics*, The Clarendon Press, Oxford, 1965; and R.S. Woolhouse (ed.), Leibniz: *Metaphysics and Philosophy of Science*, Oxford University Press, New York, 1981.

[2] Gottfried Wilhelm Leibniz, *Monadology*, trans. by Paul Schrecker and Anne Martin Schrecker, The Bobbs-Merrill Company, Inc., Indianapolis, 1965, p. 148.

[3] Cited by Mates, *op. cit.*, pp. 85-86.

[4] *ibid.*, pp. 154-55.

[5] George Boole, *An Investigation of the Laws of Thought*, 1854; reprinted by Dover Publications, New York, 1958, p. 159.

[6] Plato, *Theaetetus*, 182A-B.

[7] For a general overview of Frege's thought, see Gregory Currie, *Frege: An Introduction to His Philosophy*, The Harvester Press, Sussex, 1982. Less valuable are the frequently cited works of Michael Dummett—*Frege: Philosophy of Language*, 2nd ed., Harvard University Press, Cambridge, MA, 1981; and *Frege and Other Philosophers*, Clarendon Press, Oxford, 1991. Dummett's interpretations are often tangential to Frege's actual texts. Concerning the ongoing debate over Frege's basic philosophical presuppositions, see the following: G.P. Baker & P.M.S. Hacker, *Frege: Logical Excavations*, Oxford University Press, New York, 1984; E.-H.W. Kluge, *The Metaphysics of Gottlob Frege: An Essay in Ontological Reconstruction*, Martinus Nijhoff, The Hague, 1980; Hans Sluga, *Gottlob Frege*, Routledge & Kegan Paul, London, 1980; and Joan Weiner, *Frege in Perspective*, Cornell University Press, Ithaca, NY, 1990.

[8] Rudolf Carnap, "Intellectual Autobiography" in *The Philosophy of Rudolf Carnap*, ed. by P.A. Schlipp, Open Court, 1963, p. 5.

9. Dummett, *Frege: Philosophy of Language*, p. xii.
10. Frege himself used a slightly different term for the idea, *lingua characteristica*, meaning "depictive language." See Kluge, *op. cit.*, pp. 235ff.
11. For example, see A. Musgrave, "George Boole and Psychologism" in *Scientia*, vol. 107, 1972, pp. 593-608.
12. Gottlob Frege, *Conceptual Notation and Related Articles*, 1879, trans. by Terrell W. Bynum, The Clarendon Press, Oxford, 1972.
13. Gottlob Frege, *The Foundations of Arithmetic*, 1884, trans. by J.L. Austin, Philosophical Library, New York, 1950.
14. Gottlob Frege, *The Basic Laws of Arithmetic*, trans. by Montgomery Furth, University of California Press, Berkeley, 1964, p. 4.
15. *ibid.*, p. 25.
16. *ibid.*, p. 127.
17. *ibid.*, p. 15.
18. *ibid.*, p. 14.
19. Frege, *Conceptual Notation*, p. 167.
20. Gottlob Frege, *Posthumous Writings*, ed. by Hans Hermes et al., University of Chicago Press, Chicago, 1979, p. 67.
21. Eight volumes, published by Macmillan in 1967 under the editorship of Paul Edwards, and saturated with the biases of analytic philosophy.
22. Cited in full, above.
23. Sluga, *op. cit.*, p. 14.
24. *ibid.*, 43.
25. Frege, *Posthumous Writings*, p. 9.
26. Andrea Nye, *Words of Power, A Feminist Reading of the History of Logic*, Routledge, New York, 1990.
27. Willard Van Orman Quine, *From a Logical Point of View*, 1953; revised edition reprinted by Harper Torchbooks, New York, 1963, p. 103. Quine is discussed in greater detail in chapter eleven.
28. Herbert Marcuse, *Eros and Civilization: A Philosophical Inquiry into Freud*, Beacon Press, Boston, 1966, p. 111.

Doxa, Detail
Graphite, 21" x 15", 1996

6

The Illogic of the 20th Century

SUMMARY: This chapter shows how Bertrand Russell took up the legacy of Leibniz, Boole, and Frege in formal logic. It describes how Russell failed in his efforts to trim formal logic and mathematics of their mythological elements. The result was a philosophical crisis that haunts both formal logic and mathematics to this day.

The person who most influenced the development of formal logic in the early modern period was the metaphysician Gottfried Wilhelm Leibniz, who died in 1716. As the last chapter showed, Leibniz inherited from his predecessors a Christianized version of the Parmenidean myth, first propounded by the ancient Greek philosopher Parmenides. As it came to Leibniz's hands, the Parmenidean myth consisted of three motifs: logical necessity, bivalence, and absolute objectivity. Leibniz's greatest contribution to the Parmenidean myth was to link it with his own metaphysical doctrine of the plurality of the world. In making this linkage, Leibniz validated the process of analyzing wholes into parts as the ideal method of human inquiry.

The previous chapter showed that Leibniz's approach to logic was later rehoned by the German philosopher Gottlob Frege, as part of his abortive quest to deduce arithmetic from pure logic. Frege located the guarantor of logical necessity in the abstractly-formalizable aspects of language, rather than in God. In effect, Frege was Leibniz without God.

Like most logicians before him, Frege was suspicious of the senses, artistic subjectivity, and anything conventionally associated with feminine modes of interpreting reality. Frege insisted that the world was a steely network of brute facts. He believed that these facts could best be clarified by a logical calculus that was mechanical and "rigid" (one of his favorite words). Although failing in his endeavor to deduce arithmetic from logic, Frege succeeded in completely re-formalizing logic. His success at this task made him the greatest logician since Aristotle.

This chapter will show how 20th-century formal logic built on Frege's work, just as Frege had built on Leibniz's. As in earlier chapters, the main subject will be the Parmenidean myth, in this case as it passed from Frege to Bertrand Russell. Despite Russell's great ingenuity, we will see that he too failed in freeing formal logic from the wobbliness of its mythological presuppositions. As we trace out Russell's efforts, the real underlying motive of modern formal logic will come into focus—the will to power of patriarchal-industrial civilization.

Russell Takes Up Frege's Mantle

As discussed in the last chapter, Frege's great hope of deriving arithmetic from pure logic was dashed in 1902, when Bertrand Russell pointed out a contradiction ("the Russell Paradox") in Frege's book *The Basic Laws of Arithmetic*.[1] Although Frege tried to resolve the difficulty discovered by Russell, he never succeeded. Russell in turn took up the quest anew. Although his own efforts to reduce arithmetic to pure logic also eventually failed, the power of his work in logic and mathematics eventually established him as the greatest Anglo-American logician of the 20th century, just as his overall work in philosophy established him (in my opinion at least) as the century's greatest Western philosopher. In any case, everyone agrees that Russell has been enormously influential. For this reason we will examine him in detail, first in terms of his personal biography and general philosophical development, and then in terms of his theory of logic.[2]

Although Russell assumed Frege's mantle, he was nearly the exact opposite of Frege in personal temperament, politics, and overall philosophy of life. Born in Ravenscroft, near Trelleck, Wales, in 1872, Russell was the second son of an old aristocratic English family. Russell's parents, Lord and Lady Amberly, were self-described "freethinkers" and admirers of the utilitarian philosophy of John Stuart Mill, who was Russell's godfather.

Unluckily for Russell, his mother died when he was only two years old, and his father two years later. Although his parents had provided in their will that Russell and his brother were to be raised by two free-thinking relatives, the will was broken by his paternal grandparents, who wanted to give their grandchildren a "Christian education." When Russell's grandfather, the famous political reformer John Lord Russell died a few years later, the children's rearing fell to their grandmother, Lady John, a Scottish Presbyterian who eventually converted to Unitarianism. Lady John decided that her young charges should be kept isolated at home, receiving their primary education at the hands of private tutors hired from abroad who would instill in them the proper Christian values.

In later years, Russell bitterly lamented the isolation he suffered during his adolescent years under Lady John's tutelage and the parochial views she tried to force on him. Nonetheless, some of his incidental comments reveal that he enjoyed at least some of the usual class privileges for a person of his station:

> There was no Sabbatarianism beyond a suggestion of avoiding cards on Sunday for fear of shocking the servants.[3]

In 1890 Russell entered Cambridge University to study mathematics. In 1894, his last year as an undergraduate at Cambridge, he turned to the study of philosophy, which eventually led him to some unresolved questions in the philosophy of logic and mathematics. In 1895, he was elected a fellow at Cambridge.

An early influence on Russell during his early Cambridge years was his fellow-student G.E. Moore. Moore's interest in a new technique of philosophic analysis encouraged Russell to move away from the idealist philosophy of F.H. Bradley.

A Fateful Encounter with Leibniz

In 1899 a chance development at Cambridge prompted a major intellectual turning point in Russell's life. In that year the idealist philosopher John McTaggart took a leave of absence from Cambridge to visit his family in New Zealand. In McTaggart's place, Russell was asked to lecture on the philosophy of Leibniz. Quickly mastering the subject, Russell successfully delivered the lectures and published them in book form in 1900 in *A Critical Exposition of the Philosophy of Leibniz*.[4]

Although at the time, Russell opposed many of Leibniz's ideas, he later returned to them. Eventually he made some of them the cornerstone of his own philosophy of logic and mathematics. The Leibnizian dogmas that had the most lasting influence on Russell's later thought were these: it is possible to develop a universal formal language for all the sciences; all truth can be divided into the mutually exclusive categories of empirical fact and abstract reason; mathematics can be deduced from pure logic; all reality can be analyzed into logical atoms; and analysis is the golden key to knowledge.

Even in cases where Russell held ideas contrary to Leibniz's, he typically did so with the acknowledgment that Leibniz's arguments were the important ones to be answered. The pole around which Russell's fully developed mathematical world always turned was Leibniz, both where Russell agreed and where he disagreed with him.

A number of important circumstances in Russell's life worked to reinforce each other in lifting Russell into a Leibnizian orbit. In addition to Moore's emphasis on an analytical approach to philosophy, mentioned above, Russell attended the International Congress of Philosophy in Paris in 1900. There he met the renowned Italian mathematician, philosopher, and linguist Giuseppe Peano, who was an admirer of Leibniz. Using a new logical symbolism that he had invented for the purpose, Peano argued that arithmetic could be deduced from a small number of arithmetic axioms and definitions. Russell, inspired by the force and clarity of Peano's methods, began to speculate that Peano's axioms and definitions could themselves be further reduced to purely logical notions as Leibniz had dreamed.

While developing these ideas in his book *The Principles of Mathematics*, Russell rediscovered the largely neglected works of Gottlob Frege, who had himself been much influenced by Leibniz.[5] Russell quickly realized that Frege, despite the contradiction that Russell uncovered in his work, had advanced far beyond even Peano in achieving the Leibnizian dream.

Fusing the notation of Peano with the insights of Frege, Russell proposed to his philosopher-friend Alfred North Whitehead that the two collaborate on a great work endeavoring to prove the thesis that arithmetic can be strictly deduced from pure logic. Whitehead agreed, and for the next ten years Russell and Whitehead worked on the three-volume classic *Principia Mathematica* ("Mathematical Principles"), which was published between 1910 and 1913. Although failing in its prime objective (see chapter three), the work was a great turning point in the history of mathematics and established the lasting renown of both Russell and Whitehead.

A Fateful Encounter with Wittgenstein

In early 1912, while the volumes of *Principia Mathematica* were being published, an intense young Austrian engineering student named Ludwig Wittgenstein came to Cambridge to study mathematics and logic, becoming Russell's pupil. The two eventually became friends of sorts, strenuously debating issues in mathematics, logic, and philosophy, and influencing each other's points of view.

Despite their common interests, however, Russell and Wittgenstein had very different personalities: the former was renowned for his polished congeniality and wit; the latter, for his moodiness and irascibility. In late 1913, during one of his famous mood swings, Wittgenstein abruptly withdrew from Cambridge and moved to Norway. There he decided to live in seclusion in a peasant's hut, although still keeping in contact with Russell by letter.

After the outbreak of World War I, Wittgenstein volunteered in the Austrian Army, and he and Russell lost contact. After the war, in 1919, Wittgenstein re-emerged from a prisoner-of-war camp in Italy, sending Russell a copy of a short work he had written in German during the war. Always generous in his friendship with Wittgenstein, Russell arranged to have an English translation of the work published in 1922 under the Latin title of *Tractatus Logico-Philosophicus* ("Logical-Philosophical Treatise"). This small book later became one of the most influential works in Anglo-American academic philosophy. (Wittgenstein's book is discussed in detail in chapter eight.)

In 1929, sixteen years after his withdrawal, Wittgenstein returned to Cambridge and submitted his *Tractatus*, written ten years before, as a dissertation for the doctoral degree. His old friends G.E. Moore and Bertrand Russell served on his examining committee. After a congenial conversation, the dissertation was quickly approved.

In their later years, Russell and Wittgenstein had a falling-out. Russell, who always prized clarity of communication, objected to Wittgenstein's verbal murkiness, and also disagreed with many of Wittgenstein's later philosophical views.

From God to the Absolute

Russell lived for 98 years, dying in 1970. He was also a prolific writer. As a result, his opinions naturally underwent much change. This change was encouraged by his view that philosophy should model itself after the sciences, and so be tentative and piecemeal, depending on the emergence of new evidence.

From his early adolescence until his death, Russell's thought went through five phases.[6] In the beginning, until he went to Cambridge, Russell was in his religious phase, a result no doubt of the Christian education he received at the hands of Lady John. After going to Cambridge in 1890, Russell entered his idealist phase, influenced by John McTaggart and Francis H. Bradley, who were then in vogue in England. Both McTaggart and Bradley were followers of the German philosopher Georg Hegel, who had developed a metaphysical system based on belief in "the Absolute."

Although Russell was initially impressed by idealism, when he turned to Hegel's views on mathematics, he was shocked to find that the great master did not seem to know what he was talking about. Eventually, Russell came to view the idealists' Absolute as God under a philosophical veil.

From the Absolute to Atoms, Logically

After successively giving up religion and idealist philosophy, Russell entered his third phase, critical realism, which he embraced around the turn of the century. During this phase, he came to the conclusion that the universe is populated with an irreducible variety of entities—minds, spatial points, instants of time, particles of matter, qualities, relations, propositions, classes, and the basic laws of logic. The classic expression of the views of this phase is his book *The Principles of Mathematics* (not to be confused with the later *Principia Mathe-*

matica), which was written in 1900 and published in 1903.

Around 1912 Russell entered his fourth and most important phase, logical atomism. Reflecting on his research on Leibniz, and drawing on his discussions with Moore and Wittgenstein, Russell came to the following three conclusions: (1) the essential feature of the world is its radical plurality; (2) the best means of gaining knowledge of the world is through analysis; and (3) the end result of analysis is uncovering the "logical atoms" out of which the world is constructed.

Russell presented these views in a series of public lectures, "The Philosophy of Logical Atomism," delivered in 1918. Subsequently they appeared in a journal entitled, ironically, *The Monist*. In the published version, Russell credited the ideas to his discussions with Wittgenstein, with whom he had lost contact because of World War I. In fact, however, the great intellectual source behind both Russell and Wittgenstein in these matters was Leibniz, as Russell himself acknowledged 41 years later when reflecting on the overall course of his intellectual history:

> Most of this [Leibniz's theory of monads] can be applied with little change to exemplify the theory that I wish to advocate.[7]

Like Leibniz, Russell was inspired by the effectiveness of the atomic theory of matter in explaining purely physical interactions. Again like Leibniz, he speculated that underlying all reality there must be a vast array of indivisible somethings that are even more basic than the physical atoms of matter. These Russell called "logical atoms." They are "logical," not in the sense that they're composed of some underlying logical stuff, but in the sense that they're what's left after logical analysis has finished its job.

Unlike Leibniz, however, Russell rejected the traditional Western notion that "substance" must be something imperishable. To the contrary, Russell argued that material reality ultimately consists of things that are only momentary. Relative duration pertains, rather, to what is constructed out of these logical atoms. As examples of his logical atoms, Russell gave patches of color, bursts of sound, etc., which he later called "sense-data." To account for the structure of things, he also recognized relations and "completely general facts" (which ground the laws of logic).

Russell regarded everything else besides these logical atoms (or sense-data) as "logical fictions." In his use of this term, Russell played on the double meaning of the word "fiction" as both "construction" and "deception." (The Latin verb *fingere*, from which "fiction" comes, means both "to form" and "to feign.") For example, Russell argued that the furniture of the world is constructed from sense-data, relations, and the laws of logic. This constructed furniture is real; nonetheless, it's not quite as real as the underlying logical atoms from which it's constructed.

In making this distinction, Russell retained the famed dichotomy between "appearance and reality" of the idealist philosopher F.H. Bradley, but with an empiricist twist. Bradley, starting with appearances, had searched for reality by moving upward and inward to the One. Russell, also starting with appearances, searched for reality by moving outward and downward to the Many.

Previous chapters have shown that both approaches are partly right and partly wrong. The reason: "one" and "many" are correlative terms. They depend for their applicability to data scenes on the decisions of some interpreter or some group of interpreters.

Neutral Monism

In the 1920s Russell entered his last philosophic phase, neutral monism, which consisted of a number of refinements to logical atomism. One of the loose-ends in his logical atomist phase was the question of what to do with minds. Although Russell did not hesitate to interpret other people's minds as logical fictions, he paused when it came to his own. Am I immediately aware of my own mind? If so, what does it look like? Is it a patch of color, a burst of sound, a pushing sensation on the surface of the skin, an odor, a sexual urge? Apparently it is none of these, or even all of them. Therefore, Russell eventually came to the same conclusion as had the Scottish philosopher David Hume in the 18th century: we never immediately apprehend our own minds. If that is the case, then who or what has the sense-data out of which the world is constructed?

To answer this thorny question, Russell turned to the theory of "neutral monism," invented by the American pragmatist philosopher William James. According to James, the dichotomy between mind and matter is a false one. The universe really consists of but one underlying stuff (hence "monism") which is neither mind nor matter (hence "neutral"). When the underlying stuff of reality is arranged in one way, we call it matter; when another, mind. In both cases, the universe remains the same stuff, only differently arranged.

Russell embraced James' neutral monism, regarding the underlying stuff as sensations. Arranged one way, sensations become minds; arranged another, matter. As a result, the distinction between the process of having sense-data (sensation), the thing having sense-data (the mind), and the thing referred to by the sense-data (the object) collapses. Strictly speaking, we cannot admit a real distinction between brains and minds. With admirable logical consistency, but no common sense, Russell boldly proclaimed that all we can ever know are our own brains.

Soon after adopting neutral monism, Russell amended it by admitting the existence of "sensibilia" (unsensed sensations, which is as contradictory as it sounds) and other people's minds. In fact, Russell never resolved the underlying problems raised by neutral monism to his own satisfaction. Although giving lip service to neutral monism, Russell gutted it with qualifications and exceptions.

Russell regarded his earlier critical realism and his later neutral monism as different stages of logical atomism. His motivation throughout was to disclose the universe's basic plurality by means of analysis, admitting as few kinds of entities as possible. It is for this reason that Russell called himself a logical atomist as early as 1899 and as late as 1959.[8]

The Two Bertrand Russells

Russell's fame among professional philosophers rests on his contributions in logic and mathematics; however, his fame among the general public rests more on his writings about politics and ethics. Russell himself regarded his political and ethical works as not really philosophical. Since politics and ethics are still far removed from scientific rigor, he saw his own writings in these areas as simply the personal views of another intellectual. His conclusions in logic and mathematics, on the other hand, he felt were objectively grounded.

There was another reason why Russell separated his writings on logic and mathematics from those on politics and ethics: his thinking in these two separate areas was based on divergent assumptions. We will see later in this chapter that there were actually two different Bertrand Russells. They maintained an uneasy intellectual truce with each other throughout the long life of that philosopher.

War Intrudes on Logic

On June 28, 1914, Russell's life, and that of the entire planet, was forever changed by the assassination of the Austrian Archduke Francis Ferdinand and his wife Sophie in Sarajevo. The quick outbreak of hostilities that followed shocked Russell, now rudely shaken from his logical studies as if from a dream. Filled with foreboding, he watched as his countrymen reacted with a festive spirit to the news of what they thought, and which he doubted, would be a short and splendid war.

Although not opposed to all war, Russell concluded that this particular one was unjustified. His stance prompted animosity by both Cambridge University and the British government. In 1916, he was fined for writing a pamphlet defending a conscientious objector who had been sentenced to prison. Later in the same year, he was fired from his lectureship at Cambridge, largely through the efforts of his erstwhile teacher, the idealist philosopher John McTaggart. In 1918, Russell was sentenced to six months in prison for writing an article criticizing the American army for its strike-breaking role in the United States. While imprisoned, he wrote *Introduction to Mathematical Philosophy*, a popularized account of *Principia Mathematica*.[9]

After the war, Russell continued to write extensively on political questions. He became known for his ringing defense of individual democratic rights and his strong condemnation of all authoritarian systems, both right and left. In the 1920s, he shocked other liberal intellectuals by condemning the new communist regime in Russia, saying the country was turning into a vast prison camp. Later, he supported British involvement in World War II, warning that civilization itself was in the balance.

After World War II, Russell became a leading advocate of nuclear disarmament and the establishment of a world government. In 1961, at age 89, he was arrested for participating in a peaceful sit-in for nuclear disarmament. He was sentenced to serve one week in jail, the same in which he had been imprisoned 43 years earlier. He was treated with kid gloves, not because of his age or fame as a philosopher, but because he was now the third Earl Russell, having inherited the title in 1931 on the death of his brother. Later in the 1960s, Russell became a vociferous critic of the American atrocities committed in Southeast Asia. His last book, *War Crimes in Vietnam*, was published three years before his death in 1970.[10]

The Cramping of Love by Institutions

In addition to politics, Russell was also outspoken in ethical, religious, and sexual matters. He said that religion was a regrettable hangover from a more primitive form of human existence. On questions of sex, he became a prominent defender of free love. He supported birth control, experimental marriages, and repeal of the laws against homosexuality, declaring:

> The cramping of love by institutions is one of the major evils of the world.[11]

As Socrates in 399 B.C. was charged with corrupting Athenian youth and disbelieving in the state gods, so Russell in 1940 A.D. was attacked as unfit to teach college students because of his sexual and religious views. In that year, the Board of Higher Education of New York had offered, and Russell had accepted, a contract to teach philosophy at the City College of New York. Local church officials, however, vociferously attacked the appointment. The mass media joined in. Finally, a Brooklyn housewife filed a taxpayer's suit against the Board of Higher Education, demanding that Russell's contract be annulled.

The judge who heard the case, particularly upset that Russell would have the laws against homosexuality repealed, ruled in favor of the outraged taxpayer. Fortunately for Russell, however, some progress had been made since 399 B.C. He was not condemned to death like Socrates, but only forced to move on to lecture in Philadelphia instead. And so the good students of City College of New York were spared the danger of being exposed to the author of *Principia Mathematica*.

As Certain As 1, 2, 3

Russell's logical writings occupy a very distinctive band in his overall development. Over a period of ten years or so, beginning around the turn of the century, he developed a compact, sharply defined philosophy of logic. It was initially occasioned by certain problems in mathematics, particularly the question "What are numbers?"

As noted earlier, Russell's theory of logic and mathematics blossomed with his discovery of the works of Gottlob Frege. Although Russell had done some work independently of Frege, he later shifted the structure of his own system of mathematical logic onto a Fregean foundation. However, he modified this foundation to avoid a contradiction, "the Russell paradox," that he had unearthed in Frege's assumptions (see chapter five). Despite the Russell paradox, Frege continued to exercise a paramount influence on Russell and Whitehead, as attested by the opening pages of *Principia Mathematica*:

> In all questions of logical analysis, our chief debt is to Frege. Where we differ from him, it is largely because the contradiction [the Russell paradox] showed that he, in common with all other logicians ancient and modern, had allowed some error to creep into his premises; but apart from the contradiction, it would have been almost impossible to detect this error.[12]

Frege and Russell shared a common trait: both were obsessed with finding a source of absolute certainty in the world, believing that it was located, if anywhere, in logic and mathematics. To demonstrate this certainty, both undertook to prove that arithmetic can be strictly deduced from elementary principles of logic, which they regarded as self-evident. To bridge the gap between logic and mathematics, both relied heavily on the concept of *class*, which had previously been studied independently in both mathematics and logic.

According to Russell, numbers are classes of those classes that are "similar." By "similarity," Russell meant, *à la* Frege, that the individuals in the various classes under consideration could be exactly paired off. For example, the number four, in Russell's view, actually consists of nothing more than the class of all those classes that happen to be quartets. Russell then defined classes in terms of "propositional functions." These, he believed, could serve as substitutes for classes in deducing arithmetic from numbers.

Although Russell avoided the fatal paradox that infected Frege's assumptions, his own work contained numerous other flaws (discussed in greater detail in chapter three). For example, if numbers are nothing but the classes of classes that are "similar," then there would be no number four if at least four objects did not happen to exist. Most working mathematicians, however, maintain that pure mathematics has nothing whatever to do with what may or may not happen to exist at any given moment.

In his attempts to deduce arithmetic from logic, Russell was forced to assume a number of principles and axioms unknown to Frege. Some were quite complex; none was self-evident. Among these assumptions: "the axiom of infinity" (there exists an infinite number of objects); "the theory of types" (the permissible values of a variable in a propositional function depend on the type of entity referred to by the values of the variable); and "the axiom of reducibility" (certain propositional functions of unlimited generality can be replaced in crucial deductive sequences by certain propositional functions of lesser generality). Russell acknowledged that these assumptions were not self-evident. Still, he felt they were justified because they allowed for the deduction of "many propositions which are nearly indubitable."[13]

In offering this justification, Russell undermined his original intention of basing the certitude of mathematics on that of logic. Now it was the presumed certitude of mathematics that determined what were to be the validating axioms of logic. Nonetheless, Russell still claimed to have deduced arithmetic from logic.

Russell's quest for absolute certitude was later dealt a death blow by the Czech-born mathematician Kurt Gödel (1906-1978). In 1931, Gödel proved that in any formal deductive system powerful enough to deduce the basic notions of arithmetic, there will always be true arithmetic propositions that cannot be deduced from any given finite number of consistent axioms.[14]

In other words, the prime motivating force behind Leibniz, Frege, and Russell—the assumption that there is a kind of certitude equivalent to formal deducibility—is false. Let us assume that some things are certain, and also that some things can be logically deduced from a finite set of self-evident axioms. Nonetheless, there's no guarantee that these two classes of things will coincide. Whatever certitude may be, it is not identical with formal deducibility. Whatever mathematics may be, it is not just logic in disguise.

Who Was the Author of *Waverley*?

Although Russell failed to deduce numbers from logic, he succeeded in clarifying certain knotty problems in formal logic. Among these was the question of how to analyze "definite descriptions." These are phrases of the form "the so and so," as in "the author of *Waverley*."

The meaning of definite descriptions seems to be the particular object they pick out. What, then, is the meaning of a definite description when it picks out an object that does not exist, as in "the present King of France"?

Frege had said a phrase like "the present King of France" refers to the null class (the class that has no members). The Austrian philosopher Alexius Meinong had claimed that such a phrase refers to a thing that has "subsistence" but not "existence." Russell proposed an alternative explanation in his famous paper "On Denoting," published in 1905, which he rightly regarded as one of his greatest philosophical achievements.[15]

As an example, Russell took up the statement "Scott is the author of *Waverley*," which contains the definite description "the author of *Waverley*." This statement, said Russell, appears to be in simple subject-predicate form, and the definite description appears to pick out an object. However, Russell cautioned, logical analysis would show that both these impressions are false.

Although the proper name "Scott" does refer to a definite object, Russell argued that there is no object that the definite description "the author of *Waverley*" refers to. If there were, then the question "Is Scott the author of *Waverley*?" would mean the same as the question "Is Scott Scott?" This question, however, is not at all what King George III had in mind when, on hearing about *Waverley*, he asked whether Scott was its author. In Russell's parlance, the definite description as such has no meaning (denotation), although the statement in which it occurs does.

Russell argued that the phrase "the author of *Waverley*" is an "incomplete symbol." That is, the phrase has a proper use only when joined with certain other symbols, analogous to the use of the mathematical symbol "d/dx" in differential equations. Russell concluded that the statement "Scott is the author of *Waverley*" should actually be analyzed as "One and only one entity wrote *Waverley*, and Scott was identical with that one." This latter statement can be formalized in logical notation as follows: "At least one x wrote *Waverley*, no more than one x wrote *Waverley*, and for all x, if x wrote *Waverley*, then x = Scott."

This last formulation is striking because the definite description "the author of *Waverley*" has completely disappeared. However, the reformulation has accurately captured the meaning of the original statement. Russell presented this reformulation as a striking example of how grammatical form can disguise logical form, which can be brought to the surface through correct logical analysis.

Now consider statements like "The present King of France is bald." This statement, said Russell, should be analyzed as follows: "At least one x is the King of France, no more than one x is the King of France, and for all x, if x is the King of France, then x is bald." Russell concluded that this statement is meaningful, but false, for two reasons: (1) the troublesome definite description can be eliminated; and (2) the statement contains the false sub-statement "At least one x is the King of France." By using logical analysis in this way, Russell argued, we can clarify the meanings and truth conditions of statements that contain definite descriptions without any appeal to either null classes or unreal individuals.

The clarifying power of Russell's methods in "On Denoting" deeply impressed Anglo-American academic philosophers. In fact, the publication of this paper may be regarded as the beginning of what has come to be called "analytic philosophy." Russell himself strongly promoted this development, for he saw in his analysis of definite descriptions an example of what should be the ideal method in logic and philosophy as a whole.

Spurred on by his success in analyzing definite descriptions, Russell drew ever closer to the pluralist metaphysics and analytic methodology of Leibniz, despite misgivings in his earlier book on Leibniz. In the end, Russell accepted Frege's version of Leibniz (Leibnizian metaphysics minus God); he rejected, however, Leibniz's emphasis on the subject-predicate form of propositions and his theory of internal relations. The world is a radical plurality just as Leibniz said, Russell concluded, and analysis is the best way to understand it.

Ockham's Razor and Russell's Hatchet

Russell adopted another motif from Leibniz, "Ockham's razor," named after the 14th-century English logician William of Ockham (discussed in chapter four). Ockham's razor is a principle that says philosophers should not assume unnecessary entities in order to explain things. Russell wielded Ockham's razor with relish, calling it "the supreme methodological maxim in philosophizing."[16]

Russell eagerly shaved off ever larger quantities of what he regarded as excessive metaphysical growth. Indeed, each of his philosophic phases may be viewed as a successive narrowing of the kinds of minimal entities he was prepared to admit as necessary to explain the world. His goal was to find the simplest of simples, then use these to reconstruct the known world, without appealing to any sort of unknown entities. With this goal in mind, Russell rephrased Ockham's razor thus:

> Whenever possible, substitute constructions out of known entities for inferences to unknown entities.[17]

In practice, Russell could never settle on the alleged simples out of which everything else was supposed to be a "logical fiction." Each kind of alleged simple seemed to evaporate into another, and that one into yet another. For example, he originally thought that numbers are classes of classes. Then he argued that classes themselves are logical fictions constructed from propositional functions, which are fictions constructed from propositions, which are fictions constructed from multiple relations whose terms are constructions from sense-data, or sensibilia, or sensations, or habits, or *something*.

Although Russell said simples should be "known entities," none of his own postulated simples fit that bill. For example, the simples he proposed in his middle period—"sense-data"—are as metaphysical, strange, and complicated as "souls." Contrary to Russell, the things that human beings spontaneously apprehend in daily life are *objects*, such as cigarettes, guns, drug dealers, etc., not sense-data, such as patches-of-red-here-now. It is only with a strained effort (or the help of a hallucinogen) that we would ever say that we saw a burst of silvery colors coming at us, instead of the automobile that in fact came crashing through the cafe window near where we were sitting. If any human being ever did go through a whole day seeing nothing but patches of color and hearing nothing but bursts of sound, he or she would be very quickly killed.

Russell would counter that "real objects" are constructs that ordinary people make as a result of sensing their sense-data. But one could equally well argue that "sense-data" are constructs that philosophers make as a result of seeing objects. Even by Russell's own standards, "objects" must be preferred to "sense-data," since they are far more familiar than the latter; however, Russell could never bring himself to concede this point, because objects are obviously complex, and only simples (so he thought) are the really real things.

In his later years, Russell admitted that he was never able to find anything that was unconditionally simple. The reason, as demonstrated by earlier chapters, is that "simple-complex" is just another facet of "one-many." These distinctions are correlative, not absolute, depending on the decision of some interpreter or group of interpreters.

Russell turned Ockham's razor into a philosophical hatchet. When confronted with macro-entities like persons, nations, and ideals, he would take out his logical hatchet and chop away until they were pulverized into a pile of relative simples. These splinters he would then chop again, hoping to find the ever-elusive ultimate simples.

Russell claimed that his resulting heaps of splinters were equivalent to the original objects. But that's as if one were to take an ax to a piano, then claim that the pile of chips and wires is the same as the instrument on which someone had just played *Gymnopédies*.

Russell was right to insist that analysis tells us something about the world but wrong to claim that it tells us what is most important. *Gymnopédies* is no less revelatory of reality than *Principia Mathematica*. Throughout his life, however, Russell scoffed at the idea that there could be a variety of roads to the palace of knowledge:

> If it [philosophy] is dry and technical, it lays the blame on the universe, which has chosen to work in a mathematical way rather than as poets or mystics might have desired.[18]

Despite Russell's biases, the universe has not decided to give a favored view of itself to Western logicians and mathematicians, just as no god ever decided to make the earth the center of the universe. Russell rightly derided the old, earth-centered astronomy yet failed to see a parallel to this provincialism in his own statement quoted above.

"The lord whose oracle is at Delphi neither reveals nor conceals," said the ancient Greek philosopher Heraclitus, "but gives a sign." The same may be said of every human interpretive activity, from mathematics to mysticism.

Structure Amid the Splinters

Even if the universe consists of heaps of simples, it clearly also has some kind of structure. In order to account for the structure amid the heaps, Russell turned to the Parmenidean myth as he had inherited it from Leibniz and Frege.

At first, Russell postulated the existence of logical and mathematical forms, in the style of Plato. He claimed the mind could directly apprehend their reality with the same vividness as it did the taste of pineapples. Other philosophers agreed with Russell that they could taste pineapples; they had a greater difficulty, however, with logical forms.

Later, Russell appealed to the universally-formalizable aspects of language, but unmoored from Frege's divine-like dyad of the True and the False. This truncated version of Frege left Russell feeling uncomfortable, however, for it implied that logical necessity is just a linguistic convention.

At other times, Russell claimed that generality and necessity were based on "completely general facts." He tried to buttress this account with a behavioristic analysis of why people assent to propositions. He acknowledged, however, that his account was unconvincing:

> Clearly the question of our knowledge of general propositions involves difficulties as yet unsolved.[19]

To appreciate the length of Russell's journey over the years in dealing with the question of logical necessity, one need only compare his earliest with his latest writings on the subject. In 1907, at the age of 35, he wrote a small essay acknowledging that his interest in logic was not just a matter of scholarship, but something akin to a mystical quest. After approvingly quoting the opinion of Plato, to the effect that mathematics displays a kind of "divine necessity," Russell added:

> Mathematics takes us still further from what is human, into the vision of absolute necessity, to which not only the actual world, but every possible world must conform; and even here it builds a habitation, or rather finds a habitation eternally standing, where our ideals are fully satisfied and our best hopes are not thwarted.[20]

Fifty-two years later in 1959, at the age of 87, Russell dismissed his earlier view as "largely nonsense."[15] Although acknowledging that his work had been motivated by a quest for transcendent certainty, Russell finally concluded that the question of logical necessity tugged at the very frontiers of human knowledge. In the end, he conceded that he could give no definitive answer to this question. The best he could come up with was this: the concept of logical necessity seems to be required by the existence of the great body of scientific knowledge.

In offering this justification, Russell returned, ironically, to a view suggested to him nearly a century before by G.E. Moore. The degree to which any truth approaches necessity, said Moore, is proportional to the number of true propositions it implies.[21] Inverting Moore's argument, one might say this: Logically necessary propositions are those general propositions that must be presupposed in order for the conclusions of the various sciences to be true. This argument presupposes, in turn, that science provides a privileged window on reality. (Chapter twelve will follow the resurgence of this argument in Willard Van Orman Quine, an American admirer of Russell's.)

The Russell Irony

Russell's career shows a great irony: He began with the claim that the certitude of mathematics could be assured by deriving mathematics from logic. He concluded his career by justifying the supposed necessary truths of logic and mathematics in terms of the certitude of empirical science. In the intervening years, he had done a complete about-face. Contemplating these changes, Russell observed:

> My philosophical development, since the early years of the present century, may be broadly described as a gradual retreat from Pythagoras.[22]

The reference to Pythagoras is telling. As discussed in chapter four, Pythagoras founded a religious cult in ancient Greece based on the belief that reality ultimately consists of numbers. His views, as modified by Plato, came to influence most subsequent Western mathematical theorists, down to Bertrand Russell.

Pythagoreanism, when combined with the Parmenidean myth, reinforced the notion that logic, mathematics, and the formalizable aspects of language are ultimately grounded in a kind of divine necessity. By the end of his life, Russell had come to recognize that such a notion is mythical. He could not justify, short of a last-ditch appeal to the overall veracity of the empirical sciences, the alleged logical necessity that was at the root of his entire philosophy of logic and mathematics.

Russell's admission of failure was of great significance. The Parmenidean myth, for the first time since its inception more than two millennia before, displayed a gaping crack, emanating from its very core. Not even the greatest logician of the age could patch it over.

The Logical Machine Stalls

Russell's mythical presuppositions about logic landed him in hot water in *Principia Mathematica*. For example, Russell believed in the absolute objectivity of logic. But once any logical system admits that it has rules in addition to axioms, it also acknowledges that it is not completely objective, for a rule is whatever

CHAPTER SIX

some rule-giver says it is. So Russell tended to assimilate rules to axioms. (Axioms are true presuppositions within the system; rules are stipulations outside the system decreeing how theorems shall be deduced from axioms.) Unfortunately for Russell, a logical system that does not distinguish between rules and axioms generates paradoxes.

An example of such a paradox is Russell's theory of types, which Russell was forced to adopt in order to avoid a fatal flaw in Frege's logic ("the Russell Paradox"). The theory of types stratifies entities and propositional functions into a hierarchy, limiting the scope of general propositions. But when stated as an axiom, the theory of types becomes self-canceling, because it specifies that no proposition can state what is true of all propositions. This fact became scandalously clear when Russell tried to state the theory of types as a proposition. For example:

> Genuine general statements about all true propositions can not be made.[23]

This proposition, however, is itself a genuine general statement about all true propositions. Or, again:

> All phrases containing the words "all propositions" or "all functions" are prima facie meaningless.[24]

But this proposition itself begins with the phrase "all phrases containing the words 'all propositions.'"

Not only is the theory of types self-canceling as an axiom, it also implies that any proposition expressing a law of logic is meaningless. Russell's mythology of logic, however, assumed the truth of these same laws of logic. To get around this glitch, Russell tried to define basic logical operations by examples, not by propositions. For example, instead of stating the law of the excluded middle as a proposition, said Russell, all we have to do is resolve to use the following "schema" as a model:

q	=	p	or	not-p
T		T		F
T		F		T

There is a fallacy here, however. Although this approach does not state the law of the excluded middle as a proposition, it nonetheless drags it in with the schema itself, which simply *assumes* that there are only two truth-values, "*T*" and "*F*."

There was a great irony in Russell's entire approach to logic: Because of the paradoxes his mythology of logic generated, he was unable to use the system to formally express the primary assumptions (namely, the Parmenidean myth) that motivated his interests in logic in the first place.

This difficulty was not only an irony but also a contradiction, for Russell believed with Frege that logical necessity is that which is universally formalizable in language. His own system, however, was incapable, by deliberate design, of formally expressing such allegedly universal features of language.

Like Frege before him, Russell was so saturated with the Parmenidean myth that he just took it for granted. Indeed, he boasted that his approach to logic was mythology-free:

> It is presented for acceptance on the ground that it accords with what can be empirically observed, and that it rejects everything mythological.[25]

The Mythology of Facts

In the last chapter, we saw that Frege took the second part of the Parmenidean myth—bivalence—and made it the foundation of the remainder. The key was his theory of the True and the False, which he combined with his theory of sense and reference. All propositions, Frege argued, refer to only two objects, the True and the False. Russell, by contrast, denied that the True and the False are *objects* to which propositions *refer*. Instead, he argued that propositions either *correspond*, or not, to *facts*—being true in the first case, and false in the second.

Russell knocked out the True and the False as foundations for the rest of the Parmenidean myth. To build a new foundation after this change, he turned to its third component, the myth of absolute objectivity, which he reformulated and strengthened by his theory of "facts."

In his early years, Russell often equated facts with propositions. Later, he distinguished between the two, viewing language as a kind of mirror of the world of facts. Descriptive language, he argued, consists of three kinds of propositions: (1) atomic or basic propositions, which directly express the reports of the senses;

(2) the laws of logic, which express "completely general facts"; and (3) complex propositions, which are deduced from the former two kinds of propositions. When the logical form of a basic proposition corresponds to that of some atomic fact, and when the elements of the proposition correspond to the elements of the fact, the proposition is true; and when a complex proposition is deduced from true basic propositions, the complex proposition is true. Otherwise, propositions are false.

Russell developed this "correspondence theory of truth" in collaboration with Ludwig Wittgenstein. Its merits are evaluated in greater detail in chapter one; for our purposes here, we will concentrate on the notion of "fact," which is the hinge on which this entire theory turns.

According to Russell, the world, as that which true propositions mirror, is ultimately composed of simple objects and external relations (relations that do not affect the natures of the things related). Through sensation, we apprehend the simples, and through the mind, relations. When entities combine with other entities according to relations, the complex that results is what Russell calls a "fact."

Russell maintains that the structure of any complex is absolutely determinate. Simply put:

> Facts are what they are, without ambiguity.[26]

It was through his theory of absolutely determinate facts that Russell sought to re-secure the Parmenidean myth, and with it, his concept of logic as necessary and absolutely objective. Briefly, he argued that the basic laws of logic are necessary and objective because of a certain *fact*: the fact that certain structures are shared by the most general facts in the world and by the most generalizable features of language.

"But how do we know what the facts of the world are?" one might ask. Through the scientific method, Russell would answer. "And the most generalizable features of language?" Through logical analysis. The scientific method, according to Russell, is the single most reliable means we have to reveal the facts of the world. But the scientific method itself necessarily uses artificial languages. These are based on certain very general theoretical presuppositions, revealed through logical analysis. These presuppositions, Russell argues, turn out to be what are conventionally called the laws of logic, and they correspond to the most general facts of the world.

In the end, then, Russell justifies both the Parmenidean myth and empirical science by invoking the existence of absolutely determinate "facts." Although seemingly simple and innocuous, this assumption about facts actually masks a snake's nest of metaphysical biases.

From Factum to Fact

Let us begin with the etymology of the word "fact," which is derived from the Latin word *factum*, meaning "that which has been done or made." This word is the perfect participle of the verb *facere*, meaning to make or do.

The use of the perfect tense is significant here. In Latin, that tense commonly denotes what has been completed in the past, but whose effects continue into the present. For example, the common Latin expression *vixi*, which is in the perfect tense. Literally, this word means "I have lived," but more fully, because of the use of the perfect just mentioned, "I am dead." The implication here is that a thing is determinate *because it is in the past*. As such, it is beyond any further change.

This idiomatic use of the Latin perfect tense has affected the meaning of the word *factum*. The word not only *denotes* "that which has been done or made" (the dictionary definition) but also *connotes*, as a result of the idiomatic use of the perfect tense, "that which is determinately given *because* it has been done or made in the past." Indeed, it is because of this connotation that the English expression "a fact" has come to mean, not "a deed," as one might expect from the literal root, but rather "a given reality," which is due to the idiomatic use of the Latin perfect tense.

The upshot is that the simple English word "fact" connotes something that is not still occurring in time, for otherwise it would not be determinate. Pastness bestows determinateness.

The Messiness of Time

These etymological observations are relevant to Russell's concept of "fact." Not only does he assume that a fact is always determinate, but also that determinateness is connected to pastness or timelessness. For example, he says that any proposition expressing factual knowledge, if well stated, should not have a truth-value that is a function of time. So the proposition "I am now in Dallas" is poorly stated. Even if true right now, it may be false two days from now. This proposition is better stated as "So and so was in Dallas at such and such a time." This formulation refers to what is determinate—because it is impersonal and past.

Russell dislikes ordinary language because its sentences are often time-dependent, so he dismisses it with an aristocratic sweep of the hand:

> The occurrence of tense in verbs is an exceedingly annoying vulgarity due to our preoccupation with practical affairs.[27]

Again, Russell recognizes a whole class of facts, such as the fact that two and two make four, where there is no question of any time reference at all. They are determinate for that very reason,.

Russell insists that artificial languages can be constructed that are entirely tense-free (like the language he invented in *Principia Mathematica*). He scoffs at the idea that something important might be lost when human experience is translated into such an artificial language. We saw above, however, that the artificial language of *Principia Mathematica* could not even express Russell's own tense-free presuppositions about logic; hence his scoffing is misplaced.

This, then, is Russell's justification for the Parmenidean myth, after ditching Frege's dyad of the True and the False: *Facts* constitute objectivity; objectivity in turn justifies a timeless model of knowledge, logical necessity, and bivalence.

In retrospect, we see a progressive sliding-down the ontological pole from Leibniz to Russell in their accounts of the Parmenidean myth. For Leibniz, the linchpin of the entire logical juggernaut was God, conceived as the great cosmic validator of logical necessity. After pulling out God, Frege reached for the common, formalizable aspects of language, which he grounded on the divine-like dyad of the True and the False. Russell kept Frege's formalizable aspects of language, but rejected Frege's transcendent objects. Said Russell: Propositions correspond, or not, with "facts"; these are the bedrock of the entire logical structure.

Frozen Facts in the Heat of Time

If formal logic (and therefore science) is ultimately based on frozen facts, how can it ever be true to reality, which is always astir under the thawing influence of time? This question is the great pitfall into which Russell's elaborate logical juggernaut eventually tumbled and from which he was never able to extricate it, although he resorted to every conceptual pulley he could think of.

To understand how Russell found himself in this predicament, we have to take a brief look at the way he analyzed the relationships between three different kinds of entities: classes, properties, and predicates. As it turns out, a crucial part of his attempted deduction of arithmetic from logic (his axiom of reducibility) rests on a fallacy in his handling of these three entities. This fallacy in turn results from false assumptions he makes about the determinateness of class membership. Our elucidation of these matters will begin with his concept of classes, then consider his treatment of their relationship to properties and predicates via the axiom of reducibility.

Since Russell equated facts with determinateness, he naturally assumed that the question of whether any given object is a member of some class or not is also determinate. He held this to be true regardless of which of the two usual methods is used in defining classes, the *extensional* or the *intensional* method, as they are conventionally called. In regard to the extensional method, a class is defined simply by enumerating some finite list of objects. For example, if I take three eggs out of the refrigerator and designate them a class, then a class they remain, to the exclusion of all other objects.

As soon as I define such a class, I know immediately, for any given object in the universe, whether it is a member of this class or not. I don't have to inquire further into any additional properties of the object.

Russell also held that class membership is determinate where classes are defined by specifying a certain property (the "intensional" class definition). For example, suppose I take the property "homophobic male" and use it to define a class. Then all objects in the universe that happen to be homophobic males are members of this class. But in contrast to a class that is defined extensionally, I cannot know immediately, for any given object in the universe, whether it is a member of an intensionally defined class or not. I must investigate whether it possesses the property in question.

This analysis of class and class membership is actually based on a tacit assumption that is by no means obvious: an entity that is a member of some class is what it is unchangingly. To see how this assumption works, let us use the example above, where we extensionally defined a certain class as consisting of three eggs taken from the refrigerator. Let us call this class E, consisting of the three eggs a, b, and c. Now suppose, after we define E, that a rolls off the table and breaks on the floor. Is the gooey yellow and white mass on the floor still a? If not, then E, by our definition, no longer exists. And if that is the case, then neither a nor E is a time-independent entity. You might object that the gooey mass on the floor is still a, only that it now has a different form. But what if my roommate's pet ferret runs into the room and gobbles up the goo, eventually converting most of it to ferret feces? Does a still exist? Clearly not, and therefore neither does E.

The correct description here is this: "Class E, consisting of a, b, and c, existed for such and such a time." This formulation is determinate, since it refers to the past. But there is a glitch: In order to derive numbers from classes, Russell insists that classes are timeless; they cannot be functions of the past, like historical events. Moreover, his system of formal logic, because of its adherence to bivalence, is not powerful enough to handle the truth-value "true at such and such a time." Because of these complications, Russell rejects any tense-bearing formulation about classes as poorly made and, indeed, vulgar. But we have just seen that without such a tense-bearing formulation we cannot talk about our class E. Conclusion: the existence of E is an anomaly in terms of Russell's understanding of classes and determinate facts.

An analogous problem arises for Russell with *intensionally* defined classes. In the case of the class defined above by the property "homophobic male," suppose there is a certain urban teenage American male, whom we shall call Closet. Let us assume that Closet enjoys joining with packs of other males his own age in the common American pastime of hunting down, cornering, and battering gay men. If we designate the class of homophobic males by H, then Russell would say it is a determinate fact that Closet is a member of H. But what if Closet undergoes a change of consciousness? Suppose he comes to the following realizations: (1) like most human males, he himself has certain homosexual desires; (2) he has come to associate these desires with degradation because of a superstitious Christian upbringing; and (3) his attacks on gay men are an acting-out of his own self-loathing stimulated by his superstitious upbringing. In this case, Closet may cease to be homophobic and hence no longer be a member of H. Conclusion: except for eternal objects having changeless qualities, intensionally-defined classes are also at odds with Russell's requirement for the determinateness of classes.

Russell always assumed that existing entities in the real world could be treated as class-members according to his theoretical understanding of class membership, whether for extensionally or intensionally defined classes. In fact, however, the question always remains open for any given existing entity whether such a theoretical class treatment is appropriate, and this question usually comes down to one involving time-relevance. If the egg does not roll off the table or is not eaten by a ferret during some relevant time frame, then it can be treated as a member of a class in Russell's sense. The same goes for the homophobic male if he does not undergo a change of consciousness. But when time changes become crucial, Russell's analysis breaks down.

In the case of entities like abstract numbers, no time change is relevant, and it is here that Russell is on his firmest ground. Even so, however, Russell's account of class is applicable to numbers only insofar as that account is *purely hypothetical*, saying nothing about objects in the real world. In fact, however, Russell sought to give an account of how numbers are actually used in counting real objects. It was this lunging at real butterflies in real trees with only hypothetical nets that caused him to trip over the tangled clump of *ad hoc* assumptions known as the axioms of infinity and reducibility.

The Axiom of Reducibility

As we saw above, Russell originally developed his theory of types in order to avoid a fatal contradiction that had plagued Frege. But the adoption of the theory of types raised a new problem for Russell: it prevented him from using propositions of unlimited generality, since now a proposition could only generalize about propositions of a lower type than itself. To get around this glitch, Russell introduced the axiom of reducibility; it says that certain propositional functions of unlimited generality can be replaced in crucial deductive sequences by propositional functions of lesser generality.

This strategy, however, brought with it another problem. Because of his adoption of the axiom of reducibility, flaws inherent in Russell's concept of class determinateness eventually infected and debilitated his entire logical system. To understand the bind in which Russell found himself, we need to look in greater detail at this troublesome axiom.

To define formally what he meant by the term "the axiom of reducibility," Russell introduced the notion of "predicative function." By this term, he meant a function that predicates of its variable that which is of a type immediately higher than the variable.

An example is the propositional function "x is homophobic," where x is understood to be a place-holder for the names of individual human beings. This propositional function generates specific propositions that predicate the property of being homophobic to the individuals named. (For example, "Pope John-Paul II is homophobic.")

Higher-order propositions are in effect *descriptions of statements*, whereas lowest-order propositions simply state facts about objects. As we will see below, Russell trips when he attempts to slide over the wide gap between description and fact.

Russell formally defines the axiom of reducibility thus: for any given higher-order function of x there is always some predicative function of x that is true when the higher-order function of x is true, and false when the higher-order function is false.[28] In other words: whenever we correctly describe statements concerning objects, our doing so is equivalent to the fact that the objects in question have some specific property, and vice-versa.

The axiom of reducibility serves as a bridge between general predicates of statements on one hand and specific properties of objects on the other. As such, it provides a detour for someone using a truth-functional logical calculus to get around the prohibition against using propositional functions that unqualifiedly refer to "all," which is prohibited by the theory of types. By virtue of the axiom of reducibility, we can always say that whenever such a forbidden general predication seems necessary to complete a proof, there must be some formally-equivalent property-statement that can be put in its place, permitting the proof to proceed despite restrictions imposed by the theory of types.

At this point, an interesting question arises: How can we be certain that there is always some property-relation involving x that is formally equivalent to some given general predication about statements about x? Russell admitted that the axiom of reducibility is not obviously true, but presented a number of arguments intended to show that it is a reasonable working supposition. His strongest point was to demonstrate (as he thought) that the denial of the axiom of reducibility would lead to impossible consequences. If we deny the axiom, he claimed, then it would be possible for us to truly describe all the possible situations concerning some object x, and at the same time find that object x itself did not have some property corresponding to each such true description of its situations. But if that were the case, Russell continued, then there could conceivably be a difference between an object's having some property and our truly predicating something of the object. And if *that* were the case, then it would be possible for two objects to have all the same predicates, but not have all the same properties. This consequence would mean that it would be possible for two supposedly different objects to have all the same predicates, and yet not be one and the same object. This conclusion Russell rejected as patently absurd, invoking Leibniz's famous principle of "the identity of indiscernibles" (if we can't find any difference between two things, they're the same). In other words, if the axiom of reducibility is false, then the identity of an object is something that transcends all that is truly predicated of it.

The Identity of Frozen Fish

Despite Russell's best arguments, however, the axiom of reducibility is in fact false, as is Leibniz's principle of the identity of indiscernibles, of which the axiom of reducibility is merely an updated version. The fallacy for both Russell and Leibniz lies in a hidden assumption: The identity of any object is closed rather than open (that is, the identity of an object is determinate). This hidden assumption *is* true for objects that existed in the past (such as historical events) or objects that are timeless (such as hypothetical numbers); however, this assumption is false for any object that continues to unfold in the present (such as you, the reader).

The predicates of any object that continues to exist in the present do *not* exhaust its properties, and for a very simple reason: Any predication we make concerning such an object can at best truly describe properties the object has already displayed in the past or approximately predict properties it may yet display in the future. However, the object is not yet finished (*factum*); therefore, its properties are not yet all determinate.

Suppose we may have said, up to the present moment, everything there is to say about an object that will still continue to exist; nonetheless, the predicates asserted at any given point of time for such a continuing object cannot *in principle* exhaust all its properties, since the object is not yet finished. Therefore, the identity of any object that continues to exist is something that transcends all that is truly predicated of the object, which Russell incorrectly thought was impossible. So it is a mistake to conclude, as Russell did, that because denial of the axiom of reducibility implies that an object's identity transcends its predicates, denial of the axiom must be false. In fact, as we have just seen, denial of the axiom turns out to imply something which is quite true, although Russell could not understand how that could be so. Like all previous systems inspired by the Parmenidean myth, Russell's logic founders when it comes to objects whose existence is still unfolding in time.

The ineptitude of Western logic in dealing with temporal realities is what the existentialist philosophers meant to castigate in their famous motto "existence precedes essence." They rightly insisted that the identity of any living being is an ongoing existential process that cannot just be delivered up, like a frozen fish in cellophane, through some kind of formal definition. Their insights, however, never moved Russell. He looked down his nose at existentialism, as witnessed by his curt response to a question about it on British television in 1959:

> I don't think myself that there's anything very important in all that.[29]

Now the fact that denial of the axiom of reducibility does not entail a false proposition about identity does not mean that the axiom is false, only that Russell's attempted proof of it is off the mark. Nonetheless, it is clear that one of Russell's most basic philosophical assumptions—that the identity of any and every object is a determinate—is false, and that this assumption first helped motivate him in articulating the axiom of reducibility. Even so, however, the veracity of any proof is independent of the motives of the person proposing it.

The Fallacy of Reducibility

This is how we can disprove the axiom of reducibility: The axiom states that for any given function F_1 of x, there is a formally-equivalent predicative function F_2 of x. Now let F_1 be the function "x has no predicates of the type immediately higher than the type of the values of x." If F_1 is true, then there is no F_2, since there can be no predicative functions where there are no predicates of a type immediately higher than that of the object to which they apply. Hence the axiom of reducibility is false in this case, and therefore not an axiom after all. (F_1 does not violate the theory of types, since F_1 is of a higher type than both the type of predicates that it mentions and the individuals that may be substituted for x.)

One might object here that it is impossible to conceive of an object that has no predicates of the type immediately higher than the object. That would mean that the object has no properties, and an object without properties is a contradiction in terms. But this objection assumes that properties and predicates are interconvertible. In fact, however, a predicate is an *asserted* property, and it is quite possible for an object to have properties that have never been asserted of it, and hence for it to be an object without predicates.

Russell erroneously assumed that a logical calculus could be developed without any reference to an interpreter (that is, that the calculus can be absolutely objective). Consequently, he repeatedly confused predicates with properties. For example, he explicitly states in *Principia* that the predicates of an object are among its properties.[30] But in fact the relation of an object to its properties is of an entirely different order from the relation of an object to its predicates. The former relation involves two terms (object-property), whereas the latter involves five (object-property-interpreter-language-predicate).

Once you start talking about an object's predicates, you have undertaken what Willard Van Orman Quine calls "semantic ascent," and that flight is not at all the same as walking in the realm of objects. The difference is that whenever discourse is about predication, there is always an implicit reference to some language and some interpreter (the predicator). Discourse about properties and objects, however, is independent of language and interpreters (subject to the qualifications discussed in chapter one). Therefore, it is possible for an object to have many properties, but no predicates, since predicates are formulations in some language, and objects can exist independent of any and all language.

At one time Russell claimed that the axiom of reducibility could be proven if the reality of classes were assumed, but that he preferred instead to view classes as logical fictions composed of objects and propositional functions. However, the same fallacy—that of the determinateness of the identity of temporal objects—infects both his axiom of reducibility and also his concept of classes. Precisely because the identity of temporal objects is not a "fact" as Russell understands the word, predicates for such objects cannot be reduced to properties, nor can class membership be absolutely determinate. Therefore, the axiom of reducibility remains false even if one were to assume that classes are real.

Russell's whole system is a theoretical tripod, resting on the theory of types, the axiom of infinity, and the axiom of reducibility. The collapse of this third foot, due to Russell fallacious view of the determinateness of identity and class membership, results in the overthrow of the entire system.

Russell the Fundamentalist

Guided by the Parmenidean myth, Russell wrongly believed that *Principia Mathematica* was like a great philosophical X-ray. It revealed, he believed, the objective logical boniness that underlay both natural reality and human speech. In reality, however, his logic, like any system grounded on the Parmenidean myth, can never realize such an ideal. At best, it can provide a logical description of only certain objects, namely those where temporal changes are "irrelevant" for the purposes at hand.

Resolution of this very question of what is temporally relevant or not itself presupposes the existence of some interpreter or some group of interpreters with specific purposes acting in specific contexts. In sum: Russell's logic contains an ineradicable subjective element, which he never acknowledged.

Indeed, *Principia* fails even in its analysis of *numbers*, which are completely atemporal objects. As noted in chapter three, this failure has generated a still-unresolved crisis in 20th-century mathematics. In a new preface to the second edition of *Principia Mathematica*, published in 1927, Russell tried to patch over some of the more obvious cracks in the original edition, but without lasting success.. To date, no one has realized the dream—proclaimed by Leibniz, attempted and abandoned by Frege, taken up anew by Russell—of deducing arithmetic from pure logic.

To the end of his life, Russell remained a philosophical fundamentalist. He believed in the existence of a few simple objective principles from which all the complexes of reality could be constructed. We could find them all, he insisted, if only we used the right analytic technique! In the same way, the religious fundamentalist regards religious truth as an objective fact revealed once and for all in some holy book, if only we interpret it in the right way. Replace the holy book with a formalized language, and seize on philosophical analysis as the inspired method, and you get Bertrand Russell.

Although hoping to analyze his way back to sure and simple principles, Russell ironically found that he had to introduce notions of ever increasing complexity and doubtfulness in order to save his system. Despite all its spectacular hoots, whistles, and flashes, the *Principia Mathematica* juggernaut eventually lurched to a standstill, unable to bring off the long hoped-for miracle of giving birth to arithmetic.

As it left Russell's hands, the Parmenidean myth encompassed the following doctrines: (1) there is a common necessity that rules both human discourse and the external world, grounded on the existence of completely general facts; (2) propositions, if meaningful, are either true or false; and (3) a timeless, static model of knowledge is the ideal because reality consists of atemporal facts, analyzable into patterns of external relations, and expressible in terms of formalized languages.

Despite Russell's revisions to the Parmenidean myth, it remains liable to the following three objections: (1) the doctrine that a common necessity rules reality, thought, and language is merely a supposition, ultimately derived from patriarchal religious belief; (2) propositions can have many truth-values besides "true" and "false"; and (3) a static, impersonal model works for only certain aspects of reality.

The most that can be reasonably claimed for any system based on the Parmenidean myth is that it is useful for certain interpreters in certain contexts; it is *not* reasonable to claim that such a system is ideal for all human cognitive endeavors. Yet throughout his life Russell repeatedly made this very claim, as when he praised scientific and mathematical knowledge with these words in 1931:

> The most that can be known, and that only on the most hopeful view, is that there are certain relations in the physical world which share certain abstract logical characteristics with the relations that we know. The characteristics which they share are those that can be expressed mathematically.[31]

Logic and the Will to Power

Russell claimed that human societies that are committed to logico-scientific thought are superior to those that are not; he believed that the former are justified in conquering the latter if the conquest furthers the spread of the scientific mentality. For example, he usually referred to the members of nature-oriented tribal societies as "savages." Again, he said that the great destruction and suffering caused by Alexander the Conqueror was justified because it resulted in the spread of the Greek language and Greek culture. Finally, he argued that the triumph of the scientific world-view justified the European conquest of North America:

> Now take a war that had no justification whatsoever in the legal sense; that is, the occupation of the North American continent by white men. I should say that on the whole that was a good thing, although it had no legal justification.[32]

Russell always viewed the quest for knowledge as part of the human will to power. So he found it easy to extend the objectifying implications of the Parmenidean myth toward the whole of nature. Humans must come to understand, he argued, that nature is a great common enemy to be subdued. The weapons for doing so are provided by logic, mathematics, and the sciences. He urged educators to promote this view in schools in order to redirect aggressive human instincts away from wars against other humans toward a great common war against nature:

> You might regard Mother Nature in general as your enemy, and envisage human life as a struggle to get the better of Mother Nature. If men viewed life in this way, co-operation of the whole human race would become easy.[33]

Russell's dogmatic commitment to the Parmenidean myth, and the implications that he draws from that myth in regard to the treatment of human beings, animals, and nature in general, constitute the classic example of the illogic of modernity. I say *illogic*, because this view is based on fallacies ultimately derived from religion; *classic*, because it was articulated and emphasized by the greatest Western philosopher of the 20th century; and *modern*, because it is characteristic of patriarchal-industrial civilization, of which it has become a principal ideological prop.

Politics vs. Logic

As indicated earlier, Russell actually developed two conflicting philosophical systems, which he was never able to reconcile: on the one hand his philosophy of logic and mathematics; on the other his philosophy of politics, ethics, and social criticism.

A good example of the conflict between Russell's two philosophies lies in the theory of relations presupposed by each. As a logician and mathematician, Russell insisted that the world consists of simples held together in complexes by purely external relations. (In purely external relations, the nature of each thing is independent of its relations to other things.) As a political and ethical philosopher, however, Russell passionately entreated other human beings to change the way they live, think, and view the world. In making these appeals, he assumed that through rational argument and emotional exhortation, he could change other people. This assumption presupposes the reality of internal relations. (In internal relations, the nature of each thing is affected by its relations to other things.)

Another example: As a logician, Russell argued that most of the things encountered in ordinary life are logical fictions, ultimately reducible to some kind of simples, such as qualities, or sense-data, or sensations, etc. These underlying simples are "the really real things" (*ta ontos onta*, as Plato would say). What, then, is the status of human minds? These are either logical fictions or inferred entities; in either case, passive. But as a political advocate, Russell assumed that minds have a direct apprehension of themselves and other minds. He also believed that they are active forces causing events to happen in the real world.

A similar dilemma confronted Russell in his theory of the emotions. As a logician and behaviorist, he insisted that each person's emotions are strictly private, and that the most one person can know of another's emotion is an inference based on the other person's objective behavior. In his political and ethical polemics, however, Russell acknowledged that emotions are immediately sharable. Indeed, he argued that attempts to change another's ethical values are really appeals to influence another's feelings by exposure to one's own.

Again, Russell as a logician insisted on the value of *analysis* as the golden key to understanding reality, but as an ethical and political philosopher he insisted on a holistic world-view. The moral goal for every individual, he argued, is to expand his or her sense of self beyond one's own skin and bones, to one's family, then nation, then biological species, then planet, and then to the cosmos as a whole. But if I identify my true self with the human race or the cosmos, what becomes of the notion that every object is an impenetrable logical atom only externally connected with other atoms? And if that notion fails, what justification can there be for regarding analysis as a privileged window on reality? Isn't holistic insight just as important as analysis? Although Russell himself possessed holistic insight in his moral and political views, there was no place for such a thing in his philosophy of logic.

Finally, Russell justified his doctrines of logic on the grounds that they were necessary to validate science. One of the main reasons he esteemed science was his belief that it had, on the whole, made life much better for humankind. But when, as a political and ethical philosopher, he looked around at the actual conditions in the modern world, conditions that could not possibly have emerged without science, he regarded them as "horrible, horrible, *horrible*."[34]

Russell and Neoscholasticism

As noted earlier, Russell's famous paper "On Denoting," published in 1905, marks the beginning of the analytic movement in Anglo-American academic philosophy. Although Russell initiated this movement with "On Denoting" and further inspired it with *Principia Mathematica*, he later chastised it in his popular writings.

Russell's criticism began with an early version of analytic philosophy, logical positivism, that came into its own in the 20s in Vienna. Influenced by the earlier views of Ludwig Wittgenstein, who had been influenced by Russell, the logical positivists argued that propositions are either formulations of pure logic or else empirical descriptions, and that the meaning of any proposition lies in its method of verification. Russell, rejecting the verifiability theory of meaning, was disturbed to see the logical positivists becoming increasingly preoccupied with linguistic analysis as an end in itself:

> There is, I think, a danger that logical positivism may develop a new kind of scholasticism, and may, by being unduly linguistic, forget the relation to fact that makes a statement true.[35]

Russell's fears were confirmed with the rise of a new style of analytic philosophy practiced at

Oxford University, which continues to set the tone in the philosophy departments of many Anglo-American universities to this day. Stressing the importance of the logical analysis of ordinary language, Oxford's analytic philosophy regards the quest for substantive answers as the prerogative of science. Henceforth philosophy's role is merely to aid us in being clear about our questions, but without presuming to offer any substantive answers. Russell objected that the ordinary language that these philosophers claim to analyze is really nothing but the talk of people of their own class and educational status.

Russell delighted in lampooning Oxford's new style of analytic philosophy with an anecdote about an experience he once had while bicycling toward Winchester. Having lost his way, he stopped at a shop to ask for directions. When he asked for the shortest way to get to Winchester, the man behind the counter, scratching his head, relayed his questions on to a knowing person in the back room, who was heard but not seen:

> "Gentleman wants to know the shortest way to Winchester."
> And a voice came back, "Winchester?"—
> "Aye"—
> "Way to Winchester?"—
> "Aye"—
> "Shortest way?"—
> "Aye"—
> "Don't know."
> And so I had to go on without getting any answer. Well, that is what Oxford philosophy thinks one should do.[36]

Russell's warnings about the implosion of analytic philosophy into a kind of neoscholasticism proved to be correct. Although Russell protested this tendency, he was himself, ironically, one of the principal causes of it. He had popularized the fad of dismissing as muddled-headed metaphysics any effort in philosophy that did not seem to be properly scientific in spirit.

Once science is taken for granted as the supreme arbiter of rational knowledge, then philosophy itself must stand before the bar of science, rather than vice-versa. Since philosophy is definitely *not* a scientific undertaking, it can enter only a very feeble plea when so judged. In fact, however, *everything*, including the "scientific method," is open to critical examination by philosophy. As we will see in chapter twelve, science, when so examined, does not fare nearly so well as is commonly believed.

A second cause of the implosion of analytic philosophy has been the progressive professionalization of philosophy in the 20th century. Throughout history, only a minority of the world's great philosophers lived out their days as functionaries in some academic institution. Among those who did, most lived in an environment far different from that of the career-humping bureaucratic wasteland that today passes for a university. The Academy of Plato and the Lyceum of Aristotle, for example, were also spiritual institutions, welcoming those who were motivated by the desire for wisdom for its own sake; they were not large, impersonal degree-mills run by petty bourgeois climbers worried about their career tracks.

Bertrand Russell was on the cusp of both the old and the new ways of doing philosophy: although a product of the university system, he was also a fiery rebel against it, even to the point of several times losing his appointments. His rebelliousness, which was the great impetus behind his philosophical insight, has rarely been emulated by the hacks who succeeded him in the field.

Modern-day professionalization has reduced philosophy to a set of professional skills that can be quantified, tested, and controlled in a bureaucratic context. Accordingly, that system of philosophy has thrived which stresses logical technique at the cost of philosophic insight and substance. The same thing happened after the rise of universities in the Middle Ages, when philosophy was also reduced to logical analysis. To find the innovative philosophers in that, as in this, epoch, one has to turn to heretics and mystics.

Russell and Wittgenstein

A modern philosopher whose work (as commonly interpreted) promoted the professionalization of philosophy was Ludwig Wittgenstein. He influenced both earlier logical positivism and the later Oxford style of philosophy. As noted above, Wittgenstein had originally been Russell's pupil at Cambridge. His first book was *Tractatus Logico-Philosophicus*, published through Russell's efforts in 1922.

Although Russell was originally Wittgenstein's teacher and patron, he later bitterly denounced his former pupil as a kind of philosophic fraud. The reason is easy to see. Although Wittgenstein shared certain philosophic interests with Russell, he sorely lacked his teacher's good-natured humanitarianism and urbane wit. Moreover, Wittgenstein expressed his views in a dense, pretentious style, and became the center of an adoring academic cult. In watching the rise of Wittgenstein, Russell saw the triumph of what he viewed as a garbled version of himself. It was not a pleasant spectacle for him to behold.

By virtue of the great scope and inventiveness of his inquiries and theories, Bertrand Russell was the greatest Western philosopher of the twentieth century. Many in the literate public at large are aware of this fact; nonetheless, one of the great academic scandals of our age is that most Anglo-American philosophy departments today have scant regard for his work. Instead, they have lavished their attention on the works of Russell's star pupil, Ludwig Wittgenstein. The supreme irony in all this, however, is that these academics have grossly misunderstood the message of their esteemed master, as succeeding chapters will amply demonstrate.

The Illogic of Patriarchy

In the last four chapters we have watched as generations of logicians successively transmitted a great myth from one era to the next, beginning with Parmenides in the 5th century B.C. and continuing until Bertrand Russell in the 20th century A.D. Although succeeding generations made various alterations to this myth, its core dogmas remained intact.

This dogmatic core, which is both mythical and false, has been at the very heart of the illogic of antiquity, the illogic of early modernity, and the illogic of the twentieth century. Moreover, underlying this dogmatic continuity has been a social and sexual one, which is its real source of historical staying-power. That social continuity has been the violently-imposed rule of human males over the rest of humanity and the entire planet. Indeed, the several illogics that we have traced out in these pages are but various phases of but one great illogic, the illogic of patriarchy. The Parmenidean myth has survived for millennia because it constitutes the core set of assumptions underlying the way in which certain kinds of patriarchal men think.

In the end, after all the dust had settled from millennia of disputation over the merits of the Parmenidean myth, Bertrand Russell seemed to have presented the final argument in its behalf. The presuppositions of the Parmenidean myth are worthy dogma, he argued, because they justify science, and because science is a supreme good. In the next four chapters, we will see what happened when one world-renowned logician realized not only that the Parmenidean myth is fallacious but also that the merits of science itself are open to question.

---

[1] Gottlob Frege, *The Basic Laws of Arithmetic*, first vol. originally published 1893, trans. by Montgomery Furth, University of California Press, Berkeley, 1964.

[2] For overviews of Russell's thought, see Elizabeth Eames, *Bertrand Russell's Dialogue with His Contemporaries*, Southern Illinois University Press, Carbondale, 1989; Peter Hylton, *Russell, Idealism, and the Emergence of Analytic Philosophy*, Clarendon Press, Oxford, 1990; Ronald Jager, *The Development of Bertrand Russell's Philosophy*, Humanities Press, New York, 1972; C.W. Kilmister, *Russell*, The Harvester Press, 1984; Paul Kuntz, *Bertrand Russell*, Twayne Publishers, Boston, 1986; and Paul Schilpp (ed.), *The Philosophy of Bertrand Russell*, Tudor Publishing Co., 3rd edition, 1951.

[3] Bertrand Russell, *The Basic Writings of Bertrand Russell*, ed. by Robert E. Egner and Lester E. Denonn, Simon and Schuster, New York, 1961, p. 31.

[4] Bertrand Russell, *A Critical Exposition of the Philosophy of Leibniz*, 1900, George Allen & Unwin, 1958.

[5] Bertrand Russell, *The Principles of Mathematics*, 1903, 2nd Edition, W.W. Norton & Company, Inc., New York, n.d.

[6] See Jager, *op. cit., passim.*

[7] Russell, *My Philosophical Development*, p. 25. Peter Hylton correctly notes that after Russell rejected idealism, he embraced the following view: "The world is made up of objects: *object* is a fundamental metaphysical category, into which everything falls. Objects are not intrinsically spatio-temporal but just atemporally *are*. Each object is quite distinct from and independent of every other; objects are related, but not intrinsically" (Hylton, *op. cit.*, p. 279). Hylton errs, however, by calling this view "Platonic Atomism." It is rather, as Russell himself acknowledged, a modification of Leibniz's theory of monads.

[8] Russell, *My Philosophical Development*, p. 11; and Bertrand Russell, *Bertrand Russell Speaks His Mind*, The World Publishing Company, New York, 1960, p. 15.

[9] Bertrand Russell, *Introduction to Mathematical Philosophy*, G. Allen & Unwin, London, 1960.

[10] Bertrand Russell, *War Crimes in Vietnam*, Allen & Unwin, London, 1967.

[11] Russell, *Basic Writings*, p. 349.

[12] Alfred North Whitehead and Bertrand Russell, *Principia Mathematica*, vol. 1, 2nd edition, Cambridge University Press, 1960 reprint of 2nd edition of 1927, p. viii.

[13] *ibid.*, p. 59.

[14] Kurt Gödel, "Über formal unentscheidbare Sätze der Principia Mathematica und verwandter Systeme I," *Monat-

shefte für Mathematik und Physik, vol. 38, 1931, pp. 173-198.

[15] Bertrand Russell, "On Denoting," 1905; reprinted in *Logic and Knowledge*, ed. by Robert Charles Marsh, George Allen and Unwin, London, 1956; 7th impression 1984.

[16] Russell, *Logic and Knowledge*, p. 145.

[17] *ibid.*, p. 326.

[18] Russell, *Basic Writings*, p. 274.

[19] Bertrand Russell, *An Inquiry Into Meaning and Truth*, W.W. Norton & Co., New York, 1940, p. 113.

[20] Bertrand Russell, *Mysticism and Logic*, W.W. Norton & Co., Inc., New York, 1929, pp. 60 & 69.

[15] Russell, *My Philosophical Development*, p. 211.

[21] See the essay "Necessity" in G.E. Moore, *G.E. Moore. The Early Essays*, ed. by Tom Regan, Temple University Press, Philadelphia, 1986, pp. 81ff. The classic objection to this view is that *every* true proposition implies an infinite number of true propositions.

[22] Russell, *My Philosophical Development*, p. 208.

[23] *ibid.*, p. 74.

[24] *ibid.*, p. 79.

[25] Russell, *Logic and Knowledge*, p. 307.

[26] Russell, *Inquiry Into Meaning and Truth*, p. 102.

[27] Russell, *Logic and Knowledge*, p. 248.

[28] See the discussion in *Principia Mathematica*, vol. 1, pp. 56ff.

[29] Russell, *Bertrand Russell Speaks His Mind*, p. 17.

[30] Russell, *Principia Mathematica.*, p. 56.

[31] Russell, *Basic Writings*, p. 625.

[32] Russell, *Bertrand Russell Speaks His Mind*, pp. 35-36.

[33] Russell, *Basic Writings*, p. 475.

[34] Quoted by Paul Edwards, "Bertrand Russell," in *The Encyclopedia of Philosophy*, vol. 7, The Free Press, 1967, p. 256; original's emphasis.

[35] Russell, *Logic and Knowledge*, p. 380.

[36] Russell, *Bertrand Russell Speaks His Mind*, p. 16.

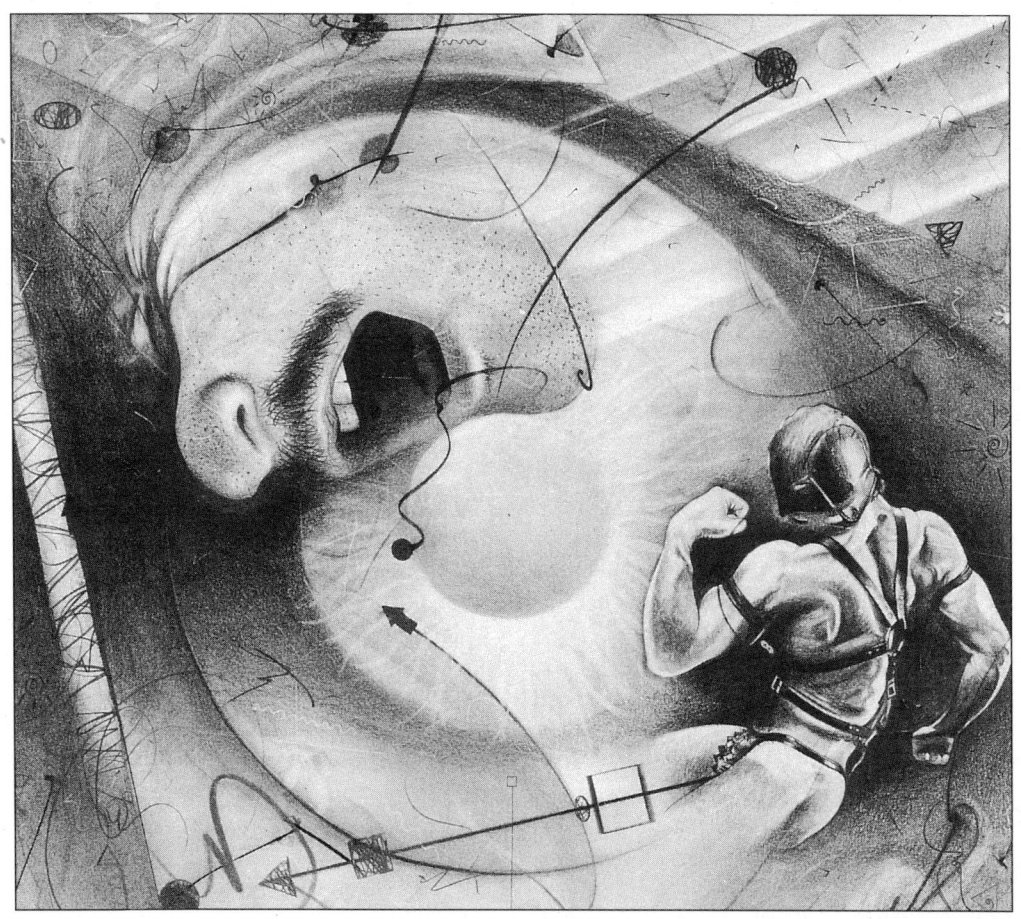

Hey Bud Xerox That Head, Detail
Graphite, 30" x 22", 1990

7

Logic and Misogyny

SUMMARY: This chapter takes up Ludwig Wittgenstein, Bertrand Russell's star pupil. Wittgenstein succeeded Russell in guiding the debate over the nature of formal logic. The chapter exposes the hysterical efforts taken by Wittgenstein's executors to conceal the fact that he was gay. It also reveals how the young Wittgenstein was influenced by protofascist values.

A certain continuity has existed in Western philosophy from the ancient Greek philosopher Parmenides in the 5th century B.C. to the modern British philosopher Bertrand Russell in the 20th century A.D. Throughout these two and a half millennia, generations of philosophers succeeded each other as intellectual carpenters laboring on a common task, the construction of the great tower of formal logic. The tower's creators proudly placed this structure atop the highest hill in their intellectual terrain. Surveying the world from the tower's pinnacle, they congratulated themselves for having constructed a platform worthy of the brightest beacon they could shine, calculative male reason.

Unfortunately for the ambition of its builders, however, the tower's foundations eventually proved unable to bear the great weight laid upon them. As previous chapters have shown, these foundations were spongy, embodying three fallacious motifs first propounded in a myth by Parmenides. These motifs, uncritically accepted in varying forms by Parmenides' successors, were logical necessity, bivalence, and absolute objectivity.

In the last two chapters, we watched both Gottlob Frege and Bertrand Russell as they were forced to confront unsolvable contradictions resulting from their adherence to the Parmenidean myth. Although each philosopher concluded his life aware that the foundations of formal logic were cracking from the core out, neither was able to do more than temporarily patch over the ever widening gaps.

In this and the next three chapters, we will see the great, unified logical tower, like its mythical prototype at Babel, finally sag under its own weight into a heap of mutually unintelligible tongues. An important philosopher who first tried mightily to prevent this collapse, but who later came to terms with it, was Ludwig Wittgenstein. This chapter and the next will show that Wittgenstein's earlier effort to save the tower sharply highlights the patriarchal, misogynist mentality that has always lain just under the surface of the Parmenidean myth. The two chapters after that will show that Wittgenstein's later effort to come to terms with the collapse of formal logic foreshadows, but never quite realizes, a post-patriarchal sensibility. As the four chapters dealing with Wittgenstein unfold, we will also discover an unexpected link between logical and sexual fantasy systems.[1]

Anti-Semitism and Self-Estrangement

Ludwig Wittgenstein was born in 1889 in Vienna, then the cultural and political hub of the Austro-Hungarian Empire.[2] His family, residing in a palatial mansion in one of Vienna's most exclusive neighborhoods, was one of the richest in Austria, comparable in wealth to the Krupps of Germany, the Carnegies of the United States, and the Rothschilds of England. His father was a powerful self-made industrialist who profited from steel-making and the armaments industry; his mother was a noted patron of classical music, hosting salons attended by the likes of Johannes Brahms and Gustav Mahler.

Although rich, influential, and cultured, the Wittgenstein family had a secret vulnerability: they were descended from Jewish forebears, and lived during an era of rising anti-Semitism. In the face of this historical crunch, the family repudiated their Jewish roots, passing as Germanic Christians. Hermann, Ludwig Wittgenstein's paternal grandfather, converted to Protestantism, adopted the middle name "Christian," espoused anti-Semitic views, and forbade any of his children to marry Jews. Karl, Ludwig Wittgenstein's father, married a Catholic, Leopoldine Kalmus (although she too was partially of Jewish descent).

Ludwig Wittgenstein, raised as a Catholic along with his seven other siblings, took pains to hide the Jewish identity of his forebears throughout much of his life. Indeed, like the German logician Gottlob Frege before him, Wittgenstein expressed rabidly anti-Semitic views in his personal diaries, at times sounding like Hitler in *Mein Kampf*. By coincidence, both Hitler and Wittgenstein, being almost exactly the same age, attended high school at the same time in Linz, Austria, although it is not known if they were acquaintances.

In his early years, Wittgenstein identified himself with Germanic culture and political aspirations. Although exempt from conscription because of a minor medical problem, he volunteered to fight on behalf of the German alliance during World War I. When it became apparent that Germany and her allies would lose, he became despondent, declaring:

> The thought that our race will be defeated depresses me tremendously, because I am German through and through.[3]

Although an anti-Semite, Wittgenstein was later disgusted by the Nazis, whom he regarded as gangsters, and he served as a volunteer medical worker for the British during World War II. But even so, he was not above collaborating with the Nazi regime financially. When Germany annexed Austria in 1938, both Wittgenstein and his brother Paul happened to be abroad. Fearing for the safety of his sisters, still living in Vienna, Wittgenstein helped conclude a financial deal with the regime in Berlin in order to save them, although his brother Paul, living in the United States, at first resisted. According to the deal, the sisters were to be exempt from the Nuremberg laws stigmatizing people of mixed Jewish descent if the family transferred its vast liquid assets from foreign accounts into the central German bank. With Wittgenstein's help, the deal was concluded, the money transferred, and the sisters saved. Ironically, while negotiations were underway to save them from anti-Semitism, the sisters themselves were suspicious of a lawyer hired in the United States by Paul because he was Jewish.

There thus existed within the Wittgenstein family an ongoing anxiety about self-identity, rooted in the desire (understandable under the circumstances) to preserve their safety, comfort, and wealth. Whatever may have been its practical merit in allowing the family to escape anti-Semitism, this practice fostered the negative psychological side-effects that always accompany living a lie. The members of the Wittgenstein family survived, but at the price of self-estrangement and spiritual atomization.

Such a corrosive family tradition perhaps contributed to the fact that three of Wittgenstein's brothers committed suicide. In any case, it provided a pernicious precedent for both Wittgenstein and his brother Rudolf (one of the three suicides) when they came to deal with their identity as homosexuals. In Ludwig Wittgenstein's case in particular, as we will shortly see, his morbid self-estrangement in sexual matters, reinforced by the precedent of his family's self-estrangement in dealing with their Jewish roots, deeply colored his basic view of the world, including his philosophy of logic.

From Engineering to Logic

Wittgenstein's early formal education was technical, not humanist, and certainly not philosophical. After private tutoring at home followed by high school in Linz, Austria, he studied engineering at a technical school in Berlin and later at the University of Manchester in England. A turning point came when he encountered Bertrand Russell's work *Principles of Mathematics* (first published in 1903), stimulating him to think about the logical principles underlying mathematics. At the suggestion of Gottlob Frege, Wittgenstein decided to apply to study mathematical logic under Russell at Cambridge University, where he was admitted in 1912. Thus began a long, tumultuous, love-hate relationship with a mentor who was his diametrical opposite in personal character and general outlook on life.

Ever moody and irascible, Wittgenstein abruptly withdrew from Cambridge a year after his admission and went to live in a small village in Norway. In 1914, with the outbreak of World War I, he volunteered to serve in the Austrian Army, eventually being taken prisoner by the Allied Forces in Italy. After the war's end, Russell managed to coax a publisher to print a small book on logic that Wittgenstein had completed while in the army, *Tractatus Logico-Philosophicus* ("Logical-Philosophical Treatise"). Together with a short follow-up essay on logic and a little dictionary for German elementary schools, this was the only material Wittgenstein ever published during his lifetime. Except for the dictionary, he later repudiated these works.

The period from 1919 to 1929 has come to be known as Wittgenstein's "lost years," partly because he was out of the orbit of philosophic debate in this period, and partly because his later academic followers knew virtually nothing about his personal life at this time. In fact, when Wittgenstein came back to Vienna in 1919 after the war, he was a changed man. He had resolved to make a complete break with the previous course of his life and to become an elementary teacher in poor public schools. Moving out of the spacious Wittgenstein mansion, he rented a room for himself in a less elegant section of Vienna near the teachers' college where he would study for his credentials. This new home was situated not far from the Prater, a public park that will concern us later.

After getting his teaching certificate, Wittgenstein departed for the Austrian back-country, where he undertook to teach peasant children in public schools in several small villages. Despite his initial high hopes, however, the endeavor turned into a disaster for everyone due to Wittgenstein's sadistic classroom methods—boxing boys on their ears and pulling out girls' hair, especially if they were slow to learn mathematics, Wittgenstein's favorite subject. In one notorious incident in 1926, he repeatedly hit a sickly boy (later to die of leukemia) until the boy fell unconscious. At an inquest into the matter, Wittgenstein lied about what happened.

Disgusted with his students, their parents, and himself, Wittgenstein returned to Vienna. There he assisted an architect-friend on the design of a new mansion for one of his sisters. After completion of the house, he had a business card made describing himself as an architect, even though he had no architectural training and his only experience was assisting his architect-friend on his sister's house.

In the meantime, Wittgenstein's small book on logic, *Tractatus*, was beginning to create a stir. It especially impressed an obstreperous new group of logical-positivist philosophers known as "the Vienna Circle," then in full revolt against the ossified dogmatism of German idealist philosophy. Although inspired by certain ideas in *Tractatus*, however, some members of the Vienna Circle were put off by Wittgenstein himself. He affected an oracular and pretentious style of speaking when questioned, which intimidated questioners into silence. For example, the logician Rudolf Carnap made this observation about Wittgenstein:

> The impression he made on us was as if insight came to him as through a divine inspiration, so that we could not help feeling that any sober rational comment or analysis of it would be a profanation. ... [He] tolerated no critical examination by others, once the insight had been gained by an act of inspiration.[4]

After his failure as a public school teacher, Wittgenstein played on Russell's great influence in order to return to Cambridge in 1929. Largely through Russell's doing, Wittgenstein received a doctoral degree for *Tractatus*, published eight years earlier, and a stipend for further research and teaching. His examiners for his oral examination on *Tractatus* were his old friends Russell and G.E. Moore. They treated the whole affair as a sort of casual, back-slapping favor done for any old buddy, providing Wittgenstein with what was probably the easiest doctoral exam in the history of philosophy. Thus spoiled academically by his colleagues in his maturity as he had been spoiled financially by his family in his youth, Wittgenstein became renowned at Cambridge for his petulance. He continued teaching on and off at Cambridge until a few years before his death in 1951.

As Wittgenstein shattered academic precedent with the ease of his doctoral examination, so he broke the famous rule of publish-or-perish by bringing out only one work in this entire period, a small essay dealing with logical form. This essay appeared in the year of his return in 1929, and he repudiated it by the time it was printed.

Despite Wittgenstein's reclusiveness, a number of his ideas received garbled public currency through the impact they were having by word of mouth on other philosophers. But when others credited Wittgenstein for these ideas, he would typically rebuke them for misrepresenting him; and when others happened to assert similar ideas, he would accuse them of plagiarism.

The truth is that although Wittgenstein dearly wanted to write a great philosophic work of his post-*Tractatus* views, he found that he simply lacked the ability to do so. In his notebooks, he admitted that sustained philosophical argument was an agony for him, adding this confession:

> My style is like a bad musical composition.[5]

Wittgenstein succeeded, however, in filling up numerous notebooks over the years with voluminous collections of notes to himself about a wide array of topics; these notes, however, lacked an overall structure, and were filled with ambiguities and inconsistencies. He died regretting that he had never succeeded in fashioning any large body of this material into a sustained, coherent, publishable philosophical work. Nonetheless, he hoped that some of his devoted followers might gain flashes of philosophical insight by perusing the material after he died.

The Unspeakable and the Murky

Wittgenstein's inability to write sustained, coherent philosophical prose (a weakness that I call "arrhesia," from the Greek word *to arrheton*, meaning "the unspeakable") may have been related to a characteristic obsession of his philosophy: the notion that there is something unspeakable in human experience, and that philosophy largely consists in warning people not to trespass too far with language. Both these phenomena may in turn be related to the fact that Wittgenstein at one time suffered from some sort of speech defect. For example, Wittgenstein's architect friend Paul Engelmann made this observation when he first met Wittgenstein in 1916:

> Wittgenstein suffered from a minor defect of speech which, however, disappeared later on. He used to struggle for words, especially when he was trying to formulate a proposition.[6]

Wittgenstein himself confirms Engelmann's observation when he says:

> Often my writing is nothing but "stuttering."[7]

Whatever the reasons for Wittgenstein's arrhesia, its harmful consequences for his work were compounded by his petulance. Reacting with oracular opacity, hostility, defensive sarcasm, and wild mood swings to any serious criticism, he repeatedly scared away anyone who might be willing to work with him in an editorial capacity.

When Wittgenstein died in 1951, his cadre of adoring followers, by then an established academic cult, believed him to have been the greatest Western philosopher of the 20th century—a view that is still held by many academic philosophers. In seeking to share Wittgenstein's philosophic insights with others, however, his followers were embarrassed by the fact that he had published nothing since 1929. Accordingly, his official literary executors turned to his vast collection of notebooks and typescripts, now under their control, in the hope of extracting and publishing comprehensible fragments. As a result, in 1953 there appeared, under Wittgenstein's name, the work *Philosophical Investigations*.[8] Although *Investigations* is his most widely read work after *Tractatus*, Wittgenstein himself never intended it to be published in this form; in fact, *Investigations* contains two large, unfinished extracts from different parts of Wittgenstein's literary remains.

After the publication of *Investigations*, Wittgenstein's executors authorized the publication of an ever-growing list of books in their master's name. Yet *all* of these books, just like *Investigations*, resulted from wide-ranging selections made by editors out of the great mass of Wittgenstein's literary remains or from the notes of his students; *none* of these works represented a consistent, finished body of philosophical prose that Wittgenstein himself felt was ready for publication.

In many cases, Wittgenstein's editors scanned through his various notebooks and typescripts, picked out fragments that in their judgment were conceptually connected to each other, and strung the results together in a book published under Wittgenstein's name. Only recently have the first volumes appeared of a critical edition of Wittgenstein's collected works.

As noted earlier, Wittgenstein suffered from arrhesia, used a pretentious, oracular style of lecturing to fend off criticism, and drove away any potential editors of his works. These facts, combined with the piecemeal posthumous publication of his works, have had the combined effect of making him one of the murkiest philosophers in Western history.

Ironically, but not unexpectedly, this very murkiness made Wittgenstein seen even more attractive and profound to the members of his academic cult, who have vied with each other over the correct interpretation of his works. To others, however, it had exactly the opposite effect. For example, Bertrand Russell, no longer able to stomach Wittgenstein's petulant obscurantism, declared with exasperation:

> He, himself, as usual is oracular and emits his opinion as if it were the Czar's ukase, but humbler folk can hardly content themselves with this procedure.[9]

Although members of the Wittgenstein cult continued to insist that their hero was the greatest Western philosopher of the 20th century, independent commentators have fallen into a furious debate with each other over the years concerning what it was that Wittgenstein advocated. Not only have the commentators bitterly hacked away at each other, but even (ironically following Wittgenstein's own precedent) at their own earlier writings. For example, P.M.S. Hacker, one of the most well respected of Wittgenstein scholars, recently put out a second edition of a celebrated book on Wittgenstein that he first published in 1972. In the second edition, Hacker hacks away at his original interpretation, calling it a "distorted picture," and uses the bulk of the second edition to correct errors he himself made in the first edition.[10]

Only in the last few years has the general outline of Wittgenstein's overall philosophy become clear. It turns out to be something quite different from what many of his most avid followers originally thought. If their high estimation of Wittgenstein was based on what they thought his philosophy to be, it is now left hanging in mid-air. And if it was not based on his philosophy, then on what?

High Priests

After Wittgenstein's death in 1951, access to his papers was jealously guarded by his literary executors. These included Elizabeth Anscombe, an adult convert to Catholicism, and Rush Rhees. They seemed to have viewed themselves as high-priests of the cult that had formed around their master. Anyone who wished to do research on Wittgenstein, especially on the circumstances of his private life, was carefully screened, given only limited access to information, and sometimes made to grovel for the privilege.

An example of the executors' haughty attitude was their treatment of Paul Engelmann, Wittgenstein's architect-friend. Having in his own possession a cache of letters received from Wittgenstein over the years, he wrote to the executors for permission to publish them in book form with commentary. (Although the physical letters were his, the copyright belonged to the executors.) In response, Elizabeth Anscombe said she would consent, but with reluctance. She did not want to permit Wittgenstein, when seen through the eyes of any of his friends, to become "infected with one's own mediocrity or ordinariness or lack of complexity." Ominously, she added:

> If by pressing a button it could have been secured that people would not concern themselves with his personal life, I should have pressed the button.[11]

The irrationality of this remark is striking because Anscombe conceded to Engelmann that she herself had never fully understood Wittgenstein's philosophy. Hence the obvious question: if still in the dark as to her master's teachings, how could she even think of suppressing information about his personal life? Might not such personal information help other people gain insights about Wittgenstein's thought that had escaped *her*? Anscombe forgot that, as the first duty of a physician is to do no harm, so the first duty of a philosopher is not to block the road to inquiry.

Engelmann did not challenge Anscombe on this point. Forced to grovel for the printing rights, he said he would show that any ordinariness or mediocrity was his, not Wittgenstein's. He concluded his introduction to the letters by saying "my heartfelt thanks are due to her for this kindness." Published thus with Anscombe's reluctant *imprimatur*, the letters turned out to fall within Wittgenstein's "lost years." They reveal him as a man deeply tormented by what he elusively calls "a particular fact."[12]

The Hysteria of the Philosophers

Among Wittgenstein's papers was a large body of material dealing with his personal life, written in a simple code, which his executors refused to reveal. Disgusted with their secretiveness, one scholar decided to bypass the executors and instead travel to Austria in order to interview people who had personal memories of Wittgenstein. In 1969, William Bartley, a fellow at Stanford University's Hoover Institution, set out on this quest. His resulting biography of Wittgenstein, first published in 1973, with a second, amplified edition in 1985, blew the lid off Wittgenstein's private life and drove the high priests of his cult into a state of near hysteria.[13]

On his visit to Austria, Bartley discovered ordinary people had been acquaintances of Wittgenstein's. They did not know that he had later become a famous philosopher. (At the time, Wittgenstein's renown was limited to English-speaking academic circles.) As part of the project, Bartley followed up on rumors that Wittgenstein was gay, going into gay bars in Vienna and speaking to some of their more elderly patrons. Promised anonymity by Bartley (homosexuality was still illegal in Austria), they confirmed not only that Wittgenstein was gay but that during his "lost years" he was wont to cruise the Prater, a large public park near where he lived. There he sought out "rough young men" as sexual partners, a practice he would renew on his later return visits to Vienna as well as in London pubs. His sources also told Bartley that when Wittgenstein engaged in these practices he felt "possessed, as he put it to friends, by a demon he could barely control." Based on these interviews, Bartley concluded:

> Throughout his life, Wittgenstein was tormented by intense guilt and suffering over his sexual desires and activities. Like many of his contemporaries, Wittgenstein had become convinced that the sort of high spiritual and intellectual creativity that he craved was virtually incompatible with sexual activity.[14]

The amount of space that Bartley devoted to Wittgenstein's sex life was only a small portion of his book; moreover, Bartley's tone was always sober and intelligent in analyzing Wittgenstein's philosophy and highly respectful in commenting on Wittgenstein's personality. In fact, if Bartley can be faulted on any grounds, it is that he erred in trying to *excuse* Wittgenstein in the face of certain failings that he uncovered. For example, although Bartley was the first to discuss in detail Wittgenstein's disastrous experience as a public school teacher in rural Austria, he put the blame on the peasants. They were hostile to Wittgenstein, says Bartley, because Wittgenstein was an advocate of a new, liberal school-reform movement. In fact, however, as later research has shown, Wittgenstein was a sadist in the classroom, lied about his behavior, and opposed the spirit of liberal school reform.

Despite Bartley's sober, even exculpatory, approach, members of the Wittgenstein cult, on learning that he would discuss Wittgenstein's sex life, attacked him as a sensation-mongering fraud. They urged the people named in his acknowledgment page to dissociate themselves from the work, threatened lawsuits, and tried to suppress the book's publication.

When Bartley refused to back down, a flurry of letters appeared in the pages of *The Times Literary Supplement* of London. In the exchange, Wittgenstein executor Elizabeth Anscombe, without actually denying that her idol was gay, attacked Bartley for not naming his sources. In response, Bartley noted that if he had done so, they might have been arrested or harassed, since homosexuality was then illegal and stigmatized in Austria.

Backing up Anscombe, Maurice Drury, a long-time friend and former pupil of Wittgenstein's who had become a psychiatrist, solemnly denied that Wittgenstein was gay. He added that Wittgenstein had no sex life whatever:

> I was a close friend of Wittgenstein's for over twenty years. I am also a consultant psychiatrist. ... It has therefore been in the nature of my work to be alert to problems [sic] of homosexuality whether latent or active. ... Those of us who knew Wittgenstein knew that sensuality in any form was entirely foreign to his ascetic nature.[15]

Unfortunately for Drury's supreme self-assurance, his pontification was immediately followed in the very same issue of the paper by a brief, matter-of-fact note from Irma Strickland. She said that in May of 1952 Bertrand Russell had confided to her that Wittgenstein was a witty homosexual.

In fact, we now know that Wittgenstein had several homosexual male lovers in the course of his life, and that he was secretly infatuated with several young male heterosexuals whom he indulged as travel companions. The question of whether Wittgenstein also liked to go cruising in public parks for rough sex is more complicated. We will see below, however, that Bartley was probably right on this score as well, although Ray Monk's more recent biography demurs on this point.

Despite threats and remonstrances, Bartley's book was published. In response, Wittgenstein executor Rush Rhees wrote one of the most astonishing book reviews in the history of philosophy.[16] Fixating on the section in Bartley's book dealing with Wittgenstein's homosexuality, Rhees vehemently argued that a person's sex life is irrelevant to understanding his or her intellectual work. He added that even if what Bartley said was true it would be "foul" to repeat it. He insisted that for us to know of a person's sex practices only "cheapens" us in evaluating the person's work. In Rhees' mind, sex was clearly a kind of dirty excrescence, like having a bowel movement. Indeed, he approvingly quoted a remark of Wittgenstein's comparing sexual pleasure to dung (*Dünger*).[17]

Even more remarkable, Rhees appended to his review a statement by John Stonborough, Wittgenstein's nephew. Although implying that he had not even read Bartley's biography, Stonborough indignantly claimed that both the author and the publisher were seeking to "pee on the graves of men whom honest and upright people admire and respect." He called the book a "farrago of obscenity and lies," and denounced Bartley himself as "slovenly" and "prurient."[18]

Although more circumspect in language than Stonborough, Rhees was actually the more reprehensible. Here was a professionally-trained philosopher arguing that one can be certain, without even looking at the evidence, that a person's sexuality has nothing to do with his or her world-view. Contrary to Rhees, however, we can never *know* whether such a connection exists or not until we actually look and see. Rhees and Anscombe resembled Galileo's doctrinaire enemies. Not only did they refuse to look through the telescope offered them, they also wanted to make sure that no one else did either.

Bartley rightly regarded Rhees' review as an example of hysteria. More importantly, he pointed out that previous biographical sketches of Wittgenstein were all fatally flawed, for none of them mentioned that he was gay; in fact, they implied he was straight. In view of what has come out since Bartley's book, we can see how these earlier accounts failed to do justice to several important personal relationships in Wittgenstein's life. For example, they either made no mention of Francis Skinner, Wittgenstein's sometime lover at Cambridge, or if referring to him at all, called him Wittgenstein's "friend." Bartley deserves credit for his courage in standing up to the hysteria of the philosophers. His book opened up a whole new perspective on Wittgenstein's life and thought that has yet to be fully explored.

Damage Control

After the publication of Bartley's book, many Anglo-American academic philosophers continued to be upset by his claims about Wittgenstein's homosexuality, especially the part about cruising in public parks for rough sex. Their anxious reactions showed that they regarded such behavior as reprehensible and degraded, or at least as something inconsistent with the philosophic life. (Apparently they had never heard of Socrates!) Rather than examine their own Victorian assumptions about sex, however, they murmured darkly among themselves in academic corridors, incredulous that such things could be true of their hero Wittgenstein.

In the meantime, pressure began to build on the Wittgenstein executors to allow full access to the personal papers in their possession, including the coded remarks in his diaries. Eventually they chose to grant access to all the material to a certain Ray Monk, who in 1990 published the fullest account to date of Wittgenstein's life.

Monk himself acknowledges that while he was conducting his research, the question he was most frequently asked was "What are you going to do about Bartley?"[19] But oddly, although this was the question most immediately on readers' minds, Monk decided to cloister the whole matter into an appendix. It doesn't begin until page 581 of his book and bears the opaque title "Bartley's *Wittgenstein* and the Coded Remarks." Oddly again, the word "homosexuality" does not appear in Monk's index, although references to Wittgenstein's homosexual behavior are scattered throughout the text. Finally, the word "homophobia" is completely absent from the book. (Imagine a biography of a great black thinker that never mentioned racism.)

In his appendix on Bartley, Monk attacks the claim that Wittgenstein cruised a Viennese park looking for sex with rough young men. For one thing, argues Monk, there is no mention of such behavior in any of Wittgenstein's extant notebooks, even though Bartley claimed (so Monk says) that the notebooks would confirm this practice. In addition, Bartley refused to disclose his sources. Finally, judging by what we *do* know of Wittgenstein, Monk says "one would rather get the impression that he was incapable of such promiscuity."[20] In Monk's eyes, these considerations suffice to show that "there is no evidence" for Bartley's claim.[21]

All of Monk's objections to Bartley are weak. In regard to the notebooks, Bartley never claimed that they would confirm Wittgenstein's cruising, only his homosexuality, which proved to be correct. Furthermore, Wittgenstein ordered several of his notebooks destroyed in 1950, the year before he died, apparently including some notebooks for his "lost years." Nor should we forget that in Elizabeth Anscombe's letter to Paul Engelmann, quoted above, she alluded to the possibility of pushing buttons in order to keep people from knowing about Wittgenstein's personal life. How do we know she didn't push some?

As to his refusal to divulge his sources, Bartley rightly pointed out that they could be harassed or arrested if publicly revealed as gay. Monk casts a blind eye to the special difficulties involved in the writing of gay and lesbian history. Because of pervasive homophobia, much of that history has been irretrievably lost. The little that has been salvaged has commonly depended on the protection of sources.

The issue of methodology in gay historiography is a delicate one. Simply to rule out of court all testimony from protected sources is a heavy-handed approach; rather, the value of such testimony in each case must be assessed in terms of many circumstantial factors. Much depends, of course, on the credibility of the author.

Bartley was a distinguished scholar affiliated with a prominent scholarly institution. As shown by his handling of Wittgenstein's disastrous school-teaching efforts, he sought to present Wittgenstein in a positive light even in the face of compromising evidence. Finally, Bartley never flinched in the face of hysterical personal attacks. Under the circumstances, I for one find him credible.

The fact that many people viewed Wittgenstein as ascetic means little. Monk himself admits that Wittgenstein was lovers with Francis Skinner, and that he was also infatuated with David Pinsent, to whom he dedicated *Tractatus*. Moreover, as every sexually active gay person well knows, there are a great many high-placed men in the church, the government, the university, and the business corporation who—completely unknown to their closest friends, professional colleagues, wives, and children—regularly have furtive, compulsive sexual encounters with other men in public places. It happens all the time! Their colleagues, as the last to know, are typically the most dumbfounded when they find out.

I have been an upfront activist in the gay/lesbian movement for nearly 30 years. One lesson these decades has taught me is this: the more closeted any gay man is, the more likely he is to have a secret, compulsive sex life that reflects fetishes, fantasies, and behavior wildly at odds with his professed values and public image.

This bifurcated behavior pattern is especially common among those who internalize a sex-negative religious viewpoint. The many closeted and conflicted gay members of the Roman Catholic hierarchy are prime examples. As we will shortly see, Wittgenstein, in addition to being closeted, also had such a sex-negative viewpoint.

Rather astonishingly, Monk claims that Wittgenstein did not live in the closet. Yet when Bartley's book mentioned that Wittgenstein was gay, many of the philosopher's friends and associates indignantly insisted that such a thing was impossible. Especially noteworthy was Maurice Drury's vehement denial, quoted above. Yet Drury was a close friend of Wittgenstein's for twenty years. If Wittgenstein did not live in the closet, how could such a denial be possible?[22]

In fact, only a few close associates within the relative seclusion of Cambridge University knew that Wittgenstein was gay. Beyond that, most others assumed that he was straight or nonsexual, or else simply never gave the matter any thought. Wittgenstein was no more out of the closet than J. Edgar Hoover.

A Particular Fact

Monk challenges Bartley's claim that Wittgenstein's homosexual behavior was a source of torment to him; nonetheless, we find circumstantial evidence alluding to this torment in Wittgenstein's letters to Paul Engelmann, written during his "lost years." The letters show that Wittgenstein was tormented by what he called his "lack of decency" [*Unanständigkeit*], his being a "swine" [*Schweinehund*], and his "baseness and rottenness" [*Niedrigkeit und Gemeinheit*]. Moreover, he says he is seeking to avoid the state where "all the devils in Hell break loose inside me" and expresses fear that "the devil will come and take me one day. I am not joking!"[23]

In this context, Wittgenstein tells Engelmann that there is one "particular fact" that he cannot come to terms with:

> I am in a state of mind that is terrible to me. I have been through it several times before: it is the state of *not being able to get over a particular fact*. It is a pitiable state, I know. But there is only one remedy that I can see, and that is of course to come to terms with that fact. But this is just like what happens when a man who can't swim has fallen into the water and flails about with his hands and feet and feels that he *cannot* keep his head above water. That is the position I am in now.[24]

In considering this remarkable passage, Monk argues that "unfortunately, there is no possible way of knowing what fact he is here talking about."[25] Monk doesn't even mention that in 1978 Albert Levi had set off a scholarly debate by arguing that this paragraph refers to Wittgenstein's role as "a guilty homosexual."[26] Levi argued that although the above passage does not specify what the words "a particular fact" refer to, nonetheless the context of the letters, together with the sexual innuendo of some of the pejorative terms, points to gay guilt.[27]

Although previous commentators, including Levi, have overlooked it, one of the letters contains an allusion that bears on this matter. As noted above, Wittgenstein decided to make a drastic change in his life during this period. Abandoning Vienna, he went out into the Austrian back-country to work as a public school teacher in poor peasant schools. What needs to be remembered is this: Wittgenstein took this step at a time when he was absorbed in reading the New Testament, devoting himself to prayer, studying the ascetic writings of Leo Tolstoy, and even thinking about becoming a monk.

After resolving to abandon worldly Vienna for the Austrian back-country, Wittgenstein wrote to Engelmann with a sense of relief, saying—

> I have carried out several operations which were *very* painful but went off well. I.e. I may miss a limb from time to time—but better have a few limbs less and the remaining ones sound.[28]

Anyone familiar with Christian lore will at once hear a familiar bell here. This puzzling reference to the surgical removal of limbs brings to mind the notorious passage in the New Testament where Jesus recommends self-mutilation in the face of intractable sexual feeling:

> What I say to you is: anyone who looks lustfully at a woman has already committed adultery with her in his thoughts. If your right eye is your trouble, gouge it out and throw it away! Better to lose part of your body than to have it all cast into Gehenna. Again, if your right hand is your trouble cut it off and throw it away! Better to lose part of your body than to have it all cast into Gehenna.[29]

For Wittgenstein, sexual attraction meant sexual attraction to other men. Moreover, he wrote this letter while afflicted with Christian values. These facts suggest that Wittgenstein understood his drastic change of life as a kind of ascetic mutilation, carried out as Jesus enjoined.

Once the Biblical reference of this letter is understood, all the references throughout these letters to indecency, rottenness, and fear of possession by the Devil come into focus. The "particular fact" with which Wittgenstein could not come to terms was his homosexual lust. He viewed manifestations of this lust as a kind of demonic possession from which he sought to free himself by a drastic, self-mutilating change of life. Seen in this light, the letters to Engelmann provide independent corroboration for what Bartley's gay sources had confided to him: Wittgenstein felt he was "possessed...by a demon he could barely control."[30]

Wittgenstein's letter is hardly a smoking gun. The evidence is only circumstantial and open to interpretation. But for all that, the letter cannot be simply dismissed as no evidence at all. To the contrary, the letter gains weight when viewed against the whole context of Wittgenstein's life. Throughout much of that life, Wittgenstein manifested patterns of behavior that are recognized today, thanks to insights gained from the gay liberation movement, as classic for the self-hating gay male: closetedness; belief that one's sexual feelings are alien or demonic; guilt over masturbation; compulsive, furtive sexual encounters with "rough trade"; great difficulty in combining sex and love; a need to test and prove one's masculinity; emotional abuse of one's lovers; a brooding sense of loneliness; and recurring fantasies of suicide.

The evidence is there. The question is how to interpret it. Monk has offered one interpretation; this book offers another. Perhaps you, the reader, have yet another. The important thing is to deal with this issue in a forthright and open manner.

The Missing Link of Sex

Throughout all of the sphincter-tight resistance to dealing with Wittgenstein's sexuality, few have dared pursue a broader question: Did Wittgenstein's sexual attitudes have any connection to his philosophy? As we will soon see, sex provides the context in which Wittgenstein sought to combine the seemingly antagonistic themes of logic and mysticism in *Tractatus*, a combination that has bedeviled generations of commentators.

To understand the connection between sexual attitudes, logic, and mysticism in Wittgenstein, the rest of this chapter will make a bit of a detour. This detour is necessary because there was a thinker who greatly influenced the young Wittgenstein but whom modern commentators have generally ignored. When we take into account this thinker's life and views, we will find anticipations of some of the most distinctive doctrines that Wittgenstein later put forth in *Tractatus*. Indeed, we will see that many of the most puzzling aspects of *Tractatus* fall into place. They will do so precisely because the missing link of sex will find its proper place in Wittgenstein's chain of reasoning about logic and mysticism.

Sex and Character

The thinker who influenced the young Wittgenstein was a protofascist Austrian philosopher, little known today, named Otto Weininger. (By "protofascism," I mean a specific historical phenomenon: that body of reactionary thought which developed in German-speaking Europe at the start of this century, and to which Hitler consciously appealed during his rise to power.)

Although Wittgenstein was poorly read in philosophy, one of the few philosophers he read avidly was Otto Weininger, a Viennese contemporary who was born in 1880 (nine years before Wittgenstein) and who committed suicide at the age of 23 in 1903.[31] Weininger made an early mark on Wittgenstein, for Wittgenstein personally attended Weininger's funeral, even though Wittgenstein was only fourteen years old at the time.[32] Later, Wittgenstein mentioned in his notebooks that Weininger was an important influence on his early work. Even after becoming disenchanted with Weininger, Wittgenstein recommended him as reading to his Cambridge colleagues.

Despite Wittgenstein's own statements about Weininger's importance, few commentators have paid much attention to him. An example is P.M.S. Hacker, whose book *Insight and Illusion* is one of the best scholarly accounts in English of Wittgenstein's philosophy. Although a meticulous researcher, Hacker mentions Weininger only once, in a footnote, stressing instead the alleged importance for Wittgenstein of the German philosopher Arthur Schopenhauer.[33] Contrary to Hacker's claims, however, Wittgenstein himself called Schopenhauer "quite a *crude* mind."[34]

Although today few people have ever heard of him, Otto Weininger was better known to the Europeans of his age than his now-famous Viennese contemporary Sigmund Freud. Like a shooting star, Weininger's fame shot across the European intellectual firmament after his death in 1903, following publication of his book *Geschlecht und Charakter* ("Sex and Character").[35] An instant success, the book went through 29 printings between 1903 and 1947, including an anonymous English translation made in 1906, still the only one available in English.[36] (Unfortunately, the English version is a sloppy paraphrase of the original.)

What was Weininger's relevance to Wittgenstein's thought? In previous chapters, we have seen that Western formal logic for a long time implicitly reflected a misogynist mentality. As we are now about to see, the significance of Weininger's *Sex and Character* is that it took these implicit misogynist presuppositions of logic and made them absolutely explicit. Indeed, Weininger's philosophical goal was to ground both ethics and logic on a misogynist philosophy of sex. Precisely this linkage of ethics and logic in a misogynist context is what so endeared Weininger to Wittgenstein.

First we will take a look at the character of Weininger himself, examining the link between his psychology on one hand and his philosophy of logic on the other. Then we will show how Weininger is the key to unlocking the mysteries of Wittgenstein's *Tractatus*.

Self-Hatred, Twice Over

Until his suicide in 1903, Otto Weininger was at odds with himself for being gay and for being Jewish. In a letter written two years before the fateful event and cryptically referring to some kind of injections, he said–

> My method of struggle against homosexuality seems to have had success.[37]

A year later he converted to Lutheranism. The following year, only a few months after publishing *Sex and Character*, he rented a room in the house where his hero Beethoven had died, and shot himself to death. Some time later, friends published two additional collections of his writings entitled *On the Last Things* and *Notebook and Letters to a Friend*. They detail his fascination with sadomasochistic sex and murder.

Although Weininger was little known when he shot himself, the sensational circumstances of his death gave him the aura of a tragic hero, and the sales of his book took off. In the following decades, the book appealed to rising reactionary elements in Europe who resented Jews and who feared the nascent political movements lobbying for civil rights for women and gay people. With such a following, the book helped lay the ideological groundwork for the rise of Nazism. Indeed, Adolf Hitler, approving a remark once made to him by Dietrich Eckart, commented that Weininger was the only "good Jew" he had ever heard of.[38]

The Nazis borrowed from *Sex and Character* in their propaganda, as witnessed by David Abrahamsen, a biographer of Weininger's:

> It may be of interest to note that as late as 1939 I heard in Norway a radio broadcast beamed from Nazi Germany, which used some of Weininger's attacks upon the Jews.[39]

Weininger's hatred of himself as a homosexual and a Jew derived from his hatred of women and anything conventionally associated with women. In his eyes, women were genetically inferior to men; indeed, he felt they had no souls. He believed that Jews and homosexual males were genetically inferior because he saw them as embodying female elements. Being himself both a homosexual and a Jew, he felt he was blemished twice over, since both identities placed him near the lowest category of all, that of women.

Weininger's beliefs clearly show how certain strains of European anti-Semitism and fascism were rooted in misogyny and internalized homophobia. This circumstance is often overlooked by historians of the period, although Bernardo Bertolucci brilliantly exposed it in his film *The Conformist*.[40]

The disparagement of Jews as an unmanly race has continued into certain European circles to this day. The 1996 election for President of Russia provided a vivid example. During the first round of voting, incumbent President Boris Yeltsin had failed to receive a majority. Consequently Yeltsin appointed one of his opponents, a tough-talking former general named Alexandr Lebed, as Russia's National Security Advisor. In return, Lebed agreed to drum up support for Yeltsin from the country's pro-military elements. As Lebed undertook to make good on his promise, the following exchange occurred:

> At a meeting with supporters in Moscow today, Mr. Lebed spoke in his usual unbridled manner. When a Cossack stood up and began to speak apologetically, Mr. Lebed stopped him. "You say you are a Cossack," Mr. Lebed said. "Why do you speak like a Jew?"[41]

As with Weininger, Lebed's disgust for men he regards as not sufficiently masculine is connected to his contemptuous attitude toward women. Lebed proved the point a few months after the election. Yeltsin, urged on by his own daughter, fired the strident Lebed from his new position as National Security Advisor. Scorning Yeltsin's daughter as a gullible tool of his political enemies, Lebed proclaimed:

> There is no woman who cannot be persuaded.[42]

Although Otto Weininger expressed his misogyny in stark and quirky terms, he merely put into bold relief an underlying assumption widely taken for granted in every patriarchal culture: women are inherently inferior to men; therefore, if anything conventionally associated with women appears in men, it represents a deformity or a disgrace. Motivated by this assumption, heterosexual men in patriarchal societies routinely deride, assault, and kill homosexual men. In addition, many homosexual men themselves (as we see in contemporary urban gay ghettoes) take pains to pump up their muscles in gyms, adopt military-style haircuts, wear uniform-like clothes, practice butch-posturing, and deride other gay men who are not "straight-appearing." Finally, men of every sexual orientation invoke this assumption to justify the economic, political, and sexual battering of women, who bear on their backs the entire weight of the patriarchal pecking-order.

Are You More M than F?

Although contempt for women is an attitude common to all patriarchal societies, Weininger's uniqueness lay in deliberately honing it into the linchpin of an intricate metaphysical juggernaut. Unknown to him at his death, the philosophical system he patched together was destined to leave a deep mark in the history of logic by virtue of its influence on the young Ludwig Wittgenstein. But the great extent of this influence would not become clear until many years after Wittgenstein's death because of the closetedness of his personal life, the occluding mentality of his literary executors, and the dense, oracular style of *Tractatus*.

In his metaphysics, Weininger argues that all human beings are to some extent bisexual. Each individual person, he says, is genetically a combination of two kinds of "plasms," one male, the other female. The male plasm he calls *arrhenoplasma* (his own coinage from ancient Greek, meaning "male plasm"). This plasm, he maintains, is responsible for primary and secondary male sexual characteristics (such as having a penis and facial hair). In addition, it is the source of those "tertiary" and "quaternary" traits that he regards as typical of the male character (such as an aptitude for formal logic). The female plasm, on the other hand, he calls *thelyplasma* (again his coinage, meaning "female plasm"). This plasm he believes is responsible for a woman's vagina, absence of facial hair, and lack of ability in formal logic.

For Weininger, if there existed a human being who was saturated with male plasm and totally lacking in female plasm, he would be the embodiment of the ideal male type, which he calls M. The female counterpart he calls F. As it is, every human being's *body* involves a combination of male plasm and female plasm; therefore, every human being's *character* can be scientifically analyzed into some blend of M and F. This blend, claims Weininger, can be expressed in a mathematical formula or table involving the symbols M and F.

This move that Weininger makes from body constituents, understood in sexual terms, to character analysis, expressed in quantitative formulas, is the crux of the book; indeed, it accounts for the title, *Sex and Character*. The fallacy of this approach is that it simplistically reduces socially-created sex-roles to physical factors.

From this theory, Weininger draws certain ethical conclusions: the more M and the less F any person is, the more he or she expresses the best possibilities of what it means to be a human being, whereas the opposite tendency is debasing. At the pinnacle of human social pyramid, then, there stands the muscled, emotionally controlled, rationally-calculating male. He rightly dominates the hierarchies of home, business, and state. At the bottom is the fleshy, emotionally volatile female. Her purpose in life is to serve men's needs and breed new offspring.

A Familiar Bivalent Melody

As noted above, Weininger hoped to give this misogynist bias a quantitative expression. He believed that it was possible to give a depiction of any human being's character by means of a table or formula that showed how much F or M the person embodied. Accordingly, his book includes odd-looking formulas and tables consisting of arrays of the letters F and M. These arrays purport to display the character of the persons for whom they are constructed.

Those who have read previous chapters in this book will recognize a familiar melody in Weininger's F-M song: his notation is yet another manifestation of the old myth of bivalence. But there's more: Weininger's claim that a bivalent F-M notation can formally display the personal character of individuals has a parallel in modern logic, which claims that a bivalent T-F

notation can formally display the logical character of arguments. In the next chapter, we will see how Wittgenstein drew on Weininger's bivalent notation in order to develop what many have regarded as Wittgenstein's most significant contribution to logic, his so-called "truth tables."

Butch, Butcher, Butchery

In regard to male homosexuality, Weininger distinguishes between what he calls the "homosexual" and the "pederast." Modern readers are likely to misunderstand him here, because "pederasty" usually means the love of an older for a younger male. But this is not Weininger's point. By "homosexual," he means a man who is sexually attracted to feminine men; by "pederast," a masculine man who is attracted to other masculine men.

Weininger regards "homosexuals" as lower in status than heterosexual males but higher than women. However, concerning "pederasty," he says that it "remains completely unresolved by this investigation."[43] The implication in terms of the rest of Weininger's theory is this: very masculine men who are sexually attracted to very masculine men constitute a kind of supermen, for they have rid themselves, as much as humanly possible, of everything feminine. The upshot is that Weininger views gay men as falling into two types: (1) feminine weaklings who are genetically inferior to heterosexual men; and (2) supermen who have only the most minimal of feminine traits.

Since Weininger viewed homosexuality in both cases as a matter of genetics, he opposed laws that make it a crime. But he regarded such behavior as inferior or even pathetic to the degree that it reflected any femininity. In his eyes, feminine-appearing gay men were congenital cripples.

Weininger Meets Calvin

Weininger's metaphysics of sex was a kind of ideology of predestination. In theory, all such ideologies stress what is unalterable. In practice, they commonly motivate their adherents to make Herculean efforts to change their behavior. For example, John Calvin's theology of predestination motivated his followers to prove through their voluntary behavior that they were predestined to be saved. Similarly, Weininger's metaphysics of sexual plasms encouraged his homosexual admirers to prove through their behavior that they were very masculine, not feminine weaklings. In the case of Calvin, the natural result was to generate a class of self-righteous religious hypocrites. In the case of Weininger, the result was to create suicidal neurotics. The next chapter will show that the most famous of these was Ludwig Wittgenstein.

A Certain Physiognomy

In addition to being deterministic, Weininger's metaphysics of sex exemplified the popular interest of his age in "physiognomy." This is the notion that a person's character can be read-off from his or her bodily features. Otto Weininger firmly believed that physiognomy could be developed into an exact science. *Sex and Character* sought to demonstrate this belief in regard to sexual matters.

In the next chapter, we will see that the grand assumption behind physiognomy—that to understand the expressiveness of physical features is to understand meaning—later seized the imagination of Wittgenstein. As a result, Wittgenstein sought to develop a physiognomy, not of the human body, but of human language.

The Nuisance of Women's Liberation

One further implication of Weininger's philosophy has to do with lesbians. He believed that they are superior to heterosexual women, since (as he thought) they are more like men. Indeed, he argued that lesbians should be permitted greater scope for their special creativity. But the dark side of this tolerance (if it can be called that) was his belief that feminine-identified heterosexual women should be kept in political bondage. In his view, the women's liberation movement was largely a smoke-screen created by lesbians, and something inappropriate to the lives of the great mass of ordinary women. Give the lesbians what they want for themselves, Weininger in effect argued, and the nuisance of women's liberation will evaporate.

The Cult of Patriarchal Reason

Because Weininger assumed that M is always superior to F, he stigmatized spontaneous emotional expressiveness as a low form of human interpretative ability, indeed as almost bestial. On the other hand, he glorified abstract logical analysis as the crowning achievement of what it means to be a human being.

Previous chapters have shown that earlier proponents of the Parmenidean myth implicitly made similar assumptions. Weininger, however, was the first to explicitly articulate them within the context of a world-view whose whole purpose was to denigrate women. In effect, he took that aspect of interpretational ability which patriarchal societies associate with domineering males and made it into humanity's most exalted window on reality. In the whole history of Western philosophy, no other writer provides a more succinct example of reducing rational human dialogue to patriarchal reason than does Weininger in the following passage:

> The logical axioms are the principle of all truth; these establish an *essence* by which cognition is governed, toward which it strives. *Logic* is a law which shall be heeded, and *man is first entirely himself when he is entirely logical. Indeed, he is not* until he is thoroughly and everywhere only *logic*.[44]

Because women are not adept at logic, says Weininger, they represent a sort of shrunken human being:

> The logical axioms constitute the principle of all conceptuality, and these are lacking in women; for them the principle of identity is not a strict standard by which alone a concept can attain its perspicuous determinateness, nor do they avail themselves of the *principium contradictionis* [principle of contradiction] as a norm for uniquely marking off a concept and thoroughly establishing it in its own right against all other things, both possible and actual. This lack of conceptual determinateness in all feminine thinking is the basis of that "sensitivity" in women by which they give unlimited free play to vague associations and so frequently drag in far-fetched things in making comparisons.[45]

To the extent that a man relies on feeling rather than concepts to express himself, says Weininger, to the same extent he degrades himself to the level of a woman. Weininger even felt the same about art, regarding expressionism, for example, as a debased form of feminine-like moodiness. Both misogyny and artistic boorishness have historically been common traits of the logicians. In Weininger's case, we see clearly how the two are connected.

Ascent to the Masculine

Weininger connects logic and ethics; indeed, he says they are but two different names for the same thing. The connecting factor is Truth, conceived as transcendent. In its role as the norm for right speaking and thinking, Truth grounds logic; and as a norm for right acting, ethics. Since, then, there is but one absolute logic and but one absolute ethics, and since both converge in the common source of Truth, it follows that to think or speak illogically is a *moral* offense:

> It is perhaps the deepest thought that *Descartes* ever expressed (and one, no doubt, for that reason so little understood and so often depicted as a dreadful misconception) that *all error is sin*.[46]

The full implications of this view become clear when we understand that for Weininger ethics means "duty to oneself," and that by "oneself" he means a super-sensible reality. That is, he regards one's true self *not* as the fullness of one's life experience, both sensual and intellectual, both masculine and feminine. Rather, one's true self is a transcendent entity on whose behalf the feelings of the empirical self must be subordinated and even sacrificed:

> Truth, purity, fidelity, uprightness in regard to oneself: that is the only conceivable ethics. There is only duty to oneself, duty of the empirical to the intelligible ego.[47]

Weininger's ethics advocate the rising up, as much as humanly possible, to one's higher self, which he understands as a process of *masculinization*. The ascent to the masculine requires the foregoing of sensual, subjective, space-and-time-dependent forms of human interpretation for those that are logical, objective, and absolute.

In effect, Weininger's ethical system takes the Christian moral dualism of soul and body, fuses it with the Platonic philosophical dualism of thinking and feeling, and regrounds both on a thorough-going misogyny. No wonder that any homosexual man who would strive to live by these ethics would end up regarding his sexual feelings as a debasing form of demonic entrapment, as did Wittgenstein, or else commit suicide, as did Weininger himself.

Weininger's insistence that logic and ethics are ultimately identical, having their common roots in a transcendent Truth, influenced the young Wittgenstein. The next chapter will show

how the "mystical" side of Wittgenstein's *Tractatus* draws out the full implications of Weininger's underlying assumption about the connection of ethics and logic in a transcendent One. We will also see how this concept motivated Wittgenstein to suppress both his sensuality and his femininity in the name of a supposed duty to his higher logical and ethical self.

The Male Ego, Writ Large

As just noted, Weininger follows Plato in dividing the self into two radically different parts, the sensible and the intelligible. His argument, in effect, is this: My lower animal functions pertain to my sensible self. But when I make a judgment in logic or ethics, my doing so presupposes the existence of an "I" who cannot be part of the sensible world, for how could such a conditioned being apprehend the absolute and eternal? There must then be an intelligible self. He nowhere appears in space and time, but his timeless existence must be presupposed in order to explain the possibility of logical and ethical judgments.

One can easily expand this view of the self into a form of "solipsism." This term is derived from the Latin words *solus ipse*, meaning "myself alone." It represents the doctrine that only I exist and that everything else in the world is merely some aspect of me. In order to reach a solipsistic conclusion based on Weininger, one need add the additional premises: all reality is a form of consciousness, and I am the only consciousness. In fact, Weininger himself seems at times to embrace these assumptions. An example is the following passage, which celebrates a kind of male solipsism:

> Man is *alone* in the universe, in eternal, immense *isolation*. ... He has no goal outside himself, nothing else for which he lives. ... he is alone, *alone*.[48]

Whether Weininger intended to be taken as a solipsist is unclear, although remarks such as the above give that impression. But interestingly, his apparent solipsism, if strictly carried out, can be construed to lead to its opposite, realism. This is the doctrine that an objective world really exists independent of any and all observers.

We can follow this reversal when we remember that Weininger argues, again in the style of Plato, that everything sensual or temporal is infected with a degree of unreality. The really real is a timeless absolute that only the intellect, itself a timeless absolute, can apprehend. On the basis of such assumptions, Weininger draws this conclusion: When I ascend from the material to the immaterial realm via the exercise of my logical and ethical powers, I shed my empirical trappings. In this way, I become ever more real by being ever more assimilated into that absolute Truth which is the source of logic and ethics.

In other words, the "I" to which at times Weininger seems to reduce the world is not this miserable piece of flesh that sees and feels. Rather, it is my higher, intelligible self insofar as it has expanded into the Truth. The more my intelligible self expands, the more my sensible self, existing in its own separate subjectivity, shrinks away. The final result is that only the objective Truth itself remains.

So one can easily read Weininger as implying a kind of solipsism, but one that ultimately turns into realism. The next chapter will show that Wittgenstein's *Tractatus* presents a similar view of the reversible interconnection between solipsism and realism.

Mystical Silence

Transcendent Truth, says Weininger, does not itself fall within the realm of logic, although it makes both logic and ethics possible. Since the realm of logic contains everything that is speakable or thinkable, transcendent Truth therefore must be unspeakable.

Believing in an unspeakable fount of logic, Weininger presents a novel view of the so-called "propositions of logic" (such as the principle of identity, "*A is A*"). These logical propositions, he says, are empty, and add nothing to our knowledge:

> The norm of thinking cannot be in thinking itself. The proposition of identity adds nothing to our knowledge, contributes nothing to our riches. Rather, it is their entire prior foundation.[49]

According to Weininger, the propositions of logic in effect show us something about logical necessity, but without really saying anything. Hence the man who ascends to the Truth through logic and ethics eventually reaches a pinnacle of mystical seeing, devoid of all speech. Reading his own notion of mystical ascent back into Immanuel Kant, Weininger lyrically praises the male loner-hero who has reached this pinnacle of solitary, speechless vision:

> Kant's solitary man laughs not, nor dances, shouts not, nor rejoices. For him, no need to make a noise, so deeply does the world-expanse its silence keep.[50]

Weininger's notion of mystical ascent through logic and ethics to a kind of speechless, mystical beholding of the world-expanse [*Weltraum*] impressed the young Wittgenstein. As the next chapter will show, *Tractatus* makes a stunning break with Gottlob Frege and Bertrand Russell in its view of the propositions of logic. These propositions, says *Tractatus*, are empty tautologies that say nothing; nonetheless, by virtue of them we can see the unspeakable basis of logic.

This motif of assimilating logic to ethics, culminating in a mystical ascent to the One, reverberates throughout *Tractatus*. Despite all the technical discussions of logic in the book, the basic thrust is *ethical*. It nudges the reader along, through logic and language, toward envisioning that which cannot be captured in language and logic. As Wittgenstein himself explained in a letter to Ludwig von Ficker:

> The book's point is an ethical one. ... My work consists of two parts: the one presented here plus all that I have *not* written. And it is precisely this second part that is the important one.[51]

Here Come the Fascists

Most historians have ignored Weininger's importance for European intellectual history. An exception is Jacques Le Rider, who in 1982 published his ground-breaking book *Le Cas Otto Weininger: Racines de l'antiféminisme et de l'antisémitisme* ("The Case of Otto Weininger: Roots of Anti-feminism and Anti-Semitism"). Le Rider convincingly argues that turn-of-the-century Vienna had become a center for a growing body of reactionary sentiment that resented Jews, self-affirmed women, and open homosexuals. Otto Weininger's significance is that he tapped into this resentment, offering conservative bourgeois Austrians what they regarded as a scientific and philosophical justification for their worst prejudices.[52]

As we have seen, at the very heart of Weininger's program was a relentless misogyny. It lauded masculine, rationally-calculating males as paragons of humanity. It disdained women as soulless, and male homosexuals and Jews as genetically inferior. These misogynist biases were actually a kind of fantasy system about sex-roles. Although Weininger never drew out the political implications of his views, his fantasies served to feed the hunger of growing reactionary sentiments in Europe. They longed for a powerful male authority-figure to appear on the scene and settle all their problems. As the supreme living embodiment of male decisiveness and authority, this hoped-for leader would put uppity women, homosexuals, and Jews in their place, and reestablish an order of manly virtue in the body-politic. Later, after the economy of Europe disintegrated and great masses of people became desperate for any kind of political solution, both Mussolini and Hitler played on such fantasies in plotting their paths to power.

Le Rider astutely points out that although Weininger furthered a fascist mentality about sex and power, he was not unique in patriarchal civilization. The line between patriarchy and fascism is a fine one indeed:

> Exaltation of the heroic self and the self of genius, disdain of sexual desire and anguished struggle against "the trace of femininity in himself"—these characterize Weininger as a fascist type. But we cannot avoid the awkward question: "What distinguishes fascist from 'non-fascist'?" Fascist virility can point with pride to the patriarchal domination that lies at the source of our civilization, having its own illustrious tradition in idealist philosophers, in artistic depictions of male/female polarity, in scientific rationality. The fascist character belongs to every age. It yet lies dormant in every man today.[53]

To notice the affinity between patriarchy and fascism is not to justify the latter; rather, it should make us examine more critically a form of fantasizing about sex and power that most people unthinkingly take for granted simply because it has been long established. The second volume in this series, *Sex and Power*, will be devoted to such a critical examination.

As we have seen, the great irony in Weininger's protofascist fantasies is that he himself was both Jewish and homosexual. Hence his whole life's work was actually an elaborate exercise in hypocrisy and masochistic self-flagellation. But this behavior, although ironic, is not unprecedented. A similar case was that of the American lawyer Roy Cohn, who was to American politics during the Cold War what Weininger was to Germanic philosophy at the turn of the century. And, as we will see in the next chapter, the tradition was carried on by Weininger's most illustrious admirer, Ludwig Wittgenstein.

From Weininger to Russell

In eagerly devouring Otto Weininger's *Sex and Character*, the young Ludwig Wittgenstein feasted on an abundant metaphysical fare. The following seven dogmas were the top items on this metaphysical menu: (1) the quest for fulfillment as a human being is a quest for ever greater masculinization; (2) masculinization means mystical ascent away from the sensual and the feminine toward a transcendent fount of logic and ethics; (3) this transcendent fount escapes all description, and can only be apprehended in speechlessness; (4) meaning is a kind of physiognomy which can be displayed through graphic tables of bivalent symbols; (5) the truths of logic *say* nothing, but *show* the way to a higher reality; (6) solipsism and realism are but two sides of the same coin; and (7) enlightenment consists of "the flight of the alone to the Alone" (to borrow the classic phrase of Plotinus).[54]

Having imbued these metaphysical dogmas from Weininger, Wittgenstein went to Cambridge in 1912 to study mathematics and logic with Bertrand Russell, who was about as far removed from Weininger as one could get. Worldly, witty, sexually exuberant, anti-authoritarian, anti-religious, and pro-feminist, Russell exemplified the opposite of everything that Weininger stood for. No doubt it was a jolting experience for the young Wittgenstein.

Over the years, Wittgenstein and Russell maintained an uneasy on-again, off-again relationship, until it eventually collapsed in undisguised mutual hostility. Their differences on social and political matters were enormous: Wittgenstein was a misogynist who opposed the right of women to vote, while Russell ran for parliament on the women's suffrage ticket; Wittgenstein believed in strict educational methods including corporal punishment, while Russell founded an alternative elementary school run on liberal principles; Wittgenstein volunteered to fight for the German alliance in World War I, while Russell was jailed for opposing the war; Wittgenstein admired Stalinism, while Russell warned that the Bolsheviks were turning Russia into a huge prison camp; Wittgenstein was a closeted homosexual who criticized Russell for advocating freer sexual mores, while Russell, a heterosexual, lost a teaching position in New York City partly for advocating repeal of the laws against homosexuality; Wittgenstein denounced those who advocated nuclear disarmament as "the *scum* of the intellectuals," while Russell went to jail for demonstrating on behalf of just that.[55]

Despite their social and political differences, however, Wittgenstein and Russell managed to maintain a civil dialogue, at least for a few years, on matters of logic. But here, as well, the gap proved unbridgeable. A notable eruption occurred early, when Wittgenstein found that he couldn't get his *Tractatus* published unless Russell wrote a laudatory preface to the work. Russell obliged, but in the process incorrectly stated that *Tractatus* dealt with the conditions needed to be satisfied by a logically perfect language. Chagrined at needing an introduction by Russell in the first place, Wittgenstein angrily responded that the book in fact dealt with the logical conditions needed to be satisfied by *any* language, not just a logically perfect one. Although Wittgenstein was right on the matter, Russell's error is easy to understand. *Tractatus* argues that any indeterminateness of sense in a language is due to lack of precision, and calls for the creation of a sign-language governed by a strictly-logical grammar.

The conflict over Russell's introduction to *Tractatus* was but the tip of a massive iceberg of jagged philosophical and personal differences. As we will see in the next chapter, much of *Tractatus* consists of forays against *Principia Mathematica*, written by Russell and Whitehead, and also against Russell's book-in-progress *Theory of Knowledge*. In addition, parts of Wittgenstein's later book, *Philosophical Investigations*, were a veiled attack on Russell's book *The Analysis of Mind*, published in 1921. Having irreconcilable personalities and worldviews, Wittgenstein and Russell were at odds on nearly everything, from sex to logic.

Of the two philosophers, Wittgenstein gained the most from their tumultuous relationship.

Wittgenstein used Russell to learn mathematical logic, publish *Tractatus*, obtain his academic degree, receive university stipends, and obtain British citizenship. In return, he offered Russell very little public thanks. Russell, on the other hand, lost from the relationship. He became demoralized in his own work as a result of Wittgenstein's harsh, oracular style of criticism. Initially believing that Wittgenstein's objections were offered in good faith, Russell found he simply could not understand many of them. Wittgenstein, speaking with moody condescension, disdained to offer clarifications. In the end, Russell came to view Wittgenstein as a philosophic fraud, while Wittgenstein thought Russell had become a philosophic antique.

In the next chapter we will examine in detail the indebtedness of Wittgenstein's *Tractatus* to Weininger's *Sex and Character*. This comparison will reveal that nearly everyone has misinterpreted Wittgenstein's real motives in writing the book.

---

[1] The secondary literature on Wittgenstein's philosophy is enormous. Most of it, however, is of little value, for the reasons discussed in this book. Among the more influential or provocative of recent commentaries on Wittgenstein are the following: Gordon Baker, *Wittgenstein, Frege and the Vienna Circle*, Basil Blackwell, Oxford, 1988; G.P. Baker & P.M.S. Hacker, *Wittgenstein: Understanding & Meaning*, The University of Chicago Press, 1980; G.P. Baker & P.M.S. Hacker, *Wittgenstein: Rules, Grammar and Necessity*, Basil Blackwell, 1985; Derek Bolton, *An Approach to Wittgenstein's Philosophy*, The Macmillan Press, Ltd., London, 1979; Raymond Bradley, *The Nature of All Being: A Study of Wittgenstein's Modal Atomism*, Oxford University Press, New York, 1992; Gertrude Conway, *Wittgenstein on Foundations*, Humanities Press International, Inc., Atlantic Highlands, NJ, 1989; P.M.S. Hacker, *Insight & Illusion: Themes in the Philosophy of Wittgenstein*; revised ed., Clarendon Press, Oxford, 1986; S. Stephen Hilmy, *The Later Wittgenstein*, Basil Blackwell, Oxford, 1987; Merrill Hintikka & Jaakko, *Investigating Wittgenstein*, Basil Blackwell, 1986; B.F. McGuinness, "The Mysticism of the *Tractatus*," vol. 75, 1966, pp. 305-328; Russell Nieli, *Wittgenstein: From Mysticism to Ordinary Language*, State University of New York, Albany, 1987; Philip Shields, *Logic and Sin in the Writings of Ludwig Wittgenstein*, The University of Chicago Press, Chicago, 1993; Joachim Schulte, *Wittgenstein: An Introduction*, trans. by William H. Brenner & John F. Holley, State University of New York Press, Albany, 1992; Ashok Vohra, *Wittgenstein's Philosophy of Mind*, Open Court, La Salle, IL, 1986; and Eddy Zemach, "Wittgenstein's Philosophy of the Mystical" in *Essays on Wittgenstein's Tractatus*, ed. by Irving M. Copi & Robert Beard, Routledge and Kegan Paul, London, 1966, pp. 359-375.

[2] The most comprehensive biography of Wittgenstein is by Ray Monk, *Ludwig Wittgenstein: The Duty of Genius*, The Free Press, New York, 1990. Monk's book is an invaluable resource, rich in anecdotal detail and meticulously researched. Unfortunately, however, the book sags in dealing with Wittgenstein's sexuality, as discussed later in this chapter.

[3] *ibid.*, p. 114.

[4] Rudolf Carnap, "From his *Autobiography*" in *Ludwig Wittgenstein: The Man and His Philosophy*, ed. by K.T. Fann, Dell Publishing Co., Inc., New York, 1967, p. 35.

[5] Ludwig Wittgenstein, *Culture and Value*, ed. by G.H. von Wright and Heikki Nyman, trans. by Peter Winch, Basil Blackwell, Oxford, 1980, p. 39.

[6] Paul Engelmann, *Letters from Ludwig Wittgenstein*, With a Memoir, ed. by B.F. McGuinness, trans. by L. Furtmüller, Basil Blackwell, Oxford, 1967, p. 94.

[7] Wittgenstein, *Culture and Value*, p. 18e.

[8] Ludwig Wittgenstein, *Philosophical Investigations*, ed. by G.E.M. Anscombe and Rush Rhees, trans. by G.E.M. Anscombe, The Macmillan Co., New York, 1953.

[9] Bertrand Russell, *My Philosophical Development*, Simon and Schuster, New York, 1959, p. 118.

[10] P.M.S. Hacker, *Insight & Illusion*, p. vii.

[11] Engelmann, *op. cit.*, p. xiv.

[12] *ibid.*, pp. xv & 33.

[13] William Bartley, *Wittgenstein*, Open Court Press, La Salle, IL, first edition 1973, second edition 1985.

[14] *ibid.*, pp. 40 & 26.

[15] Maurice Drury, letter, *The Times Literary Supplement*, February 22, 1974, # 3755, p. 186.

[16] Rush Rhees, Review of Bartley's *Wittgenstein* in *The Human World*, vol. 14, February 1974, pp. 66-85.

[17] *ibid.*, p. 77, footnote.

[18] *ibid.*, pp. 78-83.

[19] Monk, *op. cit.*, p. 581.

[20] *ibid.*, p. 584.

[21] Ray Monk, letter in *White Crane* [journal of gay male spirituality], no. 17, Summer 1993, p. 17.

[22] Monk characterizes Drury's book, *The Danger of Words*, as "more truly Wittgensteinian than almost any other secondary text." Monk, *Ludwig Wittgenstein*, p. 403.

[23] *ibid.*, pp. 11, 33, 37, & 29.

[24] *ibid.*, p. 33; original's emphasis

[25] Monk, *op. cit.*, p. 187.

[26] Albert Levi, "The Biographical Sources of Wittgenstein's Ethics," *Telos*, No. 38, Winter 1978-79, p. 67. See also Steven S. Schwarzschild, "Wittgenstein as Alienated Jew," *Telos*, No. 40, Summer 1979, pp. 160-165; Thomas Rudebush & William M. Berg, "On Wittgenstein & Ethics: A Reply to Levi," *Telos*, no. 40, Summer 1979, pp. 150-160; and Albert Levi, "Wittgenstein Once More: A Response to Critics," *Telos*, No. 40, Summer 1979, pp. 165-173.

[27] Against Levi, another critic claimed that Wittgenstein was writing as a Jew estranged from Christian society. This critic did not know about Wittgenstein's rabid anti-Semitism. Other critics claimed the letters referred to Wittgenstein's depression over not getting *Tractatus* published. This explanation fails to account for Wittgenstein's allusion to devils and his calling himself a "swine." Although Levi's argument was not conclusive, the objections made to it by other critics were weak. In any case, Monk should have at least mentioned this debate.

[28] Engelmann, *op. cit.*, p. 39; original's emphasis.

[29] Matthew, 5:28-30; *The New American Bible*, P.J. Kenedy & Sons, New York, 1970.

[30] Bartley, *op. cit.*, p. 40.

[31] On Weininger's life and works, see David Abrahamsen, *The Mind and Death of a Genius*, Columbia University Press, New York, 1946, and, most important of all, Jacques Le

Rider, *Le Cas Otto Weininger*, Presses Universitaires de France, Paris, 1982. A disappointing book on Weininger is Allan Janik, *Essays on Wittgenstein and Weininger*, Rodopi, Amsterdam, 1985. Janik wrote this book at the behest of Weininger's brother, in order to improve Weininger's historical image. As an example of the twisted thinking in this book, Janik calls Weininger a "humanist" because Weininger (in Janik's opinion) had "a benevolent attitude to those whom he considered inferior" (p. 87).

[32] Le Rider, *op. cit.*, p. 37.
[33] Hacker, *op. cit.*, p. 88.
[34] Wittgenstein, *Culture and Value*, p. 43.
[35] Otto Weininger, *Geschlecht und Charakter*, Wilhelm Braumüller, Vienna, originally published in 1903; 9th printing, 1907.
[36] Otto Weininger, *Sex and Character*, anonymously translated, G.P. Putnam Sons, New York, 1906.
[37] Le Rider, *op. cit.*, pp. 18-19.
[38] Adolf Hitler, *Monologe im Führerhauptquartier*, ed. by Werner Jochmann, Hamburg, 1980, p. 148.
[39] Abrahamsen, *op. cit.*, p. 122.
[40] Bernardo Bertolucci, *Il Conformista* (movie), Mars/Marianne/Maran, Italy, 1970.
[41] Alessandra Stanley, "In the Kremlin, Chickens Still Come Home to Roost," *The New York Times*, June 28, 1996, p. 8.
[42] Allesandra Stanley, "New Close Yeltsin Aide: His Daughter," *The New York Times*, November 3, 1996, p. 4.
[43] Weininger, *Geschlecht und Charakter*, p. 62.
[44] *ibid.*, p. 205; original's emphasis.
[45] *ibid.*, p. 244.
[46] *ibid.*, p. 192-193; original's emphasis.
[47] *ibid.*, p. 206.
[48] *ibid.*, p. 210; original's emphasis.
[49] *ibid.*, p. 200; original's emphasis.
[50] *ibid.*, p. 211.
[51] Engelmann, *op. cit.*, p. 143; original's emphasis.
[52] Le Rider, *op. cit.*, p. 114-115. See also John Lauritsen and David Thorstad, *The Early Homosexual Rights Movement (1864-1935)*, Times Change Press, New York, 1974.
[53] *ibid.*, pp. 216-217.
[54] Plotinus, *Enneads*, VI, 9, 11.
[55] Wittgenstein, *Culture and Value*, p. 49, original's emphasis.

Sacra 3, Detail
Graphite, 30" x 22", 1990

Documents, Detail of Installation
Salt and Text on Floor, 1996

Logic on Stilts

SUMMARY: This chapter takes up Ludwig Wittgenstein's famous book on logic, *Tractatus Logico-Philosophicus*. The chapter reveals a sex-related aspect to the book that most commentators have overlooked.

As noted in the last chapter, Ludwig Wittgenstein volunteered to fight for the German alliance during World War I. After the war he presented his mentor, Bertrand Russell, with a little book on logic that he had completed while in the trenches.

Thanks to Russell's encouragement, Wittgenstein in 1921 witnessed the publication of his new book, *Logisch-philosophische Abhandlung* ("Logical-Philosophical Treatise"). The following year, the book was translated into English, but with a Latin title, *Tractatus Logico-Philosophicus* (same meaning).[1] In this chapter, we will first explore the partial dependence of *Tractatus* on the thought of Bertrand Russell, and then show how the book goes off on an anti-Russell tangent, inspired by the works of the protofascist Otto Weininger. In the process, we will uncover a surprising connection between logical and sexual fantasy systems in Wittgenstein's early philosophy. Once this connection comes into focus, we will see that most of Wittgenstein's later admirers have misconstrued his intent in writing the book.

The Ghost of Leibniz, Again

Although at odds with Russell on many matters, the young Wittgenstein nevertheless shared with him certain assumptions that Russell had derived from the German philosopher Gottfried Wilhelm Leibniz. As shown in chapter five, Leibniz believed that analysis is the golden key to knowledge. When analysis goes as far as it can, said Leibniz, it finds the basic building blocks of reality, which Leibniz called "monads." Influenced by Leibniz, Russell also believed that to know is to analyze, and that analysis eventually ends with some bedrock of elemental units. Russell likewise shared Leibniz's dream of creating a "universal sign-system" (*characteristica universalis*). This was to be an artificial language that would clearly depict by its structure the logical form of any argument expressed in it.

Wittgenstein himself rarely mentioned Leibniz in his own writings and appears to have read little about him. Through his early apprenticeship with Russell, however, Wittgenstein unknowingly inherited three Leibnizian doctrines: (1) knowing is principally a matter of analyzing; (2) logical atoms are the building blocks of reality and the guarantors of the determinateness of sense in language; and (3) it is possible and desirable to construct a universal sign-system. Unaware of the details of Leibniz's sophisticated philosophy, Wittgenstein struggled mightily on his own to work out anew the implications of these three doctrines.

The fruit of Wittgenstein's struggle was *Tractatus*. In many respects, this book was merely a re-invention of the wheel which the master metaphysician Leibniz had already constructed far more elegantly over two centuries before. Because many later members of the Wittgenstein cult shared their master's aversion to philosophical history, they too failed to recognize the crucial indirect influence of Leibniz in Wittgenstein's *Tractatus*. As a result, they overestimated the novelty and importance of Wittgenstein's ideas. Moreover, the thing that *was* novel in *Tractatus*, namely the engrafting of the protofascist metaphysics of Otto Weininger onto a Leibnizian root, has still largely escaped their notice.

From Monads to Definite Descriptions

Leibniz's emphasis on logical analysis inspired Russell in 1905 when he published his famous paper "On Denoting."[2] This essay, a landmark in the history of formal logic, later inspired Wittgenstein when he was struggling to understand how languages are able to have determinate meaning. To appreciate the evolution in thought that took place from Leibniz to Wittgenstein, we will take a brief look at Russell's 1905 paper.

As discussed in chapter six, Russell's paper addressed itself to a sentence that is now famous in philosophical lore: "Scott is the author of *Waverley*." This sentence includes the definite description "the author of *Waverley*." (Definite descriptions are phrases that have the form "the so and so.") At the time, logicians could not translate sentences that contain definite descriptions into logical notation. Russell showed how to do it.

According to Russell, "Scott is the author of *Waverley*" means this: "At least one x wrote *Waverley*, no more than one x wrote *Waverley*, and for all x, if x wrote *Waverley*, then x = Scott." Here the troublesome definite description, "the author of *Waverley*," is gone. What remains is the variable "x," along with several propositional functions, as in "x wrote *Waverley*." Formal logic can easily handle such propositional functions, but not the original, unanalyzed definite description.

Russell enjoyed a rush of praise for his analysis of definite descriptions. This success, reinforced by the analytic imperative he had inherited from Leibniz, motivated Russell to regard an ever growing number of things as subject to the same sort of reductive analysis. Eventually he came to view most of the things of the world as "logical fictions," that is, as derivative complexes, constructed out of simpler, more real, entities.

The question naturally arose, then, as to what constitutes the ultimate simples. Russell's answer: "sense-data"; that is, the immediate, fleeting, uninterpreted reports of the senses.

Ironically, although Russell was influenced by Leibniz, he was loath to accept the answer about ultimate simples that Leibniz had himself offered. Leibniz had argued that the really simple things of the world do not *appear* at all. Rather, they are entities ("monads") that must be presupposed. Russell disliked this answer because he was influenced by British empiricism. Although Russell conceded that there were things that the mind could apprehend in its own right, his departures from empiricism were always made grudgingly, as if he were betraying a beloved parent. Wittgenstein, by contrast, felt no filial reverence for British empiricism.

Facts and Objects

Influenced by Russell's adaptations from Leibniz, Wittgenstein argued in *Tractatus* that what we call "the world" is nothing but a big heap of "facts." Each fact is a kind of chain, completely analyzable into concatenated simples. These simples are the ultimate constituents of reality.

Wittgenstein conceived of each of these fact-chains as flat and horizontal, in contrast to the medieval view of "the great chain of being." The medievals viewed all reality as a sort of grand ladder reaching from the humblest bits of matter below to the heights of the hierarchy of heaven above.[3] Wittgenstein's concept of facts, on the other hand, is what results when the great chain of being that links heaven and earth is broken. All that's left is the earthly realm. This is conceived as a flat, horizontal panel of side-by-side slides, to be examined serially under a microscope. In effect, Wittgenstein removed the upper tip of the medievals' great chain of being from its lofty perch in the heavens, and unceremoniously laid the whole thing on its side on the ground. Thus shifted, the interconnectedness of reality could no longer function as a ladder reaching to something higher. We will shortly see, however, that Wittgenstein still wanted to reach the higher realm—but with a different kind of ladder!

What, then, are the ultimate simples from which "facts" are concatenated? In his informal writings, Wittgenstein toyed with different answers to this question: visual points, color patches, sound-moments, point-masses, properties, relations, etc. By the time he wrote *Tractatus*, however, Wittgenstein had adopted another way of looking at the matter. From a strictly logical point of view, he reasoned, it is *irrelevant* what the simples are. All that we need know is that if there is to be a world and if language is to have determinate sense, then there must be a residue of *some sort* of simples left over, after analysis has been carried as far as it can go. These ultimate simples, the last residue left after analysis, Wittgenstein simply called "objects" (*Gegenstände*).

In speaking of "objects," Wittgenstein broke with Russell, who regarded "sense-data" as the ultimate simples. Wittgenstein returned (apparently without even being aware of it!) to Leibniz's original line of reasoning. As noted above, Leibniz had concluded that simples do not *appear*; rather, we are forced by *logic* to postulate their existence if our concepts of reality and the meaningfulness of language are to have any coherence. Similarly, Wittgenstein also viewed his "objects" as a sort of logical atom. Indeed, if one substitutes the word "monad" in many places in *Tractatus* where Wittgenstein speaks of "object," the result reads like passages written more than 200 years earlier by Leibniz. For example, Wittgenstein says this:

> Objects make up the substance of the world. That is why they cannot be composite. ... The substance of the world *can* only determine a form, and not any material properties. ... In a manner of speaking, objects are colourless. ... Objects are what is unalterable and subsistent; their configuration is what is changing and unstable.[4]

Atomic Facts

According to Wittgenstein, when "objects" combine, they form the most elementary kind of fact there is, which he calls a *Sachverhalt*. An earlier English translation of *Tractatus* rendered this word as "atomic fact"; the newer, currently favored, translation renders it as "state of affairs." Each translation has some merit, because each conveys half of the word's meaning. A double translation has occurred because Wittgenstein's concept of *Sachverhalt* covers two separate claims: (1) there is a kind of *atomic fact*, resulting as the last residue from the analysis of other facts; and (2) this atomic fact is a *state of affairs*, in that it is an ordered set of "objects."

The fact that *Sachverhalt* has the double meaning of "atomic fact" and "state of affairs" reflects Wittgenstein's assumption that analysis cannot go on indefinitely. Otherwise, he claims, the world would have no ultimate building blocks, and so the elements of language would be unable to hook onto reality. Because these ultimate building blocks cannot be further analyzed, they cannot be facts. (A fact is that which can be determinately analyzed by language.) These ultimate building blocks are "objects." Their existence must be presupposed in order for language to be meaningful. What, then, is this cusp at which facts and objects meet? It is the *Sachverhalt*, which is both a "state of affairs" (a combination of objects) and an "atomic fact" (a fact that cannot be analyzed into more facts).

Fallacies About Facts

Contrary to Wittgenstein, earlier chapters have shown that what is "simple" is so only in some context for some interpreter or some group of interpreters. Therefore, there is no such thing as ultimately-simple facts, only facts that are relatively simple in some context. Analysis can go on for ever.

There is also a problem with Wittgenstein's objects. As noted, these are "colourless." That is, they are mere focal points for possibilities of combination; they don't have any actual material characteristics. But how can a mere focal point for possibility ever generate something *real*? No matter how many colorless pieces of glass you put in front of each other, you never get any color. (Leibniz faced a similar difficulty in trying to distinguish between possible and real monads.) Russell's sense-data, which give material characteristics to the elements of reality, have more explanatory power than Wittgenstein's colorless objects.

Truth, Pictured

Wittgenstein used his theory of facts and objects to account for how propositions can be meaningful, and, if meaningful, true or false. Inspired by a court case where a small model was used to depict the scene of an accident, he argued that the simplest propositions we use are "pictures" of reality. But how can a proposition, he asked himself, make a picture? By being arrayed against some state of affairs. When the names match, one-on-one, the elements of a state of affairs that actually exists, and when the names exhibit the same form among themselves as do the elements of the state of affairs, then the proposition is true; otherwise false. Strictly, this arraying process occurs with only "elementary propositions." However, Wittgenstein maintained that *every* proposition can be generated by combining or separating out some group of elementary propositions.

The merit of this theory is that it can explain how propositions can be both meaningful and false. Like Frege and Russell, Wittgenstein assumed that the meaning of an elementary proposition was some entity associated with it. But if so, how can such a proposition assert that the entity associated with it does not exist? For example, the proposition "The present king of France is bald." This proposition is meaningful, even though there is no present king of France. As discussed above, Russell analyzed propositions like this into propositional functions and the variable "x". But what about the values of "x"? Don't they have to exist? Doesn't that just bring up the same old problem on a deeper level?

No, said Wittgenstein. Elementary propositions are the last residue that remains after a complete analysis of language. They picture states of affairs, which are *possible facts*, not actually existing objects. Objects themselves exist *below* the level of states of affairs, whether actual or possible. The entity that corresponds to a false but meaningful elementary proposition is not any object, but rather a possible configuration of objects (a *Sachverhalt*, or state of affairs). If this possible configuration actually exists as pictured, then it is a fact, and the proposition is true. If not, the proposition is false—but still meaningful.

Wittgenstein's picture theory is a classic example of the correspondence theory of truth, discussed in chapter one. As noted there, advocates of the correspondence theory usually adhere to the principle of bivalence (a proposition is either true or false, and nothing else). However, the correspondence theory suggests that a proposition can be true or false by *degrees*, depending on how much the proposition-picture corresponds to the fact-model. Advocates of the correspondence theory almost always overlook this implication. The reason is that a myth is at work here, the Parmenidean myth.

Truth, Tabled

Wittgenstein believed that any given proposition could be analyzed into elementary propositions. Each of these is either true or false, depending on whether the described state of affairs exists or not. Therefore, he concluded, if we know under what conditions the elementary propositions are true or false, we can also know the same for any proposition compounded from them.

Acting on these assumptions, Wittgenstein created various "schemata" ("schema" in the singular). Schemata are tables that display the relationship between elementary propositions and the propositions compounded from them.[5]

For example, let "p" and "q" be any elementary propositions, and let "r" be the compound proposition "p & q." Here "&" means that the propositions on both sides of it are true. In this case, "r" is true if, and only if, both "p" and "q" are true. This relationship can be expressed by the following schema ("T" = True, and "F" = False):

p	q	r
T	T	T
F	T	F
T	F	F
F	F	F

According to Wittgenstein, the proper propositional sign (that is, the best set of symbols) for expressing the compound proposition "r" *is* the above schema itself. Why? Because the schema tells us neither more nor less than all of the truth-conditions of "r."

Among the schemata considered by Wittgenstein is one type with a special property: the truth-value in the last column is always a "T." For example, let "r" be the proposition "p or not-p." Here "or" means that at least one of the propositions on either side of it is true. In this case, the schema for "r" is as follows:

p	not-p	r
T	F	T
F	T	T

This schema shows that it is *irrelevant* what truth-values are assigned to "p" and "not-p," since "r" is always true. Such a schema is the propositional sign for a "tautology," that is, a proposition that is true by virtue of its form alone. The opposite of a tautology is a contradiction; the truth-values it generates are always false (as in "p & not-p"). Tautologies and contradictions share a remarkable trait: both wear their truth-values on their sleeves, independent of what may or may not be the case in the real world.

With schemata, said Wittgenstein, we can know by mere inspection whether any constructed proposition is a tautology, a contradiction, or neither. Schemata thus show the importance of using the right kind of notation, which Wittgenstein believed he had found once and for all.

Wittgenstein's admirers generally call the above schemata "truth tables" (a phrase that does not actually occur in *Tractatus*). They regard these truth tables as their master's most important contribution to logic. His originality, they say, was that he used them as strict *definitions* of logical connectives like "&" and "*or*."

This interpretation misconstrues the way Wittgenstein conceived of the relationship between propositions in general and schemata. As noted in chapter six, Bertrand Russell also used the word "schema," based on Frege's "courses of value" (*Werthverläufe*). Wittgenstein's novelty, as P.M.S. Hacker has demonstrated, was his insistence that the proper sign for *any* kind of proposition, regardless of how general, is some schema. This emphasis on the global role of schemata follows from Wittgenstein's very definition of "proposition":

> A proposition is an expression of agreement and disagreement with truth-possibilities of elementary propositions.[6]

As a result of this global view of schemata, Wittgenstein thought that a truth-table calculus would be adequate for the whole of logic. In particular, he discounted the need for any stipulated rules in addition to schemata:

> The rules of logical syntax must go without saying, once we know how each individual sign signifies. ... "Laws of inference," which are supposed to justify inferences, as in the works of Frege and Russell, have no sense, and would be superfluous. ... In a suitable notation we can in fact recognize the formal properties of propositions by mere inspection of the propositions themselves.[7]

After *Tractatus* was published, logicians showed that schemata (or truth tables) are actually rather limited. For one thing, they can't see inside the p's and q's they use. So they can't handle any argument whose truth depends on the internal structure of its propositions. In addition, stipulated rules have turned out to be essential to logic after all.

When Wittgenstein later realized that he was wrong to discount stipulated rules, he abandoned the schema-concept of propositions. Instead, he spent much of his subsequent philosophical life trying to understand what rules and rule-following are. In the end, he came to a radical conclusion: rules always reflect some particular life-form and mythology.

Many of Wittgenstein's latter-day followers have down-played the full implications of this conclusion. The reason is that Wittgenstein's later view undermines the Parmenidean myth and the Western logical tradition. It also has awkward consequences for mathematics and the natural sciences as well. Despite back-pedaling by many of his self-proclaimed followers, however, Wittgenstein fully intended the explosive implications of what he was saying. But more of this in following chapters.

Bipolarity

As discussed, *Tractatus* views all propositional signs, when properly analyzed, as truth-functional schemata of elementary propositions. Since he permits only "*T*" and "*F*" to be truth-values in these schemata, his whole view of the nature of the proposition hangs on the principle of bivalence.

In chapter five, we saw that Frege re-honed the Parmenidean myth, as he inherited it from Leibniz, by giving bivalence a special prominence. Eliminating Leibniz's appeal to God as the ultimate guarantor of logic, Frege grounded both logical necessity and the static ideal of knowledge on what he called "the True" and "the False." These he regarded as transcendent objects, reminiscent of the divine "dyad" found in the ancient Pythagoreans. In chapter six, we saw that Russell rejected both the God of Leibniz and the transcendent objects of Frege. Instead, Russell appealed to what he called "completely general facts" as the ultimate foundation for logical necessity; moreover, he viewed bivalence psychologically, as a disposition to assent, or not, to propositions.

Wittgenstein sided with Frege against Russell in one respect: he insisted that bivalence is the foundation of everything else in logic, and rejected any psychological account of it. However, Wittgenstein followed Russell against Frege in rejecting the concept of the True and the False as *objects*.

Wittgenstein outlined his own views on the matter in a set of notes dictated in 1913, before writing *Tractatus*. In the notes, he argued that "bipolarity" (as he called it) is the very essence of the proposition. Using an earlier version of truth tables with "*W-F*" notation (German for "*T*" and "*F*"), he stated:

> To every molecular function a WF schema corresponds. ... These two letters are the poles of atomic propositions.[8]

Wittgenstein continues and reinforces the same concept in *Tractatus*. At one point he even reverts to a modified version of his older schemata of 1913, saying that when we use "*p*," "*q*," and "*r*" to stand for propositions, we could equally well use the symbols "*TpF*," "*TqF*," and "*TrF*."⁹ If we do so, he continues, we can graphically trace out the connecting lines between the various *T*'s and *F*'s, and so see the logical relationship of "*p*," "*q*," and "*r*."

The implication is that every logical proof is merely a deconstruction of some molecular proposition into an aggregate of atomic propositions. The deconstruction shows how the propositions' poles are related to each other, and *that* is the proof.

This approach to logic sweeps away Leibniz's God, Frege's transcendent objects, and Russell's "completely general facts." In effect, logic reduces to a kind of *character study*, namely, the study of the character of signs that are properly expressive of bipolarity. Anything that logicians may drag in as an addition to this bare character study of bipolar signs is needless, and even contaminating. "Logic," as Wittgenstein was fond of saying, "must look after itself."¹⁰

Bipolarity/Bisexuality

We have seen that Wittgenstein's concept of logic as the character study of bipolar signs, together with his concomitant "schemata," emerged as a reaction to the earlier views of Russell, Frege, and Leibniz. What is commonly overlooked is that Wittgenstein's notion of bipolar logical character was influenced by Otto Weininger's notion of bipolar sexual character.

As discussed in the last chapter, Weininger absorbed the faddish interest of his time in "physiognomy" (the pseudo-science that holds that a person's character can be read-off from his or her physical attributes). Regarding sex as the most basic of human physical attributes, Weininger argued in his book *Sex and Character* that every human being is bisexual.¹¹ Much of a person's character, insisted Weininger, can be simply read-off from the particular proportional mix of "male-plasm" and "female-plasm" in his or her body. To the extent that a person's body is dominated by male-plasm, he or she embodies the ideal male type, which Weininger called "*M*" (for *Mensch*, meaning "Man"). To the extent that a person's body is dominated by female-plasm, he or she embodies the ideal female type, "*W*" (for *Weib*, meaning "Woman"). Weininger also believed that the particular mix of male-plasm and female-plasm for any person could be scientifically expressed through a formula or table. Accordingly, his book includes several curious formulas consisting of combinations of the signs "*M*" and "*W*," which he intended as schematic depictions of kinds of human character.

Weininger's elaborate metaphysics of sex boils down to two basic claims: (1) the study of character can be reduced to the study of bodies (understood as *signs* of character); and (2) a person's character can be scientifically depicted by a formula or table showing the relationship of two essential factors, "*M*" and "*W*."

The parallels between Weininger's physiognomical approach to human character and Wittgenstein's physiognomical approach to human language are striking. Weininger says the study of human character can be reduced to the study of physical bodies in their capacity as signs. Wittgenstein says the study of the logical character of language can be reduced to the study of the use of the physical signs that express logical connections. Weininger says that any given person's individual character can be scientifically depicted by a formula using the symbols "*M*" and "*W*" (for "Male" and "Female" in German). Wittgenstein says the logical character of any given compound proposition can be depicted by a formula using the symbols "*W*" and "*F*" (for "True" and "False" in German).

Both Weininger and Wittgenstein insist that the essential thing to understand in their respective fields is the working-out of an underlying "polarity" (*Polarität*). For Weininger, to understand the character of a person is to understand the exact structure of an interplay of "*M*" and "*W*." For Wittgenstein, to understand the logical character of a compound proposition is to understand the exact structure of the interplay of "*W*" and "*F*." For both Weininger and Wittgenstein, the important thing is the study of character (in the one case personal, in the other, logical). Again for both, *character is a matter of the physiognomy of an underlying bipolarity.*

Wittgenstein's work with truth tables was indebted to Russell's schemata and Frege's courses of value, as we have seen. But for all that, Wittgenstein's truth tables give to his predecessors' notions an unexpected (and usually unnoticed) twist: they draw on unstated assumptions about physiognomy and bipolarity that Wittgenstein extracted from Weininger.

Chapter Eight

Mysticism and Logical Necessity

Wittgenstein's successors in logic have regarded his truth-table concept as a sort of entablature. With this entablature, they say, Wittgenstein sought to crown the great columns of formal logic that were first rough-hewn by Gottlob Frege and later re-engineered by Bertrand Russell. In reality, however, Wittgenstein actually sought to overthrow these columns and to build an entirely different kind of structure. For the purpose, he used as his intellectual mortar a concoction of Otto Weininger's that was as far removed as possible from any of Russell's philosophical recipes. To understand this point, we need to trace out the close connection between Wittgenstein's concept of truth tables and his theory of logical mysticism.

Earlier chapters have shown that logicians throughout the ages have been stumped by the problem of logical necessity, which they have assumed to exist but have never been able to adequately explain. Most logicians have asserted that logic describes some kind of reality that grounds and validates logical necessity. Various candidates for this grounding reality have been the goddess far-constraining Order (Parmenides), the mind of Zeus (the Stoics), the Logos-Christ (medieval Christian philosophers), the True and the False (Frege), and completely general facts (Russell). Wittgenstein, by contrast, draws on Weininger's *Sex and Character* to argue that logic does not *describe* anything. Rather, says Wittgenstein, the imperatives of logic (like those of ethics) are revealed only through a kind of mystical insight into the unspeakable.

Wittgenstein's logical mysticism involves the connection of his schemata ("truth tables") to logical proof. As noted above, Wittgenstein holds that a logical proof, correctly understood, does not involve any stipulated rules. Rather, a logical proof can be seen as a kind of compound proposition. It is reducible, like any other compound proposition, to some set of elementary propositions or their denials.

Accordingly, to carry out a logical proof is to use an adequate notation (schemata) to construct some compound proposition from certain elementary propositions or their denials. Using such a construction, we can *see* the overall patterns that exist among the various bipolar truth-values. This seeing *is* the proof.

What sort of thing do these patterns among truth-values refer to? A describable reality? Surely not, says Wittgenstein. How could we possibly describe that which must be presupposed as the ground of the possibility of describing? Does that mean that nothing real answers to the patterns of truth-values? Surely not, says Wittgenstein again. In that case, how could logical discourse occur? We are able to utter meaningful propositions that describe things; therefore, that which is logically necessary for such utterances to occur must be real. So the relational patterns among truth-values do not point to some describable thing—yet they are related to something that is real! What is it?

This is the old question about the nature of "logical form"—What it is in reality and language that enables combinations of signs to mirror combinations of real objects? By the time Wittgenstein wrote *Tractatus*, this old question had become the question of what Russell called the "logical constants."

Building on Frege's work, Russell had argued that we can use variables—say "p" and "q"—into which we can plug individual propositions as needed. But consider the compound proposition "$p \& q$." Here "$\&$" means that the propositions on both sides of it are true. Although we can substitute different propositions for "p" and "q," we can't substitute anything for "$\&$." This symbol is a constant. What's more, it's a *logical* constant, because it stands for a logical relation.

The symbol "$\&$" seems to represent something that is in both language and the world. What is it? Russell offered various answers to this question over the years. Most of his answers assumed that the logical constants are descriptive and representative.

Wittgenstein rejected Russell's whole approach to the problem. Instead, Wittgenstein argued that the symbols "$p \& q$" are merely a convenient abbreviation that obscures what's logically important. Drawing on the precedent of Russell's own analysis of definite descriptions, Wittgenstein said the whole situation can be re-analyzed in such a way that the troublesome symbol "$\&$" just disappears. Wittgenstein claimed that when we say that "$p \& q$" is a proposition, all we really mean is that there is some proposition "r" that satisfies the following schema:

p	q	r
T	T	T
F	T	F
T	F	F
F	F	F

The above schema does everything that the propositional sign "*p & q*" was intended to do, but without even using the symbol "&." Therefore, the symbol "&" does not stand for some *thing*.

Russell had shown that you could never find anything in the world that you could tag with the name "definite description." Likewise, Wittgenstein argued, you can never find anything that you can tag with the name "logical constant." Conclusion: the logical constants do not represent or describe. Wittgenstein calls this conclusion the "fundamental idea" of *Tractatus*:

> My fundamental idea is that the "logical constants" are not representatives [*nicht vertreten*]; that there can be no representatives of the *logic* of facts.[12]

As noted earlier, Wittgenstein regards all language as a kind of description or representation of objects or collections of objects. Since he now maintains that the logical constants do not describe or represent, it follows that logical form—that which makes language possible in the first place—is itself unspeakable. In the beginning, in Wittgenstein's gospel, there was not the Word, but the Unspeakable.

Although expressed in logical jargon and buried deep within *Tractatus*, this "fundamental idea" reflects a deep mystical impulse on Wittgenstein's part. We will soon see this impulse break through the thin shell of logical jargon that encases it here. Like the branches of a mighty oak, it will reach out into the entire firmament of Wittgenstein's thought, affecting his views on ethics, religion, and sex.

Show and Tell

For the moment, however, we must remain content to ask ourselves a question of more limited scope: if logical form is an indescribable reality, as Wittgenstein insists, how can we communicate about it? In answer, Wittgenstein argues that every meaningful propositional sign both "says" (*sagt*) and "shows" (*zeigt*) something about the world. What the propositional sign *says* is that some particular state of affairs exists, as in the sentence "A majority of men are misogynists." What this propositional sign *shows*, on the other hand, is that *if* what it describes is true, *then* certain other things either are or are not true. For example: if it is true that a majority of men are misogynists, then it is *not* true that a majority of men are *not* misogynists. This implication is true by virtue of what we see *must* be true, regardless of any particular facts in the world; otherwise, language would be impossible.

The core thesis of Wittgenstein's *Tractatus* is that logical form can only be *shown*, not *said*. The reason: language and logic are possible only by virtue of a realm of reality that is in itself indescribable. This thesis suggests that certain kinds of logical notation may be better than others for making such revelations. Wittgenstein offers his schemata as the finest example to date of a notation that can best show (but not describe) this higher reality. In effect, his schemata become a kind of privileged window on the unspeakable realm of logical necessity.

In developing his theory of the unspeakable—solemnly delivered in a condensed, oracular style, in a book bearing a Latin title—Wittgenstein presents himself to his readers as a kind of hierophant. In ponderous cadences laced with odd-looking symbols, he intones the message that logical form, although unspeakable, is nonetheless directly viewable—thanks to the schema, a new notation that he himself has invented. As the favored priest who has succeeded in mastering the symbolic clues, he leads us on through the twists and turns of the logical labyrinth to the very threshold of the unspeakable mysteries. In this sacred journey, the work of all others (a profane lot—think of Bertrand Russell!) is now exposed for what it is, mere preparatory window-dressing. Indeed, no serious logical problems any longer remain, for he has at least succeeded in solving them all:

> The *truth* of the thoughts that are here set forth seems to me unassailable and definitive. I therefore believe myself to have found, on all essential points, the final solution of the problems.[13]

The Emptiness of Logic

Wittgenstein's views of the nature of logical form have important implications for what have been called "the truths of logic." Many previous logicians had assumed that there were certain privileged compound propositions that were self-evidently true (such as "Not both p and not-p"). These were thought to describe an unchanging realm of truth, and to provide the necessary basis for all deduction. Breaking with this tradition, Wittgenstein argued that all the truths of logic are empty tautologies. They indeed *show* something about logical necessity, but they *say* nothing at all about the world. Indeed, they are not even necessary for licensing other deductions. For example, the so-called truth of logic "Not both p and not-p" (known as the law of contradiction) is merely the following schema:

p	not-p	r
T	F	F
F	T	F

The schema of the so-called law of contradiction is no more special than any other. *All* schemata are mere displays of relationships among bipolar truth-values. Moreover, the construction of other schemata do not depend on this one. Every schema counts as its own proof. When we look at any particular schema, we can just *see* whether it is tautologous, contradictory, or neither. This discrimination constitutes the whole business of logic. In sum, logic is flat, not a hierarchy, and the so-called truths of logic are merely empty tautologies.

One might object here that Wittgenstein just re-introduces the law of contradiction through the back door, by the way he constructs schemata. To say that only a "T" or an "F" can occur as the truth-value for any given proposition implies that no proposition can have both "T" and "F." This is just another way of saying "Not both p and *not-p*," especially since Wittgenstein says that to assert "p" is merely to assign the truth-value "T" to "p."

Wittgenstein would respond by saying that the real issue here is bipolarity, not the so-called law of contradiction. For Wittgenstein, the fact that something is a proposition *means* that it is bipolar. From the nature of this bipolarity flows not only the so-called law of contradiction but also all other tautologies, which are all on the same level. Why does Wittgenstein regard bipolarity as the essence of the proposition? Because only bipolarity, he argues, can explain how it is possible for language to hook onto the world. That is, states of affairs either exist or not; elementary propositions either assert their existence or their non-existence. This is the simple, bipolar basis of all language.

Despite Wittgenstein's claims, however, we saw earlier that bipolarity is just the old myth of bivalence in a new guise. Even more, we saw that bipolarity is undermined by Wittgenstein's own picture theory of the proposition. Using his new truth tables, Wittgenstein does succeed in de-mythologizing the law of contradiction, as he claims, but only at the expense of recasting and reinforcing the old wobbly myth of bivalence.

Wittgenstein's argument that the truths of logic are empty shocked Bertrand Russell. He compared his reaction to that of a pious Catholic when he or she discovers that there have been wicked popes. Russell had good reason for shock. If Wittgenstein was right, Russell's agenda of deducing arithmetic from logic was off the mark. Logic, Wittgenstein said, can never describe *anything*. Therefore, it cannot be used to prove that such things as numbers exist, with such and such properties.

As noted in chapter six, Russell acknowledged that he had been forced to introduce certain non-logical premises (such as the axiom of reducibility) in order to derive numbers from logic. Nonetheless, he felt that these were mere temporary expedients, to be removed after further progress in logical technique. In *Tractatus*, Wittgenstein mercilessly criticized these *ad hoc* premises. Logic is an empty hat, Wittgenstein insisted. Despite Russell's attempted sleight of hand, no *thing* can ever be pulled out of that hat, not even something as airy as a number.

Russell, uncomfortable with Wittgenstein's mystical bent, used his introduction to *Tractatus* to challenge the notion that there is anything unspeakable in logic. Even if the structure of the language we are considering cannot be described, argued Russell, we can nonetheless create a higher-level language in which we can talk about the structure of the first, lower-level language. Russell's suggestion foreshadowed the concept of "metalanguage" later developed by Alfred Tarski and David Hilbert.

Wittgenstein could respond, however, that whatever the highest-level metalanguage might be, it must also have some logical form, and so the problem just repeats itself at this higher level. But there is an embarrassing irony for Wittgenstein in this response. His *Tractatus* itself is just such a highest-level metalanguage.

Therefore, on Wittgenstein's own assumptions, *Tractatus* cannot describe logical form. Despite these restrictions, however, the book manages to say a lot about logical form—that it exists, that it is unspeakable, that it is the ground of meaning, that propositional signs display it through their bipolar relations, etc. If Wittgenstein can say all these things about logical form, why can't Russell say everything he wants to as well?

Although rejecting Wittgenstein's mystical streak, many later commentators have praised his contention that the truths of logic are mere tautologies, viewing this claim as an original contribution to the history of logic. As noted in the last chapter, however, this idea comes right out of Otto Weininger, who had argued that any so-called truth of logic "adds nothing to our knowledge, contributes nothing to our riches."[14]

Like Wittgenstein, whom he influenced, Weininger linked the emptiness of logic to the concept of an unspeakable Truth that grounds both logic and ethics. In addition, Weininger made an implicit distinction between the propositional roles of *saying* and *showing*. Wittgenstein's contribution did not lie in inventing this distinction, but in making it explicit and systematic, and in collapsing the entire hierarchy of logical truths down to the sub-basement structure of his schemata.

Though important, Wittgenstein's changes were refinements to a peculiar, mystical vision of logic that he had extracted from Weininger. Had Wittgenstein's commentators not had an anti-historical bias, they would have read Weininger, and so given a more accurate appraisal of Wittgenstein's alleged originality in *Tractatus*. Wittgenstein himself ruefully admitted in his personal diaries that he was not a very original thinker. The real originality of *Tractatus* lay with Weininger. Wittgenstein sought to save as much as he could of Weininger in the face of the opposing world-view pushed by the atheist-materialist Bertrand Russell. Although the logical jargon in *Tractatus* came from Bertrand Russell, its soul belonged to Otto Weininger.

God is Not In the World

Some commentators have tried to dismiss Wittgenstein's mystical view of logic as a sort quirky, *ad hoc* tangent. However, his effort to ground logic on mysticism reflects the deepest current in *Tractatus*. Evidence for this current is the way Wittgenstein deals with ethics, acting (again) under the influence of Weininger. Indeed, although much of the book ostensibly deals with technical logical questions, Wittgenstein himself confided in private that the book should actually be understood as a work on *ethics* (which for Wittgenstein included theology).

In order to fathom Wittgenstein's deepest aim in *Tractatus*, we need to be aware of his underlying religious motivation. Although carefully shrouded in logical gauze, this disposition is no shriveled mummy, but rather the book's core animating force.

Near the end of *Tractatus*, Wittgenstein makes a short, two-sentence statement. The second sentence of this statement, an aphorism, constitutes the single most important assertion in the book. At first, it might seem odd to make such a claim for this aphorism. After all, Wittgenstein explicitly says what his "fundamental idea" is, namely the thesis that the logical constants do not stand-in for any thing. However, there is no conflict here, for the latter aphorism is actually a more concise reformulation of his "fundamental idea." The key to understanding *Tractatus* lies precisely in seeing that his earlier statement about logical constants is a foreshadowing of his later statement, which runs as follows:

> How things are in the world is a matter of complete indifference for what is higher. God does not reveal himself *in* the world.[15]

Wittgenstein's earlier statement about logical constants maintains that logical form is inaccessible to descriptive language. The statement above implies that there is a realm that is "higher." Behind both statements lies a common assumption: the world that is accessible to descriptive language is just a flat fact. The really important things in life (of which logical form is one) are in another realm altogether.

The context in which Wittgenstein delivers this aphorism clarifies its meaning. The aphorism is part of a brief, penultimate section in *Tractatus* dealing with *ethics*. This ethical section is the concluding part of an overall explanation of an abstract principle of *logic*. The aphorism shines forth like a bright flash, encapsulating the entire preceding section on ethics. The ethical section, for its part, encapsulates the much longer section on logic, from which it springs. Above both the logical and ethical sections there stands this over-arching logical principle, one of the seven major theses of *Tractatus*:

> The general form of a truth-function is $[\bar{p}, \bar{\xi}, N(\bar{\xi})]$. This is the general form of a proposition.[16]

Decoded and unpacked, this over-arching principle says that all meaningful language consists either of elementary or compound propositions, and that every compound proposition is nothing but a collection of certain elementary propositions or their negations. This principle is the linguistic mirror of Wittgenstein's claim that the world is a mere collection of independent facts, which are ultimately aggregates of objects, and nothing more.

Now if the world is just a collection of facts, then logical form cannot be something *in* the world, because logical form is neither an object, a collection of objects, a fact, nor a collection of facts. Logical form, although real and immediately intuitable, is unspeakable. By the same token, ethical meaning (in the sense of the purpose or value of one's life) is also not *in* the world. If we did a complete inventory of all the separate things in the world, we would never find some object or state of affairs that we could tag as "ethical meaning," just as we would never find anything that we could tag as "logical form." So ethical meaning is like logical form: although real and immediately intuitable, it is unspeakable.

In the aphorism above, Wittgenstein condenses into the word "God" all of reality that is not a flat fact describable by language. He especially has ethics in mind, because he conceives of the usual questions asked about God as questions about ultimate purpose and value. In Wittgenstein's eyes, when people think they are debating about the existence and nature of God, what they are really doing is asking themselves questions like "What is the meaning of my life?" and "Why does the universe exist?"

In the aphorism, as well as in his personal musings of the time, Wittgenstein makes it clear that for him meaning, value, and God are all very real. They are not, however, facts describable in language. One simply *experiences* meaning, value, and God, without ever being able to *say* what they are, just as one simply *sees* logical form, without being able to describe it in language. For this reason, he says, those who have uncovered the meaning of life find they can never put in into words. Even so, however, they are not deluded:

> What is unspeakable is there. It *shows* itself, it is the mystical.[17]

Zeus Against Prometheus

"God does not reveal himself *in* the world"—this aphorism is the grand conclusion of all the tortuous logical meanderings in *Tractatus*, the condensation into a few words of all the doctrinal mist that suffuses the book. The same idea is restated in the book's final sentence (thesis number seven): "That whereof we cannot speak, over that must we pass in silence." Although some commentators have viewed this last sentence as an extraneous after-thought, Wittgenstein himself attests to its importance at the very beginning of the book:

> One might perhaps express the whole meaning of the book in the words: What can be said at all, can be said clearly; and that whereof we cannot speak, over that must we pass in silence. Therefore the book aims to give thought a boundary, or rather—not thought, but the putting of thoughts into words.[18]

Wittgenstein's primary purpose in writing *Tractatus* was to limit language, in order to allow safe space for "what is higher." Despite the gleaming new linguistic scalpels applied to the body of philosophy by the atheist Bertrand Russell, God would remain safe—because God transcends *language*.

The publication of *Tractatus*, then much misunderstood, contributed to Wittgenstein's reputation as the philosopher of language par excellence. The ironic truth, however, is that he regarded himself as the defender of that which *cannot* be expressed in language. In fact, Wittgenstein combats language in *Tractatus*, attempting to chain it immobile to the worldly rocks below, acting like a latter-day Zeus against Prometheus.

To this day, many still portray Wittgenstein as an early player in the much heralded "linguistic turn" in philosophy. As noted in chapter six, the linguistic turn was initiated earlier, when Gottlob Frege cut God out of the Parmenidean myth. According to Frege, logical necessity can be explained without any mystical appeals to God; instead, all we need do is invoke the formalizable nature of language itself, which is anchored on two objects, the True and the False. Contrary to Frege's efforts, however, Wittgenstein staged a retrograde maneuver in *Tractatus*, once again introducing mystical appeals to God. The earlier philosophical tradition that Frege had found so useless in logic— because of its messy mysticism—was the very tradition that Wittgenstein enthusiastically clasped to his breast.

Although widely hailed as the intellectual heir of Frege and Russell, the early Wittgenstein was in reality a revanchist for idealist philosophy. His over-riding goal was to surround the citadel of "what is higher" with an impassable moat of silence. Thus would the loquacious new breed of irreverent philosophers lose their easement rights into the higher realm.

In view of Wittgenstein's real intentions, we can now appreciate the close connection in his mind between logic and ethics. Inspired by the mystical metaphysics of Otto Weininger, Wittgenstein tacitly (literally so!) made four crucial assumptions: (1) there are absolute imperatives of logic; (2) there are absolute imperatives of ethics; (3) both these imperatives are grounded in a Truth that transcends the world; (4) none of these imperatives can be put into words.

Although unspeakable, the imperatives of logic *show* themselves by the way in which we have to use signs in order to communicate meaningfully. Likewise, the imperatives of ethics *show* themselves by the way have to act in order to have a clear conscience. We can *see* the most basic principles of what is right and wrong, just as we can *see* the most basic principles of what is logical and illogical, but without being able in either case to put those ultimate principles into words. And above both sets of principles we gain a distant glimpse of that Truth which is their common divine source.

Error and Sin

In the end, the boundary line between logic and ethics collapses for Wittgenstein: to be good is to be logical, and vice-versa, as Plato had argued over 2,000 years before. Through Weininger, who was influenced by Plato on the matter, Wittgenstein became convinced that "all error is sin."[19] This conviction reinforced his personal predilection (as it does with all who hold it) of regarding anyone who disagreed with him as tainted.

Wittgenstein's assumptions about ethics in *Tractatus* explain the abrupt change in his life after he returned to Vienna following World War I. As noted in the last chapter, he underwent a kind of psychological self-mutilation, renouncing his previous life and going out into the Austrian back-country to teach peasant children. This behavior is consistent with the implicit assumption underlying *Tractatus* (examined below) that one has a higher self that stands in stark moral isolation from the world. Convinced, thanks to Weininger, that there were absolute, world-denying moral imperatives that could only be shown, not described, Wittgenstein strove to exemplify them through his change of life. By his abandonment of Vienna for the Austrian back-country, he hoped that people could see, without his having to tell them so, that he had abandoned his lower for his higher self.

Alas for Wittgenstein, the experiment proved to be a moral disaster for him and everyone around him, as we saw in the last chapter. His disillusionment from this experience, and not certain abstract problems in logic, was the beginning of his disenchantment with the worldview of *Tractatus*. The book was principally about ethics, and when Wittgenstein realized that those ethics no longer worked for him, he was forced to re-examine the book's assumptions.

Circling in Vienna

Now that we understand the real purpose of *Tractatus*, we can better understand Wittgenstein's bumpy encounters with the Vienna Circle. As noted in the last chapter, Vienna at the turn of the century had become a center for protofascist intellectual currents. They found their classic expression (prior to Hitler) in the anti-Semitic, homophobic, and misogynist metaphysics of Otto Weininger. But intellectual life in Vienna had also witnessed currents of thought moving in exactly the opposite direction. The most noteworthy example of these counter-currents appeared in the Vienna Circle, an informal group of intellectuals founded in 1922 by Moritz Schlick, a professor at the University of Vienna.

Members of the Vienna Circle felt that European philosophy after Immanuel Kant had degenerated into a kind of ersatz-religion, using the concept of "the Absolute" as a thinly veiled substitute for God. They sought to liberate philosophy from the religious and metaphysical manacles that then restrained it, and so develop a new kind of philosophy that was scientific in spirit. Those in the Circle who had political interests tended toward socialism.

The Vienna Circle greatly admired the atheist Bertrand Russell, whose writings on logic, mathematics, and science vibrated with the same new obstreperous spirit. Hence they reacted with excitement when they heard that Russell's star pupil, a certain Ludwig Wittgenstein from their own Vienna, had published a small treatise demonstrating that the so-called truths of logic were nothing but empty tautologies.

In the eyes of the Vienna Circle, such a demonstration, if valid, would be a great feat. The idealist philosophical tradition, against which they were in revolt, had maintained that abstract reason in and of itself could reveal truths about the world that transcended the reports of the senses. Members of the Circle, by contrast, wanted to believe that all knowledge was derived from empirical observation, and that any claim to knowledge that was not so derived was a metaphysical impostor. If Wittgenstein had indeed proved what they hoped for, then idealism would have the foundation blown out from under it, and the ground would be cleared for them to build their own new philosophy.

On reading *Tractatus*, members of the Circle were delighted to find Wittgenstein saying that logical truths were empty tautologies; however, there was much in the book that they did not understand or else simply ignored. Partially as a result of their interpretation of *Tractatus*, they promoted the development of a new philosophical tradition, logical positivism. This tradition held that logic says nothing about the nature of the world, that all positive knowledge is derived from the senses, and that the meaning of any empirical statement is the manner in which it is verified (the "verifiability principle"). Invoking these principles, the logical positivists hoped to sweep away the entire post-Kantian idealist tradition as a misuse of language.

As we have seen, however, Wittgenstein was actually trying to *constrain* the Russell-inspired world-view that stimulated the Vienna Circle. Although Wittgenstein did say that the truths of logic are empty tautologies, he did *not* do so with the intent of abolishing the notion of a higher truth. To the contrary, Wittgenstein was inspired by Weininger, who was saturated with the very idealist philosophy that the Circle loathed.

Wittgenstein did not regard German idealist metaphysics as a puffed up mass of nothing, as did the Vienna Circle, but rather as a misguided effort to say what could only be shown. The idealists, Wittgenstein believed, were right in what they meant, but wrong to think they could actually put it into words. But even so, Wittgenstein felt that language did have some role to play in the matter, contrary to the logical positivists. Even though one can never *describe* the higher realm postulated by idealism, one can nevertheless attempt to "elucidate" (*erläutern*) it; that is, one can use language as a kind of gesturing, prompting others to orient their eyes in the right direction, toward the mystical. If others catch on to these language-gestures, they'll finally realize the inadequacy of the words being used, step out beyond them, and glimpse with their own eyes the unspeakable Truth; and if not, they won't, and that will be the end of the matter. And, in fact, this is exactly how Wittgenstein viewed the use of his own language in *Tractatus*:

> My propositions serve as elucidations in the following way: anyone who understands me eventually recognizes them as nonsensical, when he has used them—as steps—to climb up beyond them. (He must, so to speak, throw away the ladder after he has climbed up it.) He must transcend these propositions, and then he will see the world aright.[20]

The effort of the Vienna Circle to build their new philosophy of logical positivism on foundation blocks borrowed from Wittgenstein's *Tractatus* represents one of the most hilariously ironic misunderstandings in the history of philosophy. The irony became even richer when members of the Circle sought to have Wittgenstein himself speak before the group, ostensibly to encourage them in their new directions. To their dismay, they found him aloof or hostile to their initial entreaties and oracular in his responses to their questions. When they finally cajoled him into appearing, he amazed them by turning his back on them and reading passages from the Indian religious mystic Rabindranath Tagore. At the time they dismissed his behavior as the eccentricities of a genius. As we have seen, however, there was much more to it than that. Consistent with his theory of ethics, Wittgenstein was trying to *show* them what he felt he could not *say* to them: your whole world-view is wrong.

The Awful Truth

Members of the Vienna Circle weren't alone in their misreading of *Tractatus*. Mistaken notions about Wittgenstein's basic intent in writing the book persisted for decades. To this day, in fact, many Anglo-American academic philosophers still entertain the following erroneous beliefs on the matter: that *Tractatus* was primarily a technical work on logic; that it sought to contribute to the basic approach to logic first inaugurated by Gottlob Frege and later buttressed by Bertrand Russell; that it was part of the linguistic turn in philosophy; that the Vienna Circle understood the basic thrust of the book; and that the book reflected a spirit kindred to that of contemporary analytic philosophy, whose historical development it furthered.

Unfortunately for Anglo-American academic philosophers, however, the awful truth is actually quite different: *Tractatus* was written in the mold of medieval philosophy, being primarily a work on ethics and theology that used logic as a handmaiden in the service of these higher ends; what was new and important in the work was inspired by the metaphysics of the protofascist Otto Weininger; the book sought to constrain, if not actually derail, the new logic that had been developed by Frege and Russell; it used the concept of the unspeakable as a shield in order to deflect the new linguistic turn in philosophy; its major points were lost on the Vienna Circle; and it's spirit is profoundly hostile to that of contemporary analytic philosophy, which has misconstrued both the meaning of *Tractatus* and the course of its own history.

The great failure of many analytic philosophers in understanding *Tractatus* stems from two sources: (1) their anti-historical bias; and (2) their sexist presuppositions about the nature of human reasoning. Supremely confident that contemporary analytic philosophy is the *crème de la crème* of Western thought, they have typically disparaged earlier philosophical developments. Indeed, they view earlier philosophies either as misguided fumblings or else as a kind of audience warm-up for their own appearance on the stage of history. (*The Encyclopedia of Philosophy*, edited by Paul Edwards, is a classic display of these prejudices.) This combination of historical provincialism with sectarian hubris has repeatedly led Anglo-American analytic philosophers into making egregious errors in understanding the arguments of philosophers whom they themselves consider important (Gottlob Frege, Bertrand Russell, and Ludwig Wittgenstein).

Analytic philosophers typically assume that philosophical reasoning (by which, in effect, they mean a certain type of reasoning favored by patriarchal males) is exempt from historical and cultural peculiarities. In fact, however, all human reasoning, including philosophical reasoning, is done by interpreters who have a history and a culture. When philosophers close their eyes to their own historicity, not only do they come to view the prejudices of their own epoch as the all-time standards of rationality, but they also fail to see how their thinking has been influenced by historically conditioned sex-roles and class-roles. Since most Western philosophers have been males living in the privileged strata of hierarchical societies, the cumulative effect of these biases has been predictable: they have come to see the nature of reality and language through patriarchal lenses.

When we behold the great spectrum of human experience that we call reality, such lenses may indeed serve quite well for a certain band of the spectrum. A fatal error occurs, however, when we assume that there must be no other colors in the rainbow but these.

Despite the assumptions of patriarchal philosophers, when we think we do not function like disembodied ghosts. A better metaphor would be to imagine our thinking-activity as a kind of glowing energy-stream emanating from our bodies, like the light from a candle. As with candles, so with minds: the quality and intensity of the light produced is affected by the history and ingredients of the source. When it comes to our most basic assumptions about anything (the special province of philosophy), how and what we think is always, in part, an outgrowth of how we have lived. Yet consider the number of philosophers (usually men) who would go to any length to *disguise* the way in which their most abstract thoughts reflect the most intimate circumstances of their lives.

Every time we think, we do so motivated by personal feelings, and influenced by the peculiarities of our species, sex, class, and ambient cultures. The concept of "pure reason" is as illusory as the concept of absolute objectivity. Both are self-serving fantasies invented by male philosophers to dress their own mummified patriarchal prejudices in the cloth of absolute truth.

Standards of right reasoning certainly exist and play an important role in our lives; nonetheless, they are always relative to some interpreter or some group of interpreters, who always have a history. Philosophical issues are certainly not reducible to mere historical observations; nonetheless, we err if we spurn the gifts brought by Clio, the muse of history, to Athena, the patron of philosophy. What we call reality is certainly not a mere creation of the peculiar way we happen to experience it; nonetheless, reality is not completely independent of who we are. We are human beings; therefore, we think like human beings, and deal with human realities.

Sex and Mysticism

Despite foot-dragging by analytic philosophers, a number of works have appeared in recent years stressing the mystical side of Wittgenstein's *Tractatus*.[21] The value of these books is that they highlight the oft-neglected spiritual dimension of Wittgenstein's thought; their weakness is that they overlook the link between Wittgenstein's mysticism and his sexuality.

For example, Russell Nieli, who sees *Tractatus* as primarily a religious work, discounts any relevance of Wittgenstein's sex life to his religiosity. Indeed, Nieli castigates biographer William Bartley, who first drew attention to Wittgenstein's closeted and compulsive sex life, for "speculative license and imagination worthy of the worst tabloid press writers."[22]

As we saw in the last chapter, however, Bartley's work was in fact an important breakthrough in understanding Wittgenstein's personal life. The tabloid-press mentality lay rather on the side of Bartley's Victorian detractors. They hysterically charged Bartley with every demonic motivation they could think of, and without a shred of evidence to back up such charges.

Although Nieli is convinced that nothing could be so far removed from mysticism as sex, such a link in fact existed in the case of Ludwig Wittgenstein. To understand how this is so, we need to explore Wittgenstein's concept of the self (or "the subject," as he calls it) in *Tractatus*. Coming late in the work, this concept weaves together into one coherent philosophical fabric the separate threads of logic, ethics, and mysticism that we have thus far detected. It also provides a revealing window for looking into the state of Wittgenstein's soul.

I Am an Eye

In propositions 5.62 through 5.641 in *Tractatus*, Wittgenstein presents a highly condensed, oracular discussion of what he calls "the metaphysical subject" (*das metaphysische Subjekt*). Touching on issues of the self, language, ethics, and logic, these cryptic remarks have long puzzled many commentators. However, when these remarks are viewed in light of parallel doctrines in Otto Weininger (who borrowed from Kant and Leibniz), their meaning comes into focus.

In the passages in question, Wittgenstein says that when he looks around *in* the world, he nowhere finds the subject who is experiencing the world. Yet even though he cannot see it, Wittgenstein knows that the subject must be real, because he knows there is something that is looking around in the world, expressing a will towards the world; this beholding and willing entity is what is meant by the term "the subject." But what is it?

To answer this question, says Wittgenstein, we must address another: what is it that makes a blur of undifferentiated experience into a coherent picture? The fact, he replies, that to some eye various objects have their own places within a coherent visual field. And what is the world itself, if not the bounded totality of such a visual field?

What, then, of the subject? It is, says Wittgenstein, none other than the set of boundaries that encloses and defines the great visual field we call "the world"—

> The subject does not belong to the world: rather, it is a boundary [*Grenze*] of the world.[23]

For Wittgenstein, the subject's act of seeing is implicated in the overall coherence of the world, which is like a large visual field. This concept is an old chestnut in German rationalist philosophy. Its classic predecessor was Leibniz's concept of the eye of God as contemplating, and thereby unifying into one universe, the otherwise hermetically sealed monads that are the basis of all reality. This Leibnizian concept was taken over by Kant, who changed the eye of God into what he called "the transcendental unity of apperception" (the subject that unifies experience, but which nowhere appears in experience). Kant also changed Leibniz's disparate monads into what he called "the sensual manifold of experience" (the chaos of pure, preinterpreted experience from the senses). A version of Kant's idea later resurfaced in the idealist philosophy of Weininger, who spoke of the subject as "a perpetual self" and a "center of apperception" that transcends the entire material world.[24] From Weininger the idea passed to Wittgenstein. He collapsed the transcendental subject into the boundaries of the world, analogous to the way in which he collapsed all logical truths into schemata.

Whereas the subject was ontological in Leibniz, epistemological in Kant, and both in Weininger, Wittgenstein recasts the whole matter in linguistic terms. He does so by taking the crucial additional steps of associating the seeing subject with the "boundaries" of the world, and then identifying these with the boundaries of *language*:

> The boundaries of my language refer to [bedeuten] the boundaries of my world. Logic pervades the world; the boundaries of the world are also its boundaries.[25]

I am an eye, says Wittgenstein. My seeing consists in containing things with language. The totality of what I linguistically contain is my world.

Wittgenstein's commentators generally view these remarks as evidence of his commitment to the linguistic turn in philosophy. It's true, as his commentators claim, that Wittgenstein defines the relationship of the subject *vis-à-vis* the world in terms of language. But his motivation in doing so is to *limit* the sphere of language and the world. Indeed, for Wittgenstein, the world is a world precisely because it is *limited*, and language is the thing that limits it.

Wittgenstein's description of the metaphysical subject in terms of linguistic containment does not *exhaust* the subject; rather, it defines what the subject is only in terms of its relationship to *the world*. The subject also has immediate visions of a higher realm that transcends both language and the world ("God"). This higher aspect of my "I" does not involve any kind of containment; to the contrary, it surpasses all boundary marks ("it is the mystical").

I contain the world with my language, but I transcend both language and the world in my personal relationship with God. This sentiment, reflected in Wittgenstein's personal life, his private writings, and *Tractatus*, rings with the spirit of German idealism (and even Lutheran pietism!). It is a view far removed from the linguistic turn in philosophy. Once again, Wittgenstein pulls a card from the idealists' deck to trump the hands played by Frege and Russell.

I Am a Lonely Eye

Wittgenstein's concept of the metaphysical subject implies a form of solipsism (the doctrine that only I exist and that everything else in the world is merely some aspect of me). His concept is solipsistic because it admits of only one eye and only one visual field, namely *my* eye and *my* visual field. Although Wittgenstein also admits the reality of "what is higher," this higher realm transcends all language. Insofar as reality is describable, it is part of my world and falls within the limits of my language. Outside this limited field lies either nothing or the indescribable.

But, Wittgenstein hastens to add, this solipsism is not as dire as it first appears: when its full implications are understood, it leads to its exact opposite, realism (the doctrine that an objective world exists independent of any and all observers). This result follows, says Wittgenstein, because "I" can be reduced to the linguistic boundaries of the world. The primary reality that is there is the world itself. The world's boundary is just the edge of its meaningfulness, not some kind of independent thing on which it depends for its existence:

> Here one sees that solipsism, strictly carried out, coincides with pure realism. The "I" of solipsism shrivels away to an exten-

sionless point, and all that remains is the reality coordinated with it.²⁶

In effect, Wittgenstein asks this: What do we mean by the term 'the world'? Answer: that which I describe with my language. What do we mean by the word "I"? The boundaries of discourse about the world. Both "I" and "the world" are but two aspects of something even more basic—language engaging reality. Looking at this engagement from one point of view (its boundaries), we find the "I" ; from the other point of view (what it describes), "the world." Language has boundaries; therefore, I am. Language has a content; therefore, the world is.

Although Wittgenstein claims that his solipsism turns into realism, the fact remains that *Tractatus* always treats of language as *my* language, never as *our* language, never as the language of a group, tribe, or culture. Indeed, any recognition of genuine social interaction is strikingly absent from *Tractatus*.

Wittgenstein's metaphysical subject is a lonely eye. It looks out into a flat world that it delimits by virtue of its own seeing. Nowhere in this world does it find other subjects, or even itself, except in the boundaries of the language it uses.

In a brief preface to his discussion of solipsism, Wittgenstein warns, in typical *Tractatus* fashion, that it cannot be described. I just *see*, he argues, that the limits of my language mean the limits of my world:

> For what solipsism *means* is quite right, only it cannot be *said*, but it shows itself.²⁷

Having delivered this warning against talking, Wittgenstein proceeds forthwith to ignore it, developing the solipsistic doctrine of the metaphysical subject, as outlined above. Here, as elsewhere in *Tractatus*, he speaks from definite metaphysical assumptions, but only obliquely indicated through tight-lipped oracular pronouncements.

Wittgenstein's contorted argument that solipsism, rightly understood, converts into realism is reminiscent of parallel tendencies in Weininger. As noted in the last chapter, Weininger sees man as alone in the universe. The more, however, man's higher, intelligible self expands, the more it encompasses the unspeakable whole. In the end, solipsism is swallowed up in realism.

Wittgenstein turns Weininger's concept on its ear, then gives it a linguistic twist. Instead of the higher, intelligible self expanding into the Truth, Wittgenstein speaks of the linguistic self shrinking away to the thinness of a membrane of meaning around the world-egg. Although Weininger uses the metaphor of expansion and Wittgenstein that of shrinkage, both philosophers try mightily to reach some absolute objectivity beginning with only "I." Despite their best metaphysical leaps, however, neither manages to escape the gravity of his own philosophical egocentrism. For both Weininger and Wittgenstein (as with all patriarchal males), the world in the end remains essentially **ME**.

I Am a Resigned Eye

Wittgenstein draws stark ethical implications from these metaphysical suppositions about the subject. As noted, he believes that the subject cannot be found in the world. Since he also views the will as part of the subject, it follows that the will cannot change what occurs in the world. Therefore, the notion that we can make a difference in the world as a result of having a good will is an illusion. Indeed, Wittgenstein maintains that the phrase "freedom of the will" is empty; it merely means that it is impossible to know what will happen in the future.

Although the will can't affect what happens in the world, says Wittgenstein, it nevertheless remains important. The reason: having a good will makes one happy, whereas having a bad will makes one unhappy. The will has this result because it *does* involve the way the subject (the eye) sees the world (the visual field) as a whole. The man who is moral and happy is he who accepts the world as a whole; the immoral and unhappy man is he who rebels against the world as a whole. Even though the individual facts in the world are the same for both men, each one's disposition determines what kind of world he lives in:

> The world of the happy man is a different one from that of the unhappy man.²⁸

The Duty of Genius

Wittgenstein's stark ethical doctrine needs to be understood in the context of his conflicted personal life. As noted in the last chapter, he was troubled in his earlier years by his homosexual desires. While dealing with this torment, he fell under the sway of the self-hating Otto Weininger and then, later, ascetic Christian ideology.

Weininger, using a philosophical sickle borrowed from Plato, cut a swath between material nature on one side and spirit on the other. According to Weininger, reality is cleft in twain by what he called "the frightful dualism between nature and spirit."[29] In his view, women and animals belong entirely to the lower world, that of nature, where femininity has its stronghold. This is a realm dominated by the drive for giving birth, which Weininger regarded as disgusting. Men, on the other hand, and especially very masculine men, are able to participate in the higher realm, that of spirit and masculinity. This is the realm where logic and ethics reign, grounded in a transcendent, unspeakable Truth.

Weininger regarded every man as having a higher, intelligible "I" and a lower, sensible "I." The more each man's intelligible "I" dominates his being, the more he proves his masculinity, and so approaches the level of the "genius."

That man who has succeeded in subordinating his sensible to his intelligible "I" fulfills what Weininger called one's duty to oneself, which he regarded as the sole basis of ethics. He touted the alleged superiority of his I-centered sense of duty to the "social ethics" of the various schools of socialism that were then on the rise. Their insistence that morality be understood in terms of group or class represented to him a slavish herd mentality (a sentiment also found in his contemporary, Friedrich Nietzsche).

In Weininger's eyes, morality finds its epitome in the genius, the man who stands in stark moral and intellectual isolation against the rest of the world. Dominating his sensual nature with logic and ethics, victorious over every feminine tendency in his character, free of the need for any kind of community, the genius ascends to a lonely pinnacle of visionary insight, far above the profane speech of the mob. There he contemplates in silence the unspeakable mysteries of being:

> He has no goal outside himself, nothing else for which he lives—he has flown far above wanting-to-be-a-slave, being-able-to-be-a-slave, being-obliged-to-be-a-slave: all human society having faded deep away beneath him, all *social* ethics having sunken; he is alone, *alone*.[30]

Weininger's understanding of duty to oneself influenced Wittgenstein's view of ethical duty in *Tractatus*. As noted above, Wittgenstein conceives of the metaphysical subject as a kind of lonely, resigned eye that beholds the world, but which nowhere finds itself *in* the world. The great quest of this eye is to raise its sights above the scenes enacted out in the profane world below, and to behold, in stark isolation and silence, the mystery which illuminates it from above. As with Weininger, so with Wittgenstein: the self by its very nature is cut off from other humans and from nature, finding its greatest solace and fulfillment in solitary encounters with the unspeakable.

So deeply does Wittgenstein in *Tractatus* associate the metaphysical subject with stark isolation that he regards language itself (which is the creation of the metaphysical subject) as something essentially non-social: *I* use *my* language; its limits are the limits of *my* world. Only after Wittgenstein became disenchanted with Weininger did he come to appreciate the view of anthropologists and socialists that language is inherently a social phenomenon.

Wittgenstein's Ladder

We have watched Otto Weininger's self-absorbed, emotionally-isolated, misogynist, logic-dominated male pursue his mystical ascent above language and the slavish herd. The imagery and feeling of this ascent find parallels in the final pages of Wittgenstein's *Tractatus*.

After his brief discussion of ethical obligation in terms of duty to one's higher self, Wittgenstein turns to the topic of the mystical, insisting that there are things that show themselves but which cannot be said. He reminds the reader that his own propositions in *Tractatus* should not be taken as descriptions. Rather, they are "elucidations" to stimulate the reader to look to those places from which the unspeakable things show themselves. Those who catch a glimpse of the mysteries will understand the inadequacy of the propositions Wittgenstein himself has used. Tossing these propositions aside like a ladder that is useful only to a point, they will at last behold the world aright. Then follows Wittgenstein's famous proposition seven, the last sentence in the book:

> That whereof we cannot speak, over that must we pass in silence.[31]

Rungs on the Ladder

In order to understand the full impact of proposition seven in the context of what has gone before, readers need to appreciate the numerical structure that Wittgenstein uses in the book. Instead of composing a flowing, sequential narrative, he has designed the book as a list of separate propositions, each of which is preceded by a number. Further, the exact rung that each proposition occupies in the conceptual ladder of the book as a whole is shown (but not said!) by the same number.

The seven major theses of the book are each preceded by a single digit; every proposition that elucidates this first proposition is preceded by the same digit, a decimal point, and a further digit; a proposition that elucidates this second proposition is preceded by the same digit as the second proposition, plus an additional digit, and so on. For example, proposition five is "A proposition is a truth-function of elementary propositions." This proposition is elucidated by proposition 5.1, which says "Truth-functions can be arranged in series." This proposition is elucidated by another, proposition 5.11, etc.

Consequently it is a serious mistake to read *Tractatus* sequentially, as is usually done, like an article in a philosophy journal, without regard to the hierarchy of numbers. Instead, one gets a much better feel for what Wittgenstein is attempting to show (but not say!) if the book is read hierarchically: that is, if all the major propositions are read first, then each major proposition is read separately with its first sub-level of commentary, then each first sub-level commentary is read again with its sub-sub-level commentary, etc. A help in reading the book the way Wittgenstein intended is to color-code the different levels of commentary for each of the seven principal propositions, and then read down along the scale of colors for each of the seven.

When one reads *Tractatus* hierarchically, following Wittgenstein's numbering system, one gets the distinct feeling of going up and down a ladder. Moreover, the impression conveyed is not so much that Wittgenstein is giving a description of something, but rather that he is nudging one along, saying something like this: Let's go up here and look at the matter from this vantage point; now let's try the view from down here; now from over there. Don't you *see*?

Read in this way, *Tractatus* displays a definite inner momentum in its arguments. Up the ladder, then back down a bit, then up a little higher—the reader is nudged along, getting higher and higher off the ground, almost without being aware of it. Eventually one can *see* that the force of all the arguments converge on proposition seven. This, unlike all the other principal propositions in the book, is not followed by any subsidiary propositions. In fact, when reading *Tractatus* hierarchically, one *feels* on reaching proposition seven that he or she has in fact climbed up beyond a tangled mass of—language!—there to stand illuminated on a refreshing pinnacle of silence. However it may be assessed philosophically, *Tractatus* is an artistic accomplishment in terms of its structure.

Some commentators, ignorant of Wittgenstein's debt to Weininger and insensitive to the hierarchical structure of *Tractatus*, have brushed aside proposition seven as an irrelevant coda to the rest of the book. After all, they argue, it's not followed by any subsidiary arguments like the other six major propositions. But that, as should now be clear, is Wittgenstein's whole point! In proposition seven, he himself finally takes literally what he has been indirectly suggesting all along: the mystical is there; it shows itself, but it cannot be said. Don't you see it too?

The manner in which the entire structure of Tractatus reaches up like a ladder to proposition seven, only to be discarded, shows what Wittgenstein meant, but felt he could never say: despite the likes of Bertrand Russell, the basic vision of Otto Weininger's idealist philosophy remains true, only it cannot be put into words.[32]

Portrait of the Philosopher As a Young Protofascist

Like Wittgenstein's eye in the latter part of *Tractatus*, we too are now in a position to have an encompassing view. This is the picture that emerges: the earlier Wittgenstein was a self-conflicted, suicidal closet-homosexual who regarded his sexual lust as both irrepressible and demonic. Moreover, he had been raised by a rich anti-Semitic family of Jewish descent who made denial of personal authenticity into a family tradition. Tormented by the gulf between his espoused moral values and his inner sexual desires, and raised in a home that rewarded hypocrisy in matters of personal identity, he fell at a very young age under the spell of the self-hating philosopher Otto Weininger.

Weininger, like Wittgenstein, was Jewish and anti-Semitic, gay and homophobic, developing an elaborate philosophy of life based on misogyny and bolstered by elaborate theories of logic, ethics, and mysticism. In addition, *fin-de-siècle* Vienna had become increasingly polarized between authoritarian and progressive strains of thought. Weininger's work provided the principal ideological framework for Austrian fascism prior to the rise of another native Austrian, Adolf Hitler, Wittgenstein's high-school contemporary.

Inspired by the works of Weininger, Wittgenstein went off to study logic at Cambridge with Bertrand Russell, who turned out to be Weininger's diametrical opposite. Shocked and offended by Russell, and unhappy in general at Cambridge, Wittgenstein abruptly withdrew from his studies. Moving to the seclusion of a small Norwegian hut, he later volunteered to fight on behalf of the German alliance in World War I, during which time he put the final touches to *Tractatus*. Inspired by the logical and ethical doctrines of Weininger, the work was intended as a definitive rebuttal to Russell's new logic and to the linguistic turn in philosophy.

After his return to Vienna following World War I, and acting in accord with the ethics of *Tractatus*, Wittgenstein attempted a kind of psychological self-mutilation. He repudiated his secretive, compulsive gay life, and moved into the Austrian back-country to teach peasant children. As a result of his sadistic classroom methods and his lies in the face of parents' protests, he returned to Vienna disheartened, regarding himself as a moral failure. By manipulating Russell, he was able to secure for himself both the publication of *Tractatus* and a position at Cambridge. There he continued teaching on and off until a few years before his death in 1951, surrounding himself with a cult of adoring followers, and publishing only one essay in the entire period.

As the pieces of the puzzle fall into place, we can see that much of Wittgenstein's early life was one of loneliness and alienation, associated with his own internalized homophobia and anti-Semitism, and reinforced by his family's tradition of hypocrisy in matters of personal identity. As commonly happens with self-hating closet-homosexuals who are both intellectually developed and emotionally repressed, his principal sexual outlet became a series of hidden, compulsive encounters. These he regarded as both fascinating and *unspeakable* ("the love that dare not speak its name").

Seeking balm for the pain of his division against himself, Wittgenstein tried the classic strategy of flight from the flesh through spiritualization of the intellect. He read ascetic writings, considered becoming a monk, and eventually attempted a kind of psychological self-mutilation. Hence his mystical quest for a higher meaning above the flat world known to science was no mere intellectual endeavor. Hidden behind this flight lay a context of powerful emotional needs. He hints at these needs in his notebooks, where he speaks not merely of "the mystical" but also of "the drive to the mystical" (*der Trieb zum Mystischen*).[33]

This kind of strategy—trying to overcome erotic impulses by redirecting them into allegedly higher paths—is an old chestnut for emotionally isolated closet-homosexuals with spiritual aspirations. Not surprisingly, those who take this tortured path are often drawn to authoritarian ideologies, while yet engaging in secretive, compulsive, and guilt-ridden sexual encounters on the sly. (The Catholic hierarchy is a magnet for men thus divided against themselves; for example, the late Francis Cardinal Spellman.) In Wittgenstein's case, maturing as he did in pre-war Vienna, the particular authoritarian ideology to which he turned was that of the protofascist Otto Weininger.

Wittgenstein was not alone among his compatriots in showing a sexual context to fascist interests. A number of self-hating (because misogynist) homosexuals of his generation later flocked to Hitler for similar reasons. Among these men the most notorious was the butch-posing, uniform-loving Ernst Röhm of the S.A. Hitler found such admirers useful for a while, until he personally led a band that killed many of them on "the Night of the Long Knives" (June 30, 1934). Despite their initial appeal to certain masculinist homosexuals, the Nazis suppressed the nascent gay-rights movement in Germany. Nazi authorities rounded up large numbers of homosexuals and sent them to death camps, where they were forced to wear a pink triangle. It should not be overlooked that Wittgenstein, although viewing the Nazis as gangsters, never publicly condemned their treatment of Jews and homosexuals.

The parallels between Wittgenstein's personal life and certain themes in *Tractatus* are striking. Consider, for example, the lonely, alienated eye through which the young Wittgenstein saw things and people around him, but in which he could nowhere find himself. This is the same isolated, disembodied, and resigned eye which, under the name of "the metaphysical subject" in *Tractatus*, looks out into the world, but without being able to see itself.

As in Wittgenstein's personal life, so in *Tractatus*: I am all alone, face-to-face with a world in which I do not fit and over which I have no power. What can be publicly known in this world is a matter of language, but language can never get to what's really important because that's *unspeakable* (although if you know how to look, you may just catch a glimpse of it). I can gain a kind of moral victory over this world by withdrawing my energy from it, and by ascending to a peak of speechless isolation.

Both the facts of Wittgenstein's personal life and their parallel doctrinal implications in *Tractatus* have political and cultural implications. In the context of the great polarization that was then occurring in Vienna (and in much of Europe), Wittgenstein in *Tractatus* threw himself firmly on the side of reaction. Following Weininger's lead, Wittgenstein rejected the view, suggested by the socialists, that language is essentially a social phenomenon. He rejected Russell's progressive critique of politics, culture, education, and sexual mores. He rejected the new logic and the linguistic turn in philosophy. He rejected the Vienna Circle's enthusiasm for demolishing idealist philosophy and for creating a new philosophic method inspired by the sciences.

Resentful of women, Jews, and open homosexuals, inspired to fight in battle for the Germanic alliance, committed to the idea of absolute imperatives in ethics and logic, and believing in the reality of an unseen world that is totally inaccessible to language, Wittgenstein used *Tractatus* to blunt the new ideas that were everywhere tearing away at the old Europe. "God" (that is, the inspiration for Otto Weininger's basic world-view) can be saved from the profanity of the socialists and the scientists and the new logicians because the name of God is unspeakable—*that* is the core doctrine of *Tractatus*.

Despite the fog of misunderstanding first generated by Wittgenstein's own closetedness and later reinforced by the obscurantism of his literary executors, the true contours of *Tractatus* have at last appeared, thanks to increased knowledge of his personal life and the social milieu in which he lived. With such a backdrop in place, *Tractatus* now comes clearly into view on the stage of history for what it really was—the spiritual self-portrait of a tormented, protofascist mind.

The great irony in all this is that *Tractatus* never accomplished its revanchist agenda for idealist philosophy because nobody could understand it. In fact, as a result of Russell's commendatory introduction to the work, most later readers misguidedly viewed it as a continuation of the spirit of Russell's own *Principia Mathematica*, and as a precursor of the Vienna Circle's logical positivism. As a result, the name of Ludwig Wittgenstein became associated with a movement in philosophy that he himself regarded as an abomination. But he was willing to trade on this misunderstanding in order to obtain a position at Cambridge for himself through Russell's efforts on his behalf. The bind in which he found himself as a result—secretly holding to a world-view that ran counter to the spirit of the colleagues who furthered his career—no doubt contributed to his abiding sense of alienation at Cambridge, to the oracular, cult-like manner with which he instructed his students, and to his reluctance to having his views published.

And the Word Fled the Flesh

Wittgenstein's alienation from the world, from the flesh, from his own femininity, from his Jewish heritage—from *himself*—all disposed him to look toward an unspeakable, transcendent realm above as a source of spiritual solace. Driven by his own self-alienation to an otherworldly spirituality, and intellectually inspired by the transcendent idealism of Otto Weininger, Wittgenstein naturally tended to look to that higher realm as the source of all *meaning*. In the face, therefore, of the new spirit of no-nonsense scientific inquiry, which insisted that the world was a flat fact of "how's," not "why's," he undertook to try and save all the "why's" by carrying them up to a spiritual attic and stashing them away in a closet of the unspeakables. There they would remain safe, free from the profane speech of the Bertrand Russells on the lower floors of the house of intellect. Although unspeakable, these higher truths would nonetheless still be directly intuitable to closeted idealists. Following Wittgenstein's train of clues, they could climb up the stairs to the attic and so *see* just what Wittgenstein really *meant*.

As with sexual, so with philosophical, closets: one solicits one's partners by *showing* with clues, not *saying* with words. Those who are "in the know" understand, and approach. Wittgenstein's *Tractatus* is distinctive precisely because of its furtive cue-giving to other closeted philosophical idealists, analogous to the way in which closeted male homosexuals display guarded cues in cruising potential sexual partners in public parks and toilets. Unfortunately for Wittgenstein, however, his cue-giving in *Tractatus* was so well guarded that nobody even knew he was cruising.

Wittgenstein's flight from himself and the world affected his treatment of logic: he elevated it to the heights on the stilts of mysticism. As a result of this move, the old, thorny question of the nature of logical necessity, which nobody from Parmenides to Russell could answer, simply disappears—the question itself is ruled out of court! When we use language, says Wittgenstein, we can only talk about facts that can be described. But logical form is not a describable fact. At some point we just *see* how words mirror reality, and that's the end of the matter.

Previous chapters have charted the development of the Parmenidean myth over the centuries. In light of that history, we can now see that Wittgenstein's *Tractatus* was a giant step *backwards* in the endeavor to create a foundation for formal logic. Frege had cut the Parmenidean myth's umbilical cord to the divine; Russell had purged Frege's account of its vestigial transcendentalism. *Tractatus* erases both these developments. As in the writings of the medieval scholastics, so in *Tractatus*: the pages always exude a theological odor, even when the subject is pure logic.

Schma, Yisroel

Perhaps the most remarkable thing about Wittgenstein's logical mysticism is how *un-*Christian it turned out to be—despite the fact that Wittgenstein was steeped in the New Testament, considered becoming a monk, and publicly declared himself "Catholic." The core defining doctrine of Christianity appears in the famous prolog to the fourth gospel:

And the Logos became flesh (*kai ho Logos sarx egeneto*).[34]

This passage was influenced by the old Stoic notion that the universe is one great living being whose mind is divine. The passage implies that the natural world is not just a dead fact, but a living word, something that addresses us and prompts us to respond with dialogue. ("Under the wind," as Archibald MacLeish somewhere says, "there was a word.") Wittgenstein's mysticism, on the contrary, insists that God is nowhere *in* the world, which for him is just a flat, meaningless fact. In the gospel according to Wittgenstein, the Logos has fled the flesh into the unspeakable realm above.[35]

Just as, despite all his internalized homophobia, Wittgenstein remained gay throughout his life, even so, despite his rabid anti-Semitism, he remained faithful to the core Jewish principle that the name of God is unspeakable. The unspeakableness of the name of God is the very doctrine that the author of the fourth-gospel prolog sought to supplant with his new notion of the incarnation of the Logos (which means, among other things, "speech" in Greek). Despite all of Wittgenstein's efforts to pass as a Christian, *Tractatus* rings, ironically, with the transcendental mysticism of the Jewish tradition, not with the immanent mysticism of the prologue to the fourth gospel.

The Scandal of Formal Logic

In chapters four and five we saw that the underlying presuppositions of Western formal logic ultimately derived from patriarchal religious sensibilities. Later, in chapter six, we watched as first Gottlob Frege and then Bertrand Russell struggled mightily to demythologize logic, while yet dogmatically clinging to the basic tenets of the Parmenidean myth. Unsuccessful in resolving contradictions that arose from Parmenidean assumptions, Russell concluded his career in logic dissatisfied with his own suggestion that completely general facts can explain logical necessity, but unable to come up with anything better.

In this chapter, we have seen that Ludwig Wittgenstein rejected the notion that logical necessity reflects any kind of *fact* at all, whether general or otherwise. In attempting to ground logic in a higher, unspeakable realm that transcends the world of facts, Wittgenstein was largely driven by his own personal religious sensibilities ("the drive to the mystical"). These religious sensibilities reflected his own peculiar kind of self-alienation and world-alienation.

The upshot is that with the publication of *Tractatus* we witness a scandalous full-circle return once again to an unabashedly mythological and even religious grounding for formal logic. I say "scandalous," because the publication of *Tractatus* in 1921 A.D. proves that as of that date the West was still unable to provide a coherent, rational account of the foundations of formal logic.

Despite this lack, however, Western philosophers since the time of the ancient Greeks had been vaunting Western formal logic as a sign of Western civilization's alleged superiority over so-called "barbarian" or "primitive" societies. Moreover, within the West itself, logicians had typically prided themselves (and still do) on the superiority of their own way of interpreting reality, compared to that of women, artists, sexual adepts, and mystics. In addition, Western philosophers in general have claimed that formal logic is the crown jewel in philosophy as profession. As should by now be clear, however, as of 1921 the *most* that these philosophers could have reasonably claimed is this: "My myths are better than your myths." Subsequent chapters will show that even this more modest claim is false.

Rules Drag In Rule-Givers

As noted earlier, a crucial part of Wittgenstein's mystical concept of logic was his claim that stipulated rules are irrelevant to logic. According to *Tractatus*, any given proof in logic is a kind of compound proposition, which consists of an aggregate of elementary propositions or their denials. The proper propositional sign for any such compound proposition is some schema. The schema simply *shows* whether the compound proposition that it signifies is tautologous, contradictory, or neither. This showing is the proof; stipulated rules do not enter into the picture.

Wittgenstein wrote *Tractatus* in the wake of the logical work of Frege and Russell, neither of whom had made a systematic distinction between axioms and rules. In the first volume of *The Basic Laws of Arithmetic*, appearing in 1893, Frege spoke only of "basic laws," a term that straddled both axioms and rules. In the first volume of *Principia Mathematica*, appearing in 1913, Russell spoke of "primitive propositions," by which he meant axioms, but one of which he called a "rule of inference." Significantly, Russell conceded that he was unable to express this "rule of inference" by means of the symbolism he had used to express the other "primitive propositions." This concession represents the first awareness on his part of the crucial difference between axioms and rules.

Russell's awareness of the difference gradually increased with the years. In his 1922 preface to the English version of *Tractatus*, Russell criticized Wittgenstein's logical mysticism, suggesting as an alternative the seminal idea of a "hierarchy of languages." The idea was developed further by Alfred Tarski, Rudolf Carnap, and David Hilbert. Eventually logicians came to realize that the higher-order language actually *prescribes* (not *describes*) the formal nature of the lower-order language. In the wake of this realization, contemporary formal logic now routinely insists on the systematic difference between axioms and rules.

Acknowledging stipulated rules in logic ran counter to the commitment that Frege, Russell, and Wittgenstein had all made to the Parmenidean myth: they wanted to believe that logic reflected a realm of absolute objectivity, valid for any and all interpreters. The gradual emergence of stipulated rules undermined this belief system because stipulated rules can always be otherwise than they are, depending on the decisions of the rule-makers. This variability is not the case with propositions, which are either true or false, depending on what happens to be the case.

Mind Your P's and Q's

By the time Wittgenstein returned to Cambridge in 1929, his disastrous experience as a rural school teacher had shaken him from the ethical presuppositions of *Tractatus*. In addition, he had begun to realize that *Tractatus* was fatally flawed in terms of strictly logical matters. For example, the book assumed that the truth-value of any given elementary proposition is independent of the truth-values of other elementary propositions. But Wittgenstein came to realize that there are simple propositions whose truth-values are not independent of each other. (For example, the truth of "I see green here" is not independent of the truth of "I see red here".)

Wittgenstein eventually realized that one can never know for certain whether the truth-values of the p's and q's in any given schema are independent of each other unless one already knows what p and q mean. Therefore, formal logic is always partially meaning-functional, never purely truth-functional. This fact completely undermines the notion that logical deduction can ever be a mere matter of mechanical calculation. (To this day, college textbooks in symbolic logic continue, shamelessly, to slide over this embarrassing fact.)

In addition, the logical system in *Tractatus* cannot look inside the p's and q's used in its schemata. Accordingly, it cannot develop a logical calculus where validity of inference depends on predicates. This limitation is just another aspect of the fallacy of assuming that there are indivisible propositions whose truth-values can be known when their meanings are unknown. All these problems stem from the basic philosophical fallacy that Wittgenstein had inherited from Leibniz: the dogma that both language and the world are divisible into ultimate simples. This, the fallacy of absolute analysis, is the root assumption behind *Tractatus*'s entire program of logical atomism. When this assumption fell off the axle of Wittgenstein's thought, his entire philosophical juggernaut went into the ditch.

The End of a Myth

The Parmenidean myth reached the last of its many grand historical incarnations in Wittgenstein's *Tractatus*. Drawing on the protofascist philosophy of Otto Weininger, the book was a classic spiritual self-portrait of an emotionally-conflicted, authoritarian closet-homosexual. That the Western logical tradition should so easily have lent itself to this type of portraiture does not speak to its credit. But as previous chapters have shown, much of the philosophical tradition that reached its culmination in Wittgenstein's *Tractatus* was the work of patriarchal males having a twisted, crippling view of reality. Otto Weininger made explicit, indeed celebrated, the worst misogynist presuppositions of that previous logical tradition. Wittgenstein built on Weininger's efforts, hoping to keep patriarchal reason shrouded in mystery.

In the next two chapters, we will follow Wittgenstein as he broke out of the mold of the Parmenidean myth, eventually reaching extraordinary conclusions. We will also see how little, in certain respects, he really changed. Through contemplating Wittgenstein's overall life and work, especially against the backdrop of the Parmenidean myth, we will be in a position to open anew the windows of Western philosophy, lately closed tight by institutionalized academics. With freshly seeing eyes, we will peer out once again toward the great mysteries of what it means to be human.

---

[1] Ludwig Wittgenstein, *Tractatus Logico-Philosophicus*; translated anew by D.F. Pears and B.F. McGuinness, Routledge & Kegan Paul, London, 1961.
[2] Bertrand Russell, "On Denoting," 1905; reprinted in *Logic and Knowledge*, ed. by Robert Charles Marsh, George Allen and Unwin, London, 1956; 7th impression 1984.
[3] See Arthur Lovejoy, *The Great Chain of Being*, Harper Torchbooks, New York; originally published 1936, Harper reprint 1965.
[4] Wittgenstein, *Tractatus*, 2.021, 2.0231, 2.0232, 2.0271. All passages are cited by Wittgenstein's proposition numbers.
[5] *ibid.*, 4.31-4.442.
[6] *ibid.*, 4.4.; and P.M.S. Hacker, *Insight & Illusion: Themes in the Philosophy of Wittgenstein*, revised edition, Clarendon Press, Oxford, 1986, pp. 45 ff.
[7] Wittgenstein, *Tractatus*, 3.334, 5.132, 6.122.
[8] Ludwig Wittgenstein, "Notes on Logic, 1913" in *Notebooks 1914-1916*, p. 94.
[9] Wittgenstein, *Tractatus*, 6.1203.
[10] *ibid.*, 5.473.
[11] Otto Weininger, *Geschlecht und Charakter*, Wilhelm Braumüller, Vienna, originally published in 1903; 9th printing, 1907.
[12] *ibid.*, 4.0312; original's emphasis.
[13] *ibid.*, p. 5; original's emphasis.
[14] Weininger, *op. cit.*, p. 200.
[15] Wittgenstein, *Tractatus*, 6.432; original's emphasis.
[16] *ibid.*, 6.
[17] *ibid.*, 6.521 & 6.522; my translation; original's emphasis.
[18] *ibid.*, p. 2; my translation.
[19] Weininger, *op. cit.*, pp. 192-193.
[20] Wittgenstein, *Tractatus*, 6.54.
[21] For example, see Russell Nieli, *Wittgenstein: From Mysticism to Ordinary Language*, State University of New York, Albany, 1987, and Philip Shields, *Logic and Sin in the Writings of Ludwig Wittgenstein*, The University of Chicago Press, Chicago, 1993. Also the earlier essays by B.G. McGuinness, "The Mysticism of the *Tractatus*," in *The Philosophical Review*, vol. 75, 1966, pp. 305-328; and by Eddy Zemach, "Wittgenstein's Philosophy of the Mysti-

CHAPTER EIGHT

cal" in *Essays on Wittgenstein's Tractatus*, ed. by Irving Copi and Robert Beard, Routledge & Kegan Paul, London, 1966, pp. 359-375.

[22] Nieli, *op. cit.*, p. 163, n.3.

[23] *ibid.*, 5.63 & 5.632, reading "boundary" instead of "limit" for *Grenze*.

[24] Weininger, *op. cit.*, p. 195 and note 5; original's emphasis. The Scottish skeptic and empiricist David Hume had also spoken of the inability to observe the self in the empirical world. From this same observation Hume drew conclusions quite different from those of Weininger and Wittgenstein.

[25] Wittgenstein, *Tractatus*, 5.6 & 5.61; my translation; original's emphasis.

[26] *ibid.*, 5.64; my translation.

[27] *ibid.*, 5.62; my translation; original's emphasis.

[28] *ibid.*, 6.43.

[29] Weininger, *op. cit.*, p. 216.

[30] *ibid.*, p. 210; original's emphasis.

[31] Wittgenstein, *Tractatus*, 7; my translation.

[32] Marjorie Perloff argues that Wittgenstein's ladder metaphor can be made to yield "a distinctively Wittgensteinian poetics." Maybe so. Still, she is wrong to claim that climbing the ladder leads to no "vision." See her *Wittgenstein's Ladder*, p. xiv.

[33] Wittgenstein, *Notebooks 1914-1916*, p. 51.

[34] John, 1:14.

[35] Wittgenstein is not the only professed Christian to espouse views contrary to the prolog to the fourth gospel. Every nature-fleeing movement within Christianity offends the doctrine that the world is God's body.

Being of Service, Detail
Acrylic on Paper, 30" x 22", 1989

"Ron," Oil on Canvas, 24" x 30", 1981

9

The Descent to Language

SUMMARY: This chapter shows how the later Ludwig Wittgenstein turned against the mythology underlying formal logic, as he increasingly emphasized the importance of language over logic. Nonetheless, he was slow to abandon the idea of an essence in language, as shown by his argument against the possibility of a private language.

The effect of publishing *Tractatus Logico-Philosophicus* in 1921 was hardly what its author, Ludwig Wittgenstein, had intended. As noted in the last chapter, the prose of this famous work proved to be so dense and oracular, and Wittgenstein's own real values so shielded, that virtually everyone mistakenly regarded the book as a continuation of the work of Bertrand Russell. Far from shoring up the foundations of Russell's logic, however, Wittgenstein sought to protect "what is higher" from the profanation of the new breed of irreverent philosophers, especially Russell. According to *Tractatus*, the world that is accessible to the scalpels of scientists, logicians, and philosophers is merely a flat fact. "God," on the other hand, is located in an unspeakable realm of higher meaning, safe from the analysts.

In the last chapter, we saw that the early Wittgenstein's mystical approach to logic was connected to the personal circumstances of his life. Conflicted over his homosexuality and his Jewish ancestry, he fell under the influence of the protofascist mysticism of Otto Weininger. Building on Weininger's theories, Wittgenstein intended *Tractatus* to serve as a revanchist force for idealist philosophy in the great intellectual debates that were then engulfing Europe.

Compounding readers' misunderstanding of *Tractatus*, Wittgenstein published no other philosophical works throughout his life except for a small essay on logical form, which he repudiated by the time it was printed. After his death in 1951, his literary executors, assuming the role of high priests in a personality cult, concealed the details of his personal life.

In the years since 1951, the executors authorized the publication of an increasing number of extracts from Wittgenstein's personal notebooks or from those of his students. But *all* these works reflected the editorial choices of Wittgenstein's editors or the viewpoints of his students; *none* was a finished philosophical book executed by Wittgenstein himself. Only recently have the initial volumes of a critical edition of all Wittgenstein's work begun to appear in print.

As a result of Wittgenstein's occult style, the secretiveness of his executors, and the piecemeal publication from his notebooks, much of what has been previously written about him is a distortion. Today, nearly a half-century after his death, Wittgenstein's life and philosophy are finally coming into focus—and both appear to be quite different from what most of his followers previously assumed.

Goodbye to Augustine

Wittgenstein's best known posthumous work is *Philosophical Investigations*. Published in 1953 by his executors, the book actually consists of two separate extracts from Wittgenstein's notebooks, "Part I" and "Part II," as the executors call them.[1]

Wittgenstein begins Part I with an excerpt from Augustine's *Confessions*, where Augustine attempts to explain how mere noise differs from spoken language. Focusing on the naming process, Augustine says that a noise becomes a name by being associated with some object, which is the object's meaning. He implies that using language is the process of combining names.[2]

The view that Wittgenstein here attributes to "Augustine," and which he now undertakes to rebut, is actually the view he himself had propounded in *Tractatus*. The world is a collection of facts, said the earlier Wittgenstein, and facts are concatenations of objects. To these objects there correspond individual names, whose meanings are the objects associated with them. As the world reduces to objects combined in facts, so language, the great mirror of the world, reduces to names combined in propositions.

Although Wittgenstein invokes the name of Augustine in *Investigations*, he actually derived this doctrine of naming from the logical atomism of Bertrand Russell. The meaning of language, Russell had argued, ultimately stems from the objects for which names stand. Russell's view suggests that logic might be able to boil down reality to some group of absolute simples that answer to the simplest of names. Russell had adapted this view from Leibniz's theory of "monads," which *are* such absolute simples.

After publishing *Tractatus*, Wittgenstein became skeptical of the notion that objects are the meanings of names. But what, then, enables mere sounds to become meaningful words? This is the great question that preoccupies *Investigations*.

In searching for an answer, Wittgenstein suggests that we examine more carefully the thing that before had seemed so simple—the naming process. Naming is actually a complex phenomenon, he now argues. It is never a matter of some isolated, culturally-disembodied ego attaching names to transparently-predefined objects (his old *Tractatus* view).

Wittgenstein's new approach stresses language as a *social* phenomenon. This approach represented a sharp break with the heroically individualistic view that Wittgenstein had inherited from the protofascist Otto Weininger. The most important stimulus for this change was the Italian Marxist economist Piero Sraffa, who had fled from Italy to Cambridge after criticizing Mussolini. Sraffa befriended the loner Wittgenstein, and in conversations with him over the years stressed the traditional socialist concept of language as a social construction. Sraffa also criticized Wittgenstein's notion that every human communication, in order to be meaningful, had to embody "logical form." One oft-reported anecdote about their exchanges reflects both Sraffa's insight and his wit:

> Sraffa made a gesture, familiar to Neapolitans as meaning something like disgust or contempt, of brushing the underneath of his chin with an outward sweep of the fingertips of one hand. And he asked: "What is the logical form of *that*?"[3]

In his preface to Part I of *Investigations*, Wittgenstein testified to the importance of his conversations with Sraffa:

> I am indebted to that [criticism] which a teacher of this university, Mr. P. Sraffa, for many years unceasingly practised on my thoughts. I am indebted to *this* stimulus for the most consequential ideas of this book.[4]

As discussed in the last chapter, Wittgenstein's earlier views in *Tractatus* reflected protofascist influences. Likewise, his later views in *Investigations* reflected socialist influences. Not that Wittgenstein ever became a socialist politically, just as he had never been a fascist politically. Nonetheless, he navigated the high seas of philosophy using light that emanated now from the one, now from the other, of these two ideological constellations.

The shift from *Tractatus* to *Investigations* could be described as the replacement of Weininger by Sraffa as Wittgenstein's guiding Muse. Under both Muses, Wittgenstein's philosophical pronouncements were the surface-film of deeply running psychological currents, churning under the influence of the great historical upheavals of his epoch. It is precisely this deep connection between the philosophical, psychological, and epochal aspects of Wittgenstein's life that must be appreciated in order to understand his thought. This connection has been neglected, however, and even scorned, by many Anglo-American analytic philosophers.

What's In a Name?

Sraffa's emphasis on language as a social construction helped Wittgenstein see the error of his individualistic account of naming in *Tractatus*. Once Wittgenstein abandoned this notion of naming, his entire concept of language underwent a revolutionary change.

In *Investigations*, Wittgenstein says that naming is *impossible* apart from social conventions. This is true even if naming is just a matter of "ostension." ("Ostension" means pointing at something, and saying "I call that a ... .") Consider, says Wittgenstein: apart from social conventions, no posture could ever be interpreted as *an act of pointing*. (Would a lion recognize my outstretched arm as an act of pointing?) In addition, pointing is useless unless people know what *aspect* of the object is being singled out. If they don't know, they must possess at least enough language to ask. These social conventions presuppose, in turn, the social group that has created them. Conclusion: there is no naming without community.

Naming My Pain

To buttress his argument, Wittgenstein takes up the case where the very opposite would seem to be true: the naming of private sensations, in particular the naming of a private sensation of pain. Contrary to what we might think, Wittgenstein contends, it is inconceivable that a person could create a name, for strictly private use, of a sensation that could be manifest only to the person in question.

To show that such private naming is impossible, Wittgenstein challenges us to try and imagine the actual details of how we might do it.[5] Suppose, he says, I experience a painful sensation that cannot be known to other people, and for which there is no existing word. Suppose, further, that my behavior in no way manifests this pain, except for this action: I write the letter "S" on a calendar for every day on which I experience the sensation.

Surely I can do this, you might say, and isn't this exactly what is meant by private naming? Yes, Wittgenstein would respond, this is indeed private naming—only if you stop and think about it, this act will get you nowhere.

In the first place, how do you know that the sensation that prompted you to write "S" on today's calendar is the same sensation that prompted you to write "S" two days ago? My memory, you would say, is certainly good enough to cover two days. But by what right, Wittgenstein would insist, do you apply the words "sensation" and "same" to that which you designate by the sign "S"?

These words—"sensation" and "same"—are part of a public language that you have learned by interacting with other people in common situations. The criterion of whether you understand the meaning of these words is that you actually use them as taught by others. So you know no more about the meaning of these words than other people do. Isn't it paradoxical, then, that you can know that these words rightly apply to that which is designated by "S," but that other people cannot?

The situation is not only paradoxical, says Wittgenstein, but impossible. Consider: you use a word rightly if you use it in the way it is publicly taught to be used in the common language of which it is part. There's no other test. So if others cannot know whether *any* publicly taught word correctly applies to what you call "S" (not even the word "it"!), then you can't either. All you are left with is this odd sign "S," dangling uselessly in the air. A sign that has no connection to the use of other signs in a language is not a part of that language; therefore, this sign cannot be a name in that language.

One might object here that this restriction applies only to languages that are learned in common with other people. Why couldn't I simply invent a whole new language of my own? Even if "S" had no role to play in others' language, it would in mine, and therefore it would be a name after all. In response, Wittgenstein argues that the concept of a private language is as incoherent as that of private naming, an argument to which we will return at the end of this chapter. For now, it is sufficient to note that Wittgenstein attacks *in toto* the individualistic concept of naming that was the basis of his philosophy of language in *Tractatus*. No longer is language to be viewed as a mere concatenation of pre-created names. In fact, the reverse is now true: names emerge out of language, which emerges out of community.

A Stake Through Russell's Heart

Again contrary to *Tractatus*, Wittgenstein says that there can be no such things as names that are simple in and of themselves. Simplicity is a *relative* notion, depending on the purposes of language-users. What may be simple in one context, may be complex in another. The important thing is to look at the actual language-in-use situation.

Because the simplicity of names is relative, so too must be the simplicity of the objects named. Now suppose someone, like the earlier Wittgenstein himself, balks at this answer. Suppose the objector persistently asks "But what are the *real* elements?" Says Wittgenstein—

> Does it matter which we say, so long as we avoid misunderstandings in any particular case?[6]

With this simple response, Wittgenstein drives a stake through the heart of Russell's logical atomism. Contrary to Russell, the world cannot be unambiguously reduced to a heap of objective simples.

In the next chapter, we will find a connection between Wittgenstein's desire to discredit logical atomism and his view that modern science and the society it has created are deformities. Wittgenstein hints at these larger social views in the motto he places at the beginning of *Investigations*. The motto is a sarcastic quip about progress from a 19th-century musical farce, *The Protégé*, by Viennese satirist Johann Nestroy:

> Of course it's just like progress to seem much greater than it really is.[7]

Language-Games

In the above example with the sign "S," Wittgenstein examined the way language might work in some concrete situation. Based on what the simple case showed, he gained an insight into language, but without becoming entangled in abstract philosophical disputes.

This method—of imagining concrete cases of language use—is a favorite one of the later Wittgenstein. The method is related to his conviction, inspired by Piero Sraffa, that we never encounter language as some kind of abstract essence (the view in *Tractatus*). Rather, what we find are a multiplicity of uses embedded in specific human situations. These specific uses *are* the nature of language.

To do justice to the link between linguistic phenomena and their social contexts, Wittgenstein coined the phrase "language-game." The closeness between the two words is more evident in the original German, *Sprachspiel*. The practice of stringing nouns together into one word is common in German. In good English, however, a hyphen must be used, which unfortunately dilutes the effect of Wittgenstein's coinage.

Readers will get a better feel for Wittgenstein's meaning if they visualize the phrase as if written "languagegame." Overlooking the intimate word-act connection in Wittgenstein's mind can easily lead readers to misunderstand his remarks about language. In fact, the word "language" in *Tractatus* and the same word in *Investigations* refer to two entirely different orders of phenomena: in the former case, to a disembodied essence; in the latter, to an aspect of concrete human social interaction.

According to the latter view, every attempt to strip language of its social contexts in the hope of finding its essence (as *Tractatus* did) destroys the very thing that enables language to be meaningful, namely, the fact that language is imbedded in some "game." Wittgenstein himself criticizes his earlier view in this way:

> In order to find the real artichoke, we divested it of its leaves.[8]

In his later writings, Wittgenstein introduces various examples of language-games. One, already noted, is that of imagining simple contexts in which certain common word-functions (such as naming) actually occur. Others are: to examine the way children first learn certain kinds of words; to speculate how imaginary peoples, which have entirely different kinds of life, might use different kinds of words; to study the contextual history of the creation of artificial languages, such as mathematics, etc.

Although Wittgenstein's examples of language-games are varied, in each case he stresses the same point: it is only because of certain ambient modes of interaction that any sign has a meaning (which is its life). Mere noises never become words unless they are part of some game; remove the game, and the words collapse back into being mere noises. Therefore, you can never understand the meaning of any sign (including those used in artificial languages like mathematics) unless you attain a detailed survey of the actual games that the sign-users are playing. Indeed, if the games being played are of an entirely different order from ours, as in those of another species, we can't even know if such beings are using signs. As Wittgenstein quipped:

> If a lion could talk, we could not understand him.[9]

Family Resemblances vs. Essences

In developing his concept of language-game, Wittgenstein sharply criticizes the traditional philosophical concept of essence. This concept, as classically developed, holds that there are real entities, or essences, by virtue of which particular objects fall into distinct classes.

Because an essence is shared by particulars, it itself is not a particular; therefore, the argument goes, it must be something that is *common*. In the past, a great debate has raged over the nature of these supposed commonalities (or "universals" as the medievals called them). As discussed in chapter one, some philosophers have argued that universals are transcendent archetypes; others, that they are eternal, but immanent in particulars; others, that they are eternal, but existing in the mind of God; and yet others, that they reflect nothing but our own arbitrary names (nominalism).

Against this debate, Wittgenstein simply observes that whenever we encounter things, they are always individual and variable; and that whenever we compare groups of things, there is always some similarity and some difference among the groups. Just because we happen to use a certain word to refer to a group of particulars doesn't mean that there must be some essence that all the particulars in this group share, and which justifies our use of this common word to refer to them. But neither is it the case that the only commonality shared by the particulars is our word for them; to the contrary, there are *reasons* why we apply words in certain ways.

To explain the matter, Wittgenstein points to his own use of the word "game" in the phrase "language-game." Although the word "game" has definite meanings in various contexts, we would be hard put to come up with a suitable definition to capture the one and only thing that all games supposedly have in common, and which everything that is not a game lacks.

In fact, Wittgenstein argues, the things we call "games" do share something, but it is not an essence. Rather, it is a complicated network of similarities of various kinds and degrees, which he calls "family resemblances" (*Familienähnlichkeiten*). Our concept of a game derives from these family resemblances, like a thread that is spun from various fibers twisted one to another:

> And the strength of the thread does not reside in the fact that some one fibre runs through its whole length, but in the overlapping of many fibres.[10]

The essentialists err, says Wittgenstein, by viewing a concept as a kind of reality in its own right; the nominalists err by reducing the concept to a mere word. Both essentialists and nominalists are committed to the same fallacy: that it makes sense to speak of the nature of a concept apart from the particular interactions where the word that refers to the concept is used.

If a word works well enough in some context, then it is meaningful—in that context. To insist on more, as essentialists do, is to chase after ghosts. But to reduce the meaning to the mere word, as nominalists do, is to overlook the interactions with reality that ground all words.

Wittgenstein's view undermines the radical dichotomy between subjectivity and objectivity. The ultimate ground for every use of signs is neither subject nor object as such, but rather some *game*, which always involves both subjectivity (the language-user) and objectivity (that with which the language-user interacts). This interactive situation is what makes signs meaningful. Remove it, and language ceases.

Wittgenstein thus challenges the old intellectualist bias that "In the beginning was the Word [*Logos*]." To the contrary, he argues that *interaction* is the primary thing, calling to witness a line from Goethe's *Faust*:

> The origin and the primitive form of the language game is a reaction; only from this can more complicated forms develop. Language—I want to say—is a refinement; "in the beginning was the deed."[11]

Wittgenstein's attack on essence, together with his stress on the interactions of actual language-users, is reminiscent of the cry of the existentialists that existence precedes essence. And in fact Wittgenstein was sympathetic to their cry. However, he preferred to express it in linguistic terms.

Good Essence vs. Bad Essence

Wittgenstein's view of family resemblances does not preclude every kind of essence, as incorrectly believed by many of his followers. For example, he acknowledges the role of stipulative definitions in science. These *create* essences for certain kinds of applications (as in the concept of "a perfect vacuum"). Essences stipulated by definition are not things that exist in their own right; they are tools that can always be further re-honed as the need arises. They are valuable as part of our framework for interpreting reality, so long as we do not make the mistake of confusing the framework with that which it seeks to frame.

Wittgenstein also acknowledges a role for essence in language. For example, he speaks of "the essential thing about private language" and says that "*Essence* is expressed by grammar."[12] This type of essence has to do with *sense*.

Every language, Wittgenstein says, has an implicit understanding as to what makes sense. For example, suppose someone says "I see an object that is all red." Regardless of whether this statement is true or false, the following statement must always be true: "If that person is seeing an object that is all red, then that person is not seeing the same object as all green." The certainty of the truth of this second statement differs from the certainty of the truth of the first, if the first is in fact true. If the second statement were false, it would not make sense, which is not true of the first.

The certainty of the second statement, Wittgenstein argues, is a matter of essence, namely the essence that is determined by the boundaries of sense in our language. This essence does not result from some stipulative definition, as in science, but rather is given by what Wittgenstein calls our language's "grammar." To Wittgenstein, this latter essence is the real McCoy, in contrast to both the stipulative essences created by science and the ghostly essences believed in by traditional philosophy. (We will further explore this concept of grammar later, when we take up Wittgenstein's theory of rules.) Despite impressions to the contrary given by certain passages in *Investigations*, Wittgenstein remained committed to essence throughout his life. What changed was where he looked for it.

From Chess to River Beds

Wittgenstein originally patterned his new word "language-game" after the word "chess" (*Sprachspiel* and *Schachspiel*, respectively, in German). But more was involved than a play on words. Wittgenstein was fascinated with chess as a model of the way language works.

The fact that chess is a game with definite rules, Wittgenstein argued, is precisely what allows its constituent parts to have a certain kind of *meaning*. For example, if I look at this horse-shaped piece of wood in front of me, I know that it will continue to be a Knight even if, say, its ears break off. Why? Because it still has a role to play that is defined by the rules of chess. In the same way, he says, an uttered sound becomes a word because it represents a pattern of possible moves in a certain kind of game. In a nutshell:

> The question "What is a word really?" is analogous to "What is a piece in chess?"[13]

Chess is an example of a *calculus*. That is, anyone can *calculate* the possible moves available to players at any given stage in the game, based on a knowledge of two things: (1) the rules of the game; and (2) the sequence of all moves made prior to the move in question.

In *Tractatus*, Wittgenstein had argued that formal logic is a special kind of calculus. After completing *Tractatus*, he realized that all calculuses are games, analogous to chess. Still influenced somewhat by *Tractatus*, he used the words "calculus" and "language-game" interchangeably. All language, he continued to believe, involves a kind of calculation.

But what happens when the rules of a game *change*? Who is making the changes? And why? Questions like these opened Wittgenstein's eyes to broader horizons. Eventually, he was forced to come to terms with a factor that formal logic had overlooked—the cast of characters who actually create and play the games.

And so Wittgenstein developed his notion of "form of life" (*Lebensform*). The spoken part of a language-game, he reasoned, is like the small, visible part of an iceberg. The larger, hidden part is the historical pattern of interactions among those who create, teach, and use the words. This pre-existing process possesses a unity in its own right; it is the game's form of life.

Wittgenstein's concept of form of life has a varying scope. At times it seem quite narrow, as with many of his examples in *Investigations*. Consequently, some commentators argue that the concept was never meant to cover an entire culture or civilization.[14] However, Wittgenstein also describes cases where a form of life corresponds to a language in its entirety, as when he remarks:

> To imagine a language is to imagine a form of life. ... [Humans] agree in the *language* they use. That is not agreement in opinions but in form of life.[15]

At times, Wittgenstein even uses the concept to refer to the common history and behavioral patterns of an entire species. An example is his explanation of why hope means one thing for a dog and another for a human being. Although a dog can hope for the return of his master, he cannot hope that his master will return the day after tomorrow. The reason is that the dog has a different form of life:

> The phenomena of hope are modes of this [humans'] complicated form of life. (If a

concept refers to a character of human handwriting, it has no application to beings that do not write.)[16]

Forms of life can be narrow and limited, but they can also be as wide as a culture or even an entire species. In any case, they are the bases of all language:

> What has to be accepted, the given, is—so one could say—*forms of life*.[17]

Many commentators have overlooked the importance that Wittgenstein puts on forms of life. As a result, they have erroneously concluded that Wittgenstein regards language as "autonomous."[18] To the contrary, however, Wittgenstein sees language as a tool created by some human group interacting with reality. As such a tool, language reflects not only the passing conventions of its users but also the realities with which they are engaged.

Language for Wittgenstein is always answerable to the nature of the world. The answering process, however, is so embedded in the conventions of the language-users that it is impossible to know with absolute clarity where convention ends and where reality begins. It is precisely this sophisticated notion of the fusion of convention and reality at the very roots of language that characterizes the genius of Wittgenstein's later view of language.

Any form of life, argues Wittgenstein, always contains certain aspects that are more durable than others. The most durable aspects have the most influence on the language-games that emerge in that form of life. To these durable aspects there corresponds a core of judgments that language-users take for granted. This core of judgments Wittgenstein calls a "mythology," a concept he develops in writings outside of *Investigations*.

Wittgenstein sees this core as mythological for two reasons: (1) it is a social construct, rather than a brute fact given by nature; and (2) it contains the culture's basic canons for deciding what it makes sense to say about reality, resulting from their struggles with reality. The core thus reflects on the deepest level the subtle fusion of convention and reality that Wittgenstein sees at work at every level of language.

The role of this mythological core in language is analogous to that of the rules of chess. Just as in chess the rules define what is a permissible move, so in language a core mythology defines what is a meaningful combination of words. An example is the proposition "If I see an object that is all red, then I do not at the same time see the same object as all green." If someone were to deny this proposition, we would say that he or she does not understand the meaning of the words used. We would confidently say this without looking at any particular object or color. Why? Because this proposition is part of the mythology of our language; it corresponds to some deep aspect of our form of life.

Wittgenstein points out that there is no sharp distinction between propositions that express fluid, as opposed to relatively static, aspects of a form of life; the form of life itself may change over time. Therefore, even though there is always some core of durable judgments, this core is not exempt from change (witness the Copernican revolution!). Even so, however, a core change is of an entirely different order of magnitude from that of other judgments in the language. Wittgenstein sums up the matter with the striking metaphor of a river bed:

> It might be imagined that some propositions, of the form of empirical propositions, were hardened and functioned as channels for such empirical propositions as were not hardened but fluid; and that this relation altered with time. ... The mythology may change into a state of flux, the river-bed of thoughts may shift. But I distinguish between the movement of the waters on the river-bed and the shift of the bed itself; though there is not a sharp division of the one from the other.[19]

Another Copernican Revolution

This view of language has a number of sensational implications. Among other things, it implies that formal logic—lauded for millennia by Western philosophers as the very map of the structure of reality—is simply part of the mythology of a particular form of life. Such a map may be useful for some form of life because it is reflective of reality for them; but it is also partly conventional.

It is just this startling implication—that there is an ineradicable conventional element at the very heart of logic—that Wittgenstein had in mind when he described his new view of language as creating a kind of Copernican revolution. Contrary to what we have all been taught to believe, he argues, reality does not revolve around Western formal logic; rather, Western formal logic is simply one among many possible constellations into which the firmament of human experience can crystallize.

Unlike Athena, the patron goddess of philosophy, formal logic cannot boast of a pedigree from the head of Zeus. Rather, the most it can claim for itself is that it has been useful for interpreting reality for a certain kind of society. As we will soon see, Wittgenstein mercilessly criticizes even this more modest boast.

I Obey Blindly

As discussed above, Wittgenstein stresses the importance of interactive social contexts to language. This stress is evident in his concept of *Praxis* ("practice" in German). Questions as to the nature of rational explanation, certainty, and logical necessity all eventually find their answer for Wittgenstein in the role played by *Praxis* in language.

The ordinary German word *Praxis* has three overlapping meanings: (1) a practice or exercise; (2) an established social custom; and (3) that which contrasts with the purely theoretical or mental. Hence this word tugs anyone who uses it toward a certain bias: something is a technique because it is part of an established social custom, having little to do with one's private mental life. Later, when we examine Wittgenstein's argument against the possibility of a private language, we will see that he draws on this bias.

In Wittgenstein's philosophy, *Praxis* is the learned technique of using signs in order to communicate, conveyed through existing social institutions and practices. He maintains that language-users can be tested for their mastery of this technique without any regard for their subjective mental states. As in chess, he argues, so in any language-game: we learn the correct moves (the correct word usages) as part of some ongoing tradition. The question of whether we "understand" the game is simply the question of whether we make certain kinds of permissible moves, which has nothing to do with what we may be privately thinking. To justify the legitimacy of any contested move, we appeal to rules that are apparent to all experienced game-players. When it comes to the question of justifying the rules themselves, we may speculate about different ones. But at some point the quest for further justification of the rules becomes pointless, and we just say "We play this game."

In the case of our native language, as opposed to a pastime like chess, our acceptance of the basic rules happens when we first learn how to use signs in order to communicate. As a result, we never deliberate about whether to adopt such rules; we just do so. These rules become definitive for what it makes sense for us to say in our language. As a result, they are endowed with a kind of certainty.

Once we are actually playing some game, we don't deliberate about whether to obey the rules; we just follow them. As Wittgenstein says:

> When I obey a rule, I do not choose. I obey the rule *blindly*.[20]

This insight into rules illuminates the nature of doubt. If I express a doubt, I am obeying the rules that underlie the language in which I express myself. I cannot reject the very rules that make it possible for me to express doubt. In order to express my rejection of the rules of some language-game, I must construct another language-game that does not presuppose them. Even so, however, this new language-game will have some other rules of its own. Therefore, there cannot be a doubt that is truly universal, as the French philosopher René Descartes believed. If Descartes had truly doubted everything, he could not have expressed his doubt in any language.

The source of all our smaller, *ad hoc* language-games, Wittgenstein argues, is the one great, all-encompassing language-game he calls "ordinary language." All smaller language-games are so many outgrowths from this common trunk, and presuppose its underlying rules, which are its roots. These rules lie solidly below all the doubt that might sprout and wither anywhere in the wind-driven branches above. To renounce these roots is to forfeit the capacity to speak.

A Certain Physiognomy

The certainty of any language-game springs from the *Praxis* that instills it. Where there is a question as to whether a particular rule applies to some case or not, the final appeal is always to the *Praxis* that underlies all rules. *Praxis* permits of no further interpretation because it creates the conditions for the possibility of interpretation:

> Not only rules, but also examples are needed for establishing a practice [*Praxis*]. Our rules leave loop-holes open, and the practice has to speak for itself.[21]

In the last chapter, we saw Wittgenstein arguing in *Tractatus* that the signs we use in order to communicate must in the end speak for themselves. Once we have a system of signs that accurately displays the possibilities of bivalent combinations for elementary propositions, we see displayed the bedrock structure of language, beyond which there is no appeal. The later Wittgenstein still seeks to find something that speaks for itself as the bedrock of language, but now he locates it in the *Praxis* of a form of life. This shift from signs that speak for themselves to a *Praxis* that speaks for itself constitutes the principal change in the theory of language from the earlier to the later Wittgenstein.

In both periods, when Wittgenstein finally reached the bedrock that could speak for itself, it turned out, ironically, to be unspeakable. In *Tractatus*, he had argued that an adequate sign system can only *show*, not *describe*, the structure of possibility that underlies both language and the world. Near the end of his life, he came to hold a similar view about *Praxis*:

> Am I not getting closer and closer to saying that in the end logic cannot be described? You must look at the practice of language [*die Praxis der Sprache*], then you will see it.[22]

In both periods, Wittgenstein associated the bedrock with a kind of physiognomy. In his earlier period, the physiognomy of adequately designed propositional signs sufficed to reveal the essential nature of language. In his later period, that role is played by the physiognomy of some culture's method of teaching the use of signs (which is exactly what Wittgenstein's *Praxis* amounts to). The following sentiment expressed in *Investigations* points to a deep bias that influenced him in both periods:

> An 'inner process' stands in need of outward criteria.[23]

Wittgenstein's later philosophy largely consists of drawing out the consequences of abandoning the occult metaphysical subject as the creator of language. In effect, Wittgenstein demoted the hidden private mind of *Tractatus* from its office of language-creator, replacing it with the manifest and public form-of-life of *Investigations*. What remained unchanged was his conviction that the outward use of signs in and of itself displays the whole inner character of language, much as 19th-century physiognomists believed that a person's character is completely manifest in his or her body.

As noted in the last chapter, Wittgenstein was much influenced by 19th-century physiognomy, which he encountered while reading Otto Weininger's *Sex and Character*. Wittgenstein's innovation was to pry this concept out of its sexual context in Weininger and apply it to language. First, in *Tractatus*, Wittgenstein applied physiognomy to propositional signs; later, in *Investigations*, he applied it to the *Praxis* that creates propositional signs. In both his earlier and later periods, Wittgenstein took the bedrock of language to be some kind of physiognomy, beyond which lay the unspeakable. And that is exactly how Otto Weininger felt about the nature of the human soul. The following statement from Wittgenstein's *Philosophical Investigations* could just as easily have been written by Weininger in *Sex and Character*:

> The human body is the best picture of the human soul.[24]

Wittgenstein's interest in physiognomy was reinforced by his readings in behaviorist psychology, in which he took a special interest. But behaviorism itself was indebted to 19th-century physiognomy.

Cultural Solipsism?

Wittgenstein's emphasis on forms of life and *Praxis* has given numerous commentators the impression that he advocates a thorough-going social relativism. Our basic views about the nature of reality, they take him to say, are determined by our cultural conditioning. These commentators maintain that Wittgenstein replaced the transcendental solipsism of *Tractatus* with a kind of "cultural solipsism."[25]

This style of interpreting Wittgenstein has been rightly criticized by other commentators as a "caricature."[26] But even so, these other commentators have had difficulty in explaining in a succinct way why Wittgenstein is *not* an out-and-out cultural relativist. After all, he *does* say that understanding the nature of numbers is simply a matter of being trained to use number *symbols* in a certain way.[27] If understanding mathematics merely means being trained to use certain kinds of symbols, then what else is mathematics but a peculiar linguistic convention? And if that is the case, then doesn't culture determine reality for the later Wittgenstein in the same way that the metaphysical subject did for the early Wittgenstein? So he would seem to be a cultural solipsist after all!

The Great Community of Humanity-in-Nature

The answer is that the later Wittgenstein undergirds his theory of language with a major assumption that has nothing to do with language as such. This assumption, which serves like an elusive off-stage prompter to the actors in every scene in Wittgenstein's later thought, is this: there exists a great community of humanity-in-nature, which constitutes the final context for deciding all human questions about the nature of reality and possibility.

Wittgenstein sees this community as the deepest of all our forms of life, generating a *Praxis* that transcends every other *Praxis*. Precisely because this great community of humanity-in-nature exists, Wittgenstein argues, language is able to fuse the conventional and the natural.

In *Investigations*, Wittgenstein alludes to this assumption only obliquely; yet the allusions are there. For example, he repeatedly warns that he should *not* be taken as an out-and-out cultural relativist, as in the following passage:

> "So you are saying that human agreement decides what is true and what is false?"—It is what human beings *say* that is true and false; and they agree in the *language* they use. That is not agreement in opinions but in form of life.[28]

Wittgenstein denies he is a simple cultural relativist—and appeals to his concept of form of life to prove it! This appeal seems contradictory only to commentators who take "form of life" to mean cultural organization and nothing more. However, the above passage distinctly *contrasts* "form of life" to mere social convention ("agreement in opinions"). The implication is that nature is somehow involved in this equation.

Another instance of his rejection of simple cultural relativism occurs in his discussion of the role of "grammar" in language. He fears that some will accuse of him saying that logic is merely an arbitrary contrivance:

> "So does it depend wholly on our grammar what will be called (logically) possible and what not,—i.e. what that grammar permits?"—But surely that is arbitrary!—Is it arbitrary?—It is not every sentence-like formation that we know how to do something with, not every technique has an application in our life.[29]

The fact that something is *conventional*, argues Wittgenstein, does not necessarily mean that it is *arbitrary*. To the contrary, he suggests another alternative: that something can be necessary (even logically necessary!) and at the same time be partly conventional, especially if it is rooted in "our life." The reason: language does not exist in a vacuum; rather, it is a set of tools for dealing with the world. If a certain tool works well, then that fact tells us something not only about our own conventions but also about reality.

Other passages in *Investigations* allude to what Wittgenstein calls "our natural history." He describes the purpose of *Investigations* with these remarkable words:

> What we are supplying are really remarks on the natural history of human beings [*Naturgeschichte des Menschen*]; we are not contributing curiosities however, but observations which no one has doubted, but which have escaped remark only because they are always before our eyes.[30]

As noted earlier, Wittgenstein in certain other writings says that language has a deep mythology. This mythology reflects what is taken for granted in the language and is rooted in the least changing aspects of a form of life. The above passage from *Investigations* associates this mythology of the-taken-for-granted with the natural history of humanity [*Naturgeschichte des Menschen*]. These considerations suggest that Wittgenstein is working under the following assumptions: (1) there is something common to all the varied individual forms of human life, a basic form-of-life of humanity; and (2) nature exists, in which the form-of-life of humanity is implicated.

Other hints of this assumption in *Investigations* are his remarks about "general facts of nature." Consider, for example, the following passage, which amplifies the one immediately cited above:

> What we have to mention in order to explain the significance, I mean the importance, of a concept, are often extremely general facts of nature: such facts are hardly ever mentioned because of their great generality.[31]

This passage brings to mind Bertrand Russell's argument that "completely general facts of nature" serve as the ultimate grounds of logical necessity (discussed in chapter six). As readers will recall, it was in part to *discredit* this notion of Russell's that the younger Wittgenstein originally wrote *Tractatus*. Now in *Investigations* we find the older Wittgenstein seemingly making an appeal to something that sounds like this old idea. In fact, as we will soon see, Wittgenstein did return to Russell—but with a new twist.

On the other hand, some might argue that Wittgenstein at times draws back from such an approach. For example, the following passage seems to repudiate any appeal to nature as a ground for understanding linguistic form:

> We are not doing natural science; nor yet natural history—since we can also invent fictitious natural history for our purposes.[32]

But this passage is not the impediment it seems. Wittgenstein's point here is merely that whenever we imagine a certain language-game in order to exemplify some aspect of language, we presuppose (or invent) certain facts of nature. In our speculating, we can imagine other natures and other language-games than those that actually exist. So we are not limited, in examining the way language works, to the actual way nature happens to be (as the natural scientist is limited). Accordingly, we can understand concepts that might otherwise seem unintelligible to us—which is his main point in the section of *Investigations* where the above passage occurs (Part II, § xii).

Those who examine language do not operate like natural scientists, says Wittgenstein; but for all that, language is possible only because nature exists, and because nature has engendered a certain human form of life. Language is both conventional and natural because it is the *nature* of human beings to live in some *society*, and because an essential part of such social life for humans is *language*.

This naturalist sentiment is an echo of a similar view articulated some 2,300 years before the publication of *Investigations* by Aristotle, whom Wittgenstein was proud never to have read, regarding him as no longer relevant. As we will soon see, an important part of Wittgenstein's later philosophy was an unknowing reinvention of Aristotle, just as part of Wittgenstein's earlier philosophy had been an unknowing reinvention of Leibniz. The Spanish-born philosopher George Santayana once remarked that those who are ignorant of history are bound to repeat it. Wittgenstein exemplified this principle throughout his philosophical life.

The Universal Language of Gestures

Wittgenstein's hidden assumption about nature is reflected in another claim in *Investigations*: that there exists a physiognomy of natural gestures. These constitute the original natural language of humankind, of which all conventional language is an extension.

Consider an observer, Wittgenstein says, who is completely unacquainted with a certain game. How can the observer tell when the players are following rather than violating the rules? Or when they are engaging in behavior that is merely incidental to the game? If the game is truly new to the observer, then he or she can't have access to any kind of pre-existing criterion within the game itself for making these distinctions.

Wittgenstein's answer: the observer can read-off the rules from the behavior itself of the participants. The observer can do this because there are certain recognizable human gestures that transcend the game in question:

> One learns the game by watching how others play. But we say that it is played according to such-and-such rules because an observer can read these rules off from the practice [*Praxis*] of the game—like a natural law governing the play.—But how does the observer distinguish in this case between players' mistakes and correct play?—There are characteristic signs [*Merkmale*] of it in the players' behaviour. Think of the behaviour characteristic of cor-

recting a slip of the tongue. It would be possible to recognize that someone was doing so even without knowing his language.[33]

Now what happens when the language being learned is one's native language? The implication of the above passage is this: there are certain innate gestures that make the acquisition of one's native language possible; we are able to read-off these gestures by virtue of participating in the human form of life.

Wittgenstein *must* resort to some such assumption in view of two other assumptions he makes: (1) there is no language without rules; and (2) there is no kind of hidden meaning behind overt behavior. Therefore, in order for us to learn the rules of our native language merely by observing the behavior of our parents, there must be some kind of behavior that is meaningful in and of itself—and that is exactly what a universally recognizable gesture is.

Earlier we saw that in Wittgenstein's view a form of life creates language through a *Praxis*. Now we see that this *Praxis* depends for the possibility of its existence on a presupposed physiognomy of a universal natural language of gestures. This physiognomy, therefore, turns out to be the deepest root of all linguistic meaning [*Bedeutung*]. As often, Wittgenstein encapsulates his entire perspective in a quip:

> Meaning is a physiognomy. [*Die Bedeutung eine Physiognomie.*]

Augustine, Refined

Investigations begins by challenging the view of naming presented in a passage from Augustine. But there is an irony here: much of Augustine's passage is actually concerned with making another point entirely—that language is possible only because it is based on a natural language of human gestures. Augustine parenthetically inserts his remarks about objects as the meanings of words into this other discussion. Wittgenstein, while focusing his entire criticism of Augustine on this interjection about naming, lets Augustine's other point go by unchallenged. The reason is that Wittgenstein himself agrees with it. Remove the part about naming, and Augustine's account of how he learned to speak from watching his parents reads just like vintage Wittgenstein:

> Their intention was shewn by their bodily movements, as it were the natural language of all peoples: the expression of the face, the play of the eyes, the movement of other parts of the body, and the tone of voice which expresses our state of mind in seeking, having, rejecting, or avoiding something.[34]

Wittgenstein's criticism of Augustine amounts to saying that Augustine did not follow through on his own physiognomical presuppositions. That is, if language is learned as Augustine says above, then it is superfluous for him to look to objects as the meanings of words. The meanings of words are simply their uses as taught. The ultimate foundation for teaching these uses is the universal language of natural gestures that is shared by a certain form of life (namely, human beings). Meaning is a physiognomy.

Extraordinary Ordinary Language

Wittgenstein's assumption that humanity is by nature a communal form of life, endowed with a universal language of natural gestures, is relevant to one of his most widely misunderstood concepts: "ordinary language" [*die gewöhnliche Sprache*]. The implication of his notion of the universal language of natural gestures, discussed above, is that this language itself is the most ordinary (*gewöhnlich*—"commonplace") of all languages.

This implication is commonly overlooked because Wittgenstein often describes ordinary usages of German or English in order to resolve philosophical puzzles in those languages. In these cases, "ordinary language" obviously means ordinary German or English. Nonetheless, "ordinary language" in the fullest sense means neither German nor English, but rather the natural language of gestures that Wittgenstein assumes all human beings know by virtue of sharing in the human form of life.

Wittgenstein demonstrates the malleability of his understanding of "ordinary language" in a book-length fragment from his notes that has never been published in full ("The Big Typescript"). Arguing that we are today still struggling, unsuccessfully, with the same basic philosophical problems as the ancient Greeks, he says:

The reason is that our language has remained the same and always introduces us to the same questions.[35]

Wittgenstein certainly knew that ancient Greek and medieval Latin are different languages from modern German and English. The fact that he saw "the same" language at work for more than 2,500 years implies that he viewed an entire historical branch of Indo-European languages as in some sense one language.

The above passage confirms what is implied, but never explicitly stated, throughout *Investigations*: Wittgenstein's "ordinary language" is a phrase of varying scope, depending on the particular community of language-users in question. To the widest community (the form-of-life of humanity) there corresponds the widest ordinary language (the universal language of natural gestures).

How does some particular national language evolve from natural gestures? As we will see later, Wittgenstein strives to answer this question solely in terms of ambient group behavior, never in terms of the private mental experiences of individuals. And therein lies the Achilles' heel of his entire theory of language.

The Sacred Oak

Wittgenstein's assumption concerning the great community of humanity-in-nature is only hinted at, never explicitly stated, in *Investigations*. Not until 1979, some 26 years after the publication of *Investigations*, did Wittgenstein's full beliefs on the matter become widely accessible. The occasion was the printing of a new Wittgenstein anthology, which included his scathing comments on Sir James Frazer, author of the monumental study *The Golden Bough*.[36] Although published late, these comments were written early by Wittgenstein, in the 1920s.

Although Frazer's work is valuable as an overview of the myths and rituals of early nature societies, it is flawed by the author's provincial attitude toward his subjects. In Frazer's eyes, early myths and rituals represent an infantile attempt at science by those who have not yet learned to reason properly (that is, like modern Englishmen). Frazer conceived of his work as part of a paean to human progress, which he saw as advancing from the bumbling methods of early savages to the shiny new scientific techniques of modern civilized Europeans.

Wittgenstein rightly rebukes Frazer for his provincialism, using some of the strongest language found anywhere in his writings:

What a narrow spiritual life on Frazer's part! As a result: how impossible it was for him to conceive of life different from that of the England of his time! Frazer cannot imagine a priest who is not basically a present-day English parson with the same stupidity and dullness. ... Frazer is much more savage than most of his savages, for they are not as far removed from the understanding of a spiritual matter as a twentieth-century Englishman.[37]

Wittgenstein attacks Frazer's view that magic is merely inept science, arguing that human beings are by nature ceremonial animals. Far from being bad science, the earliest human rituals should in fact be viewed as a form of language, developed from natural human gestures:

In the ancient rites we have the use of an extremely developed gesture-language.[38]

To elaborate, Wittgenstein draws attention to the uncanny spectacle depicted in the opening pages of Frazer's work: an ancient priest-king guards, at risk to his own life, the sacred oak of Nemi, in whose branches grows the golden bough (mistletoe). In contemplating this spectacle, Wittgenstein asks: Why did certain ancient peoples so venerate the oak? Because, he replies, it was an important part of the life of their society, uniting them with nature into a greater community:

They and the oak were united in a community of life.[39]

Wittgenstein compares the relationship of humans to the oak with that of fleas to a dog. What would happen if fleas developed language, culture, and religion? Would these creations be independent of their natural dependencies? No—

If fleas developed a rite, it would be based on the dog.[40]

As with fleas and the dog, so with humans and nature: human culture and the languages that make it possible do not exist in a vacuum. Rather, humanity is united with nature in a great community of life; therefore, language at its base always involves a fusion of the conventional and the natural, which is the great hidden premise behind all of Wittgenstein's later writings.

Wittgenstein's methods in *Investigations* and his remarks on Frazer both imply that the ability to imagine the language of any people requires the ability to imagine their form of life. This is exactly what Frazer, despite all his erudition, was unable to do.

Indeed, Frazer could not be expected to understand even his own language. To his cultural provincialism there corresponded one that was linguistic: the belief that one's native language does not affect one's perception of reality. In fact, however—

> An entire mythology is stored within our language.[41]

At the conclusion of his criticisms of Frazer, Wittgenstein makes an off-hand remark contrasting magic with science. The crucial difference between the two, he argues, is that there is "progress" in science but not in magic.[42] This is a surprising distinction for him to make here, however. On his own terms, progress is always relative to some form of life. Why can't a system of myth and ritual embody a society's growing body of knowledge?

Wittgenstein's off-hand remark is inconsistent with the whole thrust of his later-developed thought. Eventually, he reversed himself on the matter, beginning *Investigations* with Nestroy's sardonic quip about progress. In his final years, as we will see in the next chapter, he turned his heaviest philosophical guns against science, mathematics, and formal logic.

The Subversiveness of Rules

Wittgenstein's interconnected notions of language-game, *Praxis*, and form of life allowed him to answer two disturbing question that eventually broke the back of *Tractatus*: (1) Are stipulated rules essential to language and logic? (2) If so, what is the source of their binding power?

As noted in the last chapter, the earlier Wittgenstein attacked the dim, but growing, awareness that logic involves not only propositions but also stipulated rules. The use of rules disturbed Wittgenstein because it implies that logic has a subjective element.

Wittgenstein's bias against stipulated rules ran contrary to the entire thrust of later symbolic logic. Inspired by Russell's critical introduction to *Tractatus*, logicians came to stress the now famous distinction between "object-language" and "metalanguage." The former consists of strings of uninterpreted signs, which are of two kinds, axioms and theorems. The metalanguage, by contrast, consists of stipulated rules defining a well-formed formula in the object-language, and licensing (or prohibiting) how theorems may be derived from axioms.

To avoid impossible paradoxes, logicians had to resort to stipulated rules. But stipulated rules are whatever the rule-giver says they are. How, then, can formal logic claim to have any objective validity?

What Is a Rule?

Wittgenstein gives this answer in *Investigations*: formal logic is conventional but not arbitrary, relative but not just a matter of personal taste, practical but not empirical, of limited scope yet authoritative within its realm. He came to this answer by analyzing rule-following in terms of language-games and *Praxis*.

In the first place, Wittgenstein said, the question of whether someone is following a rule is always decided by an appeal to the person's *behavior*, not his or her private mental activity. (You have to move the Knight a certain way, regardless of what you may be thinking.) On the other hand, mere behavior does not constitute rule-following. (I may move the Knight the right way by chance.) What makes the difference? In a word—*Praxis*. If I move the Knight the way I have been *trained* to move it, then I understand the rules that govern the use of the Knight.

What is the connection, Wittgenstein asks, between following a rule and the words (or other symbols) that expresses the rule? *Praxis*, again. Only through training and custom do rules become associated with words and symbols.

What, then, is the *meaning* of a rule that is expressed in words? Clearly, this meaning is not some sort of occult event in the mind of the rule-follower, or some ghostly halo hanging around the words. These things simply have no bearing on whether a rule is being obeyed. Rather, says Wittgenstein, the meaning of a rule that is expressed in words is the overall behavioral relationship among the word-users, their words, and their training.

Logic and Fly-Bottles

How does Wittgenstein move from this behavioral account of rule-following to logic? By considering the power of various kinds of rules. Participants in any form of life hold to its various behaviorally-formed rules with varying degrees of tenacity. Among the most tenaciously held rules, says Wittgenstein, are those that define for any form of life the way it understands the structure of possibility. These are the rules that license or prohibit certain combinations of words on the grounds of sense. (For example: *"This green house is red all over" doesn't make any sense.*)

These rules constitute a kind of Supreme Court for judging the admissibility of other rules of less sweeping ambit. When one appeals to this high court, the quest for further justification comes to an end. If someone should challenge the legitimacy even of the high court, we would simply shrug our shoulders and say:

> If I have exhausted the justification I have reached bedrock, and my spade is turned. Then I am inclined to say: "This is simply what I do."[43]

Passages like this have misled many commentators. They see Wittgenstein as saying that whether one follows a basic rule of logic or mathematics is a matter of arbitrary personal choice, like choosing the sort of wig one might wear to a drag party. But the above passage must be considered in its context. The statement "This is simply what I do" refers to my activity as a member of a certain form of life conditioned by a certain *Praxis*. It does *not* refer to casual decisions I might make in matters of personal taste.

In the above passage, Wittgenstein is saying this: The final boundary in the quest for justification is not anything theoretical at all, but rather something quite basic in the manner in which participants in a form of life happen to live. From the natural history of their interactions with each other and with the world, they have adopted certain deep (that is, commonplace) rules about what it makes sense to say. The most important are so commonplace as to be invisible to them. But they are as real as life itself, which is their source.

Anything that is said in the language of a form of life cannot fly beyond the contours of what it makes sense to say in that language; at most, such an attempt can stretch the boundaries of sense in order to make room for itself. Trying to escape the boundaries of language simply by banging up against them is like a fly trying to escape from the fly-bottle. The only way out for the poor fly is to patiently feel its way about, bit by bit, until it attains a survey of the contours that constrain it, eventually orienting itself toward the opening. But this is not an easy task because the boundaries are invisible to the fly. And when the fly does eventually escape, its flight is into silence, for it has left the contours of meaningful speech behind. It cannot tell other flies of its experiences outside the bottle.

This Is How We Live

Drawing on the above analysis of rules, Wittgenstein gives this answer to the problem of rule-conventionality in logic: Yes, formal logic does depend on stipulated rules, which I didn't fully appreciate when I wrote *Tractatus*. And yes, rules can vary, depending on the decisions of the rule-makers. But for all that, there are limits to the spectrum through which we can vary the rules.

For example, we can't use a rule that would allow propositions to inherit all possible truth-values at the same time. The reason is practical: the whole point of having a logical calculus is to rule-out the inheritance of certain truth-values under certain conditions. A calculus that permitted them all would be useless (that is, senseless).

In actual practice, we always evaluate the efficacy of any proposed rule in formal logic by appealing to other, higher-level rules to which we are already committed in our rational discourse in general. But what about evaluating these higher-level rules? How do we judge *their* efficacy? Can we find some great rule-book of logic dictated by God? A kind of ten commandments for all rational thought? No, eventually we reach a stage where appeals to rules come to an end, and we just decide the matter on the basis of what it makes *sense* for us to say, based on our own purposes and interests.

What it makes sense for us to say is related to our natural history as a form of life. The fact that we happen to decide the matter of sense in a certain way doesn't mean that every intelligent species of life in the universe must reach the same conclusion. The contours of fly-bottles depend on the techniques and life-histories of the fly-bottle makers.

The rules of logic, therefore, involve both conventionality and necessity: conventionality, because logic needs rules, and rules are commands that might be otherwise; necessity, because the rules of logic, unlike any other kind of rule, define what it makes sense to say, and in the matter of sense, the spectrum of variability is not unlimited.

Rules that define a language's sense map out the structure of possibility for the users of that language. Such rules are relative, in that they are created by a particular form of life. But they are also absolute, in that every form of life which engages in rational discourse has a mythological core in its language that defines the structure of possibility for that form of life. If people wish to speak with each other, they must do so consistent with the core in their language that maps out what it is possible for them to say, or else change the core. Their only other alternative is silence.

Because every form of life is a part of nature, every system of logic reveals something about the nature of the world. At the same time, however, every system of logic also reveals something about the conventional habits of the form of life that has created the system. It is not possible, in principle, to tell exactly where the conventional habits end and the rule of nature begins. Like the fire that cooks food on the household hearth, logic is the joint result of both human connivance and the will of Zeus.

Grammars, Ordinary and Extraordinary

Wittgenstein links three activities together as different aspects of one and the same reality: (1) following rules that prescribe or forbid the way in which words may be combined; (2) making sense in a language; and (3) understanding the structure of possibility. Of these, he lays special stress on the first. To follow the rules that legislate how words may be combined in our language, he argues, is what it means to make sense when we speak; and to make sense when we speak is what it means to understand what is ultimately possible and impossible.

Now how can rules, which merely legislate how words may be combined, extend their sway to the structure of possibility? Because these rules, Wittgenstein argues, express the basic ways in which participants in any form of life actually live. Every language begins with a society of gesture-capable organisms interacting with their environment and each other. The limits of these interactions define the boundaries of possibility for that form of life. These boundaries are in turn reflected in the rules that they create for licensing certain combinations of words as meaningful and proscribing others as meaningless. Accordingly, meaning, possibility, and rule-following are like riders on a three-seat tandem bike. Any change in the foot-stokes of one will affect those of the others.

The pattern of meaning and possibility, as fixed by a language's basic rules for combining words, Wittgenstein calls "grammar." In adopting this usage, he insists that he is not stretching the ordinary meaning of the word. Every language, he argues, has rules that specify how words may or may not be combined. For example, English permits the combination "I am," whereas it forbids the combination "they is."

So far, Wittgenstein's concept of grammar is like ordinary grammar. However, Wittgenstein also says that the rules that outlaw "they is" are of the same type as the rules that outlaw "The red house is all green." Contrary to Wittgenstein, however, no ordinary grammar book would ever assimilate these two sentences into the same type. Clearly, a distinctly philosophical concept is at work here that goes beyond the ordinary meaning of the word "grammar."

To rule out the red/green sentence above, ordinary grammarians would not appeal to a grammar book at all, but to a dictionary or a color chart. Indeed, ordinary grammarians make a sharp distinction between syntax and meaning: the former treats of how words of certain types may be combined with words of other types, whereas the latter is a matter of what individual words stand for.

This ordinary distinction is intolerable to Wittgenstein, because in his later period he repudiates the notion that the meaning of a word is the object for which it stands. By seeking to reduce the meanings of a language's individual base-words to rules that specify how they may be combined, he is committed to assimilating all dictionaries into grammars. Whatever philosophical merit this view may or may not have, it has very little to do with the ordinary meaning of the word "grammar." To the contrary, Wittgenstein's concept of ordinary grammar is as extraordinary as his concept of ordinary language.

Essence Stages a Come-Back

Among the extraordinary claims that Wittgenstein makes for "grammar" are these: it determines sense; it shows the expanse of the possible and the impossible; and it reveals what kind of object anything is. Most extraordinary of all, he says that the opposite of a proposition that expresses a rule of grammar cannot be understood (which is certainly not the case with a proposition of ordinary grammar). Like all of his other important innovations, Wittgenstein's notion of "grammar" is highly metaphysical. Expressed in a nutshell, it comes to this:

> *Essence* is expressed by grammar.[44]

Wittgenstein was right to invoke the word "essence" here. In traditional Western metaphysics, essence has played the role of that thing by virtue of which thoughts have determinate meanings, and the world, determinate possibilities. But Wittgenstein was wrong to think that he was the first to ground essence in grammar and in humanity's status as a living organism. One finds a similar approach in Aristotle, who explicitly uses grammar as a guide for delineating both conceptual meaning and physical possibility.

Like Wittgenstein, Aristotle stresses the fact that humanity is a living organism functioning in nature, and views logic as an outgrowth of the natural use of human language. Although Wittgenstein differs from Aristotle in important details, his allegedly revolutionary concept of essence is definitely in the old Aristotelian mold.

Wittgenstein also has notable differences from Aristotle. The biggest is Wittgenstein's stress on the relativity and variability of essence (as evidenced by his discussion of "family resemblances," discussed above). Because there are all sorts of language-games, says Wittgenstein, there can be all sorts of essence, depending on the particular rules that underlie the game that is in fact being played.

Again contrary to Aristotle, Wittgenstein eventually came to deny universality to the peculiar language-game called formal logic. In taking this step, Wittgenstein broke with the entire Western logical tradition going back to Parmenides.

Can Rules Be Private?

A noteworthy consequence that Wittgenstein draws from his concept of rules and grammar is that there can be no such thing as a private rule. This consequence, buttressed by his argument that there can be no such thing as private naming (discussed above), is the crux of his famous argument that there can be no such thing as a private language.

By the word "private," as applied to rules, Wittgenstein means cut off from public use. For example, I am following a private rule, in Wittgenstein's sense, if I do the following: I show someone a piece of paper with lines drawn on it and claim that the drawing is a map that I've used to complete a recent journey. However, I cannot explain how the lines on the paper are to be correlated with the observable features of any known terrain.

In this case, says Wittgenstein, my claim is empty. Regardless of what thoughts I may have on the matter, I cannot meaningfully be said to have followed such a drawing as a map. Lines only become a map (that is, a sign for a rule) when they are in principle publicly usable. And an action only becomes an example of rule-following when it is in principle mappable (and therefore imitable). Remove the possibility of imitation and public access, and there are neither signs for rules nor the following of rules.

This argument is just a further development of Wittgenstein's notion of *Praxis*. We have seen that by "language" Wittgenstein always means specific language-games created by *Praxis*. Accordingly, learning a language is like submitting to toilet training: it depends on rules that we have been disciplined to obey through prior training by societal authorities, beginning with our parents. The question of whether we are in fact following the rules is a matter of comparing our public behavior with our public training, never a matter of examining our private mental states.

As noted above, the German word *Praxis* has three meanings: practice, established social custom, and activity that is not theoretical or mental. Once anyone becomes accustomed to describing rule-following in terms of *Praxis*, it seems ungrammatical to speak of rules that might be unique and purely personal. To the contrary, rules must be a matter of public behavior, imposed by some societal authority. Anything else is merely incidental. We will soon see that this (typically German) concept of rules is inadequate to the richness of human personal experience.

Names Minus Rules Equals Ciphers

Wittgenstein combines this argument against the possibility of privately following a rule with his earlier argument against the possibility of private naming. The result is his claim that a language that is strictly private is inconceivable.

Here are the steps to Wittgenstein's reasoning: Naming always involves connecting some symbol to other symbols according to rules. Now if I want to create a truly private name, I have to create a new symbol that will be used in accordance with rules that I have also created and which have no behavioral connection to the world. But such rules are inconceivable. Accordingly, my new symbol will be a mere cipher, not only for others, but for me as well. Since I cannot create any strictly private name, a language that is strictly private is inconceivable.

Old Wine in New Bottles

In the end, Wittgenstein allows only one avenue of connection between words and the world— some socially-created network of behavioral rules. These define for a form of life both the meaning of its concepts and the structure of possibility in its world. Essence is expressed by grammar, and grammar derives from environmentally-molded group behavior.

This concept of language is vintage Aristotle, but poured by Wittgenstein into new bottles manufactured by Charles Darwin and J.B. Watson. The merit of this approach is that it brings the source of language down from the heavens (where *Tractatus* sought to stash it away) and relocates it in the openness and concreteness of human social interaction. In this way, Wittgenstein is able to overcome the solipsism that crippled *Tractatus*.

But this approach also has a weakness: it does not go far enough in grounding language in human concreteness. Having brought language down from heaven to the level of human society, Wittgenstein stalls in advancing further within society to reach the individual interpreter. Despite his convoluted writing style—ambulatory, repetitive, suffused with diverting metaphorical flourishes—Wittgenstein pushes a simple thesis: language is just another aspect of herd behavior; therefore, all linguistic meaning is social; private mental activity is irrelevant.

Enter the Interpreter

As noted, Wittgenstein's theory implies that a strictly private language is inconceivable. As we are now about to see, however, this claim is false. Accordingly, his original theory of language must be false as well.

Wittgenstein's entire argument hangs on the alleged impossibility of private rules. To say "I know I am following a rule," he argues, always fails as evidence for establishing that I am actually following a rule. What is relevant, rather, is a comparison of my public behavior to my public training. In a nutshell—

> Are the rules of the private language *impressions* of rules?—The balance on which impressions are weighed is not the *impression* of a balance.[45]

Wittgenstein's error lies in not giving due regard to the interpreter. As shown in earlier chapters, there is no such thing as a fact in the absolute (the fallacy of absolute objectivity). To the contrary, there are only facts-for-interpreters (relative objectivity). Remove the interpreter, and you remove the facts as well. The question of whether someone is following a rule or not, is, like all questions of fact, a question for some interpreter or some group of interpreters.

Wittgenstein's argument is the strongest when second-party interpreters evaluate another interpreter's behavior in terms of rule-following. Here the interpreter's private impressions are irrelevant. For example, when I move the Knight, I am following the rules of chess in the eyes of others only if they judge that my behavior is consistent with the public training that defines the game for us all.

But not every kind of rule-following is analogous to some group watching a chess game. In particular, when *I* interpret my own behavior, the fact in question is not the-fact-for-some-group at all, but rather the-fact-for-me. Are facts-for-me any less real merely because they are not facts-for-others? Not if the only distinction between the two types of facts is simply one of group vs. individual.

Previous chapters have shown that different interpreters may know different sets of facts. These sets may turn out to be congruent, or overlap somewhat, or diverge entirely. Consequently, an ineradicable complexity lies at the heart of the interpretational process, and therefore at the heart of reality. This complexity is a perpetual thorn in the side to anyone who dogmatically insists that group consensus must be the final determinant of factuality.

When Wittgenstein insists that my judgment about my own rule-following *must* be grounded in the judgments of others, he begs the very question at issue—namely, whether one can have a purely private judgment about one's own rule-following. Wittgenstein simply *assumes* that all judgments about rule-following must be socially and behaviorally grounded in order to be judgments. This assumption is partly prompted by his fondness for the loaded word *Praxis*, especially as exemplified by the game of chess.

The most that Wittgenstein has proved is this: any language whose complete function is to be publicly descriptive of public facts cannot contain any elements that are purely private. The closest approach to such a publicly-descriptive language is the language of physics. But the jury is still out on the question of whether the complete function of every human language is to be publicly descriptive of public facts. At times, Wittgenstein himself demurs, for he insists that there is no one essence, or model, to which all human language must conform. Rather, he says, there is a great variety of language-games that must be accepted as they are.

Wittgenstein's arguments against the possibility of a private language go against the deepest grain of his entire later approach to language. In bringing language down from heaven into human society, he implicitly recognized that there could be no such thing as a transcendent objectivity for all language. Instead, he offered a new relative objectivity based on his concept of "form of life." Limits remain to the meanings of our concepts, he argued, but these are not given from on high like the ten commandments; rather, they have a bedrock in the behavioral interactions of a form of life.

Wittgenstein failed to see that one can make an analogous move from form of life to individual interpreter. As discussed in earlier chapters, our individual reality maps result partly from our genetic hardware, partly from our cultural conditioning, *and* partly from our own idiosyncratic life-experiences. As a result, there can be both consonance and dissonance among different reality maps—even within the same form of life.

Apollo's Tripod

Wittgenstein sees language as resting on two ultimate supports: the universal natural language of human gestures and patent group behavior. But language is actually a tripod whose third foot is the interpreter. Without the interpreter, how else could primal human gestures ever become articulated into sophisticated moves in language-games? Individual *interpreters*, not language-games or forms of life, actually invent and modify language-games. In so doing, interpreters bring to bear their own unique individual experiences, which may not yet be fully expressible in the language they seek to modify. As a result of this pressure from the pre-verbal experiences of individual interpreters, the boundaries of language, and therefore the boundaries of meaning, are ever changing.

If Wittgenstein were right, human language would never change and develop. It would forever remain a closed set of gestures that are innate to the human species. But genuinely new forms of meaning appear in language all the time, occasionally even in the face of overwhelming opposition by the herd. Conclusion: the private mental experiences of interpreters are *not* irrelevant to linguistic meaning.

As an example, consider the work of one of America's greatest poets, Allen Ginsberg. Although drawing on primal human gestures and contemporary social conventions, Ginsberg's poetry also expresses something else: the unique personal experience and vision of Allen Ginsberg. One of the most striking aspects of Ginsberg's poetry is its deliberate *violation* of the established rules of English syntax. But for all that, his poetry is not nonsense. In fact, quite the contrary: Ginsberg's violation of syntax actually *adds* to the meaning of his poetry. Consider the following passage, which excoriates the language of U.S. military propaganda during the Vietnam War:

> U.S. Military Spokesmen
> Language language
> Cong death toll
> has soared to 100 in First Air Cavalry
> Division's Sector of
> Language language.[46]

On Wittgenstein's terms, the idea that there could be meaning in language precisely in virtue of violating syntax is inconceivable. It would be like saying "It is permitted to say *This red house is also all green*." But despite Wittgenstein's strictures, even this forbidden sentence might actually be meaningful—as in a poem.

Wittgenstein's concept of language-game, valuable as far as it goes, does not go far enough. As Ginsberg's poetry shows, one can imagine a language-game where violations of syntax are among the very things that convey meaning. But if that is the case, then language-games cannot be entirely reducible to observable group behavior, conventional syntax, and universal natural gestures. A language-game must also involve another essential ingredient, the interpreter.

Like the divine tripod from which Apollo spoke, language rests on three, not two, feet; these, not as hard as Delphian bronze but just as important, are natural human gestures, social conditioning, and the interpreter's private experience. Remove any one of these feet, and the tripod of language overturns. Whenever anything is said, the conveyed meaning depends in part on the particular individual who happens to say it and on the particular individual who happens to hear it. As Apollo cannot be excised from his oracle, so the interpreter cannot be excised from his or her language.

Although Wittgenstein never reached the interpreter, his concept of language-game illuminated the variability of language. In the next chapter, we will see how Wittgenstein invokes this variability to criticize the claim of formal logic to be the only game in town. In so doing, he will undermine some of the most cherished presuppositions of modern Western philosophy.

---

[1] Ludwig Wittgenstein, *Philosophical Investigations*, ed. by G.E.M. Anscombe and R. Rhees, trans. by G.E.M. Anscombe, The Macmillan Company, New York, 1953.

[2] *ibid.*, p. 2; Augustine, *Confessions*, I, 8.

[3] Norman Malcolm, *Ludwig Wittgenstein, A Memoir*, Oxford University Press, New York, 1st edition, 1958, 2nd edition, 1984, p. 58; original's emphasis.

[4] Wittgenstein, *Investigations*, p. x; original's emphasis.

[5] *ibid.*, p. 89 ff.

[6] *ibid.*, p. 23.

[7] *ibid.*, p. viii; Johann Nestroy, *Der Schützling*, IV, 10: Überhaupt hat der Fortschritt das an sich, dass er viel grösser ausschaut, als er wirklich ist.

[8] Wittgenstein, *Investigations*, p. 66.

[9] *ibid.*, p. 223.

[10] *ibid.*, p. 32.

[11] Ludwig Wittgenstein, *Culture and Value*, ed. by G.H. von Wright and Heikki Nyman, trans. by Peter Winch, Basil Blackwell, Oxford, 1977 & 1980, p. 31, with punctuation correction; John, 1;1; Johann Wolfgang von Goethe, *Faust*, I.

[12] Wittgenstein, *Investigations*, pp. 95 & 116; original's emphasis.

[13] *ibid.*, p. 47.

[14] See S. Stephen Hilmy, *The Later Wittgenstein: The Emergence of a New Philosophical Method*, Basil Blackwell, Oxford, 1987, p. 179ff. He has been justly criticized by Gertrude Conway, *Wittgenstein on Foundations*, Humanities Press, International, Inc., Atlantic Highlands, New Jersey, 1989, p. 42ff.

[15] Wittgenstein, *Investigations*, pp. 8 & 88; original's emphasis.

[16] *ibid.*, p. 174.

[17] *ibid.*, p. 226; original's emphasis.

[18] An example is P.M.S. Hacker, *Insight and Illusion: Themes in the Philosophy of Wittgenstein*, revised 2nd edition, Clarendon Press, Oxford, 1986, p. 129, n. 19.

[19] Ludwig Wittgenstein, *On Certainty*, ed. by G.E.M. Anscombe and G.H. von Wright, trans. by Dennis Paul and G.E.M. Anscombe, Harper Torchbooks, New York, 1969, p. 15.

[20] Wittgenstein, *Investigations*, p. 85; original's emphasis.

[21] Wittgenstein, *On Certainty*, p. 21.

[22] *ibid.*, p. 66.

[23] Wittgenstein, *Investigations*, p. 153.

[24] *ibid.*, p. 178.

[25] Merrill Hintikka and Jaakko Hintikka, *Investigating Wittgenstein*, Basil Blackwell, 1986, p. 21.

[26] G.P. Baker and P.M.S. Hacker, *Wittgenstein: Rules, Grammar and Necessity*, Basil Blackwell, 1985, p. 171.

[27] Wittgenstein, *Investigations*, p. 57.

[28] *ibid.*, p. 88; original's emphasis.

[29] *ibid.*, p. 142.

[30] *ibid.*, p. 125.

[31] *ibid.*, p. 56.

[32] *ibid.*, p. 230.

[33] *ibid.*, p. 27. The sentiment expressed here contrasts with Willard Van Orman Quine's doctrine of "the indeterminacy of translation," discussed in chapter eleven.

[34] Wittgenstein, *Investigations*, p. 2; Augustine, *Confessions*, I, 8.

[35] Ludwig Wittgenstein, "The Big Typescript," quoted by P.M.S. Hacker, *Insight and Illusion*, p. 160.

[36] Ludwig Wittgenstein, "Remarks on Frazer's *Golden Bough*," trans. by John Beversluis, in *Wittgenstein: Sources and Perspectives*, ed. by C.G. Luckhardt, Cornell University Press, Ithaca, 1979, pp. 61-81.

[37] *ibid.*, pp. 65 & 68.

[38] *ibid.*, p. 70.
[39] *ibid.*, p. 73.
[40] *loc. cit.*
[41] *ibid.*, p. 70.
[42] *ibid.*, p. 74.

[43] Wittgenstein, *Investigations*, p. 85.
[44] *ibid.*, p. 116; original's emphasis.
[45] *ibid.*, p. 92; original's emphasis.
[46] Allen Ginsberg, "Wichita Vortex Sutra," *Planet News*, City Lights Books, San Francisco, 1968, p. 129.

Abstract Returned, Detail
Acrylic on Canvas, 20" x 24", 1993

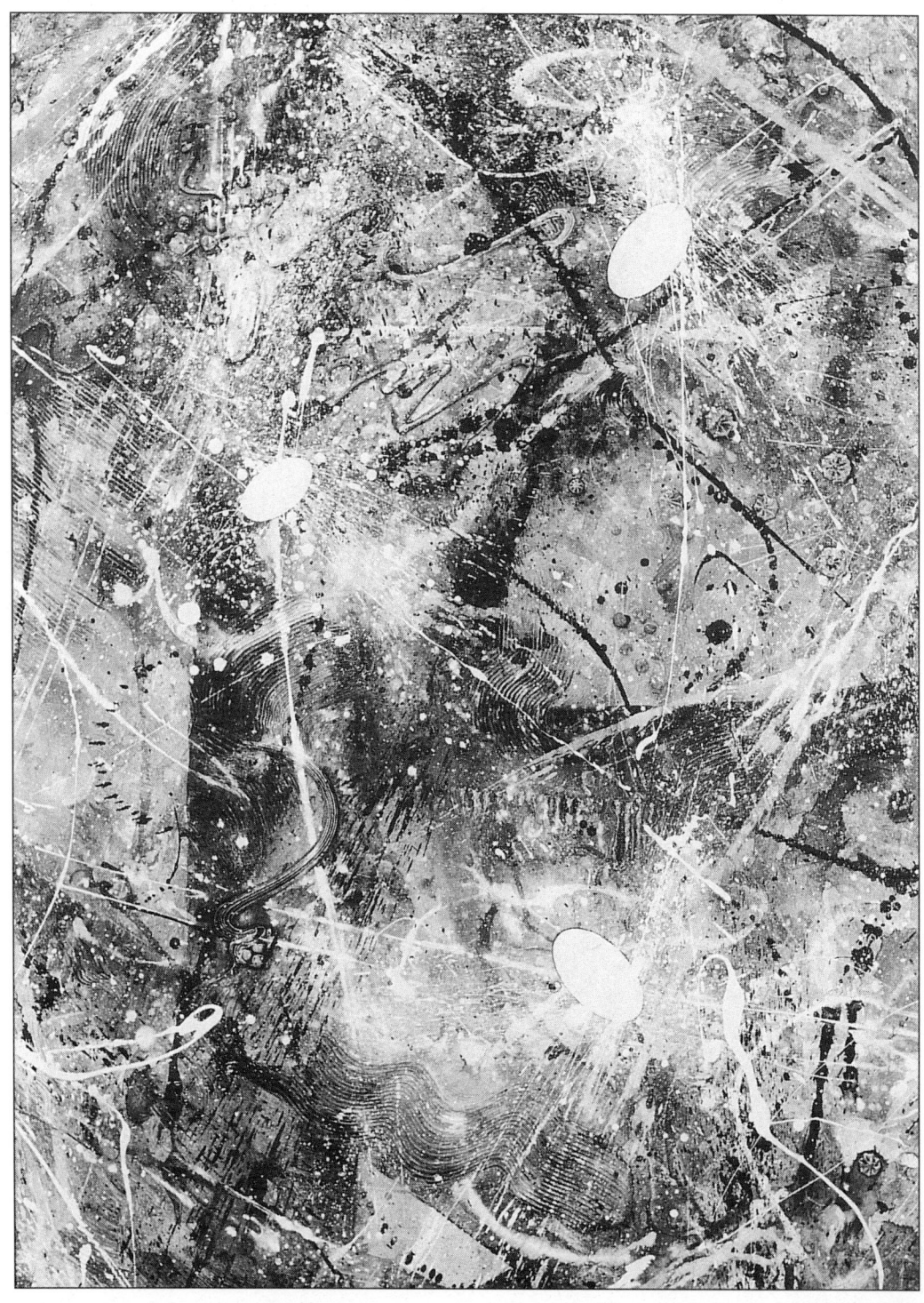

Inner Vision, Detail
Acrylic on Paper, 30" x 22", 1992

10

Logic vs. Language

SUMMARY: This chapter shows how Ludwig Wittgenstein came to view both formal logic and science as detrimental to human life. It also shows how the increasing worldliness of his later philosophy of language paralleled a like change in his sexual attitudes.

Ludwig Wittgenstein's *Philosophical Investigations*, published posthumously in 1953, sought to correct his own earlier views on the nature of language. As discussed the last chapter, a pivotal part of this corrective effort was Wittgenstein's new concept of "language-game." In this chapter, we will see how Wittgenstein brought this new concept to bear on formal logic.

In Wittgenstein's new view, there are a great many language-games, none of which may presume to set itself up as the supreme standard for all others. Among these many games is one where a calculus is used for tracing out the inheritance patterns of truth-values in arguments. Those who like to play with this type of calculus are called logicians, and their game is formal logic.

As part of their game, logicians like to compare the many uses of ordinary language to the operations of their calculus, noting degrees of similarity and difference. Such a calculus represents a kind of ideal, but not in the sense of an authoritative standard to which language must conform. Rather, a logician's calculus is like a map, elucidating the rough and variable terrain of actual linguistic usage.

Explorers of a new physical terrain would be foolish if they tried to remove a newly encountered rock formation simply because it didn't match their tentative map. They ought to redraw the map instead! In the same way, logicians are foolish to try and expunge certain language-games from the landscape of human communication just because they don't conform to their calculuses. Both the rock formation and the language-game are in order just as they are. They don't need someone's map to have validity.

The Crystalline Machine

Wittgenstein admits that he was guilty of an idealistic attitude toward logic when he wrote *Tractatus*. Reflecting on his own earlier approach, he uncovers what he calls "a tendency to sublimate [*sublimieren*] the logic of our language."[1] In using this word, Wittgenstein apparently had in mind the physical phenomenon of sublimation, whereby certain solids can convert directly into vapors without going through an apparent liquid state. For example, a layer of snow on the ground will eventually disappear into vapors even though the surrounding temperature remains below freezing. The point of Wittgenstein's analogy: logicians treat language as if it were a base solid from which they can extract some ethereal essence. Sublime logic exuded from the crassness of ordinary language!

In effect, Wittgenstein makes this admission: In *Tractatus*, I urged people to lift up their eyes to the heights, whence cometh our help. But now I realize we should rather look around at the solid features of language that are sticking out in our faces. We needn't go chasing after invisible vapors in the air after all. Enough of the alleged sublimity of logic—back to the rough and tumble of ordinary language!

When we actually look at language in the concrete, continues Wittgenstein, we nowhere find "the crystalline purity of logic."[2] In fact, he realizes that he had bought into a myth, the myth of an ideal machine whose actions are symbolized by its very structure (as in Frege's concept-script, discussed in chapter five):

> The logical machine—that would be an all-pervading ethereal mechanism.—We must give warning against this picture.[3]

Though not composed of matter, this machine seemed to the early Wittgenstein to be more real, more unyielding than anything made of metal. But what was the source of its remarkable hardness and inflexibility? Why couldn't its parts bend and break as in other machines?

The source of the logical machine's remarkable qualities was simply our own requirement. Mesmerized by the fallacy that communicating is a kind of calculating, we created the mythology of an ideal machine. But the actual usages of language are far more complicated than this picture acknowledges, says Wittgenstein. Formal logic is a highly simplified picture of how certain language-games work, useful in limited contexts. No logical calculus, however, provides a privileged window on the nature of reality.

Wittgenstein vs. Wittgenstein

The realization that communicating is not reducible to calculating did not come easy to Wittgenstein. Both his private writings and the notes kept by his students show that he was slow to depart from the calculative ideal of language that had mesmerized him while writing *Tractatus*.

Evidence for the gradualness of Wittgenstein's transition appears in the way he uses the terms "calculus" (*Kalkül*) and "language-game" (*Sprachspiel*). For some time following his return to Cambridge in 1929, he seems to have regarded these two words as equally appropriate for describing the basic way in which language works. Later, however, "calculus" gives way to "language-game."

Even so, however, the calculative ideal retained some influence. The best example of this influence is Wittgenstein's argument against the possibility of a private language. As discussed in the last chapter, Wittgenstein argued that there cannot be a private language because it would require the formation of private rules. But a rule that is private, he argued, is no rule at all; therefore, a private language is impossible.

The underlying assumption behind this argument is that communicating is a matter of calculating. We can all tell whether some noise is appropriately used (that is, has *meaning*) by calculating according to publicly accepted rules. Remove calculations according to public rules, said Wittgenstein, and you remove the entire basis of meaning.

On the one hand, however, Wittgenstein says that language cannot be reduced to one kind of game, least of all the idealized calculative game of the logicians. Indeed, near the end of his life he went so far as to say this:

> What we regard as expression [in a gesture] *consists* in incalculability.[4]

Wittgenstein in Mid-Air

Wittgenstein never succeeded in resolving his underlying ambivalence about the basis of meaning in language. On the one hand, he remained fascinated throughout his life by the ideal of the sublime crystalline machine in the sky; on the other, he realized that actual language is a mundane affair that has no need for any validation by crystalline machines. Although insisting that language is in order just as it is, he nonetheless never fully accepted his own admonitions on the matter, but periodically cast a longing glance back up to his erstwhile ideal in the heavens.

This philosophical ambivalence about meaning was not a superficial trait, but reflected a deeper psychological ambivalence that pervaded his life. This ambivalence is beautifully depicted in Derek Jarman's striking 1993 film *Wittgenstein* (using a script by Terry Eagleton). As Jarman's film shows, Wittgenstein lived much of his life suspended in psychological mid-air, pulled in opposing directions by the attractions of heaven and earth.

The penultimate scene of the film has Wittgenstein, by now dead, reappear in the guise of his early boyhood self. He wears self-concocted mechanical wings and balloons, by which he has managed to ascend into mid-air, but no higher. Through wire-rimmed glasses, he casts quizzical glances above and below. In the background, the voice of his long-time friend, the worldly economist John Maynard Keynes, remarks that Wittgenstein could never fully commit himself to the earthly realm of language, even after abandoning the icy heaven of logic:

> Something in him was still homesick for the ice, where everything was radiant and absolute and relentless. Though he had come to like the idea of the rough ground, he couldn't bring himself to live there. So now he was marooned between earth and ice, at home in neither. And this was the cause of all his grief.[5]

Wittgenstein's ambivalence about meaning paralleled his attitudes toward his own sexuality. As noted in chapter seven, the earlier Wittgenstein fell under the influence of the self-hating protofascist Otto Weininger. Fascinated with Weininger's notion of a transcendent realm that grounds both logic and ethics, and influenced by Christian asceticism, Wittgenstein concluded that his sexual nature was incompatible with a higher "duty to himself."

In later years, after his disastrous experience as a public-school teacher, Wittgenstein began moving away from this world-denying spirituality. In his personal life, he was able to establish ongoing lover-relationships with other gay men, including Francis Skinner and Ben Richards. Paralleling this change, he began to see language less as a reflection of a celestial ideal and more as a set of practical tools for animal survival. But he never came fully to terms with either the world or himself.

Are There No Standards?

As Wittgenstein descended from the celestial logical machine to mundane language-games, he had to come to grips with a thorny question: If there is no transcendent standard by which to judge reasoning, but just a collection of various language-games, how can we ever say that anybody's argument accords with, or violates, logic? And how can we account for propositions that are necessarily true?

Many of Wittgenstein's critics maintain that he barters away logical necessity for conventional agreement or personal taste. On Wittgenstein's account, the critics say, the truths of logic are true merely because we—either individually or as a society—happen to resolve that they be true. But we could just as well resolve that they be false. Consequently, Wittgenstein reduces both logic and mathematics to a matter of social convention or personal whim, which shows that his views are ridiculous.

As discussed in the last chapter, a purely conventionalist reading of Wittgenstein is an oversimplification. Throughout *Investigations*, Wittgenstein insists on the special, compelling nature of logic and mathematics, in contrast to the contingency found in factual description. Far from denying this distinction, he sets out to elucidate it. But in so doing, he foregoes the right to appeal to any kind of transcendent realm, as he had done in *Tractatus*.

A Shared Understanding of Meaning

Although we can create arbitrary new games with arbitrary rules, Wittgenstein argues, we always do so against the back-drop of some larger game that is just taken for granted. Otherwise, the new game would have no sense. The back-drop game is not as arbitrary as the new creation because it provides the standard by which to evaluate the newcomer. For any context of linguistic evaluation, Wittgenstein calls the most inclusive network of backdrop games "ordinary language."

Corresponding to every language-game is a form of life, which creates the game's grammar. Cultures and the human species as a whole constitute the most encompassing of all human forms of life. The grammars that they create define the deep contours of meaning for their members.

These deep contours of meaning, like all aspects of language, are conventional. Nonetheless, they are *not* arbitrary, for three reasons: (1) they are the bedrock for the possibility of all communication; (2) they are the standard of last appeal by which any language-game of lesser scope is evaluated; and (3) they reflect their creators' primal animal interactions with each other and with nature. If we try and dig below this bedrock, we will not find anything that is less arbitrary; instead, we will find that which is altogether beyond the scope of language. The quest for justification comes to an end in the bedrock of a form of life and its mythology (that is, its deepest grammar).

The upshot: logical necessity is a shared understanding of deep meaning, relative to some form of life. When people reason in mathematics and logic, what they really do is trace out the boundaries of what it makes sense for them to say in their language. This undertaking is quite different from deciding whether some particular description is verified by some particular fact in the world.

For example, consider the sentence "$2 + 2 = 4$." This sentence is always true for you and me, but not because either you or I have arbitrarily decided that it shall be true. Rather, if this sentence were false, that circumstance would so undermine the meaningfulness of the common language of which this sentence is an outgrowth that we would no longer be able to communicate with each other.

An appeal to logical necessity is an appeal to the shared realization that if we deny a certain sentence, we loose the ability to communicate. Faced with the alternative of adhering to some sentence or giving up the capacity to communicate, we always choose the former, at least if we want to tell anybody about it.

The shared realization among users of a language that certain of its sentences express its core contours of meaning bestows on these sentences an irrefragability that is not possessed by other kinds of sentences. Therefore, these sentences are absolute—but only for language-users in that form of life. There is no guarantee that other forms of life using other languages will follow the same patterns in their privileging of sentences.

Forms of life are also constantly changing. As they change, the basic contours of meaning in their languages may change as well. A recent example is the shift in concepts occasioned by quantum mechanics. Our descendants (if patriarchal-industrial civilization survives) will probably not understand our difficulties with these concepts.

The claim that logical necessity is based on a shared understanding of deep meaning does not undo the role of logical thinking in our language, insists Wittgenstein, nor does it reduce it to a matter of personal whim. To the contrary, it accounts for everything that logic is supposed to do in language, but without appealing to any kind of transcendent realm. Wittgenstein's famous remark on the matter, often misunderstood, is clear when considered in the context of his overall view of language:

> If language is to be a means of communication there must be agreement not only in definitions but also (queer as this may sound) in judgments. This seems to abolish logic, but does not do so.[6]

Fly-Bottles and the Meaning of Life

In grounding logical necessity in a shared understanding of deep meaning, Wittgenstein does not mean to suggest that this meaning is hidden away in some lower depth. The meaning is deep in the sense that it is ubiquitously established in practice and, for that very reason, invisible. In order to reach deep meaning, Wittgenstein argues, we needn't do any digging at all. Rather, we must carefully remind ourselves of the various uses of ordinary language right under our noses. By so doing, we will develop an overview of the basic contours of meaning in our language.

So we are like the fly in the fly-bottle. This creature, by patiently feeling its way about, gains a survey of the invisible walls on whose inner sides it walks. If meticulous and persistent, the fly will eventually maneuver itself over these invisible contours, reach the bottle's opening, and go free. Likewise, we ourselves, by patiently surveying the details of ordinary language, will eventually obtain a survey of the contours of meaning in our language from the inside out. By virtue of gaining this survey, says Wittgenstein, we too will experience a kind of release.

What kind of release does Wittgenstein have in mind? Let us recall what he has argued for so far: The only communicable meaning we have in life is embodied in language-games; language-games reflect the core mythology of their form of life; this mythology embodies the basic contours of meaning for its form of life. Conclusion: to gain an overview of the contours of meaning in our common language is to see the common meaning of our form of life.

Accordingly, Wittgenstein's metaphor of the fly escaping from the fly-bottle does not apply merely to linguistic matters, as is commonly thought. Rather, his urgency in calling for a "survey" (*Übersicht*) of ordinary language, and in equating the attainment of this survey with a kind of release, reflects an ethical and spiritual concern on Wittgenstein's part.[7]

But there's a hitch: once we leave the bottle of language, we can no longer tell others what we have discovered outside its contours. To find out, they will have to go through the same process for themselves. It is for this reason, says Wittgenstein, that people who have found the meaning of life are never able to tell others what it is. Nonetheless, someone who has reached this level of synoptic vision can give others clues as to the right method. This method consists in patiently assembling reminders of the deep meaning found in ordinary language.

In view of the ethical and spiritual implications of Wittgenstein's metaphor of the fly-bottle, we can now appreciate the full meaning he packed into his most oft-quoted quip:

> What is your aim in philosophy?—To shew the fly the way out of the fly-bottle.[8]

Considered in the overall context of Wittgenstein's thought, this quip implies that philosophy aims at spiritual release and peace of mind, using an informed approach to language as a means of personal enlightenment. As noted in the last three chapters, this is a characteristic sentiment of Wittgenstein's, to which he remained faithful in both his earlier and later periods. The quip also hints at Wittgenstein's abiding sense of personal torment in doing philosophy, which he makes explicit elsewhere, as in the following remark:

> Thoughts that are at peace. That's what someone who philosophizes yearns for.[9]

A Great Myth

On Wittgenstein's account of language, formal logic and mathematics are not some kind of super-physics; that is, they do not *describe* some super-reality that lies behind the more tangible realities that the individual sciences investigate.

What, then, is the role of logicians and mathematicians? They exhibit what belongs to our common frame of reference in interpreting reality. They do not reveal reality in and of itself. Nonetheless, frames of reference, if they work, have a connection to reality.

What of the laws of logic and mathematics? They are parts of a great myth to which a form of life has committed itself in order for its participants to be able to communicate with each other. Such a myth is necessary, for if we try to combine words or other symbols contrary to these laws, we find that we cannot communicate. But not every form of life in the universe need be committed to the same myth.

Logical necessity? It is absolute, but only for a form of life whose agreement in judgments makes it so. Logical necessity is not "the basis of all reality," if, indeed, that phrase has any meaning at all. Nonetheless, logical necessity is not arbitrary. Only certain kinds of agreement enable mere strings of sounds to function as coherent descriptions of reality.

The meaning of life? There is no one great meaning for all, but rather certain common meanings that are relative to particular forms of life. Around these limited constellations of meaning and language there turns only a vast firmament of silence.

Logical Atomism Explodes

Wittgenstein's argument that logical necessity is rooted in an agreement in judgments is his rebuttal to his own earlier view of logic in *Tractatus*. Indeed, it is his rebuttal to every theory of logic that believes reasoning can be adequately represented by some truth-functional calculus.

To the early Wittgenstein, a proposition is atomic if it is a simple, positive assertion of a fact that cannot be further analyzed into more facts. On the foundation of atomic propositions, said Wittgenstein, rests the whole weight of the great pyramid of language.

Now if certain propositions are atomic, they must have another characteristic: the truth or falsity of any one of them must be independent of the truth or falsity of the others. Otherwise, one atomic proposition could be analyzed in terms of another, but that would mean the propositions are not atomic after all. Atomic propositions, then, have two interconnected characteristics: (1) they assert independent atomic facts; and (2) they are truth-functionally independent.

These characteristics imply something important about meaning: the meaning of any given atomic proposition has nothing to do with the truth-values of other atomic propositions. This must be so because atomic propositions are, by definition, truth-functionally independent, and because every proposition has some meaning. Logical atomism, therefore, rests on a crucial assumption:

> It makes sense to say of some group of propositions that they are individually meaningful, and at the same time that there is no connection between the meaning of any one of them and the truth-values of the others.

The early Wittgenstein recognized the great importance of the above assumption. His entire theory of "objects" and "facts" (discussed in chapter eight) was an argument about what the substance of the world had to be like in order for the above assumption to come out true. In his own words:

> Objects make up the substance of the world. That is why they cannot be composite. If the world had no substance, then whether a proposition had sense would depend on whether another proposition was true.[10]

The above three sentences capture the entire theory of logical atomism in a nutshell. They say that it is possible for certain basic propositions to have sense without regard to whether any other proposition is true or false. Therefore, the world must ultimately consist of separate, unconnected atomic facts. Each of these atomic facts (consisting of an arrangement of irreducible objects) grounds the sense of some atomic proposition. If this were not so, we would have to abandon the assumption that certain basic propositions can have sense without regard to the truth-values of other propositions. But this latter assumption no rational person would ever deny—or so Wittgenstein thought at the time.

Wittgenstein's later view, however, denies the very assumption that seemed unassailable to him in his earlier years. To the later Wittgenstein, just the opposite is true—the meaning of any proposition always partly depends on the truth-values of the other propositions with which it shares some context.

Wittgenstein arrived at this conclusion by way of his view that logical necessity is rooted in an agreement in judgments, combined with his notion of the contextual nature of language-games. This new view of the relation between meaning and truth-functionality not only rebuts logical atomism but also rings the death knell for the whole tradition of formal logic as it has been practiced since the time of Gottlob Frege.

The House That Holds Up Its Foundations

To understand why the root assumption of logical atomism cannot stand, says Wittgenstein, consider the role of the Knight in chess: it depends on the rules that define the possible moves of *all* the pieces, and on the purpose for which the game as a whole is played. The same contextual considerations apply to language-games. Individual propositions, their truth-values, and their truth-grounds all have particular roles precisely in virtue of belonging to the particular language-game that constitutes their common context.

Moreover, Wittgenstein argues, games are created and played by *people*. Therefore, every proposition has a meaning ultimately in virtue of a whole range of agreements in judgments on its players' parts. These players have agreed on a mythology that grounds their "logical necessity"; agreed on the parameters of meaning for different kinds of propositions; on the truth-grounds for particular propositions; and on the assignment of their truth-values. And even when the game-players disagree on any of these matters, they have other common games that they play in order to seek resolutions for their disagreements, to the extent that they are humanly resolvable.

Logical atomism simply ignores all of these contextual and human factors. It blithely assumes that logical necessity is some kind of universal law spelled out in the heavens above, and that individual propositions exist in a vacuum, independent of particular language-users and particular language-games.

Wittgenstein might have added this argument as well: logical atomism, because it posits insuperable barriers between individual atomic propositions, always verges on having its universe of discourse dissipate into a cloud of hermetically sealed monads. In order to avert this dispersal, Leibniz brought God down from heaven and plugged him into logic, just as the early Wittgenstein inflated his own ego up to the size of the universal metaphysical self. In fact, however, propositions are able to interconnect as they do not because of God or because of anyone's ego but because they have specific roles to play in particular language-games.

Wittgenstein concludes that the meaning of any given proposition cannot, in principle, be disjoined from the truth-values and truth-grounds of other propositions in the same game. To the contrary, an essential part of the meaning of any proposition is the full context of the language-game in which it occurs as a move.

A stunning corollary of this conclusion is that the paradigm so beloved of modern logicians—the truth-table—turns out to be a subterfuge. For example, logicians typically define the logical connective "or" in the compound proposition "p or q" by means of the following truth-table:

p	q	or
T	F	T
F	T	T
T	T	T
F	F	F

In making this truth-table definition of "or," logicians simply *assume* that they can ignore the meanings of any particular propositions that might be substituted for "p" and "q." (That is, they assume that "p" and "q" function like atomic propositions.) But suppose "p" = "This book is all red" and "q" = "This book is all green." In this case, the third row down in the above truth-table does not yield a "*T*," as expected; in fact, this row, with these particular values of "*p*" and "*q*," is *nonsensical*.

Despite their grandiose claims, logicians cannot apply truth-tables to any actual instance of human reasoning without first looking at the meanings of the propositions in question, to see if they fit. The same is true for *every* attempt at representing human reasoning by a purely formal, calculative system. But if logicians have to look first, they are cheating. The much-touted claim that a truth-functional logic can do justice to human reasoning is one of the great superstitions of Western philosophy.

Because the important thing in language is always the concrete language-game, even such grand considerations as logical necessity have their validity only because they support particular games. Without these games, these grand considerations would be useless. Hence language does not depend for its validity on allegedly deeper principles; in fact, nearly the opposite is true:

> And one might almost say that these foundations-walls are carried by the whole house.[11]

An irony in Wittgenstein's rebuttal of logical atomism is that it represents, unknowingly to Wittgenstein himself, a return to the thought of the English philosopher Francis Bradley. Propositional meaning, said Bradley, cannot be atomized, but is always dependent to some degree on greater contexts. Bertrand Russell, developing his own logic in conscious opposition to that of Bradley's, ridiculed this contextual notion of meaning as nonsense. Wittgenstein, reacting in turn against Russell, convincingly argued that it was Russell's atomistic view of meaning that was nonsense. But neither Wittgenstein nor his followers ever realized that Bradley had earlier developed his own critique of logical atomism, and one of much greater depth and power. Unfortunately, largely as a result of Russell's scorn, Anglo-American academic philosophers have relegated Bradley to the ash heap. In fact, however, Bradley is a most insightful philosopher.

Wittgenstein's *Philosophical Investigations*, published nearly a half-century ago, sounded the death knell for formal logic. Most logicians since then, however, have been like the proverbial unaware monkeys, clasping their hands to their ears and refusing to believe that philosophy must henceforth be played in a new key. But despite the logicians' denial, the embalmed body of formal logic continues to move ineluctably toward its interment. In the remaining section of this chapter, we will come to Wittgenstein's aid by giving formal logic a well-deserved final shove into its grave.

The Darkness of This Time

What is the proper role of the logician? In *Investigations*, Wittgenstein does not give much attention to this question. Several tangential remarks, however, suggest that he was still willing to concede to logicians an ambit of their own, provided it be reasonable. He implies that a problem arises only when logicians presume to set themselves up as umpires for ordinary language, which is in order just as it is.

In other remarks published subsequent to *Investigations*, Wittgenstein takes a stronger stand against formal logic. By the time he died in 1951, he had come to the conclusion that formal logic obfuscates the way language actually works and sidetracks mathematical understanding. In addition, he viewed it as contributing to the debasement of life that characterizes modern technological civilization.

If one reads *Investigations* hurriedly, he or she will likely miss the pessimistic view of technological civilization that lies just under the surface. As noted earlier, a clue is Wittgenstein's motto for the book, taken from Johann Nestroy: "Of course it's just like progress to seem much greater than it really is." Again, in the preface to *Investigations*, Wittgenstein expresses hope that the book's ideas will help illuminate those living in "the darkness of this time."[12]

Ideas to which Wittgenstein only gives clues in *Investigations* come into sharper focus in subsequently published works. In particular, the extent of his critique of formal logic and science becomes clear in several volumes published by his editors during the period from 1956 to 1977.

The Cancer of Formal Logic

In *Remarks on the Foundations of Mathematics*, published in 1956, Wittgenstein argues that the idea of looking for one sure foundation for mathematics, as Frege and Russell did, is ill conceived. Mathematics is not some big contraption, like an old biplane on display at the Smithsonian, which just hangs from the ceiling without any real connection to the way we actually live. To the contrary, mathematics consists of all sorts of different kinds of games rooted in our form of life. What these various games have in common is not one idealized foundation in pure logic but rather the special ways that they discharge functions that are both practical and grammatical.

Mathematical games are practical, in that they provide us with various "forms of description" (*Darstellungsformen*) of the world; that is, they provide the root-concepts by means of which we measure, and structurally conceive of, physical objects, space, and time. But in addition, mathematical games are also grammatical, in that they trace out what it makes sense for us to say in our language; that is, if we deny a true mathematical proposition, the price we pay is that we can longer communicate with each other.

Mathematicians, accordingly, are creators, not mere discoverers. When they establish a new mathematical proof, what they do is create a new root-concept of the way we map out physical reality. They show that holding this new root-concept is connected to the capacity of our entire language to be meaningful. The meaning of the new concept is not restricted to the concept alone but lies in its proof, which is the way the concept has become an outgrowth of our whole language. The meaning of our whole language, in turn, is extended by our proving the new concept.

Mathematicians are in the business of mapmaking. But mathematicians' maps differ from all other maps because they are maps of last resort, in the sense that if we reject these maps, we lose the capacity to communicate conceptually. Hence Wittgenstein's famous remark:

The mathematician creates *essence*.[13]

As noted above, the later Wittgenstein does not reject the concept of essence, as many of his followers have wrongly believed. Rather, he relocates essence in "grammar," by which he means the basic set of rules in our language that prescribe how types of words may be combined. The mathematician, accordingly, is the grammarian par excellence. In creating new proofs, the mathematician affects the scope and nature of the rules by virtue of which we are able to communicate through concepts.

Essence, the special province of mathematicians, is created, relative, and conceptual, and lies in our language; it does not lie in reality in and of itself, whatever that may be. Nonetheless, essence is not arbitrary, because divergence from essence means abandonment of our capacity for conceptual communication.

Mathematical certainty comes to this: today we in this form of life are required to speak of reality in such-and-such terms if we want our words and symbols to be meaningful. However, these terms could change tomorrow, and other forms of life might have entirely different terms. The God of mathematics is orderly, but he is not a fundamentalist.

Wittgenstein argues that formal logic—or "mathematical logic" as it is often called now—is largely irrelevant to the way mathematics actually functions in our life. At best, formal logic can serve as an ancillary technique for highlighting certain special mathematical applications. At worst, it sidetracks mathematicians by goading them into pursuing a false ideal, and then demoralizes them when they cannot attain it.

Breaking with the dominant Western philosophical tradition since 1910, when Russell and Whitehead published the first volume of *Principia Mathematica*, Wittgenstein delivers this stern rebuke:

> "Mathematical logic" has completely deformed the thinking of mathematicians and of philosophers, by setting up a superficial interpretation of the forms of our everyday language as an analysis of the structures of facts. Of course in this it has only continued to build on the Aristotelian logic.[14]

Wittgenstein notes that Russell invented modern logical technique in *Principia* as part of his effort to resolve the contradiction that he had found in Frege's *Basic Laws*. This contradiction, in turn, was the direct outgrowth of Frege's attempt to algebracize logic. Wittgenstein castigates the whole algebracizing approach to logic as—

> a cancerous growth, seeming to have grown out of the normal body [of language] aimlessly and senselessly.[15]

As to the contradiction that Russell discovered, Wittgenstein basically says, So what? Just because some abstract contradiction has been discovered somewhere doesn't mean a practical problem exists. The germane question is always whether a contradiction will impede the practical application of some calculus. In fact, the contradiction discovered by Russell has never done so. The contradiction is only disturbing to those who believe that thinking can be reduced to calculating, but this belief is itself the grand fallacy that underlies all formal logic. On the basis of this false belief, logicians (including the author of *Tractatus*) have sidetracked entire generations of Western mathematicians and philosophers.

In order to re-acquaint ourselves with the proper aims of both mathematics and philosophy, says Wittgenstein, we need to puncture the inflated pretensions of the logicians. The way to do that is to consider the full ramifications of the fact that "logical inference is part of a language-game."[16] This fact implies that there can be a variety of different kinds of logic, corresponding to the different kinds of games that are being played. Moreover, the question of what kind of logic is appropriate to which circumstances can never be decided mechanically. This decision requires an assessment of the details of the game in question, including details about the habits of the form of life that is playing the game. Therefore, there can be no such thing as one grand logical map by means of which humans might navigate themselves over every sort of conceptual terrain. There is no substitute for thinking, not even formal logic.

The Axis of Language

Wittgenstein argues that not only did Frege and Russell misunderstand the nature of mathematics, they also misunderstood the nature of certainty. In *On Certainty*, published in 1969, he stresses that the grounds of certainty in language do not lie in anything as superficial as some logical calculus; rather, certainty is "something animal."[17] We gradually *learn* what is certain for us by virtue of being initiated while young into some community that consists of other living organisms. As part of our community initiation, a system of commonly accepted judgments, reflecting our community's deepest life-struggles, gradually dawns in our consciousness—and always as an emergent *whole*, never as individual, abstract propositions dangling in a vacuum.

Only in the context of this whole system of commonly learned judgments does it makes sense to say that some given proposition can be doubted, for doubt is inconceivable without the acceptance of some standards by which to doubt. Moreover, we cannot be said to "know" the core propositions that render possible the doubting of other propositions, because knowledge is variable, depending on good evidence and sound reasoning. Core propositions, however, stand fast, no matter what. We do not "know" them; we simply adhere to them.

In one of his most striking metaphors, Wittgenstein compares language to a massive rotating body. The propositions that stand firm for us are like its axis:

> This axis is not fixed in the sense that anything holds it fast, but the movement around it determines its immobility.[18]

The axis of certainty within our language is defined by the movements of our whole language, which itself rotates by virtue of the energy transmitted to it by the galaxy of the form of life in which it is embedded. From the axis of language, and not from any surface structure built by the logicians, come all standards of certainty. These axial standards are final because there is no deeper foundation to which we might dig; but they are also relative, because the impulse from a significant shift in the way we live can transmit itself inward to the core of our language. As with the earth itself, the axis of every language wobbles; but for all that, it doesn't cease to be an axis.

Frege and Russell, in their quest to free logic from "psychologism," concocted a Rube-Goldberg calculus that was a parody of the way humans actually communicate. Their misguided effort, triggered by their misunderstandings of mathematics and certainty, has led all subsequent philosophy down the blind alley called formal logic.

The Disaster of Science

Frege and Russell simply took it for granted that Western science was a great boon for humanity. Russell in particular disparaged 19th-century German idealist philosophy as a thinly veiled rationalization for monotheistic religiosity. He resolved that henceforth philosophy would have a new duty: polishing the logical tools that scientists needed in order to make their dissections.

Wittgenstein, by contrast, eventually concluded that science was a disaster for humanity. Many of his academic admirers, dazzled by the mystique of science, have passed over this element in their master's thought in embarrassed silence; nonetheless, it represents the logical culmination of Wittgenstein's entire later way of thinking. Indeed, it provides the best grounds for remembering him as a worthy philosopher.

The collection of Wittgenstein's remarks entitled *Culture and Value*, translated into English in 1980, reveals that his hostility toward science grew over decades, beginning with his return to Cambridge in 1929. For example, in 1930 he wrote:

> Man has to awaken to wonder—and so perhaps do peoples. Science is a way of sending him to sleep again.[19]

By the end of his life, he had become bitter about the matter. In 1946, reflecting on the development of the atomic bomb, he complained that the anti-nuclear intellectuals (particularly Russell) were "philistines" and "the *scum* of the intellectuals." They failed to see, said Wittgenstein, that the bomb was a "bitter medicine" that might lead people to question the idolization of science that had made the bomb possible:

> All I can mean is that the bomb offers a prospect of the end, the destruction of an evil,—our disgusting soapy water science. And certainly that's not an unpleasant thought.[20]

This view contrasts with Wittgenstein's earlier remarks on *The Golden Bough*, written in the 1920s. As noted above, Wittgenstein originally distinguished modern science from tribal magic on the grounds that there is "progress" in science but not in magic. In fact, however, belief in the inherently progressive nature of science is inconsistent with an implicit notion in the later-written *Investigations*: the question of whether *any* human activity is progressive is always relative and contextual, depending on the full social context in which the activity occurs. In 1947, Wittgenstein drew out the full implications of this contextualist view as it pertains science. In the process, he revealed why he had begun *Investigations* with Nestroy's sardonic remark about progress:

> It isn't absurd...to believe that the age of science and technology is the beginning of the end for humanity; that the idea of great progress is a delusion...; that there is nothing good or desirable about scientific knowledge and that mankind, in seeking it, is falling into a trap. It is by no means obvious that this is not how things are.[21]

Wittgenstein was shaken by the course of totalitarianism in the 1930s, despite his own earlier fascination with the protofascism of Otto Weininger and with Bolshevism. He eventually concluded that fascism and socialism in the 20s and 30s, like the atomic bomb in the 40s, were symptomatic of a grotesque new kind of civilization that would have been impossible without science. As early as 1930 he wrote:

> The spirit of this civilization makes itself manifest in the industry, architecture and music of our time, in its fascism and socialism ... I have no sympathy for the current [*dem Strom*] of European civilization.[22]

In 1947, continuing the same line of thought, Wittgenstein revealed that much of his later work was intended as a warning to scientists and mathematicians concerning the narrow linguistic presuppositions and the disastrous social consequences of their methods. With despair, he compared his warnings to the widely ignored notices posted by the British government during World War II:

> My reflections are like the notices on the ticket offices at English railway stations, "Is your journey really necessary?" As though someone who read this would think "On second thought *no.*"[23]

Idolatry Exposed

In light of Wittgenstein's criticism of formal logic and science in his later-published writings, *Philosophical Investigations* itself comes into focus as more than a technical treatise on the nature of language. Contrary to the narrow view held by many of its academic commentators, the book is also an exercise in civilization-critique. Its larger aim, as suggested by the sardonic motto quoted from Nestroy that begins the book, the illusion that Western scientific civilization represents progress.

Investigations undertakes this larger aim by attacking the concept of language implicitly assumed by advocates of the superiority of Western modernity. Acting on the basis of their misunderstanding of language, these advocates (especially Russell) have put forward the following arguments: formal logic is the highest exemplar of rational thinking; formal logic can account for the certainty of mathematics, which is the exemplar of certainty for all science; science is the window of choice in viewing the nature of reality; and science has been a great boon to humanity. Since modern Western civilization is unique in having created formal logic, advanced mathematics, and science, it follows that the development of modern Western civilization has meant substantial progress for humanity.

All these arguments, *Investigations* implies, are spurious. They all stem from a misconception concerning how language actually works. Contrary to the advocates of Western superiority, language does not involve some uniform, ethereal essence unconnected to the particular mores of the people who use it. Instead, language is always a matter of concrete language-games, which are designed for a wide variety of particular human purposes. Moreover, thinking is not some kind of disembodied halo hanging around words, or a transcendent abstraction. Thinking *is* the various uses of signs in these different language-games.

Wittgenstein's writings published after *Investigations* further develop these implications. Formal logic now appears as a parody, not an exemplar, of human thinking, for it ignores the variety and contextuality of human sign-usage. In addition, formal logic obfuscates the nature of mathematics and sidetracks working mathematicians. Finally, reality is not one big absolute objectivity, viewable independent of the particularity of language. To the contrary, language in part creates reality. As a result, reality comes in all the colors contained by the whole spectrum of possible language-games. Science, occupying one band on this wide spectrum, takes itself for the whole.

Wittgenstein also makes a historical pitch: the actual record of science shows that it has been the source of infinite misery and the creator of a barbaric culture. Science is in fact a great idol that devours the spiritual life of the people who worship it. Humanity needs to change the way it lives in order to throw off the despotism of the priests who serve this idol. Alas, however, such a change is improbable. Science will likely prevail, creating in the process a unified, debased world-culture driven by war:

> Perhaps science and industry, having caused infinite misery in the process, will unite the world—I mean condense it into a *single* unit, though one in which peace is the last thing that will feel at home.[24]

In Wittgenstein's spiritual condemnation of science in the 1940s one can hear a presage of Allen Ginsberg's political lamentations in the 1960s. The god of the military-industrial-scientific complex, howled Ginsberg, is like Moloch in ancient Canaan, eating its own followers' young. The great difference between Wittgenstein and Ginsberg is that Wittgenstein never imagined that by celebrating his own sexuality he might deepen his critique of modernity. For that deeper insight, we have to wait for the rise of the Beat poets in the 1950s, the countercultural prophets in the 1960s, and the movements for liberation by women and gay people in the 1970s. Nonetheless, the publication of *Investigations* in 1953 was a little foreshock of the earthquake to come. Unfortunately for visionaries then and since, Moloch has survived. But then so, too, has the vision that sees through Moloch, although not among academic philosophers. One will find that vision living still, however, in these pages.

All Things Are Full of Gods

As discussed in chapter eight, Wittgenstein in his earlier period was committed to an otherworldly, monotheistic spirituality. This spirituality viewed the world merely as a collection of flat facts. Far above the world, utterly transcending it, is "God," conceived as the single, unspeakable fount of both ethical obligation and logical necessity. Situated above all that is plural and describable, God beckons to humans to shed their entanglement in the sensuous plurality of the world below, and raise their eyes to the pure mystical vision emanating from the One above. By ascending to the One, humans not only affirm their higher selves but also gain an understanding of the meaning of life. This understanding cannot be put into words, but consists in beholding the innumerable facts called "the world" as a single, limited totality, dependent for its existence and order on a single higher being. Wittgenstein sums up this entire spiritual perspective in a single sentence near the end of *Tractatus*:

> God does not reveal himself *in* the world.[25]

When Wittgenstein abandoned the ideal of a crystalline logical machine in the sky and undertook to describe language in its mundane particularity, he began developing a new spirituality. This linguistic shift was spiritual for him because it undermined the notion that the divine is absent from the world. To the contrary, Wittgenstein now found himself in agreement with a sentiment expressed by Longfellow:

> In the elder days of art,
> Builders wrought with greatest care
> Each minute and unseen part,
> For the gods are everywhere.
> (This could serve me as a motto).[26]

Just as "God does not reveal himself in the world" encapsulates the earlier Wittgenstein, so "the gods are everywhere" encapsulates the later Wittgenstein. In making this shift, Wittgenstein turned his back on the old monotheistic bias that the world's particulars lack reality because they are particular, observable, and plural. Instead, Wittgenstein returned to the earlier pagan viewpoint that the concrete plurality of the world is real and divine in its own right. Indeed, Longfellow's poem alludes to a remark made by Thales of Miletus, the West's first notable philosopher:

> All things are full of gods.[27]

A Common Thread

Despite Wittgenstein's spiritual shift, a common thread nevertheless runs from *Tractatus* to *Investigations*: the notion that the scientific mentality trivializes what is best in human experience, and that the last protection against this trivialization is the realm of the unspeakable. In *Tractatus*, Wittgenstein accepted the claim of science to be the final arbiter of facts. To save what is best in human experience, he elevated the realm of meaning above the realm of fact, accessible only to mystical insight.

In *Investigations* and other writings, Wittgenstein challenges science's claim to be the final arbiter of fact. There are now many different kinds of facts, depending on the particular language-game being played. Some, but not all, facts are well suited to the judgments of science. In addition, a realm of the unspeakable remains, but it is no longer transcendent. Rather, this realm appears in the concrete, social *Praxis* that is the foundation of all logic and language:

> Am I not getting closer and closer to saying that in the end logic cannot be described? You must look at the practice of language [*die Praxis der Sprache*], then you will see it.[28]

Investigations is *Tractatus* turned inside-out. A transcendent, monotheistic concept of meaning gives way to one that is immanent and polytheistic. The grand pretensions of logic, mathematics, and science shrink to one band on the spectrum of human experience. But just as a glove that is turned inside-out has the same surface material as before, so there is a material continuity in Wittgenstein's conceptual turnings: the ultimate sources of meaning cannot be captured in language. Although he relocated the source of the mystery, Wittgenstein never ceased being a mystic.

Bewitched by Language

Wittgenstein's spirituality, both in its earlier and later forms, had a quietist tenor: faced with the turmoils of living, one must learn to accept his or her limited place in the cosmos through contemplation of the given order of things. For the earlier Wittgenstein, this contemplation meant seeing the world as a limited whole, dependent for its existence on the transcendent One that is the fount of ethics and logic. For the later Wittgenstein, this contemplation consisted in gaining a survey (*Übersicht*) of the various meanings expressed in one's language. In both the earlier and later views, the goal remains the same: peace of mind, achieved through contemplating the larger picture of things. If a person continues to experience personal turmoil in life, then he or she has not yet conformed to the larger pattern:

> The fact that life is problematic shows that the shape of your life does not fit into life's mould. So you must change the way you live and, once your life does fit into the

mould, what is problematic will disappear.[29]

The quietist tenor of Wittgenstein's spirituality affected his concept of the proper role of the philosopher. Contrary to the activist bent of Russell, who was always challenging everything, from God to ordinary language, Wittgenstein believed that philosophy should aim at a kind of intellectual resignation. This belief underlies his notion that philosophical problems are really pseudo-problems that arise from being bewitched by language. The way to break language's spell is calmly and patiently to trace words back to the concrete language-games whence they have first arisen. By assembling reminders of how we actually use our words, we gain a survey of the grammar of our ordinary language, and so realize that there really is no problem after all. It's not that we find the answers; rather, the questions themselves dissolve. And then we find peace of mind.

Are You a Good Witch Or a Bad Witch?

Wittgenstein's urgent call to resist the bewitchment of language is reminiscent of a similar call in Frege. As discussed in chapter five, Frege viewed that which is universally formalizable in language as divine, and all else as devilish. Wittgenstein, while preserving Frege's distinction between the divine and devilish aspects of language, characterizes each just the opposite. For Wittgenstein, it is precisely the particular, concrete usage in actual language-games that reveals "grammar" or "essence." The universally formalizable, on the other hand, is a deceiving wraith, leading philosophers down endless blind alleys. Frege was right, says Wittgenstein, to warn against the bewitchment of language. But he confused the angels with the devils!

Wittgenstein's view that all philosophical problems result from the misuse of language has a certain merit: it challenges philosophers to be on guard about the meanings of words that they import into philosophy from ordinary language, and also about using facile linguistic analogies. For example, the statement "The Absolute manifests itself in time" is *not* analogous to the statement "Assunta arrived home from the baths at 3:00 a.m." Although both statements use noun, verb, and adverbial phrase, it's questionable whether one can even speak of "the Absolute" as one speaks of an ordinary person or thing. Such careless sliding back and forth between language-games of different types only muddies the philosophical waters.

But Wittgenstein was wrong to insist that the misuse of language is the *only* source of philosophical problems. Many problems have arisen because of genuine human puzzlement about the nature of reality, not merely because of confusion about the usages of words. If all philosophical problems arose from the misuse of existing words, Plato would not have needed to invent the word "quality" (*poiotes*). The problem in this case was that the existing language was inadequate.

Contrary to Wittgenstein, the unsettling problems of philosophy will not just dissolve, if only we could gain a complete survey of our ordinary language. The problems are real, and there are no easy solutions. Life itself, apart from any consideration of language, will always challenge human thinking. Peace of mind is for the dead.

I Have a World-Picture

Wittgenstein's claim to use a purely descriptive method in philosophy has impressed many of his commentators and followers, who have taken his claim at face value. In their eyes, Wittgenstein succeeded in freeing himself from the taint of metaphysics. For example, P.M.S. Hacker, one of Wittgenstein's most influential commentators, says this:

> Wittgenstein's philosophical techniques do not rest on a *theory* of anything. ... Any suggestion that Wittgenstein's philosophical clarifications have metaphysical consequences is a sure sign that they have been misconstrued.[30]

Ironically, Hacker makes this claim while explaining how Wittgenstein's concept of linguistic survey leads to the view that philosophy should be free of theory. But to say that philosophy should be free of theory is itself a theory!

Wittgenstein's so-called descriptive philosophical method is actually embedded in a mass of metaphysical presuppositions. Wittgenstein himself consciously constructed these in order to rebut his own earlier metaphysical presuppositions in *Tractatus*. Moreover, a crucial tenet of Wittgenstein's later philosophy is that *everyone* (the philosopher included) makes a commitment to some substantive world-view by the very fact of using some language. This commitment is the thing that makes certainty possible, says Wittgenstein, because certainty can occur only within the context of an assumed world-view:

> Doubt comes *after* belief. ... I have a world-picture. [*Ich habe ein Weltbild.*][31]

Enter the Ordinary Philosophers

The later Wittgenstein contributed to the rise in the 1950s of a new philosophical movement called "ordinary language philosophy," just as the earlier Wittgenstein had contributed to the rise of logical positivism in the 1920s. As noted in chapter eight, the logical positivists had in fact misunderstood the early Wittgenstein, embracing certain surface features of his system while overlooking deeper presuppositions that were hostile to their own agenda. Thirty years later, the ordinary language philosophers repeated the same sort of mistake with the later Wittgenstein.

The turning point came when philosophers realized that Russell had failed in his effort to deduce arithmetic from logic. This failure opened the door for the later Wittgenstein, who argued that formal logic is a caricature of language. Rather than waste more time speculating about logic, Wittgenstein insisted, let's look at the ordinary language right under our noses.

This call influenced a number of other philosophers at Cambridge and later at Oxford especially. Disenchanted, like Wittgenstein, with the vaunted claims of logic, these philosophers turned their attention to what they, too, called "ordinary language." In the ensuing decades, these philosophers found imitators in the philosophy departments of many other Anglo-American universities.

The new ordinary-language philosophers heralded Wittgenstein as one of their own. On the surface there were certain parallels. For example, all had a critical attitude toward formal logic and a new respect for the workings of ordinary language. In addition, they shared an awareness that language never occurs in a vacuum but always in some concrete social situation involving human activity. So where Wittgenstein spoke of "language-games," John Austin of Oxford spoke of "speech-acts." Finally, they were all convinced that the best road to philosophical clarity lay through the field of detailed, linguistic description.

Despite these parallels, however, a gulf separated Wittgenstein from the rest. Wittgenstein's views on language were the result of an underlying spiritual vision about human life and culture. Because of this vision, Wittgenstein scorned the high regard for science as a modern form of idolatry. Again, the purpose of surveying language was for him the attainment of peace of mind; he wasn't out to create a new kind of science.

The other ordinary language philosophers had no detectable spiritual vision at all. To the contrary, they typically took pains to appear spiritually vacuous. For example, John Austin argued that the task of philosophy is to pick up the crumbs that the sciences let fall from their plates:

> I believe that the only clear way of defining the subject matter of philosophy is to say that it deals with what's left over, all the problems that remain still insoluble, after all the other recognized methods have been tried. It's the dumping ground for all the leftovers from other sciences, where everything turns up which we don't know quite how to take.[32]

After Wittgenstein's death, ordinary language philosophy ossified into just another academic fad. Bored graduate students mined it for doctoral dissertations as part of their work-out on the academic treadmill. This ossifying process was furthered by the personality cult that had formed around Wittgenstein, fostered by his literary executors. The truncated version of Wittgenstein's thought that they promoted lacked both substance and style.[33]

Another factor promoted the banality of ordinary language philosophy: the movement to professionalize philosophy. Anglo-American academic philosophers increasingly came to view themselves as professional specialists, on the model of specialists in the natural sciences. Their particular specialty was to be the conceptual clarification of language. Studying philosophy would mean mastering an inventory of testable skills for dealing with linguistic analysis, much as a podiatrist might learn how to cut corns.

Chapter Ten

Disappearance of the Interpreter

Today the question of what constitutes good philosophy in academia is decided by peer-group review, similar to the way in which medical procedures are evaluated. Just as the private spiritual visions, if any, of a surgeon are irrelevant to his or her medical performance in the operating room, so such things are now deemed irrelevant to the performance of a philosopher in the classroom.

The new academic philosophers believe that by freeing philosophy from the stain of subjectivity they have at long last freed philosophy from metaphysics, which arises from the intrusion of subjectivity into philosophy. To their relief, they no longer have to bear the humiliating reproach once hurled by scientists, that philosophy is just bad poetry.

Wittgenstein's philosophy contributed to this depersonalization. In both his earlier and later periods, he effectively cut the interpreter out of language. In the earlier period, what remained as the root of language was something unspeakable, shelved away in the mysteries of logical form above; in his later period, the root of language was also something unspeakable, but now located in the grammar of ordinary language below, and in the collective form of life that creates ordinary language. In both periods, when it comes to giving an actual account of how language manages to be meaningful, the interpreter simply falls out of the picture. The workings of language are like the physiognomy of the body; they constitute a public affair that is objectively accessible through learned techniques of either analysis (Wittgenstein's earlier period) or description (his later period).

The irony of Wittgenstein's depersonalized legacy is that it resulted from a struggle within himself to attain a personally-redeeming spiritual vision of human life and culture. His later imitators, lacking any spiritual depth of their own and ignorant of Wittgenstein's inner struggles, seized on the purely surface features of his thought. These they used as tools in their own quest to professionalize philosophy. To the detriment of both philosophy in general and the understanding of Wittgenstein in particular, they have succeeded.

Moses at the Jordan

Much of Western philosophy before Wittgenstein simply assumed that minds encounter reality directly, on the analogy of an eye beholding an object placed immediately in front of it in the clear light of day. Philosophers differed on what the objects were that minds encountered. Plato, for example, said they were "Forms"; Bertrand Russell, "sense-data." But whether "Forms" or "sense-data" or something else, these objects were generally assumed to be immediately accessible to minds, which used them, as directly presented, to gain a view of the world.

The later Wittgenstein said that this traditional picture was incomplete. The mind never has an experience that can be spoken of, he insisted, unless that experience passes through the medium of language, and this medium is not a nothing. Language is like a lens, which always has a curvature, color, and density all its own, inevitably modifying everything that passes through it.

Like a lens, language is a human artifact; therefore, language embodies what is conventional and transient. But even so, language is not an arbitrary or capricious artifact; it is adapted to the natural necessities of the culture that creates it. As a result, reality, insofar as it is communicable, cannot be cleaved utterly into a conventional half and a natural half. Any reality we can talk about is always a mix, in part created by our culture, and in part reflective of something natural beyond that. Within this mix, we can separate out the conventional and the natural halves only up to a certain point; beyond that, the separating process itself dissolves, and we are confronted by the unspeakable.

Wittgenstein also realized that formal logic is a myth-system. As previous chapters have shown, Western philosophy has assumed that there exists some sort of divinely-originated order that establishes what is logically conceivable, physically possible, and linguistically expressible. Logicians, appealing to various guises of this alleged transcendent order, have concocted various logical calculuses, claiming that these exemplify the highest standards by which to judge human thinking. In a significant twist to this tradition Frege replaced "God" with "language" (appropriately formalized) as the ultimate guarantor and source of logic. Russell, following Frege, appealed to "completely general facts." But even so, they remained committed to the dogma of one logic for all, supported by the ancillary dogmas of logical necessity, bivalence, and absolute objectivity.

In his earlier period, Wittgenstein reaffirmed the older concept of logic. Indeed more: he was a revanchist for idealist philosophy. Scandalized by the efforts of Russell (an avowed atheist!) to secularize philosophy, the earlier Wittgenstein sought to re-ground logic with a language-transcending mysticism. The ultimate fount of logical necessity, bivalence, and objectivity, insisted *Tractatus*, is nothing human, but rather an unspeakable, divine transcendence. Like Neptune's caerulean deep, this transcendence both nourishes and limits the little island of human language that it encompasses.

In his later period, Wittgenstein realized that *Tractatus*, like the entire logical tradition of which it was the culmination, was a work of myth. Insofar as human thinking can be communicated, he now argued, it consists in the practical use of signs in concrete social situations. The various instances of such action-embedded sign-use he called "language-games." Since there are a great many language-games, there are also a great many ways in which human thinking can occur. Hence it remains improbable that there would be one standard of right thinking for each and every case. When we actually look at the specific ways in which humans use language, insisted Wittgenstein, we find a great variety of different standards of right usage at work. These depend on the particular purposes involved in each language-game.

The notion of one great-logic-in-the-sky for all language-use is illusory. Even worse, it confuses us when we try to gain a survey of how language actually does its job. Logicians are tunnel-vision reductionists who try to force all human language into one tightly-packed paradigm; their influence has impaired our ability to appreciate the variegated richness of human communication. They are enemies of language.

In making these criticisms, Wittgenstein brings to mind the ancient Chinese philosopher Chuang Tzu. He summed up Chinese philosophy's traditional disdain for logicians with these words:

> They are able to subdue other people's mouths, but cannot win their hearts. This is where their narrowness lies.[34]

Wittgenstein's accomplishment lay in bringing language and logic down from the heavens, relocating them in the context of human culture. His failure was that he could not embrace the individual interpreter as well. Contrary to his own strictures against essentialism, he insisted that there was an essence after all for language as a whole. He located this essence in the contours of a language's grammar, which he maintained can only be a social, never an individual, construct. In clinging to this dogma, he mirrored Aristotle's fatal mistake, likewise derived from an analysis of grammar, that all knowledge is of the immanent group-form, and that the individual as such is unknowable. As a result, Wittgenstein closed the door on exploring how privately-spun threads of the individual might contribute to the weave of language.

In both his accomplishments and failures, Wittgenstein was like Moses. He took the lead in bringing the Anglo-American philosophical community out of the intellectual wilderness of formal logic in which it had been wandering for decades. But he himself never crossed the Jordan into the land of a fully interpreter-based philosophy. Nonetheless, he led the way up to a certain point. During the great countercultural awakening of the 1960s, the best minds of the age (most of them poets) outflew both Wittgenstein in particular and academic philosophy in general; nonetheless, Wittgenstein was a presage of what was to come.

Wittgenstein was a mediocre, but influential, philosopher. His earlier philosophy was mostly a revanchist, mystical rehash of Leibniz (via Russell) and Weininger. Its historical importance lies in the fact that it was the last significant incarnation of the Parmenidean myth. His later philosophy was important because it exposed the Western logical tradition as a myth, and because it stressed the importance of social context and language to the philosophy of mind. Even so, however, the view of language as a social construct was hardly novel, having long been advocated by linguists and anthropologists. An example is the Swiss linguist Ferdinand de Saussure (1857-1913). Long before Wittgenstein developed his later views, Saussure had argued that language is a socially structured whole, and that its parts have meanings only by virtue of their roles in that whole. Saussure even used the analogy of chess. Only academic philosophers were taken by surprise by this contextual view of language.

Another weakness in the later Wittgenstein was his inability to develop a coherent, overall statement of his views. After his death, this weakness was augmented by his literary executors, who attempted to conceal the facts of his life. His slavish academic followers, misunderstanding the master, turned their own garbled and pedestrian accounts of his views into an established academic orthodoxy.

As an added injury, the Wittgenstein cult encouraged an entire generation of philosophy students to dismiss the greatest English-writing philosopher of the 20th century, Bertrand Russell. Although still widely read among the general public, Russell's writings have found an ever-shrinking audience among academic philosophers themselves. The reason is that Russell sharply criticized both Wittgenstein himself and the Wittgenstein cult. Despite this neglect by academics, Russell's work far surpasses that of Wittgenstein's both in its breadth of vision and in its capacity for sustained and engaging philosophical argument. Russell certainly had his faults, as discussed in chapter six, but for all that, no other Western philosopher of this century comes near his level, unless it be his collaborator on *Principia Mathematica*, Alfred North Whitehead. Even from the perspective of the Wittgenstein cult, it must redound to Russell's credit that much of Wittgenstein's own work, both earlier and later, was an attempt to refute Russell. The shadow of the teacher whom he both admired and resented falls on every page of Wittgenstein's work.

Wittgenstein's critical attitude toward formal logic and science offended many subsequent Anglo-American academic philosophers. Although praising the later Wittgenstein for emphasizing the social and behavioral nature of language, they have generally passed over in embarrassed silence his view of formal logic as an intellectual cancer, and science as a spiritual decimator. But as this chapter has shown, these critical views are not to be dismissed as tangential offshoots of Wittgenstein's thought. To the contrary, they represent the logical flowering of his most deeply rooted metaphysical assumptions and ethical values. The darkly critical perspective adumbrated in *Investigations*, and presented in sharp relief in his later-published writings, is that of a soul that was alien to the modern scientific world.

Despite the monkeys-who-won't-see attitude of many Anglo-American philosophers, Wittgenstein's final views on logic and science deserve to have a full hearing in the court of philosophy: first, because they stem from the deepest level of his thought, and are essential to understanding him as a philosopher; and second, because in coming to these views he discovered something important for all philosophy.

As past chapters of this book have shown, Western formal logic is indeed a myth-system. Originally stemming from ancient patriarchal religious beliefs, this myth-system wended its way in various guises from classical Greece through medieval Christian Europe to contemporary patriarchal-industrial civilization. Throughout the course of its long historical transmission, its greatest devotees have typically been men who have been inept at non-calculative modes of human interpretation and interaction.

Although useful in certain contexts, this myth-system has often been used as an intellectual bludgeon, beating down the world-views of those who value holistic, non-calculative ways of interpreting reality. Such has been its role in discounting the visions and experiences of women, children, poets, mystics, and sexual adepts within the West; it has also been used to denigrate the world-views of so-called "primitive" societies outside the West. And as the case of Otto Weininger demonstrates, certain presuppositions of this myth-system need be exaggerated only a little in order to produce an ideology congenial to fascism.

The chief implication of Wittgenstein's entire later philosophy is this: humanity needs to expand its consciousness beyond the logico-scientific mentality, and to develop different ways of living that are less dependent on scientific technique. This conclusion is the crowning achievement of his life and philosophy. He came to it despite his own professional training as an engineer, despite his apprenticeship to Russell, despite the flattery of the logical positivists, and despite the entrenched contrary values of the entire academic world in which he lived. A rising-up against formal logic and science in the name of language—that is the heart of Ludwig Wittgenstein, and the best reason for future generations to remember him as a worthy philosopher.

Unfortunately, later logicians have largely ignored Wittgenstein's most provocative criticisms of their craft; nonetheless, some have become uncomfortably aware on their own of a certain mythological sponginess in logic. Among these is a contemporary American logician who in his younger days highlighted the conventionality of logic; in his later years, however, he reverted to an embattled dogmatism in order to shore up logic's foundations. Since many regard this logician as the greatest American philosopher of his age, we will turn to his views in the next chapter.

---

[1] Ludwig Wittgenstein, *Philosophical Investigations*, ed. by G.E.M. Anscombe and R. Rhees; trans. by G.E.M. Anscombe; The Macmillan Company, New York, 1953, p. 18. Anscombe renders *sublimieren* as "sublime," which is a bit off the mark, for the reasons discussed above.
[2] *ibid.*, p. 46.
[3] Ludwig Wittgenstein, *Remarks on the Foundations of Mathematics*, ed. by G.H. von Wright, R. Rhees, & G.E.M. Anscombe; trans. by G.E.M. Anscombe, The Macmillan Company, New York, 1956, p. 36.
[4] Ludwig Wittgenstein, *Culture and Value*, ed. by G.H. von Wright and Heikki Nyman, trans. by Peter Winch, Basil Blackwell, Oxford, 1977 & 1980, p. 73; original's emphasis.
[5] Derek Jarman, *Wittgenstein* (movie), Zeitgeist Films, Britain, 1993; Terry Eagleton, *Wittgenstein: the Terry Eagleton Script, the Derek Jarman Film*, The Trinity Press, Worcester, England, 1993, p. 142. In my opinion, Jarman's film is the single best commentary available on the life and thought of Wittgenstein.
[6] Wittgenstein, *Investigations*, p. 88.
[7] Wittgenstein's fly-bottle metaphor brings to mind Plato's metaphor of the cave. The difference is that Wittgenstein stresses the role of language in transcending the shadows of the world.
[8] *ibid.*, p. 103.
[9] Wittgenstein, *Culture and Value*, p. 43.
[10] Ludwig Wittgenstein, *Tractatus Logico-Philosophicus*, translated by D.F. Pears & .F. McGuinness, Routledge & Kegan Paul, London, 2nd impression, 1963, 2.021-2.0211.
[11] Ludwig Wittgenstein, *On Certainty*, ed. by G.E.M. Anscombe and G.H. von Wright, trans. by Dennis Paul and G.E.M. Anscombe, Harper Torchbooks, New York, 1969, p. 33.
[12] Wittgenstein, *Investigations*, pp. viii & x; Johann Nestroy, *Der Schützling*, IV, 10.
[13] Wittgenstein, *Remarks on the Foundations of Mathematics*, p. 13; original's emphasis.
[14] *ibid.*, p. 156.
[15] *ibid.*, p. 166.
[16] *ibid.*, p. 179.
[17] Ludwig Wittgenstein, *On Certainty*, pp. 46-47.
[18] *ibid.*, p. 22.
[19] Wittgenstein, *Culture and Value*, p. 5.
[20] *ibid.*, pp. 48-49; original's emphasis.
[21] *ibid.*, p. 56; *cf.* his "Remarks on Frazer's *Golden Bough*," trans. by John Beversluis, in *Wittgenstein: Sources and Perspectives*, ed. by C.G. Luckhardt, Cornell University Press, Ithaca, 1979, p. 74.
[22] *ibid.*, p. 6.
[23] *ibid.*, p. 62; clarifying comma added.
[24] *ibid.*, p. 63; original's emphasis.
[25] Wittgenstein, *Tractatus*, 6.432; original's emphasis.
[26] Wittgenstein, *Culture and Value*, p. 34.
[27] Aristotle, *De Anima*, A5, 411a7. Commentators often interpret Thales as offering a purely mechanistic account of reality; in fact, as this statement shows, he continued the established pagan tradition of regarding reality as alive in its own right, as did most of the other pre-Socratic philosophers. Even the atomists sang hymns to "bountiful Venus," by which they meant the life-energy in the cosmos.
[28] Wittgenstein *On Certainty*, p. 66.
[29] Wittgenstein, *Culture and Value*, p. 27.
[30] P.M.S. Hacker, *Insight and Illusion: Themes in the Philosophy of Wittgenstein*, revised 2nd edition, Clarendon Press, Oxford, 1986, p. 155, n. 13, & p. 335; original's emphasis.
[31] Wittgenstein, *On Certainty*, p. 23; original's emphasis.
[32] John Austin, "Performative-Constative," originally published in 1958, reprinted in *Philosophy and Ordinary Language*, ed. by Charles E. Caton, University of Illinois Press, Urbana, 1963, p. 42.
[33] See the canned essay entitled "Can There Be a Private Language?", written by Wittgenstein executor Rush Rhees, in *Philosophy and Ordinary Language*, ed. by Charles E. Caton, University of Illinois Press, Urbana, 1963, pp. 90-107. Rhees mimics the choppy style that Wittgenstein himself viewed as a *defect* in his writing.
[34] Chan, Wing-Tsit, ed., *A Source Book in Chinese Philosophy*, Princeton University Press, Princeton, New Jersey, 1963, p. 233.

11

The Logic of Dr. Strangelove

SUMMARY: This chapter focuses on Willard Van Orman Quine, the doyen of American logicians. It shows how Quine failed to save the Parmenidean myth by hitching it to another myth, that of scientific progress. The chapter also reveals how formal logic after Quine has continued to perpetuate the Parmenidean myth, despite its claim to be myth-free.

Previous chapters have shown that formal logic originally emerged from a myth-system developed by Parmenides, and consisting of three motifs: logical necessity, bivalence, and absolute objectivity. Medieval philosophers later recast this myth in Christian terms. Later still, the myth imbibed new life from the monotheistic metaphysics of Gottfried Wilhelm Leibniz. At the end of the 19th century, Gottlob Frege recast the myth again, introducing the divine-like dyad of "the True" and "the False." To Frege's chagrin, however, this addition only succeeded in generating contradictions, discovered by Bertrand Russell.

In the early twentieth century, Russell succeeded Frege as the great white hope of formal logic. Enlisting the help of Alfred North Whitehead, Russell published *Principia Mathematica*, purporting to derive arithmetic from logic. After *Principia* sputtered and stalled, the Parmenidean myth was reshaped by Ludwig Wittgenstein. In his earlier phase, Wittgenstein reached back to the old mystical notion of God as the validator and guarantor of logic. In his later period, however, Wittgenstein frankly acknowledged that formal logic is a myth system, and a harmful one at that.

Among those who have occasionally paid lip-service to Wittgenstein is the contemporary American philosopher Willard Van Orman Quine, now nearly ninety years old. From his high perch as master logician at Harvard University from 1948 until 1978, Quine exercised a great influence over modern American academic philosophy. After his retirement from Harvard, a steady stream of his books and reprints continued to bolster his reputation. Today many academics regard him as the greatest American philosopher of the second half of the twentieth century.[1]

The present chapter is an overview of Quine's life and philosophy, and of some of those who later supplanted him in formal logic. The purpose of this overview is to spotlight Quine's failed attempt to haul Russell's old logical juggernaut out of the ditch into which it fell decades ago. Quine's failure meant that the Parmenidean myth also remained in the ditch, and with it, the pretensions of formal logic.

Unaccustomedly Well Paid

Willard Van Orman Quine was born in 1908 in Akron, Ohio, the son of a prosperous manufacturer. He majored in science at a local high school, and mathematics at Oberlin College, from which he graduated in 1930. After marrying his fiancée, Naomi Clayton, he set off for graduate school at Harvard University, where he studied advanced mathematics. In 1932, after only two years in residence at Harvard, he was awarded the Ph.D. degree, having written his dissertation on certain aspects of Russell's *Principia Mathematica*.

After graduation from Harvard, Quine received a postdoctoral fellowship to study abroad. He attended a few meetings of the Vienna Circle, where the new philosophy of logical positivism made a life-long impression on him. After completion of his tour, Quine returned to Harvard, where he was inducted into the newly established Society of Fellows. The new position afforded him, as he later boasted, "three years of good stipend and no duties." Afterwards, he was appointed instructor.

During this period, Quine befriended S.I. Hayakawa, later President of San Francisco State University, and a fierce defender of the establishment against student protesters during the Vietnam-War era. In Quine's opinion, Hayakawa "behaved courageously."[2]

With the onset of World War II, Quine volunteered for the Navy. Happily, he landed a comfortable domestic assignment for himself in an office in Washington, DC, accompanied by "a bright and congenial group of scholars and mathematicians."[3] After the war, Quine and his wife separated, and he married Marjorie Boynton, who had been under his command in the Navy. Quine notes that she was helpful in typing his manuscripts.

In 1948, Quine became a full professor at Harvard, and in 1949 did a stint with the conservative Rand Corporation, where he was "unaccustomedly well paid."[4] For most of the remainder of his professional life, he stayed at Harvard, with occasional excursions to Oxford and elsewhere.

Of Bachelors and Dogmas

In 1951 (by chance the year of Wittgenstein's death), Quine published a controversial paper on logic. In the eyes of many, the paper implied that logic is a cultural construct, having only relative validity. At the time, such a claim was sensational, especially coming from a professional logician. Later, however, Quine seemed to do an about-face, closing the door to such tantalizing interpretations.

Entitled "Two Dogmas of Empiricism," Quine's paper challenges the old accepted notion that there is a cleavage between two kinds of truths, those that are "analytic" (true by virtue of their meanings alone), and those that are "synthetic" (true by virtue of particular facts in the world). The paper also criticizes a newer notion, stemming from logical positivism, that descriptive sentences are meaningful only if their individual terms can be related to particular observations.[5]

Quine's attack on the analytic/synthetic cleavage is based on the difficulty of defining what "analytic" means. A plausible approach is to define this word in terms of "sentence meaning" or "synonymy of terms." However, these words only make sense if we already understand the meaning of "analytic." We are stuck in a definitional loop!

Quine concludes that analyticity, meaning, and synonymy are but so many facets of the same underlying gem—the capacity of sentences to signify. Before simply assuming that there *must* be a cleavage between analytic and synthetic sentences, he argues, we need to examine just what it means to say that a sentence signifies.

Facing Experience Corporately

Quine approaches the question of how sentences signify by way of his criticism of the second dogma of empiricism, the claim that descriptive sentences are meaningful only if their individual terms can be related to particular observations. Ironically, Quine the atheist developed his views under the influence of Pierre Duhem, a conservative French Catholic physicist who died in 1916. According to Duhem, any sentence that appears in a scientific theory has meaning only in virtue of being part of that larger theory. You can't just pluck out individual sentences and expect them to have meaning by themselves. In fact, individual sentences in scientific theory only rarely have a direct confrontation with observational evidence. A scientific theory, said Duhem, is nothing but a practical tool for making predictions from one observation to another; it is not a window into the nature of reality, which for Duhem is provided only by metaphysics and religion.

In "Two Dogmas of Empiricism," Quine takes up Duhem's concept of the nature of meaning in scientific sentences, applies it to sentences in any system of language, and discards entirely the notion of a separate metaphysical or religious insight into reality. Every sentence, Quine argues, has meaning only in virtue of being a member of some complex of many-sentences-plus-evidence. Because of the system-dependence of sentence meaning, every bit of empirical evidence is relevant to some degree to the meaning of every sentence. The meaning of any sentence, in the fullest sense, is its overall role in the entire complex.

The upshot is that the process of empirical verification, which is the ultimate grounding-process for any theory, is never a matter of testing individual sentences in isolation from each other. As Quine says in one of his most famous pronouncements:

> Our statements about the external world face the tribunal of sense experience not individually but only as a corporate body.[6]

If this view of sentence meaning is correct, how can we justify an unbreachable wall between analytic and synthetic sentences? We can't, says Quine. No sentence is purely linguistic, entirely cut off from the world of fact; otherwise, it would cease to be relevant to reality. Nor is any fact entirely independent of language; otherwise, it would not be statable.

If all this is true, how can we know what really exists independently of our various linguistic frameworks? For example, what about souls?— they have no place in the language of physical science. Quine dismisses such questions as muddled. To choose a convenient linguistic framework, he says, is what it *means* to make a decision about what really exists. Why? Because linguistic frameworks are tools for making accurate predictions, and the making of accurate predictions is the test of knowing what there is. By constantly adapting and honing our predictive tools, we attain an ever more accurate understanding of reality; this honing process, when efficient and rational, is what we call "science."

Logic and the Survival of the Fittest

Among our linguistic frameworks, says Quine, is formal logic. Like any other linguistic framework, its value depends on its usefulness as a tool.

In the struggle to survive, humans invent and use tools, including language tools. Some of these, having an application in every cognitive endeavor, are called the truths of logic. Their value, says Quine, is that they exemplify the standard ways of using the logical particles ("and," "if—then," etc.).

Formal logic is thus part of the struggle to survive. In the long run, those who are the most logical and the most adept at experimentation are also the most successful in making predictions. Consequently, they gain the upper hand over their circumstances, and over those who have been less logical and less scientific. They also gain the best understanding of the natural world-order, says Quine, because reality is revealed by the tools we successfully use in grappling with it.

This logical/evolutionary process is reflected in the way we are socialized, says Quine. From the moment we first begin to learn, we are trained to accept certain basic uses of language as logical on the face of it, without the need of any further justification. Any point of view that runs counter to this basic usage strikes us as absurd or incoherent. Our acceptance of these matters is part of a larger way of looking at life that we just assume with the rest of our culture:

> We imbibe an archaic natural philosophy with our mother's milk.[7]

Whenever we encounter an intractable observation that runs counter to our inherited system of interpreting the world, we first tinker with the periphery of the system. If this limited attempt fails, our tinkering goes deeper. Eventually we may be forced to revise certain basic laws of science. The next to the last thing we change is mathematics, and the very last of all is logic.

In adapting our overall world-view, we can never step outside it as a whole, confronting reality nakedly. Rather, we always take a stand in one part of our natural world-view in order to modify another part, moving around from part to part as circumstances require. To illustrate this process, Quine is fond of quoting a striking simile originated by the Austrian logical positivist Otto Neurath:

> We are like sailors who must rebuild their ship on the open sea, never able to dismantle it in dry-dock.[8]

The philosopher, says Quine, has a special role to play in keeping the common, inherited world-view afloat on the churning sea of human experience. This role lies in testing and clarifying the conceptual worthiness of the ship's various planks. But in so doing, the philosopher first accepts the bulk of the given world-view as true:

> The naturalist philosopher begins his reasoning within the inherited world theory as a going concern. He tentatively believes all of it, but believes also that some unidentified portions are wrong. He tries to improve, clarify, and understand the system from within. He is the busy sailor adrift on Neurath's boat.[9]

According to Quine, then, formal logic is part of a great social fabric, namely the common world-view by means of which our society navigates the high seas of human experience. As a practical tool that helps keep that ship afloat, logic can be changed as circumstances require. But if that is so, then the cleavage that philosophers have traditionally drawn between analytic and synthetic truths is an illusion.

All sentences, insists Quine, ultimately owe their truth in one way or another to human experience, which alone buoys them up. What are called analytic truths are simply those sentences that in the long run have become the most firmly established in our overall linguistic framework. We are slow to change them because in so doing we change the way it makes sense for us to speak of our experiences, which is a momentous development. Logic has the permanence of any long-reliable human tool. But such tools can be changed with the needs of their users.

Four Dogmas of Scientism

Quine's view of logic in "Two Dogmas of Empiricism" resembles that of the later Wittgenstein. Both philosophers reject any transcendent source as a basis for logic, stressing that logic is a human tool, best understood in terms of the practical situations where it is used. Both see a continuum between the truths of logic and the rest of language. Finally, both recognize that logic can change, while also appreciating the historical and evolutionary momentum that renders logic resistant to change.

There remain, however, vast differences between Quine and Wittgenstein. By the end of his life, Wittgenstein had concluded that formal logic warps language, and that science, which formal logic serves as a handmaiden, is socially harmful. Quine, on the other hand, has continued to hold quite different beliefs in these matters.

The gulf between Wittgenstein and Quine is reflected in a philosophical retrenchment that Quine carried out after publication of "Two Dogmas." This retrenchment was directed against readers who saw the essay as advocating an attitude of cultural relativism toward logic, and perhaps even toward science. Quine has opened the door, these readers concluded, to the development of radical new logical systems, depending on cultural variations.

Although a quick scan of "Two Dogmas" can easily lead one to such conclusions, Quine himself was horrified by such a reading. Unknown to many of his readers at the time, Quine was (and is) deeply committed to four other dogmas that lie just below the surface of this essay, and which completely undercut its apparent relativistic thrust.

These four dogmas, to which Quine frequently alludes in his many later writings, are the following: (1) Euro-American civilization represents the acme of human social evolution; (2) This civilization has triumphed because of its acceptance and empowerment of the scientific method; (3) Science alone reveals the true nature of reality; and (4) There is only one true logic, that which manifests the skeleton of the body scientific.

Quine's absolutist assumptions about logic come out clearly in his own technical writings on the subject. For example, in 1950 he published a college textbook on logic entitled *Methods of Logic*. In the introduction he notes:

> Thus the laws of mathematics and logic may, despite all "necessity," be abrogated. ... No such revolution, by the way, is envisaged in this book; there will be novelties of approach and technique in these pages, but at bottom logic will remain unchanged.[10]

Much of Quine's later writing after "Two Dogmas" seeks to curb the overly holistic and relativistic reading of that essay. For example, in his famous book *Word and Object*, published in 1960, he deplores what he calls his own earlier "excessive holism."[11] Moreover, in the 1960s and 1970s, as we will later see, he became the leading academic opponent to the development of alternative logics. As a testament to Quine's great influence, his opposition resulted in the smothering within the United States of one of the most important new developments in logic since the time of Aristotle.

The unmovable foundation-stone of Quine's absolutist view of logic is his belief, at times reaching religious intensity, in the worthiness of science. This belief distinguishes Quine from Wittgenstein, who abandoned formal logic when he realized that it rested on a foundation of myth, and who regarded modern science as debasing. Quine, on the other hand, sought to find a better foundation for logic precisely in science. In the end, as we are now about to see, all Quine succeeded in doing was replacing the hoary Parmenidean myth by another myth that is equally fallacious—the myth of scientific progress.

The Illuminated Manuscript of Reality

Despite appearances in "Two Dogmas of Empiricism," Quine holds to an absolutist view: there is only one true logic, namely the system of modern formal logic originated by Gottlob Frege, refined by Bertrand Russell, and perfected by Willard Van Orman Quine. In praising the power of this logic, Quine has coined a metaphor using the archaic English verb "limn" (pronounced "lim"). This word means "to represent by a drawing or painting." It first appeared in old English as a garbled form of "illuminate," as in the phrase "to illuminate a manuscript." Drawing on these connotations, Quine describes the business of logicians as—

> limning the true and ultimate structure of reality.[12]

The religious feeling behind Quine's metaphor is reinforced by his habit of calling his own logical system "the canonical notation" or "the canonical scheme." He disparages any alternative system as "deviant logic."

Quine seeks to ground this quasi-religious attitude in empirical science. He takes up where Russell had left off, ignoring Wittgenstein's two tangential interludes, the first into transcendental mysticism, and the second into linguistic anti-logicism.

Quine's account runs like this: of all human efforts throughout history to discern the nature of reality, science has proven to be the most effective. Indeed, the development of the scientific mentality by the modern West represents the liberation of human consciousness from the "muddy savagery" and "savage theology" of earlier societies. Science has transformed humanity's "animal vestige" into the purity of theory, thereby gaining victory over "unreason" and "darkness." Every human being, in abandoning the fantasies of childhood and adopting the rationality of adulthood, recapitulates individually the collective progress of the human race in shedding its savage, pre-scientific mentality.[13]

Modern science—and not poetry, music, religion, myth, sexual ecstasy, personal intuition, or anything else—shows what reality really is:

> What reality is like is the business of scientists, in the broadest sense, painstakingly to surmise; and what there is, what is real, is part of that question. ... The last arbiter is so-called scientific method, however amorphous.[14]

Of the sciences in general, says Quine, the most truly scientific is theoretical physics. All the other sciences—psychology, anthropology, sociology, etc.—are imperfect to the degree in which they are removed from the methods and findings of physics.

For example, certain schools of psychology now talk about "minds," "intentions," "feelings," and other mentalistic entities. This regrettable terminology is necessary, argues Quine, only because of the primitive methods now current among psychologists. Eventually, such talk will be completely translatable into talk about associated bodily states:

> We can just reinterpret the mentalistic terms as denoting these correlated bodily states, and who is to know the difference?[15]

Propping Up The Eye of God

The core laws of physics, Quine continues, constitute "pure mathematics," which is not purely conceptual after all. Rather, pure mathematics maps out the basic structure of possibility in the world, as presupposed by physics. Any sort of mathematics that is divorced from this empirical basis is simply a collection of uninterpreted symbols, not mathematics at all. Within mathematics, the most firmly established part is called logic, which is faithfully captured by Quine's own "canonical notation."

Like the eye of God on the dollar bill, Quine's logic shines forth atop the apex of a great pyramid. The apex is mathematics, which rests on the boulders of physics and the other sciences, which rest on the broad foundations of the scientific method. Naturally, any God so supported is bound to endorse the props that hold him up. As the dollar bill says, *annuit coeptis* ("He has approved the foundations"). In Quinean terms, this motto translates thus: to be logical is to embrace the structure of modern science, which is the very basis and support of logic; to hanker after other structures is a sign of savagery or deviancy, like hankering after false gods.

The Neo-theology of Scientism

Quine thinks it preposterous that anyone should undertake to criticize science, which is the basis of logic, from an extra-scientific standpoint. To the contrary, he insists that science is "not answerable to any supra-scientific tribunal," and he praises "the robust state of mind" of those scientists who "have never felt any qualms beyond the negotiable uncertainties internal to science." The reason for science's exemption from extra-scientific criticism is its unmatched success in making predictions. Its success, Quine argues, has made it the touchstone in deciding whether any other view has access to the truth:

> Scientists are so good nowadays at discovering truth that it is trivial to endorse their methods and absurd to criticize them.[16]

Quine insists that the faith commonly placed by laymen in scientific experts is well founded. As proof, he cites the role of science in creating automobiles and nuclear bombs:

> The faith that we place in the scientific experts, at any rate, is well grounded in evidence. ... Even the uneducated layman must be impressed by the technological fruits of scientific knowledge, from the horseless carriage to the hydrogen bomb.[17]

During the 1960s and 1970s, Quine's facile assumptions about logic and science received a big jolt. As a result of the genocidal war then being waged by the United States in Southeast Asia, many in the American counterculture began to question the overall social and political role of science, particularly in regard to the military-industrial complex. Some, like the poet Allen Ginsberg, challenged the claim that Western logic is always logical.

These criticisms stung Quine, who stoutly rose to the defense of science and logic. At times sounding like a preacher, he fiercely denounced "false doctrine," "superstition," "belief in magic," and "defiant attacks on the scientific establishment." Gravely, he proclaimed:

> Even as light is opposed by darkness, science and reason have their enemies.[18]

In thus equating human rationality with his own particular concept of logic, Quine unknowingly followed the patriarchal precedents of his forebears in logic, going back to Parmenides. As previous chapters have shown, logicians have typically collapsed the entire spectrum of human interpretational ability into the narrow band of some logical method. Any way of relating to reality outside this narrow band they have regarded as perverse. Consequently, their philosophy of logic has often become an intellectual bludgeon for discounting those who converse with reality in another idiom, such as women, poets, visionaries, religious and sexual heretics, and the members of non-Western tribal societies. In the eyes of the logicians, it's only reasonable that such people should be discounted, or even dominated and suppressed. After all, they can't even think right!

What's Real Anyway?

As noted above, Quine believes that to use some language for the practical purpose of describing the world is to commit oneself to the existence of certain kinds of entities. For example, if I find it practical to speak of the existence of physical objects, then I am committed to the doctrine that physical objects are real. What, then, does formal logic have to say about what what's real?

To answer this question, Quine focuses on "quantifiers." These are logical symbols that roughly correspond to the ordinary English words "at least one," "none," and "all." For example, consider this English sentence: "Some men are not self-centered." Translated into the language of formal logic, this sentence becomes: "There is some x such that it is a man, and such that it is not self-centered." The quantifier is the set of logical symbols used to represent the phrase "There is some x such that... ."

According to Quine, whenever I utter the words "there is some x such that...," I commit myself to the existence of a certain object. In the example above, I commit myself to the existence of at least one man.

This view of ontology seems to be relativistic. After all, one can say the magic words "There is some x such that..." in many different contexts. For example, in discussing ancient Greek mythology, one might say "There is some x such that it is a dog, three-headed, and guards the portals of the underworld." Such a being exists in ancient Greek mythology, and even has a name, Cerberus. Therefore, the sentence is true; therefore, reality—insofar as it pertains to Greek mythology—includes the entity named Cerberus.

Quine, however, shudders at such a use of the quantifier. Despite the seeming plurality of worlds that his own analysis seems to invite, he is adamant that—

There is really only one world, and there is not, never was, and never will be any such thing as Cerberus.[19]

But why can't I have my own linguistic framework, with its concomitant ontology, and you, yours? Answer: Quine actually presupposes something far more substantial than the relative utility of various linguistic frameworks; he assumes the absolute truth of science. He also maintains that his "canonical notation," as he calls it, gives an X-ray view of the skeleton of possibility at the core of the body scientific. So Quine doesn't really tolerate various ways of saying "There is some x such that..." In fact, there is only one right way, the one used by scientists, and in particular physicists.

It is in the context of Quine's commitment to the absolute validity of science, and especially physics, that his most oft-quoted quip is to be understood:

> To be is to be the value of a variable.[20]

This quip is not just a comment on logical theory, as commonly supposed by Quine's commentators. Rather, it has a deeper meaning based on slurring together different senses of the word "variable." On the one hand, "variable" does obviously refer to the variable of logical theory, as discussed above. With this sense, the quip merely articulates, in a pithy manner, Quine's view that linguistic frameworks involve ontological commitments.

But we have seen that Quine also makes two additional claims: (1) science, and especially physics, provides the decisive linguistic framework for describing the world; and (2) his own canonical notation captures the skeleton of science's linguistic framework. Moreover, Quine believes, along with Russell, that the entire conceptual scheme of mathematics can be boiled down to logic.[21] As a result of these assumptions, he effectively stretches the notion of "variable" to include the variables used in higher mathematics and in physics.

Consequently, the full implication of Quine's quip is this: to be is to be formalizable by science, in the context of a linguistic framework whose essence is formal logic, rightly understood. In sum, what falls outside the pale of science, mathematics, and the logic of Willard Van Orman Quine is unreal.

Deviants

Fiercely devoted to his own brand of logical orthodoxy, Quine derides any alternative as "deviant." Over the years, he has hurled this epithet at the logical systems of Charles Sanders Peirce, Jan Lukasiewicz, C.I. Lewis, and (most important of all, as we will soon see) Lotfi Zadeh.

Ironically, Quine himself had once been implicitly labeled as deviant by his erstwhile teacher Rudolf Carnap. He criticized Quine's blurring of the distinction between analytic and synthetic truths because it seemed "to deviate considerably from customary ways of thinking."[22]

Quine's name-calling runs deep. He cries out in genuine anguish when major changes are proposed to what he calls "the orthodox logic." These alternative systems, he says, just muddy the water when we try to understand the language of science. His unyielding stance resembles that of a religious fundamentalist who dismisses any suggestion of doctrinal change as incomprehensible:

> It would seem that such an idea of deviation in logic is absurd on the face of it. If sheer logic is not conclusive, what is?[23]

Quine is nonetheless aware that reputable physicists and mathematicians have challenged the law of the excluded middle. In response, he argues that the law should be retained because it helps simplify and organize the body of science as a whole:

> Let us just recognize rather that the law of [the] excluded middle is not a fact of life, but a norm governing efficient logical regimentation.[24]

Now if this law is merely a tool for promoting logical efficiency, as Quine concedes, then it is singularly inappropriate to imply that thinkers who would try other kinds of tools are "deviants." The effect of brandishing such an epithet—whether in logic, religion, politics, or sexual psychology—is to impede the road to inquiry, a fatal flaw for anyone who would wear the mantle of philosopher. Throughout history, those who have been quickest to resort to such labeling have commonly been haunted by insecurities concerning their own perceived orthodoxy in logic, religion, politics, or sex. As noted above, Rudolf Carnap had once implied that his erstwhile student W.V. Quine was a philosophical deviant.

Quine's disparaging attitude toward logical alternatives prevailed in most university philosophy departments in the U.S. Not surprisingly, it produced a chilling effect on creative thought. The result was that "fuzzy logic," the single most important breakthrough in logic since the work of Gottlob Frege, was developed not by a logician but by an electrical engineer, and in the face of withering scorn from academic philosophers. Nonetheless, as we will soon see, fuzzy logic eventually carried the day, thanks to the intervention of Japanese scientists who knew nothing of Quine.

Pride and Paradox

Before disdaining the work of others, Quine would have done well to deal with certain paradoxes in his own. For example, he insists that there are such things as absolute logical truths. These he defines as those sentences that remain true when their constituent parts, except for the logical particles, are varied at will. He seems to have such sentences in mind when he asks rhetorically, "If sheer logic is not conclusive, what is?"[25]

But Quine also insists that there is no real gulf between logical truths and factual truths; rather, the sentences that are the most firmly embedded in the fabric of science constitute the truths of logic. But if there is such a continuum, how can Quine know that there exists a set of sentences in which the logical particles occur essentially, as opposed to all other sentences, where they do not? Wouldn't it seem more likely that this sort of sentence-essence would constitute a hypothetical limit, to which *every* sentence would approach in *some* degree? In his own favored logical calculus, which he presents as "canonical," Quine presupposes absolute logical truths; however, his theory of science presupposes that logical truth occurs by degrees. He never resolves the tension between these two contrary views.

One of Quine's favorite examples of an absolute truth of logic is the sentence "No unmarried man is married." Here "no," "un-," and "is" are logical particles. The logical form of this sentence can be represented by the schema "No un-M x is M," where "M" is replaceable by an adjective or descriptive phrase, and "x" by the name of an object. Quine claims that whatever adjectives or names are substituted in this way for "M" and "x," the sentence that is so formed will come out true. But despite Quine's claim, a counter-example can be easily produced. For example, let "M" = "who is short compared to randomly selected men," and let "x" = "man." The resultant sentence is "No man who is not short compared to randomly selected men is short compared to randomly selected men." Because a man can be short compared to some men but not short compared to others, this sentence is *false*. Therefore, according to Quine's own definition, the original sentence "No unmarried man is married" is *not* an absolute truth of logic.

The reason the above example fails is that the meaning of the substituted descriptive phrase involves a matter of contextual degree. In general, terms that are contextual or gradient in meaning trip-up formal logic, which requires a strictly black-or-white conceptual base in order to operate properly. If more than black-or-white is involved in the meaning of terms, there can be degrees in the manner in which one proposition negates another. The classical concept of propositional negation, based squarely on the myth of bivalence, cannot handle these gradations.

Quine just takes the black-or-white requirement for granted in presenting his definition of absolute logical truth—even though, ironically, his own theory of science presupposes that logical truth is a matter of degree. But he is unwilling to embrace the implications of this relativity in his own logical calculus because it smacks of deviancy. In fact, when he assesses the various arguments presented for multi-valued logics, he finds—

> The worst one is that things are not just black and white; there are gradations. It is hard to believe that this would be seen as counting against classical negation; but irresponsible literature to this effect can be cited.[26]

With Apologies to Plato

The conflict between Quine's philosophy of science and his philosophy of logic causes him problems in terms of ontological commitment. On the one hand, he examines the language used by physicists and mathematicians, in order to discover what they say the world really consists of. His conclusion: physical objects, classes of physical objects, and classes of classes. But when Quine writes technical essays on problems in logic, he finds he must resort to phrases like "logical forms," "forms of inference," and "logical structure." At times, he explicitly connects these terms with the magic words "there are...," as when he remarks in one of his logical manuals:

> There are forms of inference, logically no less sound than those dealt with in Part II.[27]

At one point Quine candidly admits that in order to do logic, we must semantically ascend from physical reality to the realm of human language—

> Thus whereas we can expound physics in its full generality without semantic ascent, we can expound logic in a general way only by talking of forms of sentences.[28]

So as a logician, Quine is committed to the reality of forms of sentences, but as a philosopher of science, he insists that all reality can be reduced to physical objects, classes of physical objects, and classes of classes. In fact, he is the advocate of two conflicting views about the ultimate building blocks of reality.

One tempting way to resolve this conflict would be to argue that the phrase "form of sentences" simply refers to some given class of sentences, and then hope to reduce sentences to classes of physical objects. But there is a fatal flaw with this approach. If the given class of sentences that defines the logical form is *closed*, then no additional sentences can be added to it. But the history of logic is full of cases where logicians say they have *discovered* that certain sentences exhibit a logical form possessed by other sentences (as in Russell's famous analysis of definite descriptions). If the logical form in question is indeed defined by some closed class of sentences, then it would be meaningless to say that another sentence had been discovered that had that same form. On the other hand, if the defining class of sentences is *open*, then what is it, in virtue of which, new sentences may be added to the class? Clearly, in this case, the logical form itself is already presupposed. In practice, working logicians always presuppose some logical form that becomes the defining property for creating an open class of sentences. They do not first define logical form in terms of some closed class of sentences; otherwise, the analysis of new sentences—to say nothing of the analysis of new languages—would be impossible.

Like Plato before him, Quine as the philosopher of absolute logic finds that he is forced to "ascend" to a realm of "forms." Plato, to his everlasting credit, frankly acknowledged that this ascent was laden with paradoxes; indeed, he spent most of his life trying to untangle them. Quine, on the other hand, has never forthrightly confronted the contradiction between his two views of reality.[29]

Where Do Numbers Come From?

Like Frege and Russell, Quine believes that arithmetic can be boiled down to logic. As discussed previously, Frege's effort foundered because of a fatal contradiction in his theory of classes, and Russell's stalled when he was forced to introduce a number of *ad hoc* axioms having little to do with logic.

Over the years, Quine has suggested a number of patches to Russell's system.[30] Nonetheless, serious problems remain. For example, Quine acknowledges that arithmetic requires a theory of identity (that is, rules for the use of the sign "="), and that identity theory is not reducible to classical logic. His solution? Simply introduce the necessary new axioms needed to define "=". Again, he concedes that class theory itself cannot be reduced to classical logic. His solution? Simply introduce the necessary new axioms needed to define classes. Significantly, however, he acknowledges that, whereas the axioms of classical logic are "obvious," those of class theory (or set theory as it is now often called) are not; in fact, a great controversy has been raging for some time among mathematicians as to the proper nature of classes, and no solution is in sight.

Quine's claim that arithmetic can be deduced from, or boiled down to, logic hangs on a tenuous notion of "logic." In reality, *anything* can be boiled down to "logic" if one simply adds enough *ad hoc* axioms to his or her logical calculus. A certain amount of axiomatic leeway is reasonable, but the axioms that Quine incorporates are far from obvious, as he himself admits, and some are highly controversial. Moreover,

Quine has never come to terms with Gödel's incompleteness proof, which says that regardless of how rich one's finite set of axioms may be, there will always be some true proposition of arithmetic that cannot be deduced from them.

Quine has found himself in the same boat as Russell: both started out believing that arithmetic could be deduced from obvious axioms of logic. When that proved impossible, each simply pulled un-obvious axioms out of the air as needed, justifying their introduction with the claim that they led to the obvious truths of arithmetic. But if the obvious truths of arithmetic are invoked to justify *ad hoc*, un-obvious axioms of logic, then just what is being deduced from what? Why not just accept arithmetic as true (or, better yet, *useful*) in its own right? In their efforts to generate numbers from classes, and arithmetic from logic, Frege, Russell, and Quine have been running around in circles. Their much-touted proofs are nothing but so much smoke and mirrors, prime examples of the folly and hubris of Western formal logic.

Three Dogmas of Behaviorism

As discussed above, Quine acknowledges the reality of physical objects, classes of physical objects, classes of classes, and (grudgingly) forms of sentences. What, then, of meaning in language?

Language, argues Quine, is merely stimulus-response behavior involving the use of uttered noises. "Meaning" in language is simply a matter of dispositions toward certain kinds of behavior where such noises occur. Those whose proper business it is to examine the roots of the phenomenon of meaning are behavioral psychologists.

Accordingly, Quine attacks the commonly held view that there is some kind of "meaning" that can be identified apart from any particular language that expresses it. He calls this common notion the museum myth of meaning:

> Uncritical semantics is the myth of a museum in which the exhibits are meanings and the words are labels. To switch languages is to change the labels. [But]...there are no meanings, nor likenesses nor distinctions of meaning, beyond what are implicit in people's dispositions to overt behavior.[31]

If there are no exhibits in the museum of language, but only labels, what do the labels refer to? And how can one label be related to another? In his effort to answer these questions, Quine puts forward three interconnected behavioristic dogmas about language for which he has become famous. He calls these three dogmas "the inscrutability of reference," "the indeterminacy of translation," and "ontological relativity." We will briefly examine each, and see how all three fit into Quine's overall view of science and logic.

What Are You Talking About?

What really happens, Quine asks, when we first learn our own native language, or encounter a radically different foreign language? We simply observe, he answers, people uttering noises in response to various "irritations" to the surfaces of their bodies. By observing such stimulus-response behavior over time, we make guesses as to what the people who are uttering sounds are talking about.

At what point can we move beyond behavioral guesswork and truly know what things the strange sounds refer to? Never, says Quine, as long as we focus on particular sentences. The reason is that all we have to go on is the speakers' behavior. Judging behavior in isolated cases cannot show what *aspect* of things particular sounds refer to.

To gain a better idea of what people are talking about, we need to construct a make-do parallel between ever larger patches of their language-use and ever larger patches of our own. Nonetheless, we must always be braced for unexpected misunderstandings. Only when we reach an overall fluency equal to that of the speakers themselves, will we be able to say with confidence what they are really talking about. In that case, however, we are no longer translating; we are just speaking the language. This inability to fully know what people are talking about, short of fluency, Quine calls "the inscrutability of reference."

Ways of Slicing Sentences

Another question Quine ponders: how do we know when some translation is the right one? In answer, Quine distinguishes between two kinds of sentences: observation sentences (which directly report observable evidence) and theoretical sentences (which state facts abstractly).

Observation sentences, says Quine, are the vehicles by which we first learned to speak our native language. Through them, we were taught to map our private observations about ordinary objects onto occasions of the public uses of words; therefore, the meanings of these words are public and behavioral, not private and mental.

Observation sentences, says Quine, are about as infallible as any sentence can be. In addition, an observation sentence faces the tribunal of experience singly, not corporately; it "simply stands or falls with the observation that it reports or predicts."[32] Accordingly, observation sentences are the principal exception to the holistic account of language presented by Quine in his earlier essay "Two Dogmas of Empiricism." In fact, he regards observation sentences as a necessary counterbalance to what he calls the "excessive holism" of that essay.[33]

Quine takes the distinction between observation sentences and theoretical sentences and combines it with his concept of the inscrutability of reference, discussed above. The result is his concept of the indeterminacy of translation.

This is Quine's reasoning: for any language, observation sentences, which are easy to translate, will be far less common than theoretical sentences. The meanings of the abstract terms in theoretical sentences are their overall roles in large chunks of their home language. To translate these terms is to translate the large chunks.

Here's the catch: there's usually more than one way to account in theory for any available body of observational evidence. Consequently, there can be many different theoretical chunks of the language that can all be mapped onto the same evidential base that is the fount of linguistic meaning. As a result, it's possible to have incompatible manuals of translation for any given language, all appealing to the same evidential base. Which among these various manuals is the right one?

There is no way, concludes Quine, to decide this question in the abstract. We simply have no objective standards of ultimate meaning to appeal to other than some behavioral base, which will always support various conflicting manuals of translation. Our conclusion is the indeterminacy of translation: there is no definitive way of translating any given body of theoretical sentences from one language into another.

But surely, one would object, we manage to translate theoretical sentences all the time. Quine would agree, only he would ask, What happens when we deem a translation manual good? In effect, we just take our native language at face value; whatever it can easily digest we regard as well translated. This practice, although convenient, simply ignores most of the theoretical alternatives.

Imposing Our Logic on Jungle Language

What happens when we come across parts of some foreign language that our native language can't digest? For example, suppose we confront a "jungle language" (as Quine calls it). In translating, we come up with sentences that imply that the natives believe they can act contrary to the laws of science. Or perhaps their beliefs come out as "prelogical," as some anthropologists have claimed. Quine responds that we have no choice but to suspect that such translations are amiss, and to proceed to *impose* our logic upon them:

> Better translating imposes our logic upon them... Fair translation preserves logical laws... For certainly, the more absurd or exotic the beliefs imputed to a people, the more suspicious we are entitled to be of the translations; the myth of the prelogical people marks only the extreme. For translation theory, banal messages are the breath of life.[34]

By "our logic," Quine means the logic expressed by his own canonical notation. He does not mean the deviant logics of other logicians.

In bringing everything back to "our logic," Quine highlights the most important implication of his whole theory of translation: what cannot be adapted to "our" dispositions to verbal behavior has no claim to linguistic meaning, for there are no behavior-independent meanings to which it can moor itself. Only if there were some kind of essential basis for linguistic meaning—say in the structure of the human mind as such—would it make sense to say that there could be criteria of translation that transcend our own native language. But Quine insists that all so-called mental phenomena are mere dispositions to behavior.

Theory Is Womb To Fact

Quine's third behaviorist dogma, ontological relativity, is modeled on Einstein's theory of physical relativity. Einstein rejected Newton's view that there can be an absolute measurement of position or velocity, independent of some particular measurer's frame of reference. Quine argues that the assertion of an object's existence is analogous to the measurement of an object's position and velocity. In both cases, some framework is presupposed: for position and velocity, the framework is the system of coordinates of the observer; for existence, the framework is the language of the speaker.

Quine finds it easy to appeal to this analogy because of the inscrutability of reference and the indeterminacy of translation. According to these dogmas, to say that a theoretical object is real is to say that it is part of, or translatable into, some given linguistic framework whose norms are just accepted. Hence factuality is always internal to some assumed theory; it is never unambiguously given by sheer matter. This conclusion is the principle of ontological relativity. As Quine, playing on the word "matter," puts it:

> There is no fact of the matter.[35]

The Absolute Stages a Comeback

On occasion, Quine compares the physical objects posited by modern science to the gods in Homeric poetry. Both are cultural constructs that function in their own respective myth-systems:

> Physical objects are conceptually imported into the situation as convenient intermediaries—not by definition in terms of experience, but simply as irreducible posits comparable, epistemologically, to the gods of Homer. ... The physical objects and the gods differ only in degree and not in kind. Both sorts of entities enter our conception only as cultural posits.[36]

Because of passages like this, some readers mistakenly take Quine to mean that all such myths are equal. In fact, however, Quine's relativity, like Einstein's, brings with it a new absolute of its own making.

In Einstein's case, the relativities of space and time are subsumed into a higher absolute, the space-time continuum. This he describes with new, more encompassing equations that hold for all observers, regardless of their relative positions to each other. Hence his so-called theory of relativity is a misnomer; in fact, Einstein's avowed goal was to establish a new theoretical absoluteness free of the relativity that he viewed as infecting, undetected, Newton's physics.

Likewise in Quine's case: although acknowledging various kinds of myths, Quine always hastens to add that not all myths are equal. Rather, one myth-system surpasses all the others—the myth-system created by modern science, and particularly theoretical physics. Anyone who reads Quine's relativistic remarks about linguistic systems must always bear in mind his absolutist subtext on science:

> What reality is like is the business of scientists, in the broadest sense, painstakingly to surmise; and what there is, what is real, is part of that question.[37]

Quine believes that the linguistic system used by modern science (in effect, higher mathematics and formal logic) has become our new, absolute, encompassing native language. Into it all relative questions about reference and reality are henceforth to be translated and answered. Indeed, this linguistic system, especially as captured by his own canonical notation, has the right to reach out and "regiment" any other myth-system that presumes to make claims about what exists.

In exalting the language of science, Quine returns to his claim that to be is to be the value of a variable. As discussed above, this claim has a pregnant sense: to be is to be formalizable by science, in the context of a linguistic framework whose essence is formal logic. Ontological relativity is just the flip side of this claim.

Parmenides, Repotted

Quine's whole philosophy turns on this claim: the various inscrutabilities, indeterminacies, and relativities of language and reality are all to be subsumed into a higher absolute, that of science and science's linguistic framework. Since formal logic is the skeleton of the body scientific, it follows that the traditional myths of logic—logical necessity, bivalence, and the ideal of timeless, impersonal knowledge—are all well grounded. They are, Quine insists, the very backbone of the language of science, which has triumphed as the language of languages.

In this way, Quine severs the umbilical cord between the Parmenidean myth and any alleged transcendent realm, a linkage that the early Wittgenstein tried to re-establish in *Tractatus*, in reaction against Russell's secularism. Quine, taking up anew Russell's pro-science agenda, retains the old Parmenidean myth entire, but repots it in the soil of empirical science.

The myths of formal logic are true, says Quine, not because they are guaranteed by Parmenides' Goddess far-constraining Order, or by the Stoics' Zeus, or by the Christians' Logos, or by Frege's the True and the False, or by the early Wittgenstein's transcendent One. They are true because they are deeply rooted in the language of the scientific method, which is the final arbiter of what exists and what does not exist.

How does Quine know that science is worthy of serving as such a grand arbiter? He simply makes two assumptions: science, considered theoretically, provides us with our best window on reality; and science, considered practically, has been a great boon to humanity. In the next two chapters, we will see that these assumptions cannot stand up to scrutiny. Quine himself, however, never doubted them; nor did he ever put forward any extensive argument to justify them.

Responses to Surface Irritations

As he aged, Quine became increasingly brittle and mechanistic in his application of behavioristic principles, in contrast to Wittgenstein, who always tempered his behaviorism with spiritual concerns. In the end, Quine came to view perception and cognition simply as a matter of triggering individual sense receptors. The following passages, although taken from various of his books over the years, all promote the same view:

> The stimulation of his sensory receptors is all the evidence anybody has had to go on, ultimately, in arriving at his picture of the world. ... It is simply the stimulations of our sensory receptors that are best looked upon as the input to our cognitive mechanism. ... The triggering of a receptor is what counts. ... All discourse is mere response to surface irritation. ... I have come this far in my physical mimicry of phenomenalistic epistemology without invading the percipient organism more deeply than his sensory receptors. All that has mattered is the individual's distinctive response to their activation.[38]

Quine's account is simplistic. Although it is true that perception and cognition are impossible without the triggering of sensory receptors, it is a fallacy to assume that they can be *reduced* to this triggering. Stimulations sent to our central nervous systems and brains must be processed and organized before they can be transformed into usable information. Are there genetically-given modes of formatting information that the human brain imposes on all such received stimulations? If so, they must be taken into account. Does social conditioning affect the contents of perception and cognition? If so, it must be factored in as well. Do my own unique life experiences contribute to the way I see the world? If so, they cannot be discounted.

Contrary to Quine, my ear does not hear, my eye does not see. Rather, it is *I* who hear through my ear and see through my eye. If hearing consisted of mere sensations in the ear, then the deaf Beethoven could never have written his immortal *Ode to Joy*. Though deaf in his ears, Beethoven yet heard in his soul. This is the fact that Quine cannot account for.

To put the matter in Quinean terms, the understanding of perception and cognition requires "semantic ascent" up from the level of sheer sensory input. Short of such ascent, we find only the stimulus of electrical impulses in various nerves, not that integrative response of an organism which alone constitutes information-processing.

If one acknowledges the possibility that nature and culture may both contribute essential features to perception and cognition, then Quine's dogmas of the inscrutability of reference, the indeterminacy of translation, and ontological relativity are all undermined. For example, all humans may be able to spontaneously perceive certain kinds of formal structures in things, as maintained by the Gestalt psychologists. If so, then the areas of language accessible to determinate translation would be larger than Quine acknowledges.

Quine, as the good empiricist he claims to be, should wait and see what further research may reveal, rather than simply decide the matter in the name of some alleged essence of language. As in the case of his dogmatic pronouncements against "deviant logic," the effect of Quine's brittle, mechanistic behaviorism is to close the door to further inquiry.

I Am a Physical Object in a Cosmic Machine

Quine's brittle behaviorism leads to a crude account of the self and nature. The universe, he tell us, is a giant machine consisting of physically interchangeable objects in motion. We ourselves are but so many physical objects mechanically interacting with each other and the cosmic machine. In this mechanical interaction is to be found the essence of both personhood and language:

> I am a physical object sitting in a physical world. Some of the forces of this physical world impinge on my surface. Light rays strike my retinas; molecules bombard my eardrums and finger tips. I strike back, emanating concentric air waves. These waves take the form of a torrent of discourse... All I am or ever hope to be is due to irritations of my surface, together with such latent tendencies to response as may have been present in my original germ plasm.[39]

Ironically, Quine claims that this view is scientific. In fact, however, his concept of physics has a distinctly old-fashioned, Newtonian ring to it. For example, he persists in viewing the world as a collection of separate physical objects impacting on each others' surfaces. However, modern quantum mechanics holds that the concept of "particle" is strictly correlative to that of "wave." Accordingly, the old Newtonian model of the universe as an aggregate of interacting billiard balls is false. Rather, says quantum mechanics, every subatomic particle extends to some degree throughout the entire universe. *Where* that spread-out-ness (wave) happens to be observed concretely (particle) is a matter of probability, depending on the varying intensities of the spread-out-ness in question.

Whether quantum mechanics is right remains to be seen. But one thing is certain: mechanistic metaphors are strikingly inconsistent with the wave-particle view of matter. The word "machine," as commonly used, denotes a human contrivance with distinctly separate parts that function by acting on each others' surfaces. But this absolute separateness of parts, where interaction occurs only at surfaces, is the very thing that quantum mechanics denies. So if someone claims to accept the latest findings of science, he or she cannot embrace a simple machine metaphor for describing the root nature of reality.

Philosophy Minus Wisdom

Quine believes that philosophy is a part of science, the part concerned with elucidating the language of science. This belief leads him to scoff at the traditional view that philosophy seeks not only knowledge but also meaning and wisdom. To Quine, this traditional view is just another vestige of "savage theology."

This view has significant implications in regard to how philosophy should be taught. Imparting the technical skills of logical and linguistic analysis has the highest priority; understanding the historical circumstances of past philosophical movements becomes peripheral; integrating one's own personal spiritual growth into philosophical activity becomes pointless.

Quine's view of philosophy as a technical profession typifies the attitude now prevalent in American universities. As a result, a great chasm has developed in American society between those who are concerned with questions of meaning, purpose, and value, and those who have been technically trained in philosophy. As discussed in the introduction to this book, this chasm has impoverished both sides. Considerations of meaning have been forfeited to members of the clergy, novelists, popular psychologists, and gurus of faddish new cults. Although concerned with substantive questions of meaning, they have usually lacked both the analytical skills and the historical knowledge to make important contributions to philosophy. The professional philosophers, on the other hand, disdaining the lack of professionalism of the first group, have wandered off onto jargon-filled tangents in technical sub-specialties. Their writings typically have nothing of any real substance to say about anything.

Quine has remained intractable in the face of growing criticisms of the gap between technique and substance in philosophy. In 1980 he sharply rebuked Mortimer Adler for his essay "Has Philosophy Lost Contact with People?", which pointedly raised the issue. Whatever one may think of Adler in general, his article raised a good question. In response, Quine said that the search for meaning and wisdom is actually an *impediment* to philosophy, and that students who are so motivated should be discouraged from entering the field:

> The student who majors in philosophy primarily for spiritual comfort is misguided and is probably not a very good student anyway, since intellectual curiosity is not what moves him.[40]

This response presupposes that a barrier necessarily exists between the quest for meaning and the quest for knowledge. Throughout most of the history of philosophy, however, the greatest philosophers have generally been those who have sought for *both* meaning and knowledge, as previous chapters of this book have demonstrated. In seeking to drive a wedge between the two quests, Quine and the academic philosophers who follow him have only succeeded in driving out of the field its most gifted, highly-motivated students. Those who have remained behind and risen in academic rank have rarely turned out to be great philosophers; commonly, they are institutional hacks. Exceptions exist, but they tend to be the very professors who have misgivings about academic philosophy as it is now practiced.

American academic philosophy is a dead fish in a stagnant pond. It has starved itself to death by building a barrier between knowledge and wisdom. The building of this barrier has been suicidal, for philosophy involves the examination of presuppositions. Any such endeavor necessarily prods those who participate in it to examine their own personal values, because the examination of presuppositions typically ends in questions of value. The examination of one's own values, in turn, is the first step on the path to wisdom, as Socrates rightly insisted. Herein lies philosophy's superiority to science, for science at most yields knowledge, whereas philosophy can open the door to both knowledge and wisdom.

The owl of Athena flies on the two wings of knowledge and wisdom. Deprived of either, she cannot take flight. When shorn of the quest for knowledge, philosophy becomes fanciful; when shorn of the quest for meaning, trivial. Only when propelled by both, does philosophy rise to its proper function—the transfiguration of self and society through the stimulus of worthy dialogue.

A Promise Unfulfilled

Quine made his most promising contribution to philosophy with his 1951 essay "Two Dogmas of Empiricism." With keen insight, the essay notes that science and mathematics are actually myth systems, no different in kind from the myth system of Homer, except in the degree to which they have proven useful in making predictions.

"Two Dogmas of Empiricism" was promising because it opened the door to tantalizing questions: What does it mean to say that something is "useful" in interpreting experience? Can different kinds of societies have different criteria of usefulness? Can different individuals or groups within the same society have different criteria? Are there different kinds of experience that involve different types of usefulness? Does the concept of usefulness make sense apart from the concept of an interpreter? If not, doesn't that mean that reality is in part interpreter-dependent?

In his later writings, unfortunately, Quine closes the door to these tantalizing questions. As we have seen, he dogmatically insists that the only useful approach to understanding reality is through mechanistic physics, behavioristic psychology, and bivalent logic. Any alternative approach he dismisses as "deviant."

With his increasingly bizarre talk in later years about the importance of surface irritations, the triggering of receptors, and the absorption of animal vestige into theory, the older Quine has at times sounded like Dr. Strangelove in Stanley Kubrick's film of the same name.[41] Again like Strangelove, Quine simply takes for granted science's subservience to the military-industrial complex.

Although Quine has enjoyed great popularity among American academic philosophers, his basic world-view has not gone unchallenged. In 1986, the Library of Living Philosophers, as part of its regular series, brought out an anthology of remarks by commentators on Quine's work, followed by Quine's responses.

Although most of the contributors maintain a deferential tone to the master, a notable exception is Henryk Skolimowski, who accuses Quine of having sold out philosophy to science. The dominant ethos of our times, charges Skolimowski, is that of science, on whose behalf

Quine and other leading analytic philosophers have become uncritical protagonists, not discerning critics. Quine is to philosophy, Skolimowski says, as Daniel Bell is to sociology, "a pillar of the Establishment":

> Professor Quine's once exciting philosophy has become a rendering—in sophisticated philosophical terms—of the ideology of science, which, after all, is the pervading ideology of the status quo.[42]

Skolimowski says that Quine's earlier philosophy offered the promise of a "radical conventionalism," but that the later Quine got bogged down in piecemeal investigations lacking any overall vision, except for the adulation of science. The effect has been to create a moral vacuum in philosophy.

The shallowness of Quine's thought, Skolimowski argues, is ironic in light of the fact that Quine is the product of one of the leading universities in one of the world's richest nations. Skolimowski notes that exemplars of "the technological mentality" generally have impressive academic backgrounds. Nonetheless, their thinking is usually sterile. This contradiction, he concludes—

> is a terrible indictment of a culture which has had so many powerful minds at its disposal and has produced so little in positive terms.[43]

Skolimowski's critique provided Quine a golden opportunity to defend the basic presuppositions of his thought, and indeed of his education and life. Instead, Quine chose to write a shallow response that is only two pages long. He argues that he has continued with his conventionalism in philosophy, saying it has broadened over the years. But he fails to justify his abiding commitment to behavioristic psychology, mechanistic physics, and bivalent logic. Nor does he justify his enthusiasm for the scientific method as the privileged window on reality or his dismissal of alternative points of view in logic as "deviant."

Despite Quine's short demurrer, Skolimowski's charge is entirely justified. To appreciate the full depth of Quine's reactionary bias in philosophy, we need only compare him to the later Wittgenstein.

As the previous two chapters have shown, after Wittgenstein realized that formal logic is a myth-system, he increasingly emphasized the variety of the "forms of life" that create and sustain myth-systems. This new emphasis helped him shed the ethnocentrism that has characterized Western logicians since antiquity.

Like the later Wittgenstein, Quine also came to realize that formal logic, mathematics, and science are myth-systems. But unlike Wittgenstein, Quine proceeded to use every philosophical gimmick he could think of to privilege the particular myth-system with which he himself was most familiar. The beliefs and practices of "savages" (as Quine consistently terms them) at best foreshadow the higher consciousness benignly bestowed on the world by modern science. These savage beliefs have no relevance for us (or even determinate content!) except insofar as they can be reformulated in the canonical notation, and made consistent with behavioristic psychology and mechanistic physics.

Why, in the end, does Quine regard the myths that are supportive of modern science as superior to all others? Because science, he argues, has proven to be the most useful in making predictions from observation to observation. But the deeper questions, which the later Wittgenstein clearly saw and which Quine has never addressed, are these: Useful for *whom*? And at what *cost*?

Quine never addresses these questions. In order to answer them, he would have been obliged to appeal to history and to some standard of values by which to judge history. But that would mean that the foundation of philosophy is not, after all, behavioristic epistemology, but rather what the Romans called *humanitas*—the very thing that is most glaringly absent from Quine's life and thought.

With Apologies to Russell

Quine's philosophy is a back-pedaling effort to shore up the old absolutist view of formal logic and science that he inherited from Russell, against the relativism that he himself had come to realize is a part of all language. Prior to Frege and Russell, the logicians had always appealed to some sort of other-worldly absolute as the guarantor of the Parmenidean myth. Russell wanted science itself as a this-worldly guarantor, but failed to take into account complications due to language. The early Wittgenstein, a closet idealist, reacted against his teacher Russell, attempting a return in *Tractatus* to the earlier tradition of a transcendent guarantor. Quine, rejecting all mysticism, sought to develop a relativistic theory of language that was consistent (so he thought) with an absolutist view of science.

The weakness in all this is the weakness that always appears in appeals to an absolute: if any crack appears in the brittle, monolithic base, the whole structure sags. The later Wittgenstein diligently ferreted out such cracks, discovering that no single structure of logical form undergirds all language. Formal logic, which is the language of science, turns out to be just one of many different kinds of language-games, all of which are valid on their own terms. No single notation is canonical for all. The tower of Babel collapses.

Although Quine is in the same general philosophical tradition as Russell, the two men have displayed contrasting characters. Russell was ever the great iconoclast. At the time he developed his philosophy, it was a bold challenge to established academic orthodoxies. As his relationship with Wittgenstein proved, Russell encouraged his students to develop alternative views to his own. He also had a life outside of the university, and was passionately committed to various struggles for social justice.

Quine, on the other hand, has spent virtually his entire adult life in an institutional setting. An admirer of the likes of S.I. Hayakawa and a pet of the Rand Corporation, he has been notably indifferent to calls for social justice. He put forth his own philosophy as a contribution to a larger academic orthodoxy, and disparaged attempts by others to develop alternative views. The transition from Russell to Quine is a classic example of how a philosophical tradition that begins with a burst of inspiration and vigor can end in a rut of stultifying academic mediocrity.

The Fuzzy Menace

As we have seen, Quine scoffs at arguments calling for alternative systems of logic. Of these arguments, he says—

> The worst one is that things are not just black and white; there are gradations. ... Irresponsible literature to this effect can be cited.[44]

The "irresponsible literature" that Quine has in mind are the writings of Lotfi Zadeh, a professor of electrical engineering at the University of Southern California in Los Angeles. In 1965, Zadeh published a small paper proposing a new kind of logical calculus, which he termed "fuzzy logic."[45] Because Zadeh was an engineer, not a logician, and because he questioned the presuppositions of Quine's "canonical notation," American academics branded his views as "deviant." The Japanese, however, ever eager for new ideas and knowing nothing of Quine's strictures, took up Zadeh's system of logic with alacrity and gave it practical applications in industry. The result was that while fuzzy logic languished in its homeland, it generated a whole new generation of technological breakthroughs in Japan, far beyond the existing capabilities of American technology, both civilian and military. Not surprisingly, this practical accomplishment by foreigners eventually forced American academics to re-examine their biases.

Lotfi Zadeh's fuzzy logic breaks the dominant trend in Western formal logic. At the same time, however, it also reinforces certain core features of patriarchal thinking. In the remainder of this chapter, we will briefly examine the double-sided nature of Zadeh's breakthrough.

The Road to California

Lotfi Zadeh was born in 1921 in Baku, the capital of what was then Soviet Azerbaijan; his mother was a Russian doctor, and his father, a prosperous Iranian merchant.[46] In 1931, the family returned to the father's home city of Teheran, where they continued to live in luxury under the reign of the murderous Shah, Reza Pahlevi. Zadeh graduated from the University of Teheran in 1942 with a degree in electrical engineering. Using connections with the U.S. military, he moved to the United States in 1944 to do graduate study at MIT and Columbia University, obtaining his Ph.D. degree from the latter school in 1949. His parents subsequently followed him to the United States. In 1959 Zadeh, comfortably ensconced in the United States, became a professor of electrical engineering at the University of California in Berkeley, and in 1963, the head of the department.

Zadeh first published his new view of logic in a 1965 article dealing with set theory. Set theory (or class theory) is related to logic because to say "Object x is such-and-such" is to attribute membership in a certain set to object x. For example, to say "Mick is a self-centered slob" is to say that Mick is a member of the set of all self-centered slobs. Traditional logic creates a parallelism between two dichotomies: on the one hand, membership or non-membership in a set; on the other hand, the truth or falsity of some statement. In our example, Mick either belongs to the set of all self-centered slobs or he doesn't; the statement that asserts this class membership is either true or false.

Zadeh's new view of logic attacks bivalence on both scores. It's an oversimplification of things, he argues, to say that an object either belongs to some set or it doesn't. In terms of our example, there are different *degrees* to which any given person is a self-centered slob. Accordingly, there are degrees of truth to any statement ascribing this trait to someone. We might say, for example, that the statement "Mick is a self-centered slob" is 65% true.

Zadeh deliberately chose the provocative name "fuzzy logic" because he knew that a host of philosophical prejudices about the nature of clarity had come to infect orthodox logic. As exemplified by the smug Willard Van Orman Quine, orthodox logicians ridiculed alternative logics as the makeshift devices of people who were too mushy-minded to think straight. Although Zadeh did not use the phrase "Parmenidean myth," he rightly sensed that a myth-system was at stake in the debate, as witnessed by his remark:

> The concept of a fuzzy set has an upsetting effect on the established order.[47]

Zadeh's choice of name is actually a misnomer, however, for there is nothing at all fuzzy about the new system. A less provocative name would be "gradient logic," since Zadeh's system is specifically designed to handle matters of degree. But Zadeh's name does have the merit of rattling the cages of the orthodox, which is always a worthwhile accomplishment whenever philosophical thought has become ossified.

Zadeh seems to have come to his idea by reflecting on the use of electrical circuits in computers. At the time of Zadeh's writing, information-flow in computer circuits was a matter of binary switches: the current in any part of the computer was either on or off, and a piece of information consisted in some on-off sequence. This binary use of electrical circuits to store information had developed in tandem with the bivalent truth-tables of orthodox logic.

In order to come up with the root concept of fuzzy logic, all one need do was realize that information might be stored in a computer by *gradations* in the intensity of the current. Then reasoning backwards to truth-tables, one comes up with an infinite variety of truth-values, corresponding to the infinite variety of levels of current. Combining this realization with the common-sense assumption (accepted by everyone but logicians) that things fall into categories by degree, not absolutely, one has the whole recipe for fuzzy logic.

The Japanese Go Fuzzy

The fact that fuzzy logic bombed in the United States did not deter Japanese engineers. They realized that a computer programmed with fuzzy logic could detect varying degrees of likeness and unlikeness in the data it was fed, and so generate new rules by which to categorize the data. In short, it could learn from its own experience. It could accomplish this feat because the act of deciding what is more or less alike within a cloud of data is the same as the act of inferring a rule from the data. By contrast, computers programmed with orthodox logic doggedly persist in applying the same old rules even when these rules become irrelevant to new data.

In the 1980s, Japanese engineers, programming microchips with fuzzy logic, brought out whole new generations of machines whose performance-levels far exceeded comparable products in the United States. A typical example is a clothes washer that continually varies the amount of electricity and detergent it uses, depending on changes in the amount of dirt it senses in the water. Although a plethora of such inventions now exists in Japan, most Americans still remain blissfully ignorant of the tremendous jump in technology that the Japanese have made by implementing fuzzy logic.

Japanese engineers did not work in a vacuum. The Japanese government, realizing the great potential of fuzzy technology, helped create two institutes for the study of the subject: the Laboratory for International Fuzzy Engineering Research, established in 1989 in Yokohama; and The Fuzzy Logic Systems Institute, established in 1990 at the Kyushu Institute of Technology. As a result of these developments, American engineers and academics finally decided to take a new look at fuzzy logic. They held the first U.S. national conference on the subject in Austin, Texas, in 1991, an event that would have been inconceivable when Quine was at the height of his influence.

The Fuzzy World-View

Although Zadeh's greatest practical influence has been in Japan, he has not been wanting in disciples in the United States. In the late 1980s, one American admirer, Bart Kosko, emerged as a forceful new advocate on behalf of Zadeh's work. Building on Zadeh's initial insights, Kosko has expanded fuzzy logic from a modest proposal for a new logical calculus into an aggressive new program for criticizing conventional mathematics and science, and for articulating a new world-view.

Kosko confidently claims that his work in fuzzy logic is helping to create a "paradigm shift" in the way people view reality (invoking a term coined by the philosopher of science Thomas Kuhn).[48] As we are about to see, Kosko is right to make such a grand claim—up to a point.

Bart Kosko was born in Kansas City, Kansas, in 1960. In the 1980s he earned various degrees in the University of California system, culminating in a Ph.D. in electrical engineering in 1987. He now directs the Signal and Image Processing Institute of the University of Southern California in Los Angeles. In addition to his academic work, he boasts of many athletic interests, including hunting, fur trapping, fly-fishing, scuba diving, karate, and weight lifting.

In 1984, Kosko met Lotfi Zadeh at a conference on artificial intelligence. Although intrigued by Zadeh's new ideas, Kosko was disappointed with Zadeh's lack of aggressiveness (as it seemed to Kosko) in taking on his critics. After some initial doubt, Kosko was converted to Zadeh's views. In 1991 Kosko published a book on fuzzy logic and computers, and in 1993 he published a manifesto for a new world-view based on fuzzy principles, *Fuzzy Thinking*.

Kosko rightly points out that orthodox logic is grounded in an outmoded myth system. Especially in regard to the matter of bivalence, he aptly observes that—

> The men and women of science beg the question of bivalence... The practice looks far more like religion than science.[49]

Kosko is wrong, however, when he attributes the mythology that lies behind orthodox logic to Aristotle. As shown in chapter four, the myth was first fabricated by Parmenides, and subsequently taken up by most major Western logicians, not just Aristotle. Indeed, ancient *opponents* of Aristotle's legacy, such as the Stoics, also swallowed the Parmenidean myth. Nonetheless, Kosko deserves credit for highlighting the mythological aspects of orthodox logic, especially in contrast to conventional academics like Quine, who touch on the matter, but never draw out the full implications.

Kosko challenges those aspects of modern mathematics and science that take orthodox logic for granted, especially classical probability theory. (It presupposes ignorance, not knowledge; it's a special case of fuzzy logic.) Kosko also points out that modern science, far from encouraging new ideas, at times acts as an inquisition to suppress them.

Despite these criticisms, however, Kosko remains faithful to mathematics and science. His complaint is that individual mathematicians and scientists do not always follow the highest standards of their own professions, as witnessed by their irrational commitment to outdated logical myths.

Kosko maintains that a fuzzy model can approximate, with ever increasing accuracy, *any* dynamical system that changes in a continuous manner. The fuzzy model can do this because it's not stuck in a black and white mode. It adapts itself to shades of gray in the data, creating an ever more precise set of rules for describing the operation of the system.

Despite the hostility of academic logicians, fuzzy logic is proving to be the most important development in the history of logic since the work of Gottlob Frege. Its strong point is its devastating critique of the myth of bivalence, combined with the development of a practical alternative to bivalence that can exceed the technological capabilities of bivalent systems.

Gray vs. Color

Despite the achievements of fuzzy logic, however, it is not so revolutionary as it advocates claim. In certain of its theoretical presuppositions, as well as in the personal values of its leading proponent, Bart Kosko, it displays a familiar underside.

Although fuzzy logic rejects bivalence, it retains two other shibboleths of the Parmenidean myth: the myth of absolute objectivity and the myth of logical necessity. Kosko, for example, believes in an absolute determinism in nature, which he maintains can be objectively mirrored by logic, provided it be of sufficient subtlety. Indeed, he argues that quantum mechanics is wrong to postulate an element of genuine contingency in reality. Fuzzy logic, he believes, will eventually prove that contingency can be peeled away from quantum mechanics, and therefore from nature. He's not phased by the fact that Einstein spent the last 25 years of his life vainly trying to prove the same thing.

Like generations of logicians before him, Kosko assumes that unpredictable change and the interpreter's personal circumstances are peripheral in creating the best description of reality (the myth of absolute objectivity). Previous chapters have shown, however, that this assumption is false. Contrary to the logicians, reality is not a dead fish wrapped in cellophane, not even a dead gray fish. As every artist knows, and as the logicians have yet to appreciate, the universe is brought to us in living color.

You Just Have To Take It

Kosko's belief in absolute objectivity and logical necessity is matched by confidence in the veracity of his own logical deductions. He proudly proclaims:

> My theorems are false if and only if 2=3. So you don't have to like it. You just have to take it.[50]

Kosko's claim brings to mind the boasts of earlier logicians and philosophers. For example, Immanuel Kant had supreme confidence in the Aristotelian logic of his own day, declaring:

> It is remarkable that to the present day it [Aristotelian logic] has not been able to make one step in advance, so that to all appearance, it may be considered as completed and perfect.[51]

Alas for Kant, the following century witnessed the development of a whole new approach to logic. The new symbolic logic dismissed Aristotle's earlier work as both cumbersome and erroneous, a judgment that would have dumbfounded Kant.

Another example is the case of Gottlob Frege. In 1893, Frege published volume one of his book *The Basic Laws of Arithmetic*. At the time, he thought he had provided an unassailable logical foundation for arithmetic. He insisted that his deductions could not be reasonably challenged by anyone who understood the concepts involved. With great bravado he dared anyone to do a better job:

> As a refutation in this I can only recognize someone's actually demonstrating either that a better, more durable edifice can be erected upon other fundamental convictions, or else that my principles lead to manifestly false conclusions. But no one will be able to do that.[52]

Alas for Frege, Bertrand Russell shortly thereafter derived a contradiction from one of Frege's axioms. Frege's house of logical cards collapsed.

The early Ludwig Wittgenstein shared the hubris of Kant and Frege. Wittgenstein confidently proclaimed that his deductions in *Tractatus* had solved the principal outstanding logical problems of his time:

> The *truth* of the thoughts that are here set forth seems to me unassailable and definitive. I therefore believe myself to have found, on all essential points, the final solution of the problems.[53]

Alas for Wittgenstein, logicians shortly thereafter proved that his system of logic was incapable of handling important kinds of generalizations. Later, Wittgenstein himself came to the conclusion that *Tractatus* was grounded in a host of dubious metaphysical assumptions.

In the same confident spirit of Kant, Frege, and the early Wittgenstein, Bart Kosko now proclaims that his deductions are unassailable, and that anybody who disagrees simply can't think straight. Time alone will tell whether he is right. But even if his particular deductions hold up, the spirit of rational inquiry is never helped by boasts of "You just have to take it."

Let's suppose that Kosko is right on this theoretical question. Even so, a practical obstacle remains. To appreciate this obstacle, remember that Kosko has proven (at most) that fuzzy logic can increasingly approximate any continuous mathematical function.[54] But is it true, as a practical matter, that the most interesting and important phenomena can be captured by continuous mathematical functions? That is, is it true that all reality can be reduced to mathematical factuality? Kosko simply assumes so. Previous chapters, however, have provided ample reasons for doubting this dogma.

Kosko himself acknowledges a related problem. When fuzzy logic approximates any dynamical system, the number of rules that it uses increases exponentially with the number of system variables. In order to keep calculations manageable, the fuzzy logician must *decide* which few of the many aspects of the system are relevant to the purposes at hand. But this maneuver reflects the basic weakness of all formal logic: it oversimplifies nature and human experience for the sake of the logician's convenience. Contrary to the claims of logicians, such an oversimplification does not provide a privileged window on reality.

This much may be granted to Kosko: fuzzy logic is a promising new tool that works in certain circumstances. To claim more is dogmatism.

Testosterone and Formal Logic

Kosko is effusive in describing the technological benefits he expects from fuzzy logic. Some of these predictions (like some of Quine's later writings) bring to mind the fantasies of Dr. Strangelove. For example, Kosko predicts that fuzzy technology will make possible the creation of "sex cyborgs." These will be robotic sex-toys that closely simulate the feel of human flesh as well as the sounds and movements of a body having sex:

> Just imagine if someone in Kyoto comes up with flesh that, if you did a Turing test, people said "Yes, that's flesh," and you just put in a little water and warm it up and so forth, and it makes all the sounds.[55]

More is involved than toys, however. Kosko predicts that fuzzy technology will allow humans and machines to become more like each other. As a result, they may even reproduce, in a master-slave sort of way:

> Man's future with smart machines will involve new variations on the old theme of master and slave. We will control our machine-intelligent superiors. We will live with them, create with them, adapt with them, maybe even reproduce with them. We will hold their strings while they hold ours, both masters and both slaves. The question will be to what degree.[56]

Kosko predicts that future surgeons, using fuzzy microtechnology, will be able to replace people's brains piece by piece with tiny computer chips. Thus will technology deliver what monotheistic religions have only dreamed of, personal immortality:

> The nanosurgeons [microsurgeons] open your skull and you are wide awake. ... At first they cut out a small gray chunk of your brain. ... They replace your brain chunk with a tiny nanochip wrapped in sponge and studded with nanotendrils. ... Next they cut out a second brain chunk and replace it with another neural-net chiplet. ... Then they cut out a third brain chunk and replace it. ... The electrochemical cloud of patterns you call you need not die... You can get out of the meat car before it wrecks.[57]

Hoping to cash in on these future benefits, Kosko has ordered that when he dies his head be cut off and frozen (cryonics). It will be thawed and resurrected on that glorious Easter morn when the new fuzzy technology finally triumphs.

Kosko's writings and remarks over the years reflect a familiar masculinist theme: adulation of the aggressive, loner male—the type of man who ever proves his valor through heroic struggles with nature and all comers. For example, Kosko boasts of his prowess in muscle-building, karate, trap-shooting, and hunting (including wild boar, with bow and arrow). He admires a Japanese colleague in fuzzy logic, Takeshi Yamakawa, who expresses contempt for "soft men," taking Kosko to the shrine of a Samurai warrior who reputedly killed 1,000 men. In his disputes with other logicians and mathematicians, Kosko likens himself to a champion boxer or warrior, boasting—

> I'll fight anyone, on any conditions, any terms. ... I don't walk into battle without a sword on.[58]

In the classroom, Kosko believes that his students draw their best flow charts in fuzzy logic when dealing with questions of sex and power. Outside the classroom, he has done contract work for the Air Force and encouraged the military to develop "smart weapons" based on fuzzy logic. Finally, he relates that the most creative ideas in logic come to him while he soaks in a hot-tub after hard, sweaty workouts because that's "when the beta-endorphins really flow."[59]

It would be easy to laugh off this type of fantasizing as a personal quirk, were it not for the precedent of Otto Weininger. As discussed in chapter seven, Weininger believed that the real man is the self-centered loner who proves his masculinity to himself and to the world through heroic struggles in the quest for power and knowledge. Dissociating himself from everything that is soft, and toughened by his heroic struggles for what is hard, the real man develops an inner strength by which he gains both a panoptic vision of the nature of the world and a kind of immortality for himself. To understand this process, Weininger argued, is to be logical; to master it, ethical.

Kosko differs from Weininger in important respects. For example, Kosko locates ego-immortality in worldly technology, not in a realm above. In addition, Kosko is not authoritarian in politics. To the contrary, he advocates "libertarian pragmatism." Nor does Kosko denigrate Jews and women. Nonetheless, Kosko and Weininger have this in common: both embed a philosophy of logic in a network of masculinist fantasizing.

After Weininger died, others used his fusion of bivalent logic and masculinist fantasy to buttress the Nazi mystique. What will happen after Kosko dies? Will others use his fusion of multivalent logic and masculinist fantasy to create a new high-tech testosterone mystique? The precedent of history shows that this question is not a trivial one.

Kosko denies that his philosophy has anything in common with Weininger's. In addition, he condemns this whole discussion of his personal circumstances as an unprincipled *ad hominem* attack that is philosophically irrelevant.[60] But if Kosko's personal fantasies and circumstances are irrelevant to his philosophy, why does he himself take such pains to advertise them to his readers?

Philosophies of logic do not just pop out of the air. They reflect the personal circumstances, fantasies, and characters of those who create them (usually men). Kosko is right when he says that philosophical ideas cannot be reduced to personal circumstances; nonetheless, knowledge of these circumstances can contribute to our understanding of philosophy, as his own case proves.

Oh Brave New World That Has Such People In It

As we have seen, Kosko at times criticizes other logicians, mathematicians, and scientists for using inquisitorial methods to stifle dissent. But Kosko makes it clear that his target is not science itself, but rather the foibles of some of its practitioners, especially those who overlook the value of his own new fuzzy logic. In language strikingly similar to that of Quine's, Kosko praises the scientific method in and of itself. He argues that it is the final criterion of what is true, having supplanted religion, philosophy, and even ethics. All of these, he claims, now have the same low status as astrology:

> Science is the measure of all things. ... Science has all but ended astrology and philosophy and religion. They live on as shells of what they once were. ... Fuzzy logic is a part of science. ... Science disposes of ethics.[61]

Both Quine and Kosko practically fall over themselves in praising the brave new world that science has created. Its successes, they say, show that science is worthy of our trust. Moreover, formal logic—whether the old bivalent version (Quine's) or the new fuzzy version (Kosko's)—is grounded in science; therefore, formal logic deserves our trust as well. The logicians don't need to rely on Parmenides' old myths anymore. Now they are hitched to the proven realities of modern science!

In the end, the justification that both Quine and Kosko offer for formal logic boils down to two interconnected claims: (1) science, considered theoretically, provides humanity with its best window on reality; and (2) science, considered practically, has been a great boon to humanity. In the next two chapters, we will examine in detail these two grand claims.

---

[1] For various views of Quine's philosophy, see Roger Gibson, *The Philosophy of W.V. Quine: An Expository Essay*, University Presses of Florida, Tampa, 1982; Lewis Hahn & Paul A. Schilpp (eds.), *The Philosophy of W.V. Quine*, Open Court, La Salle, IL, 1986; Christopher Hookway, *Quine: Language, Experience and Reality*, Stanford University Press, Stanford, CA, 1988; Alex Orenstein, *Willard Van Orman Quine*, Twayne Publishers, Boston, 1977; and

George Romanos, *Quine and Analytic Philosophy*, The MIT Press, Cambridge, MA, 1983.
[2] Willard Van Orman Quine, "Autobiography of W.V. Quine" in Hahn and Schilpp (eds.), *op. cit.*, pp. 14 (stipend) & 19 (Hayakawa). Quine misidentifies Hayakawa's school as the University of San Francisco, which is a Catholic institution.
[3] *ibid.*, p. 24.
[4] *ibid.*, p. 27.
[5] Willard Van Orman Quine, "Two Dogmas of Empiricism," first published in 1951; reprinted in Quine's *From a Logical Point of View*, 1953; 2nd revised edition, 1961; Harper Torchbooks reprint, New York, 1963, pp. 20-46.
[6] *ibid.*, p. 41.
[7] Willard Van Orman Quine, *The Ways of Paradox and Other Essays*, Harvard University Press, Cambridge, MA, 1st edition, 1966, revised edition, 1976, p. 229.
[8] Otto Neurath, "Protocol Sentences" in *Logical Positivism*, ed. by A.J. Ayer, The Free Press, New York, 1959, p. 201.
[9] Willard Van Orman Quine, *Theories and Things*, The Belknap Press, Cambridge, MA, 1981, p. 72.
[10] Willard Van Orman Quine, *Methods of Logic*, Holt, Rinehart and Winston, New York, 1st edition 1950, 2nd edition 1959, pp. xiv-xv.
[11] Willard Van Orman Quine, *Word and Object*, The M.I.T. Press, Cambridge, MA, 1960, 11th printing, 1979, p. 13, n.5.
[12] *ibid.*, p. 221.
[13] Willard Van Orman Quine, *Ontological Relativity and Other Essays*, Columbia University Press, New York, 1969, pp. 134-35; also *Word and Object*, pp. 123-124; and (with co-author J.S. Ullian) *The Web of Belief*, Random House, New York; 1st edition, 1970; 2nd edition 1978, p. 4.
[14] Quine, *Word and Object*, pp. 22-23.
[15] Quine, *Theories and Things*, p. 19
[16] Quine, *Theories and Things*, p. 72; *The Web of Belief*, p. 32.
[17] Quine, *The Web of Belief*, p. 62.
[18] *ibid.*, pp. 4-6.
[19] Quine, *Methods of Logic*, p. 201.
[20] Quine, *From a Logical Point of View*, p. 15.
[21] In his most recent book, Quine says that Russell was wrong to think that all of mathematical truth could be deduced from self-evident logical truth. Nonetheless, Quine still insists that "the whole conceptual scheme of classical mathematics boils down to" truth functions, quantification theory, and class membership. (Willard Van Orman Quine, *From Stimulus to Science*, Harvard University Press, Cambridge, MA, 1995, p. 9.)
[22] Rudolf Carnap, "Empiricism, Semantics, and Ontology" in *Meaning and Necessity: A Study in Semantics and Modal Logic*, Phoenix Books, The University of Chicago Press, Chicago, 1947; 5th printing, 1967, p. 215, n. 5.
[23] Quine, *Philosophy of Logic*, pp. 80-81.
[24] Quine, *Theories and Things*, p. 36; and Willard Van Orman Quine, *Quiddities*, The Belknap Press of Harvard University Press, Cambridge, MA, 1987, p. 57.
[25] Quine, *Philosophy of Logic*, p. 81
[26] *ibid.*, p. 85.
[27] Quine, *Methods of Logic*, p. 120.
[28] Quine, *Word and Object*, p. 273.
[29] Alex Orenstein describes Quine as "a reluctant Platonist." (Orenstein, *op. cit.*, p. 61.)
[30] For example, see his "New Foundations for Mathematical Logic" in *From a Logical Point of View*, pp. 80-101. As noted above, his most recent view is that, although mathematics cannot be deduced from logic, "the whole conceptual scheme of classical mathematics" can be boiled down to logic (Quine, *From Stimulus to Science*, p. 9).
[31] Quine, *Ontological Relativity*, pp. 27 & 29.
[32] Quine, *The Web of Belief*, p. 22.
[33] Quine, *Word and Object*, p. 13, n.5
[34] *ibid.*, pp. 58, 59, & 69.
[35] Quine, *Ontological Relativity*, p. 47.
[36] Quine, *From a Logical Point of View*, p. 44.
[37] Quine, *Word and Object*, p. 22.
[38] Quine, *Ontological Relativity*, pp. 75, 84, 159; *The Ways of Paradox*, 233; *From Stimulus to Science*, p. 19.
[39] Quine, *The Ways of Paradox*, p. 228.
[40] Quine, *Theories and Things*, p. 193; Mortimer Adler, "Has Philosophy Lost Contact with People?" *Newsday*, 11/18/1979.
[41] Stanley Kubrick, *Dr. Strangelove, or How I Learned to Stop Worrying and Love the Bomb* (movie), Columbia, Britain, 1963.
[42] Henryk Skolimowksi, "Quine, Ajdukiewicz, and the Predicament of 20th Century Philosophy" in Hahn and Schilpp, *op. cit.*, pp. 473-474.
[43] *ibid.*, p. 490.
[44] Quine, *Philosophy of Logic*, p. 85.
[45] Lotfi Zadeh, "Fuzzy Sets," *Information and Control*, vol. 8, 1965, pp. 338-53. See also his article "Fuzzy Logic and Approximate Reasoning," *Synthese*, vol. 30, 1975, pp. 407-28.
[46] The best overall account of fuzzy logic is Daniel McNeill's & Paul Freiberger's *Fuzzy Logic*, Simon and Schuster, New York, 1993. See also Bart Kosko, *Fuzzy Thinking; The New Science of Fuzzy Logic*, Hyperion, New York, 1993.
[47] McNeill & Freiberg, *op. cit.*, p. 50.
[48] Kosko, *Fuzzy Thinking*, p. xvi; Thomas S. Kuhn, *The Structure of Scientific Revolutions*, 2nd edition, The University of Chicago Press, Chicago, 1970, p. 89.
[49] Kosko, *Fuzzy Thinking*, p. 15.
[50] Quoted by McNeill & Freiberger, *op. cit.*, p. 192.
[51] Immanuel Kant, *Critique of Pure Reason*, 2nd Edition, trans. by Max Müller, Macmillan, New York, 1925, p. 688.
[52] Gottlob Frege, *The Basic Laws of Arithmetic*, trans. by Montgomery Furth, University of California Press, Berkeley, 1964, p. 25.
[53] Ludwig Wittgenstein, *Tractatus Logico-Philosophicus*, trans. by D.F. Pears & B.F. McGuinness, The Humanities Press, New York, 1963, p. 5; original's emphasis.
[54] Bart Kosko, "Fuzzy Systems as Universal Approximators," *IEEE Transactions on Computers*, vol. 43, No. 11, November 1994, pp. 1329-1333.
[55] McNeill & Freiberger, *op. cit.*, p. 241; Kosko, *op. cit.*, p. 283.
[56] Kosko, *Fuzzy Thinking*, p. 285.
[57] Bart Kosko, "Chipping Away at Your Brain," *Free Inquiry*, Winter 1994, p. 96.
[58] McNeil and Freiberger, *op. cit.*, p. 194.
[59] Kosko, *Fuzzy Thinking*, p. 61.
[60] Bart Kosko, unpublished letter to author, November 1, 1996.
[61] Kosko, *Fuzzy Thinking.*, pp. 255-262.

Technophilia, Detail
Acrylic on Canvas, 24" x 33", 1991

12

The Metaphysics of Science

SUMMARY: This chapter addresses the effort by modern logicians and mathematicians to save the Parmenidean myth by buttressing it with the myth of scientific progress. The chapter exposes fatal weaknesses in the presuppositions of the scientific method. It shows how formal logic and science each cling to each other in order to justify their own poorly-grounded theoretical claims.

In the last chapter, we saw that Willard Van Orman Quine and Bart Kosko claimed to reject all mysticism in finding a ground for formal logic. Nonetheless, they both retained much of the old Parmenidean myth. What could provide non-mystical support for this myth? Following the precedent of Bertrand Russell, they turned to science for an answer. Science has a unique capacity, they said, to bring the true nature of reality into focus. Because formal logic provides an X-ray of the conceptual skeleton within the body scientific, formal logic is well grounded. Science saves Parmenides!

As noted in the last chapter, this justification for formal logic rests on two interconnected assumptions: (1) science, considered theoretically, provides humanity with its best window on reality; and (2) science, considered practically, has been a great boon to humanity. As we are about to see in this and the following chapter, both these claims are as far-fetched as Parmenides' ancient appeal to the goddess far-constraining Order.

Science vs. Observational Knowledge

Before assessing the value of science, we have to be clear about the meaning of the term. The Latin root of the word is *scientia*, which is a translation of the Greek *episteme*. Both words originally meant knowledge, skill, or expertise. This linguistic fact parallels a historic one: the popular mind has generally associated science with reliable knowledge, especially that sort of knowledge whose reliability derives from observation. Hence the genuinely puzzled look on many people's faces when anyone would dare to challenge science's credentials. "Challenge science?" they think. "Well, you might as well challenge careful observation. After all, isn't that what science is—knowledge derived from careful observation?"

Despite this common reaction, however, science in the modern sense involves much more than knowledge derived from careful observation. Consider, for example, the original residents of North America and Africa prior to the white invasions from Europe. There is no question that these tribal societies had developed great systems of reliable knowledge about animals and plants, cumulatively developed from generations of careful observation. Yet historians of science are unanimous that such tribal societies are "prescientific." But if science equals reliable knowledge based on careful observation, how could historians of science come to this conclusion?

The answer is that what we call "modern science" is actually a very peculiar phenomenon; however, it has become so much a part of the fabric of modern life that its peculiarity is now lost on us, just as the peculiarities of Christian dogma were lost on devout Christians during the Middle Ages. To comprehend this peculiarity, we will take a brief look at certain historical circumstances in the evolution of modern science. Once we have this perspective, we will be able to give a correct definition of the term.

Revolution in Heaven

The great turning point for the development of modern science occurred in 1543. The Polish astronomer Nicolaus Copernicus, realizing that his approaching death would protect him from persecution, permitted publication of his revolutionary scientific treatise *De revolutionibus orbium caelestium* (*On the Revolutions of the Celestial Spheres*). In contrast to the received view of astronomy, dating from the Egyptian astronomer Ptolemy in the 2nd century A.D., Copernicus argued that the planets and the stars do not revolve around the Earth as they appear to. Instead, Copernicus maintained that it is the Earth that rotates, first around its own axis, and then, together with the planets, around a stationary sun.

Although not widely realized today, the condemnations of Copernicus were of two types—those of the clergy and those of the astronomers—who each had their own reasons. Most people now remember only the first type, the ecclesiastical condemnations. Church hierarchs, jealous of their prerogatives as the arbiters of higher truth, resented the fact that some upstart would map out the abode of God and the angels by methods beyond their own institutional control. Their self-serving condemnation of Copernicus richly deserves the scorn that all succeeding generations have heaped on it.

The case is not so simple, however, with the other group, the astronomers. Their argument against Copernicus was that his system contravened *observations*. For one thing, any fool can see that the Sun, stars, and planets rise in the east and set in the west. Furthermore, we can all feel with our own feet that the Earth is stationary, not moving. If Copernicus were right, there would be a constant wind from the east, as the Earth turned into it, and if you threw a stone straight up into the air, it would always fall down some distance behind, to the west. Finally, the claim that the Earth rotates around the Sun is disproved by the fact that we observe no stellar parallax. That is, if the Earth really traveled such a huge distance around the Sun, we should be able to detect differences in the positions of the fixed stars at each end of the Earth's orbit. (The same way that a stationary house appears in different positions of our field of vision, when we view it at each end of a long passing road.) However, we observe no such stellar parallax. Furthermore, we know that the amount of observed parallax for any remote object decreases the further the object is from us. Therefore, one of two things must be true: either Copernicus is wrong, or else the fixed stars are at such mind-boggling distances from us as to render parallax undetectable. But this type of mind-boggling distance has never been *observed*.

The astronomers had other objections as well. Copernicus' system, when depicted with a map, looks nearly as complicated as Ptolemy's. (Copernicus wrongly thought the orbits of the planets were circles, not ellipses; hence he was forced to use epicycles in the style of Ptolemy.) Finally, both systems were about equally accurate for predicting the actual observed positions of the planets. The cumulative weight of such objections prevailed with those thinkers who regarded careful observation as the foundation of knowledge. As the historian of science Edwin Burtt rightly observes:

> Contemporary empiricists, had they lived in the sixteenth century, would have been the first to scoff out of court the new philosophy of the universe.[1]

Despite these objections, Copernicus eventually won the day. Why? Because his system harmonized better with observations? No. Rather, Copernicus' system won because it was more *scientific*. By understanding what it was that made his system more scientific, compared to Ptolemy's, we will find our sought-for definition of modern science.

God Geometrizes

Copernicus' method proved to be scientific because he was *not* concerned with merely giving an account of observations. Rather, he sought to render a special kind of account of observations, the kind that would embody the simplest mathematical reduction possible. In part, he sought this reduction because he found it esthetically pleasing; but more than that, he was convinced that the ultimate nature of reality itself is both mathematical and simple, regardless of how it may appear to the senses.

Copernicus' mathematical attitude represented a break with the dominant philosophy of the high Middle Ages, especially as represented by Thomas Aquinas's revised version of Aristotle. The empirical, unmathematical tenor of Aquinas's philosophy is reflected in the famous dictum *Nihil in intellectu quod non prius fuerit in sensu* ("there is nothing in cogitation that was not first in sensation").

Influenced by a revival of Platonic thought in the early Renaissance, Copernicus believed that God is the great geometer, and that the human mind can behold mathematical concepts as such. He insisted that his account was the simplest mathematical schematization of all the available evidence, and *therefore* that his system truly depicted the nature of reality. He rightly predicted that only mathematicians would be able to fully appreciate the power and elegance of his system, and that it would be due to mathematicians that his system would eventually prevail.

Some decades later, another great mathematical thinker, Galileo Galilei, confirmed Copernicus' forecast with these words of praise for his predecessor:

> With reason as his guide he resolutely continued to affirm what sensible experience seemed to contradict.[2]

Although Copernicus embraced the Platonic view that mathematics reveals the nature of reality, he rejected the other-worldly cast that Plato had given to mathematics. Copernicus insisted that material reality is precisely where the mathematical essence of the world manifests itself. We must approach sensory evidence, said Copernicus, with the same attentiveness that Plato had lavished on the ethereal realm of the Forms. By bringing mathematics down from the heavens, Copernicus succeeded in explaining the movements of the heavens.

Copernicus' mathematicization of observational knowledge established a precedent that was followed by Galileo Galilei and Johannes Kepler. This new approach yielded its most dazzling results at the hands of Isaac Newton, whose monumental book of 1687 was called, significantly, *Philosophiae naturalis principia mathematica* (*The Mathematical Principles of Natural Philosophy*). This work, drawing on the research of Copernicus, Galileo, and Kepler, integrated the principles of both terrestrial and celestial mechanics into one elegant mathematical whole, rooted in Newton's own insights into gravitation. The world's admiration for this feat was captured by Joseph Lagrange. The nature of physical reality could be discovered but once, he observed, and it was Newton's good fortune to have done so.

Why did mathematics and empirical observation join hands in the works of Copernicus, Galileo, Kepler, and Newton? Historian Stephen Mason shows that it was because the Renaissance witnessed the fusion of two previously separate phenomena, the craft tradition and the scholarly tradition.[3] Previously, craft workers lacked a literary tradition for recording their techniques in a way scholars would take seriously. Scholars, on the other hand, recorded their own theoretical findings in a literary tradition that was inaccessible to craft workers. During the Renaissance, the two paths crossed. As a result, mathematics, previously an ethereal part of the scholarly tradition, was brought to bear on practical observations made by craft workers. This cross-fertilization is especially clear in the case of Galileo. Through conversations with Italian plumbers, for example, he discovered that water will rise only a certain distance in a pipe. Significantly, he recorded the results of his empirical experiments in Italian, and his theoretical principles in Latin.[4]

1, 2, 3, What Do I See?

Every human society has had some body of knowledge, either written or otherwise, that was derived from careful observation. Renaissance history shows that the peculiar phenomenon called "modern science" does not consist in having such knowledge. Rather, modern science involves something more: the mathematicization of knowledge derived from careful observation.

What, then, is the meaning of this clumsy word "mathematicization"? The examples of Copernicus, Kepler, Galileo, and Newton tell us. First, individual observations are translated into impersonal propositions about measurable quantities. For example, instead of "I see green now," we get "A spectroscope records a certain frequency of electromagnetic radiation at a certain time in a certain place." Next, the whole body of quantitative propositions is organized into a formal deductive system so that a great number of these propositions can be deduced from a smaller number of axioms by means of rules of inference. Additional quantitative propositions are then deduced from the axioms and tested against additional observations. If the deduced propositions clash with observations, the axioms are revised accordingly.

From this cyclical process, an important consequence follows: Because the mathematicized system generates the specific predictions to be tested by observation, the system defines, in part, the questions asked. What is the meaning of a question asked of experience? What constitutes an observation that is relevant to answering the question? How is the answer to be interpreted? The way in which these questions are answered is influenced by the presuppositions of the mathematicized system that is supposedly being tested.

In short, experiment does not occur in a vacuum. What the scientist sees is in part defined by the scientific system he or she presupposes while looking. This fact, as we will see shortly, is of great importance in evaluating the claim of modern science to be a privileged lens on reality. For now it will suffice to note that mathematicization blurs the line between conceptualization and observation. This blurring explains why nearly every great scientist has rejected Aquinas' dictum that all cogitation derives from sensation; in science, sensation is in part determined by the manner of cogitation.

The Male Will to Power

Modern science, as we have just seen, is not the same as knowledge derived from careful observation. Rather, science involves something more: the mathematicization of knowledge derived from careful observation. But even this definition is not quite accurate. It fails to take into account the *motivation* behind such mathematicization, especially in recent centuries.

In antiquity, the philosophers of nature were divided into a large number of competing schools. Nonetheless, they generally agreed that the principal goal of their investigations was knowledge for its own sake, or esthetic satisfaction, or spiritual fulfillment, or some combination of these. Unlike modern scientists, they rarely thought of their goal in terms of the subjugation of nature or the domination of other nations. The nearest example to this type of thinking was the 3rd-century B.C. mathematician and mechanic Archimedes. Like Galileo, Archimedes delighted in using higher mathematics for the sake of solving this-worldly problems. Working as a military engineer for the tyrant of Syracuse, he was killed during the Roman siege of that city in 212 B.C. He was thus an early example of that marriage of militarism and science which, some 2,000 years later, would become a hallmark of patriarchal-industrial civilization.

Presages of the modern scientific notion of knowledge for the sake of power appeared in the thinking of two Englishmen who, by coincidence, shared the same last name, Roger Bacon and Francis Bacon. Roger Bacon (1214-92) was an unconventional Franciscan who was eventually suppressed by his order because of his (then) unorthodox ideas. In language worthy of Galileo, Bacon proclaimed the principle that "all things are known through the application of mathematics." He insisted that humanity, by mathematicizing empirical knowledge, would achieve great technical breakthroughs in the quest to dominate nature. With remarkable foresight, he predicted that such a new science could create mechanically powered cars, ships, submarines, airplanes, and other "unheard of engines."[5]

Roger Bacon's dream was amplified three-hundred years later by his namesake, Francis Bacon (1561-1626), a wily English politician and philosopher. In the intervening centuries, the Renaissance had witnessed a revolution in many of the traditional crafts. Consequently, the later Bacon found a more sympathetic audience for his ideas.

After the appearance of Francis Bacon's writings, scientists increasingly came to view the quest for knowledge as a quest for power. That Bacon should be the one to make such an idea stick was no accident, for much of his personal life was colored by his own unscrupulous will to power. For example, he promoted his early career by gaining the patronage of Robert Devereux, the Earl of Essex, who became one of his best friends. In the great quarrel between Essex and Queen Elizabeth, however, Bacon betrayed Essex, personally directing the crown's prosecution of Essex on a charge of treason. After Essex's execution, Bacon attempted to serve as a confidant to the Queen, who nonetheless remained leery of him. After Elizabeth's death, Bacon became a toady to King James I, defending the king's absolutist claims against a growing tide of democratic sentiment in parliament. While serving as Attorney General under King James, Bacon carried out the king's wish to have a prisoner tortured in order to force a confession. This torture, contrary to the law, he carried out over the objections of the famed jurist Edward Coke. Grateful for this favor, King James promoted Bacon to the position of Lord Chancellor and then raised him to the peerage. At the peak of his career, however, Bacon fell into disgrace, when he was caught accepting a bribe in a judicial proceeding. Despite a lifetime of self-serving political intrigue and influence-peddling, he died deeply in debt.

In his writings on science, Bacon is preoccupied with questions of power. He advocates what he calls a "great instauration." By this term he means both a theoretical and practical renewal of science. The theoretical renewal is to be his own newly proposed methodology of research. The practical renewal is to be a program of economic and political support given to science by the state, preferably a state that is highly centralized under one sole ruler like King James.

Bacon's recommendations for improving scientific method stress the importance of applying deductive rigor to empirical observation but, ironically, have little to say about mathematics. As a result, his views in this area are actually *less* innovative than those of Roger Bacon, and so have had little historical influence. But his call for the centralization of state power and for the state's endorsement of science as an ongoing institution has been enormously influential.

In contrast with the contemplative attitude expressed by the ancients, Francis Bacon says that philosophers follow nature in their experiments with the greater goal of conquering nature for their nation and their species. As Carolyn Merchant has demonstrated, Bacon's favorite metaphor for nature is as a rebellious female adversary who must be forced into subjugation and obedience. Such views marked the beginning of a relentless objectifying assault on nature by European males.[6]

Bacon's ideas first bore fruit in 1662, when King Charles II, acknowledging Bacon's influence, issued a charter creating the Royal Society. This was a state-supported institution for promoting "useful" scientific research, that is, research that might be useful to the state. Other nations followed suit. These state-supported institutions have grown cancerously into the gargantuan industrial-military-scientific complexes of the present day.

Modern Science

Drawing on the brief historical sketch above, we see that the three defining marks of modern science are careful observation, mathematicization, and the will to power (largely on the part of men). Accordingly, we arrive at this definition: modern science is the mathematicization of knowledge that has been derived from careful observation, motivated by the (primarily male) will to power.

Among the fields that are today loosely called sciences, this definition fits most closely that of theoretical physics. Psychology, on the other hand, presents the case of a much looser fit. But this divergence matches what most physical scientists themselves would, in a rough and intuitive way, regard as science. They generally view theoretical physics as the ideal of rigor to which all the sciences should in principle aspire, whereas they regard psychology as a discipline that is still striving to enter the scientific club, and which, at its worst, is but a step or two above voodoo.

Is Science Metaphysical?

We are now in a position to evaluate the oft-made claim that modern science, considered theoretically, provides us with the best window on reality. Over the last few centuries, many people have made this claim. Of this number, one of the most informed and articulate has been the historian of science A. d'Abro. In 1927, d'Abro published *The Evolution of Scientific Thought from Newton to Einstein*.[7] This book outlines the revolutionary changes that occurred in physics between the appearance of Newton's *Principia* in 1687 and Einstein's papers on the theory of relativity published in 1905 and 1916. As part of his historical overview, d'Abro includes a 99-page chapter entitled "The Methodology of Science." This chapter is a spirited and closely-reasoned defense of the claim that modern science is the window of choice for apprehending reality.

D'Abro wrote his defense of science as a rebuttal to another book, written a few years earlier, that was highly critical of the modern scientific mentality. This earlier book was *The Metaphysical Foundations of Modern Physical Science* by Edwin Burtt.[8] Reviewing the revolution that occurred in science from Copernicus to Newton, Burtt had argued that the new science uncritically absorbed a number of crude metaphysical assumptions that have ever since distorted the human understanding of reality.

Although it occurred some decades ago, the debate between d'Abro, the defender of science, and Burtt, the critic, set the general tone for most later arguments on the subject. More recent critiques have focused on science as a social construct embodying historical and gender biases. More recent defenses have attacked social constructivism and feminism as ill-informed and misguided. In terms of core arguments about the scientific method, however, recent works on both sides have not advanced much beyond d'Abro and Burtt. Accordingly, we will use the d'Abro-Burtt debate as a springboard for considering the issue.⁹

The Question of Metaphysics

Burtt's critique of science, published first, claims that Isaac Newton violated his much-vaunted claim of following empirical evidence, free of preconceived hypotheses. Burtt notes that Newton wrote as many works on theology as he did on science. He argues that Newton's quirky theological view of space as the *sensorium Dei* (God's sense organ) led him to the conclusion that space exists as an absolute frame of reference for all physical events, a view later attacked by Einstein.

Of even greater importance, says Burtt, is the distinction between "primary qualities" and "secondary qualities" that Copernicus, Galileo, and Newton all to some degree endorsed, and which has continued as a keystone of scientific thought ever since. According to this distinction, a "primary quality" is one that is quantitative, as opposed to qualitative, and that pertains to material things independently of the circumstances of any observer; for example, mass, acceleration, etc. A "secondary quality," on the other hand, is one that is qualitative, as opposed to quantitative, and that is affected by the state of the observer; for example, color, odor, etc.

Burtt notes, correctly, that the whole trend of modern science has been to regard primary qualities as more real than secondary qualities, a point with which most historians of science would agree. But Burtt adds his own controversial note to this accepted melody. The overall effect of this dichotomy between primary and secondary qualities, he argues, has been pernicious, for it twists our understanding of what is important in the natural world and marginalizes our personal mental experience:

> The world that people had thought themselves living in—a world rich with colour and sound, redolent with fragrance, filled with gladness, love and beauty, speaking everywhere of purposive harmony and creative ideals—was crowded now into minute corners in the brains of scattered organic beings. The really important world outside was a world hard, cold, colourless, silent, and dead.¹⁰

D'Abro, as noted, rejects Burtt's claims on all points. D'Abro insists that science is purely phenomenological, not metaphysical. That is, scientists simply make observations, and then frame tentative hypotheses to coordinate the observed phenomena with the maximum of simplicity. Next, they make predictions based on their tentative hypotheses. If the predictions turn out true, the hypotheses are retained; if not, new hypotheses are framed.

D'Abro concedes that in the short run scientific findings may reflect some particular scientist's belief-system. In the long run, however, he says the impersonal, phenomenological method of science weeds out such biases. Without mentioning Burtt by name, d'Abro scoffs at the view that modern science as a whole is driven by any sort of metaphysical assumptions:

> Opinions of this sort have been expressed by numerous philosophers who have devoted their attention to what they call the "metaphysics of science"; but we may hasten to say that the opinion appears to be entirely unwarranted. It is solely the criterion of simplicity of co-ordination [of phenomena] which decides on the orientation of science.¹¹

Of Metaphysics and Water Buckets

D'Abro attacks Burtt's criticism of science in detail. First he challenges Burtt's treatment of Newton's concept of absolute space; next, d'Abro defends the value of the distinction between primary and secondary qualities.

On the first point, d'Abro denies that Newton derived his scientific concept of absolute space from his religious concept of space as God's sense organ. On the contrary, says d'Abro, Newton's concept of absolute space evolved solely as a result of his reflections on certain phenomena of motion. Newton came to the conclusion that there must be absolute space, argues d'Abro, because of his famous water-bucket experiment. This experiment suggested to Newton that there must be some kind of absolute motion, and hence absolute space.

In this famous experiment, Newton took a bucket, partially filled with water, and suspended it by a rope from the ceiling. Next, he turned the bucket until the rope was twisted tight. With the water and bucket both at rest, Newton then released the bucket, giving it a sharp thrust in the direction opposite to that in which he had twisted the rope. Newton observed that the water gradually began to rotate in the unwinding direction. As it did so, the water receded from the bucket's axis of rotation, and climbed the walls of the bucket.

Eventually the water came to rest—*relative to the containing bucket*. But even when at rest relative to the bucket, the water still endeavored to retreat further from the axis of rotation, pressing up against the walls of the bucket with a measurable force.

This pressing motion of water away from the axis of rotation does *not* exist merely relative to the bucket, for the water continues to seek to move beyond the bucket even when it is at rest relative to the bucket. Now motion is always motion in the context of some presupposed framework; therefore, there must be some absolute framework to account for the retreating motion of water in the rotating water bucket, even when the water is at rest with respect to the bucket. This absolute framework, concluded Newton, is what we mean by the phrase "absolute space."

D'Abro concludes that Newton was driven to postulate the existence of absolute space because Newton realized that all rotatory motion involves a sort of *acceleration*, and not just *uniform velocity*. Newton knew that it is impossible to relativize acceleration in the same way as uniform velocity.

D'Abro accuses Burtt of making a major scientific blunder in his discussion of Newton's concept of absolute space: Burtt failed to note the essential distinction between *the absoluteness of acceleration* and *the relativity of uniform velocity*, the very distinction that was at issue in the water-bucket experiment. Burtt's work, d'Abro caustically remarks, is an example of what happens when philosophers with a school-boy knowledge of physics attempt to criticize science.

God's Presence

Although Burtt does at time muddy the distinction between acceleration and uniform velocity, there is more to the picture. D'Abro ignores another argument for absolute space in Newton's *Principia* that is based, not on acceleration at all, but on uniform velocity.

Consider the uniform movement of a body on a ship, says Newton, which is moving uniformly on a sea on the earth, which is moving uniformly through space. What is the true motion of the body? Newton argues that there must be some absolute uniform motion in regard to some absolute space, which he obtains by adding up the constituent uniform velocities, *disregarding entirely any considerations of acceleration*:

> If the Earth also moves, the true and absolute motion of the body will arise, partly from the true motion of the Earth, in immovable space, partly from the relative motion of the ship on the Earth; and if the body moves also relatively in the ship, its true motion will arise partly from the true motion of the Earth, in immovable space, and partly from the relative motions as well of the ship on the Earth, as of the body in the ship.[12]

This notion—that there must be some absolute space against which all relative uniform velocities can be measured—later became the focus of Einstein's fierce assault on Newtonian physics. This notion of absolute space, said Einstein, is a complete fiction. Why? Because the only possible way to measure uniform velocity (as opposed to acceleration) is against some object arbitrarily taken as a standard of reference. A space that is empty of all objects cannot serve as a standard for the measurement of any uniform velocity. Absolutely empty space is absolutely nothing!

As Burtt rightly points out, Newton could not bring himself to entertain this conclusion. On the basis of his personal religious convictions, Newton was convinced that space is God's way of being present to all things at once. He makes explicit this hidden hypothesis in the famous "General Scholium" appended to the second edition of *Principia*:

> He [God] endures for ever, and is everywhere present; and by existing always and everywhere, he constitutes duration and space. ... He is omnipresent, not virtually only, but also substantially... In him are all things contained and moved.[13]

Burtt also notes that Newton probably inherited this metaphysical doctrine from his mathematics teacher at Cambridge, Isaac Barrow, who also believed that space is God's presence. Indeed, the idea seems to have been in vogue in certain intellectual circles in 17th-century England as the result of the influence of Henry More, the Platonist philosopher ensconced at Cambridge. More, reacting against the mechanistic views of Thomas Hobbes, and reviving certain ancient Stoic notions, argued that spirit is actually something extended, and that God's presence is identical with space.

The fallacious notion of absolute space, once entrenched in the Newtonian canon, helped reinforce an allied fallacy, the notion of "the aether." This was a subtle substance, supposedly spread throughout space, that could account for electromagnetic phenomena. Einstein overthrew the aether as well as absolute space.

As a simple calculation shows, Newton's metaphysical beliefs influenced a substantial percentage of the life of science. The beginning of the modern scientific era was 1543, when Copernicus published his new astronomy. Newton published *Principia* in 1687. Einstein overthrew Newton's concepts of absolute space and the aether in 1905. Accordingly, Newton's metaphysical concepts had prevailed for about 60% of the whole life of modern science by the time Einstein overthrew them. So d'Abro is wrong when he claims that metaphysical assumptions in science do not long outlive the particular scientists who use them. Moreover, as we will see later, Einstein acted out of his own metaphysical assumptions in overthrowing Newton.

Contrary to d'Abro, science is *not* just a matter of constructing the simplest system from the broadest collection of observations. Like every human conceptual system, science rests on broad, unproven presuppositions. When scientists pretend otherwise, they delude both themselves and others. Worse yet, they obstruct the critical examination of such presuppositions, which is the business of philosophy, and especially metaphysics. A scientific system that will not tolerate the examination of its first premises merely ends up, in Burtt's perceptive words, as "the objectification of the mood of an age."[14] Science is no excuse for not thinking.

The Complexity of Scientific Simplicity

The argument that science merely seeks to create the simplest theoretical whole from observed data has a fatal flaw: it fails to recognize that the concept of "simplicity" is by no means a simple one. What is regarded as simple in any particular historical epoch is affected by complicated cultural factors. We have already come across an example in the case of Copernicus. As noted, astronomers in the time of Copernicus were unable to detect any stellar parallax. Hence they were faced with an alternative: either Copernicus was wrong, or else the spatial structure of the universe was far more complicated than any of them dared imagine. They concluded, based on the argument from simplicity, that Copernicus was wrong. Copernicus also appealed to simplicity—the simplicity of his mathematical model, despite the complexity of its empirical consequences. It took several decades for Copernicus's contemporaries to understand this complicated new concept of simplicity. In order to do so, they had to have some understanding of higher mathematics, which is hardly a simple matter.

Since the time of Copernicus, the scientific concept of simplicity has become even more complicated. Consider the paradoxical complexities that follow from the simplifying theory known as "quantum mechanics." If we use the ordinary meaning of the term, there is very little that is "simple" in the world of modern physics.

Contrary to the concoctions of scientists, the simplest hypothesis of all is that things are what they appear to be. This assumption, however, led to the conclusion that the heavens revolve around the Earth. Getting people to think otherwise was no simple matter.

Science does employ a concept of simplicity, as d'Abro maintains, but this concept is not the same as ordinary simplicity. Scientific simplicity is an ideal methodological construct, created and adhered to by various experts engaged in specialized scientific pursuits. To claim that a scientific system is well suited to reveal truth because it adheres to such an ideal of simplicity is circular because this ideal itself is a creation of the scientific method whose purpose it is to regulate. D'Abro's concept of simplicity overlooks all these complexities.

Burtt is right, then, to maintain against d'Abro that the ship of science rides on metaphysical waters. His book amply documents his contention not only for the new astronomy of Copernicus, Galileo, and Newton, which we have discussed above, but also for Johannes Kepler (astronomy), René Descartes (analytic geometry), William Gilbert (magnetism), and Robert Boyle (theory of gases). Moreover, Stephen Mason, in *A History of the Sciences*, documents how various metaphysical beliefs influenced the rise in the 19th century of the theory of evolution, cell theory, embryology, and the study of electromagnetic phenomena.[15]

In the 20th century, the most famous example of metaphysical motivation in science was Albert Einstein. In the style of Benedict Spinoza, Einstein believed that the universe is governed deterministically by one all-powerful God, in accordance with mathematical simplicity. This dogma motivated Einstein at the turn of the century to mount a devastating attack on the cumbersome, *ad hoc* explanations that the Netownians had put forward to explain electromagnetic phenomena. The result was Einstein's theory of relativity, which revolutionized physics.

Alas, however, the very same metaphysical bias also led Einstein to *reject* the second great revolution of 20th-century physics—statistical quantum theory, which holds that pure chance is forever intertwined in the roots of reality. Clinging to his famous dictum that God does not play dice with the universe, Einstein wasted the last decades of his life vainly trying to come up with a deterministic super-theory that would swallow up chance into the will of God. Despite Einstein's best efforts, however, the overwhelming consensus of contemporary physicists is that chance is here to stay. God may still exist, but if statistical quantum theory is right, there always remains a real chance that God's will may be thwarted. Therefore, God cannot be all-powerful in the manner supposed by Spinoza and Einstein.

A New Way of Ideas

Of the various metaphysical presuppositions that underlie science, the most important and persistent is the doctrine of primary and secondary qualities. As noted earlier, a primary quality is one that is quantitative and independent of the particular circumstances of the observer, whereas a secondary quality is qualitative and affected by the state of the observer (color, odor, etc.). Those, like d'Abro, who claim that science is our best lens on reality usually rest their claim on the close connection between science and primary qualities. Primary qualities are more real than secondary qualities, the argument goes. Because science is the technique that measures, analyzes, and coordinates primary qualities, science provides us with the best view of reality.

The actual terms "primary quality" and "secondary quality" came into prominence with the English philosopher John Locke (1632-1704). In his famous *Essay Concerning Human Understanding*, first published in 1690, Locke attempted to give a new account of reality and knowledge based on atomism and empiricism. His great philosophical adversary was the ancient Greek philosopher Plato and those later philosophers, like Descartes, who had been influenced by Plato.

Locke attacked Plato's claim that both knowledge and reality presuppose a realm of immaterial "Forms" (*ideai*) that are superior to the senses. With a droll twist typical of his character, Locke introduced what he called his "new way of ideas," which consisted of turning Plato's own terminology on its head. Locke took the Greek word *idea*, which to Plato meant a transcendent paradigm of reality, and gave it the opposite meaning of a subjective mental content. (A bit earlier, Thomas Hobbes had given the word a similar subjective twist.) Yes, Locke said, Plato was right to say that all knowledge is a matter of ideas, but ideas are not paradigms in heaven. They are merely representations in our own minds, derived from sense experience.

Apart from ideas that we have in our minds, said Locke, reality consists of atoms and combinations of atoms. The qualities that matter has due to the atoms are primary qualities, which to Locke were solidity, extension, figure, and mobility. On the other hand, matter has the power to produce in our minds, via the ideas stimulated in us by the various motions of atoms, certain other qualities, such as colors, sounds, and tastes. These are secondary qualities. They have no reality in themselves:

> The particular bulk, number, figure, and motion of the parts...may be called *real* qualities, because they really exist in those bodies. But light, heat, whiteness, or coldness, are no more really in them than sickness or pain... Take away the sensation of them...and all colors, tastes, odors, and sounds, as they are such particular ideas, vanish and cease, and are reduced to their causes; i.e., bulk, figure, and motion of the parts.[16]

Although Locke regarded his system as something new, it actually represented the latest phase of a long philosophical tradition going back to classical antiquity. A close equivalent of the doctrine of primary and secondary qualities existed in ancient Greece, and was likewise associated with atomism and empiricism. Its leading exponent was the 5th-century B.C. philosopher Democritus, the great philosophical adversary of Plato.

Among the few fragments that have survived from Democritus's work is one where he makes a distinction between qualities that exist "by convention" and those that exist "in reality":

> After Democritus had attacked sensation by saying that colour exists by convention, bitter by convention, [but] atoms and void exist in reality, he lets the senses say the following words against the mind: "Miserable mind, you get your evidence from us and do you try to overthrow us? The overthrow will be your downfall."[17]

This fragment shows that Democritus was aware of a *paradox* involved in making a distinction between the two kinds of qualities: if all knowledge comes from sensation, then how can any quality pretend to be more real than the lowest sense quality? Later philosophers after Democritus, in taking up the distinction between primary and secondary qualities, have often overlooked this important paradox. Unfortunately, we do not know from Democritus' surviving fragments how he resolved the problem.

Among the many thinkers who were later influenced by Democritus' distinction between primary and secondary qualities were Epicurus and Titus Lucretius Carus in antiquity; Galileo Galilei, John Locke, and Isaac Newton in the Renaissance; and, most important for our present purposes, A. d'Abro. Ironically, as we are now about to see, d'Abro's spirited defense of the theoretical value of science, frankly grounded on the hoary distinction between primary and secondary qualities, is as metaphysical as anything in the history of philosophy.

Stripping Reality of the Personal

D'Abro begins his defense of science with the dichotomy between private personal experience on one hand and common knowledge of the objective world on the other. Private experience as such, d'Abro urges, is illusory, for only the methodological comparison of many private experiences can create a common standard by which to distinguish the real from the non-real:

> It is never the private views considered in isolation that give us the objective world. It is solely a certain construct or synthesis of the private views which can be deemed to represent objective reality.[18]

What private experiences, then, are to be compared in constructing the common, objective world? And what methodology is to be followed in constructing their synthesis? It is here that d'Abro appeals to the dichotomy between primary and secondary qualities, and also to what I have called mathematicization. Primary qualities, he says, are best suited to represent impersonal objects because they are quantifiable; that is, they can be easily subsumed into a deductive system of applied mathematics. Hence primary qualities are "entities to which an impersonal existence may be conceded, if for none other than methodological reasons."[19]

But why is mathematicization a good method for revealing the nature of reality? Because, answers d'Abro, the use of mathematics in empirical science always occurs in tandem with careful observation. Scientists first ascertain a large body of empirical facts, which they express in terms of primary qualities. Next, they coordinate these facts mathematically into a system. Finally, they use the system as a deductive tool for predicting further facts. If the predictions prove to be accurate, the system is confirmed; if not, the system is altered to account for the variation between fact and prediction.

What do we mean, asks d'Abro, when we say that we know the nature of reality? The real test is whether we can make accurate predictions about what will happen. And what do we mean when we say that some body of knowledge constitutes a science? We mean that we have a great mound of quantitatively-expressed empirical facts, organized into a simple mathematical system, and effectively honed into a predictive tool. And what has proven more effective than such a tool for making predictions about what will happen? Nothing. Therefore, we may conclude, says d'Abro, that science is our best window on the nature of reality.

Whose Reality?

D'Abro's entire argument for the theoretical validity of science rests squarely on a metaphysical assumption, namely that reality is something objective, and therefore something common and impersonal. Acting on this assumption, d'Abro regards secondary qualities as poor indicators of reality because they depend on the particular circumstances of the observer; they do not strip reality of the personal. To the extent that any judgment about reality is idiosyncratic, subjective, and personal, to the same extent, says d'Abro, is that judgment poorly suited to determining the nature of reality. Science, on the other hand, shows what reality as it is: colorless, odorless, soundless, tasteless, and devoid of all feeling.

But why must we assume with d'Abro that reality is limited to what is objective? How do we know that subjectivity is not also constitutive, at least in part, of reality? After all, even d'Abro concedes that objective primary qualities are extracted from subjective secondary qualities.

Contrary to d'Abro, let us consider the question of whether the uniquely personal and subjective might not also contribute to reality. But what is it, d'Abro would likely insist, that subjectivity reveals about reality? The very fact that d'Abro's question is in order here is the crux of the whole matter. The reason: our broadened inquiry *invites* d'Abro to pose this very question, whereas his own narrower inquiry bars this question as irrelevant from the outset. In short, his argument is question-begging.

The important question is this: *Whose* definition of reality shall we use in judging science? And *why*? Clearly, this question is not a scientific one. To the contrary, this is a *philosophical* question, if ever there was one.

How, then, shall we answer this philosophical question? Philosophy shows us: by an inclusive, rational dialogue that has the right to call on every aspect of human experience as witness. Neither history, nor art, nor language, nor theater, nor sex, nor poetry, nor common sense, nor religious ecstasy, nor tribal magic, nor personal biography can be excluded when this question is on the table.

Admittedly, such a dialogue can become quite complicated, as the history of philosophy amply proves, but with good reason, for this question is quite difficult, perhaps the most difficult of all. Nonetheless, life itself calls upon us to make some sort of answer, however tentative. If we fail to do so, we will never be able to make a rational evaluation of anyone's claim about what is real and what is not. We will just accept unthinkingly what everyone else around us says.

But perhaps there is no one great answer to the question of the nature of reality. Perhaps the complexity of nature and human experience requires us to use one make-do concept of reality in one context, and another in others. Fine. But if so, then the most that science can reasonably claim for itself is that it reveals certain *aspects* of reality. Most scientists, however, are loath to make this concession. It opens up the possibility of a debate with non-scientists (and, in particular, with philosophers) as to where to draw proprietary lines on the map of reality. Like most insular specialists, scientists are territory-conscious. But is reality?

Our conclusion: d'Abro is entitled to his peculiar metaphysical assumption about the nature of reality, but he is not entitled to claim universal validity for it. The most that d'Abro has proved is this: insofar as reality is something objective, and insofar as objectivity is a matter of the mathematicization of primary qualities, to that extent, science is our best lens on reality. But the important questions remain: How much of reality is objective? Is objectivity just a matter of mathematicizing empirical knowledge?

D'Abro's overall argument for the theoretical superiority of science is clearly circular. The scientific method, he says, reveals reality because reality is a matter of mathematicized objectivity. But how do we know that reality is like this? It has to be in order to be accessible to the scientific method.

Pragmatic Pitches

D'Abro attempts to break out of this dogmatic loop by various pragmatic pitches. One is to what he calls "commonplace knowledge." In our ordinary lives, he argues, we first attain knowledge by having perceptions of things, and then by coordinating these perceptions into systematic wholes. Science is just a more sophisticated version of this same game. So if the process is valid in the case of ordinary life, why not for science?

As noted earlier, this argument is superficial. The simplifications of science are of an entirely different order from those of commonplace knowledge. You might as well say that a marble is like the moon because both are spheres. There is a certain analogy between the two, but it won't bear much weight.

Another of d'Abro's pragmatic pitches: nothing beats science in the business of making accurate predictions. Drop both a lead ball and a feather from a great height in a vacuum, and not all the poetry, religion, theater, or tribal magic in the world will tell you that both will reach the bottom at exactly the same moment. Science, however, will tell you this fact, as well as the velocity of both at the moment of impact. What human technique can compare to this predictive power?

The flaw in this appeal is that it overlooks the *overwhelming* use made by humans of non-scientific techniques in order to make successful predictions. As an example, consider your own behavior during any ordinary day of your life. When was the last time you consulted a scientific journal in order to know how to cross the street, chat with your neighbors, make love, or perform any of a day's scores of personal activities? We constantly make successful predictions based on instinct, habit, common sense, and hunches. If we had to rely on the findings of science alone, none of us would survive for one day.

In addition, consider the overall course of human history. Assuming that the human species reached its present form, say, 150,000 years ago, and dating the rise of modern science from 1543 A.D., we see that the human race has been bereft of the predictive power of modern science for 99.698% of its entire life as a species. If the predictive power of science is so important to humanity, how could humanity have survived this long without science?

Science is unsurpassed at making *certain types* of predictions. But if overall utility in making accurate predictions is important, then science comes way down the totem pole after instinct, habit, common sense, and hunches.

Cornering the Market on Progress

Another of d'Abro's pragmatic pitches: science is cumulatively correctable. Each generation of scientists corrects the errors of its predecessors. The overall result is that science approaches ever more closely to reality as a limit.

D'Abro is right, up to a point: science does progressively approach ever closer to a *certain kind of reality*. But d'Abro is wrong to think that this process is unique to science. In fact, cumulative correctability also occurs in many non-scientific endeavors.

Consider, for example, the role of ritual and myth in indigenous tribal societies. White imperialists typically regard nature peoples as ignorant savages who need to be conquered by scientized societies for their own good. But in fact, indigenous tribal societies usually possess a great mass of detailed knowledge concerning their physical environment, their psychic and spiritual needs, and their collective history. They transmit this information from one generation to the next through myth and ritual, which are the great teachers in tribal society. Each generation receives this cultural largesse with great reverence, adds insights to it derived from their own unique experiences, and hands the treasure on to the next generation. The result is that the cumulative knowledge of the tribe follows close on the contours of reality as the tribe encounters it.

Partisans of science dismiss this sort of tribal knowledge because it fuses subjective emotional expressiveness with objective descriptions of fact. As we have seen above, however, this scientific reaction is based on a doubtful metaphysical dogma, namely that reality is identical to objectivity, and that objectivity consists in the mathematicization of primary qualities. Once we begin to question this dogma, we can look at tribal myth and ritual with freshly-seeing eyes.

What do we see?—the members of such societies usually insist that they live close to the heart of reality. In addition, many of these societies have survived for enormous lengths of time. Their greatest danger, in fact, has historically come from scientifically-empowered white imperialists. And how have the natives typically regarded their white conquerors? As savages.

Nonetheless, say the partisans of science, tribal myth and ritual are static when compared to science. Tribal societies make only peripheral changes in their knowledge systems once they enjoy a stable relationship with their environment. Science, however, always pushes ahead, delving deeper and deeper into the nature of reality.

Here the partisans of science have a point. Science has, indeed, proven to be restlessly energetic in a way that is unprecedented among tribal societies. But to claim, as the partisans of science do, that this restless activity represents progressive movement into the nature of reality begs the very question at issue.

To understand this point, consider developments that have taken place in atomic theory in the 19th and 20th centuries. Inspired by the ancient belief of Democritus that matter ultimately consists of *atoma* (that is, indivisible particles), John Dalton in the early 19th century gave a detailed analysis of chemical reactions in terms of atomic weight. Later scientists, building on Dalton's theory, discovered that atoms are not indivisible after all, but consist of other sorts of allegedly indivisible building blocks, electrons and protons. Scientists yet later, again building on this theory, discovered that there are in fact hundreds of so-called elementary subatomic particles. Yet another generation of scientists, again adding to the theory, concluded that many of these subatomic particles are actually composed of sub-subatomic particles, which they have named quarks. Not to be outdone, the latest generation of scientists has uncovered the existence of a great profusion of sub-sub-subatomic particles, which they call "strings." If science follows historical precedent, the strings themselves will eventually decompose.

Has the ever deeper penetration of the atom by scientists during the past 200 years, motivated by a hunger to find the ultimate constituents of matter, represented an ever closer approximation to the nature of reality? Nuclear physicists would certainly say so. But one could equally well argue that this entire two-centuries-long endeavor is a prime example of science obsessively lurching off on a tangent.

Who is to say that a modern nuclear physicist gazing at a spectrograph in a laboratory sees more of reality than an ancient tribal hunter scanning a familiar jungle habitat? Have nuclear physicists, simply because they have been *busy* for 200 years, advanced closer to reality than the tribal society that has enjoyed a stable existence in the Amazon jungle for time out of mind? To give the palm to the nuclear physicists begs the two questions at issue: What is reality? and What is progress in knowledge?

Scientists say that reality is identical to objectivity. Progress in knowledge, therefore, consists in the increase of known primary qualities, and then in the more elegant mathematicization of these primary qualities. But as we have seen, both these assumptions are highly questionable. Once we realize how shaky the theoretical foundations of science really are, science can no longer sustain its grand pretension to be cumulatively correctable in a uniquely privileged way.

The most that can be said is this: science, like every human cognitive endeavor, augments and refines its store of knowledge. In so doing, science reveals some aspects of reality. Likewise, other human cognitive endeavors augment and refine their particular stores of knowledge. In so doing, they reveal other aspects of reality. All of these cognitive endeavors have some contribution to make to human enlightenment, but none is king of the hill. Science has no monopoly on either truth or progress.

The Logic of All Normal Men

As noted above, d'Abro claims that scientific knowledge is like ordinary knowledge, but organized in a more rational way. For the sake of argument, let us grant this claim. Even so, a question remains as to the nature of this so-called "rational way" that guides the operations of science.

Did this "rational way" appear among the residents of North America before the coming of the white European invaders? Apparently not, for d'Abro disparages indigenous tribal societies for their failure to develop science, regarding their ways of thinking as primitive, superstitious, and savage. Where, then, shall we find this "rational way"? D'Abro tell us:

> By "a rational way" we mean primarily "according to the rules of logic." Irrespective of whether these rules are assumed to have been derived from experience or to reduce to *a priori* judgments, all normal men appeal to them, and all scientific theories, even the most revolutionary ones, are based on their acceptance.[20]

The reader who has read the previous eight chapters on the history of logic will at once see how naive such a response is. Contrary to d'Abro's assumption, "the rules of logic" have hardly been transparently clear to "all normal men." On the contrary, there have been conflicting schools of logic in the past 2½ millennia. Moreover, those logical principles that have been most widely lauded as "laws" are both mythical and false, reflecting tunnel-vision thinking by patriarchal males.

The irony of d'Abro's argument is that it makes an appeal to logic in order to validate science. However, the logicians themselves have been at a loss for millennia as to the rock on which they might build the church of logical necessity. In the last half of the 20th century they believe they have finally found their long-sought foundation—*science*. The principles of logic are secure, the argument goes, because they elucidate the conceptual skeleton of the body scientific. But science is secure, d'Abro now tells us, because it follows the principles of *logic*. Each discipline, although quick to make categorical claims for its own validity, grabs at the other for the support that it cannot find within itself. As should by now be obvious, the root principles of neither formal logic nor modern science are secure. Both are based on metaphysical presuppositions of a highly questionable nature.

One might object that many human endeavors rest on questionable presuppositions, yet they still have some value. True, but not every human endeavor pretends to be a supreme embodiment of a certain form of human consciousness. Both formal logic and modern science make such exalted claims for themselves, the one for the realm of reasoning, the other for the realm of fact. Despite such pretenses, however, there is a higher court to which both logic and science must yield: the full complexity of human experience, which refuses to submit to any partial law, least of all one decreed by patriarchal males.

The Fear of Subjectivity

Why is d'Abro so resistant to acknowledging a subjective aspect to reality? He fears that subjectivity will undermine the possibility of having a criterion by which to distinguish illusory from veridical experience. But here the old paradox of Democritus rears it head: if primary qualities are abstracted from subjective secondary qualities, and if primary qualities are real, then there must also be something of reality in secondary qualities as well. Otherwise, where does the reality of primary qualities come from?

In the end, d'Abro's entire argument hangs on his belief in the possibility of absolute objectivity. Earlier chapters have shown, however, that the concept of objectivity cannot be disjoined from the concept of the interpreter. Any attempt to do so renders the concept of objectivity incoherent. Contrary to what the partisans of science and formal logic are quick to assume, there simply is no such thing as absolute objectivity. But that doesn't mean that everything must then dissolve into pure subjectivity, as many fear. Rather, objectivities do exist, but they are *relative* objectivities. Any given objectivity always presupposes some interpreter or some group of interpreters to which it is strictly correlative. The interpreter is here to stay; therefore, subjectivity is too.

Pragmatic Reality vs. Reality

At times, d'Abro claims that he has no interest in reality itself, whatever that may be, but rather in what he calls "pragmatic reality." By this phrase he means the reality that emerges as the result of the simplest scientific coordinations of observed data:

> What the nature of this real world of things in themselves may be, whether it could ever be described in human language, whether it is identical with the idea we have formed of it, are questions which are probably meaningless, and in any case insoluble. ... In this chapter, the word reality will therefore be held to connote scientific reality, which means the simplest co-ordination of scientific facts, hence, ultimately, of sense impressions. ... For him [the scientist], reality is identified with simplicity of co-ordination, and he states his views explicitly, realising full well that a reality of this type is far from being absolute and that it is essentially pragmatic.[21]

D'Abro's easy slide from reality to pragmatic reality is a greasy one, for the whole question is whether pragmatic reality may serve as a reasonable substitute for reality. Although d'Abro is eager to make this substitution, his own terminology betrays a reticence to leaving science hanging in mid-air unconnected to the real world of things in themselves. For example, d'Abro cannot bring himself to let go of the word "reality" altogether. But why not? After all, he could just as easily have spoken of "scientific fantasy," saying "In this chapter, the word reality will therefore be held to connote scientific fantasy." Why doesn't d'Abro say this, but instead insist on retaining the word "reality"?

Put another way: How can d'Abro know that science pragmatically approximates reality if he doesn't believe in the existence of that which science approximates? On the other hand, if this approximating relationship does not exist, how does science differ from being just another theoretical construct hanging in the air?

Despite his disclaimers, d'Abro is committed to the existence of an independent reality to which science approximates pragmatically. But how can he know that science has access to the most important aspects of this independent reality? Only by embracing the fallacy of absolute objectivity, as noted above.

Despite d'Abro's best efforts, science remains just one of the many tools available to humans in the quest for knowledge. Where quantification of observed phenomena is called for, science is appropriate; where the qualitative experience of the moment is important, however, science can actually be a detriment. So-called "pragmatic reality" or "scientific reality" can never establish that what it captures is the most important or interesting aspect of reality. Conclusion: the claim that science provides humanity with its best window on reality remains unproven.

Domination and Pragmatism

Many people who admire science would give short shrift to the whole idea of seeking theoretical validation for their attitude. If they bothered to read d'Abro at all, it would be his incidental pragmatic pitches that would impress them most. "Who cares about all these theoretical quibbles?" many would ask. "The plain fact is that science, considered practically, has immeasurably benefited the human race. Anything that has been so useful must be good at reflecting reality; otherwise, how could it have worked so well?"

This notion—that if something works, it must reflect reality—certainly has some truth to it. If we try to build a house but use a plan that ignores the laws of physics, the house will not stand. On the other hand, if we know of a particular sort of house that people have been successfully building for generations, we are justified in surmising that the plans for such a house are realistic. Reality, we might say, is what slaps you in the face when you're out of touch with it. If you don't get slapped, if in fact your plans work, especially over the long haul, you must have some understanding of reality.

All this is reasonable enough, but there's a catch: we have to be clear about what we mean when we say that something "works." That is, we have to understand the distinction between working and merely having some effect. To understand this distinction, consider the following case. Suppose a drunken, testosterone-driven male is speeding down an old country road in a jalopy. As he flies over the bumps, he is unaware that gas is leaking from the old, frayed gas hose where it fits onto the nozzle of the engine's fuel pump. Suppose further that he rams his way over a deep rut in the road, jolting the engine, and causing the hot wire that comes from the ignition coil to slip out of its worn, cracked seat in the distributor cap. At this point, when the sputtering sparks from the wire encounter the collected cloud of gas vapor, a predictable result occurs: the engine explodes.

Here the frayed gas hose and the ignition wire both had a noticeable effect in the world. But did they "work"? No, and for an obvious reason: the purpose of a gas hose and an ignition wire is not to blow up the engine but to make the car run smoothly. As this example demonstrates, to say that something works is not merely to say that it has an effect, but rather that it has an effect in accordance with some *purpose*. Without a reference to purpose, we may say that things have an effect in world, but not that they *work*.

Those who are impatient with theoretical arguments concerning science make a pragmatic pitch: science is good at revealing the nature of reality because science works. But we have just seen that to say something works means that it has an effect in accordance with some purpose. What, then, is the purpose of science? To find the truth, you might say. But how do we know that science finds the truth? Because it works. But works for *what*?

Here pragmatists have a problem. If they say, "for finding the truth," their answer is clearly circular. To be non-circular, the answer must indicate something for which science works, and this something must be other than merely "finding the truth," while yet being a plausible indicator of the latter.

One possible answer is, "for making accurate predictions." More fully: "science works for consistently making accurate predictions, and consistently making accurate predictions is a practical indicator of knowing the truth." But as discussed earlier, science is hardly unique in being able to make accurate predictions. In fact, if predictive power is to be the criterion of success in the discovery of truth, then science must come far down the totem-pole, after instinct, habit, and common sense. At most we can say, on this basis, that science is good at revealing certain aspects of reality.

At this point our pragmatist would likely invoke the concept of overall human welfare: "That which works in the long haul to promote human survival, happiness, and well-being is for all practical purposes true for humans. And why not? After all, humanity encounters reality only insofar as reality is humanly accessible. Science doesn't just have effects. Science, on the whole, promotes human welfare; therefore, science truly reflects the reality that humans live with."

This metaphysical assumption, that what works on the whole to promote human welfare also reveals reality, is dear to the American school of philosophy known as pragmatism. This assumption—conjoined with a cheery attitude toward science—appears in the American philosophers Charles Sanders Peirce (1839-1914), William James (1842-1910), and John Dewey (1859-1952).

Pragmatism has had a positive impact on philosophy, for it challenges theorists with their heads in the sky to show how their ideas make a practical difference. However, pragmatism has weaknesses when taken too far. One of the worst is its ethnocentric view of human intelligence.

In practice (which is the important thing!), pragmatists view human intelligence as the smarts that are needed to survive and thrive in the modern world. This attitude was expressed in its most crass form by William James, when he defined truth as "the cash value of ideas." Such an attitude implies that all those human cultures that did not manage to survive and thrive in the modern world were out of touch with reality. How much wiser and happier they would have been if only they had bought into the cash value of ideas!

But consider the indigenous Indian tribes of North America. They were nearly annihilated by white European invaders, who used the latest scientifically-devised means of slaughter to achieve their goals of conquest and expropriation. Was white European culture more in touch with reality because it had the smarts to drive the Indians out of their lands? Could it be possible that the Indians saw important aspects of reality to which the white invaders were blind—and blind precisely because they had the smarts to drive the Indians out of their lands? On pragmatist assumptions, this last question is paradoxical, if not impossible. Anyone, however, who regards this question as meaningful and important cannot remain satisfied with pragmatism. Technological might does not make ontological right.

For the sake of argument, however, let us grant the pragmatist assumption that what works on the whole to promote human welfare reveals reality. Even so, the question remains—Has science, on the whole, benefited humanity? Many, no doubt, will be nonplused to find anyone seriously raising this question, just as many in the Middle Ages simply assumed that Christianity was good for everybody. Nonetheless, as we will see, this is a reasonable question.

Technology vs. Technique

How does science translates itself from pure theory into a practical historical force? The answer is summed up in one of the most revered words of our time, "technology."

Beginning with the Renaissance, theoretical developments in science increasingly engendered parallel developments in the productive crafts, which reacted back on science itself, especially through the creation of new tools. To the extent that the scientific method has influenced the productive crafts, to the same extent have these crafts become "technological," as opposed to merely "technical."

In the centuries since the Renaissance, science and technology have grown ever closer together. Indeed, the last decades of the 20th century have witnessed the near fusion of science and technology, as the two have become aspects of a larger historical reality that might be called "sci-tech." Without this technology that it has engendered, science would be just a cloud of theory hanging in the air. Hence to evaluate the overall practical impact of science means to evaluate the historical impact of scientific technology.

Before we begin this evaluation, we must be clear about our terms. Most people today use the word "technology" in a loose way, as a rough equivalent for "a system of practical techniques." For example, contemporary historians sometimes speak of "ancient Chinese technology." But such a usage is anachronistic, for the word "technology" and its equivalents did not occur with the present meaning until the 18th century.[22]

The original source of our modern word "technology" is the ancient Greek word *tekhnologia*, which means the study of the rules common to a craft. The prime example of *tekhnologia* to the Greeks was grammar. Clearly, this limited meaning of *tekhnologia* is much different from that of "technology" in modern languages. No one today, if asked to give an example of technology, would ever think of mentioning grammar.

Why this big difference in meanings? As noted above: the ancients maintained a sharp distinction between the scholarly and the craft traditions. The former was the sphere of free citizens; the latter, of slaves and freedmen. The idea of fusing the two would have been preposterous.

This fusion of the theoretical inquiry into nature with the practical production of commodities is one of the distinguishing characteristics of modernity and the source of the uniquely modern word "technology." Only in the last few hundred years have human beings come to judge the practical value of theoretical knowledge in terms of its efficacy for the mass production of commodities.

"Technology," in the modern sense of the word, means the social ordering of productive techniques according to a scientific model. But what is a scientific model? As discussed earlier, science distinguishes itself from mere knowledge by being the mathematicization of knowledge. Analogously, technology distinguishes itself from mere technique by being the mathematicization of technique.

Technology applies to the productive process the same mentality that science applies to the cognitive process. Behind both science and technology lies the same motive: to reduce some given system (in the one case, theoretical, in the other, productive) to a collection of interchangeable, quantitative units, ordered according to rigid rules. In the case of science, the interchangeable, quantitative units are the individual elements from which the entire world-system allegedly emerges; for example, atoms, electrons, quarks, etc. In the case of technology, the interchangeable, quantitative units are the individual products that are produced by the system; for example, cigarettes, TV sets, liquor bottles, hand guns, etc. Science's rigid rules are the principles by which the elements create the system; for example, natural laws, quantum generalizations, etc. Technology's rigid rules are the dictates according to which the system manufactures its products; for example, the requirements of assembly lines and factories, the law of supply and demand, etc.

Dear to both science and technology is the assumption (or rather metaphor) that reality, whether cognitive or productive, is a machine. Whatever fits into the overall machine-picture of reality and of the productive process is held to be real, important, lasting, and objective; whatever does not fit into the machine model is viewed as illusory, trivial, ephemeral, and subjective. Scientists doing research in their laboratories, workers laboring in their offices and factories—thus is the world to be known, thus are human needs to be satisfied. But what kind of a world, what kind of a human being, is created when productive techniques are socially ordered according to a scientific model? In other words, what has been the overall historical impact of science? To this great question we will turn our attention in the following chapter.

---

[1] Edwin Burtt, *The Metaphysical Foundations of Modern Physical Science*, Doubleday Anchor Books, Garden City, New York; first published 1924; revised 1932; paper edition, 1954, p. 38.

[2] Galileo Galilei, *Dialogue Concerning the Two Chief World Systems*, trans. by Stillman Drake, quoted by Shmuel Sambursky, ed., *Physical Thought from the Presocratics to the Quantum Physicists*, Pica Press, New York, 1974, p. 224.

[3] Stephen Mason, *A History of the Sciences*, first published 1956, revised edition by Collier Books, New York, 1967, pp. 11-12 & 108 ff.

[4] Sambursky, *op. cit.*, p. 262; Mason, *op. cit.*, p. 224.

[5] Roger Bacon, *Opus maius*, trans. by Susan Hall, and *Epistola de secretis operibus*, trans. by Lynn Thorndike; both quoted by Sambursky, *op. cit.*, pp. 156 & 160-161.

[6] Carolyn Merchant, *The Death of Nature: Women, Ecology, and the Scientific Revolution*, Harper & Row, San Francisco, 1980, p. 189.

[7] A. d'Abro, *The Evolution of Scientific Thought from Newton to Einstein*, first edition, 1927; revised edition, Dover Publications, New York, 1950.

[8] Edwin Burtt, *The Metaphysical Foundations of Modern Physical Science*, Doubleday Anchor Books, Garden City, New York; first published 1924; revised 1932; paper edition, 1954.

[9] A recent defense of science is Paul Gross's and Norman Levitt's *Higher Superstition: The Academic Left and Its*

Quarrels with Science (Johns Hopkins University Press, Baltimore, 1994). This book is strongest in its criticism of recent social-constructivist theory; however, it lacks d'Abro's detailed and closely-reasoned defense of science's positive points. See also their recent anthology *The Flight from Science and Reason*, Annals of the New York Academy of Sciences, vol. 775, 1996. Many recent feminist critiques of science are valuable for their socio-historical insights but lack Burtt's focus on epistemology and ontology in their own right. Such is the case, for example, with two books by Sandra Harding, *The Science Question in Feminism* and *Whose Science? Whose Knowledge?* (Cornell University Press, Ithaca, NY, 1986 & 1991 respectively). Although Harding navigates the waters of epistemology, her guiding star is always political correctness. Another example is Susan Bordo's *The Flight to Objectivity: Essays on Cartesianism and Culture* (State University of New York Press, Albany, NY, 1987). Bordo seeks to give a "psychocultural" account of modern scientific epistemology. When she is not playing the psychologist, her views on epistemology and ontology reflect an indebtedness to Burtt, as she herself acknowledges.

[10] Burt, *op. cit.*, pp. 238-39.
[11] D'Abro, *op. cit.*, p. 403.
[12] Isaac Newton, *Principia*, quoted by Sambursky, *op. cit.*, p. 300.
[13] Isaac Newton, "General Scholium," quoted by Burtt, *op. cit.*, p. 258.
[14] Burtt, *op. cit.*, p. 304.
[15] Mason, *op. cit.*, *passim*.
[16] John Locke, *An Essay Concerning Human Understanding*, VIII, 17, original's emphasis; in *The English Philosophers from Bacon to Mill*, ed. by Edwin Burtt, The Modern Library, New York, 1939, p. 267.
[17] Citation of Democritus in *Die Fragmente der Vorsokratiker*, ed. by H. Diels, 68 B 125; quoted and trans. by Sambursky, *op. cit.*, p. 57.
[18] A. d'Abro, *op. cit.*, p. 446.
[19] *ibid.*, p. 391.
[20] D'Abro, *op. cit.*, p. 359.
[21] *ibid.*, pp. 367 & 374.
[22] Donald Cardwell, *The Norton History of Technology*, W.W. Norton & Co., New York, 1995, p. 107.

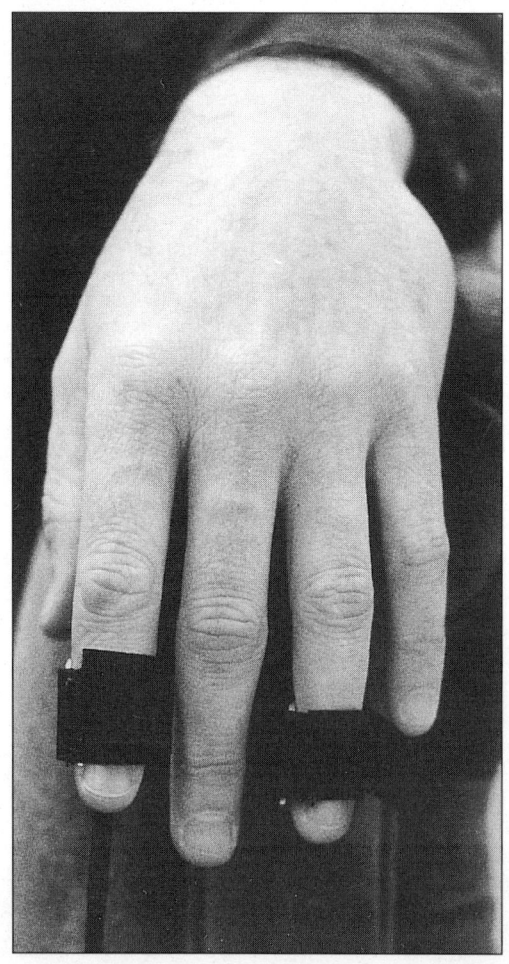

Hey Faggot, Performance with Polygraph Equipment, 1995

13

The Science of Dr. Frankenstein

SUMMARY: This chapter shows that the myth of scientific progress is bankrupt; therefore, it cannot save the equally bankrupt Parmenidean myth, as logicians have hoped. The chapter concludes with a new, appreciative assessment of Mary Shelly's novel *Frankenstein*.

Logicians have long sought some absolute foundation for formal logic. Previous chapters have followed their quest from the time of Parmenides in ancient Greece to the time of Willard Van Orman Quine and Bart Kosko in the late 20th-century United States. As we have seen, the latest twist in this old quest is a scientific one. Formal logic is an absolute, logicians now argue, because it provides an X-ray of the conceptual skeleton of the body scientific. Science is held to be a worthy foundation for two reasons: (1) considered theoretically, science provides humanity with its best window on reality; and (2) considered practically, science has been a great boon to humanity.

In the last chapter, we took up the first of these two claims, and found it wanting. In this chapter, we will take up the second. The historical evidence will show that this claim fares no better than the first.

Our evaluation will begin by highlighting peculiar conditions in Medieval and Renaissance Europe that were necessary for science to take root. As we will see, these conditions were partly religious, involving the triumph of a whole new way of looking at nature. Next, we will examine the areas of global change in which science has manifested its greatest influence: the European voyages of discovery, the spread of European power around the globe, the creation of whole new societies in the Americas and elsewhere, and the triumph of industrialism. Finally, we will assess the view of science as it appears in a classic work of modern fiction, Mary Shelley's novel *Frankenstein*.

Exit Oberon and Titania

In writing histories of Europe, institutionalized academics commonly focus on only a tiny minority of Europeans—kings, popes, warlords, philosophers, city-dwellers, and the literate classes. Until well into the 19th century, however, the overwhelming majority of Europeans were illiterate peasants whose world-views and lifestyles differed markedly from those of their masters. This other Europe has fallen below the threshold of observation for academic historians, who have themselves generally been literate, urban, and bourgeois.

The distinction between the two Europes was pronounced in the area of religion, a fact that is relevant to the later rise of science. In pre-Christian times, people viewed all nature as filled with autonomously-acting spirits whom humans might personally address and venerate. To approach nature always meant to respect the powers and demands of these spirits. Accordingly, pagans resisted the later view that nature is reducible to a mere collection of dead or non-living elements.

Christianity, on the other hand, adores one supreme God who dominates and uses nature as a mere created resource. Only insofar as nature reflects the glory of its creator is it to be an object of veneration. Hence Christians are more receptive to the impersonal objectification of nature as a valid path to knowledge. Because of this receptivity, the Christian religion paved the way, albeit unwittingly, for the scientific method that would supplant it.

What made Europe become Christian in the first place? In a nutshell—coercion. When it was first introduced into early Europe, Christianity encountered stiff popular resistance, a fact often lost sight of today. The new religion's earliest enthusiasts were not the peasant masses, but kings, chieftains, and other petty officials. They saw in the new religion, with its authoritarian claims to universal acceptance and obedience, a convenient means of maintaining control in a time of social fragmentation and decay.

During much of the period from the fall of Rome in 476 A.D. to the crowning of Pope Innocent III in 1198 A.D., both the church and the state were weak in Europe. The peasants, who constituted the vast majority of the people, continued to openly practice various forms of pagan nature worship, to the chagrin of their Christian rulers.

By the 12th century, the church and the state had made significant progress in consolidating their powers. In consequence, the established authorities turned their attention to eradicating "heresy." By this term they usually meant any religious movement that combined both pagan and Christian practices. In later centuries, the Holy Inquisition and its Protestant counterparts undertook to exterminate "witchcraft," which often consisted of various broken-down strains of the old paganism under a Christian veneer. It was through their ongoing onslaught against heresy and witchcraft that European officialdom finally Christianized Europe, and in so doing unwittingly prepared a soil that was conducive to the rise of science.

The Christian onslaught against supposed heretics and witches lasted for hundreds of years, peaking in the period from the 13th to the 17th centuries. By the time it played itself out, it had turned into a holocaust in which Christian authorities horribly tortured and killed millions of people. During the bloodiest episodes, the majority of victims were women, which is not surprising, inasmuch as women were the principal transmitters of the old nature-focused religion.[1]

More often than not, the authorities were sincere in fomenting this persecution. They genuinely feared the broken-down strains of the old paganism that everywhere confronted them in the countryside. Such practices, they believed, were a great plot by Satan himself to overthrow Christian civilization.

The practitioners of the old rites generally regarded themselves as casual participants in age-old folk traditions, or even as faithful Christians who happened to be following locally-colored liturgies. When arrested by Christian inquisitors, however, they were commonly tortured until they confessed to worshipping "the Devil."

There was, ironically, a certain truth to these forced confessions. What the inquisitors meant by "the Devil" was a distinct form of pre-Christian, nature-oriented spiritual consciousness that lay just under the surface of the old peasant customs. Although many illiterate peasants called themselves Christians, their belief in the autonomous divinity of trees, animals, sex, and the cosmos was at odds with established Christian doctrine. The inquisitors sensed that an un-Christian religious sensibility was pervasively entrenched in the very bosom of European Christendom.

The oft-made claim that the persecution of heretics and witches was a mere "mass delusion" falls flat in view of its length, some four hundred years. The persecutions began as soon as the church and the state were in a position to suppress surviving pagan practices. Moreover, the persecution reached its acme during the enlightened Renaissance, not the Middle Ages. As H.R. Trevor-Roper rightly observes:

> The most ferocious of witch-burning princes, we often find, are the most cultured patrons of contemporary learning. ... It [the witch-burning] was forwarded by the cultural popes of the Renaissance, by the great Protestant reformers, by the saints of the Counter-Reformation, by the scholars, lawyers and churchmen.[2]

Although paganism died out among the privileged urban classes by about 1000 A.D., the situation was otherwise for the peasants. First-hand reports continue into the late Renaissance telling of seasonal peasant rites. Participants costumed themselves as animals, wore clothes of the opposite sex, engaged in public sexual practices, and paid homage to a goat-footed figure. More recent are the remarkable first-hand accounts of 18th and 19th-century witnesses during their visits to the remoter parts of the European hinterland.

For example, in the 1870s the Frenchmen Édouard Piette and Julien Sacaze noted pagan survivals in the remote Luchon region of the French Pyrenees.[3] Near the town of Poubou, in the vicinity of ancient megaliths, they reported the following:

> Till not long ago, on the night of Mardi Gras, the young men of this village used to go out in a procession in order to build a big straw fire on the rock. They marched in single file, each one holding the backside of the one in front of him, advancing with postures and gestures that were both burlesque and obscene. After the fire was lit, they danced around the rock, *penem manu proferentes* [holding the penis out with the hand]. The rites of this nocturnal feast,

which people still celebrated some thirty years ago, calling it the feast of the *gagnolis*, offend decency too much for me to describe them in complete detail.[4]

Piette and Sacaze reported that men and women still visited this rock in order to increase their fertility, using a phallic projection as a dildo. They realized that these practices reflected a religious consciousness after their conversations with Augustin Germès, age 84, the former mayor of the local town of Jurvielle. Germès insisted that old people still worshipped the megaliths and that he was upset with the younger generation for abandoning the older ways:

> In the old days, when people were upright, everybody had a great faith in these stones; everybody worshipped them and addressed their prayers to them. As for myself, I've always believed in them; I'll die believing in them.[5]

On several occasions, local priests tried to destroy the megaliths. During the night, however, the locals would sneak back to the sites and reassemble the fragments together into a pile. On one such occasion in 1871, the priest at Portet hired someone to re-scatter the stones and plant a cross on the spot. By chance, the hired hand fell ill and died soon thereafter. Some of the locals regarded his death as an act of divine retribution for sacrilege.

With the conclusion of the witch hunts around the year 1700, the Christian world-view, in one form or another, finally triumphed in most of Europe. The institutions in society that benefited most from this bloody triumph were the same ones that had pushed it in the first place—the state, the church, and the university.

As a result of the final triumph of Christianity, a revolutionary new way of looking at nature penetrated the consciousness of Europe. No longer were natural phenomena filled with spirits and gods who spoke directly to people. Now there was just one God, far away in Heaven. To encounter this God, one had to leave the forests and the meadows, and enter a church. There the new God's priests and ministers, in carefully scripted scenes, opened and closed the institutional shutters through which alone the divine mystery of life was henceforth permitted to shine. Nature, deprived of the host of uncanny spirits who had animated and protected her, steadily declined in status to a mere resource, and then, finally, to a mere machine.

Only after this revolutionary change in attitude toward nature had occurred could scientific thinking become a historical force in Europe. Because of its emphasis on primary qualities, science requires that all subjectivity be peeled away from one's encounter with nature. The old paganism, however, insisted that dialogue with nature involves a spiritual dimension and, therefore, subjectivity. In rejecting the subjectivism of paganism, science turned human dialogue with nature into an objectifying assault.[6]

The holocaust against the pagan-inspired peasants of Europe was a necessary (although not a sufficient) precondition for Europe's massive endorsement of the scientific mentality. In deliberating on the question of whether science has been a great boon to humanity, we cannot close our eyes to this awful price and pretend that it was never paid. Science has been expensive from the very start.

The Great Devastation

In the Renaissance, while inquisitors were busy attacking paganism, a momentous development was under way: the craft tradition and the scholarly tradition crossed paths.[7] Classical antiquity, as we saw in the last chapter, had kept these two traditions apart. Now for the first time, a large number of innovative thinkers came forward who studied in common such diverse subjects as plumbing, higher mathematics, ballistics, and classical Latin literature. The greatest of these new hybrid thinkers was Galileo, who laid the groundwork for what was later to be called the scientific method.

At first, the church tried to suppress this new viewpoint because it appealed to a style of proof that dismissed scripture and ecclesiastical authority as irrelevant. Ironically, however, the church itself had eviscerated the one great historical force that in previous societies had succeeded in keeping the lid on science—animistic spirituality.

By draining nature of its own indwelling fund of spirits and banking all the world's spiritual capital in one God above, Christians found they had no counterweight to the arguments of the new breed of Renaissance thinkers. How does such a spiritually-depleted nature, the new thinkers asked, differ from a machine? Why not, then, use a machine model in order to gain knowledge of nature? Surely God won't mind; after all, he's far above nature anyway. The Christians could not reply, as the pagans once did, that the gods who live in the trees, the rivers, and the hills would mind.

All this would have been of merely academic interest, had not the new methods of Renaissance science quickly wrought a stunning practical impact on the whole world. The first great historical application of science, and the one that opened the eyes of European rulers everywhere to the enormity of its power, was its role in the chain of events now euphemistically called "the voyages of discovery."

Science, Ships, and Guns

The turning point came in 15th-century Portugal. Prince Henry the Navigator, son of King John I of Portugal, wanted to wrest the lucrative gold trade of Africa away from Islamic middle men, who transported the gold by camel across the Sahara Desert to north African port cities. Henry hoped to send Portuguese ships down the western coast of Africa in order to intercept the gold at its source, a string of prosperous African kingdoms then located in the vicinity of the Niger river. He also had visions of eventually circumnavigating Africa and reaching India.

To further these ends, Henry founded a school of navigation, the first ever to be based on scientific principles, as opposed to craft technique. Although not realized at the time, Henry's decision was a milestone in the history of science and technology. The newly designed ships and methods of navigation revolutionized travel on the seas, eventually opening up the entire world to European "exploration."

After Henry's death in 1460, Portugal continued his policy of imperialist expansion empowered by scientific methodology. In 1487, Bartholomeu Dias, a patron of the new sciences, circumnavigated the southern tip of Africa; and in 1498, Vasco da Gama reached the Malabar Coast in India. Seeing these impressive results, Spain and other European promoted the new technologies of shipbuilding and navigation.

At the same time they were revolutionizing sea travel, Europeans applied their new scientific methods to another area that would change the course of world history: the design and production of firearms. Primitive guns made of metal, little more than toys, first appeared in China in the early 14th century. Europeans, taking up these curiosities and developing them scientifically, quickly created two new deadly kinds of weapon, the arquebus and cannon.

Thanks to the practical application of science, Europeans now possessed not only ships that could take them around the world but also weapons that no non-European society could withstand. As a consequence, European males inflicted on the world one of the most ghastly sustained episodes of violence in history. First, the Portuguese seized a number of coastal enclaves and inland gold mines in Africa. They soon realized that they had won access to a commodity far more valuable than gold: living human bodies. Black Africans were forced into slavery, first to work Portuguese enterprises in Africa, and later as an export commodity to sell to other Europeans who were conquering and colonizing the Americas.

Over the next several centuries, Europeans, and later Americans, seized and sold untold millions of Africans into slavery. About half the number shipped out died from the brutalizing conditions of the journey. The remainder lived out their days in forced labor, laying the foundations for the brave new economy that would eventually emerge in the Americas.

The expansion of European power over the rest of the world, empowered by the new sciences, was rapid and devastating. The Portuguese, once secure in Africa, reinforced their position in the Indian Ocean, destroyed Calicut, conquered Goa, and laid the foundations for centuries of European imperialism in the Far East. At the opposite end of the globe, Christopher Columbus, after traveling on the Atlantic Ocean for 61 days in 1492, stumbled onto islands in the Caribbean, mistakenly thinking he had reached India. Following Columbus came the Spanish adventurer Hernando Cortés, who destroyed Aztec civilization in Mexico in 1521. Following Cortés came Francisco Pizarro, who destroyed Inca civilization in Peru in 1532.

In North America, European powers competed with each other in a race to expropriate the various native Indian tribes of their lands. Later, the United States Government, created in 1789, applied the latest technology in a century-long program aimed at annihilating the Indians entirely.

In the meantime, the new white masters of the Americas created a global economic cycle based on the labor of millions of African slaves. Ships from New England carried foodstuffs, lumber, and animals to the West Indies. From there they returned with sugar and molasses, from which manufacturers made rum. Traders then took the rum to the coast of Africa, with which they bought slaves. On their return, traders sold the slaves in the West Indies and the colonies, thus completing the cycle.

From its beginning with Prince Henry's school of navigation, most of the principal instigators of the Great Devastation were men who were eager to apply the latest methods of science to their endeavors. They readily accepted the new astronomy, pouring over the new mappings of the heavens in order to better navigate their way to new markets; supported new research in ballistics in order to have better weapons for defeating their competitors; and encouraged research in metallurgy in order to better exploit their slave-worked mines. Like their spiritual heirs who gave the world the Vietnam War in the 1960s, the instigators of the Great Devastation were the brightest and the best of their times.

The Great Devastation, beginning in the middle of the 15th century, thus represented the first sustained practical application of the new sciences. Adventurous European males, drawing on the intellectual labor of Europe's brightest and best, reduced millions of Africans to slavery, destroyed the great indigenous civilizations of Central and South America, laid the groundwork for the annihilation of the native residents of North America, and began a centuries-long pattern of imperialist domination in the Far East.

This cascade of historical rape, which would have been impossible without the means provided by the new sciences, followed the horrors of the great witch-hunts, which paved the way for the triumph of the scientific mentality in the first place. From its very start, therefore, modern science, considered as a practical historical force, has been a terrifying plague to innumerable human beings.

Supply-Side Economics

What was the historical benefit for which this great suffering was the historical cost? Within Europe, a minority of warriors, landlords, and entrepreneurs saw their power and profits skyrocket, while the Catholic Church harvested a bountiful crop of newly-forced converts in Africa and the Americas. In addition, as a result of increased trade and the flow of gold and silver from the Americas, the overall economies of Portugal and Spain underwent a temporary surge, and then a slump, followed by longer-lasting improvement in the economies of the Low Countries, France, and England.

Throughout many areas of Western Europe, cities grew larger, and literacy spread among the population. In the countryside, the condition of the peasants was mixed. Many gained because of the expansion of markets, but many also lost because of the increased economic and political power of landlords. Peasant revolts were not uncommon in this period, and were brutally repressed.

In regard to urban wage-earners, although an overall economic improvement occurred in many parts of Western Europe, benefits did not easily trickle down. To the contrary, from 1450 to 1550, real wages in Spain, France, Germany, and England fell 20-50%. As usual, those profiting the most from exploitation were the least willing to share the plunder. In addition, the great influx of gold and silver from the New World caused a general price rise. As one group of historians has aptly noted:

> For wage workers the price rise meant economic regression and a serious fall in living standards. For manufacturers, however, higher prices meant larger profits, and the price revolution was a profit inflation from which they emerged with a larger share of the community's wealth than ever before.[8]

The terrible costs of the Great Devastation clearly outweighed its modest and unevenly distributed benefits—if, indeed, one may ever say that terrible oppression is "historically justified." Inasmuch as the Great Devastation represented the first sustained impact of science as a historical force, the same judgment may be rendered against science as well.

The Industrial Revolution

The partisans of science object that this initial impulse of European expansion was not the end of the story. From the economic and social conditions created by this impulse, there eventually grew a great tree, industrial civilization, with all its benefits and conveniences. Despite regrettable early losses, the argument goes, science in the long haul has greatly benefited humanity because science was indispensable to the rise of the industrial system.

The underlying assumption here is that industrial civilization has, on the whole, been a boon to humanity. Let us now examine this commonly accepted assumption.

Imperialism & the Rise of Industrialism

As the Great Devastation spread around the globe, the European powers fought among themselves like a pack of snarling dogs, seeking top position in devouring the economic carcasses of the defeated non-European societies. In 1815, after the defeat of Napoleonic France, Britain emerged as the world's greatest imperialist power. A revolutionary consequence followed: Britain undertook a massive effort to apply scientific methods to its economy, just as the British bourgeoisie, rich from imperialism, consolidated its final control over the state. The result was the onset of the industrial revolution. Eventually, all of Europe began moving in some degree toward the new industrial era.

On the positive side, the new economic system produced standardized commodities in ever greater quantities, at ever cheaper prices. The negative side was catastrophic. Landlords, industrialists, and politicians colluded to drive tens of millions of peasants off their ancient common lands and into the cities, where cheap labor was needed to run the new, scientifically-designed factory machines. The great extended families of the European peasantry, anciently anchored to their ancestral rural communities, were uprooted and nuclearized, corresponding to the nuclearization of the productive process itself.

The new urban poor worked most of their waking hours at subsistence wages under filthy and dangerous conditions. Factory smoke-stacks and drain-pipes, largely unregulated by government, poured forth a steady stream of strange new toxic pollutants into the air, the rivers, and the earth. The great forests of Europe were denuded of their ancient trees. The massive extinction of animal species and the carbonization of the atmosphere, hallmarks of the industrial epoch, had begun.

Hungry for cheap raw materials for their new factories, the bourgeoisie pushed for greater exploitation of the lands conquered during the Great Devastation. European states became economic vampires, deliberately draining their own colonial possessions of economic vitality. The colonies were forced to become dependent providers of raw materials to the mother country, which alone had the privilege of manufacturing finished articles, to be purchased back by the colonies.

The long-term effect of this policy was to destroy the economic infrastructure of the colonies and to reduce their residents to abject poverty. Thus was created the global morass known today as "the Third World." A classic example was India. In the 17th century, bloody battles between Moslems and Hindus had exposed the Indian subcontinent to predatory expeditions by competing European powers. After decades of war, British troops eventually overwhelmed most of the subcontinent, which became a British Crown Colony in 1858. In 1877, Queen Victoria of England assumed the title Empress of India. In the meantime, British agents strove to create an elite English-educated ruling class, discouraged the study of native languages and culture, and undercut the economic autonomy of independent villages by the massive importing of British industrial goods. The results were catastrophic for the natives. Bengal, for example, which before the British conquest had been quite prosperous, ended up as Bangladesh, one of the world's most impoverished countries.

Even China, long successful at resisting colonialism, eventually succumbed, as the industrialized nations, including by now the United States, forced their way in. With China's doors forced open to foreign trade, its local crafts and trades crumbled before an onslaught of cheap goods imported from the great industrial powers. Poverty increased in rural areas, the overall quality of life fell, and an urban proletariat influenced by revolutionary intellectuals began to form.

The First World Wide Web

Events in India and China demonstrate the degree to which imperialism benefited by the continuing advance of science. In the earliest days of the Great Devastation, imperialist incursions had often been limited to coastal areas. Although the European states had the ability to travel almost anywhere on the high seas, they often lacked the technical means to maintain a system of communication and control over large inland areas, especially if the invaded country had a well organized army. By the end of the 19th century, however, this limitation fell. Thanks to new scientific breakthroughs in transportation and communication, the great industrial states expanded their colonial reach, now having the ability to invade and occupy almost any type of terrain.

The United States, for example, in a systematic program of deliberate genocide, succeeded in killing off nearly all the Indians that blocked its westward expansion, not to mention tearing off a sizable chunk of Mexico. The result was a continental empire that stretched "from sea to shining sea."

A similar phenomenon occurred in Russia. In 1558, Ivan the Terrible dispatched groups of merchants and Cossacks eastward into Siberia to open that vast area to Russian hegemony and trade. Small bands of roving Russian forces pushed their way ever further eastward. The invaders, though few in number, overcame the native Buryats, Tunguses, Yakuts, and Chukchi. After crossing the Bering Sea, they subdued the Inuit of Alaska and established trading posts within striking distance of San Francisco.

As science advanced, the great European powers, later joined by Japan, divided up the remainder of the world into competing empires. By the outbreak of the First World War in 1914, 82% of the world's population had fallen subject to some form of colonial domination.[9]

Without the practical tools supplied them by science, the European bourgeoisie would never have been able to decimate Africa, the Americas, and the Far East. And without the new capital and markets generated by imperialism, the bourgeoisie would never have been able to pay for the creation of the industrial system.

The world-wide scenes of carnage created by imperialism and industrialism everywhere bear the bloody handprints of applied science. In weighing the question of the overall historical impact of science, we cannot fail to put these facts on the scales of judgment.

Scientific Socialism

Although science-empowered imperialism brought ever greater wealth to the ruling classes of industrial states during the 19th century, the burgeoning numbers of the working class often suffered horribly. In reaction, various popular protest movements arose. The most important proved to be the socialist movement, which contained many different varieties.

At one end of the socialist spectrum were those who criticized the triumph of science and the new industrial state. They called for maintenance of the craft tradition, direct control of businesses by their immediate employees, decentralization of the state, emancipation of women and homosexuals, and restoration of the ancient pagan reverence for nature.

An example of this version of socialism was the gay English philosopher and poet Edward Carpenter (1844-1929). Appalled by the barbarities perpetuated in the name of scientific progress, Carpenter predicted that industrialism would eventually discredit and undermine itself, leading to a return of the lost wisdom of the pre-industrial period:

> And when the Civilisation-period has passed away, the old Nature-religion—perhaps greatly grown—will come back. ... Man will once more feel his unity with his fellows, he will *feel* his unity with the animals, with the mountains and the streams, with the earth itself and the slow lapse of the constellations, not as an abstract dogma of Science or Theology, but as a living and ever-present fact. Ages back this has been understood better than now.[10]

At the other end of the socialist spectrum were the Communists. Scorning the idea of a craft-dependent, nature-revering society as "infantile" and "utopian," the Communists called for the rapid industrialization of the economy and the application of the scientific method to all areas of life. In 1917, just after the Bolsheviks came to power in Russia, Lenin said that the new industrial society would require totalitarian control. Only in this way, he claimed, could economic production conform to his ideal model for social efficiency, the clock:

> Neither railways nor transport, nor large-scale machinery and enterprise in general can function correctly without a single will linking the entire working personnel into an economic organ operating with the precision of clock-work.[11]

Lenin, not Carpenter, proved to be the voice of socialism's future. The Bolsheviks, ruthlessly violent in pushing their agenda against an equally ruthless European establishment, carried the day in Russia. Once secure in power, they murdered their enemies, both real and imagined, *en masse*, and relentlessly pushed both industrialism and science. Stalin in particular was as effective in decimating the peasantry of Russia as had been the entire enclosure movement against the peasants of England.

After the triumph of the Bolsheviks in Russia, industrial civilization broke into two warring camps, the Capitalists and the Communists. After World War II, these camps became identified with the imperialist ambitions of two competing super-states, the U.S.A. and the U.S.S.R. The American Capitalists placed final economic control in the hands of the few hundred super-rich families who owned the largest corporations, although the American public continued to exercise indirect political influence through representative democracy. The Soviet Communists, on the other hand, placed both economic and political control in the hands of a dictator and a small clique of high party apparatchiks, who ran the entire country as one giant business corporation. Despite these differences, however, both camps agreed on two major points: (1) industrialism is the best way to satisfy humanity's economic needs; and (2) the practical application of science is essential to industrial success.

The Loss of Leisure

The partisans of science have a response. Despite the dark undersides of imperialism and industrialism, they say, the industrial system eventually stabilized in a more humane form, at least in the West. When it did, it brought to humanity a great boon—relief from the ancient burden of meaningless toil.

As with many of the claims made for science, this one too is false. Although not widely realized, industrialism actually increased the amount of time that human beings must work in order to satisfy their basic needs, as demonstrated recently by economic historian Juliet Schor.[12]

Schor points out (as anthropologists have long known) that people in so-called "primitive" societies generally work far less than the members of so-called "advanced" societies. When modern Europeans first encounter such societies, they typically denounce the natives as "lazy," although the natives do not see themselves that way at all. Factory owners in particular have been vexed at the difficulty of getting tribal natives to work in their new colonial factories. Unless forcibly restrained and constantly watched, the natives flee as soon as possible back to their old haunts. Even when the Europeans succeed in destroying these old haunts, the natives do not flock into the factories; more often, they collapse into a life of alcoholic despair.

In ancient Greece and Rome, the amount of time devoted to work, even for many slaves, was far less than that of the modern wage-earner. The numerous pagan gods all had their special days that the people celebrated with festive processions and revels. At Athens, there were 50 to 60 holidays a year; at Tarentum, half the year was devoted to holidays; Rome under its old calendar had 109 holidays in a year of 355 days.

The Middle Ages continued the same attitude toward work. Many of the ancient pagan gods survived under the guise of Catholic saints, each having his or her special feast day. The actual work day was about eight hours long in the Middle Ages, in the context of many holidays. For example, in 14th-century England, the actual working year for the servile class was 175 days, and in medieval Spain, holidays took up five months of the year.[13]

All this changed with the triumph of the industrial revolution in England and its spread to other countries. Masses of peasants, thrown off their ancient lands by the enclosure movement, were reduced to the status of urban proletarians. Lacking a means of survival in the cities, they contracted to work as factory workers for a set amount of wages for "the day." When the advance of science made extensive indoor lighting possible, "the day" came to mean as long as workers could continue at their stations without collapsing, often up to 16 hours at a time. In addition, the workers lost all their old holidays except for Good Friday and Christmas.

By the mid-nineteenth century, factory workers in Britain and the United States were working an average of 3,150 to 3,650 hours per year.[14] Eventually, through the formation of trade unions that were willing to strike, workers improved their circumstances. In the face of fierce opposition from factory owners, unions succeeded by the 1920s in scaling back the daily work period to eight hours, as it had been over four hundred years earlier in the Middle Ages.

Those who boast that industrialism reduced human labor to the eight-hour day conveniently forget that this accomplishment was the work of unions, who had to fight industrialists for what was once the established norm. They also forget that the hours that the industrialists themselves had introduced and fought unsuccessfully to keep "were probably the longest and most arduous work schedules in the history of humankind."[15]

Science played an important role in the determination of industrialists to keep workers on the job as long as possible every day. The factory, which was the result of the application of scientific methods to the productive process, was basically a system of machines working in tandem as a super-machine. The machines generated the most profit when they ran constantly and steadily, with the least interruption from troublesome humans. Constantly having to train bevies of new workers and coordinate frequent shift changes was inefficient and costly from the point of view of the machine (and therefore of the machine owner). Consequently, the captains of industry held out for the smallest possible work force with the longest possible hours. Until 1923 (when it was finally forced to change by unions), the U.S. steel industry had a seven-day work week of twelve hours a day.

In more recent years, the quickening pace of technological change has not promoted the lessening of human work, as commonly believed. To the contrary, during the last few decades the work week in the United States has actually *increased*. Through overtime and moonlighting on the part of wage-earners, and extra hours imposed by bosses on salaried employees, the average American worker is now on the job longer than at any time since the 1920s, when the old eight-hour day of the Middle Ages was re-established. From 1969 to 1987, in particular, annual leisure time for the average American worker fell 47 hours.[16] During this same period, the real purchasing power of American workers also fell significantly. As a result, Americans find they have to work ever longer hours just to stay in place.

The oft-made claim that technology reduces human labor is also refuted in another area of human labor, often overlooked—housework. During the last sixty years or so, there has been an extraordinary technological revolution within the home: indoor plumbing, electrification, introduction of new devices like vacuum cleaners, micro-wave ovens, etc. Despite all these changes, however, the work week for the average American housewife has remained fairly constant at around 50 hours per week.

The labor-saving argument for technology also fails for Japan, which is just now overtaking the United States as the world's leading technological innovator. Despite technological gains in their country since the end of World War II, most Japanese workers put in a work week of 6-6½ days, and as many as one-half decline to use their accrued vacation time. Among Japanese men who work on salary, a new phenomenon has appeared called *karoshi*, or "death by overwork." A growing number of these men are collapsing and dying at their desks, typically following long periods of high-stress work.

In contrast to both the United States and Japan, Western Europe has seen a steady decline in the work week since World War II (although modern Europeans still work more than people in so-called "primitive" societies). The difference is not due to technology but economics, politics, and culture. European trade unions continue to have greater clout than their American counterparts, and Europeans in general place a higher value on the leisure necessary for personal cultural development. Faced with the choice of more leisure or more money, most modern Americans would take the money, especially in light of the steady decline in their purchasing power since 1973.

These historical facts clearly confound the common claim that science, in making possible the rise of industrialism, has helped reduce the burden of labor. In fact, the opposite is true: the early period of the industrial revolution brought with it the greatest increase in the volume of work known to history. Only after determined resistance by workers *against* the industrializers did the work week shrink back to its previous level in the Middle Ages. Moreover, since World War II (an age of breath-taking technological innovation), the work week has again been expanding.

Thank God It's Friday

Industrialism has also affected the quality of work. In most so-called "primitive" societies, humans felt a positive emotional investment in their work. The North American Indians, for example, typically experienced in their labors of hunting and gathering a powerful sense of bonding with their own sex, their tribe, and nature, which they celebrated through collective song, dance, and myth. Work was under their own immediate control, for their own immediate benefit, and imbedded in their emotional relationships to each other and to nature.

An emotional involvement in work is also found in many non-industrial societies that are not "primitive." Evidence is the astonishing beauty and loving care that typically appear in many artifacts made by craftspeople during the pre-industrial era, and which are conspicuously rare in the mass-produced commodities of the Steel Age.

Industrialism—which is the systematic application of scientific methods to the productive process—killed off the last vestiges of the craft tradition, and with it, the meaningfulness of human labor. Just as science scorns the subjective experiences of the individual observer as an obstacle to the pursuit of knowledge, so industrialism scorns the subjective experiences of the individual worker as an obstacle to the production of commodities. Industrialism and science, by peeling away subjectivity and meaning from life, have reduced the economic system to a machine, workers to cogs, and work itself to rote.

Today the overwhelming majority of people in "advanced" societies spend forty hours or more a week working at monotonous, soul-killing jobs that have little or no relevance to their own personal lives. Most workers would quit these jobs on the spot if only they could find some other way to meet their life expenses. But they can't. Wearily dragging themselves through their assigned chores day after day at assembly lines, offices, sales counters, and laboratories, they look up repeatedly at the clock for the approach of their next coffee break, or lunch hour, or quitting time.

At the close of a typical work day, industrial workers inch along in cars or overcrowded buses through congested traffic, finally reaching home irritated and fatigued. In the few free hours remaining before sleep, they squeeze in some personal interaction with spouse and children, and then a slot for television. Sleep follows, followed by the next day, which brings the same routine again. On weekends, workers struggle to deal with all the household chores and shopping they couldn't find time for during the week. And so on, day after day, year after year, until the departure of their children, retirement, confinement to an old-age home, and death.

From the Barrel of a Gun

By far, the most baneful influence of science, briefly touched on in our discussion of industrialism and imperialism, has been war. A close connection with war existed from the very beginnings of modern science. For example, the largest industrial establishment in Europe in the first half of the 16th century was the Venetian Arsenal, owned by the Venetian state. It was here that Galileo set the opening scene of his great scientific treatise *Dialogue on the Two Chief Systems of the World*. This setting was no accident. The new technology of cannon-making required an increased theoretical knowledge of ballistics, in order to provide the cannon with better aim. So the cannon-makers turned to the new scientists. Galileo, one of those consulted, subsequently hit upon the analogy of viewing the heavenly bodies as if they were fired projectiles moving in an arc. On the basis of this analogy, he began to clarify the difficult new concept of momentum. Later, Isaac Newton, further developing the same analogy, created his grand synthesis of terrestrial and celestial mechanics.

The occupation of engineer, vital in forging the link between science and technology, began with warfare. The very word "engineer" originally meant the military officer in charge of maintaining and using siege engines in war. The first published description of an industrial machine tool was *De la pirotechnia* by Vannoccio Biringucci in Venice in 1540, describing cannon-boring techniques. He was a military engineer who later became director of the pope's munitions supply.[17]

The factory model of production, later one of the defining features of the industrial system, took its rise from the state-owned, science-empowered munitions plants that arose during the Great Devastation:

> It is characteristic of the early modern period that until far into the seventeenth century the best examples of large-scale industrial organization were state-owned factories producing war materiel.[18]

The close historical connection between science, industrialism, imperialism, and war has served to intensify the horror of war in many ways. First, new breakthroughs in science resulted in the design of more deadly weapons. Second, the application of scientific methods to the productive process made it easier to manufacture such weapons in massive numbers. Finally, breakthroughs in the technologies of communication and transportation made it easier to use the deadly weapons over larger areas.

These technological developments have mutually reinforced each other to produce a profound change in the societies themselves that engage in war. To avoid future defeats on the battlefield due to technological inadequacy, governments find they have to be in a constant state of war-readiness; that is, they have to develop an "integrated-systems approach" to governing. Otherwise, they may not be able to get their factories to produce the necessary war materiel when needed, or mobilize sufficient numbers of trained soldiers, or coordinate complicated military maneuvers by air, land, and sea, or sustain the requisite level of war hysteria in the civilian population. The result is that the modern nation-state has increasingly come to resemble a huge machine whose principal function is to engage in, or at least prepare for, war.[19]

Priming the Great Trigger

As noted earlier, by the eve of World War I, a few imperialist states had divided four-fifths of the globe into colonial areas and spheres of economic exploitation. In most cases, the imperialist powers owed their success to their long-standing development and use of the tools of institutionalized violence. These tools were both physical and cultural. They consisted of the following: scientifically developed weapons-systems; historically conditioned obedience to centralized bureaucratic authority; regimentation of sexual feeling; culturally enforced enthusiasm for competitive male violence; and separation of thought from feeling in hierarchically controlled education processes.

Since the beginning of the Great Devastation in the 15th century, these were the tools to which European states, and later the U.S. and Japan, repeatedly resorted in order to implement their agendas of domination. Not surprisingly, when there were no longer any significant "undeveloped" societies left to conquer, the dominating societies—so long emotionally primed for mass violence, so long trained in violence's latest scientific techniques—turned at last against each other in a grand paroxysm of war.

Today, when faith in science's shiny new methods leads many simply to ignore the lessons of history, the awful significance of this science-empowered paroxysm of violence usually passes unnoticed. In order to counteract this neglect, we will pause here to consider in some detail a recent historical chain of events that enthusiasts for science would prefer not to mention. Let anyone who has ever praised the beneficence of science and technology squarely face the dreadful facts that follow.

A Century of Mass Male Horror

On June 28, 1914, a young Serbian nationalist named Gavrilo Princip assassinated the heir to the Austrian throne, Archduke Francis Ferdinand, and his wife, Duchess Sophie Chotek of Hohenberg, when the imperial pair were visiting the Bosnian city of Sarajevo. The assassin's act set off a cache of historical gunpowder that had been accumulating for centuries. The released energy eventually enveloped much of the planet in the flames of three great successive, interlocked wars, running from 1914 to 1990 (World War I, World War II, and the so-called "Cold War"). Because of this ongoing convulsion, the last half-millennium—long touted as an era of ever greater "progress"—ended with the violence of nearly a century of total war.

The bomb quickly exploded after Gavrilo Princip lit the fuse. Prodded by Germany, Austria-Hungary declared war on Serbia. A few days later, Germany itself declared war on Russia, and France invaded Belgium. In the Far East,

Japan, seeking to expand its influence over China and seize German possessions in the Pacific Islands, declared war on Germany. Eventually the war reached an unprecedented size, with a host of countries fighting against an alliance consisting of Germany, Austria-Hungary, Turkey, and German colonial possessions in Africa and the Pacific Islands. By November 11, 1918, when World War I ended with the defeat of Germany and its allies, nearly eight and a half million soldiers had been killed in combat (an average of more than 6,900 deaths per day) and an additional twenty-nine million had been wounded or were missing (more than 23,500 per day).

Although Europe stopped fighting by 1918, the underlying hunger for nationalist expansion persisted, along with the technological means to act on this hunger. By the late 1930s, aggressively authoritarian regimes emerged in Germany, Central Europe, the Soviet Union, the Balkans, Turkey, Italy, Portugal and Spain. In Japan, the army gained increasing political power, assassinating advocates of democracy at home and leading the country into a policy of religiously-tinged nationalist expansion abroad.

At the time, Germany was one of the planet's most technologically advanced nations, although suffering economically. On March 5, 1933, a great turning point occurred: the Nazi party of Adolph Hitler and its ally, the German Nationalist Party, together received 52% of votes cast in free elections for the German parliament. The Nazis' major financial backing came from rich German industrialists.

Hitler, who had already been named Chancellor a few months before, moved quickly to create a totalitarian state that institutionalized rabid militarism and anti-Semitism, and glorified the worst patriarchal fantasies of male power. Before the monumentally chiseled presence of *der Führer*, German troops goose-stepped to their appointed national destiny. Endlessly they marched, by the tens of thousands, all scientifically equipped, with right arms outstretched in collective phallic salute.

On September 1, 1939, after obtaining the secret consent of the Soviet Union, Hitler's forces invaded Poland, prompting a declaration of war on Germany by Britain and France. Pursuant to its secret understanding with Germany, the Soviet Union seized eastern Poland and later Estonia, Latvia, Lithuania, and southeastern Finland. Within a few years, much of the world was once again at war. On one side were Germany, Italy, Japan, Finland, the nationalist Chinese regime operating out of Nanking, and various states in Southeastern Europe (Hungary, Romania, Bulgaria, *et al.*). On the other side were the democratic regimes of Western Europe, and later the U.S.S.R. and the U.S.A.

By the time the war ended with the surrender of Japan on September 2, 1945—six years and one day after its beginning—the world had witnessed the greatest single episode of human carnage in its history, with an estimated 55 million dead and 35 million wounded, many of them civilians. Among the casualties were these: 6,000,000 Jews and thousands of homosexuals and Gypsies murdered in Nazi extermination camps; tens of thousands of German workers and refugees killed by the Allied bombing of working-class quarters in Dresden; and hundreds of thousands of Japanese killed and maimed by the American dropping of atomic bombs on Hiroshima and Nagasaki. In addition, millions of people around the globe had suddenly become refugees, flocking to squalid camps in strange new lands, where they succumbed to starvation and disease.

The Hot "Cold War"

Like World War I that preceded it, World War II likewise failed to resolve the underlying question of world domination, and so it gave rise to yet another cycle of global conflict. On June 24, 1948, Soviet forces occupying the eastern part of Germany shut off all land and water access to the sectors of Berlin that were occupied by French, British, and U.S. forces. Although intended to strangle the Western-occupied areas of Berlin, the blockade eventually failed because of a sustained airlift of supplies.

In mounting the Berlin blockade, the Soviet Union broke with its former World War II allies, thus beginning what came to be called "the Cold War." Contrary to its name, however, this struggle was in fact a decades-long hot war. On the one hand was the Soviet Union with its satellites, representing itself as the standard-bearer of the long-suppressed working class now rightfully come into its own. On the other hand was the United States with its satellites, representing itself as the defender of democracy and personal freedom.

Despite these ideological pretenses, however, the Cold War was a naked power struggle between the two principal victors of World War II. At stake was the domination of world markets and the creation of spheres of political and economic influence. The Soviet Union devoured the nations of Eastern Europe that it had wrested from Germany and turned them into bleakly subsisting satellites dominated by ruthless, Soviet-tethered bureaucrats. In addition, the Soviets financially supported cadres of terrorists around the globe in an attempt to co-opt, wherever possible, indigenous resistance movements to Western imperialism. At home, after having been decimated by German invasion and Stalin's murderous political paranoia, the Soviet nation degenerated into a bleak, totalitarian society dominated by a new ruling class of one-party bureaucratic hacks.

The United States, for its part, gave eager financial and military support to many of the planet's most oppressive, even fascistic, regimes. Driven by hunger for cheap raw materials for the American industrial system, the American government sponsored systematic programs of torture and assassination in Third World countries, established a great loop of American military bases on strategic foreign soil, and acted everywhere to suppress indigenous movements fighting for political and economic reform.

At home, after the death of President Franklin Roosevelt on April 12, 1945, U.S. society took a sharp turn to the right, similar to the situation after World War I. Big business gained a lasting strangle-hold on the economy, politicians stirred up mass hysteria against "Reds" and homosexuals, black-listing and censorship spread in the arts, racist sentiments underwent a resurgence, and a pervasive banality and morose conformity overtook national intellectual life.

The principal hot episodes in the Cold War occurred in the Far East, largely in the shadow of the Chinese revolutionary Mao Zedong. In 1949 in Beijing, after a protracted civil war, Mao proclaimed the creation of the People's Republic of China, as the defeated right-wing Nationalist Party, supported by the U.S., fled to Formosa. On June 25, 1950, the armed forces of North Korea, encouraged by Mao, invaded South Korea, then under American hegemony. When the southern regime began to falter, U.S. President Harry Truman dispatched American troops in its support. Shortly thereafter, the United Nations condemned North Korea for aggression and authorized an international army of resistance in the area, consisting mainly of Americans, under command of the American general Douglas MacArthur. When MacArthur's forces crossed into North Korea and approached China, a mass of Chinese troops burst across their border and drove the Americans back into South Korea. In July 1953, the superpowers recognized that a military stalemate existed in Korea and so divided the country into two dictatorial regimes, the North under the thumbs of China and the Soviet Union, and the South under the U.S.

Although a stalemate in military terms, the Korean War was nonetheless a boon to the U.S. economy. Public spending on the war forestalled the period of economic recession that typically follows the termination of great wars in capitalist societies. The war also stimulated development of "the military-industrial complex," as U.S. President Dwight Eisenhower first called it.

With the Korean War, the U.S. began to assume the mantle of the old European imperialist regimes as self-appointed arbiters of world history. The Europeans had been forced to drop this mantle as a result of their mutual exhaustion in World War II.

Vietnam

The U.S. continued further in the same vein in regard to Indo-China. After the conclusion of World War II, French and English troops tried to maintain foreign control over Vietnam, but were rebuffed by a major defeat of French forces at the Battle of Dien Bien Phu in May 1954. As a result of this defeat, the great powers decided to partition Vietnam into a northern and southern sector, with provisions for free elections to be held throughout the country in 1956.

As the election date approached, U.S. President Dwight Eisenhower, fearful that the Communists would win, supported the establishment of a right-wing dictatorship in the South under Ngo Dinh Diem. In response, the Communists began a guerrilla war of national liberation. Later, Diem, having fallen out of favor with the

U.S. because of his resistance to Washington's "advice," was killed in a U.S.-backed military coup in 1963. New governments—the military dictatorships of Marshal Ky and Nguyen Van Thieu—subsequently came to power in South Vietnam with U.S. blessing.

In 1964 U.S. President Lyndon Johnson falsely declared to Congress that Communist forces had, without provocation, fired on U.S. ships in the Gulf of Tonkin. Through this ruse, Johnson gained Congressional backing for an expanded U.S. war in the region. Repeatedly rebuffed, however, by an unexpectedly tough resistance, the U.S. under Presidents Johnson and Nixon eventually resorted to a war of mass, indiscriminate terror against civilians, including the saturation bombing, with napalm, of civilian areas in Vietnam, Cambodia, and Laos.

At home in the U.S. itself, extensive media reports of U.S. atrocities in Indo-China, combined with protests from the rising American counterculture, brought pressure on Washington to end the war. A military turning point occurred in January 1968 ("the Tet Offensive"), when guerrilla forces mounted a stunning attack from which the Americans and their puppet South Vietnamese forces never fully recovered. Seven and a quarter years later, on April 30, 1975, Communist guerrillas swept to unconditional victory throughout the country. The last American forces withdrew in haste and humiliation from Saigon, thus marking the U.S.'s first defeat in war.

Afghanistan

The Soviet Union experienced a similar rebuff to imperialist ambitions in its guerrilla war in Afghanistan. As with the U.S. in Vietnam, so the U.S.S.R. sought to fill the shoes of a retreating Western European imperialist power, in this case Great Britain. After World War II, when an exhausted Britain retreated from the area, Soviet interest in Afghanistan, including financial aid and the sending of "advisors," was rekindled.[20]

In July 1973, a relatively bloodless palace coup by left-leaning military officers, led by Prince Mohammed Daoud, overthrew the monarchy and proclaimed Afghanistan a republic. Five years later, in April 1978, Daoud and his entire family (including his grandchildren) were killed in a second military coup. This coup produced a Communist regime, eventually dominated by the ruthless Soviet client Hafizulla Amin. Because of Amin's widespread use of torture and mass arrests, an existing popular Islamic guerrilla movement continued to spread, winning control of much of the countryside. Amin responded, in the style of the government of South Vietnam toward its rebels, with a policy of terrorism against the civilian populace, bombing villages with napalm and burning fields of crops.

The Soviets became disenchanted with Amin, as the U.S. had become disenchanted with their puppet Ngo Dinh Diem in South Vietnam. Amin began to resist "advice" from Moscow and proved inept in bringing the resistance under control. On Christmas Eve, 1979, Soviet troops poured into Afghanistan, claiming that the Afghan government had asked them to intervene. The Soviets had Amin and several of his family members killed, replacing him with Babrak Karmal, probably a KGB agent. Babrak appointed Soviet citizens to run many government offices, while Soviet troops attacked the Islamic guerrillas in the countryside using chemical warfare and a "scorched earth" policy.

The Afghan resistance continued, as the Soviets found themselves bogged down in an expensive, unwinnable guerrilla war, just as the Americans had in Vietnam. In November 1986, the new Soviet leader Mikhail Gorbachev, looking for a way to disengage the U.S.S.R. from a losing situation, nudged Karmal out of office and replaced him with his own protégé, Najibullah Khan. Najibullah managed to hold on to power until 1992, when he finally fled for protection to a U.N. compound in Kabul, the capital.

Rival Afghan guerrilla factions, using weapons taken from the Russians or supplied by the Americans, fought each other for control of the country. The Taliban, a mélange of armed Islamic religious fanatics, eventually prevailed, taking the capital in September 1996. Breaking into the U.N. compound, they seized and killed Najibullah and his brother.

The conflicts in Korea, Vietnam, and Afghanistan were not the only ones to result in great suffering and death during the "Cold War." Throughout the period, competing agents of the U.S. and the U.S.S.R. engineered conflicts in many countries around the globe. These machinations often resulted in assassination, economic disruption, governmental collapse, famine, and civil war. In Africa in particular, the super-powers hired and trained professional provocateurs to inflame local tribal conflicts until they exploded into hideous political and ecological catastrophes. The combined effect of the Great Devastation, European imperialism, and Cold War intrigue was to turn much of Africa into a political and economic wasteland.

Perhaps the most devastating result of the Cold War emerged in Cambodia. There manipulations by the U.S., the U.S.S.R., and China resulted in the triumph in the late 1970s of the fanatical, Chinese-backed Khmer Rouge. They systematically killed millions of Cambodian citizens in one of the worst atrocities ever recorded in human history.

Science & The Second Hundred Years War

The horrifying wars that succeeded each other between the assassination of the Archduke Francis Ferdinand in 1914 and the disintegration of the Soviet Union in the 1990s were all interconnected. They were parts of an ongoing struggle among the technologically developed powers for economic and political domination of the globe.

The avalanche of violence that overwhelmed the world between 1914 and 1990 (the Second Hundred Years War, as I call it) was ghastly because it was empowered by scientific technology. Science made possible new weapons, new forms of communication, new modes of travel, new productive processes, and new means of state control. These technologies reinforced each other toward a common violent end.

Back in the U.S.

The final victors of the Second Hundred Years War were the U.S. and the U.S.S.R. And what was the grand payoff from all these decades of technologically-empowered violence? During the Cold War, both the U.S. and the U.S.S.R. squandered much of their national economic assets on military-related technology. Each country vied with the other in acquiring the latest weapons-systems and in creating the most technologically sophisticated armies.

In the short run, these military expenditures stimulated the economies of each super-power; in the long run, however, the effects were disastrous to both. National resources that otherwise would have gone into laying the foundations for future domestic production went instead into immediate military needs that were economically unproductive in the long haul, however much they might stimulate the economy for the moment. For example, billions would be spent on missiles that, when completed, would sit idle in their silos for years, completely unconnected to the rest of the economy. Had the same resources been devoted to creating new peace-time business ventures, they would have continued to generate new products and services for decades.

Because military pump-priming provided an intense short-run rush to the economy during the Cold War years, many Americans proudly spoke of their country as "the affluent society," holding it up as an economic model for the rest of the world. A small minority of observers, however, thought otherwise. They warned that the intensive spending on military technology would have devastating consequences for peacetime economic productivity in years to come.

The most prominent of these critics was Columbia University professor Seymour Melman. Writing in 1964, at the peak of the euphoria over American affluence, Melman shocked many of his fellow citizens when he argued that the U.S., because of its great investment in military technology, was on its way to becoming a depleted society:

> A process of technical, industrial, and human deterioration has been set in motion within American society. ... This deterioration is the result of an unprecedented concentration of America's technical talent and fresh capital on military production. ... More than two thirds of America's technical researchers now work for the military. ... The combination of financial success and decaying productive capability has become a far-ranging pattern that threatens the viability of the American industrial system at its base.[21]

Melman surmised that a similar process of deterioration was under way in the Soviet Union. He also argued that the U.S. and the U.S.S.R. had become poor role-models for the developing countries of the Third World. Following American and Soviet examples, many of these struggling nations were pouring their limited national assets into military technology, thereby paving the way for long-term economic and ecological catastrophe.

Although dismissed at the time, Melman eventually proved to be right on all counts. On the surface, the U.S. economy flourished during the Cold War years, especially under the presidency of Ronald Reagan, who orchestrated the largest single peace-time military build-up in the nation's history. Under the surface, however, contrary trends were at work. Technological superiority in civilian industry was passing to Germany and Japan; they had been forbidden by their terms of defeat in World War II from developing a significant military establishment. At the same time, a growing number of America's civilian-oriented factories were closing their doors, unable to keep up with foreign competition.

When the burgeoning federal debt eventually reduced the flow of lucrative government contracts to the American defense industry, these factories found that they lacked the technical expertise to redirect themselves to productive peace-time ventures. Burdened with formidable foreign competition in civilian products and a limping defense industry, the American economy stalled, entering a protracted period of "downsizing," as it was euphemistically called.

Although wealthy American defense contractors enjoyed great profits during the Cold War, workers found that their purchasing power steadily declined after 1973, requiring them to work ever longer hours just to keep in place. During the same period, economic inequality greatly increased in the U.S. By the 1990s the U.S. had the widest class gap of any Western industrial nation, with the richest one percent of American households owning 40% of the nation's wealth.[22] At the same time, there were roughly 3,000,000 homeless Americans.[23]

Corresponding to the overall decline in workers' purchasing power has been a steady deterioration in social well-being. This deterioration is documented in a comprehensive statistical study conducted by the Institute for Innovation in Social Policy of Fordham University. The Institute found that between 1973 and 1994 (the last year for which statistics are available), the overall index of social well-being in the United States fell by 40%. Disturbing statistical trends involving young people stand out. For example, from 1970 to 1994, the teen suicide rate increased nearly 100%.[24]

Throughout the later years of the Cold War, drug and alcohol addiction spread widely among all segments of the American public, literacy rates dropped, and the American public-education system in large urban areas all but collapsed. By the 1990s, most Americans' largest single daily activity next to working and sleeping was watching TV. At the same time, 75% of all commercial network television was paid for by the country's 100 largest corporations. They exposed the average American television viewer to 21,000 commercials a year.[25]

Most disturbing of all is the pervasiveness of depraved behavior among American males. In 1989, there were 30,000 murders in the U.S., the overwhelming majority committed by men. One in five women reported having been raped in their lifetimes, and one in three, sexually molested in childhood.[26]

American incarceration rates fell overall from 1961 to 1972. From 1972 to 1995, however, the rates increased by almost 350%, corresponding to the drop in purchasing power of the average American worker during the same period. By mid-1995, the U.S. prison population (mostly male) had reached 1.6 million, the highest per capita incarceration rate of any major country in the world. Among blacks, the overall incarceration rate was 18 times higher among men than among women; among whites, 16 times higher among men. Contrary to common opinion, the easy availability of firearms in the U.S. is not the principal factor affecting the high homicide rate; in fact, the *non*firearm homicide rate in the U.S. is greater than the total homicide rates in most other major countries.[27]

Behind these statistics lies a stark picture that every discerning observer during the past decades has commented on: the overall quality of life in the U.S. is plummeting. A sizable segment of the public who wish to work remain permanently unemployed, having simply given up. Many more who do have jobs are chronically underemployed. Those who hold down regular jobs find it increasingly hard to make ends meet, having to work more hours each week at jobs they hate just to stay in place. Workers spend their declining leisure time watching television. Public services, especially in education, are falling apart. Mass homelessness is now an accepted part of the urban American landscape. Egregious forms of male violence are pervasive.

Most political leaders are whores in the pay of big corporations and special interests. Nearly everybody knows somebody who has a serious drug or alcohol problem. Organized religion has become either irrelevant or some form of racket. Life has lost its meaning.

Back in the U.S.S.R.

So much for the grand prize won by the U.S. for coming out on top at the close of the Second Hundred Years War. The U.S.S.R., as runner-up, won an equally noteworthy prize. When the Soviet system finally collapsed despite President Mikhail Gorbachev's best efforts to save it, Russia lost nearly of all its economic and political satellites. As a result, food, clothing, and fuel became scarce in Russia. Elderly and disabled pensioners found that they could not survive because of the plummeting value of the ruble. Public order and safety became virtually non-existent in many regions; others were on the verge of civil war. In certain cities, organized crime took over the function of government. Alcoholism became rampant, penetrating to the highest levels of state. The average life span fell. The Communist world-view became irrelevant, both personally and nationally. Life lost its meaning.

Back in the Third World

Although the decline in the quality of life in America and Russia at the end of the alleged age of progress is daunting, the worst situation exists in the Third World. Having been repeatedly gang-raped by Europe during the Great Devastation, and later by the U.S., the U.S.S.R., Japan, and China during the Industrial Dark Age, much of the globe now lies politically and economically prostrate. In many such places, the only means of public order that remain are competing rag-tag military cliques armed to the teeth with weapons recently provided by American, Russian, and Chinese technology. The overwhelming majority of the world's inhabitants now live under conditions of mass squalor, famine, plague, civil war, and ecological collapse.

Testosterone and Technology

Many people, without actually examining the historical record, continue to insist that science, on the whole, has greatly benefited both humanity and the planet. As we have seen, however, the historical evidence proves otherwise: the single greatest practical impact of science during the past 500 years has been to magnify and institutionally empower the violence of human males. Science and technology, the peculiar inventions of a certain type of patriarchal mentality, have enabled militarists, industrialists, and political leaders to engineer horrifying episodes of imperialist exploitation, genocide, war, fascism, and environmental devastation. When judged in terms of its overall historical impact, "modern science" is just another term for rape.

Sanitation

"But what about the positive side?" the partisans of science ask. As an example, they typically point to modern advances made in public health. In this spirit, technology historian Donald Cardwell denounces the critics of science and technology as promoters of "a state of Gothic ignorance," adding—

> You cannot enjoy the benefits of modern medicine and public health—of which the most determined critics would surely approve—without accepting the rest of science and technology.[2]

Contrary to Cardwell, however, the situation is not so simple. For one thing, his remark assumes that science and technology constitute one seamless fabric that we must either accept or reject *in toto*. Cardwell will not permit the luxury of a third option, that of critically evaluating the different strands in technology, with the intention of rejecting some while accepting others. This sort of all-or-nothing thinking is common among people who are dogmatic enthusiasts.

Cardwell's remark is off the mark in another regard: it misrepresents the actual history of the modern public-health movement. Contrary to Cardwell, the great improvement in public health that began to occur in the West in the latter part of the 19th century had little if anything to do with science and technology. In fact, most of those who were responsible for this turn of events were critics of the type of society that science and technology were then creating. Inasmuch as many people today share Cardwell's ignorance of this subject, we will pause here briefly to review the historical facts.

The sanitation movement, which engendered the single greatest improvement in modern European health, derived its principal inspiration from a strain of thought that later came to be called, disparagingly, "back-to-nature romanticism." Its ideological roots derived from German *Naturphilosophie* (nature philosophy) and from the writings of the Swiss-born philosopher Jean-Jacques Rousseau (1712-1778). Both these sources had been highly influenced by descriptions of native societies made by European invaders during the initial phases of the Great Devastation.[29]

As the Great Devastation got under way, Europeans reaching the Americas, Greenland, and the South Sea Islands published a stream of first-hand accounts describing the nature-oriented tribal societies they encountered in these strange new places. In general, these reports depicted the natives as possessing meager material possessions (as judged by European standards) but as long-living, robustly healthy, and happy. Today, many commentators scoff at the positive depictions of natives in these early accounts, claiming that the Europeans "romanticized" what they saw. However, such scoffing overlooks an important fact: the Europeans, far from being sentimental, were generally hard-bitten adventurers eager to find any way they could to exploit the newly found societies.

These first-hand accounts made a sensational impact on the European intelligentsia. In contrast to the good health and the concern with cleanliness found among "primitives," European life in the Middle Ages and the Renaissance was positively filthy; moreover, Europe had a long history of recurring episodes of mysterious diseases and plagues, and short life-spans had long been the rule. These conditions resulted from the chaos that followed the collapse of Greco-Roman civilization and were later reinforced by Christianity. In contrast to ancient paganism, medieval Christianity regarded nudity as sinful and concern with bodily cleanliness as a sign of the Devil's influence. The more pious of Christians boasted that they had never removed their clothing or taken a bath in their entire lives.

This morbid mentality contrasted not only with that found among "primitives" but also with the practices of other "civilized" societies. For example, when the Chinese began interacting with Europeans as a result of Marco Polo's trip, they were shocked at how dirty the Westerners were. The situation was later aggravated by the rise of industrialism, which drove the European peasantry off the land, forcing them to live in filthy tenements in overcrowded cities that lacked any standards of public sanitation.

The European intelligentsia also learned that native societies often underwent a catastrophic decline due to disease after contact with the Europeans. For example, Bartholomew Gosnold explored the New England coast in 1602 in an area today called "Martha's Vineyard." He described the Indians as "people of a perfect constitution of body, active, strong, healthful, and very witty." Within a few years of Gosnold's visit, more than 90% of the Indians in the area died from diseases contracted from their European visitors.[30]

Many of the European intellectuals who read these accounts were critics of the political order of their day. They noted that native peoples were not only more healthy than contemporary Europeans but that they were also free from exploitation by decrepit bureaucratic structures of state and church. The European writers concluded (wrongly) that the natives, at least originally, did not live in any kind of structured society but in "a state of nature." In fact, the great complexity and variety of native societies tended to be invisible to the observers. Nonetheless, native culture in general did contrast to European culture in being emotively immediate and nature-affirming, as opposed to bureaucratically remote and nature-hostile.

Rousseau

As mentioned above, Jean-Jacques Rousseau was one of the influences on the later sanitation movement. Explorers' descriptions of native tribal societies provided him (and many others) with a model for criticizing the artificiality and oppressiveness of contemporary European society. "Man is born free, and everywhere he is in chains," declaimed Rousseau in the first line of the first chapter of his book *The Social Contract*, published in 1762. Much of the existing European social order should be swept aside, he argued, for it perverted the innate goodness that all human beings have in a state of nature. In making this appeal, *The Social Contract* added its weight to a growing body of revolutionary European thought that clamored for reform in the name not only of utility but also of nature.

At the same time, paradoxically, *The Social Contract* also reinforced a different line of thought, one that validated state power. When invoked for certain types of higher purposes, Rousseau maintained, coercion by the state is morally justified. But how could this be, if the state of nature, where all are free and independent, is of a higher order than the civil state? Rousseau responded that the state, far from being a mere mechanical contrivance, is a natural outgrowth of human need, manifesting a given people's deepest collective interest, which Rousseau called "the general will." As such a natural outgrowth, the state alone provides the means whereby human beings can fully develop the moral potential that is theirs only inchoately in the state of nature.

Combined with the attack on the artificiality and oppressiveness of European society, this second line of thought easily led to a double-barreled concept: personal health is a matter of public policy, involving active participation by the power of the state. And it is legitimate to criticize existing public policy by an appeal to nature; that is, by an appeal to the practices of societies that live close to nature. And this is exactly the twofold tack taken by the sanitation movement in the 19th century.

Building on Rousseau's view, partisans of the sanitation movement challenged the new group of *laissez-faire* industrialists. This group, busily covering the European landscape with scientifically designed factories, claimed that the common good is best served when each person is most free to satisfy his or her own individual appetites, with the least possible interference from the state.

Personal health is primarily a public matter, insisted the sanitationists, and the best public health policy is to follow the practices of nature societies around the world. That is, the state should enable people to keep themselves *clean*, with easy access to pure food, water, earth, and air, and a safe and easy method of disposing of waste. Acting on these beliefs, sanitationists demanded that factories have adequate ventilation and standards of cleanliness; that cities improve their water-supply and waste-disposal systems; and that the average person be taught how to practice good personal hygiene. Their new approach eventually gave wide currency to the saying "Cleanliness is next to godliness." Although taken for granted today, this saying was revolutionary when first introduced, for it ran counter to traditional Christian thinking, as noted above.

Significantly, many of the sanitationists *rejected* the germ theory of disease, first propounded in scientific form in 1857 by Louis Pasteur. And, in fact, Pasteur himself questioned whether large concentrations of microbes might not be a characteristic symptom, rather than a cause, of disease. The basic attitude of the sanitationists was summed up in a remark by Florence Nightingale. Rejecting the germ theory of disease, she said—

> There are no specific diseases. There are specific disease conditions.[31]

The sanitationists' voices were heeded, for wherever they put the new methods into effect, the health of the people improved immediately and dramatically. As a result, Europe witnessed the greatest single improvement in health and longevity since the days of the Roman Empire. All this was accomplished by people who were indifferent to the latest findings of science on the matter; indeed, they opposed many basic features in the new type of society that scientific industrialism was creating. As René Dubos rightly observes:

> The conquest of epidemic diseases was in large part the result of the campaign for pure food, pure water, and pure air based not on a scientific doctrine but on philosophical faith. It was through the humanitarian movements dedicated to the eradication of the social evils of the Industrial Revolution, and the attempt to recapture the goodness of life in harmony with the ways of nature, that Western man succeeded in controlling some of the disease problems generated by the undisciplined ruthlessness of industrialization in its early phase.[32]

In their struggle to bring European health standards up to those of nature societies, the sanitationists played a historical role similar to that of the trade unionists, who struggled to reduce the modern work-day back to its medieval length. In both cases, real human progress meant *restraining* the social and economic momentum that science had introduced into the productive process.

Modern Medicine's Double Edge

At this point, the partisans of science are likely to back-track. "Very well," they will say, "the achievements of the sanitation movement can't be chalked up to modern science. But what about later developments in medical science? For example, the role played by antibiotics in controlling infection and by vaccines in preventing communicable disease, as well as the development of new surgical techniques. As for your much-admired 'nature societies,' just look at the way medical science has helped improve the wretched lot of primitive groups living in India and Africa. These achievements have to be put in the scale when we assess the historical merit of science."

Here we must concede that the partisans of science have a point, but with a qualification. Although it's true that modern medical science has made great strides in treating certain kinds of diseases, we must not overlook a salient fact: the *types* of diseases that have appealed to medical science for relief are largely those that have been caused or seriously aggravated by the development of patriarchal-industrial civilization, of which science itself has been a prime promoter.

For example, it's true that modern medical science has been of help to many people living in wretched squalor and poverty in Africa and India. But how did it happen that so much of the Third World has been reduced to abject squalor? We saw earlier: from the beginning of the Great Devastation until the Cold War, the great powers, empowered by science, deliberately crushed the economic, political, and social substructures of the societies they overran. The former colonies, on finally gaining independence, were often only pathetic caricatures of their former selves.

Modern medical science deserves credit for helping to heal some of the wounds in these afflicted societies. Science as a whole, however, deserves a roaring reproach for having continually empowered the imperialists throughout their long history of crippling conquest. The overall historical role of science here is like that of a rapist who nearly kills his victim and then returns to bring her some bandages. He deserves credit for this help, but it is far outweighed by the blame he bears for the original assault.

Scientifically Created Disease

An analogous situation exists in the case of the victorious imperialists. As just noted, one of the great boasts of modern medical science is that hard-nosed scientific research, not mushy nature romanticism, is responsible for creating antibiotics.

Those who make this boast, however, overlook a terrible historical irony: medical science, by the very act of creating miraculous antibiotic drugs, has also inadvertently created new strains of deadly bacteria for which no known treatment exists. Only now are the full implications of this development making themselves felt. Those who understand the implications are trembling.

The best over-all account of this situation is the eye-opening 1994 book *The Plague Makers* by Jeffrey Fisher. He's a medical pathologist and researcher who monitors health technology for the World Health Organization.[33]

Fisher points out a terrible irony: regardless of how effective any given antibiotic is, it always leaves behind some bacterial strain that is resistant. When the bacteria that are vulnerable to the antibiotic disappear from the body, the surviving, resistant strains proliferate, for they now have far fewer competitors in the struggle for essential nutrients. In addition, a new generation of bacteria appears about every 20 minutes. Consequently, the effects of genetic mutation appear far more quickly among bacteria than in other forms of life. Finally, bacteria have a unique genetic ability called "conjugation." One bacterial strain can pass its newly mutated genes on to an entirely different strain by mere physical contact. For example, a newly mutated bacterial strain that proliferates among hogs (fed antibiotics by agribusiness to increase their weight) can pass their drug-resistant genes on to an entirely different strain that resides in human beings.

As a result, hospitals have become breeding grounds for newly mutated strains of deadly bacteria that are resistant to all known antibiotics. Every year approximately two million Americans come down with an infection in a hospital that they didn't have when they entered. Most chilling, every year more than 80,000 Americans die from hospital-caused effects, a number greater than the casualties in either the Korean or the Vietnam War.[34]

So far, whenever a new antibiotic-resistant bacterium has evolved, medical science has succeeded in developing a more potent antibiotic before the bacterium could reach plague proportions. However, there's a catch; the virulence and reach of the new bacteria are steadily growing:

> They [physicians] know that hospitals are in jeopardy of once again being overwhelmed with untreatable infectious diseases such as pneumonia, tuberculosis, meningitis, typhoid fever and dysentery. ... The infections that are cutting a wide swath through our hospitals today are completely resistant to the antibiotics we have come to blindly rely on. We are standing on the brink of catastrophe.[35]

The worst danger exists in the Third World, where regulation of medicine is less strict than in the United States. Third-World drugstore clerks and street hucksters dispense antibiotics for every conceivable ailment, whether bacterial or not. This practice, encouraged by drug companies, has promoted the emergence of dangerous, antibiotic-resistant bacteria on an unprecedented scale. The potential for a dangerous mutation is evident when one considers that one-third of the world's population are passive carriers of tuberculosis.[36]

Those who appeal to the new antibiotics in order to prove the beneficence of science as a whole are jumping the gun. The historical record of antibiotics is not yet concluded, and may turn out to be quite different from what most would have anticipated. In 1969, at the height of American smugness, U.S. Surgeon General William Stewart confidently testified before Congress that American medical science had at last won the battle against bacteria. It was time, he said, to "close the book on infectious diseases."[37] Today, a generation later, the most informed authorities on the matter are fearful of new, untreatable global plagues made possible by these very same advances in medical science.

Without doubt, modern medical science has helped a great many people. Infectious disease, traumatic injury, and pain have all been amenable to the new scientific methods. But whether the overall historical impact of medical science will prove to be benign remains to be seen. The problem with antibiotics shows that science may yet come to rue that record.

In any case, those who automatically equate health with modern medicine overlook an important fact: the denizens of many human societies, both past and present, have enjoyed the blessings of longevity and a healthy life, even though they lacked the interventions of modern medical science. The crucial consideration for any society seems to be the total way its people lives:

> Medical geography, the history of diseases, medical anthropology, and the social history of attitudes towards illness have shown that food, water, air, in correlation with the level of sociopolitical equality and the cultural mechanisms that make it possible to keep the population stable, play the decisive role in determining how healthy grownups feel and at what age adults tend to die.[38]

The Spoils of War

The partisans of science have one final argument to make. "Although great suffering has regrettably marked the transition to modernity," they say, "science has nonetheless made it possible for us to enjoy innumerable conveniences in our daily lives, from the way we clean our bodies to the way we deliberate on national policy. Although any one of these conveniences by itself may seem trivial, all of them together add up to a revolutionary qualitative improvement in what it means to live as a human being. This ongoing, interconnected system of practical conveniences not only makes life more bearable but also frees us to develop more fully the higher parts of our human potential. In any case, there is simply no possibility of going back to living in a cave and feeding on wild asparagus. Even the members of nature societies prefer the system of scientifically created conveniences once they have access to it."

This argument slides over two questions: Convenient for *whom*? And at what overall *cost*? For example, U.S. consumers in recent decades have taken for granted the ease of buying television sets, vacuum cleaners, washing machines, automobiles, hair dryers, computers, etc. However, their easy access to such conveniences is a direct result of war and environmental devastation.

As a result of its smashing victory in World War II, the U.S. inherited the global spheres of economic influence that European imperialist powers had spent centuries creating. The result was the transformation of the U.S. into a global imperialist power, comparable to the transformation of Rome after its victory over Carthage in the second century B.C. As with Rome, so with the U.S.: the conquered were bled in order to glut the victorious.

In the 1950s, the U.S. Government established a military protectorate over more than 40 nations covering 15 million square miles of territory and more than 600 million human beings.[39] Entire countries became the playthings of giant American corporations, who collaborated with C.I.A. torturers and assassins to keep "the right people" in control of bullied foreign governments. As a consequence, American factories enjoyed an unprecedented windfall of cheap raw materials from around the globe as well as privileged trading relations with dozens of America's satellites.

The spoils of war continued to pour into the homeland. By the late 1960s the U.S. reached its zenith, vaunting itself as "the affluent society." At the same time, it continued to bleed the nations whose exploitation made possible this American economic miracle. Not surprisingly, rebellions and wars of national liberation broke out around the world against American imperialism. The most important was the War in Vietnam, where the tide of history turned against the U.S. in its humiliating defeat of 1975.

By the late 1980s, the U.S. had lost a substantial part of its world-wide hegemony. Many countries revolted. Others (like Japan), although remaining allies in name, poured their resources into the needs of their non-military infrastructure. Through such investments, they eventually outpaced the U.S. in peace-related technologies. In addition, huge multi-national corporations emerged that dwarfed the power of American-controlled enterprises.

As the American empire sagged after the War in Vietnam, so did its economic well-being. As noted earlier, the purchasing power of American workers has fallen significantly since the mid-1970s, and American life everywhere shows signs of decay.

Another Used-Up Country

Ironically, U.S. society today shows many of the same characteristics found in the Third-World countries whose exploitation fueled American affluence after World War II. Like the client-states it exploited, America itself is now well on the way to becoming a used-up country, both economically and spiritually. As America rusts, a growing national subculture of squalid aimlessness continues to wend its way, like a burgeoning intestinal parasite, through the bowels of its urban underbelly. Non-mainstream artists have been in the forefront of calling attention to this development. An example is filmmaker Jim Jarmusch, whose 1984 movie *Stranger than Paradise* is a classic portrait of the newly emerging America.

The parallel between the new America and the Third World is no mere coincidence. Just as the exploited Third-World poor made possible *la dolce vita* in the U.S. in the 50s and 60s, so today the economic "downsizing" of the U.S. by multi-national corporations is enriching a new international class of investors and entrepreneurs. And the costs? Yesterday, Tijuana; today, Detroit; tomorrow, perhaps your home town.

The erstwhile affluence of the U.S. enabled its middle and upper classes to gorge themselves with new gadgets and conveniences of every imaginable sort, just as the newly found affluence of Japan and other Asian nations is now enabling their new middle classes to gorge themselves. All the while, however, global hunger, poverty, and disease have been steadily on the increase, and the health of the planet's natural environment is on the verge of collapse.

The Whole Picture

Although a minority of people today are quite comfortable due to mass-produced conveniences, the triumph of industrialism during the last two centuries has greatly augmented overall human suffering and environmental deterioration. To congratulate industrialism under these circumstances is like giving a productivity award to a company after examining only the income column in its ledger. You don't have to be an accountant to know that the expenses column is also relevant; yet such a one-sided attitude is typical of the promoters of the industrial system.

The enthusiasts of science claim that industrialism's conveniences, although distributed unevenly around the globe, have nonetheless improved the overall quality of life for those societies lucky enough to enjoy them. This claim also flies in the face of the historical evidence. As an example, consider the course of events in the U.S. during the last century and a half. As industrialism came into its own after 1850, it brought about a radical re-definition of American culture. Among the industrially-conditioned events contributing to this re-definition were these: the final phase of the Indian wars, which forever expunged the Indian nations as viable contributors to American history and culture; the Civil War, the bloodiest in the nation's history, which enabled big business to emerge as the preeminent force in American politics; the annihilation of nearly all of the nation's magnificent virgin forests, an ecological catastrophe comparable to what is now occurring in the Amazon rain forest; the poisoning of most of the nation's rivers and lakes and the befouling of the nation's air; the shredding of the nation's rich tapestry of independent family farms; the absorption of the nation's myriad independent businesses and shops by huge corporate conglomerates; the cancerous growth of blighted cities; and grotesque overpopulation.

Along with these degradations, industrialism also provided a benefit: an ever growing cornucopia of new gadgets and conveniences for the middle and upper classes. But having come into possession of these conveniences, Americans also found they had to live and function in the redefined culture that the same industrial system had created along the way. What, then, is the overall quality of life in this technologically-defined culture?

The Lost Magic of Life

The destruction of the spirituality of the Indians, the cooption of government by big business, the decimation of the natural environment, the subversion of independent farmers, craftsworkers, and shopkeepers, and the drive toward over-urbanization and overpopulation have all worked to the same effect: the United States today is a great cultural and spiritual wasteland. Despite a glut of radios, TVs, VCRs, CD players, camcorders, personal computers, modems, cellular telephones, satellite dishes, and information highways, the average American today (as poll after poll has amply demonstrated) does not know the most elementary facts of history, geography, politics, or literature. Despite the hundreds of millions of dollars invested by Hollywood during the last several decades in high-tech films, a first-rate Hollywood movie appears as rarely in the U.S. as a sighting of the Aurora Borealis. Despite universal public high-school education and perhaps the largest network of private and public universities in history, most American adults who regularly read books (a distinct minority in itself) rarely read anything other than work-related manuals, cookbooks, or pulp fiction. Although raised in a country that has led the world in applying high-tech methods to farming, few Americans under 30 know what a vine-ripened fruit tastes like.

Most Americans do not know how to have sex, raise children, care for the elderly, grieve, or die. Most Americans have no understanding of the concept of meaningful work. Most have never experienced any type of emotionally-integrative communal life beyond that of the nuclear family. Most have lost all feeling for the mystery, power, and beauty of nature. In terms of the practical wisdom of how to live a sound and centered human life, modern Americans as a whole are among the most ignorant people in the history of the human race.

To this picture of technological culture, compare, say, the situation in classical Greece. The geographical area was small, consisting of a string of small cities and towns scattered throughout the Balkans, the Cyclades, Asia Minor, Sicily, and Italy. Although bereft of all the conveniences and gadgets of modern science, ancient Greece within the span of a dozen generations gave the world the poetry of Homer, Sappho, Alcaeus, Hesiod, and Pindar; the histories of Herodotus and Thucydides; the speeches of Lysias and Demosthenes; the theater of Aeschylus, Sophocles, Aristophanes, and Euripides; and the philosophy of Parmenides, Heraclitus, Empedocles, Democritus, Socrates, Plato, and Aristotle. Nor should it be forgotten that after Greece fell subject to Rome, the most technically-oriented society of classical antiquity, its bloom of creativity faded.

Contrary to the partisans of science, gadgets and conveniences in themselves have little to do with the overall quality of life. A people living on a materially slim level of existence can enjoy full and happy lives, just as a people surfeited with material luxuries can lead empty and unfulfilling lives. The crucial consideration in all cases is the whole pattern of life by which a people satisfies its own needs and relates to the rest of humanity and the planet. When judged on these inclusive terms, industrialized societies stand exposed for what they really are: impoverished forms of human life.

The Termite People

"If industrial society is as impoverished as you claim," the partisans of science retort, "why is it that primitive people around the globe, once they get a real taste of its conveniences, want to jump on the bandwagon?" Like many other historical claims made for science, this one too is an out-and-out falsehood. From the founding of Jamestown at the beginning of the 17th century until the Battle of Wounded Knee at the end of the 19th, the American Indians had ample opportunity to observe the new civilization that was spreading across what is now the United States. Once they realized what was happening, the Indians resisted with all the violence they could muster, sparing no one in their attacks, regardless of age or sex. True, many surviving Indians in the United States today have resigned themselves to the victorious culture. But resignation to overwhelming force is one thing, free acceptance another.

The struggle by so-called "primitive people" against scientific modernity has not ended. Today there are some 3,000 native societies within the borders of 200 or so countries. Among many of them, including reservation-bound remnants of the American Indian nations, the survivors are struggling as best they can to protect their old ways from "progress." Rarely do those involved in such a struggle have good things to say about the new way of life that confronts them. The Xingu Indians of the Amazon, for example, call whites "the termite people."[40]

The Judgment of History

To anyone who considers the whole pattern of the evidence, the verdict is clear: science has not proved to be a great boon. To the contrary, the overall historical impact of science has been catastrophic, although science has made life easier for certain privileged classes.

As a historical force, modern science was at its best during its gestation, in the hundred years between the death of Copernicus and the death of Galileo. Then, to its credit, science undermined the stifling hold that the Christian religion had long exercised on Western thought. In the intervening centuries since Galileo, however, science as a historical institution has increasingly come to resemble the Christian juggernaut it displaced. Like medieval Christianity, so modern science has become a highly stratified and privileged machine, lubricated by vast amounts of money, and professionally piloted by sycophants serving society's ruling interests. Using a language understood only by the initiated and appealing to methods held to be sacrosanct, the hierarchs of science presume to define the true nature of reality for the entire society.

As we saw in the last chapter, science can at most claim to have privileged access to certain colors in the spectrum of reality, not the whole rainbow. But like medieval Christianity before it, modern science is by nature intolerant. It dogmatically insists that there is but one world and but one true way of beholding it. Anyone who challenges these claims is guilty of "superstition" or a "flight from reason."[41]

Frankenstein

Throughout the last several centuries, voices critical of science have not been wanting. As might be predicted, many of the most eloquent and perceptive of these voices have belonged to artists, poets, novelists, and dramatists, not to scientists and industrialists. Equally predictable (although less excusable) has been the scandalous neglect accorded these artistic voices by Western academic philosophy. Rarely does a modern university course in the philosophy of science even mention them.

Of all the critiques of modern science written by novelists in the past two centuries perhaps the most powerful is one of the earliest, Mary Shelley's novel *Frankenstein; or, the Modern Prometheus,* published in 1818 when the author was 21 years old.[42] Critics and commentators (usually men) often underestimate the intellectual power of this novel because it was written by a young woman. Although Shelly's writing reflects the personal circumstances of her life, it is a mistake to psychologize-away her critique of science. As we are about to see, that critique is both informed and prescient.[43]

Mary Shelley (*née* Godwin) was born in England in the summer of 1797. Her mother, who died from complications in giving birth to Mary Shelley, was the celebrated feminist writer and political radical Mary Wollstonecraft, who in 1792 had written the ground-breaking *A Vindication of the Rights of Woman*. Mary Shelley's father was the equally-celebrated anarchist philosopher William Godwin, who in 1793 had published *Enquiry Concerning Political Justice*.

In 1808, at the age of ten, Mary Shelley published her first book, *Mounseer Nongtongpaw*. By the time she reached late adolescence, she was widely read in the Greek and Roman classics, history, the sciences, philosophy, religion, and contemporary letters. In 1814, at age 17, she eloped with her future husband, the poet Percy Bysshe Shelley, joined by her half sister Jane ("Claire") Clairmont. The three traveled across the European continent in search of new adventures. Within a few years, Shelley gave birth to two children, the first of whom died not long after birth.

In 1816, at age 19, while staying at Lord Byron's house in Geneva, Mary Shelley began writing *Frankenstein*, which she completed in 1817, and published anonymously in 1818. Her husband, Percy Shelley, whom she had married two years after their elopement, later died in a boating accident in Italy in 1822. She lived her remaining years quietly, out of the public eye, producing a number of travel journals and novels. In 1826, she published *The Last Man*, the story of the destruction of humanity by a plague, and in 1831 brought out a revised edition of *Frankenstein*. She died in 1851, never having remarried.

The feeling of Mary Shelley's *Frankenstein* is quite different from what appears in most of the movies her book later inspired. The book is a series of pensive letters written by a certain R. Walton to his sister in England. Walton is the skipper of an exploratory ship slowly making its way north into the frozen Russian Arctic.

Beginning with Walton's very first letter, Shelley draws a contrast, which she sustains throughout the book, between the coldness of the external environment and the repressed inner-burning passion of its male, nature-challenging protagonists. Shelley reinforces the ice-metaphor with the protagonists' deeds and words. As his ship slowly penetrates deeper into the frozen north, Walton confides in a letter to his sister that he is a lonely man who cannot make emotional contact with the men under his command, adding:

> I desire the company of a man who could sympathize with me; whose eyes would reply to mine. You may deem me romantic, my dear sister, but I bitterly feel the want of a friend.

Some time later, as if in answer to his prayers to find a friend, Walton beholds a remarkable sight out on the ice floes: a huge man-shaped creature, but of monstrous proportions, rapidly driving by on a dog sled, then disappearing into the distance. The next morning, Walton's ship makes another surprising encounter, this time with an ordinary-sized man on a dog sled. The stranger, nearly dead from exhaustion, takes refuge on Walton's ship, introducing himself as Victor Frankenstein. He says he has been chasing someone on the ice floes who has escaped from him, calling him "the daemon."

During the course of long, brooding nighttime conversations with Frankenstein, Walton discovers that the newcomer is a man with a character similar to his own. The captain confides to his sister that he is coming to love his new companion like a brother, adding "Will you laugh at the enthusiasm I express concerning this divine wanderer?" Under coaxing from Walton, the reluctant Frankenstein gradually unfolds the strange tale of how he came to be chasing a huge demon on the Arctic ice floes, beginning his long account with this melancholic warning:

> You seek for knowledge and wisdom, as I once did; and I ardently hope that the gratification of your wishes may not be a serpent to sting you, as mine has been.

Frankenstein recounts that in his early adolescence he marveled at the wonders and beauty of nature, which led him to read the nature mystic Agrippa, the alchemist Paracelsus, and the theologian of nature Albertus Magnus. Later, at age 17, Frankenstein entered the University of Ingolstadt in Germany to study science and medicine. There his professors ridiculed his mystical and emotional attitude toward nature, urging him to develop a more "modern" attitude. Although at first averse to viewing nature in cold, analytical terms, the young Frankenstein eventually adopted the modern viewpoint promoted by his teachers. Withdrawing from interaction with most other people, he maniacally devoted himself to the study of mathematics and the natural sciences, especially chemistry. After an immense effort, working in total seclusion, he uncovered the secret of how to animate lifeless matter. Because of the hellish experiences that followed this discovery, he tells Walton that he will never reveal the secret to any man:

> Learn from me, if not by my precepts, at least by my example, how dangerous is the acquirement of knowledge, and how much happier that man is who believes his native town to be the world, than he who aspires to become greater than his nature will allow.

Realizing that he could animate dead matter, Frankenstein undertook the project of creating a living man from body parts assembled from the dead. In his fanatical devotion to this task of conquering nature by means of science, he became insensitive, ironically, to the very beauty of nature that had first inspired his interest in science:

> It was a most beautiful season; never did the fields bestow a more plentiful harvest, or the vines yield a more luxuriant vintage; but my eyes were insensible to the charm of nature.

Shelley uses Frankenstein's account of creating the creature as a means to express her basic argument in the book: any human pursuit, including even the pursuit of knowledge, when cut loose from one's simple feelings of affection for nature, family, and friends, brings havoc to humanity. At times, in her eagerness to make this point, Shelley finds she has to restrain herself from preaching through the mouth of her characters, as in Frankenstein's following exhortation to Walton:

> If the study to which you apply yourself has a tendency to weaken your affections, and to destroy your taste for those simple pleasures in which no alloy can possibly mix, then that study is certainly unlawful, that is to say not befitting the human mind. If this rule were always observed; if no man allowed any pursuit to interfere with the tranquillity of his domestic affections, Greece had not been enslaved; Caesar would have spared his country; America would have been discovered more gradually, and the empires of Mexico and Peru had not been destroyed. But I forget that I am moralizing in the most interesting part of my tale; and your looks remind me to proceed.

Frankenstein tells Walton that the creature he assembled was monstrously ugly. When the creature twitched with the first spasm of life, Frankenstein ran in fear from his apartment, unwilling to assume responsibility for the effects of his science. Later, when Frankenstein returned to the scene with a friend, the creature was gone. With relief, Frankenstein thought that he was rid of his creation, but events were soon to prove otherwise.

Sometime after he recovered from the shock of his creation, Frankenstein received a letter from his father in Switzerland with terrible news: while the family was on an outing in the country, Frankenstein's younger brother was murdered by an unknown assailant. After reading the letter, Frankenstein rushed home, filled with foreboding. While visiting the scene of the murder at night during a lightening storm, he beheld the silhouette of the creature fleeing into the distance.

As a result of this tragedy, the Frankenstein family decided to go into seclusion in a remote area of the Swiss Alps. During the retreat, Frankenstein climbed up a slope to the edges of a glacier. There amid the cold, icy crags, his creature suddenly appeared and confronted him.

In a story within a story, Shelley has the creature take Frankenstein to a cave and tell him of his experiences since he was created. Although physically ugly, the creature is literate, eloquent, philosophical, and (at first) good. He accuses Frankenstein of not loving him as God loved his creation, Adam; instead Frankenstein heartlessly abandoned him to a world in which he was totally unsuited to live.

The creature tells Frankenstein that after fleeing the apartment where he was created, he hid in a hovel by a rural German cottage. By observing the occupants of the cottage—French refugees who were then teaching a young Arabian woman named Safie their language—the creature learned to read and write. The creature was especially affected when they read to Safie from Constantin Volney's *Ruins of Empires* about the destruction of the American Indians:

> I heard of the discovery of the American hemisphere, and wept with Safie over the hapless fate of its original inhabitants. These wonderful narrations inspired me

with strange feelings. Was man, indeed, at once so powerful, so virtuous, and magnificent, yet so vicious and base?

After the creature disclosed himself to the occupants of the cottage, they chased him out, horrified by his appearance. While traveling in the countryside near Geneva, the creature chanced upon a young boy wondering alone. He approached the boy, hoping he would be his companion, but the boy screamed out in fear. The creature, trying to silence his cries, inadvertently killed him, not realizing his victim was Frankenstein's younger brother, William. Frustrated in his attempts to break out of his loneliness, the creature now bids Frankenstein make him a wife, saying "I am malicious because I am miserable."

Frankenstein tells Walton that at first he agreed to the creature's request, and betook himself to a remote building in the northern highlands of Scotland to work on the task. But when the creature's mate was nearly finished, Frankenstein had a change of heart, fearing they would breed a devilish new species. In the creature's presence, Frankenstein tore apart the nearly completed body.

The creature, furious, promised to destroy everything that was dear to Frankenstein. Later, he killed Frankenstein's best friend, and on Frankenstein's wedding night, his new bride, causing Frankenstein's father to have a fatal stroke.

Frankenstein tells Walton that, driven by the desire for vengeance, he has pursued the creature ever since, as the creature has receded further and further northward. The creature always succeeds in eluding Frankenstein at the last moment, leaving behind taunting messages, such as "My reign is not yet over" and "You live, and my power is complete." Now near the north pole, Frankenstein realizes that his death is approaching. Comparing himself to Satan in *Paradise Lost*, he cries out:

> All my speculations and hopes are as nothing; and, like the archangel who aspired to omnipotence, I am chained to an eternal hell.

As Frankenstein approaches death, the ship finds itself completely locked amid huge ice floes. Walton cries out in anguish over Frankenstein's impending death, for he realizes that he is losing the one person with whom he has been able to make an emotional bond:

> Must I then lose this admirable being? I have longed for a friend; I have sought one who would sympathize with and love me.

After Frankenstein dies, Walton hears a noise coming from the cabin where the body lies. Entering, he finds the creature leaning over Frankenstein's body, sobbing deeply at his death, and bemoaning the fact that Frankenstein never loved him. In the style of Dido of Carthage after she was spurned by Aeneas, the creature declares that he will build a funeral pyre and throw himself upon it. He rushes off the ship to his dog sled as Walton makes his last entry:

> He was soon borne away by the waves, and lost in darkness and distance.

The Scientific Character

As should be evident from the story just outlined, Mary Shelley's *Frankenstein* is no mere pastiche of Gothic fears and adolescent fantasies. To the contrary, Shelley carefully integrates mood, characterization, and plot toward one over-arching goal, the indictment of the psychological character of the modern scientist.

Victor Frankenstein clearly stands for a type: he is the driven, self-centered male who is unable to connect emotionally with the people around him, whether his father, or his best friend, or his fiancée, or the creature he makes, or Walton who loves him and wants to save him.

At most, in his earliest youth, Frankenstein makes an emotional connection with nature, which leads him to study the works of Agrippa, Paracelsus, and Albertus Magnus. Shelley alludes to these three thinkers because they all integrated their interest in nature into a larger picture of meaning, either philosophical or religious. They represent the best hope the young Frankenstein has—the possibility of reaching higher meaning through a loving embrace of nature. When Frankenstein becomes a student at the University of Ingolstadt, however, he loses even this earlier emotional bond with nature. Frankenstein's professors, ridiculing the holistic sensibility of Agrippa, Paracelsus, and Albertus, reinforce Frankenstein's fatal flaw, his emotional disconnectedness to the world about him. This is the very trait that enables him to become a great scientist.

Having come to view nature through the cold, analytical eyes of his university professors, Frankenstein maniacally devotes himself to the study of mathematics and the natural sciences, especially anatomy and physiology (like a modern medical student!). The culmination of this exercise in intellectual and spiritual autism is his creation of a living being that is a monstrous mockery of what Frankenstein intended. Shocked by the ugliness of what he has done, Frankenstein simply flees and hopes the creature will just go away (the scientist as the ultimate deadbeat dad).

Ironically, the creature turns out to be morally superior (at least in the beginning) to Frankenstein, for the creature longs to have a loving connection with all about him, and especially with Frankenstein himself. Because of his ugliness and clumsiness, however, the creature is rejected by everyone, including his maker. Furious that Frankenstein rejects him, the creature proceeds to kill all who were dear to Frankenstein. Only after this slaughter can Frankenstein muster a direct emotional connection with the monster, the connection of vengeful anger, the archetypical male emotion.

As we have seen, when Frankenstein encounters Walton on the Arctic seas, he meets someone very much like himself, that is, an emotionally-isolated male who has turned to the study of the natural sciences, motivated by the desire to conquer nature. Walton, however, was once a poet, and still retains a glimmer of outward-reaching ardor, as evidenced by his yearning for an emotional connection with Frankenstein. Walton's feeling, however, is not reciprocated. As the giant ice floes of the Arctic lock into a frigid rigidity around the two men, Frankenstein dies. The last display of human warmth comes, ironically, from the weeping creature.

The Inability to Love

Feminist commentator Anne Mellor has recently re-drawn attention to the intellectual content of *Frankenstein* as an indictment of modern science. Although deserving credit for this effort, Mellor goes off on a tangent when dealing with the homoerotic undercurrents that flicker between Frankenstein, the creature, and Walton. Mellor characterizes these currents this way:

> Victor Frankenstein's most passionate relationships are with men rather than with women. ... In place of a heterosexual attachment to Elizabeth [his intended bride], Victor Frankenstein has substituted a homosexual obsession with his creature. In his case this fixation is energized by his profound desire to reunite with his dead mother, a desire that can be fulfilled only by Victor's becoming himself a mother.[44]

Mellor's penchant for neo-Freudian theorizing is a weakness that mars many parts of her commentary, for this theorizing has little to do with the actual text. As we have seen, Victor Frankenstein has difficulty making an emotional connection with *anyone*, regardless of the person's sex. His emotional involvement with the creature, such as it is, is no "homosexual obsession" that arises from a failed heterosexuality on his part. Rather, Frankenstein's emotion toward the creature is *anger* for causing the death of Frankenstein's younger brother, his intended bride, and his father. The real homoerotic feelings in the book appear on the part of Captain Walton and the creature, both of whom love Victor Frankenstein, and both of whom Frankenstein spurns. Mary Shelley's text is clear: Frankenstein was a man who could not love *anyone*, the very failing that contributed to his prowess as a great scientist.

The Modern Prometheus

As the subtitle of her novel suggests, Mary Shelley's theme is that the scientist is the modern Prometheus. Most people today know the ancient Greek myth of how Prometheus stole fire from heaven and gave it to mortals, bringing down upon both himself and humanity the wrath of Zeus. Few know, however, that some of the ancient myths also say that Prometheus molded men and animals from clay, animating them with the fire he stole from heaven. These lesser-known myths are the basis of Shelley's allusion to Prometheus in her subtitle. The scientist, like Prometheus, violates the prerogatives of the gods. In so doing, he displays hubris (wanton violation of the order of things), which brings down the wrath of Zeus on all.

Shelley's work is remarkable in that it appeared prior to the worst horrors that resulted from the application of science to the productive process. Indeed, her book came out even before the word "scientist" was coined. At the time of writing *Frankenstein*, the term for someone who rationally explored the mysteries of nature was "natural philosopher." Shelley was keenly aware, however, that a great gap existed between the sensibilities of thinkers like Agrippa, Paracelsus, and Albertus Magnus on one hand and the methods of more-recent natural investigators. The moderns ripped the quest for knowledge of nature out of its previous context of a larger quest for meaning. Natural discoveries now stood coldly and nakedly on their own, mere tools to be used by emotionally-frigid men in their quest to dominate nature and each other.

The Re-emergence of Color

In the last chapter, we saw that formal logic and science, considered theoretically, are like two men who have but one leg each: neither can stand by himself, but only by clasping onto the other. Yet each loudly boasts that he is a pillar of strength in his own right. We will grant to this boisterous pair the right to hobble along, clinging to each other, but we will not buy into their boast to be pace-setters for all who walk the road of human consciousness.

In this chapter, we examined the claim that science, considered practically, has been a great boon to humanity. Taking the whole picture into account, we found the overall impact of science to be catastrophic. Indeed, science's greatest historical legacy has been to ramify and institutionalize the human male's capacity for violence—not a surprising result, since science is, after all, primarily a male creation.

Is there no alternative, then—must we go back to living in caves and feeding on wild asparagus? The enthusiasts of science would have us believe so. Either embrace the whole of formal logic, higher mathematics, and modern science, despite their faults, or else resign yourself to "a state of Gothic ignorance." As the reader should by now recognize, this dire warning is just another example of the type of hokey black-or-white thinking that has long dominated scientific dogmatism.

In the next chapter, we will see that it is possible to bring humanist values to bear in rationally deciding which aspects of science should be socially promoted, and which not. We will also explore some of the many rich colors that logicians, mathematicians, and scientists cannot see. These colors will provide us with glimmers of hope for extricating ourselves from the nightmare called "modern civilization."

---

[1] See my *Witchcraft and the Gay Counterculture*, Fag Rag Books, Boston, 1978.
[2] H.R. Trevor Roper, *The European Witch-Craze*, Harper and Row, New York, 1956, pp. 154 & 91.
[3] Édouard Piette and Julien Sacaze, "La montagne d'Espiaup," *Bulletins de la Société d'anthropologie de Paris*, 1877, pp. 225-251; and Julien Sacaze, "Le culte des pierres dans le pays de Luchon," *Association française pour l'avancement des sciences, compte rendu*, vol. 7, 1878, pp. 900-905.
[4] Sacaze, "Le culte des pierres dans le pays de Luchon," p. 903.
[5] Sacaze, "La montagne d'Espiaup," pp. 901-02.
[6] Concerning the evolution of modern science as an objectifying male assault on nature, see Carolyn Merchant, *The Death of Nature: Women, Ecology, and the Scientific Revolution*, Harper & Row, San Francisco, 1980.
[7] See Stephen Mason, *A History of the Sciences*, first published 1956, revised edition by Collier Books, New York, 1967, pp. 11-12 & 108 ff.
[8] Felix Gilbert et al., *The Norton History of Modern Europe*, W.W. Norton & Co., New York, 1971, p. 58.
[9] Hermann Kinder and Werner Hilgemann, *The Anchor Atlas of World History*, trans. by Ernest Menze, Anchor Press, New York, 1978, vol. 2, p. 98.
[10] Edward Carpenter, *Civilisation: Its Cause and Cure*, originally published 1889; reprinted by Tao Books & Publications, Boston, 1971, p. 55; original's emphasis.
[11] Quoted by Alec Nove, *An Economic History of the U.S.S.R.*, Penguin Books, Baltimore, 1969, p. 57.
[12] Juliet Schor, *The Overworked American: The Unexpected Decline of Leisure*, Basic Books, New York, 1991.
[13] *ibid.*, p. 6 (antiquity) & pp. 46-47 (Middle Ages).
[14] *ibid.*, p. 51.
[15] *ibid.*, p. 6.
[16] *ibid.*, p. 36.
[17] Donald Cardwell, *The Norton History of Technology*, W.W. Norton & Co., New York, 1995, p. 64.; Martin van Creveld, *Technology and War from 2000 B.C. to the Present*, The Free Press, New York, 1989, p. 143.
[18] Felix Gilbert et al., *The Norton History of Modern Europe*, W.W. Norton & Co., New York, 1971, p. 51.
[19] See van Creveld, *op. cit., passim*.
[20] For the recent history of Afghanistan, see Thomas Hammond, *Red Flag Over Afghanistan: The Communist Coup, the Soviet Invasion, and the Consequences*, Westview Press, Boulder, CO, 1984; and Raja Anwar, *The Tragedy of Afghanistan: A First-Hand Account*, Verso, NY, 1988.
[21] Seymour Melman, *Our Depleted Society*, Dell Publishing Co., New York; originally published in 1965, paperback in 1966; pp. 3, 4, & 59.
[22] Keith Bradsher, "Gap in Wealth in U.S. Called Widest in West," *The New York Times*, April 17, 1995.
[23] Jerry Mander, *In the Absence of the Sacred. The Failure of Technology and the Survival of the Indian Nations*, Sierra Club Books, San Francisco, 1991, p. 28.
[24] Nick Ravo, "Index of Social Well-Being Is at the Lowest in 25 Years," *The New York Times*, National Edition, October 14, 1996, Section A, p. 12.
[25] Mander, *op. cit.*, pp. 78-79.
[26] *ibid.*, p. 27.
[27] Uri Bronfenbrenner, et al., *The State of Americans: This Generation and the Next*, The Free Press, New York,

1996, pp. 36 & 38 (incarceration rates); and p. 32 (nonfirearm homicides).

[28] Cardwell, *op. cit.,* p. 508.

[29] For an excellent overview, see René Dubos, *Mirage of Health; Utopias, Progress, and Biological Change,* originally published in 1959; paper reprint by Harper Colophon Books, San Francisco, 1979.

[30] *ibid.,* p. 229.

[31] *ibid.,* p. 148.

[32] *ibid.,* p. 151.

[33] Jeffrey Fisher, *The Plague Makers; How We Are Creating Catastrophic New Epidemics—and What We Must Do to Avert them,* Simon & Schuster, New York, 1994.

[34] *ibid.,* p. 31.

[35] *ibid.,* pp. 10-11.

[36] *ibid.,* p. 51.

[37] *ibid.,* p. 18.

[38] Ivan Illich, *Medical Nemesis; The Expropriation of Health,* Pantheon Books, New York, 1976. pp. 17-20.

[39] Amoury de Riencourt, *The American Empire,* Delta, New York, 1968, p. 96.

[40] Mander, *op. cit.,* pp. 6 & 225.

[41] For a classic display of this attitude, see Paul Gross and Norman Levitt, *Higher Superstition: The Academic Left and Its Quarrels with Science,* Johns Hopkins University Press, Baltimore, 1994. See also their anthology, *The Flight from Science and Reason;* Annals of the New York Academy of Sciences, vol. 775, 1996.

[42] Mary Shelley, *Frankenstein; or, The Modern Prometheus,* originally published in 1818, revised edition in 1831; photo-reprint of the original 1818 edition with critical notes in *The Annotated Frankenstein,* ed. by Leonard Wolf, Clarkson N. Potter, Inc., New York, 1977.

[43] Anne K. Mellor rehabilitates the intellectual content of *Frankenstein* in her *Mary Shelley: Her Life, Her Fiction, Her Monsters,* Routledge, New York, 1988.

[44] *ibid.,* pp. 121 & 122.

Talismans, Detail
Acrylic on Canvas, 40" x 60", 1990

Epilog

Beyond Logic, Mathematics & Science

SUMMARY: This chapter points out the philosophical consequences that follow from the failure of science, and opens the door to a more encompassing vision of human rationality and experience.

Formal logic, higher mathematics, and modern science all claim thrones for themselves: the first two, as final arbiters of the structure of possibility; the last, as the final arbiter of what really exists. As preceding chapters have demonstrated, however, these grand pretenses are all hollow. The root presuppositions of formal logic and higher mathematics are mythological, derived ultimately from patriarchal religious beliefs. Like over-stretched rubber bands, these presuppositions rupture when logicians and mathematicians try to expand them into universal laws. Furthermore, modern science is parochial, dismissing broad aspects of reality just because they don't fit into its narrow methodology. Finally, the overall impact of science, considered as a historical force, has been catastrophic.

Although formal logic, higher mathematics, and modern science have all overstated their claims, each nonetheless has a legitimate role to play in certain contexts. To the extent that communication rests on timeless, impersonal structures, formal logic and higher mathematics are in their special element. And to the extent that knowledge is a matter of the mathematicization of empirical evidence, science likewise is uniquely valuable. A problem occurs, however, when each of these disciplines, in placing its hand on some particular section of the great elephant of reality, mistakes the part it encounters for the whole. Such narrowness of vision can easily harden into "scientism"— dogmatic insistence that science is humanity's best window on reality.

Logicians, mathematicians, and scientists exemplify the fallacy of scientism when they discount the value of art, religion, personal intuition, sexual ecstasy, and tribal myth as worthwhile windows on reality. Educators exemplify the fallacy of scientism when they use the sciences as models for teaching non-scientific subjects. Political leaders exemplify scientism when they legislate legal privileges for the over-industrialization of society and penalize non-industrial, craft-oriented alternatives. And philosophers exemplify scientism when they identify the life of reason with what Herbert Marcuse has called "the logic of domination."[1] All who exemplify the fallacy of scientism ignore the wise words of the 11th-century Arab philosopher and astronomer Alhazen concerning the nascent sciences of his time:

> A person who studies scientific books with a view to knowing the truth ought to turn himself into a hostile critic of everything that he studies.[2]

What Makes Something Rational?

Scientism fosters the fallacy that scientific methods define the canons of rationality. Is some given person speaking rationally? To answer this question, scientism inquires as to whether the person's statement is consistent with the rules of formal logic and mathematics, and with the factual findings of science. If so, the person is given an initial presumption of speaking rationally; otherwise, not.

In many situations this sort of assessment is entirely appropriate, but not always. Such an assessment is appropriate, for example, if someone should claim to have seen the sun rise in the west this morning. Since this claim means that a public event allegedly occurred that is inconsistent with what everyone else on the planet has observed, we are justified in challenging the rationality of the person who made it, and in bolstering our challenge by an appeal to science.

It is not appropriate, however, to assess every statement in this manner. For example, consider the following statement made by Ovid concerning Phaethon, the mortal son of the Sun, who foolishly tried to drive his immortal father's fiery chariot across the sky:

> Poor Phaethon looked down from the sky's highest point.
> Far, far below lay the earth's vast spread.
> He paled. His knees started shaking with fear.
> The glare of the light made darkness well up in his eyes. ...
> What should he do? A great stretch of sky lay behind him;
> Even more lay before. He pondered the length of each. ...
> He slackened no further the horses' reins,
> Nor was his strength enough to restrain them,
> Nor did he even know their names.
> Here and there, scattered across stretches of sky,
> He discerned, trembling in fear, astounding sights,
> The forms of monstrous beasts.[3]

When judged by the assumptions of scientism, Ovid's statement is so irrational as to verge on the insane. For one thing, the Sun does not travel around the Earth, least of all in a chariot drawn by horses that have individual names; for another, the Sun is not a living being with feelings and prerogatives, nor has it begotten a son who is human, nor are the constellations in the sky monstrous beasts.

Despite scientism's assessment, however, Ovid's statement is actually quite rational. The passage in question is his own Latin version of an ancient Greek myth that warns of the dangers inherent in humanity's quest to harness the great powers of nature. If such a quest is carried too far, the myth warns, it will overstep the prerogatives of the gods and so end by bringing catastrophe to the whole planet. In view of the subsequent sorry history of patriarchal-industrial civilization, this ancient myth stands forth not only as rational but also as eminently wise. It remains, however, completely unscientific.

We needn't appeal to exotic examples from antiquity, however, to challenge the dogma that science defines the canons of rationality. We have a counter-example right under our nose—this very dogma! Consider the paradoxical situation of any scientist who would claim that science is the best window on reality: no logician or mathematician has ever succeeded in deducing this dogma itself from the established axioms of logic and mathematics, nor has any empirical scientist ever succeeded in inferring this dogma from the data of any particular science. Whence, then, does this dogma derive the rationality of its own claim to be rational?

Clearly, this dogma is a higher-order assumption *about* logic, mathematics, and science, not something proven *within* any of these disciplines; that is, this dogma is a *philosophical assumption*. How are we to rationally evaluate this assumption's own particular claim to be rational? Only by considering it against the backdrop of some wider concept of rationality; otherwise, we're just assuming what we're trying to prove.

Scientism vs. Humanism

How, then, do human beings arrive at their wider concepts of rationality? Our discussion in chapters one and two of the nature of interpretation is relevant to this question. As noted there, groups of individual interpreters who share common reality maps constitute normative communities. That is, such interpreters agree in sharing a certain set of canons by which they judge the merits of different propositions that describe the nature of the world or express values. For example, the international community of nuclear physicists share certain common standards by which they decide whether any newly proposed atomic theory is well grounded in experimental evidence, properly expressed in mathematical notation, etc. By virtue of sharing such standards, nuclear physicists are able to agree in a great many cases as to which new findings are scientifically tenable and which not.

By consistently judging matters according to their shared canons, a normative community creates a hypothetical exemplary interpreter. In other words, their canons define a model of what a "good" member of their community is. In our example above of the nuclear physicists, the hypothetical exemplary interpreter is someone who examines nature according to certain established methods, and who expresses his or her conclusions in certain kinds of terminology. To the extent that any particular physicist embodies this hypothetical exemplary interpreter, to the same extent is he or she deemed a "good physicist."

In chapter two we saw that the more inclusive any such hypothetical exemplary interpreter becomes, the less technical are the canons that define it, and the more ethical they become. In the case of the normative community of nuclear physicists, the hypothetical exemplary interpreter is rather technical, as just noted; however, in the case of the normative community of all humanity, the hypothetical exemplary interpreter does not constitute "a good physicist" but "a good human being." Value judgments of this breadth are ethical, not technical.

The question "What does it mean to be rational?", like all questions of value, is ultimately decidable (if at all) by an appeal to some set of canons that define a hypothetical exemplary interpreter. In this particular case, the normative community is quite broad, for "rational" means "a rational human being."

Scientism is the dogmatic assumption that the hypothetical exemplary interpreter for rationality must be equivalent to the hypothetical exemplary interpreter for modern science. Accordingly, the advocates of scientism regard any critique of scientific rationality as an indication of "gothic ignorance" or a "flight from reason" or "rank superstition." This book has shown, however, just how *irrational* it is to simply identify science with rationality. The claim that formal logic, higher mathematics, and modern science reveal what is most important or basic about reality simply cannot stand up to rational scrutiny; furthermore, the overall practical impact of science has been devastating. Conclusion: *Scientists are in no position to dictate to the rest of humanity what it means to be a rational human being.*

Humanism

This verdict against science, however, can claim no absolute basis for itself; it, too, presupposes an implicit set of canons by which science is judged, both theoretically and practically. Readers of the preceding chapters of this book will have recognized that the set of cannons to which I have implicitly appealed all along in judging logic, mathematics, and science are those of "humanism." Because of the importance of humanism in rendering this judgment against science, we need to be clear about the meaning of the term.

One modern scholar who has helped clarify the original meaning of the word "humanism" is Paul Oskar Kristeller.[4] As Kristeller demonstrates, humanism was at first a limited phenomenon, referring to a change in educational and literary ideals that occurred during the Renaissance. By the end of the Middle Ages, most European universities were dominated by scholasticism, which stressed technical mastery in theology, logic, and natural philosophy, all highly colored by the teachings of Aristotle as interpreted by Thomas Aquinas. As the Renaissance advanced, however, a growing number of independent writers and researchers, spurred by the recovery of ancient Greek and Latin manuscripts, mounted an attack on the scholasticism of the universities. Invoking the great minds of antiquity, these writers called for a new approach to learning that would value not only the technical skills required for theology, logic, and science, but, even more, the literary, scholarly, and philosophical skills necessary to understand the full range of human nature.

The subjects favored by the new writers were poetry, grammar, rhetoric, moral philosophy, history, and research in Greek and Latin literature. In time, these subjects strengthened their positions in the university curriculum, becoming known as *studia humanitatis* ("studies of humanity"), and the person who taught them was called a *humanista* ("humanist").

Although Kristeller rightly points out the origin of the word "humanism," he errs by insisting on an overly-literal meaning for the word in terms of overall historical context. For example, Kristeller regards Marsilio Ficino, the 15th-century commentator on Plato, as a Platonist rather than a humanist. But this hair-splitting distinction overlooks an important fact: a whole new *spirit of inquiry* came to birth during the Renaissance, stimulated by the recovery of ancient writings, and motivated by a desire to achieve a wider understanding of human nature. Ficino's interest in Plato was part of this larger spirit of inquiry. "Humanists," then, were not just a narrow band of linguistic or rhetorical teachers, as Kristeller argues. They were also the many innovative thinkers who benefited from the new interest in language in general and from the newly recovered documents in Greek and Latin in particular. On the basis of this wider understanding of the word, Marsilio Ficino was *both* a Platonist *and* a humanist.

The great value of Renaissance humanism was that it challenged the narrowness that logic, theology, and the science of the day had inflicted on the educational process. In this regard, let it be noted, Renaissance humanism also contrasted with the later Enlightenment, which tended to identify the whole life of reason with formal logic, mathematics, and science. Modern commentators often overlook this difference between Renaissance humanism and the Enlightenment.[5]

Renaissance humanism also had a fault: it did not go far enough. By the word "human," Renaissance humanists commonly meant "upper-class European male." As a result, many Renaissance humanists failed to validate the experiences of women, the lower classes of Europe, and non-European peoples. This bias contradicted the liberal spirit with which Renaissance humanists challenged the logicians, theologians, and natural scientists of their day.

The literary and educational changes promoted by Renaissance humanism encouraged the development of new philosophical viewpoints that outlived the Renaissance. It's not enough, some philosophers eventually asserted, to live according to the dictates of theology, logic, and science; each of us also needs to develop his or her own human potential as an end in itself. The canons of judgment that are derived from the fullness of human experience, some finally argued, are sufficient to judge logic, science, and even God himself.

"Humanism," as I use the term in this book in criticizing scientism, is the value judgment that the fullness of human experience should serve as the ultimate source for formulating canons of human rationality. Acting on this value judgment, I have invoked, against the presumptions of scientists, the experiences of poets, painters, musicians, dramatists, mystics, and shamans, to list but a few. On the basis of their experiences, I have accused science of fobbing off on humanity a shrunken concept of rationality.

Whether you, the reader, concur with this accusation will largely depend on the source of your own canons of rationality. For example, if you believe that the Bible is definitive of truth, then you will have an entirely different way of handling this whole question, just as you will if you believe that the search for truth is the exclusive prerogative of the scientific method. In any case, however, I hope you will at least agree that it is important to *think* about the sources of your own canons of judgment, whether for rationality or for any other normative question. And I hope you will also agree that merely to question science's definition of reason does not automatically commit one to "Gothic ignorance" or "rank superstition" or a "flight from reason," as many enthusiasts for science claim.

Reclaiming the Whole Self

A humanist concept of reason (as opposed to scientism's concept) finds a natural ally in the richness of human language, which is why the Renaissance humanists stressed the study of grammar, poetry, rhetoric, and historical narrative against the scholastics' emphasis on logic. By devoting attention to the *studia humanitatis*, Renaissance humanists were able to reclaim for rational dialogue a vast body of human experience that simply could not be expressed in the bony language of logic. As a result, the Renaissance humanists promoted the spread of enlightenment, that is, the greater understanding of the whole self and its place in the cosmos.

Humanism Subverted

Thanks to the efforts of the Renaissance humanists, the *studia humanitatis* secured a lasting position in the university curriculum. Unfortunately, however, this academic victory entailed deleterious side-effects. As noted earlier, many of the Renaissance humanists had been independent writers and researchers; consequently, their works often glow with that spirit of freshness and authenticity that only personally-experienced struggle and growth can bestow. Their successors in the universities, however, tended to be institutional hacks who taught the *studia humanitatis* the same way they taught logic, that is, as just another hoop to make their students jump through before granting them degrees.

Later, the triumph of modern science subverted the whole original spirit of the *studia humanitatis*, for science insists on depersonalization in the knowledge-acquiring process. Benumbed by the scientific model of learning, modern educators now teach "the liberal arts" (as the historical successors of the *studia humanitatis* are called) as a matter of impersonal fact-accumulation. As a result, modern liberal-arts educators lay great stress on questions like "What is the etymology of the name 'Dedalus' in Joyce's *A Portrait of the Artist as a Young Man*?" They dismiss the importance of questions like "How does Joyce's esthetic vision relate to the personal experiences of my life?" Of course, questions of etymology are important (as this book itself on numerous occasions has demonstrated); nonetheless, it is a colossal blunder when educators denigrate, as a matter of pedagogical principle inspired by science, the importance of relating personal experience to the contents of liberal-arts courses.

The great power of the liberal arts, in contrast to science, is precisely their ability to stimulate the experiential and emotional life of one who studies them. Thereby do the liberal arts promote one's growth and freedom as an autonomously-thinking human being. In fact, that's why these subjects are called "liberal arts" (*artes liberales*—"the arts appropriate to a free citizen*").

Having suffered from academic institutionalization and then from the triumph of science, the liberal arts experienced their *coup de grace*, especially in the United States, in the collapse of the modern public-education system. The modern American public school, particularly in inner-city areas, hardly deserves the name of education. In the worst cases, which are common enough, teachers find themselves engulfed by large classes of loud, threatening students, many of whom (especially males) are armed with dangerous weapons. In such circumstances, teachers consider themselves lucky if they can keep a modicum of order throughout the day, let alone actually teach their students anything.

Even in the better-run of public schools, serious obstacles remain. Generally, buildings are inadequately maintained, and classes are large. Students learn from committee-approved textbooks, not from the independent scholarly research and personal life experiences of their teachers, who tend to be poorly trained and poorly paid. One statistic tells it all: the longer an American student remains in public school, the more likely he or she is to fall behind same-grade students in other countries.[6]

With adequately trained teachers and good facilities, textbook methods and large classes can sometimes suffice for technical subjects like woodworking or biology. No so, however, for the liberal arts. The reason is that such canned teaching lacks "transmission," as certain Buddhist schools call it. That is, the liberal arts, in order to work their proper effect, require a close personal dialogue between teacher and student wherein each strives to integrate what is being learned into the whole meaning-pattern of his or her life. When this personal transmission from teacher to student is lacking, the liberal arts degenerate into just another form of information-gathering, and so are gutted of everything that makes them unique. The recent advent of computerization in the classroom is likely to push personal transmission, and therefore the liberal arts, into even greater irrelevance. If the past history of technology is any guide, a thoroughgoing computerization of the learning process will likely produce a society of high-tech savages.

The institutionalization of learning, followed by the triumph of science, followed by the collapse of modern public education have all worked toward the same end: very few people in modern industrial societies, and particularly so in the United States, have any idea at all of what it means to have a liberal-arts education. Even many of those who sport the letters "B.A." after their names have at most experienced a process of information-gathering in non-scientific fields. They have never glimpsed what it was that so excited and inspired people like Marsilio Ficino or Giordano Bruno.

As the status of the liberal arts has declined in the modern period, so the humanist concept of reason has faded as well. In effect, reason now means the type of thinking that prevails in formal logic, higher mathematics, and science. All else is dismissed as either make-shift imitation or "Gothic ignorance." Likewise, the productive process has come to mean mass industrialization. Anything else is viewed as the equivalent of living in a cave and feeding on wild asparagus.

The call to re-affirm the value of humanist reason is a call to reclaim the whole self against the fragmentation inflicted on the self by formal logic, higher mathematics, and modern science. This call to wholeness is necessary because science pretends it can understand both human experience and the human body by dissecting them into tiny pieces. Patching together the knowledge-bits thus gained, science claims to present us with an overall model of what it means to be human. As Mary Shelley early realized, however, the real result created by such methods is a Frankenstein monster.

An appreciative understanding of the whole—the very thing that eludes the scientist's scalpel—can never come about from the mere addition of dissected parts. It can only come from a process of *dialog* wherein a whole person interacts with the entire environment and other whole persons with the goal of constructing an overall vision of commonly-lived meaning. The integrating capacity that this sort of dialogue summons forth in us is what I mean by "humanist reason." This integrating capacity is the soul that William Blake found wanting when he watched the academics and industrialists of his time lavish praise on Isaac Newton's brave new physics:

> I turn my eyes to the Schools & Universities of Europe,
> And there behold the Loom of Locke, whose Woof rages dire,
> Wash'd by the Water-wheels of Newton.

The Liberal Arts, Revived

The intellectual soil that is most conducive to the growth of humanist reason is the study of the liberal arts. Not a study modeled after science, however, but one adapted to the unique value of the liberal arts; that is, a study characterized by personal dialogue, where the participants deliberately strive to build a bridge from their inner selves to the subjects outwardly studied.

Humanist dialog as applied to the liberal arts requires that teachers give due regard to the special points of view and feelings that are unique to students in virtue of their special circumstances in life. In the case of women, for example, humanist dialog acknowledges the importance to the learning process of the personal life-experiences shared by students precisely because they are women. For gay people and members of racial minorities, humanist dialogue hears the life-experiences shared by members of such minorities. For all people, humanist dialog means embracing the full richness of human experience as the highest guiding principle to learning.

Humanist dialog in the liberal arts naturally raises the question of *which* writers and artists are to be studied. Western schools and universities generally focus their attention on works by upper-class, white, European males. This tradition certainly contains much of value (it has enriched my own life, for example). Nonetheless, the high value of this tradition does not justify a dismissive attitude toward works by women, working-class people, and members of non-Western societies. The issue becomes critical when the students in the classroom are themselves women, working-class people, and descendants of non-Western societies. Just as humanist dialog makes room in its methodology for the emotional and experiential life of its participants, so it makes room in its syllabus for writers who appeal to participants' particular intellectual interests.

Although humanist dialog has an ear for the personal interests of its participants, nonetheless a classroom is not the same as a playpen. The other half of humanist learning is rigorous training, especially in regard to languages. For this half, there is no substitute for years of intense, disciplined study. Only when disciplined study and experiential openness find their right mix does the golden light of the liberal arts display itself. To achieve this happy blend, no canned rules will ever suffice. In the end, the issue comes down to *character*, of the teacher, the students, and the larger society of which they are all members.

Politics & Humanist Education

In our day, this type of disciplined, but experientially-inclusive, study of the liberal arts has largely been lost. It will not revive without a massive rethinking and refinancing of both public and private education. Alas, any effort to bring about such changes will instantly meet overwhelming resistance, for the current crisis in education is but a symptom of a deeper rot eating away at the core of modernity—the mass accumulation of power and wealth for the few through the enforced alienation of the many from nature, meaningful work, the larger human community, and their own inner selves.

It's no accident that the decline in the liberal arts in the United States has coincided with an ever-widening gap between rich and poor, as well as a steady decline in the purchasing power of the ordinary worker. The magnates of patriarchal-industrial civilization well know that it is not in their interest to promote the widespread development of humanist reason. Otherwise, how will they keep "the little people" in their nine-to-five slots on assembly lines, offices, and laboratories? Rather, let schools and universities serve as degree mills for training workers and technicians for their proper slots in the great industrial machine. They can find spiritual enrichment on their own time, in extracurricular affairs. Now let's get on with the business of progress!

Working people, for their part, can scarcely develop their capacities for humanist reason when they have to spend most of their waking hours struggling just to pay the rent and put food on the table. This basic economic fact has an important educational consequence: the struggle to revive the liberal arts must go hand and hand with the struggle to distribute wealth on a fairer basis. Otherwise, the term "liberal arts" will just be a mask for elitism.

Autonomy and Dependency of Science

We have seen that humanist dialog has an essential role to play in the liberal arts. But what about the sciences? A little reflection will show that the closer, methodologically, any science approaches physics, the less amenable will it be to humanist dialog. After all, the scientific method *means* stripping away, as much as possible, the subjectivity of the knower from the knowing process. Although there may be some room in the social sciences for humanist dialog, any attempt to impose it on the physical sciences would only make science into nonscience.

Despite its many failings, science does occupy its own special band on the spectrum of human experience. Because of methods that are peculiar to it, science can reveal aspects of reality that are not accessible as such to other forms of human interpretation.

Accordingly, Paul Gross and Norman Levitt, two vocal defenders of science, are right to reject efforts to reground science on any nonscientific methodology. In particular, they rightly criticize efforts in this direction by certain feminists and social-constructivists:

> Feminism...is not a methodology for doing science; it does not offer any privileged insights into scientific questions.[7]

Although Gross and Levitt are right to insist on the methodological autonomy of physical science, they err when they advance a further claim: science makes a sufficient response to feminist critique if it offers equal career opportunities in science to women. Of course, we all agree that equal employment opportunity is important, but something of far greater import is at stake here. As feminist writers (and many others!) have amply shown, the scientific life is not some sort of ethereal flight, blissfully removed from the rough and tumble of practical life. To the contrary, science today is a meaty system of money and power, deeply entwined in the institutional sinews of patriarchal-industrial civilization.

Who shall hire scientists and pay for their expensive equipment? What sorts of questions shall scientists be funded to research? Who are the intended beneficiaries of this research? What have been the actual effects of past scientific research? These are the kinds of questions that arise whenever scientists seek access to a society's resources in order to underwrite their work. And it is precisely here that humanist dialog engages the scientific enterprise, for these questions cannot be answered in a way that is strictly internal to science. Rather, these questions call into play matters of history, politics, esthetics, and moral value; that is, they call into play humanist dialog.

In chapter thirteen, we saw that the principal historical effect of science during the past 500 years has been to ramify and institutionalize the human male's boundless capacity for violence. Hence we the people are entirely justified in taking an aggressively skeptical stance toward any scientist who would seek financial support from the public largesse. We are equally justified in challenging business corporations when they underwrite scientific research for products or practices that undermine the common good. Finally, we are justified in confronting individual scientists themselves when their work contributes to war, social oppression, torture (whether of people or animals), fascism, genocide, or environmental rape.

What role, then, shall science play in modern life? This question has no fixed answer. It must be continually re-addressed, as the particular consequences of various sciences are ever tested against our best values, and the sciences made to conform accordingly. The important thing is to acknowledge the priority of values over science, and to keep dialog on the matter open. Everyone affected by science has a right to be heard.

The Truth Squad

Some enthusiasts of science want to close the dialog. An example is Mario Bunge, a teacher of the philosophy of science at McGill University in Montreal. In a recent anthology sponsored by the New York Academy of Sciences, Bunge fiercely attacks the liberal-arts departments of many universities. They have become hiding places, he charges, for feminist and social-constructivist charlatans who are plotting to overthrow both science and reason:

> We should expel the charlatans from the university before they deform it out of recognition and crowd out the serious searchers for truth. ... Let all genuine intellectuals join the Truth Squad and help dismantle the "postmodern" Trojan horse stabled in Academia before it destroys them.[8]

In the best tradition of scientism, Bunge simply assumes that reason is identical to science; hence he regards any critique of science as an obscurantist assault on rationality itself. We have seen, however, that the simple identification of reason with science is irrational. Science represents but one color on the spectrum of reason; it has no right to try and expunge the other colors.

Enthusiasts of science are right to insist that science has a connection to reality. Social constructivists are also right to insist that science is socially constructed. The error of the former camp is to overlook the culturally-conditioned face of science; the error of the latter camp, to overlook the ability of science to reveal certain aspects of reality. Each camp sees part of the truth and mistakes that part for the whole.

The whole truth lies between the two camps. Like any human tool, science reveals both something of reality and also something of the conventional behavior of the tool-users. Where, then, shall we draw the line between these two aspects of science? A difficult question. Indeed, this book has shown that if we are to deal with this question in an intelligent manner, and not dogmatically, we must invoke the whole range of human experience as evidence; that is, we must appeal to the complexities of humanist dialogue. Surely, it is no answer at all to call for the formation of a "Truth Squad" in order to drive out and suppress those who hold dissenting opinions. Anyone who thinks that truth can be attained through such methods should reflect on the words of John Stuart Mill in *On Liberty*:

> Complete liberty of contradicting and disproving our opinion is the very condition which justifies us in assuming its truth for purposes of action; and on no other terms can a being with human faculties have any rational assurance of being right.[9]

The New Humanism

I advocate, then, a new version of humanism. The new humanism builds on the old by recognizing its predecessor's liberating challenge to the formal logic, religiosity, and natural science of its time. In the name of the fullness of human experience, the old humanism insisted on the importance of languages and the arts in cultivating human reason. As we saw, however, the old humanism also had its flaws, most notably its glib identification of "human beings" with white, European, upper-class males. The new humanism, by contrast, recognizes that human beings who are not part of this elite also make important contributions to the life of reason. The new humanism also recognizes the deep connection between the life of reason and the life of democracy, and so consciously identifies itself with ongoing struggles for economic and political justice.

The Limits of Reason

As we have seen, humanist reason can be a liberating force in exposing the pretensions of science and industrialism to define canons of human rationality; nonetheless, even humanist reason itself (which is reason at its most holistic and humane) represents but a limited dimension of human interpretational power. The greater crime of science and industrialism is that they have truncated not only reason but also the entire rainbow of human interpretational ability as expressed in art, meaningful work, personal spiritual development, sex, and emotive connectedness with other human beings and with the sublime powers of nature. To correct this greater wrong will require an appeal to a force greater than reason. That force is the power of interpretive self-creation that is present in some degree in every part of nature, but especially so in living organisms, and above all in the human psyche.

Everything that is alive and conscious always has the potential of redefining itself to some degree through its activities and its consciousness. Indeed, death can be viewed as the loss of the potential for such self-redefinition. Moreover, even non-living, non-conscious reality has the potential for change. Reality, then, and especially conscious reality, resists being frozen into definitions. Since all definitions say "This stays so and is not otherwise," any intellectual endeavor based on definitions (such as formal logic, mathematics, science, and philosophy) can at best be only tentative and halting. Definition-based rationality, even if practiced by the mind of God (if such a being should exist), can never do justice to the richness of reality.

To understand more clearly this inherent limit to reason, ask yourself this: What is it that makes any given rational system of concepts powerful? Answer: the ability of the rational system to convincingly explain or predict a great many phenomena on the basis of a few presuppositions. How, then, does a rational system generate such explanations or predictions? Formal logic provides the answer: arrange the propositional content of such a system *formally*; that is, arrange the whole system as a set of definitions, axioms, rules of deduction, and theorems. The scope and elegance of any such rational system when thus formally arranged constitutes its power as a system.

With this understanding of system-power in mind, we can appreciate the great importance of two theorems about formal systems proved in the 1930s by the mathematician Kurt Gödel. Given any formal system adequate for expressing arithmetic, Gödel showed: (1) there will exist a valid formula of the system that cannot be proved within the system; and (2) there can be no proof of the consistency of the system within the system itself. In effect, these two theorems mean that any deductive system that is strong enough to express arithmetic will nonetheless be too weak to prove all true arithmetical formulas. The only way for the system to prove all valid arithmetical formulas is for it to assume axioms whose logical consistency it can never establish.

An important corollary follows: if reality is at least as complicated as arithmetic, then no rational system of definitions and concepts, when cast as a deductive system having axioms known to be logically consistent, will be adequate for describing all reality. Contrary, therefore, to the pious hope of Plato and the entire rationalist school of philosophy, reason faces inherent, inescapable limitations. Reason, by its very nature, can never grasp the whole truth.

Computers Won't Save Us

Despite the inherent logical limits faced by reason, many people today have high practical hopes for computers, regarding them both as paragons of rationality and as the tools of choice for solving practical human problems. Although computers certainly have a role to play in modern life (this book was typed on one), their enthusiasts ought to remember an important limitation: a computer is nothing more than the embodiment in electrical circuitry of somebody's (usually some man's) system of formal logic. Hence computers are heir to all the objections that are congenital to formal logic. Despite this limitation, however, many scientists and mathematicians continue to insist that their new machines will eventually provide humanity with its best tool for displaying the basic contours of reality. An example of this shiny confidence is the sentiment expressed in the 1970s by Prof. John McCarthy, then head of Stanford University's Artificial Intelligence Laboratory:

> The only reason we have not yet succeeded in formalizing every aspect of the real world is that we have been lacking a sufficiently powerful logical calculus. I am currently working on that problem.[10]

Prof. McCarthy seems unaware that this sort of confidence in the power of formalization has been a regular leitmotif in the history of formal logic, as we have seen in previous chapters. In the end, confident formalists throughout history have all suffered the same fate as Icarus: the higher they have sought to fly, the more their wings have become unglued. The difference is that Icarus knew when he was falling.

In addition to the inherent logical limits faced by the flight of reason, there are also obvious practical ones as well. No human being could possibly survive one day if he or she had to limit personal actions to those validated by reason. Like all living things, human beings are constantly required to act in the absence of adequate knowledge. In the overwhelming majority of real-life situations, human action is guided by instinct, cultural conditioning, idiosyncratic impulse, and habit, not by rational thinking, whether scientific, philosophic, or otherwise. And, in fact, an undue preoccupation with conceptualizing can actually diminish the quality of one's life, leading, for example, to artistic boorishness, sexual alienation, physical weakness, nature-deprivation, and ineptitude in social interaction. If it is true, as Socrates claimed, that the unexamined life is not worth living, then it is also true, as the common street-wise rebuttal goes, that the unlived life is not worth examining.

The limitations of definition-based rationality reflect evolutionary limitations imposed on the human organism. The so-called "higher mental functions" of the species *homo sapiens* evolved late in the natural history of the hominids, who as an identifiable family evolved late in the natural history of all living beings. Corresponding to the late evolutionary development of these functions is their relative weakness in affecting human behavior. Before any human being makes a rational judgment about any matter whatsoever, a whole host of instincts, urges, and emotions have already come into play, making pre-rational interpretative judgments about what is interesting, important, desirable, or even logically possible.

Its lateness and weakness does not belittle the marvelously creative role played by reason in human experience, but it does undermine the claim that reason, especially in philosophy or science, opens our best window on reality. This claim, when reinforced by institutional coercion, typically generates a tragic lessening of the quality of life. No more dreary and oppressive ideal of society can be imagined than that advocated by Plato in his proposed rule of philosopher-kings, unless it be the Christian version of the same idea in John Calvin or the Communist version in Lenin. The proper role of human reason is to clarify and integrate one's overall interpretational life, not tyrannize it. This lesson was taught in the ancient rites of Dionysos and Demeter, but forgotten in the systems of Plato, Calvin, and Lenin.

Human beings have the ability to make preconscious or unconscious interpretations with a degree of power and elegance surpassing that of even the most profound scientific or philosophical systems. Great works of art, fabulous episodes of love-making, and transcendent religious experiences are all obvious examples attesting to the existence and power of such a reason-transcending human interpretive faculty.

Even Socrates, usually depicted as the great exponent of rationalism for its own sake, highly appreciated his own reason-transcending interpretive ability, which he called his *daimonion* (literally, "spirit-guide"). According to the written accounts left by his contemporaries, Socrates typically followed the dictates of reason as far as they would go, but even so would often come to a point where he realized that reason was inadequate. Then he would hearken to the voice of his inner *daimonion*. In fact, Socrates' belief in his *daimonion* occasioned one of the major charges in the indictment against him: namely, that he followed strange, new gods not recognized by the Athenian state. Although a principal founder of Western rationalism, Socrates recognized the human need and ability to act beyond the pale of reason.

The sciences and philosophy are important to the human experience, but so are art, religion, sex, athletics, and even day-dreaming. Each of these areas of activity is a kind of window through which we can gain some insight about what it means to be human and even, at times, a glimpse of the nature of reality. But surely part of the insight so gained is the realization of how limited any and all of these windows are.

Through our interpretations, we help create a kind of world, which becomes our familiar home, whether horrifying, banal, or sublime, and in which we experience external reality to the extent that our genetic, cultural, and individual capacities allow us. In this way, we express who we are and also gain insight, at certain moments, into the meaning of our lives. But we can never really find "the Answer" in any final and authoritative sense that some aspire to, because the living universe from which both we and our gods have emerged and into which we will again dissolve is not finished and never will be. Only what is past, static, or dead can be defined, and even then only imperfectly in tentative definitions soon outmoded. The contrivances of human reason come and go; the elusive mysteries of our common mother, the living universe, abide.

Intimations of Revolution

In criticizing the wasteland created by science and industrialism, we have invoked not only humanist reason but also the power of interpretive self-creation that transcends all reason. All such invocations, however, remain but futile gestures if limited to theoretical discussions of the nature of reality and reason. Patriarchy, science, and industrialism have all triumphed not because of any sort of theoretical misunderstanding but because their triumph has served the economic, political, and sexual self-interest of certain privileged groups and strata of society.

Understanding, although important, is not enough; action also is required. In particular, we require a practical program for challenging the basic patterns of domination that now prevail in human life. Accordingly, we will turn to such issues in this series' next volume, *Sex and Power*.

---

[1] Herbert Marcuse, *Eros and Civilization: A Philosophical Inquiry into Freud*, Beacon Press, Boston, 1966, p. 111.

[2] Quoted by Shmuel Sambursky, ed., *Physical Thought from the Presocratics to the Quantum Physicists*, Pica Press, New York, 1974, p. 139.

[3] Ovid, *Metamorphoses*, II, 178-194.

[4] See, for example, Paul Oskar Kristeller, *Renaissance Thought: The Classic, Scholastic, and Humanist Strains*, Harper Torchbooks, New York, 1961. The philosophy of Prof. Kristeller, my erstwhile doctoral advisor and political antagonist at Columbia University, has come to influence certain of my own philosophical and scholarly views to a greater degree than I at first realized; he himself would no doubt be horrified at this development.

[5] For example, Sandra Harding repeatedly conflates the two in her book *Whose Science? Whose Knowledge?*, Cornell University Press, Ithaca, NY, 1991.

[6] Urie Bronfenbrenner, *et al.*, *The State of Americans: This Generation and the Next*, The Free Press, New York, 1996, p. 198.

[7] Paul Gross and Norman Levitt, *Higher Superstition: The Academic Left and Its Quarrels with Science*, Johns Hopkins University Press, Baltimore, 1994, p. 251.

[8] Mario Bunge, "In Praise of Intolerance to Charlatanism in Academia," pp. 96-115, in Paul R. Gross, Norman Levitt, and Martin W. Lewis (eds.), *The Flight from Science and Reason*, Annals of the New York Academy of Sciences, vol. 775, 1996, pp. 110 & 111.

[9] John Stuart Mill, *On Liberty*, 1859; Appleton-Century-Crofts, Inc., New York, 1947, p. 19.

[10] Quoted by Joseph Weizenbaum, *Computer Power and Human Reason: From Judgment to Calculation*, W.H. Freeman and Co., New York, 1976, p. 201.

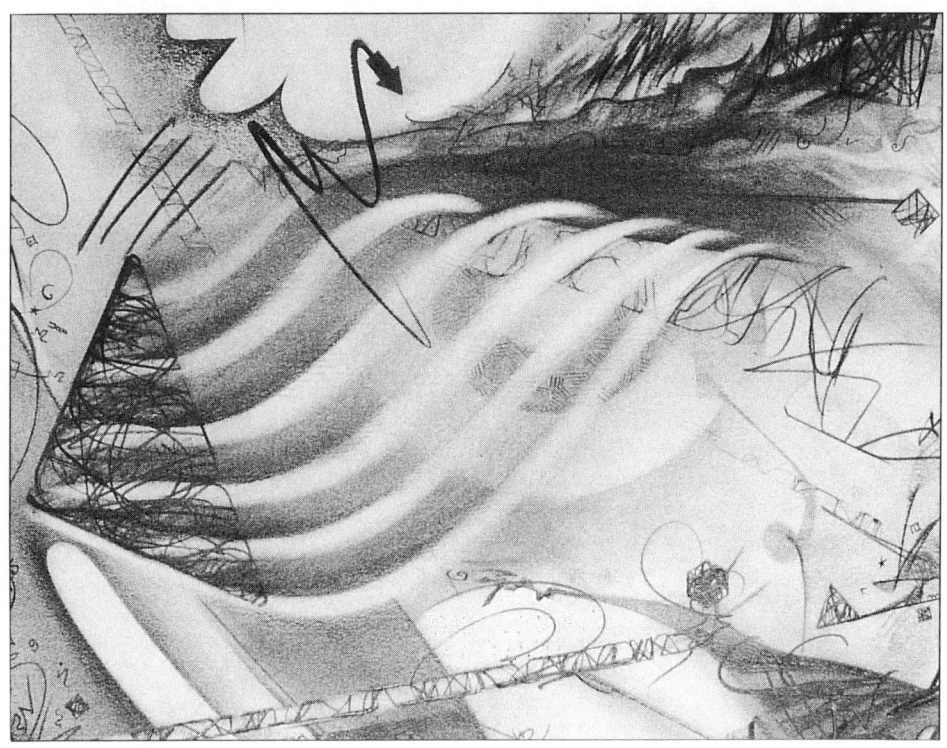

Sacra 2, Detail
Graphite, 30" x 22", 1990

"Spatial Relativity," Acrylic on Canvas, 30" x 60", 1995

Cited Titles

Books, Articles & Movies

Abrahamsen, David, *The Mind and Death of a Genius*, Columbia University Press, New York, 1946.

Adam, John, "Profile: Bart Kosko," *IEEE Spectrum*, February 1996, p. 58-62.

Adams, Marilyn McCord, *William Ockham*, vols. I & II, University of Notre Dame Press, Notre Dame, IN, 1987.

Adler, Mortimer, "Has Philosophy Lost Contact with People?" *Newsday*, November 18, 1979.

Anchor Atlas of World History, The, ed. by Hermann Kinder and Werner Hilgemanntrans, Anchor Press, trans. by Ernest Menze, New York, 1978.

Anwar, Raja, *The Tragedy of Afghanistan: A First-Hand Account*, Verso, NY, 1988.

Aristophanes, *Clouds*.

Aristotle, *Categories*, *Metaphysics*, *On Interpretation*, *On the Life-Principle [De Anima]*, *Posterior Analytics*, *Prior Analytics*.

Augustine of Hippo, *The City of God*, *Confessions*, *Ten Homilies on the First Epistle General of St. John*.

Austin, John, "Performative-Constative," originally published in 1958, reprinted in *Philosophy and Ordinary Language*, ed. by Charles E. Caton, University of Illinois Press, Urbana, 1963.

Ayer, A.J., *Freedom and Morality and Other Essays*, Clarendon Press, Oxford, 1984.

_____, *Language, Truth and Logic*, first published 1936; 2nd ed., Dover Publications, New York, 1946.

_____, *Part of My life. The Memoirs of a Philosopher*, Harcourt Brace Janovich, New York, 1977.

_____, *Philosophical Essays*, St. Martin's Press, New York, 1954, reprinted 1965.

Bacon, Francis, *Novum Organum*, trans. by G.W. Kitchin, in *Physical Thought from the Presocratics to the Quantum Physicists*, ed. by Shmuel Sambursky, Pica Press, New York, 1974.

Bacon, Roger, *Opus maius*, trans. by Susan Hall, and *Epistola de secretis operibus*, trans. by Lynn Thorndike; in *Physical Thought from the Presocratics to the Quantum Physicists*, ed. by Shmuel Sambursky, Pica Press, New York, 1974.

Baker, Gordon, *Wittgenstein, Frege and the Vienna Circle*, Basil Blackwell, Oxford, 1988.

Baker, G.P., & P.M.S. Hacker, *Frege: Logical Excavations*, Oxford University Press, New York, 1984.

_____, *Wittgenstein: Rules, Grammar and Necessity*, Basil Blackwell, 1985.

_____, *Wittgenstein: Understanding & Meaning*, The University of Chicago Press, 1980.

Bartley, William, *Wittgenstein*, Open Court Press, La Salle, IL, first edition 1973, second edition 1985.

Bentham, Jeremy, *A Fragment on Government*, Oxford University Press, 1951.

_____, *An Introduction to the Principles of Morals and Legislation*; in Edwin A. Burtt, *The English Philosophers from Bacon to Mill*, The Modern Library, New York, 1939.

_____, *Traités de Législation Civile et Pénale*, ed. by Pierre Étienne Dumont, Paris, 1802.

Bertolucci, Bernardo, *Il Conformista* (movie), Mars/Marianne/Maran, Italy, 1970.

Biringucci, Vannoccio, *De la pirotechnia*, trans. by Cyril Smith & Marth Gnudi, Basic Books, New York, 1959.

Blackstone, William, *Commentaries on the Laws of England*, 2 vols., ed. by William Carey Jones, Bancroft-Whitney Co., San Francisco, 1915-16.

Blake, William, "A Vision of the Last Judgment" in *The Poetry and Prose of William Blake*, ed. by David Erdman and Harold Bloom, Doubleday & Co., Garden City, NY, 1968.

Bordo, Susan, *The Flight to Objectivity: Essays on Cartesianism and Culture*, State University of New York Press, Albany, NY, 1987.

Copi, Irving M., & Robert Beard (eds.), *Essays on Wittgenstein's Tractatus*, Routledge and Kegan Paul, London, 1966.

Boethius, *The Consolation of Philosophy*, trans. by W.V. Cooper, The Modern Library, New York, 1943.

Bolton, Derek, *An Approach to Wittgenstein's Philosophy*, The Macmillan Press, Ltd., London, 1979.

Boole, George, *An Investigation of the Laws of Thought*, 1854; reprinted by Dover Publications, New York, 1958.

———, *The Mathematical Analysis of Logic*, 1847; reprinted by Barnes and Noble, New York, 1965.

Bradley, F.H., *Appearance and Reality. A Metaphysical Essay*, 2nd edition, 9th impression, The Clarendon Press, Oxford, 1930.

———, *Essays on Truth and Reality*, The Clarendon Press, Oxford, 1914.

———, *The Principles of Logic*, Oxford University Press, London, 2nd edition, 1922.

Bradley, Raymond, *The Nature of All Being: A Study of Wittgenstein's Modal Atomism*, Oxford University Press, New York, 1992.

Bradsher, Keith, "Gap in Wealth in U.S. Called Widest in West," *The New York Times*, April 17, 1995.

Bronfenbrenner, Urie, et al., *The State of Americans: This Generation and the Next*, The Free Press, New York, 1996.

Bunge, Mario, "In Praise of Intolerance to Charlatanism in Academia" in Paul R. Gross, Norman Levitt, and Martin W. Lewis (eds.), *The Flight from Science and Reason*; Annals of the New York Academy of Sciences, vol. 775, 1996, pp. 96-115.

Burnaby, John, *Augustine: Later Works*, The Westminster Press, Philadelphia, 1955.

Burtt, Edwin A., *The English Philosophers from Bacon to Mill*, The Modern Library, New York, 1939.

———, *The Metaphysical Foundations of Modern Physical Science*, Doubleday Anchor Books, Garden City, New York; first published 1924; revised 1932; paper edition, 1954.

Cardwell, Donald, *The Norton History of Technology*, W.W. Norton & Co., New York, 1995.

Carnap, Rudolf, "From his *Autobiography*" in *Ludwig Wittgenstein: The Man and His Philosophy*, ed. by K.T. Fann, Dell Publishing Co., Inc., New York, 1967.

———, "Intellectual Autobiography" in *The Philosophy of Rudolf Carnap*, ed. by P.A. Schlipp, Open Court, 1963.

———, *The Logical Structure of the World*, trans. by Rolf A. George, University of California Press, Berkeley, 1967.

———, *Meaning and Necessity: A Study in Semantics and Modal Logic*, Phoenix Books, The University of Chicago Press, Chicago, 1947; 5th printing, 1967.

Carpenter, Edward, *Civilisation: Its Cause and Cure*, orginally published 1889; reprinted by Tao Books & Publications, Boston, 1971.

Chan, Wing-Tsit, ed., *A Source Book in Chinese Philosophy*, Princeton University Press, Princeton, New Jersey, 1973.

Cicero, Marcus Tullius, *On Duties, On Fate*.

Conway, Gertrude, *Wittgenstein on Foundations*, Humanities Press, International, Inc., Atlantic Highlands, New Jersey, 1989.

Copernicus, Nicolaus, *De revolutionibus orbium caelestium*, 1543.

Currie, Gregory, *Frege: An Introduction to His Philosophy*, The Harvester Press, Sussex, 1982.

d'Abro, A., *The Evolution of Scientific Thought from Newton to Einstein*, first edition, 1927; revised edition, Dover Publications, New York, 1950.

de Riencourt, Amoury, *The American Empire*, Delta, New York, 1968.

Descartes, René, *Discourse on the Method of Rightly Conducting Reason and Seeking for Truth in the Sciences, Meditations on First Philosophy, Principia Philosophiae*.

Diogenes Laertius, *Lives of the Famous Philosophers*.

Drury, Maurice, *The Danger of Words*, Routledge and Kegan Paul, New York, 1973.

———, letter, *The Times Literary Supplement*, February 22, 1974, # 3755, p. 186.

Dubos, René, *Mirage of Health; Utopias, Progress, and Biological Change*, originally published in 1959; paper reprint by Harper Colophon Books, San Francisco, 1979.

Dummett, Michael, *Frege and Other Philosophers*, Clarendon Press, Oxford, 1991.

———, *Frege, Philosophy of Language*, 2nd Edition, Harvard University Press, Cambridge, 1981.

Eagleton, Terry, *Wittgenstein: the Terry Eagleton Script, the Derek Jarman Film*, The Trinity Press, Worcester, England, 1993.

Eames, Elizabeth, *Bertrand Russell's Dialogue with His Contemporaries*, Southern Illinois University Press, Carbondale, 1989.

Edwards, Paul, Editor in Chief, *The Encyclopedia of Philosophy*, 8 vols., Macmillan Publishing Co., Inc., & The Free Press, New York, 1967, reprinted 1972.

Engelmann, Paul, *Letters from Ludwig Wittgenstein*, With a Memoir, ed. by B.F. McGuinness,

trans. by L. Furtmüller, Basil Blackwell, Oxford, 1967.
Euclid, *Elements*.
Euripides, *Bakkhai*.
Evans, Arthur, *The God of Ecstasy*, St. Martin's Press, New York, 1988.
—————, *Witchcraft and the Gay Counterculture*, Fag Rag Books, Boston, 1978.
Felix Gilbert et al., *The Norton History of Modern Europe*, W.W. Norton & Co., New York, 1971.
Feyeraband, Paul, *Against Method*, Verso, New York; originally pub'd 1975, third edition, 1993.
Fisher, Jeffrey, *The Plague Makers; How We Are Creating Catastrophic New Epidemics—and What We Must Do to Avert them*, Simon & Schuster, New York, 1994.
Fleming, Victor, *The Wizard of Oz* (movie), Metro-Goldwyn-Mayer, United States, 1939.
Frazer, James, *The Golden Bough*, 12 vols., 3rd edition, Macmillan & Co., London, 1911-15.
Frege, Gottlob, *The Basic Laws of Arithmetic*, first vol. originally published 1893, trans. by Montgomery Furth, University of California Press, Berkeley, 1964.
—————, *Conceptual Notation and Related Articles*, trans. by Terrell W. Bynum, The Clarendon Press, Oxford, 1972.
—————, *The Foundations of Arithmetic*, originally published 1884, trans. by J.L. Austin, Philosophical Library, New York, 1950.
—————, *Posthumous Writings*, ed. by Hans Hermes et al., University of Chicago Press, Chicago, 1979.
Galileo Galilei, *Dialogue Concerning the Two Chief World Systems*, trans. by Stillman Drake, quoted by Shmuel Sambursky, ed., *Physical Thought from the Presocratics to the Quantum Physicists*, Pica Press, New York, 1974.
Gibson, Roger, *The Philosophy of W.V. Quine: An Expository Essay*, University Presses of Florida, Tampa, 1982.
Ginsberg, Allen, "Wichita Vortex Sutra," *Planet News*, City Lights Books, San Francisco, 1968.
Gödel, Kurt, "Über formal unentscheidbare Sätze der Principia Mathematica und verwandter Systeme I," *Monatshefte für Mathematik und Physik*, vol. 38, 1931, pp. 173-198.
Godwin, William, *Enquiry Concerning Political Justice and Its Influence on Morals and Happiness*, ed. by F.E.L. Priestly, University of Toronto Press, Toronto, 1946.
Goethe, Johann Wolfgang von, *Faust*.

Gross, Paul, and Norman Levitt, *Higher Superstition: The Academic Left and Its Quarrels with Science*, Johns Hopkins University Press, Baltimore, 1994.
Gross, Paul R., Norman Levitt, and Martin W. Lewis, eds., *The Flight from Science and Reason*; Annals of the New York Academy of Sciences, vol. 775, 1996.
Hacker, P.M.S., *Insight & Illusion: Themes in the Philosophy of Wittgenstein*, revised edition, Clarendon Press, Oxford, 1986.
Hahn, Lewis, & Paul A. Schilpp (eds.), *The Philosophy of W.V. Quine*, Open Court, La Salle, IL, 1986.
Halévy, Elie, *The Growth of Philosophic Radicalism*, translated by Mary Morris, Beacon Press, Boston, 1966.
Hammond, Thomas, *Red Flag Over Afghanistan: The Communist Coup, the Soviet Invasion, and the Consequences*, Westview Press, Boulder, CO, 1984.
Hanke, Lewis, *Aristotle and the American Indians*, Indiana University Press, Bloomington, 1959.
Harding, Sandra, *The Science Question in Feminism*, Cornell University Press, Ithaca, NY, 1986.
—————, *Whose Science? Whose Knowledge?*, Cornell University Press, Ithaca, New York, 1991.
Hilmy, S. Stephen, *The Later Wittgenstein: The Emergence of a New Philosophical Method*, Basil Blackwell, Oxford, 1987.
Hintikka, Merrill, and Jaakko Hintikka, *Investigating Wittgenstein*, Basil Blackwell, 1986.
Hitler, Adolf, *Mein Kampf*, ed. by John Chamberlain et al., Reynal & Hitchcock, New York, 1939.
—————, *Monologe im Führerhauptquartier*, ed. by Werner Jochmann, Hamburg, 1980.
Homer, *Odyssey*.
Hookway, Christopher, *Quine: Language, Experience and Reality*, Stanford University Press, Stanford, CA, 1988.
Horgan, John, *The End of Science: Facing the Limits of Knowledge in the Twilight of the Scientific Age*, Helix Books, New York, 1996.
Hylton, Peter, *Russell, Idealism, and the Emergence of Analytic Philosophy*, Clarendon Press, Oxford, 1990.
I Ching, The, or Book of Changes, trans. by Richard Wilhelm, Princeton University Press, Princeton, NJ, 1967.

Illich, Ivan, *Medical Nemesis; The Expropriation of Health*, Pantheon Books, New York, 1976.

Ishiguro, Hidé, *Leibniz's Philosophy of Logic and Language*, Cornell University Press, Ithaca, NY, 1972.

Jager, Ronald, *The Development of Bertrand Russell's Philosophy*, Humanities Press, Inc., New York, 1972.

Janik, Allan, *Essays on Wittgenstein and Weininger*, Rodopi, Amsterdam, 1985.

Jarman, Derek, *Wittgenstein* (movie), Zeitgeist Films, Britain, 1993.

Jarmusch, Jim, *Stranger Than Paradise* (movie), Goldwyn/ZDF, The United States, 1984.

Joyce, James, *A Portrait of the Artist as a Young Man*, The Viking Press, New York, reprint of 1961.

Jungius, Joachim, *Logica Hamburgensis*, ed. by Rudolf Meyer, J.J. Augustin, Hamburg, 1957.

Kant, Immanuel, *Critique of Practical Reason*, trans. by Lewis White Black, Liberal Arts Press, New York, 1956.

_____, *Critique of Pure Reason*, 2nd Edition, trans. by Max Müller, Macmillan, New York, 1925.

_____, *Foundations of the Metaphysics of Morals*, trans. by Lewis White Beck, The Liberal Arts Press, New York, 1959.

_____, "What is Enlightenment?" in *Foundations of the Metaphysics of Morals and What is Enlightenment?*, trans. by Lewis White Beck, The Liberal Arts Press, New York, 1959.

Kilmister, C.W., *Russell*, The Harvester Press, 1984.

Kirk, G.S., & J.E. Raven, *The Presocratic Philosophers*, Cambridge University Press, Cambridge, 1963.

Kline, Morris, *Mathematics. The Loss of Certainty*, Oxford University Press, New York, 1980.

Kluge, E.-H. W., *The Metaphysics of Gottlob Frege*, Martinus Nijhoff, The Hague, 1980.

Kosko, Bart, "Chipping Away at Your Brain," *Free Inquiry*, Winter 1994, p. 96

_____, "Downdraft," *Buzz*, April 1996, pp. 86-119.

_____, "Fuzzy Systems as Universal Approximators," *IEEE Transactions on Computers*, vol. 43, No. 11, November 1994, pp. 1329-1333.

_____, *Fuzzy Thinking; The New Science of Fuzzy Logic*, Hyperion, New York, 1993.

Kristeller, Paul Oskar, *Renaissance Thought: The Classic, Scholastic, and Humanist Strains*, Harper Torchbooks, New York, 1961.

Kubrick, Stanley, *Dr. Strangelove, or How I Learned to Stop Worrying and Love the Bomb* (movie), Columbia, Britain, 1963.

Kuhn, Thomas S., *The Structure of Scientific Revolutions*, 2nd edition, The University of Chicago Press, Chicago, 1970.

Kuntz, Paul, *Bertrand Russell*, Twayne Publishers, Boston, 1986.

Langer, Susanne K., *Philosophy in a New Key: A Study in the Symbolism of Reason, Rite, and Art*, Harvard University Press, Cambridge, MA; originally pub'd 1942, Third Edition, 1963.

Lauritsen, John, and David Thorstad, *The Early Homosexual Rights Movement (1864-1935)*, Times Change Press, New York, 1974.

Le Rider, Jacques, *Le Cas Otto Weininger*, Presses Universitaires de France, Paris, 1982.

Leibniz, Gottfried Wilhelm, *Leibniz: Logical Papers*, ed. by G.H.R. Parkinson, Clarendon Press, Oxford, 1966.

_____, *Monadology*, trans. by Paul Schrecker and Anne Martin Schrecker, The Bobbs-Merrill Company, Inc., Indianapolis, 1965.

_____, *A New System of the Nature and the Communication of Substances*, 1695, in his *Philosophical Papers and Letters*, trans. by Leroy Loemker, vol. 2, The University of Chicago Press, Chicago, 1956.

Levi, Albert, "The Biographical Sources of Wittgenstein's Ethics," *Telos*, No. 38, Winter 1978-79, p. 67.

_____, "Wittgenstein Once More: A Response to Critics," *Telos*, No. 40, Summer 1979, pp. 165-173.

Line, Les, "1,096 Mammal and 1,108 Bird Species Threatened," *The New York Times*, October 8, 1996, Section B, p. 6.

Locke, John, *An Essay Concerning Human Understanding*, in *The English Philosophers from Bacon to Mill*, ed. by Edwin Burtt, The Modern Library, New York, 1939.

Lovejoy, Arthur, *The Great Chain of Being*, Harper Torchbooks, New York; originally published 1936, Harper reprint 1965.

Lucretius, Titus Carus, *De Rerum Natura*.

Malcolm, Norman, *Ludwig Wittgenstein, A Memoir*, Oxford University Press, New York, 1st edition, 1958, 2nd edition, 1984.

Cited Titles

Mander, Jerry, *In the Absence of the Sacred. The Failure of Technology and the Survival of the Indian Nations*, Sierra Club Books, San Francisco, 1991.

Marcuse, Herbert, *Eros and Civilization: A Philosophical Inquiry into Freud*, Beacon Press, Boston, 1966, p. 111.

Mason, Stephen, *A History of the Sciences*, first published 1956, revised edition by Collier Books, New York, 1967.

Mates, Benson, *The Philosophy of Leibniz: Metaphysics and Language*, Oxford University Press, New York, 1986.

——————, *Stoic Logic*, University of California Press, Berkeley & Los Angeles, 1953.

——————, *The Philosophy of Leibniz*, Oxford University Press, New York, 1986.

McGuinness, B.G., "The Mysticism of the *Tractatus*," in *The Philosophical Review*, vol. 75, 1966, pp. 305-328.

McNeill, Daniel, & Paul Freiberger, *Fuzzy Logic*, Simon and Schuster, New York, 1993.

Mellor, Anne K., *Mary Shelley: Her Life, Her Fiction, Her Monsters*, Routledge, New York, 1988.

Melman, Seymour, *Our Depleted Society*, Dell Publishing Co., New York; originally published in 1965, paperback in 1966.

Merchant, Carolyn, *The Death of Nature: Women, Ecology, and the Scientific Revolution*, Harper & Row, San Francisco, 1980.

Mill, John Stuart, *On Liberty*, 1859; Appleton-Century-Crofts, Inc., New York, 1947.

Milton, John, *Paradise Lost*.

Monk, Ray, letter in *White Crane* [journal of gay male spirituality], no. 17, Summer 1993, p. 17.

——————, *Ludwig Wittgenstein: The Duty of Genius*, The Free Press, New York, 1990.

Moore, G.E., *G.E. Moore. The Early Essays*, ed. by Tom Regan, Temple University Press, Philadelphia, 1986.

——————, *Principia Ethica*, Cambridge University Press, Cambridge, 1966 (reprint of 1903 edition).

Musgrave, A., "George Boole and Psychologism," *Scientia*, vol. 107, 1972, pp. 593-608.

Nerburn, Kent, *The Wisdom of the Great Chiefs: The Classic Speeches of Chief Red Jacket, Chief Joseph, and Chief Seattle*, New World Library, San Rafael, CA, 1994.

Nestroy, Johann, *Der Schützling*, farce with song, 1847.

Neurath, Otto, "Protocol Sentences" in *Logical Positivism*, ed. by A.J. Ayer, The Free Press, New York, 1959.

New American Bible, The, P.J. Kenedy & Sons, New York, 1970.

Newton, Isaac, *Philosophiae Naturalis Principia Mathematica*, 1687.

Nieli, Russell, *Wittgenstein: From Mysticism to Ordinary Language*, State University of New York, Albany, 1987.

Nove, Alec, *An Economic History of the U.S.S.R.*, Penguin Books, Baltimore, 1969.

Nye, Andrea, *Philosophy & Feminism: At the Border*, Twayne Publishers, New York, 1995.

——————, *Words of Power, A Feminist Reading of the History of Logic*, Routledge, New York, 1990.

Orenstein, Alex, *Willard Van Orman Quine*, Twayne Publishers, Boston, 1977.

Ovid, *Metamorphoses*.

Parkinson, G.H.R., *Logic and Reality in Leibniz's Metaphysics*, The Clarendon Press, Oxford, 1965.

Parmenides, *On Nature*.

Pearson, A.C., *The Fragments of Zeno and Cleanthes*, C.J. Clay, London, 1891; reprinted by Arno Press, New York, 1973.

Perloff, Marjorie, *Wittgenstein's Ladder*, The University of Chicago Press, Chicago, 1996

Piette, Édouard, and Julien Sacaze, "La montagne d'Espiaup," *Bulletins de la Société d'anthropologie de Paris*, 1877, pp. 225-251.

Planck, Max, *Scientific Autobiography and Other Papers*, trans. by F. Gaynor, New York, 1949.

Plato, *Meno, Republic, Socrates' Defense [Apologia], Sophist, Theaetetus*.

Plotinus, *Enneads*.

Protagoras, *Contrary Arguments, On the Gods*.

Ptolemy, *Great System of Astronomy*.

Quine, Willard Van Orman, "Autobiography of W.V. Quine" in *The Philosophy of W.V. Quine*, ed. by Lewis E. Hahn and Paul A. Schlipp, The Library of Living Philosophers, Open Court, La Salle, IL, 1986.

——————, *From a Logical Point of View*, 1953; 2nd revised edition, 1961; Harper Torchbooks reprint, New York, 1963.

——————, *From Stimulus to Science*, Harvard University Press, Cambridge, MA, 1995

——————, *Methods of Logic*, Holt, Rinehart and Winston, New York, 1st edition 1950, 2nd edition 1959.

———, *Ontological Relativity and Other Essays*, Columbia University Press, New York, 1969.

———, *Philosophy of Logic*, Harvard University Press, Cambridge, MA; 1st edition, 1970; 2nd edition, 1986.

———, *Quiddities*, The Belknap Press of Harvard University Press, Cambridge, MA, 1987.

———, *Theories and Things*, The Belknap Press, Cambridge, MA, 1981.

———, *The Ways of Paradox and Other Essays*, Harvard University Press, Cambridge, MA, 1st edition, 1966, revised edition, 1976.

———, and J.S. Ullian, *The Web of Belief*, Random House, New York; 1st edition, 1970; 2nd edition 1978.

———, *Word and Object*, The M.I.T. Press, Cambridge, MA, 1960, 11th printing, 1979.

Ravo, Nick, "Index of Social Well-Being Is at the Lowest in 25 Years," *The New York Times*, National Edition, October 14, 1996, Section A, p. 12.

Rhees, Rush, "Can There Be a Private Language?" in *Philosophy and Ordinary Language*, ed. by Charles E. Caton, University of Illinois Press, Urbana, 1963.

———, Review of William Bartley's *Wittgenstein* in *The Human World*, vol. 14, February 1974, pp. 66-85.

Romanos, George, *Quine and Analytic Philosophy*, The MIT Press, Cambridge, MA, 1983.

Rorty, Richard, *Philosophy and the Mirror of Nature*, Princeton University Press, Princeton, NJ, 1979.

Rousseau, Jean-Jacques, *The Social Contract*, Chap. VIII, trans. by Gerard Hopkins, in *Social Contract; Essays by Locke, Hume, and Rousseau*, ed. by Ernest Barker, Oxford University, 1960.

Rudebush, Thomas, & William M. Berg, "On Wittgenstein & Ethics: A Reply to Levi," *Telos*, no. 40, Summer 1979, pp. 150-160.

Russell, Bertrand, *The Basic Writings of Bertrand Russell*, ed. by Robert E. Egner and Lester E. Denonn, Simon and Schuster, New York, 1961.

———, *Bertrand Russell Speaks His Mind*, The World Publishing Company, New York, 1960.

———, *A Critical Exposition of the Philosophy of Leibniz*, George Allen & Unwin, 1958.

———, *An Inquiry Into Meaning and Truth*, W.W. Norton & Co., New York, 1940.

———, *Introduction to Mathematical Philosophy*, G. Allen & Unwin, London, 1960.

———, *Logic and Knowledge*, Essays 1901-1950, ed. by Robert Marsh, George Allen and Unwin, London, 1956.

———, *My Philosophical Development*, Simon and Schuster, New York, 1959.

———, *Mysticism and Logic*, W.W. Norton & Co., Inc., New York, 1929.

——— & Alfred North Whitehead, *Principia Mathematica*, vol. 1, 2nd edition, Cambridge University Press, 1960 reprint of 2nd edition of 1927.

———, *The Principles of Mathematics*, first published in 1903, 2nd Edition, W.W. Norton & Company, Inc., New York, n.d.

———, *War Crimes in Vietnam*, Allen & Unwin, London, 1967.

Sacaze, Julien, "Le culte des pierres dans le pays de Luchon," *Association française pour l'avancement des sciences, compte rendu*, vol. 7, 1878.

Saussure, Ferdinand de, *Course in General Linguistics*, originally published in French in 1916, trans. by Roy Harris, Duckworth, London, 1983.

Schor, Juliet, *The Overworked American: The Unexpected Decline of Leisure*, Basic Books, New York, 1991.

Schulte, Joachim, *Wittgenstein: An Introduction*, trans. by William H. Brenner & John F. Holley, State University of New York Press, Albany, 1992.

Schwarzschild, Steven S., "Wittgenstein as Alienated Jew," *Telos*, No. 40, Summer 1979, pp. 160-165.

Seung, T.K., *Structuralism and Hermeneutics*, Columbia University Press, New York, 1982.

Shakespeare, William, *A Midsummer Night's Dream, Hamlet*.

Shelley, Mary, *Frankenstein; or, The Modern Prometheus*, originally published in 1818, revised edition in 1831; photo-reprint of the original 1818 edition with critical notes in *The Annotated Frankenstein*, ed. by Leonard Wolf, Clarkson N. Potter, Inc., New York, 1977.

_____, *The Last Man*, 1826, new intro. by Brian Aldiss, Hogarth Press, London, 1985.

Shields, Philip, *Logic and Sin in the Writings of Ludwig Wittgenstein*, The University of Chicago Press, Chicago, 1993.

Schilpp, Paul (ed.), *The Philosophy of Bertrand Russell*, Tudor Publishing Co., 3rd edition, 1951.

Sikes, J.G., *Peter Abailard*, Cambridge University Press, Cambridge, 1932.

Skolimowksi, Henryk, "Quine, Ajdukiewicz, and the Predicament of 20th Century Philosophy" in *The Philosophy of W.V. Quine*, ed. by Lewis E. Hahn and Paul A. Schlipp, The Library of Living Philosophers, Open Court, La Salle, IL, 1986.

Sluga, Hans, *Gottlob Frege*, Routledge & Kegan Paul, London, 1980.

Smith, Adam, *An Inquiry into the Nature and Causes of the Wealth of Nations*, 1776.

Stanley, Alessandra, "In the Kremlin, Chickens Still Come Home to Roost," *The New York Times*, June 28, 1996, p. 8.

_____, "New Close Yeltsin Aide: His Daughter," *The New York Times*, November 3, 1996, p. 4.

Thomas Aquinas, *The Disputed Questions on Truth*, vol. 1, questions I-IX, trans. by Robert W. Mulligan, Henry Regnery Company, Chicago, 1952.

_____, *Selected Philosophical Writings*, selected and translated by Timothy McDermott, Oxford University Press, New York, 1993.

Trevor Roper, H.R., *The European Witch-Craze*, Harper and Row, New York, 1956.

van Creveld, Martin, *Technology and War from 2000 B.C. to the Present*, The Free Press, New York, 1989.

Vohra, Ashok, *Wittgenstein's Philosophy of Mind*, Open Court, La Salle, IL, 1986.

Volney, Constantin, *Les Ruins*, 7th ed., Bossange, Paris, 1821.

Wagner, Jane, *The Search for Signs of Intelligent Life in the Universe*, Harper & Row, New York, 1986.

Waismann, Friedrich, "How I See Philosophy" in *Logical Positivism*, ed. by A.J. Ayer, The Free Press, New York, 1959.

Weiner, Joan, *Frege in Perspective*, Cornell University Press, Ithaca, NY, 1990.

Weininger, Otto, *Geschlecht und Charakter*, Wilhelm Braumüller, Vienna, originally published in 1903; 9th printing, 1907.

_____, *Sex and Character*, anonymously translated, G.P. Putnam Sons, New York, 1906.

Weizenbaum, Joseph, *Computer Power and Human Reason: From Judgment to Calculation*, W.H. Freeman and Co., New York, 1976.

Whitehead, Alfred North, *Process and Reality. An Essay in Cosmology*, Harper Torchbook reprint of 1929 edition, New York, 1957.

Whitman, Walt, *Leaves of Grass*.

Wittgenstein, Ludwig, "Remarks on Frazer's *Golden Bough*," trans. by John Beversluis, in *Wittgenstein: Sources and Perspectives*, ed. by C.G. Luckhardt, Cornell University Press, Ithaca, 1979.

_____, *Culture and Value*, ed. by G.H. von Wright and Heikki Nyman, trans. by Peter Winch, Basil Blackwell, Oxford, 1980.

_____, *Notebooks 1914-1916*, 2nd ed., ed. by G.H. von Wright and G.E.M. Anscombe, trans. by G.E.M. Anscombe, The University of Chicago Press, Chicago, 1979.

_____, *On Certainty*, ed. by G.E.M. Anscombe and G.H. von Wright, trans. by Dennis Paul and G.E.M. Anscombe, Harper Torchbooks, New York, 1969.

_____, *Philosophical Investigations*, ed. by G.E.M. Anscombe and Rush Rhees, trans. by G.E.M. Anscombe, The Macmillan Co., New York, 1953.

_____, *Remarks on the Foundations of Mathematics*, ed. by G.H. von Wright, R. Rhees, & G.E.M. Anscombe; trans. by G.E.M. Anscombe, The Macmillan Company, New York, 1956.

_____, *Tractatus Logico-Philosophicus*, bilingual edition by D.F. Pears & B.F. McGuinnes, The Humanities Press, New York, 1961.

Wollstonecraft, Mary, *A Vindication of the Rights of Woman*, 1792.

Woolhouse (ed.), R.S., *Leibniz: Metaphysics and Philosophy of Science*, Oxford University Press, New York, 1981.

Zadeh, Lotfi, "Fuzzy Logic and Approximate Reasoning," *Synthese*, vol. 30, 1975, pp. 407-28.

_____, "Fuzzy Sets," *Information and Control*, vol. 8, 1965, pp. 338-53.

Zemach, Eddy, "Wittgenstein's Philosophy of the Mystical" in *Essays on Wittgenstein's Tractatus*, ed. by Irving Copi and Robert Beard, Routledge & Kegan Paul, London, 1966, pp. 359-375.

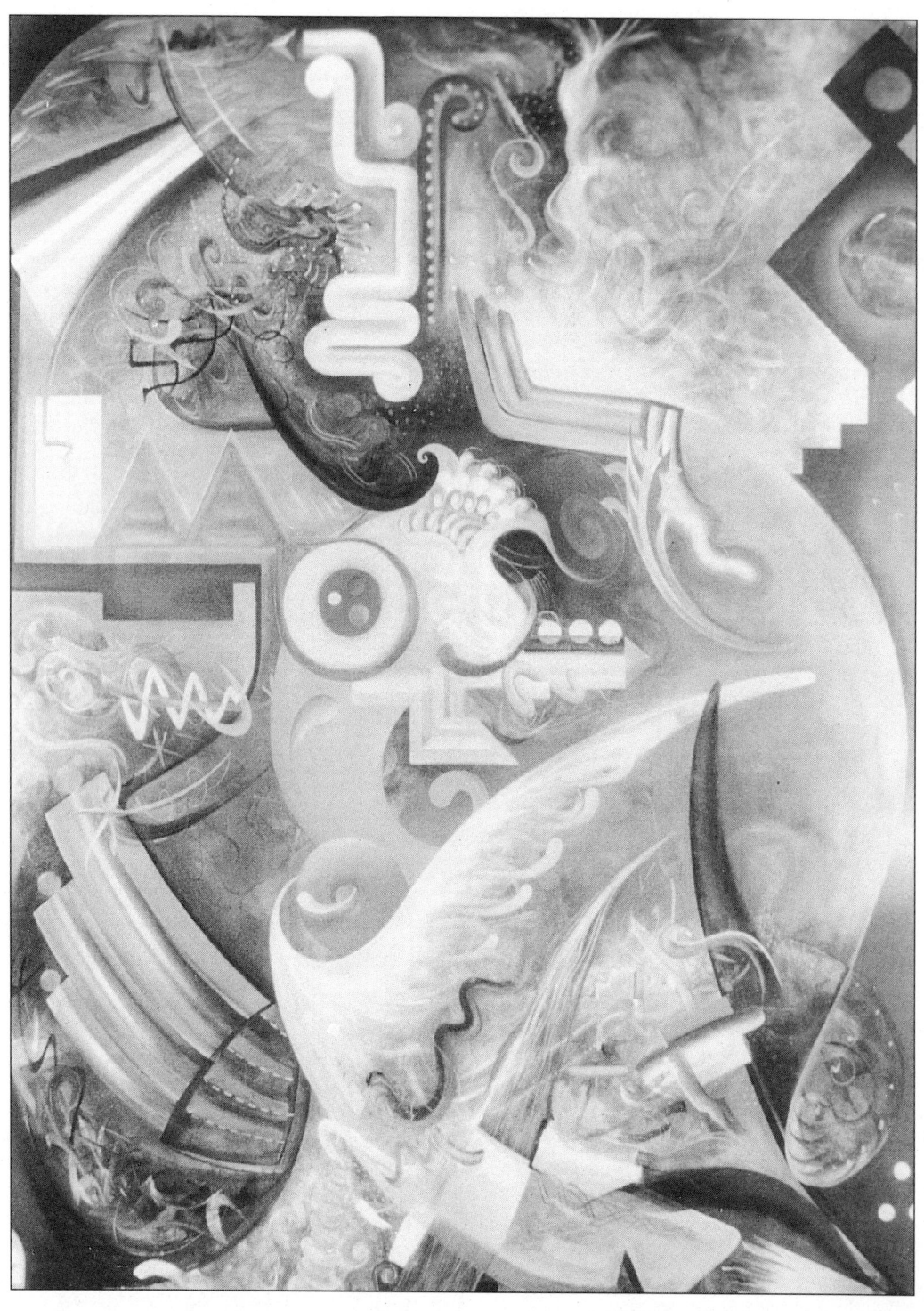

Costanza, Detail
Oil on Canvas, 72" x 48", 1987

Glossary

—A—

A Posteriori Proposition. A proposition that is judged to be true only because of particular observable facts. Example: "The mouse is in the cat." Opposed to **A Priori Proposition**.

A Priori Proposition. A proposition that is judged to be true regardless of any particular observable facts. Example: "No two different things are ever in the same place at the same time." Opposed to **A Posteriori Proposition**. See also **Analytic Proposition**. Many modern philosophers conflate *a priori* propositions and analytic propositions.

Absolute, The. In idealist philosophy, the one supreme context that encompasses and grounds all other contexts. See **Idealism**.

Acceleration. A change in the rate of change of physical position. Compare to **Uniform Velocity**.

Aether. In pre-Einsteinian science, a supposed ethereal substance spread throughout the universe.

Analytic A Priori Proposition. A proposition that is judged to be true regardless of any particular observable facts, and merely by virtue of the meanings of its terms and the way they are combined. Example: "2 + 2 = 4." Compare **Analytic Proposition** and **A Priori Proposition**.

Analytic Imperative. The conviction that analysis is the golden key to knowledge.

Analytic Philosophy. The dominant tradition in late-twentieth-century Anglo-American academic philosophy. It regards science as the highest arbiter of matters of fact, and defines philosophy as professional expertise in logical and conceptual analysis.

Analytic Proposition. A proposition that is judged to be true merely by virtue of the meanings of its terms and the way they are combined. Example: "If A is longer than B, and B is longer C, then A is longer than C." Opposed to **Synthetic Proposition**. Many modern philosophers conflate analytic propositions and *a priori* propositions. See **A Priori Proposition** and also **Analytic A Priori Proposition**.

Animism. A metaphor for viewing reality whereby most natural phenomena are regarded as living or life-like. Opposed to **Mortism**.

Anticipations of Experience. Interpretations that derive from encounters with past *interpretanda* and that prefigure encounters with future *interpretanda*.

Argument. In formal logic, a sequence of propositions in which one or more propositions are inferred from the others. See **Proposition** and also **Calculus, Truth-Functional**.

Arrhenoplasma. In the philosophy of Otto Weininger, a bodily factor that is responsible for all physical and psychological manifestations of masculinity. Contrast to **Thelyplasma**.

Arrhesia. The inability to write sustained, coherent prose.

Aristotelianism. The philosophical system of the ancient Greek philosopher Aristotle. He placed a higher value on the senses than did his teacher, Plato. See **Forms** and also **Essences**.

Artes Liberales. Literally, "the arts appropriate to a free citizen"; that is, the liberal arts.

Atomism. The doctrine that reality is ultimately made up of indivisible units (*atoma*, in Greek). Two forms: physical atomism (as in the philosophy of Democritus) and spiritual atomism (as in the philosophy of Wilhelm Gottfried Leibniz). The modern atomic theory, an offshoot of historical atomism, no longer regards atoms themselves as indivisible, although it is still searching for ultimate, indivisible particles. Compare **Monads**.

Axiom of Choice. In the philosophy of Bertrand Russell, the assumption that for any collection of classes, it is always possible to choose one object from each class in order to form a new class.

Axiom of Infinity. In the philosophy of Bertrand Russell, the assumption that the universe consists of an infinite number of objects.

Axiom of Reducibility. In the philosophy of Bertrand Russell, the assumption that for any true proposition of a high logical type a logically equivalent proposition can be found of the first-order type.

Axioms. See **Calculus, Truth-Functional**.

Axis of Language. In the philosophy of the later Ludwig Wittgenstein, the least changing core of a society's whole pattern of changing language-use.

—B—

Behaviorism. The doctrine that the investigation of patent behavior is sufficient to account for everything in human life called "mental phenomena."

Bivalence. A motif in the **Parmenidean Myth**. The myth of bivalence claims that correct thinking consists in judging reality in terms of two mutually exclusive values. More specifically, the doctrine that any proposition can have only two truth-values, true or false. See **Truth-Values** and also **Parmenidean Myth**.

Boolean Logic. The system of formal logic invented by George Boole. He depicted propositions about class relations with common algebraic symbols.

—C—

Calculus, Truth-Functional. In formal logic, a method of mechanically determining the truth-values of compound propositions and arguments. In formal arguments, assumed strings of symbols are called axioms; derived strings, theorems; and the commands that license deductions, rules of inference. See **Truth-Values**.

Canonical Notation. In the philosophy of Willard Van Orman Quine, the system of formal logic invented by Gottlob Frege, improved by Bertrand Russell, and perfected by Willard Van Orman Quine. Compare to **Deviant Logic**.

Cartesianism. The philosophical tradition founded by René Descartes. See **Res Cogitans** and **Res Extensa**.

Categorical Imperative. In the philosophy of Immanuel Kant, the ethical injunction to act only on those principles of action that one can will to be binding on all.

Characteristica Universalis. In the philosophy of Gottfried Wilhelm Leibniz, a "universal sign-system"; that is, an artificial language whose syntax transparently displays logical form. See **Logical Form**.

Closetedness. The reluctance of a gay man or lesbian to be publicly known as gay or lesbian.

Cognitive. Contributing to the acquirement of a body of knowledge. See **Knowledge**.

Coherence Theory of Truth. The doctrine that true propositions are those that, taken as a whole, give the most coherent overall account of reality. Opposed to **Correspondence Theory of Truth**.

Concept-Script. A style of logical notation invented by Gottlob Frege.

Consciousness. Awareness that is not entirely reducible to the operations of the five senses, although it may depend on them.

Contradiction. In formal logic, a proposition that is always false by virtue of its form alone. Contrast to **Tautology**.

Correlative Concepts. Concepts whose meanings presuppose each other. Example: *up* and *down*.

Correspondence Theory of Truth. The doctrine that true propositions are those that, taken individually, correspond to individual facts. Opposed to **Coherence Theory of Truth**.

Course of Values. In the philosophy of Gottlob Frege, an ordered array of truth-values that can be used to represent a propositional function. See **Truth-Values** and also **Propositional Function**.

Critical Realism. The doctrine that the basic building blocks of the universe consist of the diverse entities presupposed by the various sciences; for example, spatial points, instants of time, particles of matter, mathematical relations, etc.

Critical Relativism. A questioning attitude toward established authorities and institutions, promoted by a growing knowledge of varying customs and practices.

—D—

Daimonion. The spirit-guide that advised Socrates whenever he reached the limits of the power of reasoning.

Data Scene. That which presents itself to consciousness.

Deconstruction. A recent school of academic literary criticism, stressing the independence of the text from the conditions of its emergence, and delighting in exposing, as an end in itself, inconsistencies and paradoxes in the text.

Definite Descriptions. In the philosophy of Bertrand Russell, phrases that have the form "the so and so" and which seem to pick out one particular individual. Example: "The author of *Waverley*."

Denotation. In the philosophy of Bertrand Russell, the object or objects picked out by a noun or phrase. Compare to **Sense and Reference**.

GLOSSARY

Descriptive Judgment. An interpretation that characterizes reality. See **Reality**; **Opinion**; and **Knowledge**.

Determinate. Amenable to precise definition. See **Fact**.

Deviant Logic. In the philosophy of Willard Van Orman Quine, any system of logic that significantly departs from the system of logic used by Willard Van Orman Quine; especially systems of logic that recognize more than two truth-values. Compare to **Canonical Notation**.

—E—

Elementary Propositions. In the philosophy of the early Ludwig Wittgenstein, the simplest of propositions; they correspond to **States of Affairs**.

Emotive Theory of Ethics. In the philosophy of A.J. Ayer, the doctrine that ethical judgments are expressions of feeling, devoid of cognitive content.

Empirical Fact. That which is adjudged to be both determinate and real by virtue of systematic and critical observation. See **Determinate** and also **Real**.

Empirical Knowledge. Knowledge derived from the reports of the senses.

Empirical Verification. The process of verifying a proposition by examining physical evidence; the body of evidence that so verifies a proposition.

Empiricism. The doctrine that knowledge is the more secure the more it can be analyzed into the reports of the individual's senses. Opposed to **Rationalism**.

Enculturation. The process of learning the practices and absorbing the values of an ambient culture.

Enlightenment. Greater understanding of the whole self and its place in the cosmos, achieved by the natural maturation of a mind grounded in authentic living. Contrast to **Enlightenment, The**.

Enlightenment, The. The system of attitudes dominant among many intellectuals in 18th-century Western Europe. The Enlightenment viewed formal logic, higher mathematics, and science as the highest expressions of human reason. Not to be confused with **Humanism, Renaissance**; or with **Enlightenment**.

Epistemic. Pertaining to the acquirement of knowledge.

Epistemological. Pertaining to the question of what standards separate knowledge from ignorance or mere opinion.

Epistemology. Philosophy insofar as it addresses the question "What is knowledge?"

Error. Incorrect **Descriptive Judgments**. Contrast to **Knowledge**.

Essences. In Aristotle's philosophy, nonmaterial realities that inhere in material realities and by virtue of which material realities are amenable to definition and classification. Compare to **Forms**.

Essentialism, Semantic. In semantics, the doctrine that the meanings of words are essences or some other kind of universal. See **Essences** and also **Universals**. Contrast to **Family Resemblances**.

Ethical Community. A normative community whose standards consist of ideals of the good human being as such. See **Normative Community**.

Euclidean Geometry. The system of geometry systematized by the ancient Greek-writing mathematician Euclid. Compare to **Riemannian Geometry**.

Eudaemonistic Ethics. Ethical systems, especially in ancient Greek philosophy, that stress happiness (*eudaimonia*) as the goal of moral conduct.

Event in Process. That which is real but not yet determinate. Contrast to **Fact**. See **Real**; **Determinate**; and **Time, Progression of**.

Extensional Classes. Classes defined by enumerating a list of objects. Example: these three eggs. Contrast to **Intensional Classes**.

External Relations. Relations where the things related do not change by virtue of being put in the relation. Example: the relation indicated by the phrase "larger than." Contrast to **Internal Relations**.

—F—

Fact. That which is both real and determinate. Contrast to **Event In Process**. See also **Real** and **Determinate**.

False Proposition. A proposition that the interpreter judges as not correctly expressive of *interpretanda* or as inconsistent with the interpreter's reality map, or both. See **True Proposition**.

Falsehood. Error, expressed in language. See **Error**. Contrast to **Truth**.

Family Resemblances. In the philosophy of the later Ludwig Wittgenstein, the complex of overlapping ways in which a word is actually used. Contrast to **Essentialism, Semantic.** See also, however, **Grammar.**

Fascism. The fusion of extreme masculinism and political authoritarianism. See **Masculinism.**

Felicific Calculus. In the philosophy of Jeremy Bentham, a method of reducing all moral evaluation to a series of mathematical calculations about pleasures and pains.

Fly-Bottle. In the philosophy of the later Ludwig Wittgenstein, a metaphor for describing the limits of language and meaning.

Form of Life. In the philosophy of the later Ludwig Wittgenstein, a unitary complex consisting of some group of people and their patterns of interactive behavior. See **Language-Game.**

Formalism. The general drive in 20th-century formal logic to eliminate, as much as possible, any conceptual content ("meaning") from the symbols used in logic.

Forms. In Plato's philosophy, nonmaterial realities that exist apart from material realities and by virtue of which material realities are amenable to definition and classification. Contrast to **Essences.**

Forms of Description. In the philosophy of the later Ludwig Wittgenstein, uses of language that exemplify root-concepts for objects, space, and time.

Function. In mathematics, a formula that generates numbers according to a rule. Example: "$y = x^2$," where numbers are substituted for "x." See **Propositional Function** and **Variable.**

Fuzzy Logic. A new system of formal logic that rejects the principle of **Bivalence.** More accurately called "gradient logic." Compare to **Parmenidean Myth.**

—G—

Gödel's Theorem. The theorem that any system of formal logic that is rich enough to express arithmetic cannot be both complete and consistent.

Grammar. In the philosophy of the later Ludwig Wittgenstein, the pattern of permissible ways in which different kinds of words may be combined with each other in the same language.

Great Devastation, The. The period from 1492 until the mid 19th century, during which science-empowered European males subjugated or destroyed nearly four-fifths of all human societies. This period gave way to the **Industrial Dark Age.** See also **Modernity.**

Great Instauration. Literally, "great renewal" or "great inauguration." In the philosophy of Francis Bacon, a hoped-for renewal of humanity to be brought about by the spread of the scientific method and by the provision of state subsidies for scientific research.

—H—

Historicity. The partial dependence of the contents of philosophical ideas on the historical circumstances of their proponents.

Homophobia. Fear and hatred of the capacity to love the members of one's own sex.

Hubris. The arrogance that comes from strength or power, and by which one oversteps natural or moral limits. See **Nemesis.**

Humanism, New. The value judgment that the liberal spirit of cultural engagement that emerged during the Renaissance ought to be expanded to embrace the experiences of women, gay people, non-Western peoples, and the lower classes. As opposed to scientism, the value judgment that the canons of rationality ought to be derived from the whole spectrum of human experience. See **Humanism, Renaissance; Enlightenment, The;** and **Scientism.**

Humanism, Renaissance. The challenge mounted in Renaissance Europe to the dominance of formal logic, theology, and science in the university curriculum, in favor of an increased emphasis on poetry, grammar, rhetoric, moral philosophy, history, and research in Greek and Latin literature. Not to be confused with **Enlightenment, The.** See also **Humanism, New.**

Humanist Reason. Ideals of human rationality that draw on the whole spectrum of human experience. Opposed to **Patriarchal Reason.**

Humanista. In the Renaissance, a teacher of the **Studia Humanista.**

Humanitas. That breadth of spirit which stems from the study of the liberal arts.

Hypothetical Exemplary Interpreter. An ideal of an interpreter, implicit or explicit in the practices of a normative community. See **Normative Community.**

Hypothetical Ideal Data Scene. An *interpretandum* that is imagined by the interpreter and used by the interpreter as a standard against which to judge actual *interpretanda*.

—I & J—

Idealism. A philosophical tradition that gained ground after the death of Immanuel Kant. It maintained that both natural and historical processes reflect the workings of some kind of higher consciousness. Opposed to **Materialism** and **Positivism**.

Ideas. In the philosophy of Plato, objective, nonmaterial "Forms" existing apart from all physical reality; in the philosophy of Augustine of Hippo, concepts in the mind of God, according to which God created the world; in the philosophies of Thomas Hobbes and John Locke, the subjective contents of individual minds (the modern meaning of the word).

Identity of Indiscernibles. In the philosophy of Gottfried Wilhelm Leibniz, the doctrine that two things are the same if it is impossible to discern any differences between them.

Illogic. The irrationality of a system of false presuppositions that poses as a model of right reasoning.

Imagination. The ability of an interpreter to construct, remember, and modify hypothetical interpretational structures.

Impressions. Interactions of an entity with its environment, the results of which the entity uses for making decisions about one and many. See also **Sign**.

Incomplete Symbol. In the philosophy of Bertrand Russell, a set of symbols that has no proper use until it is joined to other symbols.

Indeterminacy of Translation, The. In the philosophy of Willard Van Orman Quine, the doctrine that there is no definitive, objective way of translating any given body of **Theoretical Sentences** from one language into another, short of a native mastery of both languages.

Industrial Dark Age, The. The present historical epoch, beginning about 1850 as an outgrowth of the Great Devastation. See **Great Devastation** and **Modernity**.

Inscrutability of Reference, The. In the philosophy of Willard Van Orman Quine, the doctrine that what particular names and phrases in any language refer to cannot be known with certainty, short of a mastery of the language as a whole.

Intensional Classes. Classes defined according to a property. Example: the class of those objects that have a thin white shell and a liquid interior. Contrast to **Extensional Classes**.

Internal Relations. Relations where the things related change by virtue of being put in the relations. Example: the relation indicated by the phrase "is transformed by." Contrast to **External Relations**.

Interpretandum (plural: **Interpretanda**). That which is to be interpreted.

Interpretation. The making of a decision about one and many; the decision so made; a decision so made that characterizes reality; a system of such characterizations.

Interpreter, The. That which, or the person who, makes a decision about one and many in regard to some *interpretandum*.

Intuitionism. In the philosophy L.E.J. Brouwer, the doctrine that mathematical operations are meaningless unless they can in principle be related to finite intuitions of space and time. Contrast to **Logicism**.

—K—

Knowledge. Descriptive judgments that are correct and adopted for good reason. See **Descriptive Judgment**. Compare to **Opinion**. See also **Truth** and **Reality**.

Knowledge by Acquaintance. In the philosophy of Bertrand Russell, knowledge stemming from immediate sensation. Example: "I feel hot." Compare to **Knowledge by Description**.

Knowledge by Description. In the philosophy of Bertrand Russell, knowledge dependent on factual descriptions. Example: "The temperature in this room is above 85°F." Compare to **Knowledge by Acquaintance**.

—L—

Language. A system of signs used by an interpreter to express feelings and desires, characterize reality, or indicate some relationship between the interpreter and reality. See **Sign** (second meaning).

Language-Game. In the philosophy of the later Ludwig Wittgenstein, a model for explaining language as a collection of games.

Law of Contradiction. In traditional logic, the alleged law that no given thing can both be and not be x.

Law of the Excluded Middle. In traditional logic, the alleged law that any given thing must be either x or *not-x*.

Law of Identity. In traditional logic, the alleged law that if any given thing is x, then it is x.

Linguistic Philosophy. Philosophy insofar as it addresses the question "What is language?"

Linguistic Turn in Philosophy, The. The effort in much modern academic philosophy to treat traditional philosophical questions as questions about various uses of language.

Literary Solipsism. The doctrine that there is no meaning outside of the text being criticized, and that I am the critic. See **Solipsism** and also **Deconstruction**.

Logic, Formal. The study of **Logical Form**; the body of knowledge created through such a study.

Logic of Domination. In the philosophy of Herbert Marcuse, the doctrine that the logic of the sciences has been used to promote emotional repression in the individual and imperialism in the world.

Logic, Symbolic. A system of formal logic that fuses algebraic symbolism with logical analysis.

Logical Analysis. In the philosophy of Bertrand Russell, the technique of analyzing concepts of physical phenomena with the same methods that formal logic uses in the analysis of arguments and propositions.

Logical Atomism. In the philosophy of Bertrand Russell, the doctrine that logical analysis will eventually come to a stop, revealing the ultimate building blocks of the universe. See **Logical Analysis** and **Monads**.

Logical Constants. Those symbols in logical formulas that admit of no substitutions (values). Example: "&" in the logical formula "$p \& q$," where "p" and "q" stand for propositions.

Logical Fictions. In the philosophy of Bertrand Russell, those things in the universe that can be analyzed by **Logical Analysis** into simpler things.

Logical Form. That by virtue of which an individual proposition or argument can be classified as an instance of a conceptual type whose properties affect validity of inference.

Logical Mysticism. In the philosophy of the early Ludwig Wittgenstein, the doctrine that both logic and ethics are grounded in a transcendent One that can only be seen, never described.

Logical Necessity. A motif in the Parmenidean myth. The myth of logical necessity claims that human thought, natural phenomena, and language are all ruled in common by some sort of divine-like force that can best be revealed through the methods of formal logic. See **Parmenidean Myth**.

Logical Particles. See **Logical Constants**.

Logical Positivism. A philosophical tradition stimulated by the Vienna Circle in the 1920s. It has two characteristic doctrines: (1) All knowledge consists of either factual propositions or formulas of logic; and (2) the meaning of any factual proposition is the manner in which it is empirically verified (the verifiability criterion of meaning).

Logicism. In the philosophies of Gottlob Frege, Bertrand Russell, and others, the doctrine that arithmetic can be derived from pure logic. Contrast to **Intuitionism**.

Logos. In ordinary ancient Greek, the word for "language," "word," "proportion," "order," and "reason." In Platonic and Stoic thought, a name for the divine source of rational order in the universe. Later identified by Christians with the second person of the Holy Trinity.

—M—

Manicheanism. A widespread ancient religious movement that fused elements of Christianity, Zoroastrianism, and paganism.

Masculinism. Glorification of male traits; in its extreme form, glorification and eroticization of male aggressiveness and brutality. See **Fascism**.

Material Implication. In formal logic, an "if-then" relation between two propositions, a and b, such that the relation is true only if it is not the case that b is false while a is true. Example: "If you are happy, then I am pleased."

Materialism. The doctrine that every existing entity consists entirely of matter. See **Matter**. Contrast to **Idealism**.

Mathematical Realism. The doctrine that numbers constitute a realm of reality in and of themselves.

Mathematicization. The process whereby a mass of individual observations is translated into a body of impersonal propositions about measurable quantities, which in turn is organized as a formal deductive system.

Mathematics. Any science that seeks for knowledge primarily through the formal analysis of quantitative relations.

Matter. That which is immediately evident to the five senses.

Meaning. That understanding which emerges from the integration of disparate experiences.

Metalanguage. In 20th-century formal logic, the language that is used to analyze (or create) the language that is being analyzed or created (the object language). See **Object Language**.

Metaphysical Subject, The. In the philosophy of the early Ludwig Wittgenstein, the world-transcending entity that uses language; that is, the soul.

Metaphysics. Philosophy insofar as it addresses the question "What are the most general assumptions underlying any given body of knowledge or belief?" The word is commonly used in a disparaging sense by each generation of philosophers to describe the root assumptions of previous generations of philosophers.

Misogyny. Fear and hatred of women or anything conventionally associated with women.

Modernity. The network of educational, economic, and political institutions that has come to prevail in much of the industrialized world during the last 150 years.

Monads. In the philosophy of Gottfried Wilhelm Leibniz, the ultimate non-material atoms that must be presupposed in order to explain the possibility of natural processes and the capacity of language to have determinate sense.

Monism. The doctrine that the whole universe is an after-effect of some unity. Opposed to **Pluralism**.

Moral Judgment. The rendering of a judgment involving the ideal of the human being as such.

Mortism. A metaphor for viewing reality whereby most natural phenomena are viewed as lifeless or dead. Opposed to **Animism**.

Myth. A system of symbols that depicts supra-empirical beings or entities, and which is socially created, historically transmitted, and explanatory of archetypal aspects of reality. Example: higher mathematics.

Mythology. In the philosophy of the later Ludwig Wittgenstein, the complex of most-firmly established judgments in any language.

—N—

Naturalistic Fallacy. The fallacious attempt to reduce moral goodness to some natural phenomenon. The classic exposé of this fallacy is by G.E. Moore.

Nemesis. The disaster brought upon oneself by overstepping natural or moral limits. See **Hubris**.

Neoplatonism. A revision of the thought of Plato by the Greek-writing Egyptian philosopher Plotinus, who advocated ascetic contemplation of "the One." See **Platonism**.

Neoscholasticism. In modern Anglo-American universities, the style of philosophical study focusing on formal logic, language, and science. Compare to **Scholasticism**.

Neutral Monism. A doctrine that Bertrand Russell occasionally advocated, adapted from William James. It holds that reality is ultimately composed of one underlying complex. When viewed one way, this complex is mind; when viewed another, matter.

Nominalism. The doctrine that universals are merely convenient names that serve as abbreviations for groupings of particulars, which alone are real. Opposed to **Realism** (second meaning).

Normative Community. A group of interpreters who share certain standards of evaluation.

Noumena. In the philosophy of Immanuel Kant, things in themselves. They can never be known as such but must be postulated in order to account for the possibility of knowledge, ethics, and religion. Example: the human soul. Opposed to **Phenomena**.

—O—

Object Language. In 20th-century formal logic, the language that is being analyzed or created. Opposed to **Metalanguage**.

Objectivity, Absolute. A motif in the Parmenidean Myth. The myth of absolute objectivity claims that a timeless, static model of reality is inherently superior to a model involving change, personal subjectivity, and feeling. See **Parmenidean Myth**.

Objectivity, Monumental. A commonly-shared interpretation of global meaning that is imposed by a dominant group on dissident groups. Examples: the belief systems of Christianity, Communism, and modern science.

Objectivity, Relative. The most commonly shared, or most deeply shared, interpretations in some group of interpreters. Opposed to **Subjectivity, Relative**. See also **Objectivity, Absolute**.

Objects. In the philosophy of the early Ludwig Wittgenstein, the ultimate, simple entities that remain after an exhaustive logical analysis of the world. Compare **Monads**.

Observation Sentences. In the philosophy of Willard Van Orman Quine, sentences that depend largely on immediate sensation for their meaning. Compare to **Theoretical Sentences**. See also **Protocol Sentences**.

Ockham's Razor. In the philosophy of William of Ockham, the doctrine that entities should not be multiplied beyond necessity; more generally, the doctrine that the simplest explanation is always the best. Compare to **Russell's Hatchet**.

Ontological. Pertaining to being or reality; pertaining to the question of what standards separate reality from unreality or illusion.

Ontological Commitment. In the philosophy of Willard Van Orman Quine, one's commitment to the actual existence of certain kinds of entities as reflected in one's use of language.

Ontological Relativity. In the philosophy of Willard Van Orman Quine, the doctrine that the understanding of what constitutes reality is always internal to some overall theory; it is never just given as such.

Ontology. Philosophy insofar as it addresses the questions "What is being?" or "What is reality?"

Opinion. Any descriptive judgment that is expressed in language. See **Descriptive Judgment**. Contrast to **Knowledge**.

Ordinary Language. In the philosophy of the later Ludwig Wittgenstein, the system of language that is presupposed as a backdrop while elucidating particular uses of language. In modern academic philosophy, the language commonly used by modern academics. See **Ordinary Language Philosophy**.

Ordinary Language Philosophy. A tradition of modern academic philosophy, particularly associated with Oxford University. It regards the conceptual analysis of ordinary language as the principal mission of philosophy. See **Ordinary Language**.

Ostension. Picking something out by pointing at it, and then giving it a name.

—P—

Paradigm. In the philosophy of Thomas Kuhn, a core system of beliefs and values about reality that are shared by a particular community of scientists.

Parmenidean Myth, The. A system of myth first fabricated by Parmenides in ancient Greece and influential in formal logic down to the present day. The myth contains three fallacious sub-myths; see **Logical Necessity**; **Bivalence**; and **Objectivity, Absolute**.

Particulars. Those entities that can have but one instance. Example: this particular tube of lipstick in my purse. Opposed to **Universals**.

Patriarchal-Industrial Civilization. The network of societies whose social relations are infused with male-supremacist values and whose economies depend significantly on factory production.

Patriarchal Reason. Ideals of human rationality that reflect male-supremacist values. Opposed to **Humanist Reason**.

Patriarchy. Systematic male domination in the family and society at large.

Phenomena. In the philosophy of Immanuel Kant, those things that are manifest to the senses and which serve as the bases for scientific knowledge. Example: the sunlight streaming through the window. Opposed to **Noumena**.

Philosophy. The art of critically and systematically examining presuppositions and implications, motivated by a passion to know; a system of thought created through such a process.

Physiognomy. A pseudo-science popular in 19th century Europe. It maintained that a person's character could be read off from his or her physical features.

Pietism. A movement in German Lutheranism that influenced Immanuel Kant. It emphasized the importance of personal piety over external ritual and dogmatic conformity.

Platonism. The philosophical system of the ancient Greek philosopher Plato. He maintained that a realm of immaterial Forms provides the basis of all knowledge. See **Forms** and also **Neoplatonism**.

Pluralism. The doctrine that the whole universe is an after-effect of some plurality. Opposed to **Monism**.

Glossary

Positivism. A philosophical tradition that gained ground after the death of Immanuel Kant. It promoted scientific measurement as the only reliable determinant of the nature of reality, and disparaged the quest for any higher meaning in nature or human life. See **Logical Positivism**. Contrast to **Idealism**.

Pragmatic Reality. In the philosophy of A. d'Abro, that understanding of reality which is constructed from the simplest coordination of the reports of the senses.

Pragmatism. The doctrine that the test of the truth of an idea is whether it "works" or "pays."

Praxis (literally, "practice"). In the philosophy of the later Ludwig Wittgenstein, the learned technique of using signs in order to communicate, conveyed through existing social institutions and practices.

Primary Quality. In the philosophy of science, a quality in an observed object that does not depend on the special circumstances of the observer. Example: mass. Contrast to **Secondary Quality**.

Principle of Sufficient Reason. In the philosophy of Gottfried Wilhelm Leibniz, the doctrine that nothing happens without some cause or reason.

Private Language. In the philosophy of the later Ludwig Wittgenstein, a language whose names and rules are created by an individual without reference to any public behavior or public sign-use.

Proposition. The meaning of a propositional sign. For example, that which is expressed by the following three different propositional signs: (1) "The Pope is misogynistic"; (2) "Der Pabst ist weiberfeindlich"; (3) "Papa mulieres odit." Compare to **Propositional Sign**.

Propositional Function. In formal logic, a formula that generates propositions or arguments according to a rule. Example: "If p, then q," where propositions are substituted for "p" and "q." See **Function** and **Variable**.

Propositional Sign. The particular symbols that a language-user uses in order to make some assertion. For example, the following string of symbols: "The Pope is misogynistic." This string of symbols is entirely different from the following string: "Papa mulieres odit." Nonetheless, both strings express the same proposition. Compare **Proposition**. See also **Sign**. Contrast to **Sentence**.

Protocol Sentences. Among certain logical positivists, those sentences that immediately report sense experience. Compare to **Theoretical Sentences**. See also **Observation Sentences**.

Protofascism. The system of reactionary thinking and fantasizing that developed in German-speaking countries in the early 20th century, and to which Hitler consciously appealed in plotting his rise to power.

Psychologism. In the philosophy of Gottlob Frege, the failure of empiricist philosophers to distinguish the objective, public content of logical concepts from the subjective, private impressions that may be associated with them. Alternatively, the mistake of basing the necessary verities of logic on empirical generalizations about the human mind.

Pythagoreanism. The philosophical system of the ancient Greek philosopher Pythagoras. He maintained that numbers are the basic elements of reality and regarded mathematics as a religious calling.

—Q—

Quantifiers. In formal logic, symbols that translate what is meant, roughly, by the English words "none," "at least one," and "all."

Quidditas. In the philosophy of Thomas Aquinas, that which makes a thing the sort of thing it is; a Latin translation of Aristotle's phrase *to ti en einai* (the defining and definable nature of a thing).

—R—

Rationalism. The doctrine that knowledge is the more secure the more it can be integrated into an encompassing system of objective concepts; opposed to **Empiricism**.

Realism. Two meanings: (1) the doctrine that the world has a given, knowable nature independent of any and all interpretation; compare to **Solipsism**. (2) the doctrine that at least some universals are real things in their own right. Opposed to **Nominalism**. See also **Universals** and **Essentialism, Semantic**.

Reality. What has the capacity to make a difference; that is, *interpretanda*.

Reality Map. The most basic set of decisions that any interpreter makes about systems, elements, and relational ranges.

Reductionism. The effort to reduce some complex phenomenon to a number of simpler phenomena.

Relational Range. The range of possibilities for interrelations among the elements of a system.

Res Cogitans. In the philosophy of René Descartes, "thinking reality," that is, human souls, angels, demons, and God; one of the two kinds of substance into which all reality is divided. Compare to **Res Extensa**.

Res Extensa. In the philosophy of René Descartes, "extended reality," that is, three-dimensional matter that is susceptible to mathematical analysis; one of the two kinds of substance into which all reality is divided. Compare to **Res Cogitans**.

Riemannian Geometry. A system of geometry invented in the 19th century by the German mathematician Georg Riemann. Compare to **Euclidean Geometry**.

Rough Trade. Men who pretend to be straight in their sexual encounters with other men; commonly, they affect a rough appearance and have violent sexual fantasies.

Rules. In formal logic, commands that license or forbid the way in which theorems may or may not be deduced from axioms. See **Calculus, Truth-Functional**.

Russell Irony, The. The turnabout in Bertrand Russell's life-quest for certainty: he began by trying to ground mathematics on logic; he ended by trying to ground both logic and mathematics on empirical science.

Russell Paradox, The. A contradiction concerning classes that Bertrand Russell derived from one of the axioms in the logical theory of Gottlob Frege. See **Logicism**.

Russell's Hatchet. In the philosophy of Bertrand Russell, the determination, pursued as an end in itself, to split any given entity into simpler entities. Contrast to Ockham's Razor.

—S—

Saturation. In the philosophy of Gottlob Frege, the generation of individual propositions from a propositional function by substituting the names of individual entities for variables in the function. See **Propositional Function**.

Schema (plural **Schemata**). In the philosophies of Bertrand Russell and the early Ludwig Wittgenstein, a tabular representation of truth-values, partly based on Gottlob Frege's concept of course of values. Later called "truth table." See **Truth-Values**, **Course of Values**, and **Truth Tables**.

Scholasticism. In medieval Western universities, a style of study focusing on formal logic, theology, and science. Compare to **Neoscholasticism**.

Science, Modern. The mathematicization of knowledge that is derived from careful observation, motivated by the (primarily male) will to power. Contrast with **Scientia**. See also **Mathematicization**.

Scientia. In Latin, a body of knowledge. Contrast with **Science, Modern**.

Scientific Progress, Myth of. The myth and fallacy that science, on the whole, has promoted human progress in terms of both knowledge and practical well-being.

Scientism. The value judgment that the canons of rationality ought to be derived from modern science. Contrast to **Humanism, New**.

Second Hundred Years War, The. The sequence of mass wars from 1914 to 1990, among the major industrial powers for world domination.

Secondary Quality. In the philosophy of science, a quality of an observed object that depends on the special circumstances of the observer. Example: taste. Contrast to **Primary Quality**.

Self-Authentication. The process of consciously rooting one's values in expanded self-awareness.

Semantic Ascent. In the philosophy of Willard Van Orman Quine, the ascent from a discussion of physical things to a discussion of the formal features of the language that talks about physical things.

Semantics. The study of how words convey meaning.

Sense and Reference. In the philosophy of Gottlob Frege, the distinction, respectively, between what a proposition asserts and the object of which it is asserted.

Sense-Data. In the philosophy of Bertrand Russell, the immediate, fleeting, uninterpreted reports of the senses, from which, in conjunction with formal logic, all knowledge is constructed.

Sensorium of God. In the philosophy of Isaac Newton, God's sense organ.

Sentence. In the philosophy of many modern logicians, any string of signs that may be said to be true or false. In effect, a conflation of **Proposition** and **Propositional Sign**.

Sign. Two kinds: (1) an impact that an *interpretandum* has on an interpreter and which the interpreter uses to refer to the *interpretandum*; and (2) a conventional symbol for the referential function of such an impact. Example of the first kind: a change in the retina caused by the impact of a photon from a light bulb. Example of the second kind: the word "light." See **Impressions**.

Signs, Flux Of. A sequence of impacts made on an interpreter as a result of the interpreter's interactions with some *interpretandum*, and which the interpreter uses to refer to the *interpretandum*.

Similarity. In the philosophy of Bertrand Russell, equinumerosity; that is, the condition wherein the individual members of different classes can be exactly paired off with each other.

Social Constructivism. The doctrine that the most important aspects of human experience are explainable as cultural constructs. In particular, the attempt to explain the sciences as mere cultural constructs.

Solipsism. The doctrine that all reality is a form of consciousness and that I am the only conscious being. Compare to **Realism**. See also **Literary Solipsism**.

Soul. That part of the human organism which creates meaning.

State of Affairs. In the philosophy of the early Ludwig Wittgenstein, the simplest of facts ("atomic facts").

Stoicism. An ancient Greco-Roman philosophical tradition that identified Zeus, the Father of the gods, with the Logos, the source of the world's rational order. See **Logos**.

Studia Humanitatis. Literally, "studies of humanity." In the Renaissance, the newly emphasized subjects of poetry, grammar, rhetoric, moral philosophy, history, and research in Greek and Latin literature.

Subjectivity, Relative. The least commonly shared interpretations in any group of interpreters. Contrast to **Objectivity, Relative**.

Substance. In traditional Western philosophy, that which is the least changing part of reality, and from which the evanescent parts of reality are constructed.

Survey (*Übersicht*). In the philosophy of the later Ludwig Wittgenstein, a detailed description of the various uses of words.

Syllogism. A model for arranging three propositions so as to yield valid arguments, devised by the ancient Greek philosopher Aristotle.

Synthetic A Priori Proposition. A proposition that is judged to be true prior to looking at any particular facts, but not merely by virtue of the meanings of its terms and the way they are combined. For example: "There are no synthetic *a priori* propositions."

Synthetic Proposition. A proposition that is not judged to be true merely by virtue of the meanings of its terms and the way they are combined. Opposed to **Analytic Proposition**.

System. Any unity that is more than the mere aggregate of its parts.

—T—

Tautology. In formal logic, a proposition that is always true by virtue of its form alone. Contrast to **Contradiction**.

Technique. The ability to create things or perform functions, personally learned in some tradition and improved through study and practice. Contrast to **Technology**.

Technology. The application of the scientific method to the productive process, aimed at the mass production of uniform commodities. Contrast to **Technique**.

Thelyplasma. In the philosophy of Otto Weininger, a bodily factor that is responsible for all physical and psychological manifestations of femininity. Contrast to **Arrhenoplasma**.

Theorems. See **Calculus, Truth-Functional**.

Theoretical Sentences. In the philosophy of Willard Van Orman Quine and others, sentences that depend on large theoretical contexts for their meanings. Contrast with **Protocol Sentences** and **Observation Sentences**.

Theory of Types. Two meanings: (1) In formal logic generally, the doctrine that certain separately made physical marks can be instances of one type-symbol; (2) In the philosophy of Bertrand Russell, the stratification of propositional functions according to degree of generality. See **Type-Symbol** and also **Propositional Function**.

Thomism. The philosophical system of Thomas Aquinas, which made Aristotelianism palatable to Christianity. See **Aristotelianism**.

Time, Progression of. Transition to determinacy. See **Determinacy**.

Transcendental Philosophy. The effort by Immanuel Kant to establish the purely formal conditions for the possibility of any kind of empirical knowledge.

Transmission. In the study of the liberal arts, the close personal dialogue between teacher and student wherein each strives to integrate what is being learned into the whole meaning-pattern of his or her life.

True Proposition. A proposition that the interpreter judges as correctly expressive of *interpretanda* and also as consistent with the interpreter's reality map. See **False Proposition**.

Truth. Knowledge, expressed in language. Contrast to **Falsehood** and **Validity**.

Truth Functional. A characteristic of a logical calculus whereby the truth-value of the form of any argument is a *function* of the relationship of that form to certain axiomatic forms. See **Function** and **Truth-Values**.

Truth-Grounds. That by virtue of which a proposition is judged to be true or false.

Truth Tables. Tabular displays of truth-values, commonly used in modern textbooks of formal logic. See **Truth-Values** and **Schema**.

Truth-Values. In formal logic, the values that propositions may have during the process of calculating patterns of valid inference. Also, the values that propositional functions may generate. Generally, only two such values are permitted, "true" and "false." See **Propositional Function**, **Variable**, and **Bivalence**. Contrast to **Fuzzy Logic**.

Type-Symbol. In formal logic, a symbol that is a universal. That is, one and the same symbol that can have more than one instance in a logical proof, as indicated by separately occurring physical marks. See **Theory of Types** (first meaning).

—U—

Uniform Velocity. Change of physical position at a constant rate. Compare to **Acceleration**.

Universals. Those entities that can have more than one instance. Examples: redness, triangularity. Contrast to **Particulars**. See also **Nominalism** and **Realism** (second meaning).

Universe of Interpretation. Any system consisting of an interpreter (or group of interpreters), *interpretanda*, and a history of interpretations. See **System**.

Utilitarianism. A system of philosophy developed by Jeremy Bentham. It recommends utility, understood quantitatively, as the highest standard in both personal morality and public policy.

—V—

Validity. In formal logic, a condition of a formal proof such that the theorems follow from the axioms according to the rules of inference and definitions of terms.

Variable. A place-holder in a function into which various values may be inserted; a place-holder for values that are so generated. Example: "x" and "y" in the function "$y = x + 2$." See **Function**, **Propositional Function**, and **Truth-Values**.

Verifiability Criterion of Meaning. The doctrine that the meaning of any factual proposition is the manner in which it is empirically verified.

Vienna Circle. A group of philosophers and scientists who met and flourished in Vienna in the 1920s. They sought to free philosophy from the dogmatism of German idealism and reground it on scientific principles. See **Logical Positivism**.

—W-Z—

World. The most inclusive system of interpretation for any interpreter or group of interpreters.

Zeno's Paradoxes. A number of paradoxes developed by Zeno of Elea, the pupil and lover of Parmenides of Elea. His paradoxes sought to prove that motion and plurality are logically impossible.

Index

—A—

Abelard, Peter, 118-119
Absolute space, 289, 290
Absolute, the, 28, 29, 30, 55, 153, 205, 253, 270
Acceleration, 289
Adler, Mortimer, 272
Aether, the, 290
Afghanistan, war in, 314 ff.
Africa, exploitation of, 304 ff., 315
Against Method (Paul Feyerabend), 6, n. 3
Agrippa, 325, 327, 329
AIDS, 106
Albert the Great, 119
Albertus Magnus, 325, 327, 329
Alexander the Conqueror, 102
Alhazen, 331
Americas, the, exploitation of, 304 ff.
Amin, Hafizulla, 314
Amores (in Augustine of Hippo), 45
Amyntas, King of Macedon, 102
Analysis of Mind, The (Bertrand Russell), 189
Analysis, 134, 169
Analytic *a priori* judgments, 147
Analytic philosophy, 3, 58, 126, 146, 158, 170
Analytic-synthetic distinction, 260 ff.
Anamnesis (in Plato), 72
Anaxagoras, 97
Anglo-American academic philosophy, 1, 2, 28, 134, 135, 137, 206, 254-257, 273
Animals, torture of, 12
Animism, 12; 258, n. 27; 301
Anscombe, Elizabeth, 177, 178, 179, 180
Anthropos (in Protagoras), 124, n. 2.
Antibiotics, 320 ff.
Anticipations of experience, 18 ff.
anti-Semitism, 137, 173-174, 183 ff., 204, 212, 213
Apatheia (among Stoics), 114
Apollo, 237
Appearance and Reality (Francis Herbert Bradley), 28
Aquinas, Thomas, 33, 45, 119 ff., 131, 284, 333
Archelaus, 97
Archimedes, 286
Aristippus, 98
Aristophanes, 97, 98

Aristotle, 31-32, 73, 93, 95, 102 ff., 107, 109-110, 112, 114, 117, 118, 119-120, 121, 124, 229, 235, 236, 248, 256, 262, 277, 278, 333
Arrhenoplasma (in Otto Weininger), 184
Arrhesia (in Ludwig Wittgenstein), 176
Artes liberales, 335
Artistic interpretation, 20-21
Artists, 100, 117, 186, 340
Asebeia (in ancient Greece), 98
Assunta, 253
Assyria, 71
Athena, 207, 226, 273
Atomic facts, 195
Atomism, 24, 72, 96, 127, 129; 258, n.27; 292, 295
Augustine of Hippo, 44 ff., 219, 230
Austin, John, 254
Axiom of choice, 81
Axiom of infinity, 81, 157
Axiom of reducibility, 81, 157, 165-166, 201
Axioma (in Stoic logic), 111
Ayer, A.J., 53 ff.

—B—

Bacon, Francis, 286-287
Bacon, Roger, 286
Barrow, Isaac, 289
Bartley, William, 177-181, 207
Basic Law V (in Gottlob Frege), 138
Basic Laws of Arithmetic, The (Gottlob Frege), 138, 147, 151, 215, 248, 278
Bedeutung (in Gottlob Frege), 141, 147
Beethoven, Ludwig, 183, 271
Begriffe (in Gottlob Frege), 137, 143
Behaviorism, 55; see also Quine, Willard Van Orman, *and* Wittgenstein, Ludwig
Bell, Daniel, 274
Bengal, exploitation of, 306
Bentham, Jeremy, 50 ff.
Bernard of Clairvaux, 118
Bertolucci, Bernardo, 183
Big Typescript, The (Ludwig Wittgenstein), 230
Bipolarity, 197, 201
Biringucci, Vannocio, 310
Bisexuality, 198
Bivalence, 94, 112, 114, 145, 173, 201, 275 ff.
Blake, William, 12, 77, 100, 336
Boethius, 117, 118
Boole, George, 134, 138
Boolean algebra, 134
Bordo, Susan, 76; 89, n.2; 299, n.9
Boyle, Robert, 290
Boynton, Marjorie, 260

Bradley, Francis Herbert, 27 ff., 152, 153, 154, 247
Britain, imperialism of, 306
Brouwer, L.E.J., 83
Bunge, Mario, 337-338
Burke, Edmund, 51
Burtt, Edwin, 284, 287 ff.
Buryats, 307

—C—

Calculus ratiocinator (in Gottfried Wilhelm Leibniz), 137
Calculus, 125-126
Calvin, John, 185, 340
Cambodia, genocide in, 315
Cardwell, Donald, 317
Carnap, Rudolf, 136-137, 146, 175, 215, 265-266
Carpenter, Edward, 307-308
Case of Otto Weininger, The (Jacques le Rider), 188
Categorical Imperative, 48
Characteristica universalis (in Gottfried Wilhelm Leibniz), 133, 137, 193
Charles II, King of England, 287
China, exploitation of, 304, 306, 307; imperialism of, 317; and the Khmer Rouge, 315
Chinese philosophy, 105, 256
Chotok, Sophie, Archduchess of Austria, 155, 311
Christ-*Logos*, 119, 123, 199
Christianity, 12, 25, 31, 37, 42, 46-47, 62, 74, 100, 115-116, 121, 284, 301 ff., 305, 340
Chrysippus, 110 ff., 114, 115
Chuang Tzu, 256
Chukchi, 307
Cicero, 43
Civil War, the, 323
Clairmont, Jane, 325
Classes, 80-81, 156, 163-164
Clayton, Naomi, 259
Cleanthes, 110, 113, 114, 115
Clio, 207
Closetedness, 180, 211, 212
Clouds (Aristophanes), 97-98
Cogito, ergo sum (in René Descartes), 75-76
Coherence theory of truth, 25
Cohn, Roy, 189
Coke, Edward, 286
Cold War, the, 308, 311, 312 ff.
Columbia University, 3
Columbus, Christopher, 304
Communism, 307
Compendia loquendi (in Gottfried Wilhelm Leibniz), 132

Completely general facts (in Bertrand Russell), 154, 160, 197, 199
Computers, 138, 335, 339
Concept-Script (Gottlob Frege), 138, 147
Concepts vs. ideas (in Gottlob Frege), 143
Confessions (Augustine of Hippo), 219
Conformist, The (Bernardo Bertolucci), 183
Conjugation (among bacteria), 320
Consequentia (in William of Ockham), 122
Consolation of Philosophy, The (Boethius), 117
Constantine, Roman Emperor, 116
Contradictions, 196, 201
Contrary Arguments (Protagoras), 96
Copernicus, Nicolaus, 74, 283 ff., 287, 290
Correspondence theory of truth, 25
Cortés, Hernando, 304
Critical Exposition of the Philosophy of Leibniz, A (Bertrand Russell), 152
Critique of Practical Reason (Immanuel Kant), 47
Critique of Pure Reason (Immanuel Kant), 4, 39 ff.
Cryonics, 279
Cultural solipsism, 227
Culture and Value (Ludwig Wittgenstein), 250
Custom, 44, 65

—D—

D'Abro, A., 287 ff.
Daimonion (Socrates), 98, 340
Dalton, John, 298
Daoud, Mohammed, 314
Darstellungsformen (in Ludwig Wittgenstein), 248
Darwin, Charles, 236
Data scene, 9-10
De la pirotechnia (Vannoccio Biringucci), 310-311
Death, 61
Declaration of the Rights of Man, 52
Deconstruction, 10, 42
Dedalus, 334
Definite descriptions, 157-158, 194, 195, 199, 200
Definition (Socrates), 98-99, 100
Demeter, 340
Democritus, 72, 96, 127, 292, 295, 296
Descartes, René, 75-76, 127, 128, 290
Descriptive Analysis, 10
Deviant logic, *see* Quine, Willard Van Orman
Devil, the, 302
Dewey, John, 298
Diairesis (in Plato), 101
Dialogue on the Two Chief Systems of the World (Galileo), 310
Diaphtheirein (Socrates), 124, n.4

INDEX 365

Dias, Bartholomeu, 304
Dionysius the Pseudo-Areopagite, 120
Dionysos, 44-45, 103, 340
Discourse on the Method of Rightly Conducting Reason (Descartes), 75
Dissoi logoi (Protagoras), 96
Donatus, 46
Downsizing, 316
Dr. Strangelove (movie, Stanley Kubrick), 273
Drury, Maurice, 178
Dubos, René, 319
Duhem, Pierre, 260
Dummett, Michael, 137, 146-147, 149
Duty, 44
Duty to oneself (in Otto Weininger), 186

—E—

Eagleton, Terry, 242; 258, n. 5
Earl of Essex, 286
Eckart, Dietrich, 183
Edwards, Paul, 206
Einstein, Albert, 29, 73, 79, 85, 270, 290, 291
Eisenhower, Dwight, 313
Ektos hypokeimenon (in Stoic logic), 111
Elbow-stroke (in Gottlob Frege), 142
Elegkhos (Socrates), 99
Elementarsätze (in Ludwig Wittgenstein), 26
Elementary propositions (in Ludwig Wittgenstein), 26, 27
Eleutheria (in ancient Greece), 95
Elizabeth I, Queen of England, 286
Emotive theory of ethics, 55
Empedocles, 93
Empirical Knowledge, 10, 11, 20, 42
Empiricism, 143, 284, 292
Encyclopedia of Philosophy, The, 146, 206
End of Science, The (John Horgan), 6, n.2
Engelmann, Paul, 176, 177, 180, 181
Engineer, origin of the occupation of, 310
Enlightenment, 62
Enlightenment, the, 47, 50, 63
Enquiry Concerning Political Justice, An (William Godwin), 325
Environmental devastation, *see* Technology
Epicurus, 292
Episteme (in Greek thought), 283
Erdmann, Benno, 137
Erläutern (in Ludwig Wittgenstein), 205
Error (in Ludwig Wittgenstein), 204
Essays on Civil and Penal Legislation (Jeremy Bentham), 50.

Essays on Truth and Reality (Francis Herbert Bradley), 28
Essences (in Aristotle), 31 ff., 36, 73, 102, 107, 108, 110, 112, 115, 121; *see also* Essentialism.
Essentialism, 30 ff.; 103, 127; *see also* Nominalism
Ethical communities, 65 ff.
Ethics, 43 ff.
Ethikos (in ancient Greece), 43
Euclid, 73; and the parallel postulate, 79
Euclidean geometry, 10, 40, 73, 78, 79, 85-86
Eudaemonistic ethics, 46
Eudaimonia (in ancient Greece), 46
Euripides, 97
Europe: class bifurcation of, 301-302; and the Great Devastation, 305, 306; and the Industrial Dark Age, 308-309
Euruproktos (in Aristophanes), 124, n.3
Evolution of Scientific Thought from Newton to Einstein, The (A. d'Abro), 287
Existentialism, 166
Expressionism, 186

—F—

Facts, theory of, 161 ff., 194, 195
Factum (in Latin), 162
Fallacies (concerning absoluteness), 27, 30, 174
Family resemblances (in Ludwig Wittgenstein), 34, 36
Far-constraining Order (as goddess), 93, 113, 115, 117, 119, 199, 271
Felicific calculus, the, 51
Feminism: 2-3, 251, 287, 337; and philosophy, 2, 3; 6, n. 4.; and science, 287; 299, n. 9; 337; *See also* Formal logic *and* Women
Feyeraband, Paul, 6, n.3
Ficino, Marsilio, 333
First interpretations, 16 ff.
Fisher, Jeffrey, 320
Flight from Reason and Science, The (Paul Gross and Norman Levitt) 299, n. 9; 330, n. 41
Flight to Objectivity, The (Susan Bordo), 89; 299, n.9
Forma corporeitatis (in John Duns Scotus), 122
Formal logic: 91 ff.; 125 ff.; 151 ff.; 173 ff.; 193 ff.; 221 ff.; 241 ff.; 259 ff.; algebracization of, 111; aristocratic bias of, 103, 117; folly of, 268; harmfulness of, 241 ff., 248-249; historicity of, 104, 115, 206; illogic of, 102, 106; opposed to ordinary logic, 92; proof in, 108-109, 199; relative objectivity of, 97, 107; and ethics, 204; and imperialism, 109, 114; and language, 219 ff., 241 ff.; and mysticism, 182, 186, 187, 188, 199, 200,

202-205; 207 ff., 212, 214-215; and women, 109-110, 117, 173 ff. *See also* Abelard, Peter; Aquinas, Thomas; Aristotle; Boethius; Boole, George; Chrysippus; Frege, Gottlob; Kosko, Bart; Leibniz, Gottfried Wilhelm; Parmenides; Plato; Quine, Willard Van Orman; Russell, Bertrand; Socrates; Weininger, Otto; Wittgenstein, Ludwig; William of Ockham; Zadeh, Lotfi. *See also* Logicism *and* Parmenidean myth
Formalism, 82, 108
Forms, Plato's theory of, 30-31, 32, 36, 72, 98, 101, 102, 110, 112, 121, 130, 255, 291; *see also* Essentialism
Foundations of Arithmetic, The (Gottlob Frege), 138
Foundations of the Metaphysics of Morals (Immanuel Kant), 47
Fraenkel, Abraham, 81
Fragment on Government (Jeremy Bentham), 50
Francis Ferdinand, Archduke of Austria, 155, 311, 315
Frankenstein (Mary Shelley): 301, 324 ff.; and the male inability to love, 328; and modern science, 327 ff.
Frazer, James, 231
Free will, 129 ff.
Frege, Gottlob, 80, 126, 136 ff., 151, 152, 156, 157, 159, 163, 167, 173, 174, 197, 199, 203, 206, 214, 246, 247, 248, 253, 255, 259, 263, 266, 267, 268, 271, 277, 278
Freud, Sigmund, 182
Functions (in Gottlob Frege), 139 ff.
Fuzzy logic: 266, 275 ff.; and Japanese engineers, 276 ff. *See also* Zadeh, Lotfi, *and* Kosko, Bart
Fuzzy Thinking (Bart Kosko), 277

—G—

Galileo, 74, 285, 286, 287, 290, 310, 324
Gama, Vasco da 304
Gandhi, Mohandas, 64
Gassendi, Pierre, 127
Gay historiography, 180
Gay people, 4, 6, 100, 101, 109, 178 ff., 183 ff., 251
Gedanken (in Gottlob Frege), 143
Gegenstände (in Ludwig Wittgenstein), 194
Gemeinheit (in Ludwig Wittgenstein), 181
Genos (in Aristotle), 103
Geometria (in ancient Greece), 73
George I, King of England, 125, 126, 134
Germès, Augustin, 303

Gesetzmässigkeit (in Immanuel Kant and Gottlob Frege), 48, 146
Gestalt psychology, 271
Gilbert, William, 290
Ginsberg, Allen, 237-238, 251, 264
Giordano Bruno, 335
God, 24, 32, 40, 41, 44, 45-46, 48, 74, 76, 114, 120, 122-123, 129, 130-131, 132, 135, 143-144, 146, 147, 148, 149, 151, 158, 163, 197, 198, 202, 203, 204, 208, 214, 219, 246, 251, 253, 255, 259, 263, 284, 291, 301, 303, 304
Gödel, Kurt, 81, 82-83, 157, 339
Godwin, William, 53, 325
Goethe, Johann Wolfgang von, 57-58
Golden Bough, The (James Frazer), 231, 250
Gorbachev, Mikhail, 314
Gosnold, Bartholomew, 318
Government, forms of, 66
Great Devastation, the, 303 ff.
Great instauration, 286
Great Reform Bill, 50
Greek logic, legacy of, 114-115
Gross, Paul, 42, n.5; 299, n.9; 330, n. 41; 337
Gymnopédies (Erik Satie), 159

—H—

Hacker, P.M.S., 177, 182, 197, 253
Hammurabi, 71
Harding, Sandra, 299, n.9; 341, n. 5.
Has Philosophy Lost Contact with People? (Mortimer Adler), 272-273
Hayakawa, S.I., 259, 275
Hedley, David, 54
Hegel, Georg Wilhelm, 28, 58, 153
Heidegger, Martin, 148
Héloïse, 118
Henry the Navigator, 304, 305
Heraclitus, 109, 159
Heresy, 302
Heteroiosis (in Stoic logic), 111
Higher Superstition (Paul Gross and Norman Levitt), 42, n.5; 299, n.9; 330, n. 41
Hilbert, David, 201, 82, 215
History of the Sciences, A (Stephen Mason), 290
Hitler, Adolph, 174, 182, 183, 188, 204, 212, 312
Hobbes, Thomas, 289, 291
Holy Inquisition, the, 302
Homer, 12
Homophobia, 42, 47, 98, 124, 178 ff., 183 ff., 204, 212
Homosexuality, 44, 54, 94, 97, 124, 148, 156, 175, 178 ff., 328

Hoover, J. Edgar, 180
Horgan, John, 6, n.2;
Humanism: and politics, 336-337; and reclamation of the whole self, 335-336; and reason, 336; and values, 329; in contrast to the Enlightenment, 334; in the Renaissance, 4, 333; vs. scholasticism, 333; vs. scientism, 332 ff.; new version of, 338
Humanista, 333
Humanitas, 274
Hume, David, 47; 217, n.24
Hylton, Peter, 171, n. 7
Hypothetical exemplary interpreter, 59-60, 83, 332-333
Hypothetical ideals, 59, 60; 67, n. 19
Hysteria of the philosophers, 177 ff.

—I—

Icarus, 339
Ideai (in Plato), 291
Idealist philosophy, 58, 205, 208
Identity of indiscernibles, 165
Illogic: of antiquity, 123-24; of modernity, 168; of patriarchy, 171
Imagination, 20, 21, 59
Imperialism, *see* Formal logic *and also* Technology
Impressions, 13, 17, 18
Incomplete symbols, 158
Indeterminacy of translation, the, *see* Quine, Willard Van Orman
India, exploitation of, 304, 306, 307
Indians, American, 14, 42, 62, 66, 109, 148, 298, 304 ff., 307, 310, 318, 323, 324, 326-327
Indigenous peoples, 324
Industrial Revolution, 306 ff., 323
Innocent III, Pope, 301
Inscrutability of reference, the, *see* Quine, Willard Van Orman
Insight and Illusion (P.M.S. Hacker), 182
Interpretandum, the, 10 ff., 18, 42
Interpretation, 9 ff., 16 ff., 21, 18, 42
Interpreter, the, 9 ff., 11 ff., 59-60, 236-237, 255
Introduction to Mathematical Philosophy (Bertrand Russell), 155
Introduction to the Principles of Morals and Legislation, an (Jeremy Bentham), 50.
Intuitionism, 83
Inuit, 307
Investigation of the Laws of Thought, An (George Boole), 134
Isonomia (in ancient Athens), 95
Ivan the Terrible, Russian Czar, 307

—J—

James I, King of England, 286-287
James, William, 155, 298
Janik, Allan, 190, n. 31
Japan: imperialism of, 311, 312, 317; loss of leisure in, 309. *See also* Fuzzy logic.
Jarman, Derek, 242; 258, n. 5
Jarmusch, Jim, 322
Jesus of Nazareth, 41, 45, 70, 181
Jews, 100, 137, 280
John Duns Scotus, 122
John I, King of Portugal, 304
John XXII, Pope, 120, 121
Johnson, Lyndon, 314
Joyce, James, 334
Jungius, Joachim, 126
Justinian, Roman emperor, 116

—K—

Kalmus, Leopoldine, 173
Kant, Immanuel, 4, 39, 47 ff., 52, 112, 139, 147-148, 187, 208, 278
Karmal, Babrak, 314
Karoshi (in Japanese society), 309
Kathekon (in Stoic ethics), 110, 114
Kepler, Johannes, 76-77, 285, 290
Ker, John, 125
Keynes, John Maynard, 242
Khan, Najibullah, 314
Khmer Rouge, 315
King, Martin Luther, 64
Kline, Morris, 78; 89, n. 1
Korean War, 313
Kosko, Bart: 277 ff., 283, 301
Kristeller, Paul Oskar, 333; 341, n. 4
Kubrick, Stanley, 273
Kuhn, Thomas, 15; 89, n. 5

—L—

Lady John, 152, 153
Lagrange, Joseph, 285
Langer, Suzanne, 6, n.3
Language, Truth and Logic (A.J. Ayer), 53, 55, 56
Language: 24-25, 99, 143 ff., 154, 203, 208, 220 ff., 241 ff.
Last Man, The (Mary Shelley), 325
Law (political), 65
Laws of logic: in Aristotle, 105 ff.; of contradiction, 105-106; of excluded middle, 83, 105, 107, 265; of identity, 105, 107. *See also* Truths of logic.
Le Rider, Jacques, 188
Lebed, Alexandr, 183

Lees, René, 54
Leeuwenhoek, Anton van, 128
Leibniz, Gottfried Wilhelm, 23-24, 30, 78, 125 ff., 132, 133, 134, 137, 143, 147, 149, 151, 152, 154, 157, 158, 159, 163, 165-166, 193, 195, 197, 198, 208, 216, 229, 256, 259
Leisure, loss of, see *Technology*
Lekton (in Stoic logic), 111
Lenin, Vladimir Ilyich, 307-308, 340
Leo XIII, Pope, 120
Lesbians, 185
Leucippus, 72, 127
Levi, Albert, 181
Levitt, Norman, 42; 299, n. 9; 330, n. 41; 337
Lewis, C.I., 265
Liar paradox, 92, 112
Libertarian pragmatism, 280
Liberum arbitrium (in Augustine of Hippo), 45
Linguistic turn in philosophy, 143, 148, 203
Lobachevsky, Nikolai, 79
Locke, John, 143, 291-292
Logic. *See* Formal logic
Logic of domination, 149
Logica Hamburgensis (Joachim Jungius), 126
Logical atomism, 154, 193, 195, 221-222, 245, 246
Logical constants, 199, 261, 266
Logical fictions, 154, 158
Logical form, 199, 202, 203, 220
Logical language, ideal of, 132-132
Logical necessity, 89, 91, 93, 94, 95, 112, 113, 114, 131, 132, 145, 159, 160, 163, 173, 199, 234, 243-244, 245, 246, 270, 278
Logical positivism, 54 ff., 126, 146, 205 ff., 254
Logicism, 137, 149, 157, 167, 267-268
Logos, 31, 111, 113, 118-119, 120, 123, 131, 144, 199, 214, 223
Longfellow, Henry Wadsworth, 252
Lucretius, 292
Ludwig IV, Holy Roman Emperor, 121
Lukasiewicz, Jan, 265
Lutheran Pietism, 47, 208
Lutterell, John, 121

—M—

M vs. F (in Otto Weininger), 184, 198; *see also* Truth tables.
MacArthur, Douglas, 313
Macedon, 102
MacLeish, Archibald, 214
Male violence, *see* Science
Manichaeanism, 44
Many, as a number, 81
Many, the, 24
Mao Zedong, 313
Marco Polo, 318
Marcuse, Herbert, 149, 331
Mardi Gras, 302
Marshall Ky, 314
Marx, Karl, 58
Masculinism, 184, 186, 188, 189
Mason, Stephen, 285, 290
Mates, Benson, 110
Mathematical Analysis of Logic, The (George Boole), 134
Mathematicization. *See* Science
Mathematics: 69 ff.; absolute attitude toward, 69; ambiguity of, 84-85; ancient history of, 71 ff.; as a myth system, 87 ff.; definition of, 70; historicity of, 83, 85, 91; proof in, 83; modern schools of, 80 ff.; quest for foundations of, 80; relativity of, 85 ff.; and René Descartes, 75; and Johannes Kepler, 76-77; and Gottfried Wilhelm Leibniz, 78; and Isaac Newton, 77; and Plato, 72-73.
McCarthy, John, 339
McTaggert, John, 152, 153, 155
Meditations on First Philosophy (Descartes), 75
Megara, school of logic of, 114
Mein Kampf (Adolph Hitler), 174
Meinong, Alexius, 157
Mellor, Anne, 328
Melman, Seymour, 315-316
Menes, King of Egypt, 71
Meno (Plato), 72
Merchant, Carolyn, 287
Mesopotamia, 71
Metalanguage, 201
Metamathematics, 82
Metaphysical Foundations of Modern Physical Science, The (Edwin Burtt), 287
Metaphysical subject, the (in Ludwig Wittgenstein), 207 ff.
Methods of Logic (Willard Van Orman Quine), 262
Military-industrial complex, 313
Mill, James, 52
Mill, John Stuart, 52, 137, 151, 338
Millennium, 4-5
Misogyny, 42, 76, 117, 149, 173 ff., 182 ff., 204, 210, 213
Moloch, 251
Monads, 23, 78, 128-129, 154, 193, 194, 195, 212, 220
Monism and Pluralism, 22 ff.
Monk, Ray, 178-182; 190, n. 2
Monodology (Gottfried Wilhelm Leibniz), 126, 131

INDEX

Moore, G.E., 60, 152, 153, 154, 160, 175
Moral judgment, 43 ff., 59 ff.; debate concerning, 61; relativity of, 62; and happiness, 64; and motivation, 63
Moralis, 43
Mortism, 12, 303
Mounseer Nongtongpaw (Mary Shelley), 325
Mussolini, Benito, 188, 220

—N—

Natural philosophy, 2, 328-329
Naturalistic fallacy, 60
Naturgeschichte (in Ludwig Wittgenstein), 228
Naturphilosophie, 318
Nazism, 100, 137, 148, 183, 188, 204, 212-213, 280, 312
Necessity, kinds of, 129-130
Neoplatonism, 44; *see also* Plotinus
Neoscholasticism, 58, 75, 169
Nestroy, Johann, 222, 232, 250
Neutral monism, 154-155
New System of the Nature and the Communication of Substances, A (Gottfried Wilhelm Leibniz), 126
New York Academy of Sciences, 338
Newton, Isaac, 29, 77-78, 125, 134, 285, 287, 288 ff., 292, 310, 336
Ngo Dinh Diem, 313, 314
Nguyen Van Thieu, 314
Niedrigkeit (in Ludwig Wittgenstein), 181
Nieli, Russell, 207
Nightingale, Florence, 319
Nixon, Richard, 314
Nominalism, 32 ff.; *see also* Essentialism
Non-Euclidean geometries, 79-80
Normative communities, 38-39, 43, 59, 83, 332-333
Notebook and Letters to a Friend, (Otto Weininger) 183
Notions and anticipations (Stoicism), 112
Numbers (in logicism), 80, 156-157, 201
Nye, Andrea, 3; 6, n. 4; 109-110, 114, 121; 124, n. 13; 148

—O—

Objectivity and subjectivity, 7, 15-16, 20, 42, 292-293
Objects (in Ludwig Wittgenstein), 26, 27, 194-196, 245
Ockham's razor, 33, 121-122, 158; *see also* William of Ockham
Ode to Joy (Ludwig van Beethoven)

Odyssey (Homer), 12
On Certainty (Ludwig Wittgenstein), 249
On Denoting (Bertrand Russell), 157, 169, 193-194
On Liberty (John Stuart Mill), 338
On Nature (Parmenides), 93
On the Last Things (Otto Weininger), 183
On the Revolutions of the Celestial Spheres (Nicolaus Copernicus), 283, 288, 324
One, the, 22-23, 117, 251, 271
Ontological relativity, *see* Quine, Willard Van Orman
Opinion vs. knowledge (in Plato), 72
Ordinary language, 135-136, 230-231, 253
Ordinary language philosophy, 169-170, 254 ff.
Ostension, 220
Ousia (in Aristotle), 32, 102
Ovid, 331-332

—P—

Paganism, survival of in Europe, 302 ff.
Panopticon, 52
Papal munitions, 311
Paracelsus, 325, 327, 329
Paradigm shift, 15; 89, n. 5
Paradox of the arrow, 94
Parallax, 284
Parmenidean myth, 92 ff., 99, 100, 101, 102, 105, 106, 109, 112-113, 114, 117, 124, 125, 131, 133, 134, 145, 159, 160, 161, 163, 166, 168, 171, 197, 203, 214, 215, 216, 256, 259, 262, 270-271, 274, 276, 277, 278, 280, 283
Parmenides, 92 ff., 102, 115, 117, 146, 149, 151, 171, 173, 214, 264, 301
Parts and Wholes, 7-8
Pasteur, Louis, 319
Patriarchal Reason, 4, 185-186, 206-207
Patriarchal-industrial civilization, 88, 337
Patriarchy, 4
Peano, Guiseppe, 80, 126, 152
Pederasty, 185
Peirce, Charles Sanders, 265, 298
Pericles, 96, 97
Perloff, Marjorie, 217, n. 32.
Phaethon, 331-332
Phallic religious rites, 303
Phantasia kataleptike (in Stoic logic), 110
Phenomena and noumena, 49
Philosophia moralis (in Cicero), 44
Philosophiae Naturalis Principia Mathematica (Isaac Newton), 77, 80, 285, 289

Philosophical Investigations (Ludwig Wittgenstein), 34, 176, 189; 119 ff., 241, 247, 250, 251, 252
Philosophy and Feminism (Andrea Nye), 6, n. 4
Philosophy and the Mirror of Nature (Richard Rorty), 6, n.3
Philosophy in a New Key (Suzanne Langer), 6, n.3
Philosophy: as an art, 5; as civilization-critique, 115, 250; as a goddess, 117; as the personal, 5; breach between technique and substance in, 3-4; definition of, 1; literal meaning of, 1, 71; two wings of, 273; and feminism, 2-3; and science, 2; *see also* Anglo-American academic philosophy *and* Analytic philosophy
Phone (in Stoic logic), 111
Physiognomy, 185, 198, 226-227, 230
Pietronigro, Frank, 5
Piette, Édouard, 302
Pizarro, Francisco, 304
Plague Makers, The (Jeffrey Fisher), 320
Plasms (in Otto Weininger), 184, 198
Plato, 30-31, 32, 58, 66, 72-73, 76, 93, 95, 96, 98, 101-102, 103, 112, 114, 117, 119, 121, 136, 159, 160, 169, 186, 204, 210, 253, 255, 266, 267, 284, 285, 292, 333, 339, 340
Plotinus, 22-23, 24, 30
Polarität (in Otto Weininger and Ludwig Wittgenstein), 198
Porphyry, 117
Portrait of the Artist as a Young Man, A (James Joyce), 334
Poubou (French town), 302
Pragmatism, 297-298
Praxis (in Ludwig Wittgenstein), 226-227, 228, 229, 230, 232, 233, 235, 252
Predicative functions, 165, 166
Primary vs. secondary qualities, 106, 288, 291-292, 296, 303
Princip, Gavrilo, 311
Principia Mathematica (Bertrand Russell and Alfred North Whitehead), 80, 81, 139, 153, 155, 156, 159, 160-161, 163, 167, 168, 169, 189, 213, 215, 257, 259
Principles of Logic, The (Francis Herbert Bradley), 28
Principles of Mathematics, The (Bertrand Russell), 152, 153, 174
Private language, 220-221, 235 ff.
Prolepseis (in Stoic logic), 110
Prometheus, 203, 328-329
Propositional functions, 157
Protagoras, 61, 96-97, 98, 124
Protégé, The (Johann Nestroy), 222
Protofascism, 182, 193, 206, 211-212
Psychologism, 135, 137, 138
Ptolemy, 73-74, 283-284
Pythagoras, 71-72, 101, 160

—Q—

Quality, coining of the word by Plato, 136, 253
Quantifiers, 264-265
Quantum mechanics, 95, 272, 290, 291
Quidditas (in Latin translations of Aristotle), 32
Quine, Willard Van Orman, 148, 160, 167; 238, n. 33; 259 ff., 280, 283, 301; absolutist views of, 270, 275; ethnocentrism of, 263; upbringing of, 259-260; and the analytic-synthetic distinction, 260 ff., 266, 273; and behaviorism, 263, 268 ff., 274; and bivalence, 270, 274, 277; and deviant logic, 263, 265, 269, 272, 273, 275, 276; and existence claims, 261, 264-265, 266, 267; and formal logic, 261ff., 271; and the indeterminacy of translation, 268, 269, 271; and the inscrutability of reference, 268 ff., 271; and logical necessity, 270; and logical particles, 261, 266; and logicism, 267-268; 281, n. 21, n. 30; and mechanistic physics, 272, 274; and observation sentences, 268-269; and ontological relativity, 268, 270, 271; and the Parmenidean myth, 270-271; and philosophy, 272-273; and quantifiers, 264-265; and relativism, 262, 269, 270; and science, 262, 263, 270, 274-275; and semantic ascent, 271; and theoretical sentences, 269; and variables, 265

—R—

Rand Corporation, 260, 275
Rationalism, 41, 132, 143, 339, 340
Reagan, Ronald, 316
Reality maps, 13 ff., 20
Reality, absolute concept of, 92, 93, 94, 100, 102, 103, 114-115, 145; *see also* Parmenidean myth
Reason, limits of, 338 ff.
Relational Range, 8, 10
Relativism, in ancient Greece, 97, 99
Relativity, theory of, 291
Religion, 41
Remarks on the Foundations of Mathematics (Ludwig Wittgenstein)
Res cogitans and *Res extensa* (in René Descartes), 127
Response patterns (of the interpreter), 11-12, 13
Revolution, 340-341
Reza Pahlevi, Shah of Iran, 275
Rhees, Rush, 179; 258, n. 33

INDEX 371

Richards, Ben, 243
Riemann, Georg, 79
Riemannian geometry, 10, 73, 85
Röhm, Ernst, 212
Roosevelt, Franklin, 313
Rorty, Richard, 6, n.3
Rough trade, 182
Rousseau, Jean-Jacques, 318 ff.
Ruins of Empires (Constantin Volney), 326
Rules of inference, 197, 215, 232-233
Russell's hatchet, 158-159
Russell paradox, the, 139, 149, 151, 156, 161, 249
Russell, Bertrand, 30, 78, 80, 81, 126, 139, 146, 149, 151 ff., 259, 263, 267, 268, 274, 275, 283; ethnocentrism of, 168; politics of, 169; upbringing of, 151; and the axiom of reducibility, 165-166; and classes, 163-164; and definite descriptions, 157; and facts, 161 ff.; and generality, 161; and pacifism, 155; and the Parmenidean myth, 160, 168, 173; and sexual liberation, 156; and the Vienna Circle, 205 ff.; and the Vietnam War, 156; and Ludwig Wittgenstein, 152, 154, 162, 169, 170-171, 174-175, 177, 189-190, 193, 197-203, 206, 219, 220, 221, 247, 251, 253, 254, 255, 256, 257; *see also* Russell Paradox.
Russell, John, 152
Russia, imperialism of, 307, 312; post-war decline of, 317

—S—

Sacaze, Julien, 302
Sachverhalte (in Ludwig Wittgenstein), 26, 195, 196
Sadomasochism, 183, 188
San Francisco, 307
Sanitation movement, the, 317 ff.
Santayana, George, 229
Sappho, 124
Saturation (of a function), 140
Saussure, Ferdinand de, 256
Schemata, 161, 196, 197, 199, 200, 201
Schlick, Moritz, 204
Scholasticism, 117 ff., 333
Schopenhauer, Arthur, 182
Schweinehund (in Ludwig Wittgenstein), 181
Science Question in Feminism, The (Sandra Harding), 299, n.9
Science: 249 ff.; autonomy and dependency of, 337; complexity and simplicity of, 290, 293-294; definition of, 287; metaphysics of, 283 ff.; predictive power of, 294; progressive correctability of, 294; transcending the limits of, 331; and Christianity, 301 ff.; and feminism, 287; 299, n. 9; 337; and formal logic, 171, 295-296; and institutional power, 324; and interpretation, 15; and male power and violence, 286, 287, 298, 311 ff., 317; and mathematicization, 285-286, 287, 292; and objectivity, 292-293, 296, 303; and observational knowledge, 283; and pragmatic reality, 296-297; and social constructivism, 338; *see also* Technology
Scientia (in Roman thought), 283
Scientific socialism, 307
Scientism, 42, 262 ff., 270 ff., 280, 331 ff.
Second Hundred Years War, the, 311 ff.
Semantic ascent, 167, 271
Sense and reference (in Gottlob Frege), 141
Sense-data (in Bertrand Russell), 154, 159, 194, 195, 255
Sensibilia (in Bertrand Russell), 155
Sensorium of God, 289
Seung, T.K., 42, n.1
Sex and Character (Otto Weininger), 182 ff., 198 ff., 227
Shelley, Mary, 301, 324 ff.
Shelley, Percy Bysshe, 325
Showing vs. telling, 200, 214
Significatio (in William of Ockham), 122
Signs, flux of, 18-19
Sin, 204
Sinn (in Gottlob Frege), 141
Sitting Bull, 66
Skeptics, ancient, 110
Skinner, Francis, 179
Skolimowski, Henryk, 273-274
Slavery, 304 ff.
Sluga, Hans, 147
Social constructivism, 15, 287; 299, n.9; 338
Social Contract, The (Jean-Jacques Rousseau), 318-319
Socialism, 205, 220, 250
Socrates, 1, 2, 30, 41, 72, 97 ff., 101, 103, 114, 156, 179, 273, 340
Solipsism, 187, 208-209
Sophist (Plato), 96
Sophists, 95 ff., 98, 102
Soviet Union, *see* Russia
Speech-acts, 254
Spellman, Francis Cardinal, 212
Spinoza, Benedict, 24, 131, 291
Sprachspiel (in Ludwig Wittgenstein), 222, 242
Sraffa, Piero, 220, 222
Stalin, Joseph, 308

States of affairs (in Ludwig Wittgenstein), 26, 27, 195
Stewart, William, 321
Stoicism, 49, 110 ff., 199, 277, 290
Stone worship, 303
Stranger Than Paradise (movie by Jim Jarmusch), 322
Strickland, Irma, 178
Strings (in physics), 295
Structuralism and Hermeneutics (T.K. Seung), 42, n.1
Structure of Scientific Revolutions, The (Thomas Kuhn), 15
Studia humanitatis, 333, 334
Substantial forms, 127, 129
Sumeria, 71
Suppositio (in William of Ockham), 122
Syllogism, 103-104, 115
Synagoge (in Plato), 101
Synonymy, 260
Synthetic *a priori* judgments, 132, 147
Systems and elements, 8 ff., 44

—T—

Taliban, the, 314
Tarski, Alfred, 201, 215
Tautologies, 196, 201, 205
Technology: definition of, 298-299; and the debasement of work, 310; and deterioration of the quality of life, 315, 322 ff.; and environmental devastation, 306, 323; and imperialism, 304 ff., 312 ff., 324; and the loss of leisure, 308 ff.; and male violence, 317; and modern conveniences, 321 ff.; and modern medicine, 320 ff.; and public health, 317 ff.; and war, 310 ff.
Tekhnologia (in ancient Greece), 299
Tet Offensive, 314
Thales, 252; 258, n.27
Theaetetus (Plato), 102, 136
Thelyplasma (in Otto Weininger), 184
Theodoric, Ruler of Italy, 117
Theodosius, Roman Emperor, 116
Theory of Knowledge (Bertrand Russell), 189
Theory of types, 81, 107-108, 157, 161
Third World, 4, 303 ff., 306, 317, 321; *see also* Great Devastation, the
Thomism, 120
Thought Experiment, 7
Times Literary Supplement, The, 178
To arrheton (pertaining to Ludwig Wittgenstein), 176
To on (in Plato and Aristotle), 92
To ti en einai (in Aristotle), 32, 103
To ti esti (in Aristotle), 99
Tode ti (in Aristotle), 31, 73
Tolstoy, Leo, 181
Tomlin, Lilly, 42, n. 6
Tractatus Logico-Philosophicus (Ludwig Wittgenstein), 25, 29, 30, 153, 170, 174, 175, 180, 182, 183, 184, 187, 188, 189, 190, 193 ff., 219, 222, 227, 229, 233, 241, 245, 249, 252, 253, 256, 271, 278
Transcendental philosophy, 39
Transvestism, 44
Trevor-Roper, H.R., 302
Trudy the Bag Lady, 21
True, the, and the False (in Gottlob Frege), 142, 144-145, 146, 148, 159, 163, 197, 199, 204, 259, 271
Truth tables, 142, 184-185, 196, 199, 246-247
Truth, 24 ff.
Truth-functional calculus, 134, 216
Truth-values, 140, 145, 199
Truths of logic, the, 200-201, 202
Truths of reason vs. truths of fact (in Gottfried Wilhelm Leibniz), 132
Tunguses, 307
Two Dogmas of Empiricism (Willard Van Orman Quine), 260 ff., 269, 273
Type-symbols, 108
Typosis (in Stoic logic), 111

—U—

Übersicht (in Ludwig Wittgenstein), 244, 252
Unanständigkeit (in Ludwig Wittgenstein), 181
Uniform velocity, 289
United States: collapse of public education in, 335; imperialism of, 304, 307, 312, 322; loss of leisure in, 309; post-war decline of, 315 ff., 323-324; 322 ff.
Universal exemplary interpreters, 40-41
Universals, 30, 35 ff., 101, 109, 118, 132, 222-223
Utilitarianism, 50 ff.
Utility, 44

—V—

Validity vs. truth, 108
Venetian arsenal, 310
Verifiability criterion of meaning, 54, 56, 205
Via antiqua (in William of Ockham), 123
Via moderna (in William of Ockham), 123
Vienna Circle, The, 54, 175, 204 ff.
Vietnam War, 313-314

Vindication of the Rights of Woman, A (Mary Wollstonecraft), 53, 324-325
Volney, Constantin, 326
Vorstellungen (in Gottlob Frege), 137, 143

—W-X—

Walton, Captain R., see *Frankenstein*
War Crimes in Vietnam (Bertrand Russell), 156
Washington, George, 66
Watson, J.B., 236
Weininger, Otto, 182 ff., 193, 198, 202, 219, 220, 242, 250, 257, 280
Weltraum (in Otto Weininger and Ludwig Wittgenstein), 188
Wertverlauf (in Gottlob Frege), 140, 142, 197
What is Enlightenment? (Immanuel Kant), 63
Whitehead, Alfred North, 80, 81, 139, 153, 257
Whitman, Walt, 109
Whose Science? Whose Knowledge? (Sandra Harding), 299, n.9
William of Ockham, 32 ff., 36, 121 ff., 130, 131, 132, 133, 143
Witchcraft, 302
Wittgenstein (movie by Derek Jarman), 242; 258, n. 5
Wittgenstein cult, the, 176-177, 254, 257
Wittgenstein, Hermann, 173
Wittgenstein, Karl, 173
Wittgenstein, Ludwig: 4, 78, 173 ff., 193 ff., 219 ff., 241 ff., 262, 263, 271, 274, 275, 278; character of, 174-176, 178, 180, 181, 211 ff., 219, 242-243; homophobia of, 177 ff., 212; homosexuality of, 174, 243; lost years of, 175, 177 ff.; philosophic stature of, 255 ff.; upbringing of, 173-174; and behaviorism, 227, 236; and certainty, 249; and chess, analogy of, 224; and the community of humanity-in-nature, 228-229, 231-232; and the correspondence theory of truth, 26-27, 28, 195-196; and essence, 223, 235, 248, 253; and family resemblances, 34-35, 222-223, 235; and fascism, 250; and the fly-bottle metaphor, 233, 244; 258, n.7; and formal logic, 241 ff., 248-249, 255; and forms of life, 224-225, 228, 233, 243-244, 274; and Gottlob Frege, 146, 173, 174, 197, 199, 203, 206, 214; and gestures, 229-230; and grammar, 224, 234-235, 253; and idealist philosophy, 205, 213, 219; and language-games, 222 ff., 242, 243, 247, 253, 256, 275; and Gottfried Wilhelm Leibniz, 126, 193, 195, 197, 198, 208, 216; and logical calculuses, 242; and logical necessity, 234, 243, 245, 246; and mathematics, 243, 247 ff.; and the metaphysical subject, 207 ff.; and modernity, 247; and mysticism, 193 ff., 259; and mythology in language, 225, 232; and naming, 220 ff., 236; and ontological pluralism, 30; and ordinary language, 230-231; and philosophy, 205, 252 ff.; and David Pinsent (infatuation), 180; and *Praxis*, 226-227, 228, 229, 230, 232, 233, 235, 252; and physiognomy, 226-227, 230; and the polytheism of meaning, 251; and private language, 215, 226, 232, 235 ff.; and Ben Richards (lover), 243; and Bertrand Russell, 174, 175, 176, 189-190, 193, 197-203, 206, 219, 220, 221, 247, 251, 253, 254, 255, 256, 257; and science, 249 ff., 254; and Francis Skinner (lover), 179, 180, 243; and socialism, 220, 250; and the survey of language, 244-245, 252; and the unspeakable, 200, 203, 213, 252; and the Vienna Circle, 204 ff.; and Otto Weininger, 182 ff., 202, 204, 207, 210, 219, 220, 242, 250
Wittgenstein's Ladder (Marjorie Perloff), p. 217, n. 32
Wolff, Christian, 126
Wollstonecraft, Mary, 53, 77, 324-325
Women, 4, 100, 109-110, 117, 183 ff., 280, 334
Word and Object (Willard Van Orman Quine), 262
Words of Power (Andrea Nye), 6, n. 4; 109

—Y—

Yakuts, 307
Yamakawa, Takeshi, 279
Yeltsin, Boris, 183

—Z—

Zadeh, Lotfi, 265, 275-276
Zeno of Citium, 110, 111
Zeno of Elea, 94-95, 96, 110
Zermelo, Ernst, 81
Zeus, 113, 114, 115, 119, 199, 203, 226, 234, 271, 328

[This page may be photocopied.]

ORDER FORM

Send me the following number of copies of *Critique of Patriarchal Reason* by Arthur Evans:

No. of Copies	Unit Price	Amounts
	$29.95 per copy	
California residents (**not** San Franciscans), add 8% sales tax—$2.40 per copy		
San Francisco residents only, add 8.5% sales tax—$2.55 per copy		
Shipping/handling costs (see below)		
	TOTAL:	

Shipping/handling costs: 1 copy-**$3.25**. 2 copies-**$4.25**. 3 copies-**$5.25**.

Please print your mailing address here:

Name: _____
Street Address: _____
_____
City: _____
State: _____ ZIP: _____

Please make your check or money order payable to White Crane Press, and mail to the following address, allowing three weeks for delivery:

Book Orders
White Crane Press
P.O. Box 170152
San Francisco, CA 94117-0152

Thank you!

Note: For information on *White Crane Journal*, lately independent of White Crane Press, address correspondence to Toby Johnson, Editor, P.O. Box 684704, Austin, TX, 78768-4704. The *Journal* is devoted to exploring issues in gay men's spirituality.